News Reporting and Writing

Eighth Edition

News Reporting and Writing

The Missouri Group

Brian S. Brooks
George Kennedy
Daryl R. Moen
Don Ranly

*School of Journalism
University of Missouri at Columbia*

Bedford/St. Martin's
Boston ■ New York

For Bedford/St. Martin's

Developmental Editor: Joshua Levy
Production Supervisor: Jennifer Wetzel
Project Management: Books By Design, Inc.
Senior Marketing Manager: Richard Cadman
Text Design: Robin Hoffmann
Photo Researcher: Alice Lundoff
Cover Design: Lucy Krikorian
Cover Photos: Before embedding with the U.S. Marines, *Dallas Morning News* corre-
spondent Jim Landers tests satellite phone computer equipment atop a Kuwait City
hotel, March 4, 2003. In the background is Liberation Tower, built to commemorate
Kuwait's liberation from Iraq in 1991. Photo by *Dallas Morning News* photographer
Cheryl Diaz Meyer; Reporter interviewing a subject at the Latin Grammys, Miami,
Florida. © Jeff Greenberg/The Image Works; Photojournalists filming a victim trapped
on the Cypress Freeway after the 1989 Loma Prieta earthquake. © Lloyd Cluff/
CORBIS.
Composition: Books By Design, Inc.
Printing and Binding: Haddon Craftsmen, an RR Donnelley & Sons Company

President: Joan E. Feinberg
Editorial Director: Denise B. Wydra
Director of Marketing: Karen Melton Soeltz
Director of Editing, Design, and Production: Marcia Cohen
Manager, Publisher Services: Emily Berleth

Library of Congress Control Number: 2004101847

Manufactured in the United States of America.

0   9   8   7   6   5
f   e   d   c   b   a

For information, write: Bedford/St. Martin's, 75 Arlington Street,
Boston, MA 02116   (617-399-4000)

ISBN: 0-312-41646-6
EAN: 978-0-312-41646-1

Acknowledgments

Acknowledgments and copyrights appear at the back of the book on pages 562–563, which constitute an extension of the copyright page.

PREFACE FOR INSTRUCTORS

Even as the information pipelines multiply, the need for our journalists to master the basics of reporting and writing grows. The eighth edition of *News Reporting and Writing* reflects the changing demands of our news rooms and re-emphasizes the basics. It matters not that a young professional can merge print, audio and visuals if the reporting is incomplete or inaccurate or the storytelling is incoherent or uninteresting.

We visited convergent news rooms in Tampa and Sarasota, talked to dozens of journalists around the country and read scores of articles. We kept asking what new skills are being required of graduates. Not surprisingly, the responses ranged from "forget teaching new technology" to insistence on mastering all the bells and whistles. But one theme emerged: Give us journalists who can report fully and write clearly; we can teach them the technology if necessary.

To help students write more clearly, we've added a new appendix, Twenty Common Errors of Grammar and Punctuation, which details the 20 most common errors found in journalism students' writing and offers strategies to correct them. In addition, this list is linked to a new Web site, Exercise Central for Associated Press Style (bedfordstmartins.com/APexercises), which includes 2,500 exercise items focusing on each of the common errors listed in the appendix.

A textbook is no place to teach new technology, but we do describe the news rooms where the technologies converge. In Chapter 1, The Nature of News, we transport your students to the *Tampa Tribune*'s news room, where the newspaper, television and Internet overlap. The changes in distribution and the effort of media companies to capture and repackage information for multiple uses are reflected frequently throughout this edition. In Chapter 2, The Changing News Business, your students will find up-to-date information about the convergence of print, radio and television and online media and how the online media are being incorporated into the news rooms. As you know, the media industry is in a significant transition, and this edition reflects that transition at the same time neither the industry captains nor we know the destination.

We do know that more of your graduates are finding jobs writing online, so we've expanded Chapter 20, Writing for Online Media, to include more on the world of online journalism, from writing for the Web to the rate of online newspaper readership, and new Web site screenshots illustrate the many uses and varieties of journalism on the Internet. The chapter is filled with practical guidelines to help your students master the differences in writing among print, radio and television and online journalism. Chances are that many of your graduates will be asked to turn in two versions of their stories even on their first job — one for the newspaper or broadcast station and one for the Web site. We trust that the exercises at the end of the chapter and in the workbook will help make shovelware a relic.

Also newly revised is Chapter 21, Writing for Public Relations. We recognize that in many journalism and communication departments, the students who are taking the beginning reporting class will enter a career in public relations. In this chapter, we discuss how to handle press releases, the work of public-relations professionals and specific approaches to writing for public relations. Students preparing for a traditional news career also will understand public relations better.

The heart of the book still is the emphasis on the basic skills: interviewing, reporting and writing. All are full of new examples and anecdotes. We have updated the computer-assisted reporting chapter (Chapter 5, Gathering Information) to reflect the advantages of using the Internet to add context to our stories. We continue to include Web sites in the end-of-chapter bibliographies so students can investigate all the chapter topics further. We suggest you create Internet scavenger hunts to encourage the students to use these resources. We elected not to create a scavenger hunt in our chapter exercises or the workbook because URLs change and the content of the Web sites changes rapidly, but you can survey them to put together a list for the scavenger hunt. Who knows? Your students might learn something without even being aware it is an assignment.

The reviewers often cite our chapter on ethics (Chapter 23) as the best in the field, and because journalism never fails to provide new examples, you will find discussions of up-to-date ethical dilemmas and how some news organizations have dealt with them.

Over the years, we have received many comments from you and your colleagues about the high quality of the examples and anecdotes. We often are asked where we find them. The answer is that we practice what we preach. We report by asking professionals for their stories and how they reported or wrote them. We all are voracious readers of both the print media and the Internet. Like your students, we have found the Internet to be a wonderful gateway to the world of the media, and we use various methods to help us find examples. We also attend professional meetings where we meet and talk to professionals. We are fortunate at Missouri that scores of journalists visit for seminars or to talk to our students, and we take good notes. Our folders are full of clippings and notes of conversations that yield nuggets for our classroom teaching and our revisions. We publish a daily newspaper and run a network television station at the journalism school, so we are never far from current practices. Among the four of us, we lead more than 50 professional seminars each year around the country, where we meet professionals and exchange information. And last, we all judge many contests, a rich source of examples.

Acknowledgments

Our colleagues and students in the approximately 30 sections of beginning reporting at Missouri give us quick feedback on the book, for which we are grateful.

We especially appreciate the contributions of Dr. Sandra Davidson, an attorney and journalism faculty colleague, who revised the law chapter, and our colleagues in our broadcast department for reviewing the chapter on writing for radio and television.

In addition, we would like to thank all of the instructors who thoughtfully reviewed the text: Joan Atkins, Morehead State University; Carol Atkinson, Central Missouri State University; Joseph Cosco, Old Dominion University; Elizabeth Fraas, Eastern Kentucky University; Byung Lee, Elon College; Bonnie McMeans, Delaware County Community College; Mia Moody-Hall, Baylor University; James Mueller, University of North Texas; Craig Sanders, John Carroll University; and John Watson, American University.

We have worked with editors at Bedford/St. Martin's for 24 years now. Each edition, they have challenged us to improve, and we appreciate their work. We would like to acknowledge the support of Patricia Rossi over the course of many editions and the gentle nudging of development editor Joshua Levy, who kept us on track and on schedule.

We want to express our appreciation to our wives — Anne, Robin, Nancy and Eva Joan — who have been wonderful partners in this undertaking.

As always, we value your comments. You can reach any of us via e-mail by addressing it to Brooksbs@missouri.edu; Kennedyg@missouri.edu; Moend@missouri.edu; or Ranlyd@missouri.edu.

Brian S. Brooks
George Kennedy
Daryl R. Moen
Don Ranly

PREFACE FOR STUDENTS

Mark Barabak, political writer for *The Los Angeles Times*, was one of hundreds of journalists covering the 2000 presidential election. Barabak and other *Times* reporters worked 70-hour weeks before the election, only to go into overtime when the outcome was too close to call. He told Narda Zacchino, the *Times'* associate editor, it was worth it.

"Two or three nights post-election, I called my 9-year-old to tell her I wouldn't be home before she went to sleep because I had to write. I explained that this had never happened before, that it was like writing history. She replied, 'Wow, it's really an honor, isn't it?'"

Added Zacchino, "Barabak, who could have been responding for the entire staff of *Times'* journalists, replied, 'Yes, it really is.'"

Journalism has always offered its practitioners an adrenaline rush, whether they are working with actors of historic events on the world scene or in their local community. If you join this profession, you, too, will experience these thrills. You will discover that you can save lives, help democracy function and help the community members know each other better.

First, though, you need to learn how to interview, report and write and learn the system in which you will apply that knowledge.

We begin our instruction, as always, where the craft of journalism begins — with consideration of what news is, who audiences are and what principles guide journalists in their efforts to supply readers, listeners and viewers with the news they need and want. You will visit a news room where journalists are working for a newspaper, television station and Web site. The first chapter sets the tone for the book. It is written clearly. It links theory to practice. It is packed with real examples drawn from the best work of journalists who are living in the real world of constant change.

The first chapter also introduces a topic that runs through the book — ethics. As both teachers and practitioners, we believe that the toughest and most important ethical issues can be understood only in the context of the realities of journalism. So we return repeatedly to those issues in preparation for a detailed discussion, which we think is the most useful in any reporting textbook, in Chapter 23.

In Chapter 2 we turn from news to news rooms, with a focus on the changing organization of the most traditional medium, newspapers. We compare structures and functions of newspaper and television news rooms. We introduce you to the convergence of print, broadcast and online media as online journalism is rapidly becoming another tool for reporting, a source of jobs for young journalists and a way of interacting with audiences.

Then you get down to work. In the next several chapters, we introduce the reporter's basic information-gathering tool, interviewing. We take you to the newest and sharpest tool, computer-assisted reporting. And we show you how to report accurately and write clearly about numbers.

On that foundation, you'll build the art of storytelling. First comes the inverted pyramid, the traditional structure that now is the basis for most print and online journalism. You'll move quickly to see the importance of good writing and learn how to achieve it. You'll move beyond the inverted pyramid to the varied structures that give room for the most satisfying storytelling. Next, you'll sharpen your skills by practicing the basic stories — obituaries, speeches and meetings, accidents and fires, crime and the courts. At every step, you'll find examples that show rather than merely tell you how and why and when to use each technique.

From the basics, you move up, just as many professional reporters do, to the coverage of major beats, ranging from local government to business to sports. Building again on what you've learned, you will explore advanced techniques, applying the tools of social science to reporting and finally to the most demanding form of journalism — investigative reporting.

We have heavily revised two chapters in this edition: Writing for Online Media and Writing for Public Relations. The first reflects the growing importance of media convergence and the online media, and the second reflects the fact that many of you enrolled in this course will be public-relations professionals rather than journalists. Both types of professionals need to know how to write clearly.

The final two chapters provide detailed discussion of laws and ethics. Throughout the skills chapters, you will have encountered practical problems involving both. The press law and ethics chapters are resources that may be brought to bear on those problems at any time.

Good writing is the hallmark of a good journalist, and a new appendix, Twenty Common Errors of Grammar and Punctuation, helps you improve your writing by identifying and correcting errors common to journalism students' writing. In addition, a new Web site, Exercise Central for Associated Press Style (bedfordstmartins.com/APexercises) includes 2,500 exercise sets that focus on each of these common errors. The Workbook also contains exercises in grammar and punctuation.

This eighth edition has been revised and updated to reflect the freshest thinking and the most relevant examples to prepare you for the changes sweeping the practice and the content of journalism. In On the Job boxes in every chapter, you'll also meet working journalists who are grappling with those changes every day.

We hope you agree that we practice what we preach. In order to teach you how to report and write clearly and interestingly, we scour the country for new examples and anecdotes. That's why we visited news rooms where radio and television, print and the Internet are converging. And when you read in Chapter 23 how Kelly McBride from the Poynter Institute has worked to create a "healthy ethical process," you know that we tracked McBride down and interviewed her. Although we aren't working on a daily newspaper anymore, we still are journalists and love reporting and writing. We're sure you will love it, too.

CONTENTS

PART TWO   REPORTING TOOLS

PART THREE   STORYTELLING

Elements of Good Writing   170

9 Beyond the Inverted Pyramid   186

The Techniques of Narration   188

How to Modify the Inverted Pyramid   193

Writing the Set-Up   199

Writing the Body   202

On the Job: Tips for Writing   203

Writing the Ending   204

Putting It Together   205

PART FOUR   BASIC STORIES

10   Obituaries   212

11   News Releases   230

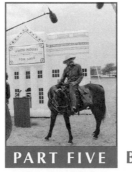

PART FIVE   BEAT REPORTING

16 Sports   356

PART SIX   SPECIALIZED TECHNIQUES

17 Social Science Reporting   374

PART SEVEN WRITING FOR SPECIFIC MEDIA

PART EIGHT RIGHTS AND RESPONSIBILITIES

Appendix 1

Twenty Common Errors of Grammar and Punctuation   525

Appendix 2

Wire Service Style Summary   535

Appendix 3

Society of Professional Journalists' Code of Ethics   541

Appendix 4

Crisis Coverage: An Interactive CD-ROM Journalism Simulation   545

Glossary   553

Index   564

News Reporting and Writing

1   The Nature of News

The attacks of September 11, 2001, the war in Iraq and the ongoing struggle against terrorism have brought unfamiliar names to America's television screens and newspaper headlines. Using the technology of laptop computers, digital cameras and handheld satellite telephones, journalists report on American soldiers at war in lands few viewers or readers can find on a map. Television networks compete to display their patriotism, while bloggers use the Internet to debate whether national security justifies restrictions on civil liberties.

A year after the attacks of September 11, a study showed that both television and print news had become more international. News directors and managing editors reported devoting more time, space and resources to stories from Afghanistan, Iraq and other distant centers of conflict. Journalism, like the world it tried to describe and explain, seemed to have changed.

But had it? When the researchers took a closer look, they realized that only the place names were different. A television news director in Chattanooga, Tenn., explained, "Nine/11 didn't change everything. This is what we do; we cover the news."

He was right. Journalists in the 21st century are doing what journalists have always done. They are telling the world its stories. How they tell those stories, however, has changed. Communication from the most remote locations is instant. The Internet gives news consumers the ability to read, watch or listen whenever they wish — and to respond. Traditional print and broadcast media are joining forces and sharing resources in the latest trend, something called convergence.

Convergence is the term that describes efforts to use the different strengths of different media to reach broader audiences and tell the world's stories in new ways. Still in its early days, convergence already demands of journalists new skills and new flexibility. Print reporters find themselves summarizing their stories into a television camera. Videographers find themselves selecting images to be published in the partner newspaper. Both print and broadcast journalists look for Web links to connect their stories to the worldwide audience and nearly infinite capacity of the Internet.

In Tampa, Fla., for example, WFLA-TV is the leading station in the market. It shares stories, staff members and even a specially constructed building with *The Tampa Tribune* newspaper and the Web site

In this chapter you will learn:

1. What news is.

2. How journalism and audiences are changing.

3. How the unchanging principles of accuracy and fairness will help you meet the challenges of permanent change.

3

TBO.com. In Lawrence, Kan., the *Journal-World* has a newspaper circulation of about 20,000 (one-tenth the size of *The Tampa Tribune*). However, it too shares a news room with a television station. Both feed the company's three Web sites. Ljworld.com carries news, mainly local. Lawrence.com focuses on entertainment, and the topic of the third, kusports.com, is fairly obvious.

Some things don't change. One constant is journalists' definition of news itself. Another is the importance of accuracy and fairness. The most fundamental is the continuing central role of journalism in a democratic society.

The basic skills required of every journalist haven't changed, either, despite the revolution in technology. Whatever the medium, the skills of news-gathering and storytelling are essential to good journalism.

WHAT NEWS IS

The criteria that professional reporters and editors use to decide what news is can be summarized in three words:

Relevance

Usefulness

Interest

Those criteria apply generally, but each journalist and each news organization uses them in a specific context that gives them particular meaning. That context is supplied by the *audience*.

Let's look at an example:

By Amos Bridges
news@ColumbiaMissourian.com

As if high school freshmen didn't have it hard enough, a recent study says only about one in three will graduate with the courses needed to get into even the nation's least selective four-year colleges.

Nationwide, only 70 percent of all students entering high school will graduate, says a study from the Manhattan Institute, a New York think tank that advocates vouchers and school choice. Fewer than half of those — 32 percent of all students — have transcripts that will get them into four-year programs with what the study defines as the least demanding course requirements.

The study, "Public High School Graduation and College Readiness Rates in the United States," says that to have "any reasonable hope of attending" a four-year college, students need to have taken four years of English, three years of math and two years each of natural science, social science and foreign language. These requirements were developed by looking at four-year institutions researchers deemed "representative of the lowest level of prestige and selectivity."

The high school graduation rate in Columbia is about 79 percent, just short of the state average of 82.5 percent, according to data from the Missouri Department of Elementary and Secondary Education, or DESE. But more Columbia students enter four-year schools the year after they graduate — 65 percent, compared to 40 percent statewide. . . .

This is the top of a story that appeared in the morning newspaper. The full story goes on to explain how local and state graduation requirements compare to the national standards and what the hometown university requires for admission. Along with it ran a box labeled "More online." That contained the Web site addresses for the national report and the state department of education. Readers could then go online and see for themselves much of the raw material on which the story was based.

Now consider this story's value to its audience. The relevance is obvious. Education touches the core of any community, especially a college town such as Columbia. Every parent, every student, every teacher has a direct stake in this subject. The story and the accompanying Web sites are useful because they allow readers to assess just where they, and those they care about, stand in relation to peers and competitors across the country. **Relevance** and **usefulness** add up to a high level of **interest.**

This story would have been a challenge for television journalists. Statistics and comparisons don't lend themselves to compelling pictures, which television demands. So the TV version would probably rely on video of students studying, on-camera interviews with experts, and charts conveying essential numbers. The presentation would be different in each medium, but the news values that make the story important and the reporting skills required to tell it would be the same. Later chapters will help you learn those skills. For now, let's look a little more deeply at news values, the criteria journalists use to decide which stories are worth telling.

Relevance, usefulness and *interest* are the broad guidelines for judging the news value of any event, issue or personality. Within those broad standards, journalists look for more specific elements in each potential story. The most important are these:

Impact — This is another way of measuring relevance and usefulness. How many people are affected by an event or idea? How seriously does it affect them? The wider and heavier the impact, the better the story. Sometimes, of course, impact isn't immediately obvious. Sometimes it isn't very exciting. The challenge for good journalism is making such dull but important stories lively and interesting. That may require relying on the next three elements.

Conflict — This is a recurring theme in all storytelling, whether the stories told are journalism, literature or drama. Struggles between people, among nations or with natural forces make fascinating reading. Conflict is such a basic element of life that journalists must resist the temptation to over-dramatize or oversimplify it.

Novelty — This is another element common to journalism and other kinds of stories. People or events may be interesting and therefore newsworthy just because they are unusual or bizarre.

Prominence — Names make news. The bigger the name, the bigger the news. Ordinary people have always been intrigued by the doings of the rich and famous. Both prominence and novelty also can be, and often are, exaggerated to produce "news" that lacks real relevance and usefulness.

Proximity — Generally, people are more interested in and concerned about what happens close to home. When they read or listen to national or international news, they often want to know how it relates to their own community.

Timeliness — News is supposed to be new. If news is to be relevant and useful, it must be timely. For example, it is more useful to write about an issue facing the city council before it is decided than afterward. Timely reporting gives people a chance to be participants in public affairs rather than mere spectators.

Notice that this list suggests two important things about news. First, not all news is serious, life-and-death stuff. Journalism has been described as "a culture's conversation with itself." The conversation that holds a culture together includes talk of crime, politics and world affairs, of course, but it also includes talk of everyday life. It includes humor and gossip. All of that can be news. Second, news is more than collections of facts. Telling the news usually means telling stories. The narrative, the humanity, the drama of storytelling is the art of journalism. To gather the facts for their stories, journalists use many of the same techniques used by sociologists, political scientists and historians. But to tell their stories so that those facts can be understood, journalists often use the techniques of other storytellers, such as novelists and screenwriters.

Differences among the news media give different weights to those criteria and require different approaches to telling stories. For example, newspapers and magazines are better than television or radio for explaining the impact of an issue or the causes of a conflict. Scholars have learned that, although most people say they get most of their news from television, few can remember very much of what they've seen or heard on a newscast. But print can't compete with television in speed or emotional power. The differing strengths and limitations of each medium make it more likely that you'll find a lengthy explanatory story in a newspaper or magazine, whereas you're more likely to learn of an event from television, radio or the Internet. The newspaper lets you read the details of a budget or a box score, but television shows you the worker whose job was cut or the player scoring the winning basket. The unique power of online journalism is that it brings together the immediacy of television and the comprehensive authority of print, with endless opportunities to pursue your interests through the Web.

> "(On television) Superficiality is not just built into the lack of time. It's that we spend a lot of time not on the phone, not in the library, but trying to show visually what we're talking about."
>
> — Sam Donaldson, ABC News correspondent

THE ROLE OF JOURNALISM AND THE CHALLENGES IT FACES

The First Amendment to the United States Constitution protects the five freedoms that the nation's founders considered essential to a democracy — the freedom of speech, religion, press, petition and assembly. In the 1830s, the French aristocrat Alexis de Tocqueville came to study the United States and wrote his classic *Democracy in America*. He was struck by the central role played by the only journalism available then, the newspapers. "We should underrate their importance if we thought they just guaranteed liberty; they maintain civilization," he wrote.

More than 200 years after they were guaranteed, the First Amendment freedoms are still essential and still under threat. After September 11, 2001, a new emphasis on national and personal security tempted government officials and citizens alike to question just how much freedom is compatible with safety. The role of journalism in guaranteeing liberty and maintaining civilization is challenged by those who make news and those who need it.

American journalism is also under threat from growing public skepticism about how well today's journalists are fulfilling their historic roles.

In a national survey conducted by the Pew Center for the People and the Press, 78 percent of those responding agreed that the news media are biased. Asked which medium is most biased, 42 percent named television, 23 percent newspapers, 17 percent magazines and 5 percent radio. (Still, when asked which source they trust most when media offer conflicting versions of a story, 34 percent named television, 27 percent newspapers, 2 percent magazines and 8 percent radio.) More than half said that increased public discontent with journalists is justified. Nearly 90 percent said sensational stories get lots of coverage just because they're exciting and not because they're important.

In that same survey, however, two-thirds said that having the press keep a close eye on politicians is a good way to prevent wrongdoing, whereas 80 percent approved of investigative reporting. Even though both daily newspaper circulation and television news viewing have declined in recent years, 79 percent in the survey said they watch local TV news on a typical evening, and 72 percent said they read a local newspaper during a typical day.

What these citizens seem to be saying is that the work journalists do is important, but it isn't being done well enough. The past decade has seen the emergence of several major efforts to improve the performance of American journalism.

One of those efforts has been driven by an informal association called the Committee of Concerned Journalists and the related Project for Excellence in Journalism. The project conducts regular research on journalism and issues reports, which can be accessed on its Web site, **www.journalism.org**. Among the reports are assessments of the quality of local television news. Another product of these reformers is a book that should be read by every student and practitioner of journalism. Written by two leaders of the committee and the project, Bill Kovach and Tom Rosenstiel, the book is *The Elements of Journalism*.

The book argues that "the purpose of journalism is to provide people with the information they need to be free and self-governing." It proposes nine principles to achieve this purpose:

1. Journalism's first obligation is to the truth.
2. Its first loyalty is to citizens.
3. Its essence is a discipline of verification.

TIPS: Audiences of the 21st century

- By 2010, married couples will no longer make up a majority of households.
- By 2025, Americans over 64 will outnumber teenagers 2-1.
- By 2050, one-fifth of the U.S. population will be Hispanic.

— All from *Undercovered: The New USA*, published by New Directions for News

4. Its practitioners must maintain an independence from those they cover.
5. It must serve as an independent monitor of power.
6. It must provide a forum for public criticism and compromise.
7. It must strive to make the significant interesting and relevant.
8. It must keep the news comprehensive and proportional.
9. Its practitioners must be allowed to exercise their personal conscience.

In these principles, you can hear echoes of the Journalist's Creed, written nearly a century before by Walter Williams, founding dean of the world's first journalism school, at the University of Missouri. Williams wrote that "the public journal is a public trust . . . that acceptance of a lesser interest than the public interest is a violation of that trust."

Williams, who was a small-town journalist before he became an educator, would have been comfortable with a second major effort to recapture for journalism the public trust. This effort, more controversial than the Committee of Concerned Journalists, goes by several names, the best-known being "civic journalism" and "public journalism." Some of its practitioners prefer to avoid labels and just think of it as journalism that seeks to strengthen democracy and citizenship.

This newest concept of journalism is based on two ideas: First, democracy isn't working as well as it should. Second, journalists have a responsibility to try to do something about that. Few observers of politics would argue with the first idea. The evidence ranges from low voter turnout to stalemates in Congress. Some scholars even argue that we are losing our basic sense of community. The second idea, however, runs squarely into the journalistic tradition of neutrality, of reporters' detachment from the events they cover. Jay Rosen, a scholar who is the leading theoretician of civic journalism, has come up with a set of contrasts in the beliefs of traditional and public journalists. Here are two that illustrate the gap:

Civic journalists believe:	Public life should work, and journalism has a role in making it work.
Traditional journalists believe:	It would be nice if public life worked, but it's beyond our role to make it work and it's dangerous to think we can.
Civic journalists believe:	Something basic has to change because journalism isn't working now.
Traditional journalists believe:	The traditions of journalism are fine; if anything needs to improve, it's the practice.

The journalist who is generally credited with — or blamed for — putting these principles into practice is Davis "Buzz" Merritt, then editor of *The Wichita* (Kan.) *Eagle*. Merritt was disgusted by the quality of journalism he saw in his paper and elsewhere during the 1988 elections. He was dismayed by the apparent lack of interest and obvious lack of involvement in public life he saw in Wichita and around the nation. So he began a series of journalistic experiments that laid the foundation for a movement.

Beginning in 1989, journalists in Wichita — and before long in dozens of other cities ranging from Charlotte, N.C., to Bremerton, Wash. — were taking polls to find out what citizens thought campaign issues should be instead of allowing candidates to set the terms of public debate. They were sponsoring public forums for the discussion of issues ranging from politics to race. In some cases, they were even assigning or hiring staff members to help citizens attack a variety of local problems. Nonprofit organizations such as the Pew, Kettering and Knight foundations contributed money and expertise. Research showed that many civic journalism projects seemed to be changing attitudes toward public life and toward the journalistic organizations.

But the critics, including top editors at *The Washington Post* and *The New York Times*, worry that civic journalists are winning goodwill at the expense of something even more important — their independence. News organizations cannot be both actors and critics, the critics argue. To them, the critic's role is the one journalists should play. When a newspaper organizes a public discussion, instead of only reporting on a discussion organized by others, it has become an actor in the drama it should be observing from a critical distance, the critics say. When journalists ask citizens what they want to know, instead of giving them what the journalists think they need to know, pandering replaces educating.

A decade after the civic journalism movement began, a study found that at least one-fifth of American news organizations had tried to put its principles into practice. Most of those found that citizens in their communities became more engaged in public life. Most also noticed that public attitudes toward journalism improved.

These efforts to reform, or restore, journalism recognize these vital functions of journalists in a free society:

- *Journalists report the news.* The first and most obvious function, it is the foundation of the rest. Reporters cover Congress and council meetings, describe accidents and disasters, show the horrors of war and the highlights of football games. This reporting takes many forms — live television, online bulletins, next-day newspaper analyses, long-form magazine narratives. No wonder journalism has been called the first rough draft of history.
- *Journalists monitor power.* Most often, Americans are concerned about the power of government. Lately, private power has become more of a worry and more a source of news. Monitoring is required even if power is used legitimately — when governments raise taxes or take us to war, for example, or businesses close plants or cut health-care benefits for employees. When the power is used illegally or immorally, another important function comes into play.
- *Journalists uncover injustice.* A television reporter learns that one brand of tires and one model of car are involved in a disproportionate number of fatal accidents. A newspaper discovers that prisoners on death row were

convicted unfairly. In those cases and thousands more, journalists bring to light dangerous or illegal abuses that might otherwise go unchecked.

- *Journalists tell stories that delight and amaze.* Some are the television mini-dramas of *60 Minutes*. Some are newspaper narratives that shape public policy, such as Mark Bowden's "Black Hawk Down," which appeared first in *The Philadelphia Inquirer* and then became a book and a movie. Some are magazine reconstructions that set the nation talking, such as William Langewiesche's *Atlantic Monthly* account of the cleanup after the World Trade Center attack.
- *Journalists sustain communities.* These may be small towns, cities or even virtual communities of people connected only by the Internet. By their reporting, monitoring, revealing and storytelling, journalists serve as the nervous system of the community. They convey information and argument. Their work is, in James Carey's phrase, the community's "conversation with itself."

Other scholars use other terms for this combination of functions. One is "agenda-setting," the placing of issues on the public agenda for discussion and decision. Another is "gate-keeping," the process by which some events and ideas become news and others do not. Now that the Internet has flooded the world with information, another role is emerging — that of "navigation," guiding readers and viewers through oceans of fact, rumor and fantasy in search of solid meaning.

Richard Saul Wurman has examined this new need in his book *Information Anxiety*, another work every journalist should read. In it, Wurman says that most news could be divided into three categories: hope, absurdity and catastrophe. Journalists typically focus on absurdity and catastrophe. Readers and viewers hunger for hope. Instead of merely pointing out problems, a journalism of hope would identify possible solutions, provide examples and tell people where to go for information or to get involved. (You'll notice a resemblance to civic journalism in Wurman's prescriptions.)

Wurman's other point relates directly to navigation. Mere information is not the most important product of journalism, he points out. Understanding is what's essential to effective communication. As journalists improve their ability to tell stories that are relevant and useful, they are more likely to convey understanding. Lacking that, citizens drift, and sometimes drown, in the ever-deepening sea of information.

"The computer is an icon for our age, but reason and imagination, which yield understanding, are yet to be programmable."

— Richard Saul Wurman

ACCURACY, FAIRNESS AND THE PROBLEM OF OBJECTIVITY

The goal toward which most journalists strive has seldom been expressed any better than in a phrase used by Bob Woodward, a reporter, author and editor at

The Washington Post. Woodward was defending in court an investigative story published by the *Post.* The story, he said, was "the best obtainable version of the truth."

A grander-sounding goal would be "the truth," unmodified. But Woodward's phrase, while paying homage to the ideal, recognizes the realities of life and the limitations of journalism. Despite centuries of argument, philosophers and theologians are still unable to agree on what truth is. Even if there were agreement on that basic question, how likely is it that the Roman Catholic Church and the Planned Parenthood organization would agree on the "truth" about abortion, or that a president and his challenger would agree on the "truth" about the state of the American economy?

In American daily journalism, that kind of dispute is left to be argued among the partisans on all sides, on the editorial pages and in commentaries. The reporter's usual role is simply to find and write the facts. The trouble is, doing that turns out often to be not so simple.

Sometimes it's hard to get the facts. The committee searching for a new university president announces that the field of candidates has been narrowed to five, but the names of the five are not released. Committee members are sworn to secrecy. What can you do to get the names? Should you try?

Sometimes it's hard to tell what the facts mean. The state Supreme Court refuses to hear a case in which legislators are questioning the constitutionality of a state spending limit. The court says only that there is no "justiciable controversy." What does that mean? Who won? Is the ruling good news or bad news, and for whom?

Sometimes it's even hard to tell what is fact. A presidential commission, after a yearlong study, says there is no widespread hunger in America. Is the conclusion a fact? Or is the fact only what the commission said? And how can you determine whether the commission is correct?

Daily journalism presents still more complications. As a reporter, you usually have only a few hours — or at most a few days — to try to learn as many facts as possible. Then, even in such a limited time, you may accumulate information enough for a story of 2,000 words, only to be told that there is space or time enough for 1,000 or fewer. The new media offer more space but no more time for reporting. When you take into account all these realities and limitations, you can see that reaching the best obtainable version of the truth is challenge enough for any journalist.

How can you tell when the goal has been reached? Seldom, if ever, is there a definitive answer. But there are two questions every responsible journalist should ask about every story before being satisfied: Is it accurate? Is it fair?

Accuracy and Fairness

Accuracy is the most important characteristic of any story, great or small, long or short. Accuracy is essential in every detail. Every name must be spelled correctly; every quote must be just what was said; every set of numbers must add

Road to a Dream Job

As politics analyst for www.washingtonpost.com, Terry Neal has a dream job. He describes it as "a bit of a strange hybrid between news and opinion." He loves it. "It allows me to bring my perspective to the political news of the day in a way that is entertaining and accessible to the masses of people who find politics interesting and important, but who don't make their living at it."

He didn't follow a straight-forward route to the top, though. In the first place, when he was in journalism school, and even after he graduated, he wasn't sure journalism was what he wanted for a career. Like many other journalism majors, he felt the lure of law school. Like many others, he was hooked on journalism by an internship, in his case at the Fort Lauderdale, Fla., *Sun-Sentinel*. "I really fell in love with journalism," he recalls.

After he graduated, a reporting job at the *Sun-Sentinel* led to an offer from *The Miami Herald.* There he began by covering local government and won a "plum assignment" to the state capital bureau in Tallahassee. "It had never been my plan in college to pursue a career as a political reporter, but I seemed to fall naturally into that niche. By this time, law school was a long-faded aspiration. I had found my calling."

After he covered Jeb Bush's first run for governor of Florida, *The Washington Post* found Terry. Three years on the metro desk, reporting on local and state politics, earned promotion to the national desk. At the age of 30, he was the *Post*'s youngest national politics reporter.

"I traveled around the country writing about congressional and gubernatorial races. I spent a lot of time on the Hill, particularly in 1998, during the whole Monica Lewinsky mess. And I got to know the White House, traveling occasionally with both President Clinton and Vice President Gore on *Air Force One* and *Air Force Two.*"

It got even better. He was assigned to cover the presidential campaign and spent a year and a half "following George W. Bush around the country, flying on his campaign plane, hanging out in Austin and filing dispatches."

But the best journalists are often restless. In Terry Neal's case, his hunger for something new led him into public relations, at Burson-Marsteller, "advising major corporate clients on media strategy and that sort of thing."

He made money, spent more nights at home, "but I always felt somewhat out of place," he realized. "I never could really wrap my mind around being an advocate. I missed journalism." So when the columnist position came open at the *Post*'s Web site, he applied.

Now, he says, "I feel like I'm back home. Sometimes you have to leave something to remind you that you miss it. . . . Sometimes you just become what you do."

up. And that still isn't good enough. You can get the details right and still mislead unless you are accurate with context, too. The same statement may have widely different meanings depending on the circumstances in which it was uttered and the tone in which it was spoken. Circumstances and intent affect the meaning of actions as well. You will never have the best obtainable version of the truth unless your version is built on accurate reporting of detail and context.

Nor can you approach the truth without being fair. Accuracy and fairness are related, but they are not the same. The relationship and the difference show clearly in this analogy from the world of sports:

The referee in a basketball game is similar, in some ways, to a reporter. Each is supposed to be an impartial observer, calling developments as he or she sees them. (Of course, the referee's job is to make judgments on those developments, whereas the reporter's is just to describe them.) Television has brought to sports the instant replay, in which a key play — for example, whether a player was fouled while taking a shot — can be examined again and again, often from an angle different from the referee's view. Sometimes the replay shows an apparent outcome different from the one the official called. Perhaps the players actually didn't make contact. Perhaps what looked like an attempted shot was really a pass. The difference may be due to human error on the official's part, or it may be due to the differences in angle and in viewpoint. Referees recognize this problem. They try to deal with it by obtaining the best possible view of every play and by conferring with their colleagues on some close calls. Still, every official knows that an occasional mistake will be made. That is unavoidable. What can, and must, be avoided is unfairness. Referees must be fair, and both players and fans must believe they are fair. Otherwise, their judgments will not be accepted; they will not be trusted.

With news, too, there are different viewpoints from which every event or issue can be observed. Each viewpoint may yield a different interpretation of what is occurring and of what it means. There is also, in journalism as in sports, the possibility of human error, even by the most careful reporters.

Fairness requires that you as a reporter try to find every viewpoint on a story. Rarely will there be only one; often there are more than two. Fairness requires that you allow ample opportunity for response to anyone who is being attacked or whose integrity is being questioned in a story. Fairness requires, above all, that you make every effort to avoid following your own biases in your reporting and your writing.

Framing Stories

The viewpoint, or perspective, from which you tell a story serves as the frame for that story. Like the frame around a picture, the frame of a story contains it, limits it and determines how much the reader sees. The changes in subjects and in sources discussed above have changed the ways journalists frame stories.

For example, the coverage of a political campaign looks very different from the perspective of the voter than it does from the perspective of the candidates.

A common complaint about today's journalism is that reporters get so caught up in the mechanics and the personalities of politics that they forget the voter's perspective — the real issues. Reporters often travel with the candidates rather than stand with the voters. Their coverage takes on an insider tone, in which the motives behind a candidate's position may seem more important than what she actually said. From the voter's point of view, substance is obscured by tactics. As in the case of basketball officials, what reporters see depends on where they stand.

The Colorado Springs Gazette undertook an experiment that shows the importance of framing. The topic was a major school bond issue. Voters in Colorado Springs had repeatedly turned down previous bond issues. Editors at the *Gazette* suspected that journalists hadn't done a very good job of explaining all sides of the issue. So they decided on an unusual step: They assigned reporters to analyze the bond issue four times — from the perspective of each of the four groups that had important stakes in the election. Separate stories were framed from the perspectives of teachers, students, parents and taxpayers with no children in school.

Steve Smith, then editor of the *Gazette*, summed up the experiment:

> As written for publication, what you had was a community of like individuals essentially arguing within themselves about the bond issue. "I like this, but I don't like that. I don't trust them to spend the money well. But my kid's school roof is leaking."
>
> We ran the four different frames over four days, borrowing a technique the Kettering Foundation folks used in the National Issues Forum issues books. We produced a grid that previewed the upcoming perspectives and summarized the perspectives that had come before.
>
> Externally, nearly all the reaction was positive. Internally, there was no consensus as to whether or not this was the right approach.

That conclusion can also apply to the whole problem of framing. Every story has several possible frames. None is perfect. Every reporter should choose the frame that seems to reveal that story most fully and fairly.

Objectivity

The rules that mainstream journalists follow in attempting to arrive at the best obtainable version of the truth are commonly summarized as objectivity. Objectivity has been and still is accepted as a working credo by most American journalists, students and teachers of journalism. It has been exalted by leaders of the profession as an essential, if unattainable, ideal. Its critics, by contrast, have attacked objectivity as, in the phrase of sociologist Gaye Tuchman, a "strategic ritual" that conceals a multitude of professional sins while producing superficial and often misleading coverage.

In his classic *Discovering the News*, Michael Schudson traces the rise of objectivity to the post–World War I period, when scholars and journalists alike turned to the methods and the language of science in an attempt to make sense of a world that was being turned upside down by the influence of Freud and Marx, the emergence of new economic forces and the erosion of traditional values. Objectivity was a reliance on observable facts, but it was also a methodology for freeing factual reporting from the biases and values of source, writer or reader. It was itself a value, an ideal.

Schudson wrote, "Journalists came to believe in objectivity, to the extent that they did, because they wanted to, needed to, were forced by ordinary human aspiration to seek escape from their own deep convictions of doubt and drift."

Objectivity, then, was a way of applying to the art of journalism the methods of science. Those methods emphasized reliance on observable fact. They also included the use of a variety of transparent techniques for pursuing truth. In science, transparency means that the researcher explains his objectives, his methods, his findings and his limitations. In journalism, only part of that methodology is usually followed.

In *The Elements of Journalism*, Kovach and Rosenstiel worry that a kind of phony objectivity has replaced the original concept. The objectivity of science does not require neutrality or artificial balance of two sides in a dispute. However, as usually practiced today, objectivity employs both devices, sometimes instead of the kind of openness that is essential in science. True objectivity, they argue, would add scientific rigor to journalistic art. Without that, journalists and audiences alike can be misled. Properly understood, objectivity provides the journalistic method most likely to yield the best obtainable version of the truth.

In 1947 the Hutchins Commission on freedom of the press concluded that what a free society needs from journalists is "a truthful, comprehensive and intelligent account of the day's events in a context which gives them meaning." The goal of this chapter is to show you how the journalists of today and tomorrow understand that need, how they are trying to meet it, and the complexity of the task. The rest of the book will help you develop the skills you'll need to take up the challenge. There are few challenges so important or so rewarding.

"You go into journalism because you can do good, have fun and learn."

— Molly Ivins, reporter and columnist

Suggested Readings

Downie, Leonard Jr. and Kaiser, Robert. *The News about the News*. New York: Knopf, 2002. This is a critical, thoroughly researched examination of current journalistic practice in all media.

Kovach, Bill and Rosenstiel, Tom. *The Elements of Journalism*. New York: Crown Publishers, 2001. This little book is packed with practical advice and inspiration, a kind of applied ethics for journalists in any medium.

Journalism reviews: Any issue of the *Columbia Journalism Review*, the *Washington Journalism Review*, *The Quill* or the *American Editor*, bulletin of the American Society of Newspaper Editors, offers reports and analyses of the most important issues of contemporary journalism.

Schudson, Michael. *Discovering the News*. New York: Basic Books, 1978. Subtitled *A Social History of American Newspapers*, this well-written study traces the development of objectivity in American journalism.

Wurman, Richard Saul. *Information Anxiety*. New York: Doubleday, 1990. This guide for consumers of information can also serve as a guide for journalists as they seek to provide understanding.

Suggested Web Sites

www.asne.org
The American Society of Newspaper Editors is the most important of the industry's professional organizations. This Web site will give you access to the society's landmark credibility project, including the results of a major study of Americans' attitudes toward, and uses of, journalism.

www.cjr.org
Columbia Journalism Review is the oldest of the magazines devoted to critical analysis of journalists' performance. You'll find critiques of major stories and essays on ethics, along with book reviews and trade news. *American Journalism Review* (**www.ajr.org**) and the newer *Brill's Content* (**www.brillscontent.com**) offer similar content.

www. journalism.org
This is the Web site of the Project for Excellence in Journalism and the Committee of Concerned Journalists. It contains relevant research and articles on the current state of journalism.

www.poynter.org
This is an excellent starting point. The Poynter Institute is the leading center of continuing professional education for journalists. On this site you'll find not only a guide to the services and resources of the institute itself but links to the sites of every major professional organization and a variety of other useful resources.

Exercises

1. Most Americans say they get most of their news from television. Watch an evening newscast on one of the major networks. Read *The New York Times* or *USA Today* for the same day. Compare the number of stories, the topics and the depth of coverage. How well informed are those television-dependent Americans?

2. Get copies of today's issue of your local newspaper, a paper from a city at least 50 miles away and a paper of national circulation, such as *USA Today* or *The Wall Street Journal*. Analyze the front page according to the criteria discussed in this chapter.

What can you tell about the editors' understanding of each paper's audience by looking at the selection of stories?

If you find stories on the same topic on two or more front pages, determine if they are written differently for different audiences. Are there any attempts to localize national stories? Suggest any possibilities you can think of.

On the basis of what you've learned in this chapter, do you agree or disagree with the editors' news judgments? Why?

3. Go to your library and look at both a recent issue of *The New York Times* and an issue from the

same date 20 years ago. Describe the differences you find in subjects and sources of stories.

4. As a class project, visit or invite to your class the editor of your local paper and the news director of a local television station. Study their products ahead of time, and then interview them about how they decide the value of news stories, how they assess the reliability of sources and how they try to ensure accuracy.

5. Choose a story topic. Now think about framing a story on that topic. How many possible frames can you imagine? What would a public journalism frame look like?

6. Take a cruise on the information superhighway. Sample some of the sources you find. Describe briefly at least five sources of information you can use as a journalist and at least five sources of news you can use as a consumer.

The Changing News Business

I n Tampa, Fla., *The Tampa Tribune* shares a news room with WFLA, a television station, and Tampa Bay Online, a Web portal. Why? Writes Gil Thelen, publisher of the *Tribune*, "Our purpose is to serve the changing needs of readers and viewers. They are ahead of us in using a combination of print, broadcast and the Internet during the day. Our rationale: Be there with news and information whenever and however our customers need and want us to be."

Adds Thelen: "For breaking news, we aim to 'publish' on the first available platform, usually television but sometimes online." A recent investigation by WFLA broke first in the *Tribune*, where the story, written by a television reporter, previewed that night's newscast and effectively teased it.

Driving the *Tribune*-WFLA-TBO collaboration is a desire by executives of Media General, the company that owns them all, to make its news operations the most effective in the Tampa market. To do so, its properties are not only sharing a news room but collaborating on news coverage. As you learned in Chapter 1, such cross-media collaboration is called *convergence,* and in the media industry it's the current rage. What's happening in Tampa is probably the most visible example of convergence yet to emerge in the United States, but it's far from the only one.

Indeed, in relatively small Lawrence, Kan., the staff of the Lawrence *Journal-World* shares a news room with staffers for the company's three Internet sites and its cable television operation (see Figure 2.1). *Journal-World* reporters make regular appearances on the local cable station, and one moderates a **blog,** or Web log discussion forum, on one of the company's online sites. Innovative publisher Dolph Simon said the company took over the city's abandoned post office building and remodeled it for the converged news operation Lawrence needs for the 21st century.

Whether convergence brings savings in staffing is not yet clear. Most insist it hasn't, but media companies still have plenty to gain from the benefits of cross-promotion. It's invaluable for a newspaper to get regular plugs on television and vice versa, and the ability to deliver the news immediately on whichever platform is best provides great opportunities.

Also driving the interest in convergence is the view of many experts that the future of the media lies in a new computer-delivered medium

In this chapter you will learn:

1. How news organizations are responding to the new technology.

2. How the various media are organized.

3. What kinds of jobs exist in those media.

4. How news is produced in each medium.

Figure 2.1
The converged news room
of the Lawrence (Kan.)
Journal-World.

capable of combining the best features of television with the best of newspapers. Many believe we are witnessing the leading edge of a major change in the media landscape. Nicholas Negroponte, founder and director of the Media Lab at Massachusetts Institute of Technology, describes the emerging **infomedium** as a home computer system capable of searching vast online databanks and displaying its results in text, audio or video form. Thus, the primary advantages of television — color, eye appeal, immediacy and low distribution costs — can be combined with the advantages of the print media — depth, interpretation and portability. Such systems depend on high-bandwidth connections to the home, and cable television and phone companies are rushing to provide just that.

Few experiments exactly like the one in Tampa can be found across the country today because current Federal Communications Commission rules limit newspaper-television cross-ownership in a single market. In Tampa, the *Tribune* and WFLA were able to merge because both were owned by Media General before the FCC rules went into effect. However, the restriction on cross-ownership hasn't dampened enthusiasm for what's happening in Tampa, and the FCC has recently voted to relax cross-ownership restrictions. Congress is balking and has the ability to block the FCC's action. If the cross-ownership rules are indeed relaxed, however, watch for a flood of Tampa-style experiments.

Common ownership isn't necessary for convergence to occur. There's no restriction on separately owned media operations combining their efforts, even to the point of co-locating their news rooms and merging their staffs.

While the end result of convergence is still uncertain, one thing is clear: The media industry is changing more rapidly than at any time in history. Newspapers, magazines, radio and broadcast television — the traditional media — face serious new challenges from Internet-based Web sites, cable television and new forms of receiving information such as **personal digital assistants** like the Palm Pilot and the BlackBerry, and **cellular telephones.** All the media owners, like Media General, are trying to figure out the best strategy for the future.

If indeed the answer is convergence, and if convergence makes sense and is here to stay, it presents a challenge for those preparing to enter the news business. How does one prepare for a career in the media industry? Is it necessary to be a **multimedia journalist** equally adept at handling a television camera and writing a magazine story? The answer, in all probability, is no. While such people will exist and will be highly valuable to the companies that employ them, most journalists will still train for work in a specific medium — newspapers, magazines, radio, television or Web sites. Even those people, however, must have some exposure to the strengths and weaknesses of both emerging media forms and the existing media. After all, convergence is all about telling a story in the best way possible — through the medium of choice and in multiple ways.

The future is difficult to predict because the existing media appear to be threatened to some degree by computer-based news and information delivery systems. Like Negroponte, many expect an eventual melding of newspapers, magazines, radio, television and news Web sites into a new information medium of the future. Whether that will happen, how fast and when is anyone's guess. That means you face a challenge as you plan your media career. Not only must you prepare for a job in one of today's media, you also must be ready to work in the media of the future. You may work in jobs that will disappear, but you may also work in jobs that have yet to be invented. Through it all, one certainty remains: Regardless of the medium, there will continue to be a demand for news practitioners who report well, write well, edit well and communicate well visually.

To illustrate the rapid transition in the media marketplace, let's look at some statistics that help us understand the changes taking place in one of the traditional media, newspapers. Consider these facts, published by the Newspaper Association of America, the newspaper industry's leading trade organization:

- The newspaper industry is shrinking. There were 1,457 daily newspapers in the United States at the end of 2002, compared with 1,745 as recently as 1980. That's 288 fewer newspapers.
- In 1970, 78 percent of the nation's adults read a newspaper daily, but by 2002 that percentage had declined to 58 percent for men and 53 percent for women. Worse, survey after survey has revealed that the biggest decline is among readers 34 and younger. That sounds an ominous note for the future; as older readers die, there is no one to replace them. Research suggests that those who fail to develop the newspaper reading habit early will not acquire it later in life.

But if the newspaper industry is dying, as some argue, it is far from dead. Consider that:

- Newspapers remain one of the most profitable industries around, helped in large part by their near-monopoly situation in most cities.
- Daily newspapers continue to capture a huge share of the U.S. advertising dollar, edging out broadcast television 18.6 percent to 17.8 percent (see Figure 2.2). And newspapers usually dominate the local news and advertising markets.

Those contradictory statistics illustrate the problem newspapers face: They are profitable for the moment but severely challenged in the long term.

Newspapers are not alone. Their traditional competitors also have serious problems. Network television, newspapers' main competitor for both advertising dollars and audience, has experienced tough financial times. The creation of more major U.S. networks (Fox, UPN and Warner Brothers) has fragmented audiences, and the proliferation and popularity of cable television programming has divided those audiences into even smaller segments. The cable channels are worrisome indeed for the broadcast industry; unlike the networks, they are ideally positioned to deliver targeted audiences to advertisers because of their focus on specific areas of information (sports, health and fitness, children, etc.). Like newspapers, network television is best able to deliver mass audiences, not the cohesive audiences that many advertisers covet. Radio does a better job of targeting specific audiences, but its impact on the media industry, as measured by its share of advertising dollars, is minuscule.

Magazines, like radio and cable television, deliver target audiences to advertisers, but they do so at a rapidly increasing cost. Like newspapers, magazines in the long term are threatened by rising production costs, and their distribution

Figure 2.2
*Media share of advertising
dollars (2003). Newspapers
edge out television as the
leading advertising medium
in the country. (Source:
McCann-Erickson Inc.,
Newspaper Association
of America)*

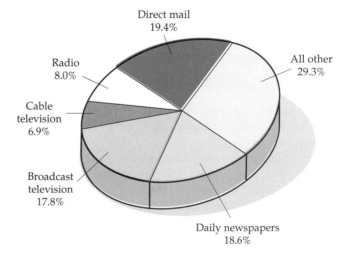

relies heavily upon ever-escalating postal rates. So no existing medium is ideally positioned for the future, and all face serious challenges. Perhaps that explains why media executives are rushing to merge and converge.

MULTIMEDIA ORGANIZATIONS

Traditional media companies are scrambling to be part of the new-media mix, as are telephone companies, the cable television industry and entertainment conglomerates. Some examples:

- Cox Enterprises Inc. (**www.coxnews.com**) began with a single newspaper in 1898. Atlanta-based Cox is one of the nation's largest media companies and, historically, has embraced new media: radio, television and cable television. In April 1996, Cox Interactive Media was formed to build Internet products in cities where Cox has significant media presence. The *Atlanta Journal-Constitution* (**www.ajc.com**) is the flagship city site (see Figure 2.3).
- Henry Luce created an empire around *Time* magazine (**www.time.com**). His successors added other successful magazines, including *Fortune* and *Sports*

Figure 2.3
The Web site of the Atlanta Journal-Constitution *also serves as Atlanta's flagship site.*

New-Media Conglomerate

Typical of the new-media conglomerate is Walt Disney Co., which gobbled up Capital Cities/ABC, now ABC Inc. The media giant now owns:

- Walt Disney Studios.
- Walt Disney amusement parks.
- The ABC television network.
- Several local radio and television stations.
- ABC Distribution, a company that distributes ABC programming worldwide.
- ESPN and its magazine.
- Buena Vista Home Video, Buena Vista Television, Buena Vista Pictures Distribution and Buena Vista International.
- The Disney Store Inc.
- The Disney Channel.
- Partial interest in several other cable television channels, including Arts & Entertainment and Lifetime.
- Partial interest in several European television channels.
- Fidelity Television.
- A multimedia group that is exploring all sorts of new ventures.
- Specialized publications, including the largest business publishing group in Mexico; Chilton Enterprises, which focuses on specialized publications for various industries; and *Los Angeles*, a city magazine.
- Fairchild Publications, publisher of *W*.
- Capital Cities Capital, a unit that exchanges advertising time and space for equity interest in growing companies.

Illustrated. Now the magazine division is a small part of a colossal media company, Time Warner (**www.timewarner.com/corp**), with entertainment, book publishing, magazine and cable television interests. It includes such diverse elements as Cable News Network (**www.cnn.com**), Warner Brothers (**www.timewarner.com**) and the Atlanta Braves baseball team. More recently, it merged with America Online (**www.aol.com**) in the largest media merger in history. That merger illustrates vividly the melding of the traditional media with newer ones. However, the merger proved shortsighted, and AOL was losing so much money the company removed "AOL" from its official name.

- Knight Ridder (**www.kri.com**), one of the United States' most respected media companies, has long seen the value of electronic delivery. It experimented in the 1940s with early versions of faxed news delivery, in the 1970s with TV-based text delivery and in the 1990s with a computerized newspaper delivered by electronic tablet, a slim but advanced version of a personal computer. You can find all of Knight Ridder's newspapers online on the Real Cities Network (**www.realcities.com**), and its *San Jose* (Calif.) *Mercury News* pioneered Internet-based news delivery with its Mercury Center (**www.mercurycenter.com**).
- Other great newspaper companies, including the New York Times Co. (**www.nytimes.com**) and the Tribune Co., publisher of the *Chicago Tribune* (**www.tribune.com**), have made major commitments to Internet-based news delivery. The *Tribune*'s reporters regularly make appearances as re-

porters on the company's television station, and it has been a leader in producing news-based CD-ROMs.

- Even small newspaper companies have entered the fray, as the *Lawrence Journal-World* (**www.ljworld.com**) convergence experiment shows. The *Journal-World*'s Web sites were early users of "push" technology, which sends information to a user based on predefined interests.
- Television companies haven't been left out of the mix, either. NBC (**home.nbci.com**) has one of the most ambitious sites on the Internet, and it has joint broadcast and Web ventures with computer giant Microsoft Corp. (**www.msnbc.com/news/default.asp**). CBS, ESPN, Fox and CNN, among others, also have major sites on the Internet.

The entry of companies such as Microsoft into the media business alarmed those who have traditionally earned their living in that sector. Many questioned whether a company such as Microsoft, with its reputation for ruthlessly working to improve the bottom line, was capable of adhering to the high standards set by media ethicists for the conduct of news operations. Yet from the moment Microsoft introduced its news-heavy Microsoft Network (**www.msn.com**), it recruited heavily from newspapers and broadcast stations, and the company's record in setting high standards for its media operations has been commendable (see Figure 2.4).

Figure 2.4
MSNBC.com represents a joint venture between NBC and Microsoft Corp.

Companies such as Microsoft simply do not enter a business unless the potential for profits is substantial. Clearly, Microsoft, Time Warner and MIT's Negroponte share a vision of the future — a melding of entertainment and news media into a new infomedium capable of delivering a choice of text- or video-based news, information and first-run movies on demand. That vision was the basis for the hectic buying and selling of media properties that occurred throughout much of the 1990s and the massive media mergers made possible by deregulation that took place after passage of the Telecommunications Act of 1996. The media landscape is changing dramatically as corporations try to position themselves for a role in the media marketplace of the future. And while no one knows the exact form the medium of the future will take, or how it will be delivered, everyone wants a piece of the action. The potential market is huge.

Included in the media mix are the computer-based **public information utilities,** which include America Online, The Microsoft Network, CompuServe and others. They offer both Internet access and lots of original and repackaged information, including news. Increasingly, they are filled with advertising. Even the Internet, once an arcane network of computers understood by only a few academicians and computer scientists, is increasingly becoming a carrier for commercial advertising targeted to specific audience segments. The World Wide Web, introduced in 1994, has transformed the Internet into an important news medium, although one that still draws only 2.1 percent of total U.S. advertising dollars.

Now, here's an observation that few newspeople like to hear: Advertising, not news, drives the media marketplace. To understand shifts in the media industry, follow the advertising dollar. Trends show more and more of the advertising dollar flowing into nontraditional media — direct mail, cable television and the Internet — and away from traditional media such as television and newspapers. So far, that shift is slight, but advertising experts expect it to accelerate as the search continues for the best way to target coveted audiences. While there is no clear picture of where the industry is headed, one certainty is that the next few years will bring accelerating change to the media mix.

As that media mix changes, so does the definition of news. As we learned in Chapter 1, traditional definitions of news don't work as well as they once did. Moreover, the definition of news is changing in ways that many news practitioners never imagined. The proliferation of electronic information services and e-mail has enabled people throughout the world to meet online. There they share their knowledge and report the latest developments about thousands of topics. Some of the most heavily traveled parts of the Internet are online forums, such as blogs, and bulletin boards where those exchanges take place. Users get information on topics about which they are keenly interested. To them, that information is every bit as much "news" as the information provided by the mass media.

That raises the question of whether we are entering an era in which the agenda-setting role of the media will diminish. Traditionally, the media have decided what the public needs to know about a given event. Further, the media have set the public agenda by ranking the relative importance of those items —

Using Newswriting Skills in Corporate Communications

As a journalism student in college, Kabby Hong didn't think he wanted the daily deadline pressures demanded of newspaper writers. As a result, he majored in magazine journalism.

Nevertheless, even as a magazine major, he was required to take courses in newswriting, reporting and news editing before he could take courses in magazine writing and editing.

Between his junior and senior years, Kabby was searching for a summer internship because his advisers had told him that nothing looked better on a journalism graduate's résumé. A couple of AT&T recruiters stopped at his school, and Kabby scheduled an interview. He won the internship, liked working in corporate communications and was hired by AT&T for what he considered a good salary as soon as he graduated.

At AT&T Network Systems in Morristown, N.J., Kabby is a writer for the internal newsletter and magazine.

Like thousands of his colleagues in corporate communications, Kabby finds that his news courses served him well. "There is an immediacy to the issues and events that we cover even within a corporation such as AT&T that demands someone who can take complicated information and tell readers what they need to know quickly.

"Newswriting skills do not just serve the 'news rooms' of major metropolitan newspapers," Kabby says. "They are essential to the success of any organization that thrives on information and the ability of its communicators to get that information out quickly, accurately and concisely."

by headline size and placement or by placement in the broadcast. In addition, by serving as gatekeepers to information, the media have helped to decide which news events get exposure at all. With the advent of online media, all that is changing. Increasingly, the public will have the ability to sort through massive amounts of information and commentary and decide for itself what is important and trustworthy and what is not. Unlike newspapers, television and magazines, online media have nearly unlimited space to carry information. Thus, the role of media practitioners as gatekeepers is diminishing.

Those changes will require an adjustment in the role of the journalist. How that adjustment will affect our society is far from clear. Many futurists believe the media will continue to play an important role in agenda-setting if not in gatekeeping. Journalists will have to help people sort through the mass of information and tell consumers what is important. Few will have the time to do that for themselves.

There will be plenty of jobs for journalists. After all, someone must still gather the news and organize it into a useful, easily consumable package. But the media services of the future will require of the journalist a broader range of knowledge — and perhaps skills. While some journalists, just as now, may be able to focus on writing, they will have to display a richer appreciation of how photos, charts, graphs and maps — and even audio and full-motion video — can complement their articles. That's because the journalist of the future will have to be literate in all forms of communication, visual as well as verbal. Many news organizations already are preaching that reality as they attempt to get reporters to think more visually and photographers and videographers to think more verbally. To provide those skills, journalism and communications schools are revamping their curricula to make it easier for students to get the necessary exposure to all media forms. Yet despite that shift, most young journalists in the next few years will enter the industry in more traditional positions.

So here's the challenge as you plan your media career: Not only must you prepare for a job in one of today's media, you also must prepare for a period of wrenching change. But while change presents problems, it also brings hope. You have a chance to participate in a media transition that is sure to open many doors of opportunity.

NEWSPAPERS

The popular misconception that newspapers are dying contradicts reality. As measured by the U.S. government, newspapers continue to rank among the leading manufacturing industries in total employment. While the industry appears to be shrinking, it is far from dead, as the existence of almost 1,500 dailies and 8,200 weeklies will attest.

Those newspapers appeal to diverse audiences. In the New York area alone, one finds not only *The New York Times*, the *New York Post*, the New York *Daily News* and *Newsday* but also dailies for many minority groups, such as the *Amsterdam News*, *El Diario* and the *Jewish Daily Forward*. For various other audiences, there are *The Wall Street Journal*, the *American Banker* and *Variety*. That diversity is mirrored elsewhere on a smaller scale.

Newspaper Organization

Because of the industry's size, it is difficult to generalize about the internal organization of newspapers. Figures 2.5, 2.6 and 2.7 show typical organizations of small, medium and metropolitan newspaper news rooms. The titles of editors found on those charts are typical, but, increasingly, organizational patterns are changing. Today's newspaper editors seek to improve ways of presenting the news, and they are reorganizing news rooms to do it. Forces driving that

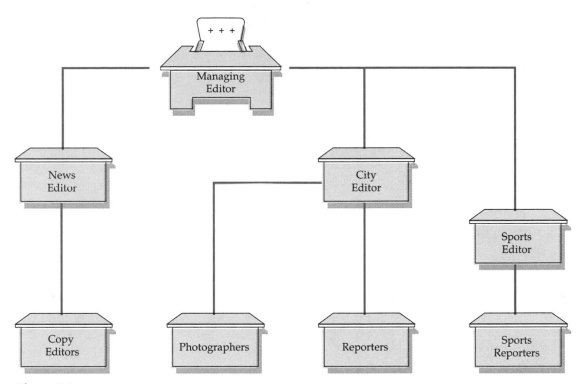

Figure 2.5
Typical news room organization of a small daily newspaper.

reorganization are an increased emphasis on graphic design and an increased emphasis on newspaper Web sites.

In the past, it was common for a reporter to finish a story before photographers or graphic designers were brought in to illustrate the piece. When that occurred, too often it was too late for the visual experts to do their best work. On major stories today, teams of reporters, photographers, graphic designers and editors are assigned from the outset. As a result, the best way to present various parts of the story is determined in a team setting. The team leader is sometimes called a **maestro,** someone who leads a reporting team just as a conductor leads an orchestra in the quest for the best possible result.

Some newspapers have taken the team concept beyond the realm of major stories and have reorganized their news rooms to make teams the basic organizational unit (see Figure 2.8). Typical is the *Star Tribune*, newspaper of the Twin Cities, based in Minneapolis. There, each reporter, writer, editor, photographer and graphic artist is part of a team responsible for specific coverage areas. In some ways those coverage areas are akin to the beats still found in most newspapers, but they are broader and reflect the newspaper's desire to expand types of content previously ignored or given short shrift.

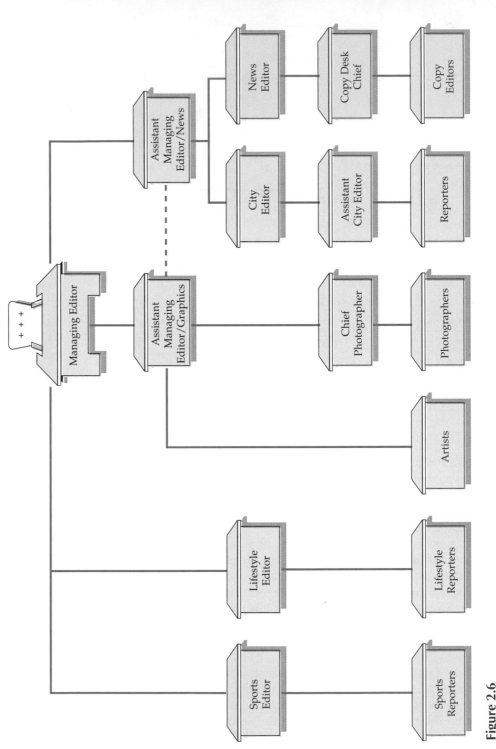

Figure 2.6
Typical news room organization of a medium-sized daily newspaper.

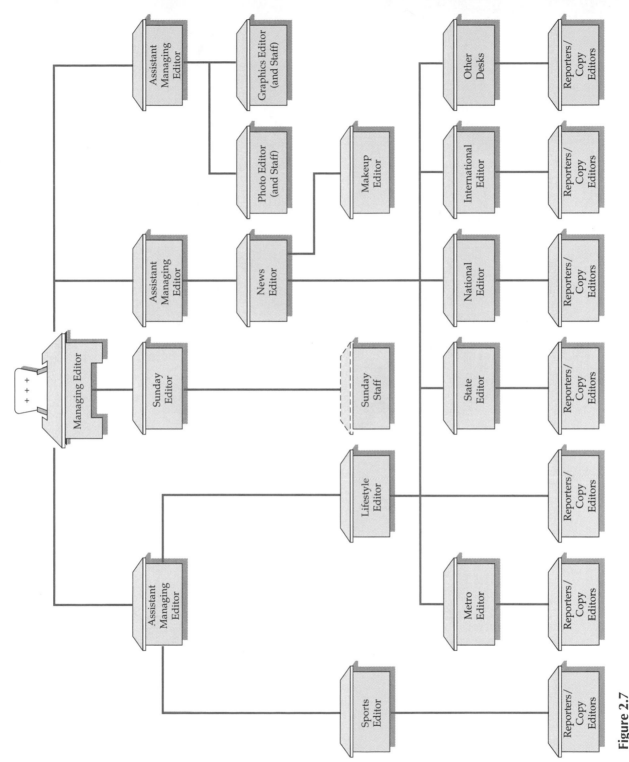

Figure 2.7
Typical news room organization of a metropolitan daily newspaper.

How decisions are made using the team concept

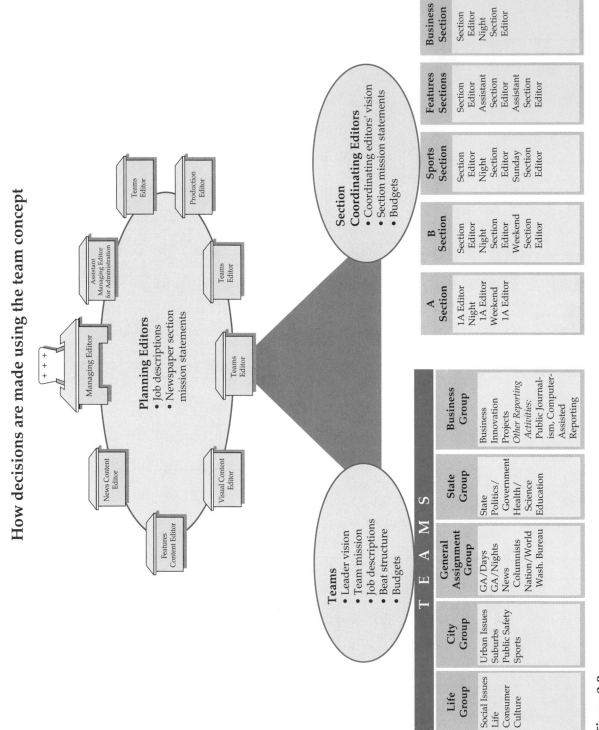

Figure 2.8
Team organizational pattern for news rooms. (Based on a model provided by the Star Tribune, Minneapolis)

Newspapers' Web sites often break news before it appears in the newspaper. In other cases they supplement and expand on what appears in print editions. Web sites, after all, have almost unlimited space.

Newspaper Production

Once you've landed that first job, ask for a thorough tour of the newspaper. The **editorial department** is just one of several departments that must work in close coordination if the newspaper is to be successful. If the **advertising department** fails to sell enough advertising, the space for news, or news hole, is small, and your department's ability to provide a comprehensive news report is adversely affected. If your department misses its deadlines, the **production** and **circulation departments** could spend thousands of dollars in overtime pay, and subscribers may not receive their newspapers on time. It's important to learn how you and your department fit into the big picture. To do so, you must fully understand the role of the other departments — advertising, business, circulation, production and perhaps others (see Figure 2.9). A newspaper is a product, and you must learn the role of each department in producing it.

Working with the Editor

Once the editorial package is prepared, editors polish it for publication. At first glance, the flow of copy through an editorial department seems simple enough (see Figure 2.10). You write your story and transfer it to the city desk queue, the electronic equivalent of an in-basket. There the city editor reads it and makes necessary changes. Then it is sent electronically to the copy desk, where it is edited again. The story is assigned a position in the newspaper, and a copy editor writes a headline. Finally, an editor sends the story or page to a typesetting machine in the composing room. This simple copy flow pattern exists at most newspapers, whether the newspaper uses computers and automated page design or still does things the old-fashioned way with pasteup of pages by hand. Indeed, electronic copy flow patterns in most cases merely duplicate the pre-computer copy flow patterns of newspapers. Despite the seeming simplicity of the pattern, decisions made along the way can make the process much more complicated than it appears.

When the city editor receives your copy, that editor must read it and make initial decisions: Is information missing? Does the story need to be developed? Does it need more background? Are there enough quotes? Are the quotes worth using? Does the lead, or opening, need to be polished? Have you chosen the right lead, or should another angle be emphasized? Is the story important? Is it useful, interesting or entertaining? Is there, in fact, some reason for publishing it? If it is important, should the managing editor and the news editor be alerted that a potential Page One story is forthcoming? Each time a city editor reads a story for the first time, these questions and more come up. The city editor is expected to answer them quickly; there is no time for delay in the fast-paced world of daily newspaper work.

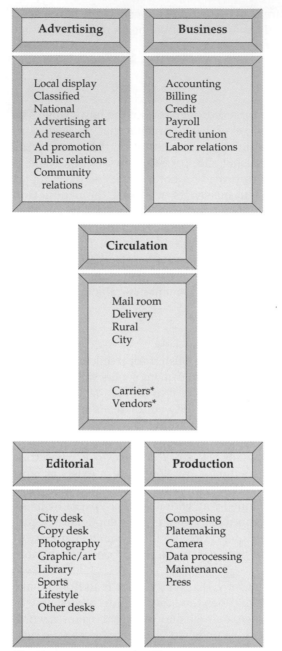

Figure 2.9
*Major departments of a
typical newspaper and
their subsections.*

*Outside contractors not employed by newspaper.

INDIVIDUAL	ACTION
Reporter	Gathers facts, writes story, verifies its accuracy, forwards to city editor.
City Editor*	Edits story, returns to reporter for changes or additional detail (if necessary), forwards story to news editor.
News Editor*	Decides on placement of story in newspaper, forwards story to copy desk chief for implementation of instructions.
Copy Desk Chief	Prepares page dummy that determines story's length, setting and headline size, forwards to copy editor. At some large newspapers, a separate design desk may play this role.
Copy Editor	Polishes writing of story, checks for missing or inaccurate detail, writes headline, returns to copy desk chief for final check.
Copy Desk Chief	Verifies that story is trimmed as necessary and that correct headline is written, transmits story to typesetting machine.

* Or assistant
Note: At any point in the process, a story may be returned to an earlier editor for clarification, amplification or rewriting.

Figure 2.10
Typical news room copy flow pattern.

After making those initial decisions, the city editor confers with you and gives direction on changes to be made. If the changes are minor ones, simply rewriting a section of the story or inserting additional information will suffice. If the changes are more substantial, involving additional interviews with sources or major rewriting, your job is more difficult.

When those changes are made, you resubmit your story to the city editor, who reads the revised version and edits it more carefully. Your work may be finished after you answer a few remaining minor questions. Or, if the city editor is still unhappy with it, another rewrite may be ordered.

You can expect frustration. Often an assistant city editor reads your story first and gives instructions on how it is to be revised. When your rewrite is submitted, the city editor or another assistant may do the editing, creating the need for more changes and yet another rewrite. This can be discouraging, but such a system has its merits. Generally, a story is improved when more than one editor handles it. Each sees gaps to be filled, and a better story results.

Working with the Copy Editor

The copy editor asks many of the same questions about your story that the city editor asks. Have you selected the right lead? Does the writing need to be polished? Have you chosen the correct words? Primarily, though, the copy editor checks for misspelled words, adherence to style, grammatical errors, ambiguities and errors of fact. The copy editor reworks a phrase here or there to clarify your meaning but is expected to avoid major changes. If major changes are necessary, the copy editor calls that to the attention of the news editor. If the news editor agrees, the story is returned to the city editor, and perhaps to you, for yet another revision.

When the copy editor is satisfied with the story, work begins on the headline. The size of the headline ordered by the copy desk chief determines how many characters or letters can be used in writing it. Headline writing is an art. Those who are able to convey the meaning of a story in a limited number of words are valuable members of the staff. The quality of the copy editor's work can have a significant impact on the number of readers who will be attracted to your story. If the headline is dull and lifeless, few will be; if it sparkles, the story's exposure will be increased.

The copy editor also may write the **cutline,** or caption, that accompanies the picture. At some newspapers, however, this is done by the photographer, by the reporter or at the city desk. Large newspapers may have a photo desk to handle cutlines as well as picture cropping and sizing.

When finished, the copy editor transfers the story to the copy desk chief, who must approve the headline and may check the editing changes made by the copy editor. When the desk chief is satisfied, the story and headline are transferred to the design desk or to the composing room, where the creative effort of writers and editors is transformed into type.

The size of the newspaper may alter this copy flow pattern substantially. At a small newspaper the jobs of news editor, copy desk chief and copy editor may be performed by one person. Some small dailies require the city editor or an assistant to perform all the tasks normally handled by the copy desk.

News room copy flow patterns have been designed with redundancy in mind. Built into the system is the goal of having not one editor, but several, check your work. Through repeated checking, editors hope to detect more errors — in fact and in writing style — to make the finished product a better one.

In this sense editors work as gatekeepers. They determine whether your work measures up to their standards. Only when it does is the gate opened, which allows your story to take the next step in the newspaper production process.

Jobs abound at newspapers for those who would edit as well as for those who would do reporting.

MAGAZINES AND CORPORATE COMMUNICATIONS

The magazine industry is vast, and generalizations about magazine publishers are difficult to make. Publishers range from conglomerates such as Time Warner, whose mass-audience magazines include *Time*, *People* and *Sports Illustrated*, to companies as diverse as Monsanto and Hewlett-Packard, which publish magazines written and designed for employees or customers or both. Many are also published by not-for-profit organizations like the Girl Scouts and trade associations.

Most magazines, even those that are commercially published, do not target mass audiences, as *Time* does, but instead target smaller audiences with a passion for the subject matter. Those include such titles as *Popular Mechanics*, *Boating*, *PC Magazine* and *Skiing*. Even more prevalent are company magazines, which usually are written and edited by corporate communications departments or public-relations staffs. Smaller magazines, those published by corporations or nonprofit organizations, are often put together by tiny staffs. Editors often write the stories, design the pages and even arrange for printing by outside vendors.

Magazine Organization

Magazines are organized much like newspapers, their print cousins. Among the various departments, only the circulation department will differ much from that of newspapers. That's because the method of distribution is dramatically different. Most magazines depend heavily on the mail and on newsstand sales for distribution; daily newspapers, in contrast, are distributed primarily by carriers. For most newspapers, mail service and newsstand sales are secondary.

In magazine and newspaper news rooms, most of the titles and job functions are the same. Still, a few titles are unique to the magazine industry. Major magazines are likely to have **senior editors** and **senior writers.** Senior editors usually edit a particular section of the magazine. At *Time*, senior editors direct the International, Arts and other sections. Senior writers, as the name implies, are the magazine's best and most experienced writers. At *Time*, they may seldom leave the office but instead take information from numerous reporters in the field and meld their reports into a well-written, coherent story.

Some magazines also have **contributing editors.** Typically, these are columnists or reporters whose work is purchased for publication. They are not employed by the magazine, and sometimes their work appears in several industry-related magazines each month.

Magazine Production

To those used to the fast-paced world of daily newspapers, the magazine production cycle looks terribly appealing from a distance. But looks can be deceiving. The deadline pressures that face magazine writers and editors are just as intense; they are merely spread over longer time periods. Still, magazine writers and editors have more time to produce their work, and as a result there is more pressure to produce a near-perfect product.

The tight deadlines of newspapers often result in less-than-perfect writing, typographical errors and similar gaffes. Those mistakes are not tolerated at the best magazines, where longer deadlines mean there is more time to strive for perfection. Additional time also allows magazine editors to expend more effort on fact-checking and polishing of writing and design.

Magazine editors also spend much more time on writing to fit. Articles often are meticulously edited to fill an exact number of typeset lines in a magazine layout. Similarly, photo captions are fine-tuned so that all lines are completely filled. Such niceties often are dismissed at newspapers, where time is more precious. The result is that most magazines have a more polished look than newspapers. That's true not only because they are printed on higher-quality paper but also because they are more meticulously edited. Unfortunately, at low-budget magazines those conditions may not exist.

Vast numbers of jobs exist for those who would work in corporate communications and public relations. The skills necessary to succeed in those jobs are the same as those needed at magazines and newspapers: the ability to write and edit well. Almost inevitably, editing a magazine will be among the jobs of the corporate communications employee.

NEWSLETTERS

One of the fastest-growing areas of journalism is the newsletter industry. Newsletters are thriving and have an economic impact in the billions of dollars. Jobs for journalism graduates abound. Oxbridge Communications publishes a newsletter directory that lists more than 21,000 newsletters of all types, including subscription newsletters. *Hudson's Subscription Newsletter Directory* lists more than 5,000 newsletters that charge subscription fees.

Those who enter this business enjoy the opportunity to write to highly targeted audiences about topics with which they can become intimately familiar. That's because newsletters typically provide more detail and analysis than the mainstream media.

Newsletter Organization

Most newsletters are small operations with a handful of employees. Sometimes they are even one-person operations. Still, a few of them have larger organizations. Newsletter journalists are able to develop a high degree of expertise in the subjects they cover, and as a result turnover is low. Those who write for newsletters enjoy working in that environment.

Too often, those who graduate from schools and departments of journalism fail to consider the many jobs at newsletters and in other sectors of what is known as "B2B," or the business-to-business press. Thousands of such jobs exist.

American Business Media, founded in 1907, is the nonprofit global association for business-to-business information providers, including providers of magazines, Web site content and service providers, trade shows, newsletters, databases and custom publishers. ABM members also stage conventions, conferences, seminars and similar events that build on the print medium. ABM member companies reach an audience of more than 47 million professionals and generate more than $16 billion in annual revenues. The skills of a journalist are needed in many of the jobs in this often-overlooked industry (see Figure 2.11).

Newsletter Production

Most newsletters are weeklies or monthlies, so the production schedule and techniques parallel those of magazines. Mail is the primary distribution medium.

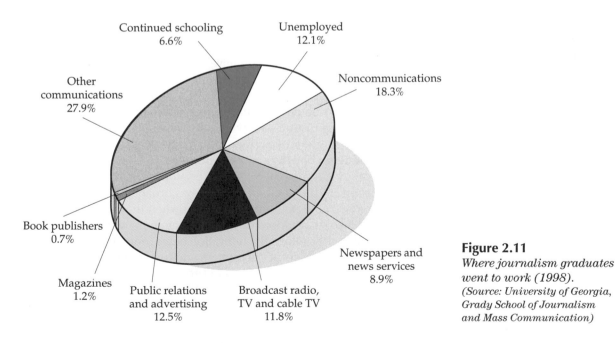

Figure 2.11
Where journalism graduates went to work (1998).
(Source: University of Georgia, Grady School of Journalism and Mass Communication)

BROADCASTING

Broadcast stations play a major role in the way the public receives its news. Increasingly, so do cable television channels like CNN, Fox News and C-SPAN, which we include in this section despite the fact that their programming is not really "broadcast." Radio, once a major player in news distribution, now is relegated to a second tier of service except for a few all-news stations in major cities and National Public Radio. Radio is used as a news medium primarily by those driving to and from work, and little of its reporting is original. Most radio news operations rely heavily on wire services for their news. Still, radio commands plenty of attention, and it attracts 8 percent of all U.S. advertising dollars.

Broadcast News Organization

The top news executive at a local television station typically is the **news director** or, at some group-owned stations, the *vice president for news*. The news director is responsible for managing news room personnel and resources and for setting news room policies. Often, the news director does not deal with details of daily news coverage. Instead, that responsibility is delegated to an *assistant news director* or *managing editor*.

"Nowhere is the impact of the new media on the old more visible than in television broadcasting. Over-the-air television is under siege these days, largely because its audiences (and its revenues) are being increasingly preempted by cable television and home videocassette recorders."

— Wilson Dizard Jr.,
Old Media, New Media

The other key management role in a television news room is that of **executive producer.** The producer determines the overall look of the station's newscasts. This includes the use of video, graphics and animation; the length and placement of stories; whether a reporter or an anchor is seen delivering the story; and how upcoming stories are "teased" going into a commercial break. Most stations also hire **show producers,** who report to the executive producer and are responsible for individual newscasts.

Producing requires an ability to see the big picture under the extreme pressure of broadcast deadlines. It is a high-stress, high-turnover job. It also is the position most in demand in local television news.

Television news, of course, requires reporters. In addition to gathering and writing the news, broadcast reporters must know how to present it in a lively and personable fashion. To be successful in large markets or at the network level, reporters must have a distinctive style and personality. In fact, **network correspondents** often do little original reporting themselves, leaving the news-gathering to **field producers** or **off-camera reporters.**

Anchors also are critical to a successful television news operation. In important ways they represent the persona of the news broadcast. Viewers know and have strong opinions about news anchors, even when they can't remember the call letters or channel of the station for which the anchors work.

Videographers play a key role in the television news room as well. TV news lives and dies by pictures. Creative videographers add to the look that often separates the top station in a market from its competitors.

In larger markets, **desk assistants** serve at the entry-level position in the television news room. They keep watch on material from the wire services, make routine beat calls, monitor fire and police scanners, and take in satellite feeds from networks or regional cooperatives.

Broadcast News Production

Viewers use television news in a fundamentally different way than they do newspapers or magazines. The audience expects and demands immediacy, so local stations program several newscasts a day and put a premium on live reporting of newsworthy events.

The frequent deadlines of broadcast news force reporters, videographers and producers to think quickly on their feet, to boil down a story to its most easily understood elements and to get on to the next assignment as quickly as possible. Broadcast journalists often find themselves "working without a net," making split-second decisions without the benefit of editors or time for reflection.

Broadcast reports are almost always team efforts. A reporter on assignment is accompanied by a videographer. Together, they collect the material that will form the basis of the report. When they finish collecting the material, they return to the station to edit it into the final form that will appear on the air. Or they edit their report in a mobile van capable of transmitting it back to the station by satellite or microwave. Editors and producers weave their material and that of other broadcast teams into the newscasts with which all are familiar.

By necessity, broadcast news focuses more on process than on completeness. While radio and television journalism are capable of great depth, analysis and perspective, those qualities are more often demanded of newspapers and magazines. (For more on broadcast news, see Chapter 19.)

ONLINE MEDIA

Today, people consume news and other forms of information in unconventional ways, and most of them involve the personal computer. Still newer information services are delivered through cell phones and personal digital assistants such as the Palm Pilot.

Among the new-media services are the public information utilities — CompuServe, America Online, The Microsoft Network and others. All PIUs carry news and other forms of information, including stories from the Associated Press and other wire services. They also provide Internet access, and their sites serve as their users' gateways to the Internet. America is tuning in. News consumers can get the news as soon as it happens; they don't have to wait for the newspaper to arrive. Nor must they wait for the nightly newscast. The public information utilities offer news on demand, 24 hours a day.

The Internet in the 1990s quickly earned a place as the most important new medium since television after the World Wide Web, an easy-to-use interface, was rolled out in 1994. Almost every daily newspaper, most major magazines, all the

Persistence Pays Off

April Eaton began her career by serving internships at *The Washington Post* and at CBS News in the Atlanta bureau. Then she served as a news room assistant at *USA Today*.

That was in 1986. "I then decided to deviate from what was slowly mounting to a newspaper career," she says.

I wanted to work in television news — not print. A contact at CBS News in New York told me either to plug away and send résumé tapes to tiny TV markets that won't pay me much, but teach me a lot . . . *or* go back to school and get my master of arts degree.

She chose the latter and after graduation worked as a general assignment reporter and fill-in anchor for three and a half years at WLOS-TV in Asheville, N.C. Now she's an education reporter at NewsChannel 5 in Nashville, Tenn.

"I'm having a ball. It's often said this fast-paced, hectic business that's riddled with deadlines is one that will burn out a person. It can happen to some reporters, but I'm not feeling it yet. Good pacing, I guess."

Eaton has a few words for "reporters-in-the-making":

1. If you really want to be in the news business, keep at it. Don't let the "there-are-no-jobs" comments slow you down.
2. Constantly work to improve your writing.
3. It's OK to know you do good work; just don't let your head get so huge you can't make it through the news room door.
4. Remember, someone helped you get to where you are, so reach back and help others.

television networks and many individual stations now have significant sites on the Web. Some include almost all the material contained in their traditional services; others tease or supplement their traditional media.

Adding legitimacy to the Web as a source for news is the presence of such major newspaper companies as the New York Times Co. and the Tribune Co. and the presence of television networks such as NBC and ABC.

Many media observers see the Web as the precursor to the infomedium of the future envisioned by MIT's Negroponte and others. Indeed, it now appears that as the Internet's bandwidth increases to permit the delivery of full-motion video, an entirely new medium is emerging.

Online Media Organization

It is a mistake to consider online media simply a new way to transmit wire service news. Each of the services maintains a news room, where at least some original material is created. Further, each buys freelance material and repackages other forms of information such as airline schedules, restaurant reviews and stock market quotations. Most allow users to download full-color pictures and sound clips.

Without a doubt, the most popular function of these media is to serve as public bulletin boards, where users with a passion for a particular topic can exchange ideas and information. Interested in tracing your ancestry? You can get plenty of help from those who share that passion on bulletin boards or newsgroups pegged to that interest. Want to know more about the latest Apple computers than was printed in your local newspaper? Go online where you'll find detailed information posted by the company, the full text of its news releases, complete technical specifications and discussion forums centered on the pros and cons of the new models. Exchanges in such forums range from irrational "flames," emotion-laden messages with little evidence of forethought or civility, to eloquent treatises on the virtues of multitasking computer operating systems.

To be sure, the news sources found on the Internet are far from being traditional media. Indeed, they are so diverse and operate so differently from other media that it is almost impossible to create a typical organization chart. But the products they produce contain plenty of news, and computer users see them as ideal sources for the news they want. Now that an estimated 75 percent of American homes have computers connected to the Internet, with the percentage climbing monthly, journalists cannot afford to dismiss computer-based news delivery as insignificant.

Also in this category are the various wire services and electronic information services. For years, the Associated Press, United Press International, Reuters and others have been viewed mainly as wholesalers of information to newspapers and broadcast stations. Through online services, their products are now going directly to consumers. More focused offspring such as the various Dow Jones online services and Bloomberg Business News (see Figure 2.12) are expanding rapidly. All of them represent new ways of delivering news into the home through the computer.

Online Media Production

Few newcomers are hired as reporters for the online media; instead, journalists are hired as online editors. That's because so far the strength of the new media lies not in the creation of new content but in the repackaging of content gathered for related traditional media. That difference also helps one understand how online media news rooms are organized. They are, in many ways, like one huge copy desk employing editors with multiple talents — computer skills, word skills and visual skills. Think of those editors as multimedia journalists.

Although that view of online media news rooms remains generally true, it is starting to change. More and more publications realize that original content is needed on online sites. As a result, some original reporting is starting to appear there. While there are still relatively few reporting jobs in the online media,

Figure 2.12
*Bloomberg.com is among
the industry's leaders for
delivering business news
online.*

some companies are pioneering the concept in recognition of the fact that this
new medium offers many possibilities other than the repackaging of old content.
As these experiments yield success, watch for others to follow. In the years
ahead, there almost certainly will be many more jobs for reporters in the online
media.

For the moment, though, most online media news rooms are filled with editors with titles not unlike those found at newspapers or broadcast stations. Editors, often called Web producers, take responsibility for certain sections of the
online service: news, sports, features and others. Content is gathered from both
traditional and nontraditional sources. Graphic displays are designed for maximum appeal on computer screens. Immediacy is paramount.

Unlike editors at a newspaper or magazine, online media editors must have
skills that more closely resemble those of the broadcast journalist. It's not good
enough to be a word editor for the online media; one must also have a good sense
of visual design. That's because the online media, like television, depend on
attractive screen presentation for impact. Journalists who work in the online
media must be competent in writing, editing and design. Increasingly, they also
will need audio and video skills; most of the online media are moving to incorporate audio and video clips into their services.

Like wire-service journalists, online journalists are constantly on deadline. Twenty-four hours a day, users log on to get the latest news and information. Thus, producing news for the online media requires journalists who thrive on deadline pressure, who have strong computer skills, who understand both written and visual communication and who are interested in pioneering a new medium. Those who can meet these requirements should have little trouble finding jobs.

OTHER CAREER OPPORTUNITIES

Journalism training is in many ways ideal training for almost any profession. The skills of writing, editing and visual communication are in great demand worldwide. The broad applications of journalism training account for the large number of journalism graduates who find themselves in jobs quite different from those they imagined.

In this chapter, we outlined the most common routes for those with journalism training to find jobs as reporters and writers of news. But there are many others, including public relations, corporate communications, advertising, ethnic newspapers, professional periodicals, union and trade publications and virtually any areas that require the skills of writing, editing or visual communication. Nationwide, the most popular majors among journalism and mass communication students are advertising and public relations. Many who receive degrees in news-editorial programs end up in other jobs, including public relations, corporate communications and online media. More than one journalism graduate has parlayed an interest in computers and journalism into a job as a newspaper systems manager. Others have found jobs training journalists to use new computer systems; vendors have learned that an understanding of how journalists work speeds the training process.

Others have gone into publications work for nonprofit organizations such as the Girl Scouts and the American Heart Association. Still others who started at newspapers have moved to television or vice versa. Because journalism and mass communications accrediting standards emphasize the importance of a broad liberal arts education, students often get the ideal mix of practical training and the ability to think. That, more than any specific skill, is the mark of a well-trained journalist.

Suggested Readings

Daly, Charles P., Henry, Patrick and Ryder, Ellyn. *The Magazine Publishing Industry*. Needham Heights, Mass.: Allyn & Bacon, 1996. A good insider's view of the magazine industry.

Dizard, Wilson, Jr. *Old Media, New Media: Mass Communications in the Information Age*. New York: Longman, 1999. A good overview of the developing media landscape.

Fink, Conrad C. *Strategic Newspaper Management*. Needham Heights, Mass.: Allyn & Bacon, 1996. The best available book on newspaper management and organization.

Martin, Chuck. *Net Future*. New York: McGraw-Hill, 1999. An excellent overview of the business of the Internet and its impact on society.

Negroponte, Nicholas P. *Being Digital*. New York: Knopf, 1996. A view of the changing media landscape by one of the industry's most prominent observers.

Picard, Robert G. and Brody, Jeffrey H. *The Newspaper Publishing Industry*. Needham Heights, Mass.: Allyn & Bacon, 1996. A good overview of the newspaper industry.

Suggested Web Sites

www.americanbusinessmedia.com
American Business Media is the trade association for the business-to-business press.

www.aol.com
America Online is the Internet service provider for millions around the world.

www.magazine.org
The professional organization for magazine journalists is the Magazine Publishers of America.

www.mediainfo.com
This site, maintained by *Editor & Publisher* magazine, provides links to many newspapers throughout North America and the rest of the world.

www.naa.org
The Newspaper Association of America, based in Reston, Va., is the newspaper industry's leading trade association.

www.nab.org
The National Association of Broadcasters is the primary trade organization of the broadcast industry.

www.newsletters.org
The Newsletter & Electronic Publishers Association is the trade organization of newsletter publishers.

www.nna.org
The National Newspaper Association represents smaller newspapers in the United States.

www.spj.org
The Society of Professional Journalists is the primary membership organization for working journalists, regardless of medium.

Exercises

1. Visit either your school newspaper or the local daily or weekly newspaper. Talk with staff members about how the staff is organized. Once you understand the system, draw an organization chart for the news department.

2. Draw a copy flow chart that shows how copy moves from reporters to the production department at the newspaper you chose for exercise 1.

3. Visit a local television station and interview the news director about how the news room is organized. Produce an organization chart that explains the operation.

4. Using the Web or one of the public information utilities, locate information on the most recent U.S. census and report the following:

   a. The population of your state.
   b. The population of your city.
   c. The range of income levels and the percentages of population that fall within those income levels in your city.
   d. The demographic breakdown of your city by race.

5. Compare the news offerings of CompuServe and America Online to those of *The New York Times* and the *San Jose* (Calif.) *Mercury News* on the Web. Describe differences in those offerings and explain which one you prefer. Why do you prefer it?

6. Make a list of at least 10 sources of information available on the Web that would be good resources for journalists. Explain your choices.

B ill Reiter knew he was onto a great story. The problem was how to *get* it. Reiter was only about a year into his first job out of journalism school. He was 22. He was from Iowa. He was white. The story was the life of Edith McClinton. Mrs. McClinton had lived through the turbulent birth of civil rights in Little Rock, Ark. She had overcome poverty, racism and blindness to achieve professional success and personal dignity. She was 89 years old and African American.

Reiter discovered immediately that telling Mrs. McClinton's story would require all the skills he had learned in school and some he would have to develop on the spot. Here's his recollection:

> Interviewing Mrs. McClinton was difficult for a number of reasons. Her age alone presented a pretty daunting challenge. Some days, she was in fine spirits and her memory was sharp as anyone's. But some days we'd be talking for five or 10 minutes and then I'd lose her. . . .
>
> Another problem was my paper. *The Democrat Gazette* does not have an excellent reputation with the black community. Early on, Mrs. McClinton and her daughter Joyce (who lives with her and takes care of her) made it clear that they didn't trust my paper and that they didn't trust me. So that's where it started.

By the time it ended eight months later, Reiter had earned the family's trust and written a seven-part, front-page narrative telling the story of race in Arkansas through the experiences of one courageous woman. The series ended with this quote from Mrs. McClinton:

> "Great things can come from freedom," she says. "I take my freedom and pass it on to my children and my grandchildren."

Not every interview is that difficult, time-consuming or important. But every successful interview begins with establishing trust and ends with telling a story.

Interviewing — having conversations with sources — is the key to most stories you will write. Your ability to make people comfortable being with you is often the difference between mediocre reporting and good reporting.

Information is the raw material of a journalist. While some of it is gathered from records and some from observation, most of it is gathered

In this chapter you will learn:

1. How to prepare for an interview.

2. How to phrase your questions.

3. How to establish rapport with a source.

4. How to ensure accuracy.

in person-to-person conversations. The skills that go into those conversations are the most basic reporting tools of any reporter for any medium. If you're interviewing for television, broadcast or webcast, your goals and techniques may be different from those of a print reporter, but the basics are the same.

BUILDING TRUST

The most basic requirement of any successful interview is a reasonable degree of trust between reporter and source. Usually, as a reporter you have to earn that trust. Here's Bill Reiter again, explaining how he broke through the barriers of race and age to earn the trust of Edith McClinton and her daughter.

> In the beginning, I would go to Mrs. McClinton's house. Without a notebook, I'd talk to her. We often talked about her story, but more than not we talked about me, about my paper, about why she should trust her story to either of us, about her concerns.
> I overcame her suspicions the same way I do with most sources. First, I'm honest. I told Mrs. McClinton that I'd be fair but that the story would be personal and honest. She might not like some of the things I wrote, I told her. . . . I guaranteed only that it was honest and accurate. We had this conversation many times. . . .
> I never understand reporters who talk to their sources like the source is some nameless bureaucrat. So I just talked to Edith the way I talk to anyone. I got to know her. More important, she got to know me. The trust came later.
> By the end, Mrs. McClinton had grown to trust me. So had her daughter, I think, and this led to honesty. It's amazing what people will tell you when they trust you. . . . And the last thing I had going for me, something I think can't be faked, was empathy. I really liked this lady, respected her, and thought her story was important. I think sources, when they're around us enough, can pick up on that.

You probably won't have months to develop trust with a source. Most times, you won't need that much time. What you will need, though, are the honesty and empathy that lead strangers to be honest with you.

PREPARING FOR THE INTERVIEW

Interviews are best used to solicit reactions and interpretations, not to gather facts. Good reporters do their fact-gathering before interviews.

How you prepare for the interview depends in part on what kind of a story you intend to write. You may be doing a news story, a personality profile or an investigative piece. In each case, you check the newspaper library and search online databases, talk to other reporters and, if there's enough time, read magazine articles and books.

To prepare for a news story, you pay more attention to clips about the subject of the story than to those about the personality of the individual to be interviewed. To prepare for a profile, you look for personality quirks and the subject's interests, family, friends, travels and habits. To prepare for an investigative piece, you want to know both your subject matter and the person you are interviewing. In all these stories, do not overlook other reporters and editors who know something about the person or subject. Let's look at each of these three types of stories more closely.

The News Story

One day Paul Leavitt made a routine telephone call to a law-enforcement source. Leavitt, then assistant city editor for *The Des Moines* (Iowa) *Register*, was working on a story. He knew the source from his days as a county government and courts reporter for the *Register*.

He expected the story, and the interview, to be routine. Polk County was building a new jail. Leavitt wanted to find out about progress on the new building. The source pleaded ignorance. He said, "Oh, Leavitt, I don't know. I haven't had time to keep up on that, what with all these meetings on the pope's visit."

Leavitt didn't say anything right away. A less astute reporter might have let the source know he was surprised. The pope in Des Moines? Are you kidding? Instead, Leavitt remembered a story he had read about an Iowan who had extended an invitation for the pope to stop in Iowa during his American visit. Leavitt didn't think the Iowan had much of a chance. When the Vatican had announced the pope's visit, people from every state were bartering for a chance to bask in the worldwide limelight.

Still, the source's slip of the tongue seemed genuine. Leavitt finally replied, "Oh, yeah, that's right. When's he coming, anyway?"

"October 4," the source said.

Before the conversation ended, Leavitt had learned of a meeting among the Secret Service, the Vatican, the U.S. State Department and Iowa law-enforcement officials to discuss the trip. He also had learned when the pope would arrive, where he would arrive, where he would celebrate Mass and when he would leave.

As a result, the *Register* stunned its readers the next morning with a copyrighted story saying the pope would speak in Des Moines. The story was printed three weeks before the Vatican released its official itinerary of the visit. Other area reporters scoffed at the story. One newspaper even printed a story poking fun at the thought of a pope hobnobbing in an Iowa cornfield.

Leavitt and the *Register* were vindicated. As scheduled, the pope arrived Oct. 4 — and celebrated Mass in an Iowa cornfield.

Remembering his conversation with the source, and how a routine question turned into a bona fide scoop, Leavitt said, "I don't even remember what the original question was."

Leavitt probably would not have gotten the story had he not remembered the earlier story about the invitation and known something else about interviewing: When a source unwittingly gives you a scoop, sometimes it is best to act as if you already know it. That may encourage the source to give you more information.

Telling Compelling Stories

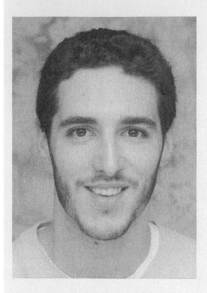

Bill Reiter is a reporter for *The Des Moines* (Iowa) *Register*. His experience at his first job after college, in Little Rock, Ark., introduces this chapter. Now he talks about interviewing, about building trust, about getting the material to tell compelling stories:

"My goal was to write a series that would take our readers inside the lives of homeless teenagers. The task seemed daunting. I had to find these young people, build enough trust to enter their world and somehow show the complex problems and dilemmas that kept them on the street.

"So, knowing they were out there but not sure where to go, I followed the first rule of reporting, the one my college professors drilled into me. . . . I left the office. I stopped folks who looked like they might be homeless. I went by a shelter. I talked to a police officer whose beat takes him to poor parts of town. It didn't take long to hear that the man to see about life on the street was a homeless-youth outreach worker named Howard Matalba."

Matalba introduced Bill to his world and to Gabrielle, a pregnant teenager. Bill again:

"I spent the next three months with Gabrielle. I wandered town with her, listened for hours to her complaining, filled notebook after notebook with quotes that never made the newspaper. I ate with her at the soup kitchen, followed her when she applied for food stamps and stuck around when she and her boyfriend snuggled up together on a bench or against a building. . . . I was there when Gabrielle applied for an apartment, when she ran out of money and food, and when she took back her boyfriend despite his abusive tendencies. I was there when she gave birth to her daughter. . . .

"My reporting came with costs. I was knocked down by a homeless man. I was punched and scratched by a homeless 19-year-old girl. I conquered my fear of heights because one of my sources, with me right behind him, scuttled over a rickety train bridge on his way to town. I worked nights and weekends, wandered for miles in the cold, and was told in no uncertain terms by a group of homeless men that they'd kill me if I came back. I went back anyway, again and again. . . .

"I looked for moments, dialogue and action that gave life to the issue I was writing about. I didn't rely on quotes that reconstructed something I wanted to write about. Instead, I wrote down what my sources actually said to each other, not what they said to me. I relaxed, acted like myself and remembered the people I was writing about had been through a lot."

His series ran on Page 1 of the *Register* and set Des Moines talking. For Bill Reiter, that's what counts.

The Profile

A reporter who decided to write a profile of a local freelance writer prepared differently. Because the reporter had used the writer as a source in an earlier story, she knew something about the writer. She needed to know more, so she looked in *Contemporary Authors* and found biographical information. She also asked the writer to send her copies of some of the articles she had written. Before the reporter went to see the freelancer, she read several of the articles. She also interviewed the editor at one of the magazines that bought the writer's material.

The reporter was prepared. Or so she thought. She had to pass one more test. The writer was an animal lover, and when the reporter arrived, she first had to make friends with a handful of dogs. Fortunately, she loved dogs. That immediately established rapport with the freelancer. The resulting story was full of lively detail:

Joan Gilbert stretches lazily to soft sunbeams and chirping birds. She dresses casually in blue denim shorts and a plaid, short-sleeved blouse. She and her favorite work companions, five playful dogs, file out the door of her little white house to begin their day with a lazy walk in the surrounding woods. When she returns, she'll contentedly sit down at her typewriter. Such is work.

Joan Gilbert is a freelance writer.

Walt Harrington specialized in in-depth profiles when he worked for *The Washington Post Magazine*. In his book, he says he spent one to three months on each profile. For profiles on George Bush and Carl Bernstein, he conducted about 80 interviews each. He also accompanied his subjects. Few journalists are afforded the luxury of three months to work on a profile, but whether you do eight or 80 interviews, the lessons are still the same: Be prepared. Be there.

The Investigative Piece

The casual atmosphere of the Joan Gilbert interview is not always possible for the investigative reporter. An adversarial relationship determines both the preparation required for an investigative piece and the atmosphere of the interview itself. An investigative reporter is like an attorney in a courtroom. Wise attorneys know in advance what the answers to their questions will be. So do investigative reporters. Preparation is essential.

In the early stages of the investigation, you conduct some fishing-expedition interviews: Because you don't know how much the source knows, you cast around. Start with persons on the fringes. Gather as much as you can from them. Study the records. Only after you have most of the evidence do you confront your central character. You start with a large circle and gradually draw it smaller.

Getting the interview is sometimes as big a challenge as the interview itself. Sources who believe you are working on a story that will be critical of them or their friends often try to avoid you. Steve Weinberg, author of an unauthorized biography of industrialist Armand Hammer, had to overcome the suspicion of many former Hammer associates. Their former boss had told all of them not to

TIPS: Before the interview

- Know the subject.
  - Seek specific information.
  - Research the subject.
  - List the questions.
- Know the person.
  - Know salient biographical information.
  - Know the person's expertise regarding the subject matter.

talk to Weinberg. Instead of calling, Weinberg approached them by mail. "I sent letters, examples of my previous work, explained what I wanted to cover and why I was doing it without Hammer's blessing," Weinberg says.

He recommends that you use a letter or an e-mail to share some of what you know about the story that might surprise or impress the source. For instance, a reference such as "And last week, when I was checking all the land records . . ." would indicate the depth of your research.

In his letter to former Hammer assistants, Weinberg talked about how Hammer was one of the most important people in the history of business. The letters opened doors to all seven of Hammer's former executive assistants whom Weinberg contacted.

Weinberg, former director of Investigative Reporters and Editors, also offers to show the sources relevant portions of his manuscript as an accuracy check. He makes it clear in writing that he maintains control of the content.

Requesting an interview in writing can allow you to make your best case for getting it. And an offer to allow your sources to review the story assures them that you are serious about accuracy. E-mail makes both the request and the offer simpler and faster.

BROADCAST INTERVIEWS

When you're interviewing someone in front of a camera, the basic rules of interviewing don't change. Some of your objectives and techniques, however, do.

The first thing to remember is that broadcast journalism is a performance. Television journalists, at least those who appear on camera, are also performers. Sure, they have to report and write, but they also have to be able to tell their stories with both words and body language to people who are watching and listening — not reading. An important part of the television reporter's performance is the interview.

Both print and broadcast reporters often interview to develop information that can be used in further reporting. Interviews on camera usually have a different goal. That goal is the soundbite, the few seconds of words with accompanying video that convey not only information but emotion. Print is a medium that mainly provides information. Television is a medium of emotion. The best interviews for television are those that reveal how a situation feels to the participants or witnesses.

Al Tompkins, the Poynter Institute's group leader for broadcast and online journalism, offers what he calls "a new set of interviewing tools" intended to produce better storytelling for television. You can find these and other tools at **www. poynter.org**. Here are some that show both differences and similarities in print and television interviewing:

- *Objective and subjective questions*. To gather facts, ask objective questions: "When?" "Where?" "How much?" But subjective questions usually produce the best soundbites. "Why?" "Tell me more. . . ." "Can you explain . . . ?"

TIPS: Set up the interview

- Set the time.
  - At interviewee's convenience — but suggest a time.
  - Length of time needed.
  - Possible return visits.
- Set the place.
  - Interviewee's turf, or
  - Neutral turf.

TIPS: Discuss arrangements

- Will you bring a recording device?
- Will you bring a photographer?
- Will you let interviewee check accuracy of quotes?

- *Focus on one issue at a time*. Vague, complicated questions produce vague, complicated, hard-to-follow answers. Remember that readers can review until they understand, but viewers can't rewind an interview. Help them follow the story by taking your interviewee through it one step at a time.
- *Ask open-ended questions*. For print, you often want a simple yes or no. That kind of answer stops a television interview. Open-ended questions encourage conversation, and conversation makes a good interview. (More on this on page 58.)
- *Keep questions short*. Make the interviewee do the talking. Tompkins points out that short questions are more likely to produce focused responses. They also keep the viewer's attention on the person being interviewed and what she or he has to say.
- *Build to the point*. The best interviews are like the best stories. They don't give away the punch line in the first few words. Soft, easy questions encourage relaxation and trust. Then move to the heart of the issue.
- *Be honest*. As true for television as for print and online, the importance of honesty is too often overlooked by rookie reporters. You do neither your source nor yourself a favor if you lead the source to expect an interview about softball when you have an indictment in mind. Tell the source ahead of time that you'll want to ask some tough questions. Say, and mean, that you want to get the whole story, to be fair. Then politely but firmly dig in. As Tompkins notes, honesty has the added benefit of helping you defend yourself against any later accusations of malice.

Other Preparatory Considerations

All this homework is important, but something as trifling as your appearance may determine whether you will have a successful interview. You would hardly wear cutoff shorts into a university president's suite, and you wouldn't wear a three-piece suit to talk to underground revolutionaries. It is your right to wear your hair however you wish, pierce your body and wear whatever clothes you want, but it is the source's prerogative to refuse to talk to you (see Figure 3.1).

Most interviews are conducted in the source's office. Especially if the story is a profile or a feature, it usually is better to get the source away from his or her work. If you are doing a story about a rabbi's hobby of collecting butterflies, seek a setting appropriate to the topic. Suggest meeting where the rabbi keeps the collection.

In some interviews, it would be to your advantage to get the source on neutral territory. If you have some questions for the provost or a public official, suggest meeting in a coffee shop at a quiet time. A person has more power in his or her official surroundings.

It is important, too, to let the source know how much time you need and whether you expect to return for further information. And if you don't already know how the source might react to a recording device, ask when you are making the appointment.

You have now done the appropriate homework. You are properly attired. You have made an appointment and told the source how much time you need. Before

Figure 3.1
*This reporter dresses to fit
in with the marchers he is
interviewing; he gains their
confidence by being friendly
and attentive.*

you leave, you may want to write down a list of questions to ask. They will guide
you through the interview and prevent you from missing important topics altogether. The best way to encourage a spontaneous conversation is to have your
questions prepared. You'll be more relaxed. The thinking you must do to write
the questions will help prepare you for the interview. Having questions prepared
relieves you of the need to be mentally searching for the next question as the
source is answering the last one. If you are trying to think of the next question,
you will not be paying close attention to what is being said, and you might miss
the most important part of the interview.

Preparing the questions for an interview is hard work, even for veterans. If
you are writing for your campus newspaper, seek suggestions from other staff
members. You will find ideas in the newspaper's electronic database. If you antic-
ipate a troublesome interview with the chancellor, you might want to seek
advice from faculty members, too. What questions would they ask if they were
you? Often, they have more background knowledge, or they might have heard
some of the faculty talk around campus. Staff members are also valuable sources
of information.

Although you may ask all of your prepared questions in some interviews, in
most you probably will use only some of them. Still, you will have benefited from
preparing the questions in two important ways. First, even when you don't use

many, the work you did thinking of the questions helped prepare you for the interview. Second, sources who see that you have a prepared list often are impressed with your seriousness.

On the basis of the information you have gathered already, you know what you want to ask. Now you must be careful about how you ask the questions.

PHRASING QUESTIONS

How questions are structured often determines the answer. Reporters have missed many stories because they didn't know how to ask questions. Quantitative researchers have shown how only a slight wording change affects the results of a survey. If you want to know whether citizens favor a city plan to beautify the downtown area, you can ask the question in several ways:

- Do you favor the city council's plan to beautify the downtown area?
- The city council plans to spend $3 million beautifying the downtown area. Are you in favor of this?
- Do you think the downtown area needs physical changes?
- Which of the following actions do you favor?
  — Prohibiting all automobile traffic in an area bounded by Providence Road, Ash Street, College Avenue and Elm Street.
  — Having all the downtown storefronts remodeled to carry out a single theme and putting in brick streets, shrubbery and benches.
  — None of the above.

TIPS: When you arrive at the interview

- Control the seating arrangement.
- Place the recording device at optimum spot.
- Warm up person briefly with small talk.
- Set the ground rules.
  - Put everything on the record.
  - Make everything attributable.

How you structure that question may affect the survey results by several percentage points. Similarly, how you ask questions in an interview may affect the response.

By the phrasing of the question, many reporters signal the response they expect or prejudices they have. For instance, a reporter who says, "Don't you think that the city council should allocate more money to the parks and recreation department?" is not only asking a question but also influencing the source or betraying a bias. A neutral phrasing would be "Do you think the city council should allocate more money to the parks and recreation department?" Another common way of asking a leading question is "Are you going to vote against this amendment like the other legislators I've talked to?"

If you have watched journalists interviewing people live on television, you have seen many examples of badly phrased questions. Many are not questions at all. The interviewers make statements and then put the microphone in front of the source — for example, "You had a great game, Bill" or "Winning the election must be a great feeling." Then the source is expected to say something. What, precisely, do you want to know?

Sometimes a reporter unwittingly blocks a response by the phrasing of the question. A reporter who was investigating possible job discrimination against women conducted several interviews before she told her city editor she didn't think the women with whom she talked were being frank with her. "When I ask them if they have ever been discriminated against, they always tell me no. But three times now during the course of the interviews, they have said things that indicate they have been. How do I get them to tell me about it?" she asked.

"Perhaps it's the way you are asking the question," the city editor replied. "When you ask the women whether they have ever been discriminated against, you are forcing them to answer yes or no. Don't be so blunt. Ask them if others with the same qualifications at work have advanced faster than they have. Ask if they are paid the same amount as men for the same work. Ask them what they think they would be doing today if they were male. Ask them if they know of any qualified women who were denied jobs."

The city editor was giving the reporter examples of both closed- and open-ended questions. Each has its specific strengths.

Open-Ended Questions

Open-ended questions allow the respondent some flexibility. Women may not respond frankly when asked whether they have ever been discriminated against. The question calls for a yes-no response. But an open-ended question such as "What would you be doing today if you were a man?" is not so personal. It does not sound as threatening to the respondent. In response to an open-ended question, the source often reveals more than he or she realizes or intends to.

A sportswriter who was interviewing a pro scout at a college football game wanted to know whom the scout was there to see. When the scout diplomatically declined to be specific, the reporter tried another approach. He asked a series of questions:

- "What kind of qualities does a pro scout look for in an athlete?"
- "Do you think any of the players here today have those talents?"
- "Whom would you put into that category?"

The reporter worked from the general to the specific until he had the information he wanted. Open-ended questions are less direct and less threatening. They are more exploratory and more flexible. However, if you want to know a person's biographical data, don't ask, "Can you tell me about yourself?"

Closed-Ended Questions

Eventually the reporter needs to close in on a subject, to pin down details, to get the respondent to be specific. **Closed-ended questions** are designed to elicit specific responses.

Instead of asking the mayor, "What did you think of the conference in Washington, D.C.?" you ask, "What did you learn in the session 'Funds You May Not Know Are Available'?" Instead of asking a previous employee to appraise the chancellor-designate's managerial abilities, you ask, "How well does she listen to

---

TIPS: The interview itself

- Use good interview techniques.
  - Ask open-ended and closed-ended questions.
  - Allow the person to think and to speak; pause.
  - Don't be threatening in voice or manner.
  - Control the flow but be flexible.
- Take good notes.
  - Be unobtrusive.
  - Be thorough.
- Use the recording device.
  - Make sure it's on.
  - Note digital counter at important parts.

the people who work for her?" "Do the people who work for her have specific job duties?" "Does she explain her decisions?"

A vague question invites a vague answer. By asking a specific question, you are more likely to get a specific answer. You are also communicating to your source that you have done your homework and that you are looking for precise details.

Knowing exactly when to ask a closed-ended question or when to be less specific is not something you can plan ahead of time. The type of information you are seeking and the chemistry between the interviewer and the source are the determining factors. You must make on-the-spot decisions. The important thing is to keep rephrasing the question until the source answers it adequately. Gary Smith wrote in *Intimate Journalism*, "A lot of my reporting comes from asking a question three different ways. Sometimes the third go at it is what produces the nugget, but even if the answers aren't wonderful or the quotes usable, they can still confirm or correct my impressions."

Every reporter seeks anecdotes, and closed-ended questions help elicit them. "What is the funniest thing you've ever done?" "The weirdest?" "What's the saddest thing that ever happened to you?" When the source talks in generalities, ask a close-ended question to get to specifics. "You say Mary is a practical joker. Can you think of an example of a practical joke she played on someone?" The answers to these types of questions yield the anecdotal nuggets that make your story readable.

ESTABLISHING RAPPORT

In her career with the Associated Press, Tad Bartimus interviewed hundreds of people. She began practicing when she worked for her hometown paper at age 14. Her assignment: interview former President Harry S. Truman. She approached him and said, "Excuse me, sir, but I'm from the local paper. Could you please talk to me?"

"Well, young lady, what would you like to know?" Truman responded.

Years later, Bartimus recalled, "For the first time in my life, I was struck dumb. What did I want to know? What was I supposed to ask him? How do you do this interviewing stuff, anyway?"

Bartimus knows the answers to those questions now. One piece of advice she offered her colleagues in an article for *AP World* was to share and care. Bartimus urges reporters to reveal themselves as people. "A little empathy goes a long way to defuse [the] fear and hostility that is so pervasive against the press," she says.

Rapport — the relationship between the reporter and the source — is crucial to the success of the interview (see Figure 3.2). The relationship is sometimes relaxed, sometimes strained. Often it is somewhere in between. The type of relationship you try to establish with your source is determined by the kind of story you are doing. Several approaches are possible.

Figure 3.2
*Establishing rapport with
interview subjects helps a
reporter to get better story
information.*

Interview Approaches

For most news stories and personality profiles, the reporter gains a great deal if
the subject is at ease. Often that can be accomplished by starting with small talk.
Ask about a trophy, the plants or an engraved pen. Bring up something humorous
you have found during your research. Ask about something you know the source
will want to talk about. In other interviews, if you think the subject might be
skeptical about your knowledge of the field, open with a question that demonstrates your knowledge.

Rapport also depends on where you conduct the interview. Many persons,
especially those unaccustomed to being interviewed, feel more comfortable in
their workplace. Go to them. Talk to the business person in the office, to the athlete in the locker room, to the conductor in the concert hall. In some cases,
though, you may get a better interview elsewhere if the source cannot relax at the
workplace or is frequently interrupted. Reporters have talked to politicians during car rides between campaign appearances. They've gone sailing with business

The "fabricated quotes" case of Masson vs. Malcolm is a bad soap opera. The lead characters are writer Janet Malcolm, the defendant, and psychoanalyst Jeffrey Masson, the plaintiff.

Here is the main scenario:

Masson became disillusioned with Freudian psychology when he was serving as projects director of the Sigmund Freud Archives in London. He was fired for advancing his controversial theories about Freud in 1981. Malcolm wanted to write about the situation. She established a rapport with him and taped more than 40 hours' worth of interviews. But she said she did not tape-record all of their conversations, especially those that occurred when they were walking or traveling in her car.

Malcolm wrote about Masson for *The New Yorker* in 1983. Book publisher Alfred A. Knopf later published a book from that material. The placement of quotation marks around certain statements in these works provoked a dispute between subject and author. Malcolm wrote that Masson said his superiors at the Sigmund Freud Archives considered him "an intellectual gigolo — you get your pleasure from him, but you don't take him out in public." Masson said he never said that. A tape recording shows that he said, "I was, in a sense, much too junior within the hierarchy of analysis for these important

training analysts to be caught dead with me."

Did he call himself an "intellectual gigolo" or not? It is a catchy phrase. Masson claimed that quote and others were fabricated. He sued *The New Yorker*, Knopf and Malcolm for libel.

In 1989, the 9th U.S. Circuit Court of Appeals ruled in favor of the defendants. The court said that an author may "under certain circumstances, fictionalize quotations to some extent." Because Masson had conceded that he was a public figure, he had to prove "actual malice" — knowledge of falsity or reckless regard (see Chapter 22).

The court said:

Malice will not be inferred from evidence showing that the quoted language does not contain the exact words used by the plaintiff provided that the fabricated quotations are either *"rational interpretations of ambiguous" remarks made by the public figure . . . or do not "alter the substantive content" of unambiguous remarks actually made by the public figure.* (Italics added.)

In 1991 the Supreme Court overturned the 9th Circuit's decision, rejecting the lower court's "rational interpretation" standard. The Court said that "quotation marks indicate that the author is not interpreting the speaker's ambiguous statement, but is attempting to convey what the speaker said."

The Court said:

Were we to assess quotations under a rational interpretation standard, we would give journalists the freedom to place statements in their subjects' mouths without fear of liability. By eliminating any method of distinguishing between the statements of the subject and the interpretation of the author, we would diminish to a great degree the trustworthiness of the printed word and eliminate the real meaning of quotations. Not only public figures but the press doubtless would suffer under such a rule.

The Court clearly was trying to protect the sanctity of quotation marks, but the Court also made it clear that not every change in a quotation is going to lead to a lawsuit. To some extent, some reporters do clean up quotes. Some reporters correct errors in grammar. Some delete "uh" or "um" without using ellipsis points. Those changes will not get a reporter into trouble. The change in words has to result in a material change in the meaning of a statement for actual malice to be present. But courts are going to look hard at cases where a writer has put words in a speaker's mouth.

The Supreme Court remanded the case. In 1992, the 9th Circuit let Knopf off the hook, saying, in effect, that Knopf relied on *The New Yorker* in concluding that Malcolm's manuscript was accurate.

In June 1993, a jury heard the case. It found two fabricated

(continued)

quotes libelous — the "intellectual gigolo" quote was not one of them. Here are the two quotes:

Malcolm quoted Masson as describing his plans for Maresfield Gardens, the home of the Freud Archives, which he hoped to occupy after the death of Anna Freud, Sigmund's child: "I would have renovated it, opened it up, brought it to life. Maresfield Gardens would have been a center of scholarship, but it would also have been a place of *sex, women, fun.* (Italics added.) It would have been like the change in *The Wizard of Oz,* from black-and-white into color." He said on tape of his meeting with a London analyst: ". . . we were going to pass women on to each other, and we were going to have a great time together when I lived in the Freud house. We'd have great parties and . . . we were going to live it up."

The second quotation involved the placement of the sentence "Well, he had the wrong man." Masson is recounting being fired by the director of the archives. The director says Masson is upsetting Anna Freud and it might kill her. Malcolm quotes Masson talking to the director:

"What have I done? You're doing it. You're firing me. What am I supposed to do — be grateful to you?" "You could be silent about it. . . ." "Why should I do that?" "Because it is the honorable thing to do." "Well, he had the wrong man."

Masson seems to be calling himself dishonorable. On the tape, the conversation, starting with the director, says:

"You could be silent about it." . . . "Why?" . . . "Because it's the honorable thing to do and you will save face. And who knows? If you never speak about it and you quietly and humbly accept our judgment, who knows that in a few years if we don't bring you back?" Well, he had the wrong man.

While agreeing the two quotes were libelous, the jury deadlocked on damages. The judge ordered a retrial on all issues — liability as well as damages. But another defendant dropped by the wayside. The jurors did not think *The New Yorker* deliberately published false quotes, so the judge dismissed the case against the magazine.

In November 1994, a jury decided in favor of defendant Malcolm.

Then, belatedly, in August 1995, Malcolm recovered a lost notebook containing her notes on some of the contested conversations.

The moral is clear. Material changes in quotations are perilous. They can lead to long court cases and expensive attorney's fees even if ultimately there is no liability for damages.

— Sandra Davidson

people and hunting with athletes. One student reporter doing a feature on a police chief spent a weekend with the chief, who was painting his home. To do a profile, which requires more than one interview, vary the location. New surroundings can make a difference.

Lisa Kremer, reporting the story of a mountain avalanche for the *Tacoma News-Tribune,* recognized that where she interviewed the rescuers was important. She approached the climbers at a restaurant and said she wanted to talk to them. They weren't sure they wanted to talk to her. "I said, 'Would you be more comfortable here at the restaurant? I could sit down right now. Or would you rather go back to the hotel?'"

They said they would meet her at the hotel. They did, and she got the interviews.

There are times when the reporter would rather have the source edgy, nervous or even scared. When you are doing an investigation, you may want the key characters to feel uneasy. You may pretend you know more than you actually do. You want them to know that the material you have is substantive and serious. Seymour Hersh, a Pulitzer Prize-winning investigative reporter, uses this tactic. *Time* magazine once quoted a government official commenting on Hersh: "He wheedles, cajoles, pleads, threatens, asks a leading question, uses little tidbits as if he knew the whole story. When he finishes you feel like a wet rag."

In some cases, however, it is better even in an investigation to take a low-key approach. Let the source relax. Talk around the subject but gradually bring the discussion to the key issues. The surprise element may work in your favor.

So may the sympathetic approach. When the source is speaking, you may nod or punctuate the source's responses with comments such as "That's interesting." Sources who think you are sympathetic are more likely to volunteer information. Researchers have found, for instance, that a simple "mm-hmmm" affects the length of the answer interviewers get.

Other Practical Considerations

Where you sit in relation to the person you are interviewing can be important. Unless you deliberately are trying to make those interviewed feel uncomfortable, do not sit directly in front of them. Permit your sources to establish eye contact if and when they wish.

Some people are even more disturbed by the way a reporter takes notes. A tape recorder ensures accuracy of quotes, but it makes many speakers self-conscious or nervous. If you have permission to use a tape recorder, place it in an inconspicuous spot and ignore it except to make sure it is working properly. Writing notes longhand may interfere with your ability to digest what is being said. But not taking any notes at all is risky. Only a few reporters can leave an interview and accurately write down what was said. Certainly no one can do it and reproduce direct quotes verbatim. You should learn shorthand or develop a note-taking system of your own.

ENSURING ACCURACY

Accuracy is a major problem in all interviews. Both the question and the answer may be ambiguous. You may not understand what is said. You may record it incorrectly. You may not know the context of the remarks. Your biases may interfere with the message.

Knowing the background of your sources, having a comfortable relationship with them and keeping good notes are important elements of accuracy. All those were missing when a journalism student, two weeks into an internship at a major daily, interviewed the public information officer for a sheriff's department about criminal activity in and around a shelter for battered women. The reporter had never met the source. She took notes on her phone interview with the deputy and others in whatever notebook happened to be nearby. She didn't record the time, date or even the source. There were no notes showing context, just fragments of quotes, scrawled in nearly illegible handwriting.

Figures stated during an interview must be double-checked. The mere statement of a statistic, even by a reliable source, does not ensure accuracy.

After the story was published, the developer of the shelter sued. Questioned by attorneys, the deputy swore that the reporter misunderstood him and used some of his comments out of context. In several cases, he contended, she completed her fragmentary notes by putting her own words in his mouth. He testified that most reporters come to see him to get acquainted. Many call back to check his quotes on sensitive or complex stories. She did neither.

When the court ordered the reporter to produce and explain her notes, she had trouble reconstructing them. She had to admit on several occasions that she wasn't sure what the fragments meant.

The accuracy of your story is only as good as your notes. David Finkel, whose story on a family's TV-watching habits became a Pulitzer Prize finalist, took extra steps to be certain his material was accurate. Observing what his subject was watching, he obtained transcripts of the shows so he could quote accurately from them. If he knew transcripts would not be available, he set his tape recorder near the TV to record the program.

Some possibilities for making errors or introducing bias are unavoidable, but others are not. To ensure the most accurate and complete reporting possible, you should use all the techniques available to obtain a good interview, including observing, understanding what you hear and asking follow-up questions. Let's examine these and other techniques.

Observing

Some reporters look but do not see. The detail they miss may be the difference between a routine story and one that is a delight to read. Your powers of observation may enable you to discover a story beyond your source's words. Is the subject nervous? What kinds of questions are striking home? The mayor may deny that he is going to fire the police chief, but if you notice the chief's personnel file sitting on an adjacent worktable, you may have reason to continue the investigation.

People communicate some messages nonverbally. Researchers have been able to correlate some gestures with meanings. For instance, folded arms often signal that someone doesn't want to be approached; crossed ankles often signal tension. Many nonverbal messages, however, may not be the same for all ethnic and cultural groups. Reporters should read more about the subject.

Understanding

Understanding what you see is crucial to the news-gathering process. So is understanding what you hear. It is not enough merely to record what is being said; you must also digest it.

Sometimes what you don't hear may be the message. The reporter who was trying to find out if the mayor was going to fire the police chief asked several questions about the chief's performance. What struck the reporter during the interview was the mayor's lack of enthusiasm for the chief. That unintentional tip kept the reporter working on the story until he confirmed it.

Asking Follow-Up Questions

If you understand what the source is saying, you can ask meaningful follow-up questions. There is nothing worse than briefing your city editor on the interview and having the editor ask you, "Well, did you ask. . . ?" Having to say no is embarrassing.

Even if you go into an interview armed with a list of questions, the most important questions will probably be the ones you ask in response to an answer. A reporter who was doing a story on bidding procedures was interviewing the mayor. The reporter asked how bid specifications were written. In the course of his reply, the mayor mentioned that the president of a construction firm had assured him the last bid specifications were adequate. The alert reporter picked up on the statement:

"When did you talk to him?"

"About three weeks ago," the mayor said.

"That's before the specifications were published, wasn't it?"

"Yes, we asked him to look them over for us."

"Did he find anything wrong with the way they were written?"

"Oh, he changed a few minor things. Nothing important."

"Did officials of any other construction firms see the bid specifications before they were advertised?"

"No, he was the only one."

Gradually, on the basis of one offhand comment by the mayor, the reporter was able to piece together a solid story on the questionable relationship between the city and the construction firm. You should end nearly every interview with the same question: "Is there anything I haven't asked that I should?"

Other Techniques

Although most questions are designed to get information, some are asked as a delaying tactic. A reporter who is taking notes may fall behind. One good trick for catching up is just to say, "Hold on a second — let me get that" or "Say that again." Other questions are intended to encourage a longer response. "Go on with that" or "Tell me more about that" encourages the speaker to add more detail.

You don't have to be stalling for time to say you don't understand. Don't be embarrassed to admit you haven't grasped something. It is better to admit to one person you don't understand than to advertise your ignorance in newsprint or on the airwaves in front of thousands.

Another device for making the source talk on is not a question at all; it is a pause. You are signaling the source that you expect more. But the lack of a response from you is much more ambiguous than "Tell me more about that." It may indicate that you were skeptical of what was just said, that you didn't understand, that the answer was inadequate or several other possibilities. The source will be forced to react.

TIPS: After the interview

- Organize your notes — immediately.
- Craft a proper lead.
- Write a coherent story.
- Check accuracy with the interviewee.

Reporters should do research after an interview to ascertain specific figures when a source provides an estimate. For example, if a shop owner says he runs one of 20 pizza parlors in town, check with the city business-license office to get the exact number.

Many dull interviews become interesting after they end. There are two things you should always do when you finish your questions: Check key facts, figures and quotes and then put away your pen but keep your ears open. You are not breaching any ethical rule if you continue to ask questions after you have put away your pen or turned off the tape recorder. That's when some sources loosen up.

Quickly review your notes and check facts, especially dates, numbers, quotes, spellings and titles. Besides helping you get it right, it shows the source you are careful. If necessary, arrange a time when you can call to check other parts of the story or clear up questions you may have as you are writing. Researchers have found that more than half of direct quotations are inaccurate, even when the interview is tape-recorded. That reflects a sloppiness that is unacceptable. Make sure you are the exception.

As a matter of courtesy, tell the source when the story might appear. You may even offer to send along an extra copy of the article when it's completed.

Remember that although the interview may be over, your relationship to the source is not. When you have the story written, call the source and confirm the information. Better to discover your inaccuracies before you print than after.

Suggested Readings

Biagi, Shirley. *Interviews That Work*. Belmont, Calif.: Wadsworth Publishing Co., 1992. A complete guide to interviewing techniques. The instruction is interspersed with interviews of journalists describing their techniques.

Burgoon, Judee K. and Saine, Thomas J. *The Unspoken Dialogue. An Introduction to Nonverbal Communication*. Boston: Houghton Mifflin, 1978. An excellent look at the subject for readers who are not acquainted with the field.

Harrington, Walt. *American Profiles*. Columbia, Mo.: University of Missouri Press, 1992. Fifteen excellent profiles and the author's explanation of how and why he does what he does.

Malcolm, Janet. *The Journalist and the Murderer*. New York: Knopf, 1990. Using the Joe McGinnis–Jeffrey MacDonald case, the author accuses all journalists of being "confidence men" who betray their sources.

Metzler, Ken. *The Writer's Guide to Gathering Information by Asking Questions*, Third Edition. Needham Heights, Mass.: Allyn & Bacon, 1997. An invaluable in-depth look at problems of interviewing.

Scanlon, Christopher, ed. *Best Newspaper Writing*. St. Petersburg, Fla.: Poynter Institute for Media Studies. Reprints of winners of American Society of Newspaper Editors Distinguished Writing Awards and interviews with the authors make this an invaluable resource. It is published annually.

Suggested Web Sites

www.poewar.com
The Writer's Resource Center offers advice on a variety of writers' concerns, including interviewing.

www.poynter.org/index.cfm
The Poynter Institute site offers an array of help for journalists. Among the lists are bibliographies on interviewing and a regular column on reporting and writing techniques by Chip Scanlan.

Exercises

1. Learn to gather background on your sources. Write a memo of up to two pages about your state's senior U.S. senator. Concentrate on those details that will allow you to focus on how the senator views the pro-life versus pro-choice issue. Indicate the sources of your information. Do an Internet search on the senator.

2. List five open-ended questions you would ask the senator.

3. List five closed-ended questions you would ask.

4. Interview a student also enrolled in your reporting class. Write a two- or three-page story. Be sure to focus on one aspect of the student's life. Ask your classmate to read the story and to mark errors of fact and perception. The instructor will read your story and the critique.

5. Your instructor will give you a news item. Prepare a list of questions you would ask to do a follow-up interview. As each question is read aloud in class, cross it off your list. See if you can come up with the most original and appropriate questions.

In Their Own Words

"**A**nd you can quote me on that." Many people who say these words don't expect to be quoted. They mean only that they are sure of what they are saying and are not afraid or ashamed to say it. Nonetheless, these are sweet words to a reporter.

Direct quotes add color and credibility to your story. By using direct quotes, you are telling readers that you are putting them directly in touch with the speaker. Like a letter, direct quotes are personal. Quotation marks signal the reader that something special is coming. Direct quotes provide a story with a change of pace, a breath of air. They also loosen up a clump of dense type.

As Paula LaRoque, writing coach and assistant managing editor of *The Dallas Morning News*, said, "The right quotes, carefully selected and presented, enliven and humanize a story and help make it clear, credible, immediate and dramatic. Yet many quotations in journalism are dull, repetitive, ill-phrased, ungrammatical, nonsensical, self-serving or just plain dumb."

Now that's a quotation worth quoting!

But not everything people say is worth quoting. You need to learn what to quote directly, when to use partial quotes and when to paraphrase. You also must learn how and how often to attribute quotations and other information. Like a researcher, you must know when information must be tied to a source. However, attributing a remark or some information does not excuse you from a possible libel suit. And, of course, you want to be fair.

Being fair sometimes is difficult when sources do not want to be quoted. For that reason you also must learn how to deal with off-the-record quotes and background information.

WHAT TO QUOTE DIRECTLY

Crisp, succinct, meaningful quotes spice up any story. But you can overdo a good thing. You need direct quotes in your stories, but you also need to develop your skill in recognizing what is worth quoting. Let's look at the basic guidelines.

In this chapter you will learn:

1. **What is worth quoting directly.**

2. **How and when to attribute direct and indirect quotes.**

3. **How to handle both on- and off-the-record information.**

Unique Material

When you can say, "Ah, I never heard that before," you can be quite sure your readers would like to know exactly what the speaker said. Instead of quoting someone at length, look for the kernel. Sometimes it is something surprising, something neither you nor your readers would expect that person to say. For example, on *Good Morning America*, Barbara Bush, the president's mother, told interviewer Diane Sawyer she would watch none of TV's coverage of the war on Iraq. Then she said, "Why should we hear about body bags and deaths and how many, what day it's going to happen? It's not relevant. So why should I waste my beautiful mind on something like that?"

When singer Dolly Parton was asked how she felt about dumb-blond jokes, she replied: "I'm not offended at all because I know I'm not a dumb blond. I also know I'm not a blond."

Striking statements like those should be quoted, but not always. *The Arizona Daily Star* did a profile of a chef who writes a weekly column. Describing his food philosophy, the chef said, "I have a food philosophy, but it's a kind of an angry one. I'd eat a baby if you cooked it right. Yeah, that's pretty much it."

The *Star*'s reader advocate wrote that at least a half dozen readers objected. Said one, "Shame on the chef for saying it, and shame on the *Star* for printing it."

There is no reason to place simple, factual material inside quotation marks. Here is a segment of copy from a story about similarities in the careers of a father and son that needed no quotes at all:

```
"My son was born on campus," says the elder Denney, 208
Westridge Drive, a professor in regional and community
affairs.

    "In fact, he was born in the same hospital that I met my
wife," he says, explaining he was in Noyes Hospital with a
fractured spine when she was a student nurse.

    Since that time, he has earned his bachelor's degree
"technically in agriculture with a major in biological
science and conservation."
```

Although the quoted material is informative, it contains nothing particularly interesting, surprising, disturbing, new or even different. It should be written:

```
Denney, of 208 Westridge Drive, is a professor in regional and
community affairs. While hospitalized in Noyes Hospital with a
fractured spine, he met a student nurse who became his wife.
Eight years later, his son was born at the same hospital.

    The son has since earned a bachelor's degree in
agriculture with a major in biological science and
conservation.
```

TIPS: Use direct quotes when

- Someone says something unique.
- Someone says something uniquely.
- Someone important says something important.

"I often quote myself. It adds spice to my conversation."

— George Bernard Shaw, playwright

The first version has 72 words; the second, with 60 words, is tighter and better.

A direct quotation should say something significant. Also, a direct quotation should not simply repeat what has been said indirectly. It should move the story forward. Here's a passage from a *USA Today* story about a proposed law that would bar health-insurance companies, employers and managed-care plans from discriminating against people because of their genetic makeup:

> Fear of insurance discrimination based on the results of genetic tests has been on the rise for years. "It stops many people cold from getting tested," says Karen Clarke, a genetics counselor at Johns Hopkins University in Baltimore.

The quotation is useful, it is informative, and it moves the story forward.

Sometimes spoken material is unique not because of individual remarks that are surprising or new but because of extended dialogue that can tell the story more effectively than writers can in their own words. The writer of the following story made excellent use of dialogue:

Avoid quotes that provide statistics. You are better off paraphrasing and attributing your source. Save quotes for reaction and interpretation.

> Lou Provancha pushed his wire-rimmed glasses up on his nose and leaned toward the man in the wheelchair.
>
> "What is today, Jake?" he asked.
>
> Jake twisted slightly and stared at the floor.
>
> "Jake," Provancha said. "Jake, look up here."
>
> A long silence filled the tiny, cluttered room on the sixth floor of the University Medical Center.
>
> Provancha, a licensed practical nurse at the hospital, glanced at the reporter. "Jake was in a coma a week ago," he explained. "He couldn't talk."
>
> Provancha pointed to a wooden board propped up on the table beside him.
>
> "Jake, what is today? What does it say here? What is this word? I've got my finger pointed right at it."
>
> Jake squinted at the word. With a sudden effort, like a man heaving a bag of cement mix onto a truck bed, he said: "Tuesday."
>
> Provancha grinned. It was a small victory for both of them.
>
> The shaggy-haired nurse was coaxing his patient step-by-step back into the world he had known before a car accident pitched him into a two-month-long coma, with its resulting disorientation and memory loss.

Here's another example of how dialogue can move the story along and "show" rather than "tell." The story is about the restoration of old cars. A father is passing on a rare technique to his son:

> When the lead is smooth and the irregularities filled to his satisfaction, he reaches for his file.
>
> "How long has it been since you've done this?" his son asks.
>
> "It's been at least 20 years."

"How do you tin it so it won't melt and all run off on the floor?"

"Very carefully."

Before the lesson is finished, a customer and two other shop workers have joined the group watching Larry at work. This is a skill few people know.

"I don't like the way this lead melts," he says.

"That's what it does when there's not enough tin?" his son asks.

"Tin helps it stick."

"Why do you pull the file instead of pushing it?"

"So I can see better."

"I would already have the fiberglass on and be done by now."

"I know, but anything worthwhile you have to work for."

Notice the careful instruction and concerned advice from a teacher/father. His last sentence contains one of life's lessons: "I know, but anything worthwhile you have to work for."

The Unique Expression

When you can say, "Ah, I've never heard it said that way before," you know you have something quotable. Be on the lookout for the clever, the colorful, the colloquial. For example, an elderly man talking about his organic garden said, "It's hard to tell people to watch what they eat. You eat health, you know."

A professor lecturing on graphic design said, "When you think it looks like a mistake, it is." The same professor once was explaining that elements in a design should not call attention to themselves: "You don't walk up to a beautiful painting in someone's home and say, 'That's a beautiful frame!'"

A computer trainer said to a reporter: "Teaching kids computers is like leading ducks to water. But teaching adults computers is like trying to teach chickens to swim."

Sometimes something said uniquely is a colloquialism. Colloquialisms can add color and life to your copy. A person from Louisiana may say, "I was just fixing to leave when the phone rang." In parts of the South you're apt to hear, "I might could do that." A person from around Lancaster, Pa., might "make the light out" when turning off the lights. And people in and around Fort Wayne, Ind., "redd up" the dishes after a meal, meaning that they wash them and put them where they belong.

Important Quotes by Important People

If citizen Joe Smith says, "Something must be done about this teachers' strike," you may or may not consider it worth quoting. But if the mayor says, "Something must be done about this teachers' strike," many papers would print the quote. Generally reporters quote public officials or known personalities in their news stories (although not everything the famous say is worth quoting). Remember, prominence is an important property of news (see Figure 4.1).

Figure 4.1
*Although quotes from
experts and public figures
are generally used to
strengthen a story's
authority, quotes from
ordinary citizens with
unique experience in a
newsworthy event may
also add credibility.*

Quoting sources that readers are likely to know lends authority, credibility and interest to your story. Presumably, a meteorologist knows something about the weather, a doctor about health, a chemistry professor about chemicals. However, it is unlikely that a television star knows a great deal about cameras, even if he or she makes commercials about cameras.

Accuracy

The first obligation of any reporter is to be accurate. Before there can be any discussion of whether or how to use direct quotations, you must learn to get the exact words of the source.

It's not easy.

Scribbled notes from interviews, press conferences and meetings are often difficult to decipher and interpret. A study by Adrienne Leher, a professor of linguistics at the University of Arizona, shows only 13 of 98 quotations taken from Arizona newspapers proved to be verbatim when compared to recordings. Only twice, however, were the nonverbatim quotes considered "incompatible with what was intended."

At a presidential campaign rally in Naperville, Ill., George W. Bush made a derogatory remark about a journalist while on stage. The remark, meant to be heard only by running mate Dick Cheney, was picked up by the microphone and several reporters' tape recorders.

The Baltimore Sun related the incident this way:

As the two candidates stood onstage, gazing out over the crowd and waving, Bush remarked, "There's Adam Clymer, major-league asshole from *The New York Times*."

"Oh, yeah, he is, big-time," Cheney agreed.

We know those quotations are accurate because Web sites such as *USA Today*'s provided an actual audio recording. *USA Today*, however, quoted the candidates differently:

Standing on a stage at the start of a rally in Naperville, Ill., Bush was heard saying to Cheney, "There's Adam Clymer of *The New York Times*, a major-league asshole." To which Cheney replied, "Yeah, big time."

Other newspapers reported censored variations of the quotes. The *St. Petersburg Times* wrote:

"There's Adam Clymer, major league a___h___," Bush told Cheney.

"Oh yeah, yeah. Big time," Cheney agreed.

The New York *Daily News* censored the quote this way:

"There's Adam Clymer — major league a___hole from *The New York Times*," Bush noted while waving to the crowd.

"Oh, yeah, he is. Big time," Cheney said, as the smiles on the two men broadened and Bush nodded while continuing to wave with both arms.

One thing's for sure. Bush and Cheney said what they said. Editors might want to censor the vulgarity, but they should not change the words. Your passion for accuracy should compel you to get and record the exact words. Only then can you decide which words to put between quotation marks.

Verification

When someone important says something important but perhaps false, putting the material in quotes does not relieve you of the responsibility for the inaccuracies. Citizens, officials and candidates for office often say things that may be partially true or altogether untrue and perhaps even libelous. Quotations, like any other information you gather, need verification.

In the 1950s, during the time of Sen. Joseph McCarthy's anti-Communism investigations, many newspapers, in the interest of strict objectivity, day after day quoted the Wisconsin senator's charges and countercharges. (It should be pointed out that some publishers did this because they agreed with his stance and because his remarks sold newspapers.) Few papers thought it was their responsibility to quote others who were pointing out the obvious errors and inconsistencies in the demagogue's remarks. Today, however, in the interest of balance, fairness and objectivity, many papers leave out, correct or point out the errors in some quotations. This may be done in the article itself or in an accompanying story.

If candidate Joe Harkness says that his opponent Jim McGown is a member of the Ku Klux Klan, you should check before you print the charge. Good reporters don't stop looking and checking just because someone gives them some information. Look for yourself. Prisoners may have an altogether different account of a riot from the one the prison officials give you. Your story will not be complete unless you talk to all sides.

"When you see yourself quoted in print and you're sorry you said it, it suddenly becomes a misquotation."

— Dr. Laurence J. Peter, author of *Peter's Quotations* and *The Peter Principle*

PROBLEMS IN DIRECT QUOTATION

By now you realize that although you should use direct quotations, they present many challenges and problems. Let's look at some of them.

"The surest way to make a monkey of a man is to quote him."

— Robert Benchley, humorist

Paraphrasing Quotes

While some quotations need verification, others need clarification. Do not quote someone unless you are sure of what that person means. The reason (or excuse) "But that's what the man said" is not sufficient to use the quote. It is much better to skip a quotation altogether than to confuse the reader.

The best way to avoid confusing and unclear quotes or needlessly long and wordy quotes is to paraphrase. You must convey to the reader the meaning of the speaker. As a reporter you must have confidence that sometimes you are able to convey that meaning in fewer words and in better language than the speaker did. You can save your editors a lot of work if you shorten quotes. Digesting, condensing and clarifying quotes take more effort than simply recording them word for word. You will not impress anyone with long quotations. On the contrary, you may be guilty of lazy writing. Here is a quote that could be cut drastically:

```
"When I first started singing lessons I assumed I would be a
public school teacher and maybe, if I was good enough, a
voice teacher," he said. "When I graduated from the
university, I still thought I would be a teacher, and I
wanted to teach."
```

A rewrite conveys the meaning more succinctly:

```
When he first started singing lessons, and even after he
graduated from the university, he wanted to be a public school
voice teacher.
```

Using Partial Quotes

It is much better to paraphrase or to use full quotes than to use fragmentary or partial quotes. Some editors would have you avoid "orphan quotes" almost altogether. Here is an example of the overuse of partial quotes:

```
The mayor said citizens should "turn off" unnecessary lights
and "turn down" thermostats "to 65 degrees."
```

The sentence would be better with no quotation marks at all.

If a particular phrase has special significance or meaning, a partial quote may be justifiable. Sometimes you may want to put a word or phrase in quotation marks to indicate that this was precisely what the speaker said. Look at this use of a one-word quote in a story about genetic engineering in *The Atlantic Monthly:*

> By all but eliminating agricultural erosion and runoff — so Brian Noyes, the local conservation-district manager, told me — continuous no-till could "revolutionize" the area's water quality.

The writer thought it important that readers should know that "revolutionize" was not his word but the word of Brian Noyes. And he was right. "Revolutionize" is a strong word.

When you do use partial quotes, do not put quotation marks around something the speaker could not have said. Suppose a speaker told a student audience at a university, "I am pleased and thrilled with your attendance here tonight." It would be incorrect to write:

```
The speaker said she was "pleased and thrilled with the
students' attendance."
```

Partial quotes often contain an ellipsis (three spaced periods) to tell the reader that some of the words of the quote are missing. For example:

```
"I have come here tonight . . . and I have crossed state lines
. . . to conspire against the government."
```

This practice at times may be justifiable, but you should not keep the reader guessing about what is missing. Sometimes the actual meaning of the speaker can be distorted by dropping certain words. If a critic writes about a three-act play, "A great hit — except for the first three acts," an ad that picks up only the first part of that quote is guilty of misrepresentation. A journalist using the technique to distort the message is no less guilty.

Capturing Dialect or Accent

Using colorful or colloquial expressions helps the writer capture a person in a particular environment. The same is true when you write the way people talk:

> "Are you gonna go?" he asked.
>
> "No, I'm not goin'," she replied.

In everyday speech hardly anyone enunciates perfectly. To do so would sound affected. In fiction, therefore, it is common to use spellings that match speech. But when conversation is written down in newspaper reporting, readers expect correct, full spellings. Not only is correct spelling easier to read, it is also less difficult to write. Capturing dialect is difficult, as these passages from a story about a Hollywood actress illustrate:

> "Boy, it's hot out theah," she started. "I could sure use a nice cold beer. How about it, uh? Wanta go get a couple beers?"

If she said "theah," wouldn't she also say "beeah"? Perhaps she said, "How 'bout it, uh?" And if she said "wanta," maybe she also said "geta."

In another passage, the author has the actress speaking "straight" English:

> "Would you believe I used to dress like that all the time? Dates didn't want to be seen with me. I was always being asked to change clothes before going out."

Then, later in the story, she reverts to less formal speech:

> "I'm tired of pickin' up checks. I've never been ta college, so I'd like to take a coupla classes. I wanta take law so I can find out who's stealing the country. And I wanta take geology. The San Andreas Fault is my hobby, y'know? I think man can beat out nature."

First the actress wanted "a couple beers." Then she wanted to take "a coupla classes." In the same passage she is tired of "pickin'" up checks, but she wants to find out who's "stealing" the country. It is unlikely she is that inconsistent in her speech.

The writer of this story tried to show us something of the character of the actress. If he wanted to convey her speech patterns, he should either have been consistent or simply reported that she talked the same off the set as on it.

Sometimes when a newspaper attempts to quote someone saying something uniquely, it betrays a bias. During the 1960 presidential election campaign, some Northern newspapers delighted in quoting Alabama Gov. George Wallace exactly, even trying to reproduce his Southern drawl. But some of these same newspapers did not try to reproduce the Boston accent of John F. Kennedy or of his brothers.

However, you should not make everyone's speech the same. Barbara King, now the director of editorial training for the Associated Press, laments "our frequent inability to write other than insipid speech" and "our tendency to homogenize the day-to-day speech patterns of the heterogeneous people we write about." She acknowledges that writers worry about exposing to ridicule the immigrant's halting or perhaps unconventional speech while the stockbroker's speech appears flawless.

King calls the argument specious. Of course, people should not be exposed to ridicule through their speech. "The point here," she says, "is simply that when the writer's intention in writing dialects, quaint expressions, nonconventional grammar, flowery or showy speech, or the Queen's English is to make a person human, that intention is not only acceptable, it's desirable."

J. R. Moehringer of the *Los Angeles Times* did this in his Pulitzer Prize-winning article for feature writing:

> "No white man gonna tell me not to march," Lucy says, jutting her chin. "Only make me march harder."

The only way you can make people human is to listen to them. King says reporters and writers usually hear but rarely listen. She advises reporters to "listen for expressions, turns of phrase, idiosyncratic talk," and to work it into their stories.

USA Today reporter James Cox did that when he wrote about multimillionaire Rose Blumkin and her Mrs. B.'s Warehouse in Omaha, Neb. Cox wrote that the 95-year-old proprietor rues the day she hired her grandsons, Ron and Irv Blumkin, to help her manage her furniture business, especially after she began to feel as if they were trying to go over her head:

> "They don't have no character. They don't have no feelings," says Mrs. B. in her thick Russian accent. "They told me I am too old, too cranky. . . . They don't know nothing. What I got in my finger they don't got in their whole heads."
>
> Mrs. B. is wonderful with customers but has no use for the hired help. "He's a dummy, my salesman. A stupe."
>
> Says salesman Jerry Pearson, "She's hell on the help but great with customers. She closes like a bear trap."

Reporter Cox was listening that day, and he worked those quotes into his story with great effect.

Mix-Matching Questions and Answers

Writers have other problems with quotes. They often agonize over whether they may use answers from one question to answer another question. Later on in an interview or in a trial, a person may say something that answers better or more fully a question posed earlier.

In the preceding Cox quotations of Mrs. B., notice the ellipsis in the quote about her grandsons. Mrs. B. probably did not say those words sequentially. The

In Their Own Words

Jo Ellen Krumm was a reporter for the *North Platte* (Neb.) *Telegraph* and a correspondent for *The Denver Post* zone sections before returning to school for a master's degree in health/medical writing and magazine journalism.

"I never thought I'd end up being an editor," she says. But after completing her degree in 1980, she was hired as associate editor of *Muscle & Fitness* magazine. Then she became research editor, articles editor and managing editor, her present position.

Both as a reporter and as an editor, Jo Ellen has had long experience with direct quotations and attribution. Here are some tips from her:

- Get it straight from the horse's mouth. Don't trust secondhand and thirdhand sources.
- Listen. Don't be so wrapped up in your preselected questions that you don't let your subject expound on his or her favorite theme or pet peeve. When your subject's on a roll, listen.
- Cultivate many sources. The more varied sources you have, the more information and points of view you'll obtain. If you rely on the same people all the time, you'll get similar quotes.
- Be nice. Remember that people don't have to talk to you. Usually they're doing you a favor. Even when you write something the source would prefer not be printed or broadcast, be professional and fair in your dealings with the unhappy subject.
- Think ahead. Remember, you may need your sources again.

words after the ellipsis may have been said hours after the previous quote. The only questions you must ask yourself in situations like this are: Am I being fair? Am I distorting the meaning? Am I putting quotes together that change what the speaker intended to say? Sentences that logically go together, that logically enhance one another and that are clearly sequential can and often should be placed together.

Correcting Quotes

The quotes from Mrs. B. bring up perhaps the most perplexing problem tied to proper handling of direct quotations. The Russian immigrant uses incorrect grammar. When do you, or should you, correct grammatical errors in a direct quotation? Should you expect people in news conferences or during informal interviews to speak perfect English?

Although quotation marks mean you are capturing the exact language of a speaker, it is accepted practice at many newspapers to correct mistakes in grammar and to convey a person's remarks in complete sentences. None of us regularly speaks in perfect, grammatical sentences. But if we were writing down our remarks, presumably we would write in grammatically correct English.

Reporters and editors differ widely on when or even whether to correct quotes. A reporter for the *Rocky Mountain News* quoted an attorney as saying, "Her and John gave each other things they needed and couldn't get anyplace else." The reporter said the quote was accurate but, on second thought, said it might have been better to correct the grammar in the written account.

A story on CNN.com about the loss of the crew in the space shuttle Columbia disaster uses these quotes:

> "As we seen (Columbia) coming over, we seen a lot of light and it looked like debris and stuff was coming off the shuttle," Benjamin Laster, of Kempt, Texas, told CNN.
> "We seen large masses of pieces coming off the shuttle as it was coming by," Laster said. "The house kind-of shook and we noticed a big sonic boom . . . and then we seen a big continuous puff of vapor or smoke stream come out and then we noticed a big chunk come over."

Did CNN.com perhaps allow these quotes to stand because Laster was on the network using these exact words? But is that a reason for not paraphrasing the quotes and avoiding making the speaker sound uneducated?

Most papers have no written policy on correcting grammatical errors in direct quotations. Because so many variables are involved, these matters are handled on a case-by-case basis. Some argue you should sacrifice a bit of accuracy in the interest of promoting proper English.

However, some would let public figures be embarrassed by quoting them using incorrect grammar. Columnist James Kilpatrick asks, "When we put a statement (of a public figure) in direct quotation marks, must it be exactly what was said? My own answer is yes. On any issue of critical substance, we ought not to alter a single word."

Yet in another matter in a different column, Kilpatrick writes, "It is all very well to *tidy up a subject's syntax* (italics added) and to eliminate the ahs, ers and you-knows, but direct quotation marks are a reporter's iron-clad, honor-bound guarantee that something was actually said."

At times it may be necessary to illustrate a person's flawed use of language. In some cases, you may wish to use "sic" in brackets to note the error, misuse or peculiarity of the quotation. "Sic," Latin for "thus," indicates that a statement was originally spoken or written exactly as quoted. It is particularly important to use "sic" for improper or unusual use of language when you are quoting a written source.

And if you think there is some agreement on the subject of correcting grammar in direct quotations, read what *The Associated Press Stylebook and Briefing on Media Law* says:

Never alter quotations even to correct minor grammatical errors or word usage. Casual minor tongue slips may be removed by using ellipses but even that should be done with extreme caution. If there is a question about a quote, either don't use it or ask the speaker to clarify.

When a reporter asked Kelly McBride of the Poynter Institute about using a quote of a child who said, "Everybody be up here," McBride answered, "Fix it." The reporter asked, "Really? I can do that?"

McBride goes on to say in her column on Poynter Online, "We fix grammar all the time, I explained. Often, we do it as we write the quotes down in our notebook. A week later, one of my colleagues told her the exact opposite. Never change anything inside the quotations marks, he said.

"If a quote contains poor grammar, the bar for using it is surpassed when the substance of the statement contains an important fact, reveals something about the character, and is relevant to the story, he said."

Correcting quotations is even more difficult for radio and television reporters. That's why they don't worry about it as much. Writers and editors for print might remember that the quotation they use may have been heard by millions of people on radio or television. Changing the quote even slightly might make viewers and listeners question the credibility of print reports. They might also ask why print writers feel the need to act as press agents who wish to make their subjects look good.

That applies to celebrities of all kinds (actors, sports figures), but it might also apply to registered political candidates and elected officials. At least, some argue, news agencies should have some consistency. If a reporter quotes a farmer using incorrect grammar, then should the same be done for the mayor or for a college professor?

A letter in *The Washington Post* criticized the newspaper for quoting exactly a mother of 14 children who was annoyed at then Mayor Marion Barry's advice to stop having babies. The quote read: "And your job is to open up all those houses that's boarded up." The writer then accused the *Post* of regularly stringing together quotes of the president to make him appear articulate. The writer concluded: "I don't care whether the *Post* polishes quotes or not. I simply think that everyone — black or white, rich or poor, president or welfare mother — deserves equal treatment."

That's good advice.

Removing Redundancies

Another question you must deal with as a reporter is whether to remove redundancies and other irrelevant material by using ellipses. Again, there is no agreement in the industry. Even though some consider it wrong to clean up quotes, they do not mind omitting words and even sentences from quotes without indicating the omission by an ellipsis. Some newspapers choose not to use ellipses because they make readers wonder what was left out or, as one editor said, "because typographically they make the paper look like chicken pox."

For most reporters and editors, the answer to the problem of correcting quotes is to take out the quotation marks and to paraphrase. However, when you paraphrase, you sometimes lose a lot. The value of quotes often lies in their richness and uniqueness.

Without question, you should know the policy of your news organization regarding the use of direct quotations. But equally without question, that policy should be that you place inside quotation marks only the exact words of the speaker. Make that your personal policy, and you can't go wrong.

Deleting Obscenity, Profanity and Vulgarity

Many news organizations never allow some things people say to be printed or broadcast — even if they are said uniquely. Obscenities (words usually referring to sexual parts or functions), profanities (words used irreverently to refer to a deity or to beings people regard as divine) and vulgarities (words referring to excretory matters) are usually deleted or bleeped unless they are essential to the story. Even on major newspapers, policy often demands that an obscenity, for example, be used only with the approval of a top editor.

Of course, there are legitimate reasons to use proper sex-related terms in health stories and in some crime stories, including child molestation stories. Unlike in the past, newspapers now routinely use words such as "intercourse," "oral sex," "orgasm" and "penis."

The Washington Post used such words in a 1998 article about Kenneth Starr's impeachment report of President Bill Clinton. The article details the controversy of explicit sexual description used in the report, which prompted wire service stories to run a warning that its contents "may be OFFENSIVE to some readers." The *Post* itself used terms in its article such as "oral sex," "sexual favors" and "phone sex."

Obviously, words such as "God" and "Jesus Christ" used in discussions of religion have always been acceptable to most people.

Nevertheless, the rules are different for words when used as what some call "swear" words in direct quotation. Some papers follow the *AP Stylebook* rule that says, "If a full quote that contains profanity, obscenity or vulgarity cannot be dropped but there is no compelling reason for the offensive language, replace letters of an offensive word with a hyphen."

The *AP Stylebook* also says not to use obscenities, profanities and vulgarities, "unless they are part of direct quotations and there is a compelling reason for them." AP style recommends flagging the story on top with a warning that the story contains language that is offensive to some.

Nevertheless, in recent years the news business has become "racier and more streetwise," writes Rita Ciolli of *Newsday*. She quotes Don Fry, of the Poynter Institute in St. Petersburg, Fla.: "There is a lot less priggishness." Fry attributes this change to entertainment programming, especially that of cable TV.

News is more likely to reflect the sensibilities of its audience. Like it or not, language that was once considered vulgar in polite society is now tolerated more widely.

In broadcasting, of course, the FCC can still fine a broadcaster or suspend a license for indecency. Though that's unlikely, audiences are quick to let a station know that it has gone too far.

At times you may wish to use vulgarities to show the intensity of someone's anger, terror, frustration or bitterness. Few inside the news media condone the casual, gratuitous use of vulgarities.

Readers and listeners don't condone them either.

Avoiding Made-Up Quotes

Fabricating a direct quote, even from general things that a source has said or from what the source might say if given the chance, is never a good idea. Even seasoned reporters are sometimes tempted to put quotation marks around words that their sources "meant to say," or to clarify or simplify a quote. The journalist reasons that it's more important to have a clear and concise quote for the reader than to be a slave to the verbose and unclear words of the source. Bad reasoning. Better to paraphrase.

An even worse idea is fabricating a quote that makes a source look bad or that is defamatory or perhaps even libelous. Doing so can result in a lawsuit.

In 1991, in Masson vs. Malcolm, the Supreme Court ruled that suits regarding quotations can proceed to trial if the altered quote "results in a material change in the meaning conveyed by the statement."

Libel or no libel, your credibility as a reporter demands that you be scrupulously exact when you place people's words inside quotation marks. Again, when in doubt, paraphrase.

Practicing Prepublication Review

A decade ago, you would not have had a city editor tell you to check the accuracy of your direct quotations with your source. Today, it is standard practice on many newspapers. Steve Weinberg, a Missouri School of Journalism professor and former head of the Investigative Reporters and Editors, calls it PPR — prepublication review — and he says, "I have practiced PPR as a newspaper staff writer, a magazine freelancer and a book author. Never have I regretted my practice. What I do regret is failing to do it during the first decade of my career because of mindless adherence to tradition."

Weinberg states candidly that it is not sensitivity to the feelings of his sources that is his primary motivator. Rather, he insists that prepublication review loosens the tongues of tight-lipped sources and gets them on the record for making their statements. Prepublication review extends also to checking the facts. Professionals insist it does not compromise their stand or make them surrender control over their stories.

Journalist Philip Weiss offers another reason why more journalists are practicing prepublication review. "The press's quiet acceptance of quote approval surely owes something to the fact that reporters are an influential elite and are themselves often the subjects of interviews," he writes. "They have had a taste of their own medicine and they don't like it."

Another reason for prepublication review is that it serves as a defense against libel. Jurors are less likely to find "reckless disregard for the truth" in an article that the source reviewed.

But what happens when sources want to change a quote? Weinberg says he makes it clear that the source is checking only for accuracy. He will consider comments about interpretation, phrasing or tone, but he retains the right to change or not to change.

And what happens if someone denies saying something that is in a direct quote? That possibility is why, Weinberg says, you need to have good notes, even if they are in shorthand. Having the interview on tape is even better.

In an article in Poynter Online about reporter Judith Miller's front-page story in *The New York Times* in which she agreed to have her story reviewed by military officials prior to publication, Kelly McBride writes: "Although the conditions for Miller's access to MET Alpha unit were unusual, they are hardly unprecedented in the world of journalism. Every day, beat reporters make deals — explicit and implicit — with their sources about what to print, when to print it, and what to leave out. Rarely do they tell their readers about these deals. Sometimes they don't even tell their editors."

Nevertheless, McBride lists some conditions for when it is appropriate "to even consider letting an outsider read a story before press time":

- Is it even possible? Does your newspaper ever allow it?
- If it's possible, circumstances should be extremely limited. It must be a last resort to getting the story.
- Is this story worth it? Exploiting PPR compromises credibility and public trust.

You need to know the policy of your news organization, and someday you may want to help develop a policy that not only allows but also demands prepublication review of the facts and quotations in a story.

ATTRIBUTING DIRECT AND INDIRECT QUOTES

Now that you've learned some of the complexities of using direct quotations, let's take a look at when and how to attribute them to a source.

When to Attribute

You should almost always attribute direct quotes — with some exceptions. You would not, for example, attribute a quotation to a 7-year-old who witnessed a

Figure 4.2
*Getting good quotes in a
television interview takes
skill and practice.*

gang shooting. You may not wish to attribute a quote to someone who saw a homicide suspect with the victim.

You should also have a good reason to allow a paragraph of direct quotations to stand without an attribution. Nevertheless, if you are quoting from a speech, an interview or a press conference and no one else is mentioned in the story, it may be excessive to put an attribution in every paragraph.

Ordinarily you should attribute indirect quotes. You should usually have a source for the information you write, and when you do, attribute the information to that source. The source can be a person or a written document. However, there are exceptions.

If you are a witness to damages or injuries, do not name yourself as a source in the story. Attribute this information to the police or to other authorities (see Figure 4.2). But if you are on the scene of an accident and can see that three people were involved, you do not have to write: "'Three people were involved in the accident,' Officer Osbord said." If you are unsure of the information or if there are conclusions or generalities involved, your editor probably will want you to attribute the information to an official or a witness. Avoid, however, attributing factual statements to "officials" or "authorities" or "sources." "Such constructions," writes journalist Jack Hart, "suggest that we are controlled by form and that we have forgotten about function."

Hart makes a plea for common sense regarding attributions. "Let's save them for direct quotations or paraphrased quotes laced with opinion," he writes. "Or for assertions likely to be especially sensitive. Or controversial." He says we should attribute only "if it matters."

"We, as journalists, know far more about the effect of the printed word than any citizen off the street who talks to us for a story, and that knowledge carries a responsibility with it. If someone is likely to get his head blown off because we run his name, we shouldn't run it without good reason."

— Bob Reuteman, city editor, *Rocky Mountain News*, quoted by Bill Hosokawa

TIPS: You need not
attribute information to a
source if you are a wit-
ness or if the information:

- Is a matter of public
  record.
- Is generally known.
- Is available from several
  sources.
- Is easily verifiable.
- Makes no assumptions.
- Contains no opinions.
- Is noncontroversial.

This is good advice for the veteran. Nevertheless, although it is possible to attribute too often and although you do not always need to attribute, when you have doubts, go with the attribution.

That goes for attributing anonymous sources, too. Even though you should seldom use them, you must attribute them. Try to preserve your credibility by giving as much information as you can about the sources without revealing their names. For example, you may report "a source close to the chancellor said." For the second reference to the same source, use "the anonymous source said."

During the Clinton/Lewinsky affair, both *The New York Times* and *The Washington Post* used anonymous sources for their stories that highlighted details of the Starr report before its release. The *Times* cited unnamed "lawyers familiar with the report," and the *Post* attributed details to "informed sources."

Sometimes, as in stories about crime victims, you may have to change some-one's name and follow it with "not her real name" in parentheses.

How to Attribute

In composition and creative writing classes, you may have been told to avoid repeating the same word. You probably picked up your thesaurus to look for a synonym for "to say," a colorless verb. Without much research you may have found 100 or more substitutes. None of them is wrong. Indeed, writers may search long for the exact word they need to convey a particular nuance of mean-ing. For example:

A presidential candidate announces the choice of a running mate.

An arrested man divulges the names of his accomplices.

A judge pronounces sentence.

At other times, in the interest of precise and lively writing, you may write:

"I'll get you for that," she whispered.

"I object," he shouted.

Nevertheless, reporters and editors prefer forms of "to say" in most in-stances, even if they are repeated throughout a story. And there are good rea-sons for this word choice. "Said" is unobtrusive. Rather than appearing tiresome and repetitious, it hides in the news columns and calls no attention to itself. "Said" is also neutral. It has no connotations. To use the word "said" is to be objective.

Some of the synonyms for "said" sound innocent enough — but be careful. If you report that a city official "claimed" or "maintained" or "contended," you are implying that you do not quite believe what the official said. The word "said" is the solution to your problem. If you have evidence that what the official is saying is incorrect, you should include the correct information or evidence in your story.

In some newspaper accounts of labor negotiations, company officials always "ask" and labor leaders always "demand." "Demanding" sounds harsh and unreasonable, but "asking" sounds calm and reasonable. A reporter who uses these words in this context is taking an editorial stand — consciously or unconsciously.

Other words you may be tempted to use as a substitute for "say" are simply unacceptable because they represent improper usage. For example:

```
"You don't really mean that," he winked.

"Of course I do," she grinned.

"But what if someone heard you say that?" he frowned.

"Oh, you are a fool," she laughed.
```

You cannot "wink" a word. It is difficult, if not impossible, to "grin," "frown" or "laugh" words. But you may want to say this:

```
"Not again," he said, moaning.

"I'm afraid so," she said with a grin.
```

This usage is correct, but often it is not necessary or even helpful to add words like "moaning" or phrases like "with a grin." Sometimes, though, such words and phrases are needed to convey the meaning of the speaker.

Learning the correct words for attribution is the first step. Here are some other guidelines to follow when attributing information:

- *If a direct quote is more than one sentence long,* place the attribution at the end of the first sentence. For example:

```
"The car overturned at least three times," the police officer
said. "None of the four passengers was hurt. Luckily, the car
did not explode into flames."
```

That one attribution is adequate. It would be redundant to write:

```
"The car overturned at least three times," the police officer
said. "None of the four passengers was hurt," he added.

"Luckily, the car did not explode into flames," he continued.
```

Nor should you write:

```
"The car overturned at least three times. None of the four
passengers was hurt. Luckily, the car did not explode into
flames," the police officer said.
```

Although you should not keep the reader wondering who is being quoted, in most cases you should avoid placing the attribution at the beginning of a quote. Do not write:

```
The police officer said: "The car overturned at least three
times. None of the four passengers was hurt. Luckily, the car
did not explode into flames."
```

TIPS: He said, she said: Punctuating direct quotations

"Always put the comma inside quotation marks," she said.

Then she added, "The same goes for the period."

"Does the same rule apply for the question mark?" he asked.

"Only if the entire statement is a question," she replied, "and never add a comma after a question mark. Also, be sure to lowercase the first word of a continuing quote that follows an attribution and a comma.

"However, you must capitalize the first word of a new sentence after an attribution," she continued. "Do not forget to open and close the sentence with quotation marks."

"Why are there no quotation marks after the word 'comma' at the end of the fourth paragraph?" he asked.

"Because the same person is speaking at the beginning of the next paragraph," she said. "Notice that the new paragraph does open with quotation marks. Note, too, that a quote inside of a quotation needs a single quotation mark, as around the word 'comma' above."

However, if direct quotes from two different speakers follow one another, you should start the second with the attribution to avoid confusion:

> "The driver must have not seen the curve," an eyewitness said. "Once the car left the road, all I saw was a cloud of dust."
>
> The police officer said: "The car overturned at least three times. None of the four passengers was hurt. Luckily, the car did not explode into flames."

Notice that when an attribution precedes a direct quotation that is more than one sentence long, wire service style requires that a colon follow the attribution.

- *Do not follow a fragment of a quote with a continuing complete sentence of quotation.* Avoid constructions like this one:

> The mayor said the time had come "to turn off some lights. We all must do something to conserve electricity."

The correct form is to separate partial quotes and complete quotes:

> The time has come "to turn off some lights," the mayor said. "We all must do something to conserve electricity."

- *The first time you attribute a direct or an indirect quote, identify the speaker fully.* How fully depends on how well the speaker is known to the readers. In Springfield, Ill., it is sufficient to identify the mayor simply as Mayor Karen Hasara. But if a story in the *Chicago Tribune* referred to the mayor of Springfield, the first reference would have to be "Karen Hasara, mayor of Springfield" — unless, of course, the dateline for the story was Springfield.

- *Do not attribute direct quotes to more than one person, as in the following:*

> "Flames were shooting out everywhere," witnesses said. "Then electrical wires began falling, and voices were heard screaming."

All you have to do is eliminate the quotation marks, if indeed any witness made the statements.

- *Do not make up a source. Never attribute a statement to "a witness" unless your source is indeed that witness.* At times you may ask a witness to confirm what you have seen, but never invent quotes for anonymous witnesses. Inventing witnesses and making up quotes is dishonest, inaccurate and inexcusable. One of the many transgressions of former *New York Times* reporter Jayson Blair was that he quoted people who never existed.

- *In stories covering past news events, use the past tense in attributions, and use it throughout the story.* However, features and other stories that do not report on news events may be more effective if the attributions are consistently given in the present tense. In a feature story such as a personality profile, when it is safe to assume that what the person once said, he or she would still say, you may use the present tense. For example, when you write, "'I like being mayor,' she says," you are indicating that she still enjoys it.

- *Ordinarily, place the noun or pronoun before the verb in attributions:*

```
"Everything is under control," the sheriff said.
```

If you must identify a person by including a long title, it is better to begin the attribution with the verb:

```
"I enjoy the challenge," says Jack Berry, associate dean for
graduate studies and research.
```

HANDLING ON- AND OFF-THE-RECORD INFORMATION

Until you are a source in a story involving controversy, you may not understand why people sometimes don't want to talk to reporters or why they don't want their names in the paper. Your job would be easy if all of your sources wished to be "on the record."

Some sources for sound reasons do not want to be named. You must learn to use professional judgment in handling the material they give you. If you agree to accept their information, you must honor their requests to remain off the record. Breaching that confidence destroys trust and credibility and may get you in trouble with the law. But it is your obligation to take the information elsewhere to confirm it and get it on the record.

Bob Woodward and Carl Bernstein, who as *Washington Post* reporters helped uncover the Watergate scandal that eventually led to the resignation of President Richard M. Nixon, were criticized for citing "high-level sources" without identifying them. Even though Woodward and Bernstein say they did not use this technique unless two independent sources had given them the same information, anonymous sources should be used rarely.

Not naming sources is dangerous for three important reasons. First, such information lacks credibility and makes the reporter and the newspaper suspect.

Second, the source may be lying. He or she may be out to discredit someone or may be floating a trial balloon to test public reaction on some issue or event. Skilled diplomats and politicians know how to use reporters to take the temperature of public opinion. If the public reacts negatively, the sources will not proceed with whatever plans they leaked to the press. In such cases the press has been used — and it has become less credible.

The third reason that not naming sources is dangerous is that once you have promised anonymity to a source, you may not change your mind without

TIPS: Three reasons for avoiding anonymous sources
1. You damage your credibility.
2. Your source may be lying or floating a trial balloon.
3. You may be sued if you then name your source.

risking a breach-of-contract suit. In 1991 the Supreme Court ruled 5-4 in Cohen vs. Cowles Media Co. that the First Amendment does not prevent news sources from suing the press for breach of contract when the press makes confidential sources public. That's why papers such as *The Miami Herald* have a policy that only a senior editor has authority to commit the paper to a pledge of confidentiality.

Some reporters make these distinctions regarding sources and attribution:

Off the record: You may not use the information.

Not for attribution: You may use the information but may not attribute it.

Background: You may use it with a general title for a source (for example, "a White House aide said").

Deep background: You may use the information, but you may not indicate any source.

By no means is there agreement on these terms. For most people "off the record" means not for attribution. For some it means that you cannot use the information in any way. Some find no difference between "background" and "deep background."

Because there is little agreement among journalists, sources may be equally vague about the terms. Your obligation is to make sure you and your sources understand each other. Set the ground rules ahead of time. Clarify your terms.

Also be sure you know the policy of your paper in these matters. For example, many newspapers do not allow reporters to use unidentified sources unless an editor knows the source and approves the usage. Other news organizations such as the Associated Press will not carry opinions, whether positive or negative, that are expressed by an unidentified source. The news agency will cite statements of fact without attribution, but only if the story makes it clear that the person providing this material would do so only on the condition of anonymity. *The New York Times* has a policy of not allowing direct quotations of pejorative remarks by an unidentified source.

Be careful not to allow a speaker to suddenly claim something is off the record. Sometimes in the middle of an interview a source will see you taking notes and suddenly try to change the rules. "Oh, I meant to tell you, that last example was off the record." With all the tact you can muster, try, without losing the source altogether, to change the person's mind. At least, tell the person to try to avoid doing that for the rest of the interview.

Nevertheless, if a city manager or police chief wishes to have a background session with you, unless it is against newspaper policy, you should not refuse. Often these officials are trying to be as open as they can under certain circumstances. Without such background sessions the task of reporting complex issues intelligently is nearly impossible. But you must be aware that you are hearing only one point of view and that the information may be self-serving.

Miles Beller, at the time a reporter for *The Los Angeles Herald-Examiner*, gave this example in *Editor & Publisher:*

Several years ago a woman phoned this reporter and "wanted to go off the record" in regard to a Los Angeles official's "secret ownership of a Las Vegas radio station" and other questionable holdings tied to this public servant. Funny thing though, the caller plumb forgot to mention that she was working for another candidate. This bit of minutia probably just slipped her mind, what with her man trailing so badly and the election a few weeks away.

Some sources make a habit of saying everything is off the record and of giving commonplace information in background sessions. Although you should not quote a source who asks to remain off the record, you may use information if one or more of the following is true:

- The information is a matter of public record.
- It is generally known.
- It is available from several sources.
- You are a witness.

So as not to lose credibility with your source, it's a good idea to make it clear that you plan to use the information because of one or more of the preceding reasons.

Knowing when and how to attribute background information is an art you will have to give continuing special care and attention to as a reporter. Remember these two important points:

1. When possible, set the ground rules with your sources ahead of time.
2. Know your newspaper's policy in these matters.

Quotations from the Internet and Other Concerns

Chat rooms are interesting to read to find out what people are saying about a particular issue, event or person. You can find bizarre and sometimes worthwhile quotations there.

May you use them without the person's permission? May you use them without attributing them?

Another question: Kelly McBride asks whether you are giving people an unfair advantage when you interview them through e-mail. Unlike people interviewed in person or over the phone, those interviewed on e-mail get to write and edit their quotes.

These and other questions surfaced after Jayson Blair, the reporter from *The New York Times* who was caught making up people, events and stories, was exposed. When you quote from man-on-the-street interviews, must you obtain phone numbers and check to see whether it really was the person with whom you spoke?

"On one of Kissinger's (then Secretary of State Henry Kissinger) sojourns, humorist Art Buchwald attributed information to a 'high U.S. official with wavy hair, horn-rimmed glasses and a German accent.'"

— Alicia C. Shepard,
American Journalism Review

Do you have special obligations when you use quotations from people who are not fully aware of how their quotes may sound on air or read in print?

What about using quotations from people interviewed by someone other than yourself? The Colorado Rockies' manager Clint Hurdle would not participate in a news conference attended by any reporter from *The Denver Post* because its columnist Mark Kiszla quoted right fielder Larry Walker from an interview by reporter Troy Renck. Jay Alves, the Rockies' media-relations director, said, "There were quotes taken out of context from a player that the columnist never talked to directly."

Denver Post managing editor Gary Clark stood by his reporter. "He did nothing wrong," he said in a *Post* story. "He (Troy Renck) did nothing wrong. He gave a quote to a colleague. The quote is accurate, and the Rockies do not dispute that."

Then the *Post* filed a formal complaint with Major League Baseball and the Baseball Writers Association of American.

Suggested Readings

Brooks, Brian S., Pinson, James L. and Wilson, Jean Gaddy. *Working with Words*, Fifth Edition. New York: Bedford/St. Martin's, 2003. The section on quotations is excellent and follows Associated Press style.

Callihan, E. L. *Grammar for Journalists*, Revised Edition. Radnor, Pa.: Chilton Book Co., 1979. This classic text contains a good section on how to punctuate, attribute and handle quotations.

Germer, Fawn. "Are Quotes Sacred?" *American Journalism Review*, Sept. 1995, pp. 34–37. Presents many views of all sides of whether and when to change quotes.

Hart, Jack. "Giving Credit When Credit Isn't Due." *Editor & Publisher*, Sept. 11, 1993, p. 2. Warns against useless attribution.

King, Barbara. "There's Real Power in Common Speech." *Ottaway News Extra*, no. 137, Winter 1989, pp. 8, 16. An excellent discussion of using real quotes from real people.

Stein, M. L. "9th Circuit: It's OK to Make Up Quotes." *Editor & Publisher*, Aug. 12, 1989, pp. 16, 30. Reactions from the press and lawyers to the court decision allowing quotes that are not verbatim.

Stimson, William. "Two Schools on Quoting Confuse the Reader." *Journalism Educator*, vol. 49, no. 4, Winter 1995, pp. 69–73. Strong arguments against cleaning up quotes.

Weinberg, Steve. "So What's Wrong with Pre-Publication Review?" *The Quill*, May 1990, pp. 26–28. Answers objections to prepublication review.

Weinberg, Steve. "Thou Shalt Not Concoct Thy Quote." *Fineline*, July/Aug. 1991, pp. 3–4. Presents reasons for allowing sources to review quotations before publication.

Weiss, Philip. "Who Gets Quote Approval?" *Columbia Journalism Review*, May/June 1991, pp. 52–54. Discusses the growing practice of allowing sources to check quotations before publication.

www.butte.cc.ca.us/services/irs/tlc/tipsheetsys/01-50/008.html
Excellent outline of rules of punctuation for direct quotations, with an exception or two regarding Associated Press style.

www.owl.english.purdue.edu/handouts/grammar/g_quote.html
A broad discussion of how to handle quotes of all kinds.

www.freep.com/jobspage/academy/king.htm
Barbara King, director of editorial training at the Associated Press, talks about using real people in stories, especially through the use of quotations.

www.journalism.indiana.edu/ethics/great.html
Discusses how much journalists should and do tamper with direct quotations.

www.poynter.org/profile/profile.asp?user=2061
Kelly McBride discusses prepublication review in her article "Wheeling and Dealing and Pre-Publications Review."

Exercises

1. Rewrite the following story, paying special attention to the use of quotations and attribution. Note the sensitive nature of some of the quotations. Paraphrase when necessary.

Christopher O'Reilly is a remarkably happy young man, despite a bout with meningitis eight years ago that has left him paralyzed and brain-damaged.

"I am happy," O'Reilly commented, as he puffed a cigarette.

He has much to be happy about. Physical therapy has hastened his recovery since the day he awoke from a 10-week-long coma. He has lived to celebrate his 26th birthday.

"I had a helluva birthday," he said. "I seen several friends. I had big cake," he added slowly.

He lives in a house with his mother and stepfather in the rolling, green countryside near Springfield.

O'Reilly's withered legs are curled beneath him now, and his right arm is mostly paralyzed, but he can do pull-ups with his left arm. He can see and hear.

"When he came back, he wasn't worth a damn," his mother said. "The hack doctors told me he would be a vegetable all his life," she claimed.

"He couldn't talk; he could only blink. And he drooled a lot," she smiled.

Now, Chris is able to respond in incomplete sentences to questions and can carry on slow communication. "He don't talk good, but he talks," his mother commented.

It all began when he stole a neighbor's Rototiller. His probation was revoked, and he found himself in the medium-security prison in Springfield. Then came "inadequate medical treatment" in the prison system. O'Reilly's family argued that he received punishment beyond what the Eighth Amendment of the U.S. Constitution calls "cruel and unusual."

"Those prison officials were vicious," they said.

As a result, he was awarded $250,000 from the state, the largest legal settlement in federal court in 10 years. "That sounds like a lot of money. But it really isn't, you know, when you consider what happened and when you consider the worth of a human life, and the way they treated him and all, we thought we should get at least a million," his mother remarked.

O'Reilly contracted the infection of the brain after sleeping "on the concrete floor" of a confinement cell, his mother maintained. He had been placed in solitary confinement because he would not clean his cell. The disease went undiagnosed for eight days, leaving him paralyzed and brain-damaged, she said.

Now O'Reilly likes watching television. "I like TV," he grinned. "And smoking."

His mother said she "never gives up hope" that "one day" her son will "come out of it."

2. Here is part of a speech by Professor Richard L. Weaver II of the Department of Interpersonal and Public Communication at Bowling Green State University. It was delivered at the International Leadership Conference, Bowling Green, Ohio. Assume the speech was given at your university and that you are writing for your school paper. Indicate the direct quotations you would use and why you would use them.

So I want to take a few moments this afternoon and look at this twofold problem that leaders face — building the proper foundation (your credibility) and motivating others. And did you know that the two are closely related? Your ability to motivate others is, according to the research, dependent mostly upon your credibility.

Let's just look briefly at what goes into credibility. Credibility is really the attitude others hold towards you at any given time. Sure, it has to do with the house you build, but as a leader you must realize that much more important than the house itself is the view that others have of the house that you build. Want to motivate others? Get your house in order first.

This might be a good self-test. Let me give you the top five components of credibility. You are all past, present, and/or future leaders. How do you measure up?

According to the research in the speech-communication discipline, the most important and first component of credibility is good, old-fashioned, sociability. Are you the kind of person others think of as friendly, cheerful, good-natured, warm and pleasant? If not, why not?

The second characteristic of credibility is competence. There is no substitute for knowledge. You have to come off as knowing what you are doing. I'm not saying that you have to be the most intelligent, well-trained, informed, expert in your area. But I want you to know right up front, others appreciate those who have done their homework, who know what they are talking about, and who seem to have a grip on what needs to be known. You have to understand that good leaders don't waste other people's time.

The third characteristic of credibility is extroversion. Now, this does not mean that all leaders are bold and verbal, talkative and assertive, or animated and dynamic. But I will tell you this: it sure helps! Extroversion often comes across as enthusiasm. Knowledge is power, but enthusiasm pulls the switch! Think of the extroverted teachers you have had and you often think of the enthusiastic teachers you have had. Why? Because the traits are similar.

The fourth characteristic of credibility is composure. Credible people are often perceived as poised, in control and self-confident. This quality helps keep the extroversion in perspective because a leader who is self-assured without being bombastic or overwhelming instills confidence in others. Are you cool under pressure? Can you retain composure when you are threatened or when your leadership ability is under attack? Composure means being able to remain relaxed, calm and cool in trying circumstances.

The fifth characteristic of credibility is character. Are you someone others view as virtuous (courageous), honest, unselfish, sympathetic, and trustworthy? In my experience, I have always related character with commitment and commitment with passion. How much do you care? There is character in commitment. You look at successful people in any field, and you'll find they're not necessarily the best and the brightest or the fastest and strongest — they are, instead, the ones with the most commitment. Have you ever heard the acronym WIT? — Whatever It Takes! Successful people are willing to do whatever it takes to succeed. Are you one who sees difficulties in every opportunity or opportunities in every difficulty?

3. Attend a meeting, a press conference or a speech and tape-record it. While there, write down the quotes you would use if you were writing the story for your local newspaper. Then listen to the tape, and check the accuracy of the quotations.

4. Interview at least two reporters, and ask them about their policies on handling sources regarding the following:

a. Off the record
b. Not for attribution
c. Background
d. Deep background

Write an essay of at least 200 words on the subject.

5. Check a library's computer database for sources of articles about journalists' use of anonymous sources. Read at least four articles, and write a 200-word report on your findings.

6. Engage a classmate in a half-hour interview about his or her life. In your story, use as many direct quotes as you think are fitting. Then check the accuracy of your quotations with your classmate.

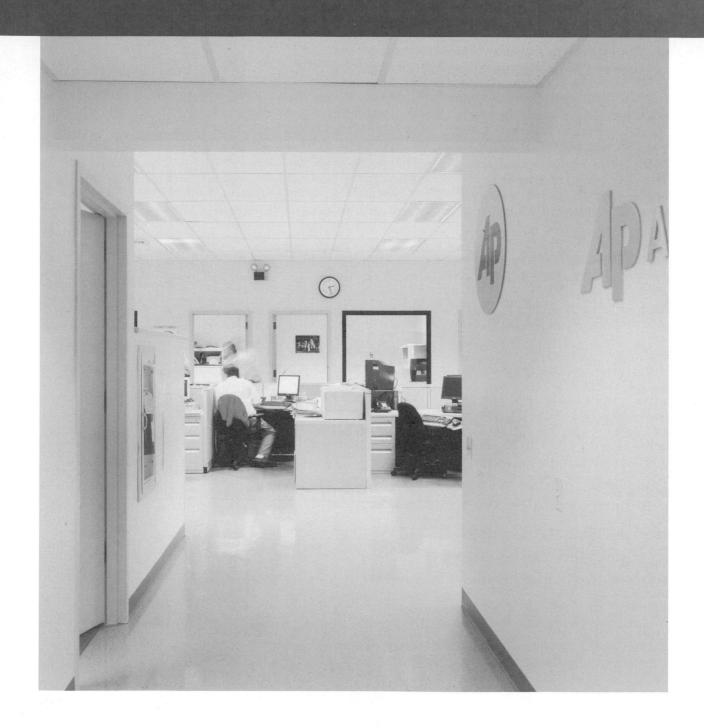

Good writing is important to journalists, as we'll explore in later chapters, but the quality of writing depends in large part on good reporting. Gathering information for a news story requires skilled interviewing, as we discussed in Chapter 3. It also requires knowing how to use the many other sources of information readily available. Make no mistake about it: There are hundreds of places to find information.

Good reporters know that the worst kind of news story is one with a single source. Rarely is such a story worth publishing. Even a personality profile should be based on more than just an interview with the source. To get a fuller perspective, it's important to talk with individuals who know the subject. Gathering information from multiple sources is one of the keys to good writing and good communication. It's also the best way to ensure accuracy. When more and more sources are checked and cross-checked, the chances of a story being accurate greatly improve.

Imagine how many sources George Dohrman of the *St. Paul Pioneer Press* checked in his Pulitzer Prize–winning story about academic fraud in the University of Minnesota basketball program:

At least 20 men's basketball players at the University of Minnesota had research papers, take-home exams or other course work done for them during a five-year period, according to a former office manager in the academic counseling unit who said she did the work.

Four former players, Courtney James, Russ Archambault, Kevin Loge and Darrell Whaley, confirmed that work was prepared for them in possible violation of the student code of conduct and NCAA regulations. Another former player, Trevor Winter, said he was aware of the practice.

James, Archambault and the office manager, Jan Gangelhoff, said

knowledge of the academic fraud was widespread.

"These are serious allegations," University of Minnesota President Mark Yudof said Tuesday. "We've called in legal counsel. I want to look into this promptly. But they are just allegations at this point."

Gangelhoff, 50, said that from 1993 to 1998 she estimates she did more than 400 pieces of course work for players, including some starters on the 1996-97 Final Four team.

"They bring in these high-risk kids, and they know that everything they did in high school was done for them," Gangelhoff said. "It's got to stop somewhere."

Gangelhoff said she "struggled for a long time" whether to disclose the allegations. When asked to prove them, Gangelhoff provided the *Pioneer Press* with computer files containing more than 225 examples of course work for 19 players, dating to 1994, that she says she wrote and players turned in. Gangelhoff said she kept only about half her files.

Gangelhoff also provided printed copies of five pieces of course work that she said had been turned in by students.

Some of the papers had grades and instructor's comments written on them. All five pieces also appeared in Gangelhoff's computer files.

Elayne Donahue, the retired head of the academic counseling unit, said she was unaware of the fraud but warned athletic department administrators that the office manager was tutoring players in violation of department policy and was ignored. . . .

Although Gangelhoff was Dohrman's primary source, there is evidence of many other sources in just the first few paragraphs of the first story in a series. Four former players confirmed the practice. A fifth said he was aware of it. The University of Minnesota president was asked to comment. Gangelhoff provided the newspaper with files of course work she produced for players. She also produced corrected copies from teachers of five of those files. Yet another source reported being aware of tutoring practices that violated athletic department policy.

As the story played out, Dohrman provided evidence of dozens of other sources that he used to get the story. In investigations, of course, dozens of sources may be necessary. But good reporters know that in any story, no matter how short, multiple sources are essential. If nothing else, multiple sources help build credibility with readers and viewers. Journalism is predicated on credibility. Without it, newspapers, magazines, broadcast stations, online sites and the rest have little to offer.

The number of potential sources of information ranges from the obvious and traditional, such as a printed almanac or encyclopedia, to online sites and computer databases. In this chapter, we explore the many possible sources of information. Good reporters make frequent use of them all.

TRADITIONAL SOURCES OF INFORMATION

The Newspaper Library

Every working reporter gets this advice from an editor early in his or her career: Check the morgue. The morgue, or newspaper library, is usually the first stop for a reporter on any kind of assignment. Occasionally there may be no time for such a check. When a fire or accident occurs, for example, the reporter rushes directly to the scene; there's no time for background preparation. But on any kind of story other than a breaking news event, the reporter's first stop should be the morgue.

Covering a speech? Look up background information on the speaker. Covering a sports event? What are the teams' records? Who are the coaches? What's the history of the rivalry? Reporters answer questions such as those, and many others, by checking the newspaper library. Today, most of those libraries are computerized, so we'll discuss them in more detail later in this chapter. In the meantime, remember this: The morgue is almost always your first stop in reporting a story.

One other note on the print or broadcast morgue: Here you can find photos of a speaker or coach you haven't met. They will help you recognize that person for a possible one-on-one interview before the speech or game begins.

Other Traditional Sources

Traditional sources of information — such as reference books, dictionaries and encyclopedias — still play an important role in the production of the daily news product. Good reporters and editors make a habit of checking every verifiable fact. Here is a list of 20 commonly used references:

- *City directories*. You can find these directories, not to be confused with telephone books, in most cities. They provide the same information as the telephone directory but also may provide information on the occupations of citizens and the owners or managers of businesses. Useful street indexes provide information on the names of next-door neighbors.
- *Local and area telephone directories*. Use telephone books for verifying the spelling of names and addresses. They usually are reliable, but they are not infallible. Remember that people move and have similar names. Almost all telephone numbers in North America are now listed on various Internet-based services, including Switchboard.com (**www.switchboard.com**).
- *Maps of the city, county, state, nation and world*. Local maps usually are posted in the news room. Look for others in atlases.
- *State manuals*. Each state government publishes a directory that provides useful information on various government agencies. These directories sometimes list the salaries of all state employees. To date, few are online.
- *Bartlett's Familiar Quotations* (Little, Brown).
- *Congressional Directory* (Government Printing Office). Provides profiles of members of Congress.
- *Congressional Record* (Government Printing Office). Contains complete proceedings of the U.S. House and Senate.
- *Current Biography* (Wilson). Profiles of prominent persons, published monthly.
- *Dictionary of American Biography* (Scribner's).
- *Facts on File* (Facts on File Inc.). A weekly compilation of news from metropolitan newspapers.
- *Guinness Book of World Records* (Guinness Superlatives). World records listed in countless categories.

- *National Trade and Professional Associations of the United States* (Columbia Books, Washington, D.C.).
- *Readers' Guide to Periodical Literature* (Wilson). An index to magazine articles on a host of subjects.
- *Statistical Abstract of the United States* (Government Printing Office). A digest of data collected and published by all federal agencies.
- *Webster's Biographical Dictionary* (Merriam-Webster).
- *Webster's New World College Dictionary*, Fourth Edition (Macmillan USA). The primary reference dictionary recommended by both the Associated Press and United Press International.
- *Webster's Third New International Dictionary* (Merriam-Webster). The unabridged dictionary recommended by AP and UPI.
- *Who's Who* (St. Martin's). World listings.
- *Who's Who in America* (Marquis). A biennial publication.
- *World Almanac and Book of Facts* (Newspaper Enterprise Association). Published annually.

These useful publications, and many others like them, enable reporters to verify data and to avoid the embarrassment caused by errors in print. Traditional sources of information other than interviews are printed government records, documents from businesses, pamphlets published by government and non-government agencies, books, newspapers, magazines and a host of others.

Be careful, though, when using material from a source with which you are not familiar. Some publications come from biased sources promoting a cause. It's the reporter's job to determine whether the information is biased or reliable. A good way to do that is to balance information from one source with information from another source with an opposing viewpoint. It may not always be possible for you to determine who's correct. Ensuring balance between two viewpoints is the next best thing.

COMPUTERIZED INFORMATION

Reporters and editors today have a wealth of information available at their fingertips. In addition to making raw data available, computers help reporters organize and analyze information.

From the news library in your local office to national databases of published newspaper, magazine and broadcast stories, the amount of online information is staggering. Primary sources of computerized information include:

- The news library or morgue maintained by your own publication or broadcast station.
- Public information utilities (CompuServe, America Online, MSN and others).
- The World Wide Web.
- Commercial database services (Dialog, LexisNexis and others).

- Government databases (city, county, state and federal).
- Special-interest databases (those created by organizations with a cause).
- CD-ROMs.
- Self-constructed databases.

Let's explore the usefulness of each.

Your News Library: The Place to Start

Computer databases are a 20th-century marvel that good reporters and editors have learned to cherish. Before they were available, doing research for a story was a laborious process that involved a trip to the newspaper, magazine or broadcast station library to sift through hundreds or even thousands of tattered, yellowed clippings. Too often, clippings had disappeared, were misfiled or were misplaced, making such research a hit-and-miss proposition. Despite those shortcomings, the library was considered a valuable asset. Reporters were routinely admonished to check there first.

You will still hear that advice in news rooms today, but many of today's new libraries are computerized, which almost always ensures that an item will not disappear and will be easy to locate. Typically, you can do a check of the computerized library from your own computer. That makes it easier than ever to do good background work on a story. Your ability to search the library is limited only by your skill with search techniques.

News libraries are what computer experts call **full-text databases,** which means that all words in the database have been indexed and are searchable. Such capability gives you incredible flexibility in structuring searches using what are known as **Boolean search commands.** Boolean operators such as AND, OR and NOT allow you to structure the search to find material most closely related to the subject being researched. For example, if you are interested in finding articles on former South African President Nelson Mandela's visits to the United States, you might issue this command on the search line:

```
Mandela AND United ADJ States
```

The computer would then search for all articles that contain the word "Mandela" and also contain the words "United" and "States" adjacent to each other. In this example, AND and ADJ (for "adjacent") are the Boolean operators. This search would produce all articles on Mandela and the United States but would exclude articles involving Mandela and, for example, the United Arab Emirates, despite the presence of the word "United" (it's not adjacent to the word "States"). The result of such a search in most cases would be a report from the computer telling you how many articles match your search criteria:

```
Search found 27 articles. Would you like to see them or
further narrow your search?
```

At that point, you would have the option of further limiting the search (by date, for example) or reading all 27 articles.

It is important to remember that computers aren't really smart. In our sample search, an article on Mandela's visit to Miami that did not contain the words "United States" would not have been found. Therefore, it is important to understand the limitations as well as the power of computer-assisted database searching. Good reporters quickly learn to take into account such possibilities and learn to recast their searches in other ways.

There are other limitations. Many library databases do not allow you to see photos, nor can you see articles as they appeared in the newspaper or magazine. Nor do most current systems permit you to hear how a broadcast story was used on the air. Instead, you have access only to a text-based version of what appeared. That limits your ability to learn how the story was displayed in the newspaper or magazine, or how it was read on the air. If necessary, however, you can always resort to looking up the original in bound volumes or on microfilm. Most newspapers save old editions in one or both of those forms. Many radio and television stations maintain tape libraries of old newscasts. While these older forms of storage may be less convenient to use, taking the time to do so is often worth the effort.

Some newer library computer systems overcome the traditional disadvantages of computerization by allowing you to display graphical reproductions of the printed page on the screen. You can view photographs, charts and maps in the same way. In broadcast applications, more and more libraries permit storage of digital video and sound clips. As such systems proliferate, the shortcomings of present computer libraries will disappear. Despite current limitations, few veteran reporters would be willing to return to the days of tattered yellow clippings. They know that computerization has made the library a more reliable source of background information.

Thus, the best reporters of today do what good reporters have always done: Check the morgue first. They simply do it with computers.

Public Information Utilities

Some might consider it strange to think of America Online, MSN and CompuServe as useful sources of information for reporters. Don't tell that to reporters who use these public information utilities.

The PIUs are accessible to anyone with a computer and an Internet connection. Designed as services for the general public, they contain forums (or electronic bulletin boards) for discussions on topics ranging from genealogy to stamp collecting to sports. Forum participants exchange messages on every conceivable topic. Some even write computer software that facilitates the pursuit of their passion, and they frequently make that software available to others interested in the topic.

Such forums provide fertile information to reporters attempting to research a story. If you are assigned to do a story on genealogy and know nothing about the subject, what better way to gauge the pulse of those passionate about the subject than by tapping into their discussions? By logging on to one of the public information utilities, you can do just that.

```
DIALOG(R)File 484:Periodical Abstracts Plustext
(c) 1998 UMI. All rts. reserv.

03824381      SUPPLIER NUMBER: 98311155    (USE FORMAT 7 OR 9 FOR FULLTEXT)
How smart liberals fail the ethics test
West, Woody
Insight on the News (IINS), v14 n26, p48
 Jul 20, 1998
 ISSN: 1051-4880       JOURNAL CODE:  IINS
 DOCUMENT TYPE:  Feature
 LANGUAGE:  English            RECORD TYPE:  Fulltext; Abstract
AVAILABILITY:  Full text online. UMIACH  CATALOG NO.: 15662.01
WORD COUNT:  840

ABSTRACT:  A report by CNN and "Time" magazine that the US used a deadly
and internationally banned nerve gas during a raid into Laos during the
Vietnam War was a sleazy piece of work by the liberal press.
       Copyright Insight on the News 1998

DESCRIPTORS:  Journalistic ethics; Liberalism; Vietnam War; Biological &
   chemical weapons
COMPANY NAMES:  Cable News Network Inc; Time Warner Publishing Inc
SPECIAL FEATURES:  Photograph
```

```
DIALOG(R)File 484:Periodical Abstracts Plustext
(c) 1998 UMI. All rts. reserv.

03824897      SUPPLIER NUMBER: 98311671    (USE FORMAT 7 OR 9 FOR FULLTEXT)
The hype report
Alterman, Eric
Nation (GTNA), v267 n4, p7
 Jul 27-Aug 3, 1998
 ISSN: 0027-8378       JOURNAL CODE:  GTNA
 DOCUMENT TYPE:  Editorial
 LANGUAGE:  English            RECORD TYPE:  Fulltext; Abstract
AVAILABILITY:  Full text online. UMIACH  CATALOG NO.: 96.00
WORD COUNT:  253

ABSTRACT:  Television newsmagazines run stories that are unfair and weakly
reported all the time, and will continue to do so despite the "Time"/CNN
debacle.  However, they now know to take on less powerful targets than the
US Army.
       Copyright Nation Co., Inc. 1998
DESCRIPTORS:  Editorials; Journalistic ethics; Reporters; Television
   programs
NAMED PERSONS:  Arnett, Peter
COMPANY NAMES:  Cable News Network Inc; Time Inc Magazine Co
?
```

```
 1/5/2
DIALOG(R)File 484:Periodical Abstracts Plustext
(c) 1998 UMI. All rts. reserv.

03824942      SUPPLIER NUMBER: 98311716    (USE FORMAT 7 OR 9 FOR FULLTEXT)
'Trust me on this'
Elvin, John
Insight on the News (IINS), v14 n27, p34
 Jul 27, 1998
 ISSN: 1051-4880       JOURNAL CODE:  IINS
 DOCUMENT TYPE:  News
 LANGUAGE:  English            RECORD TYPE:  Fulltext; Abstract
AVAILABILITY:  Full text online. UMIACH  CATALOG NO.: 15662.01
WORD COUNT:  217

ABSTRACT:  The national Drug Abuse Resistance Education group (DARE) is
suing former "New Republic" writer Stephen Glass for making up material in
articles, including one about DARE.
       Copyright Insight on the News 1998

DESCRIPTORS:  Journalistic ethics; Litigation; Drug prevention
NAMED PERSONS:  Glass, Stephen
?
```

Figure 5.1

*A search on journalistic ethics reveals several recent citations on the
subject in major newspapers from the database service Dialog.*

Or, if you are seeking to interview those who participated in World War II's Battle of the Bulge, try posting a request for names on one of these services. Chances are you will be inundated with names and telephone numbers of individuals or various veterans' groups that would be delighted to help.

The popularity of such services is almost impossible to overstate. What people like about the public information utilities is that they do what radio talk shows do — give people a forum in which to exchange ideas with those who share similar interests. Writing in *Editor & Publisher*, Barry Hollander, a journalism professor at the University of Georgia, contrasts the skyrocketing popularity of talk radio with the continuing decline of newspaper circulation:

> Newspapers used to be an important part of what bound
> communities together, a common forum for ideas and discussion.
> But as communities fragmented along racial and demographic
> lines, newspapers have done a better job of chronicling the
> decline than offering ways to offset the trend.
>
>   A sense of connection is needed. Newspapers, and [their]
> electronic editions in particular, offer one opportunity to
> bring people together in ways similar to talk radio.

Over the years, newspapers, magazines and broadcast stations have attempted to connect with their readers and listeners by doing people-on-the-street interviews. Interviewing people at random seldom produces good results because often those interviewed know nothing about the topic or don't care. By tapping into the forums on the public information utilities or on the Internet (discussed later in this chapter), you are assured of finding knowledgeable, conversant people to interview.

But the public information utilities are much more than a good source of interviewees. Most have news from various newspapers and wire services and offer information on subjects as diverse as travel and where to attend college. Most also have the full text of an encyclopedia online. Some contain photos as well.

The oldest such service is CompuServe, which contains a large number of forums and carries the archives of several major newspapers. CompuServe also was the first of the PIUs to expand outside the United States. It is quite popular in Europe and has some foreign-language services. German users abound.

These services represent efforts to explore ways to reconnect with the public. With their huge amounts of easily accessible material, they are also useful sources of information for reporters and editors.

The Internet

When a little-known California-based cult called Heaven's Gate staged a mass suicide, newspapers and broadcast stations had no trouble finding background data on the group. The Heaven's Gate site on the Internet gave reporters a mother lode of information about the sect and its leader.

News Is Information

Three years after graduation, Charles Hammer worked for Delphi, a public information utility. Earlier, he was a deputy producer at Access Atlanta, the online service of the *Atlanta Journal-Constitution* available through Prodigy. There, he was responsible for developing content, designing quizzes and surveys and creating new sections of the service.

Now he works for TheSquare, an online network for students and alumni of the world's most selective colleges and universities.

Hammer is one of the many journalism graduates discovering that the so-called new media offer an increasing number of job opportunities. He describes what attracted him to a nontraditional news job upon leaving college:

"The line between journalist and reader will blur as technology evolves. The amount of information available will be staggering. Traditional news sources will be challenged by anyone who has access to a computer, a television or even a telephone.

"To be a journalist in the new media, you must think of news as information. You must be able to present information over different media, whether it be a computer, a television, a telephone or a newspaper. But most importantly, you must not forget what you learned in your journalism classes: Present reliable, well-written information in an easy-to-read format — or the reader will go elsewhere."

That incident illustrates what a powerful source of information the Internet — and its user-friendly interface, the World Wide Web — has become.

The Internet is not a single computer network but rather a series of interconnected networks throughout the world. That arguably makes it the world's first truly international news medium.

For the journalist, the Internet serves two primary purposes:

- It is an increasingly robust source of online information, including federal, state and local government data, and information published by companies on almost any imaginable topic. Need information on a new drug? Chances are you can find it on the Internet, complete with more detail than you ever wanted to know. Need to know about Estonia? Plenty of Web sites are available to tell you what you need to know or to give you the latest news from Tallinn, its capital. Further, most North American newspapers, magazines and broadcast stations have a substantial Internet presence, sometimes complete with archives of previously published stories. Some experts, in fact, now refer to the Internet as the world's largest library. That's good stuff

Evaluating Links

The Web is a great resource for reporters, but determining the credibility of information you get there can be problematic. If the source is a respected media organization such as *The New York Times* or *The Washington Post*, chances are the information is solid. But if it is published by an organization promoting a cause, there is ample reason to be wary.

Stan Ketterer, a journalist and journalism professor, tells reporters to evaluate information on the Web by following the same standard journalistic practices that they would use for assessing the credibility and accuracy of any information:

- Before using information from a Web site in a story, verify it with a source. There are exceptions to this rule. They include taking information from a highly credible government site like the Census Bureau or when you can't contact the source on a breaking story because of time constraints. An editor must clear all exceptions.
- In most cases, information taken directly from the Web and used in a story must be attributed. If you have verified the information on a home page with a source, you can use the organization in the attribution — for example, "according to the EPA" or "EPA figures show." If you cannot verify the information after trying repeatedly, attribute unverified information to the Web page — for example, "according to the Voice of America's site on the World Wide Web." Consult your editor before using unverified information.
- If you have doubts about the accuracy of the information and you cannot reach the source, get it from another source, such as a book or another person. When in doubt, omit the information.
- Check the extension on the site's Internet address to get clues as to the nature of the organization and the likely slant of the information. The most common extensions used in the United States are *.gov* (government), *.edu* (education), *.com* (commercial), *.mil* (military), *.org* (not-for-profit organization) and *.net* (Internet administration). Most of the government and military sites have credible and accurate information. In many cases, you can take the information directly from the site and attribute it to the organization. But consult your editor until you get to know these sites.
- The same is true for many of the sites of colleges and universities. If college and university sites have source documents, such as the Constitution, attribute the information to the source document. But beware. Personal home pages have .edu extensions, and the information is not always credible.
- In almost all cases, DO NOT take information directly from the home pages of commercial and not-for-profit organizations and use it without verification.
- Check the date when the page was last updated. The date generally appears at the top or bottom of the first page of the site. Although a recent date does not ensure that the information is current, it does indicate that the organization is paying close attention to the site. If no date appears, if the site has not been updated for a while, or if it was created some time ago, do not use the information unless you verify it with a source.

for a reporter who needs to do a quick bit of research to provide background material or context for a news story.

- It is a publishing medium that offers new opportunities for media companies and journalists, and new jobs for journalism and mass communications graduates. In recent years, media companies large and small alike have rushed to establish a presence on the Web in the belief that this is an exciting new medium of increasing interest to the public and one with enormous commercial potential (see Figure 5.2). Media companies also use the Internet to attract readers and viewers to their more profitable traditional products.

Just as on the public information utilities, forums for exchange of ideas and information are the Internet's most popular item. But the Internet's forums are far more comprehensive than those on the PIUs. You can find forums on topics as diverse as journalism in the Balkan countries and the French film industry.

Some of the early limitations of the Internet have been overcome. Because the Internet is a collection of many different types of computer systems, it was not designed with ease of use in mind. In the past, users often grew frustrated as they tried to grapple with many different ways of accessing information. Then

Figure 5.2
Established by the San Jose Mercury News, the Mercury Center is a substantial Internet resource for both national news and regional coverage of Northern California.

programs such as Gopher, developed at the University of Minnesota and named for that school's sports mascot, began to simplify Internet access. Now programs such as Internet Explorer and Safari provide a consistent user interface to all Web sites that conform to standards, and they open the Web to the general public.

The Internet also serves as an excellent medium for transmitting photos and even audio and video clips. It's possible to tap into the Louvre's Web site and see paintings from that famous collection in full color.

Many observers of the media industry believe that in the future much news and information will be consumed through an information appliance in the home capable of giving the consumer a choice of full-text, full-motion video and audio. On one device you could read the text of a presidential address or see it being delivered. On that same device, you might later watch a movie or order your groceries. Indeed, all of that is possible today on the Web, and further consolidating those services into a single, practical device will happen in time.

When it does, we will truly have the "information superhighway" envisioned by so many. The wise journalist is in touch with what's possible today while waiting for the full potential of this powerful new medium to develop. Already it is the source of many jobs for computer-savvy journalists.

Commercial Database Services

When newspapers and magazines entered the computer era in the early 1970s, publishers were quick to realize the potential value of saving and reselling previously published information. Newspapers and magazines quickly began selling access to their archives by establishing alliances with companies founded for that purpose.

On many topics, searching your own news library will not be sufficient. If U.S. Rep. Barney Frank is making his first appearance in your community and you have been assigned to cover him, your morgue probably won't help; little will have been written about him in your city. It probably will be much more useful to read recent articles published in Massachusetts, Frank's home state. By doing so, you will be armed with questions to ask about recent events of interest to him. In such situations, the national commercial databases are invaluable.

One of the leading commercial database services is LexisNexis, which provides full-text access to hundreds of newspaper and magazine libraries. It is a rich source of background information for a reporter who wants to see what has already been written on a given subject.

Government Databases

For years, government agencies have maintained large databases of information as a means of managing the public's business. They cover almost every conceivable service that government offers, from airplane registration and maintenance records to census data to local court records. They are maintained not only by the federal and state governments but also by even the smallest of city and county agencies.

The growth of commercial databases is a great asset to reporters, who easily can see what has been written about a subject in other newspapers. But there are some potential problems if you use excerpts from those stories:

- Copyright laws must be obeyed. Take care not to use too much material without obtaining permission.
- Not all articles that appeared in a newspaper can be found in a database. Wire service and market reports, death notices, box scores, social announcements and items written by freelancers often are excluded.

Because most of these databases were begun many years ago, they often reside on large mainframe computers or on dedicated minicomputers. Data are stored in various file formats, and it often is difficult to access the information. Independent analyses of the data once were impossible because the data were controlled by government agencies. Further, few newspapers had the resources or the computers on which to do independent analyses. After the introduction of personal computers in the early 1980s, however, reporters began finding ways to interpret mainframe data.

A breakthrough technology involved the purchase of nine-track mainframe data tapes from government agencies and subsequent analysis on personal computers equipped with nine-track drives. Newspapers started to win Pulitzer prizes using this technique, and soon the National Institute for Computer-Assisted Reporting was established at the University of Missouri to spread the word about the technique. Suddenly, reporters had at their disposal the technology to make better use of existing open-records laws, at both state and federal levels.

Among the reporters taking advantage of the technology is Penny Loeb of *U.S. News & World Report.* When she worked for *New York Newsday,* she used a computer analysis of tax and property records to reveal an astounding story: The City of New York owed $275 million to taxpayers as a result of overpayments on real estate, water and sewer taxes. To get that story, Loeb had to analyze millions of computer records. Doing that by hand would have consumed a lifetime, but with the assistance of a computer, she accomplished the task in a matter of weeks.

Still, Loeb cautions against expecting instant stories:

> Don't just go get a computer tape and expect a great story. You need a tip that there is a problem that computerized data can confirm. Or you may have seen a problem occur repeatedly, such as sentencing discrimination. The computer can quantify the scope.

Analyses of this type usually are done with **relational database programs.** Relational database programs, unlike simpler **flat-file databases,** permit you to compare one set of data to another. A classic example would be to compare a database of a state's licensed school bus drivers to another database of the state's drunken driving convictions. The result would be a list of school bus drivers guilty of such offenses.

After the introduction of this technology, investigative reporters were among the first to use it. But once such databases are available in easily accessible computer form, you can use them in your day-to-day work just as easily. For example, you might want to analyze federal records on airplane maintenance to produce a story on the safety record of a particular airline. If the records are maintained in an easily accessible format, the next time an airplane crashes it will be possible to call up the complete maintenance record of the aircraft merely by entering the plane's registration number. Such information can be extremely useful, even in a deadline situation.

Another common use of computers has been to compare bank records on home mortgages to census data. By tracking how many mortgages are issued to

- Something may have been published, but that doesn't mean it is accurate. History is littered with incidents of newspapers quoting each other's inaccuracies.
- You don't know if the reporter who wrote an account has any real knowledge of the subject matter. If you lift information from that reporter without such knowledge, you may introduce an inaccuracy.
- Databases aren't infallible. The information in them is entered by humans, who are susceptible to mistakes. Databases occasionally are doctored in an attempt to prove a position or promote a cause.

homeowners in predominantly black or Hispanic areas, reporters have been able to document the practice of redlining, through which banks make it difficult or impossible for minorities to obtain loans.

Again, such records are useful even after the investigation is complete. Access to driver's license records, census data, bank records and other forms of data can be used daily to produce news stories, charts, maps and other graphic devices. Numbers can be useful in helping to tell a story. They can be particularly effective if used as the basis for charts to illustrate the impact of the numbers.

Special-Interest Databases

Numerous special-interest groups have discovered the usefulness of placing information in computerized databases, and they are eager to make journalists aware of the existence of that information. Some of that material may be quite useful; indeed, it may be unobtainable from other sources. But just as journalists must be wary of press releases issued by organizations promoting a cause, they must be equally wary of information in such databases. It is important to remember that organizations of this type will promote their perspective on a topic, often without any concern for balancing the information with opposing views.

CD-ROMs

During the past few years massive amounts of information stored on compact discs have become a terrific new source of reference. Encyclopedias, dictionaries, telephone directories, census data and thousands of other titles are available on CD-ROMs, which serve as an efficient and inexpensive way to store vast amounts of information. One such title is the *CIA World Fact Book*, which lists detailed information on every nation. CD-ROM titles can be quick and effective references for the journalist on deadline.

Self-Constructed Databases

When Elliot Grossman of *The Morning Call* in Allentown, Pa., tried to document abuses of parking privileges by local police officers, he sifted through thousands of paper records to prepare his story. Grossman discovered that over the years a scam had allowed hundreds of police officers to park their private cars almost anywhere simply by signing the backs of parking tickets and sending them to the Allentown Parking Authority. Any excuse, it seemed, would suffice for one of Allentown's finest.

Some data on parking tickets were available on computer, but the Parking Authority refused to release the computer tapes necessary for a quick analysis. So Grossman, with the help of a news clerk and reporting interns, decided to do it the hard way. He set out to build his own database to document the extent of the problem.

For two weeks, Grossman and his helpers sat at laptop computers in the offices of the Parking Authority and entered data on the type of violation, location of the vehicle, date and time of violation, and license plate number. In many cases, other notations were made on the officer's badge number or the reason the officer was parked at the location. The result was a body of information that allowed Grossman to confirm his suspicions that many of the tickets were dismissed without good reason. What had begun as a rule allowing the cancellation of tickets for officers on official business had grown into a local scandal, and Grossman was able to expose it.

Grossman's experience is one example of many that show how the best reporters have embraced the considerable capability of personal computer technology. Once the domain of investigative reporters, computer skills are now vital in all areas of the news business. Today, no reporter who hopes to succeed in the profession can afford to be without skills in searching internal and external computer databases and building his or her own databases and spreadsheets. These skills, in addition to more traditional library search skills, are among the essential tools of today's working journalist. Like the carpenter who must know how to use a hammer and saw, the journalist must know how to use words and computers.

Like Grossman, reporters occasionally find that the data they want cannot be obtained from government agencies or private businesses. Despite open-records laws at the federal and state levels, public officials often find ways to stall or avoid giving reporters what they want and need. Further, some things aren't available in databases.

Reporters who find themselves in that predicament sometimes resort to analyzing data after entering it by hand. That's a time-consuming process, but it can be effective. If your knowledge of computer programs is limited, consult with computer experts in your news organization. They will be able to recommend an appropriate tool.

If much of what you are indexing contains textual material, you will need a **free-form database.** A program of that type popular among reporters is AskSam, adopted by many of the nation's leading investigative reporters. Ask-Sam makes it easy to construct a database of quotations, notes or similar material. Many database programs do not handle such material so easily.

If you need to create a simple list of names, addresses and telephone numbers, a flat-file database might be best. Relational database comparisons, as we have discussed, require more sophisticated programs such as Microsoft's Fox-Pro or Borland's Quattro Pro.

Many reporters also are turning to **spreadsheet programs** to help them sort through the complexity of government or corporate financial data. A business reporter might use a spreadsheet program to spot trends in the allocation of resources or changes in sources of income. After you collect data covering several years, a spreadsheet program, which can easily create graphs from the data, makes it easy to notice trends that otherwise might go undetected. Similarly, the government reporter might use a spreadsheet to spot changes in allocations to various city, county, state or federal departments or agencies.

New uses of computers in the coverage of news are being tried daily. Today's best reporters keep abreast of technology for that reason.

TIPS: Ten sources of story ideas

- Other people.
- Other publications.
- News releases.
- A social services directory.
- Government reports.
- Stories in your own newspaper.
- Advertisements.
- Wire copy.
- Local news briefs.
- You.

COMPUTER DATA AS A SOURCE OF INFORMATION

Earlier in this chapter, we described how some reporters have used computers to produce extraordinary stories. Let's examine one such story from the *Detroit Free Press:*

By Tracy Van Moorlehem
and Heather Newman
Free Press Staff Writers

When it comes to education, the MEAP isn't everything.

It might seem that way, with all the stress in recent years on comparing and improving scores on the MEAP — Michigan Educational Assessment Program — tests, annually given to fourth- and seventh-graders in math and reading and fifth- and eighth-graders in science and writing. School districts use the scores as bragging points; real estate agents for selling points.

The tests, begun in 1969, measure the extent to which each student has learned what the state has defined as basic skills.

By the straight MEAP numbers, schools in affluent areas such as Bloomfield Hills are academic powerhouses while those in relatively poor areas such as Detroit are weaklings.

But consider those MEAP scores in light of other factors beyond the control of the schools, such as poverty, unemployment, the number of single-parent families or parents without a high school diploma in a community.

That's what the *Free Press* did in a computer analysis that produced some surprising results. Detroit schools, for example, are overcoming the odds — doing better than predicted, given the factors working against them.

The analysis shows that students in Bloomfield Hills and some other well-off, high-scoring districts could be doing even better.

The study also demonstrates how any straight-up comparison of MEAP scores is inevitably flawed. Consider: Only 49 percent of Detroit fourth-graders pass the MEAP math test, compared with 84 percent of Bloomfield Hills fourth-graders.

Consider: Seventy-one percent of Detroit students are from families poor enough to qualify for a free or reduced-price school lunch; only 2 percent of Bloomfield Hills students qualify.

Yet the test is scored without regard for educational resources, obstacles or opportunity. Educators say MEAP scores brand some schools and entire communities as inferior, creating a cycle that's hard to break.

Mary Anne Bunda, a professor of educational leadership at Western Michigan University, said comparing MEAP scores directly is like rating hospitals based solely on patient death rates: You might think the hospital with the highest numbers gave the worst care.

But what if that hospital specialized in fatal diseases, or was next door to a hospice?

Likewise, schools coping with factors such as severe poverty may be doing a superior job of educating students who start out behind wealthier counterparts. Poor parents, for example, may not be able to afford books, or home computers. Single, working parents may not have as much time to read to children. Parents who dropped out of high school may be too intimidated to approach educators about what's going on with their children in school.

Yet, distorted as MEAP scores may be, they are often used as the sole yardstick of school performance.

Realtors use them to sell one neighborhood over another. Lawyers cite them in child custody battles. State officials use them to accredit schools.

And newspapers, including the *Free Press*, publish them in rank order.

Beginning today, the *Free Press* will take a deeper look at the MEAP, filtering the scores through non-school factors that play a significant role in education.

Researchers and experts say the analysis is a step forward in thinking about the MEAP.

"What you have here is just amazing," said Catherine Taylor, associate professor of educational psychology at the University of Washington in Seattle. She said the "startling" level of correlation between poverty and test scores, especially in urban and suburban districts, illuminates the challenge facing urban educators.

But experts offered a host of cautions, too:

- Poverty and low scores are not inevitably linked.

  "As ammunition for a bigot, it's very, very dangerous," said Harvey Czerwinski, program supervisor in the Office of Research, Evaluation and Testing for Detroit schools.

- Poor schools should not cite adverse circumstances to explain low scores as satisfactory.

  "We are not where we want to be. We are not satisfied with our achievement, even exceeding your model," said Aaron Hedgepeth, also a program supervisor in Detroit's testing department.

- Finally, educators cautioned against making too much of the analyzed MEAP scores, falling into the same trap as with raw scores.

  MEAP tests capture the performance of a small segment of students on one day in a selective curriculum, they said.

"This kind of analysis is better than . . . just looking at the raw numbers, but it's far from ideal," Bloomfield Hills Superintendent Gary Doyle said of the *Free Press* study. "It takes a very limited measure and makes it a little better — but not much."

The *Free Press* story was a complex one that involved taking the raw MEAP test-score data from the Michigan Department of Education, then adjusting the results for factors found to affect school performance. Here's the paper's explanation of how that worked:

To look at MEAP test scores in light of the different challenges facing schools, the *Free Press* used a statistical analysis method called multiple linear regression.

Here's how it works:

Consider MEAP scores against a factor; for example, poverty within the school district. On a graph, you can see that as poverty goes up, MEAP scores go down.

Multiple linear regression is a way of looking at the possible effect of more than one factor. In addition to poverty, the *Free Press* found an impact from six other factors:

- The percent of single parents in a district.
- The percent of households where no one is a high school graduate.
- The local unemployment rate.
- School funds per pupil.
- The percent of students who speak English as a second language.
- Location, specifically city/suburban, midsize town or rural area.

Among city and suburban school districts, more than 62 percent of the differences in scores can be traced to such nonschool factors.

They accounted for 33 percent of the differences among districts in midsize towns, and almost 16 percent of the differences among rural districts.

By using multiple regression to project test scores based on the makeup of the community, we found some disadvantaged districts that are doing better than expected.

The story went on to show that some districts in the inner city are actually outperforming those in richer suburban districts when variables are factored out. Good reporting such as that helps readers sort out the differences between the rhetoric of political candidates and reality. But doing such stories requires reporters to have a working knowledge of statistical analysis and familiarity with basic math. In this case, the *Free Press* enlisted the help of a nearby university professor to analyze the data. Reporters still had to be able to understand the results and translate them into terms readers could understand.

Reporting such as this is known as computer-assisted reporting, and it has become the heart and soul of investigative reporting in the United States. Almost all the recent winners in the annual contest of Investigative Reporters and Editors employed this technique. So, too, did recent winners of the Pulitzer Prize for Investigative Reporting. Organizations such as IRE and the National Institute for Computer-Assisted Reporting offer seminars in computer data analysis. Today's best reporters are eager to take advantage of such offerings.

Suggested Readings

Callahan, Christopher. *A Journalist's Guide to the Internet: The Net as a Reporting Tool*. Boston: Pearson Education, 2002. A useful guide to using the Internet as a reporting resource.

Dizard, Wilson, Jr. *Old Media, New Media: Mass Communications in the Information Age*. New York: Longman, 1999. An interesting perspective, probably the best written yet, on the movement of society into the Information Age and the impact of that on existing media.

Houston, Brant. *Computer-Assisted Reporting: A Practical Guide*. New York: Bedford/St. Martin's, 2004. An excellent introduction to computer-assisted reporting by the director of the National Institute for Computer-Assisted Reporting.

IRE Journal. This monthly magazine is available from Investigative Reporters and Editors, Columbia, Mo. It offers regular articles on the use of computers in the news-gathering process.

Schlein, Alan M., Peter Weber (Editor) and Michael Sandkey (Editor). *Find It Online: The Complete Guide to Online Research*. Tempe, Ariz.: BRB Publications, 2002. Basic information on the use of Web resources.

Suggested Web Sites

www.ire.org
Investigative Reporters and Editors maintains an excellent Web site for anyone interested in investigative reporting.

www.nicar.org
The National Institute for Computer-Assisted Reporting conducts seminars for reporters in data analysis with computers.

www.reporter.org
Useful links to a variety of news support organizations.

reporter.umd.edu
Links to a variety of useful sources on the Internet. The Web site accompanies the book by Christopher Callahan listed in the Suggested Readings section.

Exercises

1. Choose any story in your local newspaper, and tell how that story could have been improved with a database search.

2. If you were interested in determining where Apple Computer Inc. is located and the name of its president, where would you look? What other sources of information might be available?

3. Write a one-page biographical sketch of each of your state's two U.S. senators based on information you retrieve from your library or a database.

4. Using the Internet, find the following information:
   a. The census of Rhode Island in 2000.
   b. The size of Rwanda in land area.
   c. The latest grant awards by the U.S. Department of Education.
   d. The names of universities in Norway that provide outside access via the Internet.
   e. The name of a Web site that contains the complete works of Shakespeare.
   f. The name of a Web site that contains federal campaign contribution data.

6 Reporting with Numbers

A llegations about racial profiling are common newspaper fodder, but *The Boston Globe* took the debate a step further. In July 2003, it unveiled the results of an analysis of 166,000 speeding tickets and warnings issued in two months by every police department and the state police in Massachusetts. They reported that whites were ticketed 31 percent of the time, while minorities were ticketed 49 percent of the time.

Backed by its exhaustive study of the numbers, the *Globe* was also able to report:

When factors of race and sex are considered together, the records reveal a tiered system of ticketing. Local police allow white women to drive faster without penalty, while reserving the harshest treatment for minority men. When drivers went 45 m.p.h. in a 30 m.p.h. zone, white women were ticketed 28 percent of the time in the two sample months; white men, 34 percent; minority women, 44 percent; and minority men, 52 percent.

The striking exception to this pattern was the Massachusetts State Police. The records show that troopers gave almost exactly equal treatment to all drivers, regardless of race, sex, or age. No local police department of any size was as fair as the State Police.

The *Globe* elevated the debate from a he-said-she-said affair to one with facts. Now police departments can no longer simply dismiss the allegations. The newspaper contributed to the community debate.

Journalists have a responsibility to understand numbers so that they are able to report clearly and accurately everything from government budgets to polling results. This chapter discusses ways you can help readers to sort through the numbers.

PROPORTION

One of the most important courtesies journalists pay to their readers is to give **proportion** to numbers in the news — explaining things relative to the size or the magnitude of the whole. A municipal budget that is

In this chapter you will learn:

1. How to use numbers that make your stories more understandable to your readers.

2. How to compute percentages and averages and other ways to make fair and accurate comparisons between places and groups.

3. The basic math principles behind such common subjects as interest, inflation and taxes.

going up by $500,000 would be a windfall for a small town in New Hampshire but a minor adjustment in a metropolis like New York, Chicago or Minneapolis.

Other figures might mean a lot or a little, depending on the context. If you know little or nothing about baseball, you might think that Babe Ruth's career batting average of .342 — 34.2 hits for every 100 times at bat — indicates that Ruth wasn't a good hitter. After all, he failed almost two out of three times at bat. When you look at the context — other players' averages — you realize that Ruth was exceptional.

Percentages and Percentage Change

Percentages are basic building blocks used to explain proportion. Batting averages explain the percentage of hits compared to the number of times at bat. The political strength of a public official is partly reflected in the percentage of the votes won at the polls. Stories about budgets, taxes, wages, retail sales, schools, health care and the environment all are explained with percentages.

To calculate a percentage, take the portion that you want to measure, divide it by the whole and then move the decimal two places to the right. Say, for example, you want to know what portion of the city's budget is allocated to police services. Divide the police budget by the city budget, move the decimal point two places to the right, and you get the percentage of the budget that pays for police services.

You can sometimes use percentages to verify whether newsmakers are accurately representing the facts. Frank Gallagher, a reporter at the *San Francisco Independent,* had the same quotes as every other reporter in San Francisco about how the city's Board of Supervisors President Barbara Kaufman had stripped another supervisor of his influential committee assignments. Kaufman said committee chairs were complaining about Supervisor Leland Yee's poor attendance. Yee told reporters that the move occurred because he voted against the board president's proposals so often. All the other media in San Francisco ran stories with the politicians' conflicting claims. Gallagher took the story one step further.

Gallagher walked down to the clerk's office and checked on the supervisors' attendance records for meetings since the beginning of the year. He discovered that Supervisor Yee attended a higher percentage of meetings than many other supervisors, and that Yee had an attendance record that was about the same as that of the political appointee who replaced him (see Figure 6.1).

"This is San Francisco, so everybody pretty much figured the real reason for the committee switch was politics," Gallagher said. "But when you put the numbers down in black and white, there's just no disputing the facts."

Precision in the use of numbers also requires that you ask the basic questions. Reporters need to be careful of percentages that might be used in misleading ways or percentages that tell only part of a story.

If someone is giving you percentages, you must ask what **population** the figures are based on. For instance, a juvenile officer told a reporter that 70 percent

TIPS: To calculate a percentage

- Portion ÷ Whole = xxx.
- Move decimal point two places right: .xxx = xx.x%.

Ranking the supes

*How often they've attended committee
and full board meetings so far in 1997:*

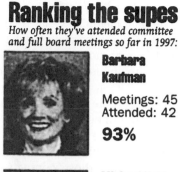

Barbara Kaufman

Meetings: 45
Attended: 42

93%

Michael Yaki

Meetings: 43
Attended: 40

93%

Susan Leal

Meetings: 40
Attended: 37

93%

Tom Ammiano

Meetings: 35
Attended: 32

92%

Leland Yee

Meetings: 53
Attended: 48

91%

Gavin Newsom

Meetings: 29
Attended: 26

90%

Sue Bierman

Meetings: 44
Attended: 38

87%

Mabel Teng

Meetings: 42
Attended: 36

86%

Rev. Amos Brown

Meetings: 45
Attended: 36

80%

Jose Medina

Meetings: 55
Attended: 44

80%

Leslie Katz

Meetings: 54
Attended: 37

69%

Figure 6.1
This graphic ran with Frank Gallagher's story in the San Francisco *Independent.
Looking beyond the finger-pointing of politicians, Gallagher investigated the
numbers and found Supervisor Yee had a strong attendance record.*

of the juvenile offenders do not have to return to his program. The reporter's first question should be "What was the population used to figure the percentage?" Was it all the juveniles in the program during the last calendar year? If so, perhaps the success rate is high because the period being measured isn't long enough. And how are the juveniles who are old enough now to be certified as adults counted? How does your source account for juveniles who may have committed a crime in another jurisdiction?

His answer may be that the figure is based on a sample of the population in the program over 10 years. A **sample** is a small number of persons picked at random so as to be representative of the population as a whole. Using common statistical tables, researchers drew a sample of the names of all juveniles who were in the program over 10 years and contacted them. From those contacts, they could determine the success rate. If the figure is based on a scientific sampling like the one just described, there would also be a **margin of error,** which would be expressed as "plus or minus x points." If the margin of error were 4, the success rate was between 66 and 74 percent.

A different base can have a significant impact on the figures. Say a colleague is making $40,000, and you make $30,000. The salary is the base. Your employer decides to give your colleague a 4 percent increase and to give you a 5 percent increase. Before you begin feeling too good about the honor, consider that your colleague's raise is $1,600, and your raise is $1,500. Your colleague won a bigger raise, and the gap between the two of you grew. You spend dollars, not percentages.

So you see that if you have different bases on which to figure the percentages, the comparisons are invalid. Here's another illustration. If you compare the amount of nuclear energy produced by countries on a percentage basis, the United States would rank near the bottom. But if you compare the actual amount of energy produced by nuclear power, the United States produces more nuclear energy than any other country. The reason you can't compare the amount of nuclear energy produced on a percentage basis is that the base — the total amount of energy produced — is different in each country.

More confusion often occurs when people talk about the difference between two percentage figures. For example, say the mayor wins the election with 55 percent of the vote and has only one opponent, who receives 45 percent. The mayor won by a margin of 10 percentage points. Notice we are talking "percentage points," in this case, the difference between 55 and 45. However, the winner won 22 percent more votes (10 divided by 45 = .22). Because the figures are based on the same whole number — in this case, the total number of voters — the percentages can be compared. But if you compare the percentage of a city budget devoted to law enforcement in consecutive years, you will need to include the actual dollar amounts with the percentages because total spending probably changed from one year to the next.

Another important aspect of percentages is the concept of **percentage change.** This number explains how much something goes up or down. If a municipal budget increases by a half-million dollars in a year, you find the percentage change by doing the following calculation: increase (or decrease)

**TIPS: To calculate
percentage change**

- (New Number) – (Old Number) = Change.
- Change ÷ Old Number = .xxx.
- Move decimal point two places: .xxx = xx.x%.
- Percentage change can be a positive or a negative number.

divided by the old budget. So, if the budget went from $1,785,500 to $2,285,500, you do the following calculation:

$500,000 ÷ $1,785,500 = .28. Move the decimal point two places to the right, and the result is 28 percent.

Notice that if in the next year the budget again increases by one-half-million dollars, you need to do a different calculation. Suppose the budget increases from $2,285,500 to $2,785,500. This time the equation is $500,000 ÷ $2,285,500, yielding a 21.9 percent increase from the previous year. It's a smaller percentage increase because the base year changed.

When changes are large, sometimes it is better to translate the numbers into plain words rather than to use a percentage figure. For example, suppose the town you are covering decides to put in its new budget $220,000 for buying park-land, while last year it spent $100,000 only. The percentage change is $120,000 ÷ $100,000, or a 120 percent increase. But the change will be easier for readers to understand if you write: "Next year the town will spend more than twice as much money as last year on parkland," and then give the actual dollar amounts.

Averages and Medians

Averages and medians are numbers that can be used to describe a general trend. For any given set of numbers, the average and the median might be quite close, or they might be quite different. Depending on what you are trying to explain, it might be important to use one instead of the other or to use both.

The **average** — also called the arithmetic mean — is the number you obtain when you add a list of figures and then divide the total by the number of figures in the list. The **median** is the midpoint of the list — half the figures fall above it, and half the figures fall below it.

To compute an average:	Step 1: Add the figures.
	Step 2: Divide the total by the number of figures: Total ÷ Number of Figures. The result is the average.
To find the median:	Step 1: Arrange the figures in rank order.
	Step 2: Identify the figure midway between the highest and lowest numbers. That figure is the median. *Note:* When you have an even number of figures, the median is the average of the two middle figures.

As a general rule, you are safe using averages when there are not large gaps among the numbers. If you took an average of 1, 4, 12, 22, 31, 89, and 104, you would get 37.6. The average distorts the numbers because the average is higher than five of the seven numbers. The mean or midpoint is 22. On the other hand, if you had numbers ranging from 1 to 104 and the numbers were distributed evenly within that range, the average would be an accurate reading.

Take a set of scores from a final exam in a class of 15 students. Students scored 95, 94, 92, 86, 85, 84, 75, 75, 65, 64, 63, 62, 62, 62, 62. Both the average and the median are 75.

The picture can look quite different when the figures bunch at one end of the scale. Take an example from professional basketball. At the beginning of the 2001–2002 season, salaries for the Minnesota Timberwolves ranged from $332,000 to $22.4 million a year. The average salary was $3.6 million, but the median was only $1.8 million. That's because the salaries of two players consumed $31.6 million of the $54.5 million annual payroll. This is an instance in which the figures bunch at one end of the scale. Of the 15 players, five made less than $1 million. Only three players made more than the average, and 12 earned less. Neither the average nor the median accurately reflects a range that varies so dramatically.

In 2003, the number of Major League Baseball players making $1 million or more dropped to 385 from 413 in 2001 and 425 in 2000. The median salary — the point at which an equal number of players is above and below — dropped to $800,000 from $900,000 at the start of last season and $975,000 in 2000.

Rates

A rate is a term used to make fair comparisons between different populations. One example of a rate comparison is **per capita,** or per person, spending, such as for school funding. Even though a big-city school budget looks incredibly large to someone in a small community, the money has to stretch over more students than it would in smaller districts. As a result, spending per capita provides a better comparison between districts with different enrollments. Suppose your school district has 1,000 students and spends $2 million, and you want to compare spending in your district to spending in another district with 1,500 students and a budget of $3 million. You would use this formula to calculate per capita spending: budget divided by the number of people:

District A: $2,000,000 ÷ 1,000 = $2,000
District B: $3,000,000 ÷ 1,500 = $2,000

TIPS: To calculate per capita spending

Divide the budget by the number of people: Budget ÷ Population = Per Capita Spending.

School district B spends $1 million more a year than district A, but both districts spend $2,000 per pupil.

In medicine, epidemiology and crime statistics, fair comparisons come in the form of rates per 100,000 people.

At the Portland Newspapers in Maine, reporters Shoshana Hoose and Kay Lazar discovered that young people in Maine were killing themselves at an alarming rate. In early 1995 they reported in the *Maine Sunday Telegram* and the *Portland Press Herald* that from 1987 through 1993 Maine had an average suicide rate among 10- to 24-year-olds of 11.94 for every 100,000 people in that age group, compared with the national average rate of 9.48 per 100,000 (see Figure 6.2). Maine's rate during those years was also much higher than it had been in the previous seven years.

4A Portland Press Herald, Tuesday, March 21, 1995

DYING YOUNG: MAINE'S QUIET TRAGEDY

Suicide prevention programs are multiplying

● According to the CDC, the most successful approach is a basketful of diverse programs.

By SHOSHANA HOOSE
Staff Writer

When a sophomore at Mt. Blue High School in Farmington killed himself in February, the second suicide there in a month, the school district acted quickly.

A "crisis team" worked through the night, making plans to break the news of the death to students and to arrange counseling for anyone who needed it.

Such teams – typically made up of guidance counselors, social workers and psychologists – have formed at many Maine schools during the past decade. They can play a crucial role in helping students cope with a suicide, and preventing one death from spawning copycat attempts.

Crisis teams are among a variety of suicide prevention programs being used in Maine. Many are relatively new and untested; some have already shown their worth. According to the Centers for Disease Control and Prevention, the most successful prevention efforts use several strategies.

Here's are some of the approaches used in Maine:

Educational programs

Maine schools teach suicide prevention in health classes.

Educational programs reach everyone in the school. That's an advantage, since there's no foolproof way of knowing which kids may be at greatest risk.

A common criticism of the programs is that merely mentioning suicide will make students think about killing themselves.

That is not borne out by research. On the contrary, experts say young people should be encouraged to share their thoughts about death and suicide.

"It gives suicidal teens a chance to let out the idea . . . that's been eating up their hearts and brains," write Richard E. Nelson and Judith C. Galas, in their 1994 book, "The Power to Prevent Suicide: A Guide for Teens Helping Teens."

But educational progams have been criticized for other reasons.

Dr. David Shaffer, a professor of child psychiatry and pediatrics at Columbia University, compared students who had attended such programs with those who had not. He found that none of the programs changed students' attitudes toward suicide or made them more willing to seek help.

'Peer helpers'

"Peer helper" programs are based on the idea that kids most often confide in their friends.

Peer helpers learn to take any suicide threat seriously and to notify an adult. They also can play a crucial role in reaching out to classmates who may feel isolated or depressed.

"If you just know one kid or two that you can talk to, it makes a world of difference," says Elizabeth Deering, a senior at Bonny Eagle High School in Standish. "Just to know that you're not alone."

Three-quarters of Maine high schools have peer helper programs. A growing number of middle schools are starting them, too.

Research shows that the programs are a good way to reach kids. A 1993 study found that they work better than any approach in curbing drug and alcohol abuse. That's significant: suicidal young people often have substance abuse problems.

But no research proves that peer programs help stop suicides directly.

And a big problem with Maine's peer helper programs is that they involve few young men. Four-fifths of the helpers are female, yet four-fifths of young suicides are male.

Sue Dreher, who trains peer helpers through a program run by the Lewiston – Auburn YWCA, acknowledges that many boys think "it's not cool" to participate. She says the fact that programs now are starting in younger grades may help to eliminate that stigma.

Communities elsewhere in the country have started peer support groups just for suicidal young people. The Portland Newspapers found no examples of that approach being tried in Maine.

Crisis hot lines

Maine has seven state-run "crisis programs" to help young people. All have toll-free hot lines and send crisis workers to the scene of a problem if necessary. Other hot lines are run by mental health agencies, hospitals and community groups.

Suicidal feelings in young people often are impulsive and short-lived. Hot lines can help them weather a crisis; they are one of the few resources available to young people out of school.

At least one study found that hot lines help prevent suicide among young women. But their effectiveness is less clear for young men, who are much more likely to kill themselves. Studies also show that many adolescents are not aware of hot lines in their area.

The Centers for Disease Control and Prevention recommends advertising hot lines more aggressively to young men, improving training for hot line workers and having hot lines do more follow-up work.

Assistance teams

Since the early 1990s, nearly half of Maine's public schools have started student assistance teams consisting of administrators, teachers and guidance counselors.

The teams look for kids with problems – failing grades, perhaps, or their parents' divorce. The teams then recommend help.

School Administrative District 9, in the Farmington area, goes a step further. When teachers or other school workers fear that a child may be suicidal, they notify the district's crisis team. It evaluates the child, contacts the family and, if necessary, makes a referral for help.

"We are very open to doing an initial evaluation on the child, no matter how minor the concern is," says Steven R. Brod, the crisis team coordinator. Each year, the team does about 50 suicide evaluations.

Suicide researchers are refining techniques to identify young people at risk of killing themselves, and screening programs are gaining a lot of attention nationally. But caution is in order.

Most programs that screen specifically for suicide risk are new and unproven. It can be costly to screen an entire school, and then refer high-risk students for treatment. Some might be referred even if they don't need help.

Other methods

Many educators and youth workers say the best way to prevent suicide is to build on kids' strengths rather than focusing on suicidal behavior.

"Most suicide prevention," says Coleman, the Muskie Institute researcher, "places too much emphasis on suicide, and not enough on the self-esteem of the child and the positive relationships they have with other people. . . . That's what saves anyone."

This strategy encompasses a wide range of programs not usually identified with suicide prevention.

At some Maine schools, health classes teach students about stress and resolving conflicts. Programs match students with a staff member who watches out for their well-being. Volunteer projects help young people feel involved in their communities.

Gauging the impact of these activities on suicide rates is very difficult since they are, by their nature, general in scope.

Staff photo by David MacDonald

Principal Bill Marston roams the school cafeteria in front of a banner promoting the PHrends peer outreach program. That and other programs in and out of school were a reaction to a student's suicide.

A 15-year-old girl's death pushed Goffstown to act

By KAY LAZAR
Staff Writer

GOFFSTOWN, N.H. – The bullet that killed Megan Pauly pierced the soul of this quiet community.

Pauly's suicide wasn't the first in Goffstown. Between May 1991 and Oct. 10, 1993, when the 15-year-old died, four other teen-agers killed themselves.

But Pauly's death was different. She left a note saying that she had been bullied by friends and that she was afraid to go back to school.

Suddenly, community confusion, anger and fear rained on Goffstown High School. The town could have crawled into a cocoon and waited for the frenzy to pass. It did not.

In the 16 months since Megan Pauly's suicide, Goffstown has pieced together an impressive array of programs aimed at teenagers, programs that are more time-intensive than costly.

It is a good example of a community tackling the issue of suicides, even though it did so only after the problem had become painfully clear.

"Megan's death brought a quick focus to the need to accelerate programs that we already had in the planning stage," says Bill Marston, Goffstown High's principal.

Many of the new programs speak directly to the two main concerns identified by a community task force after Pauly's suicide. Those concerns centered on the lack of positive after-school activities and the perceived lack of people for troubled teens to turn to.

In response, Goffstown has:

● Added a new drug and alcohol counselor at the high school and a fourth guidance counselor, at an additional yearly cost of $70,000.

● Started a high school teen counseling group called PHrends, with 23 students who are trained to listen, confidentially, to their peers' problems and assist them.

● Intensified reporting to town police of any fights or even verbal threats at the middle and high schools to see, in the words of Goffstown Police Lt. Mike French, "if a pattern of behavior is developing and deal with it before it gets to be a problem."

After 39 years as a principal – 14 of them in Goffstown – Marston says the Pauly suicide was a haunting wake-up call.

He remembers that just two days before her suicide, the freckle-faced redhead was in Marston's office, calmly assuring him that the seemingly minor tiff she had with three girlfriends was resolved.

"I'm still saying, 'What did I miss?'" Marston says. "Now I'm much more tuned-in to making sure we don't overlook anything." And part of that gnawing lesson has been woven into new training for teachers and staff.

Marton's advice: "Get your crisis intervention plans in place before a tragedy."

Yet the most powerful weapon in Goffstown's anti-suicide arsenal extends beyond school walls.

Called The Partnership, it's a comprehensive linking of community businesses, civic organizations and the high school. The aim is to introduce students to career and volunteer paths they might pursue after school hours.

Twice during the last year, students have been matched with business owners during a day-long, on-site "Shadowing Program" to learn about job opportunities.

The bulk of The Partnership's programs are scheduled to start later this month. Among them is an effort to help high school students learn about volunteer opportunities at the local nursing home, garden club and other organizations.

Goffstown hasn't had any more youth suicides since Pauly died.

Many Goffstown High students feel that town and school officials should be applauded for their accomplishments.

"We have all of these wonderful programs now, though it was possible before," says Matt Hunter, a 17-year-old senior who is the first student representative to the school board. "A little good comes out of everything bad."

Mike Ryan, a lawyer who works with juvenile offenders and who has spearheaded The Partnership plan, knows he's got a lot of hard work ahead of him.

Finding creative ways to capture teen attention – particularly kids on the fringe, the non-joiners, the ones more likely to feel suicidal – hasn't been easy.

And because of limited funds and volunteers already tapped to the brink, The Partnership has yet to come up with programs for 20- to 24-year-olds, an age group that's 36 percent more likely to commit suicide than high school kids.

Staff photo by David MacDonald

Sally Durgan of AmeriCorps chairs a meeting of The Partnership at Goffstown High School. The Partnership helps knit the school and town together in helping at-risk teens.

At 774-TALK, teens talk down other teens

● About 10 percent of last year's calls to the hot line were classified 'depressed/suicidal.'

By KAY LAZAR
Staff Writer

It was the most draining phone call Derek Absher ever had. The young woman on the other end of the line told him she was going to kill herself. She had a plan.

For 45 minutes, Absher, 16, stayed on the line with the teen-ager – listening, talking and finally convincing her to ask a friend to stay with her until more help could be found.

"It was exhausting," Absher said, recalling that early December call. "It took every idea in my head to feel I helped her."

Welcome to 774-TALK, the only crisis intervention hot line in Maine staffed by teens, for teens. Its goal: to provide a confidential service for young adults who need someone to listen when they are confused, depressed or suicidal.

There is plenty of debate about whether hot lines can stanch the rising tide of suicides among young people. Social workers and those staffing the lines are quick to relate instances of suicidal callers checking back to say, "Thanks, you talked me out of it."

But scientific evidence of such success is hard to come by. In fact, the national Centers for Disease Control said in a 1992 report on youth suicide prevention that "all we can say – and scientifically defend – is that (hot lines) may or may not prevent youth suicide."

As the experts debate, the phones at 774-TALK keep ringing.

Staffing the line are 27 teen volunteers, all of whom have received three weeks of training on crisis intervention.

The bulk of the work involves talking callers through problems. Frequently callers complain they can't communicate their angst to their parents. The volunteers are trained to suggest that callers confide in a trusted adult – a coach, teacher, neighbor or other relative the teen might not have considered.

The Portland-based hot line is run by Ingraham, one of Portland's best-known private, nonprofit social services organizations.

Teen line 12 years old

Ingraham has operated a 24-hour adult crisis hotline, 774-HELP, for 25 years. The TALK line was launched 12 years ago, when the number of kids on the brink started exploding, and Ingraham realized it needed a separate service that spoke directly to young adults. Recently, the teen line has been tied into a statewide, toll-free number: 1-800-870-9991.

"Kids are really thirsting for information," said Pamela McNally, Ingraham's hot line coordinator.

Cloaked in anonymity, teenagers often ask questions and confide problems and fears they wouldn't share with a best friend.

"I have a lot of close friends," said Tina Parsons, 15, a TALK volunteer. "But on the TALK line, people are so much more open."

What do they say?

Some are about to get kicked out of their homes and are looking for a place to live. "That's more of a problem than I ever realized," Parsons said.

Nearly a third of the calls last year concerned sexuality, according to the agency's statistics.

There are drug-related calls. "I've had 10- and 11-year-olds call," Parsons said. "At first it stuns you, like what is this 10-year-old doing with this issue?"

And there are teen-agers, already parents themselves, who are unable to handle the stress.

The line received 811 calls last year – 100 more than the year before. Roughly 10 percent of the calls last year were classified "depressed/suicidal," according to McNally, who reviews the notes volunteers are instructed to take during every phone call.

That 10 percent is an increase over 1993, when 8 percent of the calls were logged as "depressed/suicidal."

McNally said that before 1992, the agency didn't keep such detailed breakdowns on calls, so there's no way to measure whether suicide calls have gone up over the hotline's 12-year history. But McNally senses they have.

"In recent years," she said, "things have gotten incredibly more serious on the hot line."

McNally said that at least one adult is always in the office for teen volunteers to turn to if they sense the caller is slipping away from them. Only as a "last resort" are calls traced and police dispatched to intervene, McNally said. In the three years she has coordinated the teen line, that has not happened.

Staff photo by John Patriquin

Derek Absher, 16, talks to a caller on the Ingraham teen crisis intervention line.

Confidentiality a must

It's tough to get a handle on exactly who is calling the line because of it's strict adherence to confidentiality. Unless the callers offer the information, volunteers don't press to find out ages or locations. McNally said she suspects that most calls come from Cumberland County.

She also suspects the line would get a lot more calls from the generally services-poor northern part of the state if teens there were more aware of TALK's toll-free line.

Another hurdle is the TALK line's limited hours: Monday through Thursday from 2:30 p.m. to 8 p.m., and Friday from 2:30 p.m. to 5 p.m. No weekends, no late evening hours. McNally acknowledges that's like asking kids to fit a crisis into business hours. But another reality takes precedence: it's tough to get teens to volunteer on weekends and evenings.

During hours when TALK line is unstaffed, there's a recording directing callers to dial Ingraham's 24-hour adult line: 774-HELP.

TALK volunteers are instructed to encourage kids to keep in touch, and especially to call back if things still aren't working out.

And what of the young woman who dialed 774-TALK and reached Derek Absher in early December? He hasn't heard from her.

This much he knows: "When I hung up with her, I felt like she was safer than when she had called. But there's no absolute surety that you know they are."

HOT LINES

The following state-funded crisis programs serve people 18 or younger who are suicidal, mentally ill or have other severe emotional needs. All programs operate round-the-clock hot lines:

Shoreline Mental Health Center (serves Sagadahoc and parts of Lincoln and Cumberland counties), 1-800-834-4673.

Mid-Coast Mental Health Center (serves Waldo, Knox and parts of Lincoln county), 1-800-540-2072.

Tri-County Mental Health Center (serves Androscoggin, Franklin and Oxford counties), 1-800-499-9141.

Sweetser Children's Services (serves Cumberland and York counties), 1-800-660-8500.

Here's a partial list of other crisis hot lines:

Ingraham, a Portland-based social service organization, 774-TALK.

Southern Maine Medical Center Hotline, 282-6136 or 1-800-660-8500.

Portsmouth Pavilion, 1-800-221-9666.

Figure 6.2

These stories from the Portland Press Herald *were part of a series that brought attention to Maine's high suicide rate among 10- to 24-year-olds and led to government action to address the problem.*

The actual number of young people committing suicide — 219 from 1987 through 1993 — might seem low in higher-population states such as New York, Texas or California. But Hoose and Lazar were able to illustrate that those deaths constituted a startling epidemic in rural counties in Maine, which has a population of just over one million people.

Three months before the newspaper's series ran, a legislative task force had delivered its opinion on how to fight the rising tide of youth violence, including suicides. Hoose and statehouse reporter Paul Carrier showed in one story for the series how years of talk and recommendations about youth suicide had translated to nearly no action. Shortly after the series ran, however, the Maine governor appointed a new study group on youth suicide and in the following year ordered several state agencies to take new and concerted steps to help adolescents at risk.

TIPS: To calculate simple interest and total amount owed

- Express the interest rate as a decimal by moving the decimal point two places to the left.
- Multiply the principal by the interest rate: $1,000 × .05 = $50
- Add the principal to the interest owed: $1,000 + $50 = $1,050

The same result can be obtained another way. Multiply the principal by 1 plus the interest rate expressed as a decimal: $1,000 × 1.05 = $1,050

To calculate compound interest

Add 1 plus the interest rate expressed as a decimal: 1 + .05 = 1.05

Using a calculator, multiply the principal by $(1.xx)n$ (the variable n represents the number of years of the loan).

The result is the total amount owed.

INTEREST AND COMPOUNDING

Interest is a financial factor in just about everyone's life. Most people have to pay it when they borrow money, and many people earn it when they deposit money at a bank. Consumers pay interest on home mortgages, car loans and credit card balances. Individuals and businesses earn interest when they deposit money in a financial institution or make a loan. Federal regulations require the interest rates charged by or paid by most institutions to be expressed as annual percentage rates so the rates can be compared.

There are two types of interest: simple and compound. **Simple interest** is interest to be paid on the **principal,** the amount borrowed. It is calculated by multiplying the amount of the loan by the annual percentage rate.

Suppose a student borrows $1,000 from her grandfather at a 5 percent annual rate to help cover college expenses. She needs only a one-year loan, so the cost is figured as simple interest. To calculate simple interest, multiply the principal by the interest rate: $1,000 × .05 = $50. To find the amount the student will repay her grandfather at the end of a year, add the principal to the interest. The student will owe $1,050.

If the loan is made over a period longer than a year, the borrower pays **compound interest.** Compound interest is interest paid on the total of the principal and the interest that already has accrued.

Suppose the student borrows $1,000 at an annual percentage rate of 5 percent and pays her grandfather back four years later, after graduation. She owes 5 percent annual interest for each year of the loan. But because she has the loan for four years, each year she owes not only simple interest on the principal but also interest on the interest that accrues each year.

At the end of year 1, she owes $1,050. To see how much she will owe at the end of year 2, she has to calculate 5 percent interest on $1,050: $1,050 × .05 = $52.50.

Here is the formula for calculating the interest for all four years (1.05 is used instead of .05 to produce a running total. If you multiply 1,000 by 1.05, you get

1,050; if you multiply 1,000 by .05, you get 50, which you then have to add to 1,000 to get the principal and interest):

$$\$1,000 \times (1.05) \times (1.05) \times (1.05) \times (1.05) = \$1,215.51$$

A host of computer programs offer consumers interest formulas and payment plans. Because most consumers pay off student loans, car loans, mortgages and credit card debt over a period of time, and because interest is compounded more often than once a year, calculations usually are far more complicated than the example. Many financial Web sites offer such programs. For instance, select Calculator on *USA Today*'s Web site **www.usatoday.com** in the Money section.

Student loans taken out through federal programs administered by banks, credit unions and universities are a prime example of more complicated transactions. Suppose a student has a $5,000 guaranteed student loan with an interest rate of 8 percent per year. After finishing school, the student has 10 years to pay, and each year she pays 8 percent interest on the amount of the original principal that is left unpaid. If the student makes the minimum payment of $65 on time each month for the 10-year life of the loan, she will pay the bank a total of $7,800. She pays $2,800 in interest on top of the original principal of $5,000. Had she not paid down the balance each month, the interest she owed would have been higher.

Consumers get the benefits of compounding when they put money in interest-bearing accounts, because their interest compounds. The same effect takes place when people make good investments in the stock market, where earnings are compounded when they are reinvested.

INFLATION

Inflation is an increase in the cost of living over time. Because prices rise over time, wages and budgets, too, have to increase to keep up with inflation. A worker who received a 2 percent pay increase each year would have the same buying power each year if inflation rose at 2 percent. Because of inflation, reporters must use a few simple computations to make fair comparisons between dollar amounts from different years.

Let's say the teachers in your local school district were negotiating for a new contract. They claimed that they were falling behind. You knew that the starting salary for a teacher in 1990 was $25,000 and the starting salary in 2003 was $34,000. To determine whether the teachers' claim was true, you converted 1990 dollars to 2003 dollars, and you found that the starting salary in 2003 would have been $35,176 if the district had been keeping up with inflation. In other words, in constant, or "real," dollars the teachers were earning more than $1,000 less in 2003 than they had earned in 1990.

Numbers that are adjusted for inflation are called *constant*, or *real, dollars*. Numbers that are not adjusted for inflation are called *nominal*, or *current, dollars*.

The most common tool that is used to adjust for inflation is the Consumer Price Index, which is reported each month by the U.S. Bureau of Labor Statistics

TIPS: Some guidelines for reporting numbers

- Cite sources for all statistics.
- Use numbers judiciously for maximum impact.
- Long lists of figures are difficult to read in paragraph form. Put them in charts and graphs when appropriate.
- If you use figures from a graph, make sure they are precise.
- Round off large numbers in most cases — for example: $1.5 million rather than $1,489,789.
- Always double-check your math and any statistics a source gives you.
- Be especially careful with handwritten numbers. It is easy to drop or transpose figures in your notes.
- If you don't understand the figures, get an explanation.

of the U.S. Department of Labor. You can get current CPI numbers on the Web at **www.bls.gov/cpihome.htm**. To calculate inflation rapidly, turn to **www.news engin.com** and select Free Tools.

TAXES

You not only pay taxes but you also have to report on them. Governments collect taxes in a variety of ways, but the three major categories are sales taxes, income taxes and property taxes.

Sales Taxes

TIPS: To calculate sales tax

- Multiply the price of an item by the sales tax rate.
- Add the result to the price of the item to obtain the total cost.

State, county and municipal governments can levy **sales taxes** on various goods and services. Sales taxes — also known as excise taxes — are the simplest to figure out.

To figure a sales tax, multiply the price of an item by the sales tax rate. Add the result to the original price to obtain the total cost.

Take the example of a student buying an $1,800 computer before beginning school at the University of Florida. If he shops in his home state of Iowa, where the sales tax is 5 percent, he will pay a tax of $90, and the computer will cost him $1,890. If he buys the computer after arriving in Florida, where the sales tax is 6 percent, he will pay a tax of $108, and the computer will cost him $1,908.

Income Taxes

The government taxes a percentage of your income to support such services as building roads, running schools, registering people to vote and encouraging businesses to grow. **Income taxes** are paid to the federal government, to most state governments, and to some municipalities.

Calculating income taxes can be tricky because a lot of factors affect the amount of income that is subject to the tax. For that reason, the only way to figure a person's income tax is to consult the actual numbers and follow tables published by the Internal Revenue Service or the state department of taxation.

Governments use tax incentives to encourage people to undertake certain types of economic activities, such as buying a home, saving for retirement, and investing in business ventures. By giving people and businesses tax deductions, the government reduces the amount of income that is taxable.

A tax deduction is worth the tax rate times the amount of the tax deduction. The most common tax deduction is for the interest people pay on their home loans. Tax deductions are worth more to people with higher incomes. Take the example of two families who own homes. Both pay $2,500 in interest on their home mortgage in a year, the cost of which is deductible for people who itemize. The lower-income family is in the lowest federal income tax bracket, in which the tax rate is 10 percent, so they save $250 on their tax bill: $2,500 × .10 = $250.

Many journalists joke about their mathematical ineptitude. They suggest that fear of math is why they went into the profession. But even for those who are genuinely afraid of statistics, there is no avoiding numbers in journalism. Numbers are at the heart of reporting government, business, sports and investigative issues, and they can surface in areas as diverse as obituaries, food, religion and entertainment.

Journalists who have a fear of numbers these days had better learn to overcome it. That might mean learning some math. Before using figures in your writing, be sure you understand what they mean.

Say you want to describe the volume of a child's screaming. Would you say the child belted out "a 25-decibel roar"? (No. It's barely above a whisper.) Or do you know how many centimeters are in a foot? (30.5.) Or how far it is from home plate to the pitcher's mound? (60 feet 6 inches.) It is vital to check reference books when such questions arise.

Even the most respected journalists can run afoul of numbers. When reporting a Supreme Court case in 1987, *The New York Times* and other media outlets reported that defendants charged in Georgia with killing whites were four times as likely to receive death sentences as were defendants charged with killing blacks. However, reporters — and the Supreme Court itself — confused "probability" and "odds."

Probability represents the likelihood something will happen. For example, the probability of getting heads when flipping a coin is ½ (one of two possible outcomes), or .5. *Odds* represent the likelihood that one thing will happen rather than another. The odds of getting heads — figured as the likelihood of getting heads vs. the likelihood of getting tails — are .5 ÷ .5 (*even money* in betting terms), or 1.

The Georgia reports concluded that the odds of a death sentence when a white was killed were 4.3 times greater than the odds when a black was killed. That doesn't mean the same thing as "four times as likely."

The lessons from that example are that *probability* and *odds* are not synonymous and that math errors can creep into reporting even when your source is the Supreme Court.

The higher-income family is in the federal income tax bracket with a tax rate of 30 percent, so they save $750 on their tax bill: $2,500 × .30 = $750.

Income tax rates are based on your adjusted gross income. If you make $12,000 after deductions, you will pay a tax of 10 percent. If you make more than $12,000 but less than $46,701, you will pay 15 percent.

Property Taxes

City and county governments collect **property taxes.** When people talk about property taxes, they usually mean taxes on the value of houses, buildings and land. In some places, people also are taxed each year on the value of their cars, boats and other personal property.

The two key factors in property taxes are the assessed value and the millage rate. The **assessed value** is the amount that a government appraiser determines a piece of property is worth. The **millage rate** — the rate per thousand

TIPS: To calculate property tax

- Divide the assessed value by 1,000:
  $100,000 ÷ 1,000 = 100
- Multiply that result by the millage rate:
  100 × 2.25 = $225

127

dollars — is the tax rate determined by the government. You figure the property taxes by multiplying the assessed value by the millage rate. For example, owners of a house valued at $100,000 taxed at a millage rate of 2.25 would pay $225 in taxes ($100,000 \div 1,000 \times 2.25$).

Counties and cities hire professional appraisers to assess the values of land and buildings in their jurisdiction, and typically their assessments have been far lower than the actual market value of the property. Because of abuses and public confusion, most states in recent years have ordered revaluations to bring assessments into line with market values, and they have adjusted millage rates accordingly, although assessments can vary widely from appraiser to appraiser.

Appraisals are based on complicated formulas that take into account the size, location and condition of the property. Still, the government may say your house is worth $60,000, but you know you could sell it for $80,000.

MAKING SENSE OF BUDGETS

The budget is the blueprint that guides the operation of any organization, and a reporter must learn to read a budget just as a carpenter must learn to read an architect's blueprint. In either case, doing so isn't as difficult as it appears at first glance.

In many cases today, you'll be able to get the budget (and other financial information as well) for your city or school district on computer disk or tape. You can probably also view it on a local Web site, but you could not download that file into a spreadsheet database. However, once you have the budget on a disk, you can create your own spreadsheet and perform analyses that not long ago were only in the power of the institution's budget director. This is one of many ways the computer has become an essential news room tool. However, with or without a computer, first you need to know the basics of budgeting.

Every budget, whether it's your personal budget or the budget of the U.S. government, has two basic parts: revenues (income) and expenditures (outgo). Commercial enterprises earn their income primarily from sales; not-for-profit organizations depend heavily on contributions from public funding and private donors. Government revenues come from sources such as taxes, fees and service charges, and payments from other agencies (such as state aid to schools). The budget usually shows, in dollar figures and percentages, the sources of the organization's money. Expenditures go for such things as staff salaries, purchase of supplies, payment of utility bills, construction and maintenance of facilities, and insurance. Expenditures usually are listed either by line or by program. The difference is this: A **line-item budget** shows a separate line for each expenditure, such as "Salary of police chief — $50,000." A **program budget** provides less detail but shows more clearly what each activity of the agency costs — for example, "Burglary prevention program — $250,000."

Now let's see what kinds of stories budgets may yield and where to look for those stories. Take a minute to scan Table 6.1, a summary page from the annual

TIPS: Budget stories usually deal with

- Changes.
- Trends.
- Comparisons.

Table 6.1

General Fund — Summary

Purpose

The General Fund is used to finance and account for a large portion of the current operation expenditures and capital outlays of city government. The General Fund is one of the
largest and most important of the city's funds because most governmental programs
(Police, Fire, Public Works, Parks and Recreation, and so on) are generally financed wholly
or partially from it. The General Fund has a greater number and variety of revenue sources
than any other fund, and its resources normally finance a wider range of activities.

Appropriations

	Actual Fiscal Year 2003	Budget Fiscal Year 2003	Revised Fiscal Year 2003	Adopted Fiscal Year 2004
Personnel services	$9,500,353	$11,306,619	$11,245,394	$12,212,336
Materials and supplies	1,490,573	1,787,220	1,794,362	1,986,551
Training and schools	93,942	150,517	170,475	219,455
Utilities	606,125	649,606	652,094	722,785
Services	1,618,525	1,865,283	1,933,300	2,254,983
Insurance and miscellaneous	1,792,366	1,556,911	1,783,700	1,614,265
Total operating	15,101,884	17,316,156	17,579,325	19,010,375
Capital additions	561,145	1,123,543	875,238	460,143
Total operating and capital	15,663,029	18,439,699	18,454,563	19,470,518
Contingency	—	200,000	200,000	100,000
Total	$15,663,029	$18,639,699	$18,654,563	$19,570,518

Department Expenditures

	Actual Fiscal Year 2003	Budget Fiscal Year 2003	Revised Fiscal Year 2003	Adopted Fiscal Year 2004
City Council	$75,144	$105,207	$90,457	$84,235
City Clerk	61,281	70,778	74,444	91,867
City Manager	155,992	181,219	179,125	192,900
Municipal Court	164,631	196,389	175,019	181,462
Personnel	143,366	197,844	186,247	203,020
Law Department	198,296	266,819	248,170	288,550
Planning & Community Development	295,509	377,126	360,272	405,870
Finance Department	893,344	940,450	983,342	1,212,234
Fire Department	2,837,744	3,421,112	3,257,356	3,694,333

(continued)

Table 6.1

General Fund — Summary *(continued)*

Department Expenditures

	Actual Fiscal Year 2003	Budget Fiscal Year 2003	Revised Fiscal Year 2003	Adopted Fiscal Year 2004
Police Department	3,300,472	4,007,593	4,139,085	4,375,336
Health	1,033,188	1,179,243	1,157,607	1,293,362
Community Services	50,882	74,952	74,758	78,673
Energy Management	—	—	54,925	66,191
Public Works	2,838,605	3,374,152	3,381,044	3,509,979
Parks and Recreation	1,218,221	1,367,143	1,400,334	1,337,682
Communications & Info. Services	532,153	730,129	742,835	715,324
City General	1,864,200	1,949,543	1,949,543	1,739,500
Total Department Expenditures	15,663,028	18,439,699	18,454,563	19,470,518
Contingency	—	200,000	200,000	100,000
Total	$15,663,028	$18,639,699	$18,654,563	$19,570,518

budget of a small city. You can apply the skills of reading a city's annual budget to similar accounting documents on other beats — for example, annual reports of businesses and not-for-profit organizations.

The most important budget stories usually deal with changes, trends and comparisons. Budget figures change every year. As costs increase, so do budgets. But look in our sample budget at the line for the Parks and Recreation Department. There's a decrease between Fiscal Year (FY) 2003 and 2004. Why? The summary page doesn't tell you, so you'll have to look behind it, at the detail pages. There, you'll discover that the drop results from a proposal by the city staff to halt funding of a summer employment program for teenagers. That's a story.

Another change that may be newsworthy is the increase in the Police Department budget. You'd better find out the reasons for that, too. In this case, the detail pages of the budget show that most of the increase is going to pay for an administrative reorganization that is adding new positions at the top of the department. The patrol division is actually being reduced. Another story.

Look again at that Police Department line. Follow it back to FY 2003 and you'll see that the increase last year was even bigger. In two years, the budget for police increased by nearly one-third. That's an interesting trend. The same

Working with Numbers

Before graduating from the University of Maryland's master's program in public affairs reporting, Sarah Cohen worked as an economist in the federal government, producing some of the statistics journalists report on each month. Early in that job, she had to be reminded how to compute a percent change, but she learned fast.

In fact, she learned so well that she now is database editor for *The Washington Post*. She sometimes works weeks to find or compute just the right number for just the right place in a story — the number that tells the story best and most accurately.

Before joining the *Post*, she worked as training director for Investigative Reporters and Editors. There, she met many reporters who were terrified of the numbers they were seeing during the computer-assisted reporting seminars.

At a recent seminar of city editors, she heard the managers' side of dealing with numbers-phobia on deadline. Reporters who proudly say, "I don't do numbers" or "I have a problem with numbers" are sometimes viewed by editors in the same way that reporters would be if they said, "I don't do names — it's too scary to get the spelling right."

"The simple fact is, reporters have to overcome their mind-numbing fear of numbers long enough every day to get their stories done. And if they can never get over that fear, they'll find themselves hard pressed to write any stories more complex than covering a dog show or a council meeting," Cohen says.

"Many reporters had to overcome a natural reluctance to knock on neighbors' doors or call a grieving family. Otherwise they could never be reporters. They have to overcome their fear of numbers to understand the increasingly sophisticated stories expected of us."

She believes the most difficult habit to overcome is the notebook-dumping syndrome.

"We're willing to throw out quotes or anecdotes we've collected. But somehow the carefully selected quote or elegantly crafted lead is sometimes followed by three paragraphs of incomprehensible numbers. So selection of numbers is most important."

There are plenty of devices to help you select the number — you can turn to ratios, rates, percentages or per-person averages, she advises. But remembering that they are guesses, opinions and summaries is the most effective way to reduce the number bloat. Use numbers when they work, not when some other way to convey the same information might work better, she advises.

Cohen is the author of *Numbers in the Newsroom: Using Math and Statistics in News*, published by Investigative Reporters and Editors.

pattern holds true for the Fire Department. More checking is in order. With copies of previous budgets, you can see how far back the growth trend runs. You can also get from the individual departments the statistics on crimes and fires. Are the budget makers responding to a demonstrated need for more protection, or is something else at work behind the scenes?

More generally, you can trace patterns in the growth of city services and city taxes, and you can compare those with changes in population. Are the rates of change comparable? Is population growth outstripping growth in services? Are residents paying more per capita for city services than they paid five or 10 years ago? More good story possibilities.

Another kind of comparison can be useful to your readers, too. How does your city government compare in cost and services with the governments of comparable cities? A few phone calls can add perspective to budget figures. Some professional organizations have recommended levels of service — such as number of police or firefighters per 1,000 inhabitants — that can help you help your readers assess how well they're being governed.

The same guidelines can be applied to the analysis of any budget. The numbers will be different, as will the department names, but the structures will be much the same. Whether you're covering the school board or the statehouse, look for changes, trends and comparisons.

Another document that is vital to understanding the finances of local government is the annual financial report. The financial report may be a few pages long or it may be a book. In any case, its purpose is relatively simple. As its name suggests, the report is an explanation of the organization's financial status at the end of a fiscal year, which often is not the same as the end of the calendar year. Here you will find an accounting of all the income the organization received during the year from taxes, fees, state and federal grants, and other sources. You'll also find status reports on all the organization's operating funds, such as its capital improvement fund, its debt-service fund and its general fund.

Making sense of a financial report, like understanding a budget, isn't as hard as it may look. For one thing, the financial officer usually includes a narrative that highlights the most important points, at least from his or her viewpoint. But you should dig beyond the narrative and examine the numbers for yourself. The single most important section of the report is the statement of revenues, expenditures and changes in fund balance, which provides important measures of the organization's financial health. Depending on the comprehensiveness of the statement, you may have to refer to the budget document as well. You can check:

- Revenues actually received compared with budgeted revenues.
- Actual spending compared with budgeted spending.
- Actual spending compared with actual revenue.
- Changes in fund balances available for spending in years to come.

Look, for example, at Table 6.2 (see pages 133–135). This combined statement gives a picture of the city's financial health. Notice first that the General

Table 6.2

**All Governmental Fund Types and Expendable Trust Funds
for the Year Ended September 30, 2003**

	Governmental Fund Types		
	General Fund	Special Revenue Funds	Debt Service Funds
REVENUES			
General property taxes	$663,932	$530,713	$192,104
Sales tax	3,967,138	3,367,510	—
Other local taxes	3,138,904	228,718	—
Licenses and permits	253,287	5,146	—
Fines	378,207	—	—
Fees and service charges	244,356	—	—
Special assessments authorized	—	—	—
Intragovernmental	4,139,690	—	—
Revenue from other governmental units	796,292	1,164,482	—
Building rentals	—	—	—
Interest	1,314,130	196,612	6,228
Miscellaneous	53,548	—	—
TOTAL REVENUES	14,949,484	5,493,181	198,332
EXPENDITURES			
Current:			
Policy development and administration	2,328,546	291,493	—
Public safety	8,403,851	—	—
Transportation	2,387,534	—	—
Health and environment	1,617,146	—	—
Personal development	1,915,376	622,065	—
Public buildings	—	—	—
Miscellaneous non-programmed activities:			
Interest expense	273,195	—	—
Other	34,975	—	—
Capital outlay	—	—	—
Debt service:			
Redemption of serial bonds	—	—	175,000
Interest	—	—	278,488
Fiscal agent fees	—	—	758
TOTAL EXPENDITURES	16,960,623	913,558	454,246
EXCESS (DEFICIENCY) OF REVENUES OVER EXPENDITURES	(2,011,139)	4,579,623	(255,914)

(continued)

Table 6.2

**All Governmental Fund Types and Expendable Trust Funds
for the Year Ended September 30, 2003 (continued)**

Governmental Fund Types		Fiduciary Fund Type	Total (memorandum only)	
Capital Projects Fund	Special Assessment Funds	Expendable Trust Funds	2002	2003
$ —	$ —	$ —	$ 1,386,749	$ 1,961,851
—	—	—	7,334,648	4,967,691
—	—	—	3,367,622	2,923,775
—	—	—	258,433	247,608
—	—	—	378,207	346,224
—	—	1,129,784	1,374,140	328,185
—	490,159	—	490,159	359,862
—	—	—	4,139,690	3,911,418
154,919	—	901,815	3,017,508	3,087,431
—	—	172,766	172,766	175,479
23,282	—	88,428	1,628,680	1,869,874
29,226	—	—	82,774	97,593
207,427	490,159	2,292,793	23,631,376	20,276,991
—	—	3,338	2,623,377	2,285,509
—	—	—	8,403,851	6,998,232
—	—	—	2,387,534	1,996,520
—	—	1,080,811	2,697,957	1,652,809
—	—	—	2,537,441	2,084,648
—	—	371,942	371,942	336,204
—	—	—	273,195	486,031
—	—	—	34,975	4,296
1,287,520	2,357,784	—	3,645,304	1,990,648
—	—	—	175,000	155,000
—	—	—	278,488	32,435
—	—	—	758	285
1,287,520	2,357,784	1,456,091	23,429,822	18,022,617
(1,080,093)	(1,867,625)	836,702	201,554	2,254,374

	Governmental Fund Types		
	General Fund	Special Revenue Funds	Debt Service Funds
OTHER FINANCING SOURCES (USES):			
Proceeds of general obligation bonds	—	—	—
Operating transfers from other funds	3,011,358	62,974	266,711
Operating transfers to other funds	(1,292,723)	(3,348,303)	—

	Governmental Fund Types		
	General Fund	Special Revenue Funds	Debt Service Funds
TOTAL OTHER FINANCING SOURCES (USES)	1,718,635	(3,285,329)	266,711
EXCESS (DEFICIENCY) OF REVENUES AND OTHER FINANCING SOURCES OVER EXPENDITURES AND OTHER FINANCING USES	(292,504)	1,294,294	10,797
FUND BALANCES BEGINNING OF YEAR	4,195,912	3,004,533	43,645
Equity transfer to Recreation Services Fund	—	—	—
Contribution to Water & Electric Utility Fund	—	—	—
Contribution to Sanitary Sewer Utility Fund	—	—	—
Contribution to Regional Airport Fund	(200,000)	—	—
Contribution to Public Transportation Fund	—	—	—
Contribution to Parking Facilities Fund	—	—	—
Contribution to Recreation Services Fund	—	(152,000)	—
FUND BALANCES, END OF YEAR	$3,703,408	$4,146,827	$54,442

Governmental Fund Types		Fiduciary Fund Type	Total (memorandum only)	
Capital Projects Fund	Special Assessment Funds	Expendable Trust Funds	2003	2002
5,681,633	1,134,261	—	6,815,894	—
415,038	469,865	—	4,225,946	3,466,261
—	(99,667)	(527,506)	(5,268,199)	(4,401,847)
6,096,671	1,504,459	(527,506)	5,773,641	(935,586)
5,016,578	(363,166)	309,196	5,975,195	1,318,788
628,856	781,248	514,378	9,168,572	8,489,184
—	—	(1,532)	(1,532)	(292,958)
—	—	—	—	(30,395)
—	—	—	—	(71,367)
—	—	—	(200,000)	(160,191)
—	—	—	—	(4,000)
—	—	—	—	(15,489)
—	—	—	(152,000)	(65,000)
$5,645,434	$418,082	$822,042	$14,790,235	$9,168,572

Fund was overspent by $2 million. Why? Was there an unexpected one-time expenditure, or was the city unable to live within its means? The General Fund is the largest of all the budget categories, so overspending there is critical. Note, too, at the bottom of the 2002 Total column, that the city has a small surplus of $201,554. Note also that spending rose more than $5.4 million, or 30 percent — a significant increase. All these facts will lead you to good stories, so you'd better look more closely.

Other clues may lead to other stories that will require more reporting and more explanation than reporters can pull from the numbers by themselves. With document in hand, head for the budget office. The guidelines offered here should help you shape your questions and understand the answers. With financial statements, as with budgets, look for changes, trends and comparisons. And always look hard at any numbers in parentheses.

MAKING SENSE OF NUMBERS FROM POLLS

Every day, new poll results illustrate what people think about various topics in the news. And just about every day, journalists confuse readers when they try to interpret the results.

The most important thing to keep in mind about polls and surveys is that they are based on samples of a population. Because a survey reflects the responses of a small number of people within a population, every survey has a margin of error. The results must be presented with the understanding that scientific sampling is not a perfect predictor for the entire population.

Suppose your news organization buys polling services and discovers that Candidate Hernandez has support from 58 percent of the people surveyed, Candidate Jones has support from 32 percent, and 10 percent are undecided. The polling service indicates that the margin of error of the poll is plus or minus five percentage points. The margins separating the candidates are well above the margin of error, so you can write that Hernandez is leading in the poll.

Now suppose Hernandez has 50 percent support and Jones has 45 percent. The margin between them is within the margin of error, so you must report that the race is too close to call. If the margin between Hernandez and Jones were less than plus or minus five percentage points, you would only report that one candidate "appears to be leading."

Journalists faced exactly that problem in the presidential race between Al Gore and George W. Bush, which was well within the margin of error for most of the 2000 campaign. Yet print and electronic journalists routinely reported slight shifts in the polls as a lead for one candidate or the other. A closer look would have revealed that neither candidate had a lead larger than the margin of error. A typical headline or broadcast tease line said that Bush or Gore was in the lead.

One of the few exceptions occurred two days before the election when the *St. Louis Post-Dispatch* ran a front-page banner headline that accurately reported, "Two days to go, and too close to call."

The size of the margin of sampling error is derived with mathematical formulas based on the size of a sample. It is always readily available with reputable poll results. For instance, in a story on polling results for Missouri and Illinois, the *Post-Dispatch* reported that the poll showed "a slight — but statistically insignificant — tightening in Missouri's top contests." Here is how the writer carefully qualified the report:

Gov. George W. Bush of Texas, the GOP nominee for president, had the support of 46.7 percent of the 602 likely voters polled. Vice President Al Gore, the Democrat, had the support of 45.2 percent.

In Illinois, Gore had opened up his lead over Bush. Of the 599 polled, 49.4 percent backed Gore to 39.5 percent for Bush.

For both states, the margin of error was 4 percentage points, which means that any figure could be four points higher or lower. In Missouri, that margin means either major party candidate could be ahead or behind in any of the three contests.

The closeness of the contest was also reflected in the cautious wording in *The New York Times* four days before the election:

The ABC News tracking poll of 1,036 likely voters put Mr. Bush's support at 49 percent, Mr. Gore's at 45 percent, Mr. Nader's at 3 percent and Mr. Buchanan's at 1 percent. The margin of sampling error is plus or minus three percentage points.

The CBS News tracking poll of 708 likely voters showed Mr. Bush at 44 percent, Mr. Gore at 43 percent, Mr. Nader at 4 percent and Mr. Buchanan at 2 percent.

The margin of sampling error is plus or minus four percentage points.

In a tracking poll by CNN/*USA Today*/ Gallup, Mr. Bush was the choice of 48 percent of the likely voters, Mr. Gore the choice of 43 percent, Mr. Nader the choice of 3 percent, Mr. Buchanan 1 percent. The poll was taken with 2,167 likely voters and has a margin of sampling error of plus or minus two percentage points.

From the results of those three polls, you can see that the larger the sample, the smaller the sampling error. In retrospect, you can also see that the polls were within the margin of error of the actual results, although Gore, not Bush, won the popular vote.

However, in news story after news story, reporters often forget the second lesson of reporting on polls: Subgroups within a sample are subject to a larger margin of error because fewer people are in the subgroup. Fewer respondents means less accuracy. If you wanted to write about how many women supported Gore or Bush, you would have to recalculate the margin of error based on the smaller number of women surveyed. Suppose you wanted to know how women in the ABC News tracking poll were going to vote. If women were half the sample or 518 respondents, the margin of error would approximately double to plus or minus six percentage points. Being honest about figures that are so unreliable can be difficult, but doing so is the only way to keep your reporting accurate and fair.

The Associated Press Managing Editors Association recommends that you have and share with your audience the following information about any poll on which you are reporting:

Identity of the survey's sponsor. The sponsor's identity is important because it gives some clues to possible bias.

Exact wording of the questions. Question wording is important because responses often depend at least in part on how the question was asked.

Makeup of the population. Here, "population" means the total number of people in the group being studied. For an opinion survey, the population might be all registered voters in the state, black males under 25 or female cigarette smokers.

Sample size and response rate. Sample size is important because — all other things being equal — the larger the sample, the more reliable the survey results should be.

Margin of error. The sampling error or margin of error is the allowance that must be made for the possibility that the opinion expressed by the sample may not be exactly the same as the opinion of the whole population. Generally, the larger the sample, the smaller the sampling error.

Which results are based on only part of the sample. The problem of sampling error makes it important to know whether any results are based on only part of the sample. The smaller that part, the greater the margin of error.

When the interviews were conducted. When the interviewing was done may be of critical importance in interpreting the poll, especially during campaigns when the candidates themselves and other events may cause preferences to change significantly within a few days.

How the interviews were conducted. Even when your newspaper does the polling, the obligation remains to let your readers know how it was done. It is also incumbent on the paper to reveal how reliable the poll is.

MIXING NUMBERS AND WORDS

Whatever the story and whatever the subject, you probably can use numbers to clarify issues for readers and viewers. All too often, however, numbers are used in ways that muddy the water. Many journalists have some trepidation about working with numbers and often create confusion unwittingly when they work with the volatile mixture of numbers and words.

In *Mathsemantics: Making Numbers Talk Sense*, Edward MacNeal asserts that reporters and editors need to be far more careful in applying numbers in the news by questioning the accuracy and meaning of the numbers they gather and report.

For example, consider the following lead: "Each year 65,000 bicyclists go to the emergency room with injuries. Of those, 70–80 percent die because they weren't wearing helmets."

Mathematically, that means that more than 45,000 bicyclists, and perhaps as many as 52,000, are dying each year, or between about 125 and 140 each day. It's much more likely that the figures meant something else entirely — that 70 to 80 percent of the bicyclists who died of their injuries would have been spared had they been wearing helmets. With the figures given, we still don't know how many bicyclists died.

Journalists can also encourage misunderstandings by describing large increases in percentage terms. For example, a news story reported that Nigerian drivers were quitting the roads because gas prices had increased "more than 300 percent." The headline said, "Tripling of gasoline prices empties roads in Nigeria." They can't both be true. And a 300 percent increase would actually be a quadrupling of prices.

Another trouble spot for mixing numbers and words occurs when reporters calculate how much more powerful or expensive something is. For example, a class that grew from 20 students to 100 students is five times as big as it was, but it has four times more students than it had before.

The lesson to be learned from these examples is not to avoid numbers, but rather to use great care to ensure accuracy. Picking the right numbers to use and using them wisely will help your news stories have the biggest impact.

Suggested Readings

Campbell, Donald and Stanley, Julian. *Experimental and Quasi-Experimental Designs for Research.* Skokie, Ill.: Rand McNally, 1966. A classic guide to field experimentation that is also useful in providing a better understanding of scientific research.

Crossen, Cynthia. *Tainted Truth: The Manipulation of Fact in America.* New York: Simon & Schuster, 1994. An illuminating account of several instances in which public-relations executives manipulated press coverage by twisting the numbers.

Cuzzort, R. P. and Vrettos, James S. *The Elementary Forms of Statistical Reason.* New York: St. Martin's Press, 1996. A basic guide for nonmathematicians in the humanities and social sciences who must work with statistics.

MacNeal, Edward. *Mathsemantics: Making Numbers Talk Sense.* New York: Penguin USA, 1995. An entertaining and elucidating look into the semantics of numbers.

Meyer, Philip. *The New Precision Journalism.* Bloomington: Indiana University Press, 1991. A step-by-step guide to using social science research methods in news reporting.

Paulos, John Allen. *A Mathematician Reads the Newspaper.* New York: Doubleday paper, 1996. The book, structured like the morning paper, investigates the mathematical angles of stories in the news and offers novel perspectives, questions and ideas.

Seltzer, Richard A. *Mistakes That Social Scientists Make.* New York: St. Martin's Press, 1996. A useful book about the kinds of errors often made by social scientists during their research.

Suggested Web Sites

www.bls.gov/cpihome.htm
The Bureau of Labor Statistics allows you to convert for inflation. In addition, it carries CPI information for the entire nation and breaks it down by regions and types of spending.

www.math.temple.edu/~paulos
You've read his book, *Innumeracy: Mathematical Illiteracy and Its Consequences.* Get more writings from the master of numbers. Paulos is a professor at Temple University.

www.minneapolisfed.org/research/data/us/calc/
The Federal Reserve Bank of Minneapolis maintains a great Web site that helps calculate inflation. It also has a clear and simple explanation of how inflation is calculated and how to use the Consumer Price Index.

www.newsengin.com
The site converts your figures for inflation easily and quickly.

www.people-press.org
The Pew Research Center offers its own credible polls on politics and public issues. It offers all the data you need to accurately assess the polls.

www.usatoday.com/money/calculat/mcfront.htm
USA Today's site offers calculators to figure everything from interest rates to how much you will need to retire.

Exercises

1. Find out from your campus financial aid office how much the graduating class has borrowed in Stafford Loans, the largest category of student loans. Calculate how much debt the average graduate will have in Stafford Loans. Then calculate how much debt the average indebted graduate will have. (The results will probably be quite different.) Find out what the total amount of payments owed will be for the average graduate with loans.

2. Find out how much your college charged for tuition in each year since 1994. Adjust those numbers for inflation so they can be compared to this year by going to **www.bls.gov/cpi**. Write a story about the increasing cost of going to college.

3. Find a story in the paper that uses a lot of numbers. Rewrite the story to use the numbers for better effect.

4. Look up numbers in *The Chronicle of Higher Education* that show the incidence of different sorts of crimes on college campuses. Write a story about crime on your campus after comparing rates of crime on different campuses.

5. Get a copy of your city's or town's current budget and come up with 10 questions a reporter should ask about the changes, patterns and trends the budget suggests.

The **inverted pyramid** has written the first draft of history in the United States for generations. Here is the Associated Press lead on the first use of the atomic bomb:

An atomic bomb, hailed as the most destructive force in history and as the greatest achievement of organized science, has been loosed upon Japan.

And here is how the AP started its story of the first moon landing:

Man came to the moon and walked its dead surface Sunday.

Journalists have been using the inverted pyramid for generations to record the daily history of world events. When the country waited for 40 days in 2000 to learn who its next president would be, thousands of journalists recorded every step of the controversy, from the recount to the Supreme Court decision. Mark Barabak, a political writer for the *Los Angeles Times*, worked long hours nearly every day. He told Nardo Zacchino, the *Times* reader representative, "Two or three nights post-election, I called my 9-year-old to tell her I wouldn't be home before she went to sleep because I had to write. I explained this had never happened before, that it was like writing history. She replied, 'Wow, it's really an honor, isn't it?'"

"Yes, it really is," Barabak replied.

Now specialized news delivered to customers online — one of the hottest new services in the new century — relies on the inverted pyramid, one of the most traditional story forms. So do newspapers, despite many editors' emphasis on encouraging new writing forms. So do radio, television and newsletters. Business executives often use the inverted pyramid in company memos so their bosses don't have to read to the end to find the main point.

Frequently misdiagnosed as dying, the inverted pyramid has more lives than a cat — perhaps because the more people try to speed up the dissemination of information, the more valuable the inverted pyramid becomes. In the inverted pyramid, information is arranged from most important to least important. The king in *Alice in Wonderland* would never succeed in the electronic news service business. When asked where to start a story, he replied, "Begin at the beginning and go on till you come to the end; then stop." Reporters, however, often begin a story at its end. Subscribers to Reuters, Dow Jones News Retrieval and Bloomberg, for instance, react instantly to news about the financial markets to get an edge. They don't want narration; they want the news.

So do many newspaper readers, who, on average, spend 15 to 25 minutes a day reading the paper, and online readers, who spend even less time reading than newspaper subscribers. If a reporter were to write an account of a car accident by starting when the driver left the house, many readers would never read far enough to learn that the driver was killed. Instead, such a story starts with its climax:

> Two people died Thursday when a backhoe fell off a truck's flatbed and sliced the top off an oncoming vehicle near Fairchild Air Force Base.

The inverted pyramid was fairly common by the turn of the 20th century. Before then, reporters were less direct. In 1869, the *New York Herald* sent Henry Morton Stanley to Africa to find the famous explorer-missionary David Livingstone. Stanley's famous account of the meeting began:

> Only two months gone, and what a change in my feelings! But two months ago, what a peevish, fretful soul was mine! What a hopeless prospect presented itself before your correspondent!

After several similar sentences, the writer reports, "And the only answer to it all is (that) Livingstone, the hero traveler, is alongside of me."

Stanley reported the most important information so casually that today's subscriber probably would not have learned that Livingstone had been found. Today's reporter would probably begin the story like this:

> David Livingstone, the missionary-explorer missing for six years, has been found working in an African village on the shores of Lake Tanganyika.

The inverted pyramid saves readers time and editors space. It saves *time* because it allows readers to get the most important part of the story first: the climax of an event, the theme of a speech, the key finding in an investigation. It saves *space* by allowing editors to shorten stories by whacking from the bottom. But if an editor had cut Stanley's story from the bottom, we would never have had the now-famous lines that end the story:

"Dr. Livingstone, I presume?"
And he says, "Yes."

145

7/The Inverted
Pyramid

Most journalism history books attribute the introduction of the inverted pyramid to the use of the telegraph during the Civil War. Forced to pay by the word, newspapers supposedly instructed their correspondents to put the most important information at the top. Researchers at the University of Southern California have found that the inverted pyramid was used even earlier. Whatever its origins, the inverted pyramid lead is presented as simply and clearly as possible. It sets the tone. It advertises what is coming in the rest of the story, and it conveys the most important information.

The lead sits atop paragraphs arranged in descending order of importance. These paragraphs explain and provide evidence to support the lead. That's why editors can quickly shorten a story; the paragraphs at the bottom are the least important. The need to produce multiple newspaper editions with the same story running different lengths in each one makes it important that stories can be shortened quickly. The inverted pyramid serves that need well. On the Internet, space is not a consideration, but readers' time is. That's why the same inverted pyramid that is used in newspapers is the most common story structure found on such television network Web news sites as **www.CNN.com**, **www.MSNBC.com**, **www.CBSnews.com** and **www.ABCNEWS.com**.

The inverted pyramid does have some shortcomings. Although it delivers the most important news first, it does not encourage people to read the entire story. Stories stop; they don't end. There is no suspense. In a Poynter Media Institute study (**www.poynter.org**), researchers found that half of the 25 percent of readers who started a story dropped out midway through the story. Interest in an inverted pyramid story diminishes as the story progresses. But the way people use it attests to its value as a quick form of information delivery. Readers can leave whenever their needs are met, not when a writer finishes a story. In an age when time is golden, the inverted pyramid still offers value.

The day when the inverted pyramid is relegated to journalism history is not yet here and probably never will be. Perhaps 80 percent of the stories in today's newspapers and almost 100 percent of the stories on news services for target audiences such as the financial community are written in the inverted pyramid form. The trend is changing — as it should be — but it's changing slowly. Some of the new media will require other forms. For instance, tailored stories for news-on-demand services that will reach a general audience need not use the inverted pyramid, nor will sites devoted to literary journalism (**www.esquire. com**). Still, as long as newspaper, electronic and broadcast journalists continue to emphasize the quick, direct, simple approach to communications, the inverted pyramid and modifications of it will have a role.

Every journalist should master its form. Those who do will have mastered the art of making news judgments. The inverted pyramid requires you to identify and rank the most newsworthy elements in each story. That is important work. No matter what kind of stories you write — whether obituaries, accidents, speeches, press conferences, fires or meetings — you will be required to use the skills you learn here.

"Because a story is important, it doesn't follow that it must be long."

— Stanley Walker,
city editor

TIPS: The inverted pyramid

- Puts the most important information first.
- Arranges the paragraphs in descending order of importance.
- Requires the writer to rank the importance of information.

HOW TO WRITE LEADS

To write a **lead** — a simple, clear statement consisting of the first paragraph or two of a story — you must first recognize what goes into one. As you read in Chapter 1, you begin by determining the story's *relevance, usefulness* and *interest* among readers. One way to measure those standards is to ask "So what?" or "Who cares?" So what if there's an automobile accident downtown? If it's one of hundreds a month, it may not be news. Any holdup in a community of 5,000 may be news because the "so what?" is that holdups are uncommon. Residents probably know the person working at the store. Neither newspapers nor radio and television stations may report the holdup in a metropolitan area because holdups are so common. But if the holdup appears to be part of a pattern or if someone is killed, the story becomes more significant. One holdup may not be news, but a holdup that authorities believe is one of many committed by the same person may be news. The "so what?" is that if the police catch this robber, they stop a crime spree. To determine the "so what?," you have to answer six basic questions: who, what, when, where, why and how?

William Caldwell, winner of a Pulitzer Prize in 1971, remembers the best lead he ever heard. He tells the story in an Associated Press Managing Editors "Writing" report:

> One summer afternoon in 1922, I was on my way home from school and my daily stint of work as editor of the village weekly, unhonored and unpaid. Like my father and two uncles, I was a newspaperman.
>
> My little brother came running to meet me at the foot of our street. He was white and crying. A telegram had come to my mother. "Pa drowned this morning in Lake George," he gasped, and I am ashamed to be remembering my inward response to that.
>
> Before I could begin to sense such elements as sorrow, despair, horror, loneliness, anger — before all the desolation of an abandoned kid would well up in me, I found myself observing that the sentence my brother had just uttered was the perfect lead. Noun, verb, predicate, period, and who-what-when-where to boot.

The information from every event you witness and every story you hear can be reduced to answers to these six questions. If they add up to a significant "so what?," you have a story. Consider this example of an incoming call at fire headquarters.

> "Fire Department," the dispatcher answers.
>
> "Hello. At about 10 o'clock, I was lying on my bed watching TV and smoking," the voice says. "I must have fallen asleep about 10:30 because that's when the football game was over. Anyway, I woke up just now, and my bedroom is on fire. . . ."

That dialogue isn't informative or convincing. More likely our sleepy television viewer awoke in a smoke-filled room, crawled to the telephone and dialed frantically. The conversation at headquarters would more likely have gone like this:

TIPS: The six basic questions

1. Who?
2. What?
3. When?
4. Where?
5. Why?
6. How?

More questions

1. What?
2. So what?
3. What's next?

"Fire Department."
"FIRE!" a voice at the other end yells.
"Where?" the dispatcher asks.
"At 1705 West Haven Street."

When fire is licking at their heels, even nonjournalists know the lead. How the fire started is not important to the dispatcher; that a house is burning — and where that house is located — is.

The journalist must go through essentially the same process to determine the lead. Whereas the caller served himself and the fire department, reporters must serve their readers. What is most important to them?

After the fire is over, there is much information a reporter must gather. Among the questions a reporter would routinely ask are these:

- When did it start?
- When was it reported?
- Who reported it?
- How was it reported?
- How long did it take the fire department to respond?
- How long did it take to extinguish the fire?
- How many fires have been attributed to careless smokers this year?
- How does that compare to figures in previous years?
- Were there any injuries or deaths?
- What was the damage?
- Who owned the house?
- Did the occupant or owner have insurance on the house?
- Will charges be filed against the smoker?
- Was there anything unusual about this case?
- Who cares?

With this information in hand, you can begin to write the story.

Writing the Lead

Start looking over your notes.

Who? The owner, a smoker, Henry Smith, 29. The age is important. Along with other personal information, such as address and occupation, it differentiates him from other Henry Smiths in the readership area.

What? Fire caused damage estimated by the fire chief at $2,500.

Where? 1705 W. Haven St.

When? The call was received at 10:55 p.m., Tuesday. Firefighters from Station 19 arrived at the scene at 11:04. The fire was extinguished at 11:30.

Why? The fire was started by carelessness on the part of Smith, according to Fire Chief Bill Malone.

How? Smith told fire officials that he fell asleep in bed while he was smoking a cigarette.

"Writing is easy; all you do is sit staring at a blank sheet of paper until the drops of blood form on your forehead."

— Gene Fowler, author

If you had asked other questions, you might have learned more from the fire department. This was the eighth fire this year caused by smoking in bed. All last year there were four such fires. Smith said he had insurance. The fire chief said no charges will be filed against Smith. It was the first fire at this house. Smith was not injured. Have you figured out the "so what?"

Assume your city editor has suggested you hold the story to about four paragraphs. Your first step is to rank the information in descending order of importance. There are lots of fires in this town, but eight this year have been caused by smoking in bed. Perhaps that's the most important thing about this story. You begin to type:

```
A fire started by a careless smoker caused an estimated $2,500
in damage to a home.
```

Only 16 words. You should try to hold every lead to fewer than 25 words unless you use more than one sentence. Maybe it's too brief, though. Have you left anything out? Maybe you should include the time element — to give the story a sense of immediacy. You rewrite:

```
A Tuesday night fire started by a careless smoker caused an
estimated $2,500 in damage to a home at 1705 W. Haven St.
```

The reader would also want to know "where?" Is it near my house? Is it someone I know? Besides, you still have only 23 words.

Just then the city editor walks by and glances over your shoulder. "Who said it was a careless smoker?" the editor asks. "Stay out of the story."

You realize you have committed a basic error in newswriting: You have allowed an unattributed opinion to slip into the story. You have two choices. You can attribute the "careless smoker" information to the fire chief in the lead, or you can rewrite. You choose to rewrite by using the chief's exact words. You also realize that your sentence emphasizes the damage instead of the cause. You write:

```
Fire that caused an estimated $2,500 in damage to a home at
1705 W. Haven St. Tuesday was caused by smoking in bed, Fire
Chief Bill Malone said.
```

Now 28 words have answered the questions "what?" (a fire), "where?" (1705 W. Haven St.), "when?" (Tuesday) and "how?" (smoking in bed). And it is attributed. But you have not answered "who?" and "why?" You continue, still ranking the information in descending order of importance. Compare this fire story with the approach in Figure 7.1.

```
The owner of the home, Henry Smith, 29, said he fell asleep in
bed while smoking a cigarette. When he awoke about 30 minutes
later, smoke filled the room.
    Firefighters arrived nine minutes after receiving the
call. It took them about 26 minutes to extinguish the fire,
which was confined to the bedroom of the one-story house.
```

A four-vehicle accident on eastbound I-70 near Stadium Boulevard ended in two deaths on Sunday. — *What / Where / When*

Barbara Jones, 41, of St. Louis died at the scene of the accident, and Juanita Doolan, 73, of St. Joseph died at University Hospital, according to a release from Springfield police. Two other people, William Doolan, 73, of St. Joseph and Theodore Amelung, 43, of Manchester, Mo., were injured in the accident. — *Provides details*

Both lanes of traffic were closed on the eastbound side and limited to one lane on the westbound side as rescue workers cleared the scene. — *Impact*

Authorities said a westbound late-model Ford Taurus driven by Lan Wang of Springfield was traveling in the right lane, developed a tire problem and swerved into the passing lane. A Toyota pickup truck in the passing lane, driven by Jones, was forced over the grassy median along with the Taurus. The two vehicles entered eastbound traffic where the truck struck an Oldsmobile Delta 88, driven by Juanita Doolan, head on. — *How*

Wang and the one passenger in his car, Kenneth Kuo, 58, of Springfield, were not injured.

John Paul, a semi-tractor trailer driver on his way to Tennessee, said he had to swerve to miss the accident. — *Eyewitness*

"I saw the red truck come across the median and hit the blue car," Paul said. "I just pulled over on the median and called 911."

Jones, who was wearing a seatbelt, died at the scene, Officer Stan Williams said. Amelung, a passenger who had been in the truck, was out of the vehicle when authorities arrived, but it was unknown whether he was thrown from the truck or was pulled out by someone else, Williams said.

No charges have been filed, but the investigation continues. — *What's next*

Figure 7.1
Note how this story, typical of the inverted pyramid structure, delivers the most important news in the lead and provides less essential details toward the end.

```
    According to Chief Malone, careless smokers have caused
eight fires this year.
    Smith, who was not injured, said the house was insured.
```

You take the story to the city editor, who reads through the copy quickly. Then she checks the telephone book and the city directory. As you watch, she changes the lead to emphasize the "so what?" The lead now reads:

```
A smoker who fell asleep in bed ignited a fire that caused
minor damage to his home on W. Haven Street Tuesday, Fire
```

Chief Bill Malone said. It was the city's eighth fire caused
by smokers, twice as many as occurred all last year.

The lead is 44 words, but it is broken into two sentences, which makes it more readable. The importance of the "so what?" changed the direction of the story. The fire was minor; there were no injuries. However, the increase in the number of fires smokers caused may force the fire department to start a public safety campaign against careless smoking. The city editor continues:

The owner of the home, Henry Smith, 29, of 1705 W. Haven St.,
said he fell asleep in bed while smoking a cigarette. When he
awoke about 30 minutes later, smoke had filled the room.

This time, though, you have an even more serious problem. Both the telephone book and the city directory list the man who lives at 1705 W. Haven St. as Henry Smyth: S-m-y-t-h. City directories, like telephone books or any other sources, can be wrong. But at least they can alert you to possible errors. Confirm by going to original sources, in this case, Mr. Smyth.

Never put a name in a story without checking the spelling, even when the source tells you his name is Smith.

There are several lessons you can learn from this experience. They are:

- *Always* verify names.
- Keep the lead short, usually fewer than 25 words, unless you use two sentences.
- Attribute opinion. (Smoking in bed is a fact. That it was careless is an opinion.)
- Find out the who, what, where, when, why and how. However, if any of these elements have no bearing on the story, they might not have to be included.
- Write a sentence or paragraph telling readers what the news means to them.
- Report information basic to the story even if it is routine. Not everything you learn is important enough to be reported, but you'll never know unless you gather the information.

Writing for the Web

In Chapter 20, you will learn details about writing news for the Web. However, you will find that most Web news sites rely on the inverted pyramid to present information quickly. For example, when wildfires swept across California in October 2003, both MSNBC and CNN posted stories written in the inverted pyramid. MSNBC's lead was 42 words:

SAN BERNARDINO, Calif., Oct. 27 — The hot Santa Ana wind driving wildfires across parts of Southern California eased Monday, but officials warned that there was still a threat from the flames that had killed at least 13 people and destroyed more than 900 homes since last week.

Too many numbers bog down a lead. Focus on the impact of the figures in the lead and provide details later in the story.

TIPS: When writing the lead, remember

- Always check names.
- Keep the lead short, usually fewer than 25 words, unless you use two sentences.
- Attribute opinion.
- Find out the who, what, where, when, why and how. If any of these elements have no bearing on the story, they might not have to be included.
- Write a sentence or a paragraph telling readers what the news means to them.
- Report basic information even if it is routine. Not everything you learn is important enough to be reported, but you'll never know unless you gather the information.

CNN's similar lead was tighter at 32 words:

DEVORE, California (CNN) — The rapidly spreading wildfires raging through large parts of Southern California have killed at least 13 people, forced the evacuation of thousands and pushed a professional football game into a neighboring state.

The two sites emphasized different angles, but both used the traditional inverted pyramid. New means of transmitting information have not yet affected the basic news-story organization.

Alternate Leads

In the lead reporting the house fire, the what (fire) is of secondary importance to the how (how the fire started). A slightly different set of facts would affect the news value of the elements and, consequently, your lead. For instance, if Smyth turned out to have been a convicted arsonist, you probably would have emphasized that bizarre twist to the story:

```
A convicted arsonist awoke Tuesday to find that his bedroom
was filled with smoke. He escaped and later said that he had
fallen asleep while smoking.
     Henry Smyth, 29, who served a three-year term for . . .
```

That lead emphasizes the news value of novelty. If Smyth were the mayor, you would emphasize prominence:

```
Mayor Henry Smyth escaped injury Tuesday when he awoke to find
his bedroom filled with smoke. Smyth said he had fallen asleep
while smoking in bed.
```

What?, So What? and What's Next?

You know that the answer to "what?" often is the lead. The preceding examples also illustrate the "so what?" factor in news. A $2,500 fire is not news to many people in large communities where there are dozens of fires daily. Even if you crafted a tightly written story about it, your editor probably would not want to print or broadcast it.

In small communities the story would have more impact because a larger proportion of the community is likely to know the victim and because there are fewer fires.

The "so what?" factor grows more important as you add other information. If the fire occurred during a fire-safety campaign, the "so what?" would be the need for fire safety, even in a community where awareness of the problem had already been heightened. If the fire involved a convicted arsonist or the mayor, the "so what?" would be stronger. Oddity or well-known people increase the value of a story. If someone had been injured or the damage had been $250,000 instead of

"Selecting the quotes isn't so hard; it's presenting them that causes the trouble. And the worst place to present them is at the beginning. Quote leads deserve their terrible reputation. Yet they still appear regularly in both print and broadcast journalism.

"We can make three generalizations about quote leads. They're easy, lazy, and lousy. They have no context. The readers don't know who's speaking, why, or why it matters. Without context, even the best quotations are wasted."

— Paula LaRocque, assistant managing editor, *The Dallas Morning News*

$2,500, the "so what?" factor might even push the story into the metropolitan press. Once you have answered all six of the basic questions, then ask yourself what the answers mean to the reader: That is your "so what?" factor.

In many stories, it is also important to answer the question "What's next?" The City Council had its first reading of its budget bill. What's next? *Members will vote on it next month.* Jones was arrested Monday on a charge of passing bad checks. What's next? *The prosecuting attorney will decide whether there is enough evidence to file charges.*

A reader in a focus group once told researchers that she just wants to be told "what?," "so what?" and "what's next?" That's a good guideline for all journalists to remember.

No journalist relies on formulas to write inverted pyramid leads, but you may find it useful, especially in the beginning, to learn some typical types of leads. The labels in the following sections are arbitrary, but the approaches are not.

The "You" Lead

Regardless of which of these leads you use, journalists are trying to emphasize the relevance of the news to the reader. One good way to highlight the relevance is to speak directly to the reader by using "you." This informal second-person lead — the **"you" lead** — allows the writer to tell readers why they should care. For instance:

> You will make more money buying Savings Bonds starting tomorrow.
> The Treasury boosted the semiannual interest rate on Series EE Savings Bonds to 5.92 percent from 4.7 percent effective Tuesday.

Readers want to know what's in it for them. The traditional approach is less direct:

> The Treasury boosted Savings Bonds interest Tuesday to the highest rate in three years.

Like any kind of lead, you can overdo the "you" lead. You don't need to write, "You have another choice in the student president's race." Just tell readers who filed their candidacy. You may, however, use those words in writing for radio and television news as a set-up for the story to come.

Immediate-Identification Leads

In the **immediate-identification lead**, one of the most important facts is "who?" or the prominence of the key actor. Reporters often use this approach when someone important or someone whose name is widely recognized is making news. Consider the following example:

JERUSALEM (AP) — Prime Minister Ariel Sharon said for the first time Monday that Israel has no plans to kill Yasser Arafat, even as he accused the Palestinian leader of continuing to orchestrate attacks on civilians.

The prime minister's name is known throughout the world, so the writer identifies the person acting immediately. Names make news.

When writing for your campus newspaper or your local newspaper, you would use names in the lead that are known, not necessarily nationally but locally. The name of your student body president, the chancellor, the city's mayor or an entertainer who has a local following would logically appear in the lead. None of them would be used in a newspaper 50 miles away.

In any accident, the who may be important because it is someone well-known by name or position. If so, the name should be in the lead.

In small communities the who in an accident may always be in the lead. In larger communities names are not as recognizable. As a rule, if the name is well-known, it should appear in the lead.

Delayed-Identification Leads

Usually a reporter uses a **delayed-identification lead** because the person, persons or organization involved has little name recognition among the readers. Thus, in fairly large cities an accident is usually reported like this:

MADISON, Wis. — A 39-year-old carpenter was killed today in a two-car collision two blocks from his home.

Dead is William Domonske of 205 W. Oak St. Injured in the accident and taken to Mercy Hospital were Mary Craig, 21, of 204 Maple Ave., and Rebecca Roets, 12, of 207 Maple Ave.

However, in a smaller community, names almost always make news. If Domonske lived in a city of 10,000, his name probably would be in the lead.

By the same token, most people know that IRS stands for "Internal Revenue Service." But many don't know that AARP stands for "American Association of Retired Persons." An Associated Press reporter used a delayed-identification lead in a story about AARP:

The nation's largest senior citizens organization paid $135 million to settle a dispute with the IRS over the income it earns from royalties.

However, the settlement leaves open the question of whether future income earned by the American Association of Retired Persons will be taxed, said the group's spokesman, Peter Ashkenaz.

Because so many people over 50 belong to AARP, the reporter could have written the lead using "you":

If you are one of 33 million members of the nation's largest senior citizens organization, you just settled a bill with the IRS.

The American Association of Retired Persons has agreed to pay $135 million to settle a dispute with the IRS over the income it earns from royalties.

AARP, which still has $19.6 million in cash reserves, says the settlement will not affect any of your services.

There are two other occasions when the reporter may choose to delay identification of the person involved in the story until the second paragraph. One occurs when the person is not well-known but the person's position, occupation, title or achievements are important or interesting. The other occurs when the lead is becoming too wordy.

As Andy Warhol said, people have their 15 minutes of fame, but fame can be fleeting. While Terry Anderson of the AP was being held captive from 1985 to 1992 by the Islamic Jihad in Lebanon, even casual consumers of the news recognized his name. By early 2000 when a court ruled that Anderson was entitled to damages, a delayed-identification lead was appropriate:

WASHINGTON — A former AP newsman was awarded $341 million from Iran on March 24 by a federal judge who said his treatment during his nearly seven years of captivity in Beirut was "savage and cruel by any civilized standards."

U.S. District Judge Thomas Penfield Jackson ordered Iran to pay $24.5 million to Terry Anderson, $10 million to his wife, Madeleine Bassil, and $6.7 million to their daughter, Sulome. The judge also ordered the Iranian Ministry of Information and Security to pay the three $300 million in punitive damages.

A name that would appear in the lead in one city would appear in the second paragraph in another. The mayor of Birmingham, Ala., would be identified by title and name in Birmingham and by title only in Bridgewater, Conn.

Figure 7.2
When AP newsman Terry Anderson was released in Lebanon in 1992, he was a household name. Eight years later, during his court case, not many readers would have recognized his name.

Thinking in the Inverted Pyramid

Anyone who has stared at a blank screen 15 minutes before deadline knows the importance of the inverted pyramid. It's the quickest, simplest way to organize your notes and thoughts.

A posh suburban country club recently caught fire nearly an hour before the early edition's deadline. As Stacy St. Clair drove to the scene — located almost 20 miles away — she wrote a mock story in her head and made mental notes about people she needed to speak with and information she needed to gather. As she drove back to the news room she filled the holes in her prewrite. It was a classic inverted pyramid, 12-inch story, which she pounded out in about 15 minutes. She finished the piece with a few minutes to spare and used the extra time to add some color to the story.

"Because the inverted pyramid has become a natural reflex in both my reporting and writing, I had enough time to go back and tell readers about foursomes who finished their rounds rather than seek shelter and panicked members who tried to save their Great Big Berthas from a fiery locker room," she said.

St. Clair, who works at the *Daily Herald* in the Chicago suburbs, believes the inverted pyramid suffers from an unfair stereotype. "Editors and professors regularly call the writing style uninspired or elementary, but it doesn't have to be. Using the inverted pyramid does not release reporters from the responsibilities of good writing. Pacing, word choice, description, anecdotes — they all have a place in the inverted pyramid. Initial reports of the World Trade Center disaster, for example, were written in the inverted pyramid, yet they contained incredibly powerful anecdotes and heart-wrenching detail," she said.

The inverted pyramid forces you to prioritize and ask yourself, "What's important here? What's the story really about?" As St. Clair notes, "Once it becomes second nature, the inverted pyramid teaches you how to focus on a story whether it's a 60-inch feature or a 9-inch car crash story."

Now she's focusing more often on the feature stories. St. Clair is the chief narrative writer.

Some titles are bulky: "Chairman of the Federal Communications Commission" assures clutter even before you add the name. "United Nations ambassador" deprives the writer of many options. When dealing with these types of positions, writers often choose to use the title and delay introducing the name until the second or third paragraph. When the title is better known than the name, writers usually use the title and delay the name until the second paragraph.

Summary Leads

Reporters dealing with several important elements may choose to sum up what happened in a **summary lead** rather than highlighting a specific action. This is one of the few times that a general statement is preferable to specific action.

When Congress passed a bill providing family members with emergencies the right to unpaid leaves from work, the writer had to make a choice: focus on the main provision or write a summary lead. The writer chose the latter:

> A bill requiring employers to give workers up to three months unpaid leave in family emergencies won Senate approval Thursday evening.

Several other provisions in the bill are explained later in the story: The unpaid leave can be for medical reasons or to care for a new child, and employers would have to continue health insurance benefits and restore employees to their previous jobs or equivalent positions.

You can also show the readers the "so what?" with the "you" lead:

> The Senate voted Thursday to allow you to take up to three months' unpaid leave in family emergencies without losing your health benefits.

Likewise, if a city council rewrites city ordinances, unless one of the changes is of overriding importance, most reporters will use a summary lead:

> MOLINE, Ill. — The City Council replaced the city's 75-year-old municipal code with a revised version Tuesday night.

Summary leads don't only appear in reports of board meetings. A Spokane, Wash., reporter used a summary lead to report a neighborhood dispute:

> An Idaho farmer's fence apparently was cut last week. It set off a chain of events Friday night that landed three people in the hospital, killed a cow and totaled a vehicle in the eastern Spokane Valley.

The basic question you must answer is whether the whole of the action is more important than any of its parts. If the answer is yes, a summary lead is in order.

Multiple-Element Leads

In some stories, choosing one theme for the lead is too restrictive. In such cases the reporter can choose a multiple-element lead to work more information into the first paragraph. But you should write the lead within the confines of a clear, simple sentence or sentences. Consider this example:

> PORTLAND, Wash. — The City Council Tuesday ordered three department heads fired, established an administrative review board and said it would begin to monitor the work habits of administrators.

Notice that not only the actions but also the construction of the verb phrases within the sentence is parallel. Parallel structures also characterize the following news extract, which presents a visual picture of the scene of a tragedy:

"Language is a very difficult thing to put into words."

— Voltaire, philosopher

> BAY CITY, Mich. — A flash fire that swept through a landmark downtown hotel Saturday killed at least 12 persons, injured 60 more and forced scores of residents to leap from windows and the roof in near-zero cold.

We are told where it happened, what happened, and how many were killed and injured.

Some multiple-element leads consist of two paragraphs. This occurs when the reporter decides that several elements need prominent display. For example:

> The Board of Education Tuesday night voted to lower the tax rate 12 cents per $100 valuation. Members then approved a budget $150,000 less than last year's and instructed the superintendent to decrease the staff by 25 people.
>
> The board also approved a set of student-conduct rules, which include a provision that students with three or more unexcused absences a year will be suspended for a week.

This story, too, could emphasize the "so what?" while retaining the multiple elements:

> The Board of Education lowered your real-estate taxes Tuesday. Members also approved a budget $150,000 less than last year's and instructed the superintendent to decrease the staff by 25 people.

Simpler leads are preferable. But a multiple-element lead is one of your options. Use it sparingly.

Many newspapers are using graphic devices to take the place of multiple-element leads. They use summary boxes to list other actions. Because the box appears under the headline in type larger than text, it serves as a graphic summary for the reader who is scanning the page. The box frees the writer from trying to jam too many details into the first few paragraphs (see Figure 7.3).

Other council action

In other action, the council:

✓ Voted to repave Broadway Ave.

✓ Rejected a new sign ordinance.

✓ Hired four school crossing guards.

✓ Expanded bus hours.

Figure 7.3
A summary box can take the place of a multiple-element lead.

Another approach is to break the coverage of a single event into a main story and a shorter story or stories, called **sidebars.** This approach offers the advantage of presenting the information in short, palatable bites. It also allows the writer to elevate more actions into lead positions. Researchers have found that breaking stories into small segments increases readers' comprehension and retention.

Both methods of presentation have advantages over the more complicated multiple-element lead.

Danger Signals

Here are some leads that understandably raise red flags to editors:

> Breaking stories into small segments increases readers' comprehension and retention.

> "The lead should be a promise of great things to come, and the promise should be fulfilled."
>
> — Stanley Walker, city editor

1. *Question leads.* Readers don't know the subject, don't know why they are being asked a question and probably couldn't care less. So the next time you are writing, say, a weather story and are tempted to begin with "So how hot was it yesterday?" lie down until the temptation passes. Either tell readers the temperature or open with an anecdote of a specific roofer sweating on the job. That's showing how hot it is.
2. *Leads that say what might happen or what might have happened.* News organizations try to report what happened. Stay away from leads like this: "Springfield residents may be looking forward to warmer weather. . . ." Talk to people. Don't speculate.
3. *Leads that overreach.* Report what you know. You may think it is harmless to say, "Springfield residents warmly greeted spring yesterday," but you don't know that *all* Springfield residents were happy about it. Maybe the guy who runs a snow-removal business would rather see winter last longer.

Leads with Flair

Although the inverted pyramid tells readers the news first and fast, not all stories begin with the most important statement. When the news value you want to emphasize is novelty, often the lead is unusual.

When a group of suspected drug dealers was arrested at a wedding, the Associated Press focused on the novelty:

NARRAGANSETT, R.I. (AP) — The wedding guests included drug suspects, the social coordinator was a narcotics agent, the justice of the peace was a police chief, and 52 officers were party crashers.

For the unsuspecting bride and groom, the ceremony Friday night was truly unforgettable — a sting operation set up by state and local police that led to 30 arrests.

Not exactly your traditional wedding or your traditional lead. Yet the essential information is contained within the first two paragraphs. A less imaginative writer would have written something like this:

Thirty suspected drug dealers, including a couple about to be married, were arrested at a wedding Friday night.

That approach is like slapping a generic label on a Mercedes-Benz. The inverted pyramid approach is not so rigid that it doesn't permit fun and flair.

What is the difference between the two-paragraph, multiple-element lead on the board of education and the two-step lead on the wedding story? In the first, the reporter was dealing with several significant actions. In the second, the reporter was dealing with only one, so she used the first paragraph to set up the surprise in the second.

STORY ORGANIZATION

Like the theater marquee, the lead is an attention-getter. Sometimes the movie doesn't fulfill the promises of the marquee; sometimes the story doesn't fulfill the promises of the lead. In either case the customer is dissatisfied.

The inverted pyramid helps you put information in logical order. It forces you to rank, in order of importance, the information you will present. Let's see how the pros do it.

One-Subject Story

Reference to largest-ever product recall establishes the "so what?"

The first paragraph speaks directly to parents who might have the pull cords in their homes. This establishes relevance to those readers.

By DAVID HO
Associated Press Writer

WASHINGTON (AP) — In its largest-ever product recall, the government says some 500 million horizontal window blinds sold over the last decade need their cords repaired because 130 babies and young children have been strangled since 1991. It is the second such recall in the last five years.

Children can turn the pull cords — as well as the inner cords that adjust the slats — into nooses around their necks, the Consumer Product Safety Commission and an industry group, Window Covering Safety Council, said Wednesday. About 55 million horizontal blinds are sold each year.

TIPS: Checklist for assembling the rest of the inverted pyramid

- Introduce additional important information you were not able to include in the lead.
- If possible, indicate the significance or "so what?" factor.
- Elaborate on the information presented in the lead.
- Continue introducing new information in the order in which you have ranked it by importance.
- Develop the ideas in the same order in which you have introduced them.
- Generally, use only one new idea in each paragraph.

Writer uses an authority to establish the seriousness of the problem.

History.

Supports the lead.

More history introducing the human-interest element.

Convergence: The AP and many newspapers frequently refer readers to the Internet for more information.

Service journalism: how to act on the information.

"It's a horrible hidden hazard that even the best parent would never think of," Ann Brown, the safety commission's chairwoman, said in an interview. "It's a silent death — the children can't call out — and the parent comes in and finds their child hanging from the blind."

The agency first addressed the problem in 1995 by issuing a similar recall, providing repair kits to consumers and getting the blinds industry to redesign its products. While blinds sold since no longer have pull cords ending in loops, those recalled models may still be in people's homes.

Last year, another investigation found the inner cords that adjust the slats could also endanger children.

Of the 130 deaths reported, the inner cords contributed to the strangulation of 16 children, all of whom were 9 to 17 months old and in cribs placed next to windows. In most cases, the outer pull cords that raise and lower the blinds were placed out of reach, but the children pulled the inner cords into loops and strangled.

The agency launched the investigation after 16-month-old Hannah Beller of Ashburn, Va., died in a rented vacation cottage in August 1998. Her parents, Eric and Elizabeth Beller, had placed her crib in a room they had checked for safety, even making sure the pull cords from a nearby window blind were out of reach, said Mrs. Beller.

"The only thing she would have been able to reach from the crib were the bottom two slats," she said. "We found her strangled from the inside cord, which she must have reached by reaching her tiny fingers through the closed blinds."

The window coverings industry recently redesigned its products again to remove the inner cord danger. New blinds sold since September have the improvement and older ones still on store shelves have warning labels advising repair, said Peter Rush, head of the Window Covering Safety Council.

Rush said consumers can visit the council's Web site at **www.windowcoverings.org** to learn how to check blinds for safety danger.

The safety commission advises owners of blinds to call the council toll-free at 1-800-506-4636 to request a free repair kit for each set of blinds. The kits include small plastic attachments to prevent the inner cords from being pulled loose and safety tassels for pre-1995 blinds with looped pull cords.

The repairs take minutes and don't require taking down the blinds.

Multiple-Element Story

Multiple-element leads are most likely when you are reporting on the proceedings of councils, boards, commissions, legislatures and courts. These bodies act on numerous subjects in one sitting. Frequently, their actions are unrelated, and more than one action is often important enough to merit attention in the lead. You have three options:

1. *You can write more than one story.* That, of course, depends on permission from your editor. There may not be enough space.
2. *You can write a summary box.* It would be displayed along with the story. In it you would list the major actions taken by the council or decisions issued by the court.
3. *You can write a multiple-element lead and story.* Let's go back to the one we used earlier:

The Board of Education Tuesday night voted to lower the tax rate 12 cents per $100 valuation. Members then approved a budget $150,000 less than last year's and instructed the superintendent to decrease the staff by 25 people.

The board also approved a set of student-conduct rules, which include a provision that students with three or more unexcused absences a year will be suspended for a week.

Four newsworthy actions are mentioned in those two paragraphs: (1) changing the tax rate, (2) approving a budget, (3) cutting staff and (4) adopting conduct rules. In this and all stories that deal with several important elements, the writer highlights the most important elements. Sometimes several are equally important, as in the school board example. Most of the time, one action stands above the rest. When that is the case, it is important to summarize the other, lesser, actions after the lead.

If you and your editor judged that changing the tax rate was more important than anything else that happened at the school board meeting, you would approach the story like this:

Lead:

The Board of Education Tuesday night voted to lower the tax rate 12 cents per $100 valuation.

Support for lead:

The new rate is $1.18 per $100 valuation. That means that if your property is assessed at $30,000, your school tax will be $354 next year.

Summary of other action:

The board also approved a budget that is $150,000 less than last year's, instructed the superintendent to cut the staff by 25 and approved a set of rules governing student conduct.

Notice that the lead is followed by a paragraph that supports and enlarges upon the information in it before the summary paragraph appears. Whether you need a support paragraph before summarizing other action depends on how complete you are able to make the lead.

In every multiple-element story, the first two or three paragraphs determine the order of the rest of the story. To ensure the coherence of your story, you must then describe the actions in the order in which you introduced them.

Suggested Readings

Brooks, Brian S., Pinson, James L. and Wilson, Jean Gaddy. *Working with Words*, Fifth Edition. New York: Bedford/St. Martin's, 2003. A must for any journalist. Provides excellent coverage of grammar and word usage and a strong chapter on "isms."

Gillman, Timothy. "The Problem of Long Leads in News and Sports Stories." *Newspaper Research Journal*, Fall 1994, pp. 29–39. Researcher found that sentences in leads were longer than sentences in the rest of the story.

Walker, Stanley. *City Editor*. Baltimore: Johns Hopkins University Press, 1999. Originally published in 1934, reissued in 1999. Walker was city editor of the *New York Herald Tribune*. His tips about writing news remain valid.

Suggested Web Sites

www.journalism.org
Select "Research" under Resources. Click on "Reports and Studies." Open the study "Changing Definitions of News." The Committee of Concerned Journalists conducted an in-depth study of news over the last 20 years to determine if what is important has changed. The results have an impact on what would be emphasized in an inverted pyramid story.

www.poynter.org/content/content_view.asp? id=6332
Roy Peter Clark of the Poynter Institute talks about news judgment by looking at the front page of a newspaper.

www.wsu.edu/~brians/errors
Paul Brians, a professor of English at Washington State University, will answer your questions about the English language.

Exercises

1. Identify the who, what, where, when, why and how, if they are present, in the following:

   The United Jewish Appeal is sponsoring its first-ever walk-a-thon this morning in Springfield to raise money for The Soup Kitchen, a place where the hungry can eat free.

2. Here are four versions of the same lead. Which of the four answers more of the six questions basic to all stories? Which questions does it answer?

   a. What began 12 years ago with a federal staff investigation and led to hearings and a court fight culminates today with a Federal Trade Commission rule to prevent funeral home rip-offs.

b. The nation's funeral home directors are required to offer detailed cost statements starting today, a service they say they are now ready to provide despite nearly a dozen years of debate over the idea.

c. A new disclosure law going into effect today will make it easier for us to determine the cost of a funeral.

d. Twelve years after first being proposed, a federal regulation goes into effect Monday to require funeral homes to provide an itemized list of services and materials they offer, along with the cost of each item, before a person agrees to any arrangements.

3. Rewrite two of the leads in exercise 2 as "you" leads. Which are better, the third-person or second-person leads? Why are they better?

4. From the following facts, write a lead.

Who: a nuclear weapon with a yield equivalent to 150,000 tons of TNT.

What: detonated.

Where: 40 miles from a meeting of pacifists and 2,000 feet beneath the surface of Pahute Mesa in the Nevada desert.

When: Tuesday.

Why: to test the weapon.

How: not applicable.

Other information: Department of Energy officials are the source; 450 physicians and peace activists were gathered to protest continued nuclear testing by the United States.

5. From the following facts, write the first two paragraphs of a news article.

Who: 7-year-old boy missing for three years.

What: found.

Where: in Brick Township, N.J.

When: Monday night.

Why: not applicable.

How: A neighbor recognized the child's picture when it was shown after the movie *Adam: The Song Continues* and called police.

Other information: Police arrested the boy's mother, Ellen Lynn Conner, 27; she faces Alabama charges of kidnapping and interference with a custody warrant.

6. From the following facts, write the first two paragraphs of a news article.

Who: 40 passengers.

What: evacuated from a Northwest Airlines jet, Flight 428.

Where: at the LaCrosse, Wis., Municipal Airport.

When: Monday following a flight from Minneapolis to LaCrosse.

Why: A landing tower employee spotted smoke near the wheels.

How: not applicable.

Other information: There was no fire or injuries; the smoke was caused by hydraulic fluids leaking onto hot landing brakes, according to Bob Gibbons, a Northwest spokesman.

7. Describe picture and information-graphic possibilities for the story in exercise 6.

8. Cut out six leads from newspapers. Identify what questions are answered (who? etc.). Identify what is not answered. Identify the kind of lead (summary, etc.).

9. Using a database that includes several newspapers, find at least two versions of the same story. Analyze the similarities and differences between them, and decide which of the two is preferable and why.

163

Whether you are writing a newspaper story, a television script, a news release or an article for a Web site, a good story told well is important to readers and viewers and to the financial success of your company. Many journalists are getting the message. That is why we see stories like this more often:

By Blake Morrison
USA TODAY

In his nightmares, Steve Cabrera stands frozen in the aisle of Flight 1763. No one moves except Jonathan Burton, the teenager who has just kicked a hole in the cockpit door.

Burton strides toward the jet's exit row. From the back of the cabin, Cabrera's wife and son scream.

I've gotta stop him. He's trying to crash the plane, Cabrera thinks, but he cannot reach the teen. Then, as the jet rumbles thousands of feet above Utah, Burton grabs the emergency exit and pulls.

A second later, Cabrera, 42, springs from his bed and races to his son's room. There, in the dark near Wyatt's bed, he strains to hear his son's breathing over his own pounding heart.

It almost happened that way, he thinks for the hundredth time since the nightmares began. "Sometimes, I can't stop him," Cabrera says of his dreams. "Sometimes, Jonathan wins."

On Aug. 11, Jonathan Burton became the first passenger to be killed by fellow passengers aboard a U.S. commercial jet. Halfway through the hour-long flight from Las Vegas to Salt Lake City, the 19-year-old began pacing the aisles, mumbling. Then he shoved a flight attendant, ran to the front of the jet and kicked free a panel on the cockpit door. Ducking his head inside, he shouted, "I can fly this f — ing plane!"

Of those details, there seems little doubt. But other, more troubling questions remain about what transpired next aboard Southwest Airlines Flight 1763.

In airport police reports reviewed by USA TODAY and in dozens of interviews conducted by the newspaper — including the first with Cabrera and another passenger who helped restrain Burton — those aboard the Boeing 737 tell terrifying and often conflicting stories about what happened during the flight. At least three of the 121 passengers aboard recall someone jumping on Burton as he lay in the aisle. One says he believes it was Cabrera who stomped the teen to death. All tell of screaming, crying and chaos in the cabin as passengers scurried away from the melee. Some of the dozen interviewed by the newspaper say they feared for their lives.

Their accounts and others are expected to become public later this

165

week, when the FBI releases more than 500 pages of investigative documents. But with an autopsy seeming to discount drugs as a cause for Burton's outburst, investigators concede that the teen's behavior might never be explained.

That opening sits atop an in-depth investigation into the death of the passenger. The writer uses narration to place you in the plane. There, you can watch events unfold. Chances are, the writing will attract readers with even a casual interest in the event.

Readers don't see that type of writing as often as they should. Some are voting with their feet; they are abandoning newspapers and magazines. Editors are looking at clips more closely for clarity and creativity, not just in feature stories but also in news stories. There's even some research to support the idea that newspapers are not as easy to read as they should be. Using the Flesch Reading Ease formula, researchers at the University of Texas looked at a century of writing in novels and newspapers. They concluded that novels had become easier to read and newspapers had become harder.

Readability is a measurement of such things as the number of words in a sentence, the number of syllables in a word and the number of ideas in a sentence. In general, the more of them there are, the harder a sentence is to understand. Can we blame readers, then, for reeling when they encounter this typical lead?

WASHINGTON — A 10-year study of an increasingly popular surgical technique used to correct poor distance vision shows that the method is reasonably safe and effective but that it might lead to an accelerated decline in the ability to see things up close, researchers said Wednesday.

That's 45 words. Hidden somewhere in the thicket is the main idea. In case the readers were still standing, the writer followed with a 47-word second sentence.

If you are thinking that science is a complicated subject calling for complicated writing, how do you explain this lead on a government story?

Hoping to prevent a recurrence of the wrongdoing uncovered during a recent nine-month undercover investigation at one of its main work sites, the New Orleans Sewerage & Water Board plans to hire a chief of security and devise a plan to prevent crimes by employees.

> "There's nothing to writing. All you do is sit down at a typewriter and open a vein."
>
> — Red Smith, newspaper sports columnist

Writing to inform and entertain is as important for journalists as it is for novelists. Just because newspapers and broadcast reports are done and gone in a day doesn't mean that we should accept a lower level of skill. Comparing the temporal nature of newspapers to a beach, syndicated columnist James Kilpatrick challenged writers, ". . . if we write upon the sand, let us write as well as we can upon the sand before the waves come in."

If Kilpatrick's challenge to your pride is not enough, then the demands of readers and listeners and of editors and news directors who are hiring should be. Editors are looking for those unusual people who can combine reporting and writing talents. The journalist whose prose jerks around the page like a mouse trapped in a room with a cat has no future in the business. The American Society of Newspaper Editors has made improved writing one of its principal long-range

Figure 8.1
Barbara Ehrenreich and Bob Woodward have received accolades for the strength of their reporting as well as for the literary quality of their writing.

goals. Each year, in cooperation with the Poynter Institute of St. Petersburg, Fla., it awards $1,000 to the winners in several categories of the writing competition it sponsors. The winning entries are published annually by the institute in a book series titled *Best Newspaper Writing*. ASNE posts the winning entries and many of its reports on writing at **www.asne.org/index.cfm?ID=1469**.

Many well-known writers — among them Daniel Defoe, Mark Twain, Stephen Crane and Ernest Hemingway — began their careers as journalists. A more recent list would include John Hersey, Tom Wolfe and Gay Talese. The best-seller list is peppered with the names of journalists: Bob Woodward, Russell Baker, Ellen Goodman, Anna Quindlen, Richard Ben Cramer, Ron Rosenbaum, Tom Brokaw and Barbara Ehrenreich (see Figure 8.1). At newspapers around the country today, small but growing numbers of journalists are producing literature daily as they deal with everything from accidents to affairs of state. If you have respect for the language, an artist's imagination and the dedication to learn how to combine them, you, too, may produce literature.

We should all attempt to bring quality writing, wit and knowledge to our work. If we succeed, our work will be not only informative but also enjoyable, not only educational but also entertaining and not only bought but also read.

GOOD WRITING BEGINS WITH GOOD REPORTING

Without the proper ingredients, the best chef is no better than a short-order cook. Without the proper use of participant accounts, personal observation and

Sharing the Experience Through Vivid Writing

By the time she had been out of school only 10 years, Patricia Rodriguez had already worked at the *Springfield* (Mo.) *News-Leader, The Cincinnati Enquirer,*

USA Weekend and the *Dallas Times Herald.* Now she is Travel Editor of the *Fort Worth Star-Telegram.* She has freelanced for national magazines, and one of her stories was included in *A Kind of Grace,* an anthology of sports stories by women writers.

So when she talks about writing, she is speaking from experience.

"The slickest writing can't disguise shallow reporting. Besides just getting the good quotes, that means writing down descriptions, smells, sounds. I also try to write down analogies as I think of them, out in the field or even in the car back to the office. It's easier and more accurate than trying to be clever in front of the computer."

She tries to avoid the temptation to overwrite.

"Don't use stuffy phrases or overload your piece with qualifiers. Tell a story: Write with active words, use natural language, and tie everything together from beginning to end.

"After you finish your interviews, try to remember the anecdotes and facts you couldn't wait to tell your roommate or deskmate. Try to get as many of those in the story as you can, even if you thought they were asides or not the story you set out to get."

She also writes for the ear.

"Read your stuff out loud, at least your lead. Yes, you'll feel goofy, but it gives you a sense of pace and rhythm and tells you which sentences are too complex and wordy."

detail, the best writer's stories land with a thud. Good writing begins with good reporting. It was the reporting that allowed Blake Morrison of *USA Today* to open his story recreating the death aboard an airplane with narration. That type of writing requires precise detail to recreate scenes. Getting those details requires hours of reporting.

That story took some time to write, but reporters pressing for detail can do it on deadline, too. In Chapter 7 we introduced you to this lead:

> Two people died Thursday when a backhoe fell off a truck's flatbed and sliced the top off an oncoming vehicle near Fairchild Air Force Base.

Now let's look at some of the detail writer Alison Boggs of *The* (Spokane, Wash.) *Spokesman-Review* collected by being there:

The top of the Suburban, from about hood height, was shorn off by the backhoe's bucket. The front seats were forced backward, and the dashboard, roof and steering wheel were torn off.

Parts of the car lay in a heap of crumpled metal and glass under the overpass. The silver Suburban was identifiable only by a 1983 owner's manual lying in the dirt nearby.

Both victims wore seat belts, but in this case, that was irrelevant, [Sgt. Jeff] Sale said. Both suffered severe head injuries.

Sleeping bags, a Coleman cooler and fishing equipment scattered on the highway and in the back of the Suburban suggested a camping trip. Unopened cans of Pepsi were jammed behind the front seat of the car.

The writer built every sentence on concrete detail. Good reporting made good writing possible.

When you read writing brimming with detail, you can be sure that the reporter's notebook is full of detail, too. Reporters who smell — and write it down — are doing their jobs. Reporters who touch — and write it down — are doing their jobs. So are those who note that someone's eyes roll and hands gesture — and write it down. Notebooks should contain not only facts and quotes; notebooks should also contain the results of reporting with all your senses.

Specific detail gathered by observant and questioning reporters always surpasses general description. It builds credibility and generates interest. One young reporter learned that the hard way. His assignment began when the city desk heard that an elderly victim of a crime committed a week earlier had died in the hospital that evening. The reporter was sent to interview the victim's neighbors, one of whom had seen a man carrying a television out of the victim's house the night she was injured. Suspicious, the neighbor had summoned police, who arrived in time to make the arrest. They found the beaten victim inside the house.

The reporter's first draft was a dry, straightforward account of the neighbor's reactions to the woman's death and the burglary. The story obviously deserved much more.

Did the victim live alone? What was the neighborhood like? Were there many break-ins in that area? Were the neighbors friendly to her? What was her house like? Nearly every question directed at the reporter required him to return to the scene. He had failed to do his reporting.

He wrote a second draft that the city editor was moments from approving. "By the way," the reporter mentioned, "did you know the television set that guy tried to steal didn't even work?" That's when he started writing his third version:

When 11-year-old Tracy Britt visited her neighbor Rose Shock in the small, one-story house just two doors off Providence Road, they just talked, mostly, because the television set was broken.

One week ago tonight, another neighbor, Al Zacher of 300 Wilkes Blvd., heard suspicious noises. Looking outside, he saw a man carrying the television set that didn't work from Mrs. Shock's home. As the man set the television down and headed for a green station wagon, Zacher called the police.

Inside lay Mrs. Shock, battered about the face.

Sunday in Springfield County Hospital, where she worked as a dietitian for many years before she retired in 1955, 85-year-old Rose Shock died.

If Mrs. Shock's relatives had their way, she would not have been living in the house with aluminum siding and paint peeling from its window frames at 302 Wilkes Blvd. After her house was burglarized last summer, her family tried to convince her to move.

"She didn't seem to be too alarmed to be living by herself," her sister, Ruth Tremaine of 306 Harley Court, said Monday. "She'd been living there 18 or 19 years, and she was happier there than she would have been anywhere else. We wanted her to go, but she just wanted to stay in her own home."

. . . David Herron, 45, of 207 Providence Walkway, is being held in lieu of $100,000 bond in connection with the incident. He is charged with assault with intent to kill, carrying a concealed weapon and first-degree robbery.

Prosecuting attorney Milt Harper said Monday he will meet with the medical examiner Thursday before deciding whether to file additional charges. He is waiting for results of autopsy tests.

Monday night, flashing blue lights atop Springfield police cars once again lit up the Wilkes Boulevard neighborhood. Police were investigating a report of a burglary at Zacher's house.

In that account, we see dirty streets, see the aluminum siding and feel the peeling paint. We learn that Mrs. Shock died in the hospital where she worked for many years. We know, too, the sad irony that she was killed for a broken television set.

ELEMENTS OF GOOD WRITING

Good writing is precise, clear and concrete. It shows rather than tells and uses figures of speech. Let's look at each of these characteristics.

Be Precise

Words should mean exactly what you intend them to mean. You should never use "uninterested" when you mean "disinterested." Nor should you use "allude" for "refer," "presume" for "assume," "endeavor" for "try," "fewer" for "less," "farther" for "further." If you report that fire destroyed a house, you mean the home needs rebuilding, not repair. If you say firefighters donned oxygen masks to enter a burning building, you are impugning either their intelligence or yours. Oxygen is dangerous around fire; firefighters use air tanks. You can make the mayor "say," "declare," "claim" or "growl" — but only one is accurate.

Avoiding Biased Language

Even when used innocently, sexist and racist language, besides being offensive and discriminatory, is imprecise. Doctors aren't always "he," nor are nurses always "she." Much of our language assumes people are male unless it is shown they are female. Precise writers avoid "policeman" (police officer), "ad man" (advertising representative), "assemblyman" (assembly member) and "postman" (postal worker). In some situations, you can use the plural to eliminate the gender: When doctors see patients, they often first try to get them to relax.

Our language is bursting with derogatory racial terminology. You should avoid using terms such as "Chinaman," "Jap," "nigger" and "Indian giver" not only because they are offensive but also because they are imprecise. They rain inaccurate stereotypes on a class of people. To be precise, use Asian American, black or African American, and American Indian or Native American.

Some words, perfectly precise when used correctly, are imprecise when used in the improper context. "Boy" is not interchangeable with "young man," and "girl" is not interchangeable with "young woman." A young Native American is not a "young buck." Elderly women are not "blue-haired," nor are all active retired persons "spry." In that context, "spry" implies that the writer is surprised to find an elderly person who is active. "Grandmotherly" fails when you describe people in their 40s who are grandmothers.

"Dumb" as in "deaf and dumb" is imprecise and derogatory. To be accurate, use "speech-impaired." When the terms are used in tandem, use "hearing-impaired and speech-impaired" for parallelism. Because alcoholism is a disease, use "recovering alcoholic" instead of "reformed alcoholic." "Handicapped" is imprecise; "disabled" is precise.

The *Los Angeles Times* uses "lesbian" unless the source prefers "gay woman." *Times* reporters also ask sources their preference for describing their "partner," "companion," "lover," and so on. The Associated Press uses "homosexual" and "gay" and does not permit "dyke," "fruit," "fairy" and "queer."

The battle over abortion extends to the terms used in the news. One side wants to be described as "pro-life"; the other wants to be described as "pro-choice." The Associated Press prescribes the terms "anti-abortion" and "abortion rights" in an attempt to be neutral.

Some dismiss this concern for language as overly zealous political correctness. That attitude implies we are afraid to tell the truth. What is the truth about ethnic slang? The truth is that many words historically applied to groups of people were created in ignorance or hate or fear. During the world wars, American citizens of German descent were called "Krauts" to depersonalize them. Americans of Japanese descent were locked up in internment camps. Almost every ethnic group that immigrated to America and started at the bottom of the ladder was regarded as dumb or as a threat to the economic well-being of those already here. Over the years, pejorative terms have been applied to immigrants from Ireland, Poland, China and Africa. We see the same thing happening to more recent immigrants from Mexico, the Caribbean and the Middle East. The adjective "Muslim" is seldom seen or heard in news reports except to modify "terrorists" or "fundamentalists." As writers concerned with precision of the language, we should deal with people, not stereotypes.

Words are powerful weapons. They define cultures, create second-class citizens and reveal stereotypical thinking. They also change the way people think about and treat others. Writers have the freedom to choose precisely the right word. That freedom can be both exhilarating and dangerous.

TIPS: Six ways to avoid sexism

- Use a generic term (flight attendant, firefighters).
- Participate in the movement to drop feminine endings (comedian, hero, actor, poet).
- Make the subject plural. (Reporters must not form *their* judgments.)
- Drop the sexist pronoun and replace it with an article. (A reporter must not form *a* judgment.)
- Rewrite to eliminate the gender. (A reporter must not judge.)
- Write the sentence in the second person. (*You* should not form *your* judgment.)

Avoiding Carelessness in Word Choice

Freedom in word choice is exhilarating when the result is a well-turned phrase. Here's Dan Berry of *The New York Times* describing a procession one year after the World Trade Center attacks: "The photographs of the dead bobbed upon the swells of the living." Here's Julie Sullivan of *The* (Spokane, Wash.) *Spokesman-Review*: "Hand him a soapbox, he'll hand you a homily."

Freedom in word choice is dangerous when it results in nouns masquerading as verbs (prioritize, impact, maximize) or jargon masquerading as respectable English (input, output, throughput).

Precision, however, means more than knowing the etymology of a word; it means knowing exactly what you want to say. Instead of saying, "The City Council wants to locate the landfill three blocks from downtown," to be precise, you say, "Some members of the City Council . . ." or, better yet, "Five members of the City Council. . . ."

Precision means using the conditional mood (could, might, should, would) when discussing proposals:

Incorrect: The bill will make it illegal . . .

Correct: The bill would make it illegal . . .

The use of "will" is imprecise because the legislation has not been passed. By using "would," you are saying, "If the legislature passes the bill, it would. . . ."

Precision means choosing the correct sentence structure to communicate explicitly what you mean. The following sentence is technically correct but imprecise:

```
The City Council passed the ordinance, and the 250 supporters
cheered.
```

It is imprecise because the compound sentence gives equal importance to the two thoughts expressed. To show cause and effect, the writer should use a complex sentence:

```
Because (or When) the City Council passed the ordinance, the
250 supporters cheered.
```

When you write implicitly, you force the reader to make inferences. Say what you are thinking.

Achieving Precision in the Use of Numbers

To many journalists and readers, numbers are a foreign language. It is our job to learn that language and to speak it so that our readers understand.

The most important way to increase comprehension is to compare numbers and sizes. Authorities may announce that forest fires destroyed vegetation over 500 square miles. What does that mean to you? To your readers? One way to make it meaningful is to compare the numbers, the unknown, to something

TIPS: Avoiding carelessness in word choice

- Know precisely what you want to say.
- Use the conditional mood (could, might, should, would) when discussing proposals.
- Choose the correct sentence structure to communicate explicitly what you mean.

known. Even if you don't know the size of your community in square miles, you have a good idea of its size. Readers in California could understand how large an area that was if they were told the forest fire destroyed an area four times the size of San Francisco. It was eight times the size of St. Louis and 15 times the size of Springfield, Mass. Check your city directory for the size and population of your community.

You translate large budget numbers by expressing them as spending per student. You translate a tax increase by expressing it as cost per taxpayer. You translate the rate of crime by expressing it as the number of crimes each minute or hour or day in your city. One newspaper examining the lack of screening for teachers expressed the findings this way:

> Spokane cabbies and Nevada blackjack dealers face tougher screening through background checks than teachers in 42 states.

If every journalist wrote about numbers in plain English, as that one did, our readers would understand us.

Be Clear

The ingredients of clear writing include simplicity, correct grammar and coherence. The following sections give specific examples of how each contributes to clarity in stories.

Keep It Simple

The readers of one newspaper once confronted the following one-sentence paragraph:

> "Paradoxically, cancer-causing mutations often result from the repair of a cell by error-prone enzymes and not the 'carcinogenic' substance's damage to the cell," Abe Eisenstark, director of biological sciences at the university, said at a meeting of the Ad Hoc Council of Environmental Carcinogenesis Wednesday night at the Cancer Research Center.

If there is a message in those 53 words, it would take a copy editor, a lexicologist and a Nobel Prize-winning scientist to decipher it. The message simply is not clear. Although the sentence is not typical of newspaper writing, it is not unusual either. The scientist is using the vocabulary of a scientist, which is inappropriate for a general audience. The reporter should say, "I don't understand that exactly. Can you translate it for my readers?" The response may produce an understandable quote, but if it doesn't, then paraphrase it and check back with your source to be sure you have paraphrased it accurately. Too much of what is written is mumbo jumbo. For instance:

TIPS: To write clearly

- Keep sentences short.
- Keep to one idea a sentence.
- Favor subject-verb-object sentences.
- Avoid using more than three prepositional phrases in one sentence.
- Avoid using more than three numbers in one sentence.
- Use plain and simple words instead of jargon, journalese, or clichés.
  — Paula LaRocque, assistant managing editor, *The Dallas Morning News*

Approximately 2 billion tons of sediment from land erosion enter our nation's waters every year. While industrial waste and sewage treatment plants receive a great deal of attention, according to the Department of Agriculture the number one polluter of our waterways is "non-point" pollution.

The writer of that lead contributed some linguistic pollution of his own. The message may have been clear in his mind, but it is not clear in print.

One remedy for unclear writing is the short sentence. The following examples introduce the same subject:

NEW YORK — From measurements with high-precision laser beams bounced off reflectors left at three lunar sites by Apollo astronauts, plus one atop an unmanned Soviet lunar vehicle, scientists believe that the moon is still wobbling from a colossal meteorite impact 800 years ago.

NEW YORK — The moon may still be wobbling from a colossal meteorite impact 800 years ago.

The writer of the first example drags the reader through some prickly underbrush full of prepositional phrases. The writer of the second has cleared the brush to expose the flowers.

Use Correct Grammar and Punctuation

Far too often, grammar and punctuation errors obscure meaning. Consider this example:

```
They spent the afternoon at the mall, buying more clothes than
they could fit in the trunk.
```

Because the participial phrase is misplaced, it sounds as if the mall bought clothes. Write the sentence this way:

```
Buying more clothes than they needed, they spent a fun-filled
afternoon at the mall.
```

No one who aspires to be a writer will succeed without knowing the rules of grammar. Dangling participles, split infinitives, subject-verb disagreement, pronoun-antecedent disagreement and misplaced modifiers are like enemy troops: They attack sentences and destroy their meaning, as the authors of a survey discovered.

The personnel director of an Inglewood, Calif., aerospace company had to fill out a government survey form that asked, among other things, "How many employees do you have, broken down by sex?" After considering the sentence for a few moments, she wrote, "Liquor is more of a problem with us."

Sentence modification was more of a problem with the writer of the survey. Here are some typical errors and ways to correct them:

"Short is beautiful. Short and simple is more beautiful. Short, simple and interesting is most beautiful."

— Don Gibb, educator

"The real problem is that misplaced modifiers and similar glitches tend to distract readers. Introduce blunders to an otherwise smoothly flowing story and it's as though a drunk stumbled through a religious procession.

"What's more, while those errors due to carelessness may not permanently damage the language, they can damage a paper's credibility. Botching a small job sows mistrust about the larger enterprise."

— Jack Cappon,
Associated Press

Incorrect pronoun:	Each of the boys brought *their* sleeping bags.
Correct:	Each of the boys brought *his* sleeping bag.
Subject-verb disagreement:	The *mayor* together with the city council *oppose* collective bargaining by the firefighters.
Correct:	The *mayor* together with the city council *opposes* . . .
	The *mayor and city council oppose* . . .
Split infinitive:	The supervisor agreed *to promptly submit* his resignation.
Correct:	The supervisor agreed *to submit* his resignation promptly.
Misplaced modifier:	*Despite his size*, the coach said Jones would play forward.
Correct:	The coach said that Jones, *despite his size*, would play forward.

Improper punctuation creates ambiguities at best and inaccuracies at worst. For instance:

```
Giving birth to Cynthia five years earlier had been difficult
for Mrs. Davenport and the two parents decided they were
content with the family they had.
```

Without the required comma before "and," the reader misses the pause and sees this: "Giving birth to Cynthia had been difficult for Mrs. Davenport and the two parents." That's a lot of people in the delivery room.

Be Coherent

A story must have a beginning, middle and end. When put in a maze, rats make many wrong turns before they find their way out. So do writers who start a story without knowing where it is going. A coherent story is one in which the information is logically connected. Coherence results when you create logical story structures, express the relationship between ideas properly, use transitions and think clearly. For more information on achieving coherence, you can turn to an entire Web site that is devoted to the topic: **papyr.com/hypertextbooks/engl_101/coherent.htm**.

Chronology is the most easily understood of story structures. You start at the beginning and go to the end. Journalists, however, often don't have the luxury of readers' time or publication space to use chronology. That's why it is important to outline a story, even if your outline merely lists the three or four points you expect to make.

Here's a simple outline you might make for a council story:

1. Approved one-way streets.
2. Raised parking fines.
3. Bought snowplows.
4. Will study downtown parking.
5. Hired audit firm.

You rank the actions in order of importance. Then you decide whether to focus on one element or write a summary lead or a multiple-element lead. Once you have done that, your outline gets more detailed:

"But I obsess during writing to the point where I can lose sleep over the right word."

— Madeleine Blais, writer

TIPS: Writing a coherent story

- Create logical story structures.
- Express the relationship between ideas properly.
- Use transitions.
- Think clearly.

1. Single-element lead
   a. One-way streets
2. Summary of other actions
   a. Parking fines, snowplows, parking facilities, city audit
3. Support lead
   a. The vote; Jones quote; opposition
4. Support other actions in order introduced in second paragraph
   a. Raised parking fines
      Amount; reason; no opposition
   b. Buy snowplows
      Cost; when delivered
   c. Downtown parking
      Define problem; when study is due; who will do it; Dehaven quote; Chamber of Commerce request
   d. Audit firm
      Who will do it; cost; when due

Although outlining may take five minutes, it will save you much more time. The outline also creates a structure that flows logically from one idea to the next. Here's how you could start the story:

```
The Springfield City Council voted Tuesday to make four
streets in the downtown area one-way.

    The council also raised parking fines to $25, voted to buy
two snowplows, ordered a study of downtown parking facilities
and hired a firm to audit the city.

    Effective March 1, the four streets that will be one-way
are . . .
```

Within each sentence, you must express the proper relationships between ideas. One way to do this is through sentence structure. *Simple sentences* express one idea. *Compound sentences* express two or more ideas of equal importance. *Complex sentences* subordinate one idea to another. Here are some examples:

Simple:	The mayor scolded the council.
Compound:	The mayor scolded the council, and she insisted on a vote.
	(Equates two ideas.)
Complex:	After the mayor scolded the council, she insisted on a vote.
	(Shows sequence.)

Compound sentences equate two or more ideas without commenting on them. Complex sentences can show cause and effect:

Compound:	The council members were angry, and they rejected the proposal.
Complex:	Because the council members were angry, they rejected the proposal.

The meaning in the first example is implicit — that is, the reader has to infer the relationship. The meaning in the second is explicit. Each sentence is correct, but the meaning of each is slightly different. Complex sentences also show other types of relationships. Subordinating conjunctions such as "if," "since," "while," "after" and "until" each carry a different and precise meaning.

You also protect coherence by carefully choosing the proper coordinating conjunction: Observe how the meaning changes with the conjunction:

```
The mayor insisted that the council vote, and the members
ignored her.

    The mayor insisted that the council vote, but the members
ignored her.
```

The second example is more coherent because it expresses the council members' reaction more logically.

Transitions are words, phrases, sentences or paragraphs that show the logical progression of the story structure and the ideas within the structure. Transitions are road signs directing traffic on the information highway (see Figure 8.2).

The reference to "memory" in the next example directs us from the first to the second paragraph:

```
Mr. and Mrs. Lester Einbender are using their memory to
project life as it might have been.

    That memory centers around a son named Michael, a
rheumatic disease called lupus and a desire to honor one while
conquering the other.
```

The word "that" beginning the second paragraph is a demonstrative adjective. Its use is subtle, but its impact is dramatic. If you wrote "A memory," you would not link the reader to the memory already mentioned. If you wrote "The memory," you would be more specific, but by writing "That memory," you point directly to the memory mentioned in the preceding paragraph. Because "a" is good only for general references, "a" is called an indefinite modifier. Because "the" is more specific, "the" is called a definite modifier. Because "that" is most specific, "that" is called a demonstrative adjective; it demonstrates precisely the word or phrase to which you are referring.

Transitions help you achieve coherence, the logical connection of ideas. They guide you from one sentence to the next, from one paragraph to the next. Writers unfamiliar with transitions merely stack paragraphs, like pieces of wood, atop one another. Transitions keep the story, if not the woodpile, from falling apart.

Repeating a word or phrase is one way to keep the story from falling apart. In the preceding example, the writer both used a demonstrative adjective (others are "this," "these" and "those") and repeated a word.

Parallelism, repetition of a word or grammatical form, is another way to guide readers through a story. Writers frequently use parallelism to achieve coherence.

On a Monday afternoon, Dr. Glenn Billman pulled back from the autopsy he was performing on a dead girl and stared at the sight before him.

In his seven years at Children's Hospital, he had never seen anything like it. The girl's colon was severely hemorrhaged, ravaged by bacteria that normally lived in a cow's intestine.

Puzzled and quietly alarmed, Billman notified local health officials. It was the first indication that the lethal strain of bacteria, E. coli 0157:H7, was on the loose.

But Billman didn't make his discovery at Children's Hospital in Seattle. He made it at Children's Hospital in San Diego, and he made it three weeks before the E. coli epidemic struck the Northwest, killing three children and sickening about 500 people.

In December, San Diego was hit by a small E. coli outbreak that killed the 6-year-old girl and made at least seven other people sick.

It is now being linked to the Seattle outbreak, but in its early stages, San Diego health officials were slow to recognize the crisis, and they have been sharply criticized for failing to notify the public about the E. coli death and illnesses.

"I really believe we need to be safe and not sorry, and the fact is, a girl died in San Diego," said San Diego County Supervisor Dianne Jacob. "I was outraged. The only way I found out was by reading it in the newspaper" after the Northwest outbreak.

When the first Washington cases were reported in mid-January, authorities here immediately queried neighboring states, including California, but were not told about the E. coli death of the San Diego girl. That information would have alerted them about the bacteria's severity and might have pointed them sooner to the source of the contamination.

Like the patients here, the San Diego girl had eaten a hamburger at a Jack in the Box restaurant days before she got sick and died. The seven other E. coli patients had all eaten hamburgers at fast-food restaurants, among them Jack in the Box.

That information was available in early January, according to Dr. Michele Ginsberg, San Diego County epidemiologist. She would not say how many of the seven patients had eaten at Jack in the Box.

"A variety of restaurants were mentioned," she said. "Naming any one of them would create public reaction and perhaps avoidance of those restaurants."

That reticence angers Jacob, the San Diego County supervisor. "I had a follow-up meeting with county health officials, and I have to tell you, very honestly, I was not pleased with their attitude," she said. . . .

Figure 8.2

Note how transitional words and phrases maintain the coherence of the story as it moves from one paragraph to the next.

Writing about the complicated subject of nuclear-waste disposal in America, Donald Barlett and James Steele, then of *The Philadelphia Inquirer*, relied on parallelism for coherence and emphasis:

This assessment may prove overly optimistic. For perhaps in no other area of modern technology have so many experts in the government, industry and science been so wrong so many times over so many years as have those involved in radioactive waste.

They said, repeatedly, that radioactive waste could be handled like any other industrial refuse. It cannot.

They said that science had most of the answers, and was on the verge of getting the few it did not have, for dealing with radioactive waste permanently. It did not, and it does not.

They said that some of it could be buried in the ground, like garbage in a landfill, and that it would pose no health hazard because it would never move. It moved.

They said that liquid radioactive waste could be put in storage tanks, and that rigorous safety systems would immediately detect any leaks. The tanks leaked for weeks and no one noticed.

Chronology and references to time provide other ways to tie a story together. Words and phrases such as "now," "since then" and "two days later" are invaluable in helping readers understand where they have been and where they are going. Chronology is important in everything from reports of automobile accidents (which car entered the intersection first?) to recaps of events that occurred over months or even years. For instance, Barlett and Steele's stories covered 35 years of efforts to store nuclear waste.

You also enhance coherence when you figure out what you want to say and then express it positively. Enter this thicket of verbiage at your own risk:

```
The Missouri Gaming Commission has 30 days to appeal a judge's
temporary order reversing the commission's decision not to
grant a gaming license to a firm that wanted to dock a
riverboat casino in Jefferson City.
```

The writer is lost in a maze of reversals of negative findings. The lead tries to cover too much territory. Express it in the positive and strip it to its essential information:

```
The state has 30 days to persuade a judge it should not have
to license a firm that wants to open a riverboat casino in
Jefferson City.
```

The writer of this sentence also failed to think clearly:

```
Amtrak, formally the National Passenger Railroad Corp., was
created in 1970 to preserve declining passenger train
service.
```

Do you suppose Amtrak was really created to preserve "declining passenger train service"?

Use Concrete Examples

For lawyers, the devil may be in the details, but for writers, clarity is in the details. Echoing your bureaucratic sources, you can write of infrastructures or facilities or learning pods. But try touching any of them. By contrast, you ride on a highway, sit in an arena and learn in a reading group.

Be specific. The speaker is big (compared to what?). The speaker is loud (how loud?). Abstractions are ambiguous. To someone who is 6 feet tall, someone big may be 6 feet 6 inches tall. To someone who is 5 feet 2 inches tall, 6 feet is huge.

Look at the concrete details stuffed in the following lead from *The Boston Globe* about an employee who killed five co-workers:

> He was an accountant who had a chip on his shoulder and a bayonet on his kitchen table. He lived with his parents across from a llama farm in a small beige house with a sign informing visitors: "Trespassers will be shot; survivors will be shot again."
>
> As dawn broke over Ledyard yesterday, Matthew Beck, 35, left his folks' home — across town from the casino — got in his car, and drove 1½ hours to his job at Connecticut Lottery headquarters. At some point, he strapped a bandolier of bullets across his chest, over his gray pinstriped shirt but concealed by a brown leather jacket. He carried a 9mm pistol and a knife.

A student writer at Indiana University could have reported that several things were missing in the apartment. Instead, she used concrete detail:

> When she awoke the next morning, the window was completely open. Random items, including a toaster, a 15-year-old broken VCR, an empty bookbag and the remote control to a stereo, were missing.

To be concrete, you must have facts — things you can touch and examine. Lazy reporters create puffballs. Poke their stories, and your finger will go clear through them. Instead of saying, "Some council members," say, "Five council members." Instead of writing that a business is "downsizing," report that 150 workers will lose their jobs. Avoid abstractions; covet concrete detail.

Show, Don't Just Tell

As you chauffeur the reader through the scenes in your story, you can drive down the road or over the green-laced, rolling hills of Kentucky. You can report that a car hit a skunk, or you can convey the nauseating smell. A word here, a phrase there, and you can hear the plane ripping the tin roof off the house, smell the acrid tires burning on a flaming car, feel the boxing glove's leather rasp against the skin. Good writing appeals to one or more of our five senses: sight, hearing, smell, taste and touch.

In addition to years of anecdotal experience, there is also statistical support for the advice to *show* rather than *tell*. For instance, researchers constructed 10 sentences telling information and 10 showing information. College students were divided into two groups and asked to read one of the groups of sentences. Then they were asked to rate the sentences on such measurements as interesting/dull, clear/unclear, and engaging/unengaging. The authors concluded, "The experiment found strong evidence that, as many experts have implied, show sentences are seen as more interesting and engaging than tell sentences."

Writer Walt Harrington could simply have told readers that detective V.I. Smith picked up his notebook to leave on a call, but he showed us his preparation:

"Well, here we go," says V.I., in his smooth, lyrical baritone as he palms a radio, unconsciously pats his right breast coat pocket for evidence of his ID wallet, pats his left breast coat pocket for evidence of his notebook and heads out the door in his athlete's saunter, a stylized and liquid stroll, a modern cakewalk.

Readers can see and hear V.I. because the writer is showing, not telling.

Knowing when a detail enhances the story instead of making it wordy is the skill of an accomplished writer. Some details are as out of place as white tennis shoes with a black business suit. What country music singer Tammy Wynette was wearing was important in a profile of her, and reporter Leola Floren captured the scene this way:

On stage, she is surrounded by musicians in green suits and cowboy boots. Stuck there in the middle, Tammy looks like one smooth pearl in a bucket of peas. Her wavy blond hair tumbles over bare shoulders to the middle of her back. Her black strapless gown is of the kind the slightly bad girls wore to the senior prom: slit up past the knees in the back, cut so low in front there isn't any decent place to pin a corsage. When she picks up her guitar, you think it ought to be a champagne glass, she looks so elegant.

Notice Julie Sullivan's power of observation in her profile of a resident of Spokane:

Joe Peak's smile has no teeth.

His dentures were stolen at the Norman Hotel, the last place he lived in downtown Spokane before moving to the Merlin two years ago. Gumming food and fighting diabetes have shrunk the 54-year-old man's frame by 80 pounds. He is thin and weak and his mouth is sore.

Words create pictures. Picture Johnny Cash: "He moves with the grace of a little boy who has to go to the bathroom." A student reporter lets us listen in because she listened:

His voice has a thousand personalities. When he is trying to convince you of something, his voice is so low you have to lean forward to hear him. When he's mad, he spits his words out in growls. When he's happy, his voice elevates, sometimes going so high that you look behind him to see if a woman entered the room.

Another student writer used her hand to gather information: "After 40 years of working outside, his skin is as leathery as an alligator's." Did she actually touch him? "Yes," she says. "I kept looking at his skin. Finally, even though I was embarrassed, I asked him if I could touch his face. He laughed. 'You can tell I don't use no fancy lotions, can't you?'"

The writing is better because the reporters didn't just ask questions and record answers. They looked; they touched; they listened. Readers can see and feel along with the reporters.

Use Figures of Speech

Good writers also know how to use the literary device known as **figures of speech** along with other kinds of analogy. Analogies such as similes and metaphors permit writers to show similarities and contrasts. Similes and metaphors are common figures of speech. *Similes* show similarities by using the word "like" or "as." Talking about a surgeon fighting a patient's massive bleeding, Tom Hallman Jr. of *The* (Portland) *Oregonian* wrote, "If he plunges ahead, it will be like replumbing a house with the water turned on." Writing about a high school basketball coach for the girls' team, Madeleine Blais wrote, "At 6'6", Moyer looms over his players. With a thick cap of graying brown hair and bangs that flop down over his forehead, he resembles a grizzly bear on spindly legs."

Metaphor is the first cousin of simile. A simile *compares* one thing to another, but a metaphor says one thing *is* another: "Michael is a lion with gazelle legs." A metaphor is a stronger analogy than a simile. Describing the radio personality and writer Garrison Keillor, a reporter once wrote, "And there he is. A sequoia in a room full of saplings." The metaphor works on two levels. Keillor is tall enough to tower over most others in the room. Because he is known internationally, his work towers over others, too.

With similes and metaphors, writers draw word pictures. The techniques set the pages of a scrapbook of images turning in each reader's mind.

The technique of analogy is also important to every journalist trying to make dimensions and numbers meaningful. That's important whether you are writing about the national debt or the size of the offensive guard. You make numbers meaningful by translating them. Writing about the national debt, one college reporter pointed out it was large enough to operate the university for decades. No number means much unless it is compared to something else.

Instead of writing that 75 percent of the people in the United States do not know that you are innocent until proven guilty, say that three of four people do not know. When the Associated Press reported that a jury awarded a woman who was scalded by her coffee from McDonald's $2.9 million, the amount of the settlement was translated as "about two days' coffee sales for the fast-food chain."

Writing to be read is not easy. Reporters become writers by the sweat of their brows. John Kenneth Galbraith, a best-selling author who is able to make economics understandable to the lay reader, commented on the difficulty of writing well. "There are days when the result is so bad that no fewer than five revisions are required," he wrote. "In contrast, when I'm inspired, only four revisions are needed."

Trying the techniques discussed in this chapter is the first step. Mastering them will be the result of trying them repeatedly.

Suggested Readings

Barzun, Jacques. *Simple and Direct*. New York: Harper & Row, 1975. An excellent rhetoric book that explains many of the details of sentence construction.

Brooks, Brian S., Pinson, James L. and Wilson, Jean Gaddy. *Working with Words*, Fifth Edition. New York: Bedford/St. Martin's, 2003. Like Strunk and White's *The Elements of Style*, this is an excellent handbook for every writer. It covers everything from grammar and punctuation to racism and sexism in language.

Kennedy, George, Moen, Daryl R. and Ranly, Don. *Beyond the Inverted Pyramid*. New York: Bedford/St. Martin's, 1993. The authors of *News Reporting and Writing* expand on the themes in this chapter.

Kilpatrick, James J. *The Writer's Art*. Kansas City: Andrews, McMeel & Parker, 1984. An informative and entertaining discussion of writing.

Strunk, William and White, E. B. *The Elements of Style*, Third Edition. Boston: Allyn & Bacon, 1995. This little book practices what it preaches. For the beginner it is a good primer; for the pro it is a good review of writing rules and word meanings.

Tankard, James and Hendrickson, Laura. "Specificity, Imagery in Writing: Testing the Effects of 'Show, Don't Tell.'" *Newspaper Research Journal*, vol. 17, no. 1–2, Winter/Spring 1996, pp. 35–48.

Suggested Web Sites

www.neiman.harvard.edu/reports/contents.html
The *Neiman Reports* are all free online. Several issues have articles about writing and reporting, but don't miss the Spring 2002 report on the Narrative Journalism Conference.

papyr.com/hypertextbooks/engl_101/coherent.htm
Daniel Kies of the Department of English at the College of DuPage explains how to achieve coherence.

www.poynter.org
Select Writing and Editing, and you will enter a world full of advice, most of it from writers. This is a site you should check often.

Exercises

1. Choose precisely the right word.

   a. We need to (ensure, insure) a victory.
   b. Stop (aggravating, annoying) your friend.
   c. The attorney won because she (refuted, responded to) the allegations.
   d. The prisoner was able to produce (mitigating, militating) evidence.

2. Rewrite Barlett and Steele's story on page 179 to take out the parallelism. Which version, the original or yours, is better, and why?

3. Punctuate the following sentences:

   a. Government officials have come under a newly enacted censorship system and several foreign speakers have been denied permission to enter the country.
   b. It was a Monday night and for the next two days he teetered between life and death.
   c. The council approved the manager's proposals and rejected a tax increase.

4. Use an analogy to explain the following numbers:

   The student council's budget is $350,000. The university has 19,000 students. The local city budget is $3 million. The city has 70,000 residents.

5. In newspaper articles find examples of:

   a. Incorrect word usage. (Correct it.)
   b. Ambiguous wording. (Correct it.)
   c. Incorrect grammar. (Correct it.)
   d. Incorrect punctuation. (Correct it.)
   e. A nicely worded sentence or paragraph.
   f. Figures of speech.
   g. Analogies that help translate numbers.

6. Access a computer database that carries several newspapers, and find at least three versions of the same news event written on the same day. Compare the sentence lengths. Look for transitions. Find figures of speech and analogies. Which, in your opinion, is the most readable? The least readable? Why?

7. Using software that uses the Flesch Reading Ease formula or a similar measurement of readability, compare a story you have written to stories from *The New York Times* and the Associated Press. What are the readability scores? Account for scoring differences and similarities.

Beyond the Inverted Pyramid

B arney Calame, the deputy managing editor of *The Wall Street Journal*, was chatting with a group of journalists about the number of his family members who had lived long lives. Calame offered an example:

> "My grandmother, who had one leg, lost the other when she tried to flee the nursing home in a wheelchair when she was 96."
>
> He stopped. Everyone looked at him expectantly.
>
> "Well?" said one listener.
>
> "Well what?" Calame asked.
>
> "How did your grandmother lose her other leg? Why was she fleeing the nursing home?"
>
> "Grandmother decided that she didn't like living in the nursing home," Calame responded. "She took off in her wheelchair, tipped going over the curb and spilled onto the street. She developed an infection in her injured leg and later had to have it amputated."

Calame was telling stories to friends. When we tell stories, we start at the beginning, or at least close enough to the beginning so the story makes sense. The approach allows the speaker to build to the climax.

Using the inverted pyramid, we get to the point as quickly as possible. That approach saves readers' and listeners' time, but it's not the best way to tell stories. If we want to engage our readers intellectually and emotionally, if we want to inform and entertain, we must use writing techniques that promise great things to come and then fulfill that promise. To that end, we should use the devices of narration: scenes, dialogue, foreshadowing and anecdotes. Our stories also have beginnings, middles and ends. With these devices, we reward readers.

Although narration thrives in any structure, narrative writing thrives in structures other than the inverted pyramid. Some of these structures are hybrids of the inverted pyramid and chronology structures. Others are adaptations of chronology. These structures are even suitable for breaking news stories if you are able to gather enough information to re-create scenes jammed with pertinent detail, if you are able to confirm the chronology, if you are able to capture the dialogue. These structures also support investigative reports, profiles, oddities and issue stories — all genres that allow you more time to gather and write.

In this chapter you will learn:

1. The techniques of narration.

2. How to modify the inverted pyramid when reporting breaking news.

If time, detail and space are available, take advantage of these devices and structures. Whether you are writing about a car accident, the Boy Scouts, the health-care system, corruption in government or the 8-year-old running the corner lemonade stand, writing the story will be easier if you know some alternatives to the inverted pyramid.

THE TECHNIQUES OF NARRATION

Exposition is the ordering of facts. **Narration** is the telling of a story. When we arrange facts from most to least important, we are using exposition, and the resulting structure is the inverted pyramid. When we use scenes, anecdotes and dialogue chronologically to build to a climax, we are using narration, and the result is a narrative, or story. The inverted pyramid has sources; a story has characters.

Storytellers don't speak in monotone. They add inflection to maintain listeners' interest. To avoid monotony, writers re-create scenes with detail and dialogue, foreshadow the good stuff to come and tempt readers to continue reading by offering them treats in the form of anecdotes.

In exposition, the writer clearly stands between the reader and the information. In contrast, the people in a story whisper to the writer, who turns and speaks to the reader. In narration, the storyteller moves aside and allows the reader to watch the action unfold.

Scenes

Gene Roberts, former managing editor of *The New York Times*, tells about his first job at a daily newspaper. His publisher, who was blind, had someone read the newspaper to him each morning. One day, the publisher called Roberts into his office and complained, "Roberts, I can't see your stories. Make me see."

We should all try to make readers see, smell, feel, taste and hear. One way to do that is to write using **scenes** as much as possible. To write a scene, you have to be there. You need to capture the sights, the sounds and the smells that are pertinent. A student reporter at South Dakota State University was there to capture this opening:

> Don Sheber's leathery, cracked hands have been sculpted by decades of wresting a living from the earth.
>
> But this year, despite work that often stretches late into the evening, the moisture-starved soil has yielded little for Sheber and his family.

> Sheber's hands tugged at the control levers on his John Deere combine last week as rotating blades harvested the thin stands of wheat that have grown to less than a foot high. . . .

The writer steps aside and allows the reader to visit Sheber on the farm (see Figure 9.1). We can see and feel the farmer's hands. We can touch the John Deere, the stunted wheat.

Figure 9.1
"Don Sheber's leathery, cracked hands have been sculpted by decades of wresting a living from the earth." Use descriptive language to paint a vivid picture for readers and to bring a story to life.

To create such scenes, you must use all your senses to gather information, and your notebook should reflect that reporting. Along with the results of interviews, your notebook should bulge with details of sights and smells, sounds and textures. David Finkel, winner of the American Society of Newspaper Editors Distinguished Writing Award in 1986, says, "Anything that pertains to any sense I feel at any moment, I write down." Gather details indiscriminately. Later, you can discard those that are not germane. Because you were there, you can write the scene as if you were writing a play.

Because Bartholomew Sullivan of the Memphis *Commercial Appeal* was observing and listening closely at a trial, his readers were able to sit in the courtroom with him:

Helfrich banged an index finger on the rail of the jury box as he recalled Thursday's testimony in which a string of Bowers's Jones County friends testified that he was a solid businessman, a Christian — "a gentleman." One of the witnesses was Nix, who called Bowers a "real, real nice man."

"They talk of gentlemen," Helfrich whispered. Then, shouting, he said: "These people don't have a gentle bone in their bodies. They were nightriders and henchmen. They attacked a sleeping family and destroyed all they owned."

Analyze the detail: banging his index finger, the whisper, the shout. We can see and we can hear.

Another scene from another trial was written by Peter St. Onge, then of *The Huntsville* (Ala.) *Times*. By creating a scene, he allows readers to watch and listen:

"I not only lost a wife, I lost a best friend, thanks to you two," he said, looking at the boys. "My son looks for his mother to come back. I have to explain to him that his mother's in heaven. I have to explain what you two did."

Johnson rocked back and forth at the words, nodding his head and wiping his eyes. Golden stared blankly, expressionless as he had been all hearing. When Golden's attorney, Val Price, objected and the judged cautioned Wright not to speak directly to the boys, Wright smiled wryly and continued.

In both of these examples, we are transported to the courtrooms because the writers worked in scenes. Neither writer wrote his entire story in scenes, as it would be in a movie script, but both created scenes when possible. The stories were richer for those scenes.

Dialogue

- When the source tells the reporter who tells the reader, you have a quotation.

- When the reporter records the conversation of two or more people speaking not to the reporter but to each other, you have dialogue.

The use of **dialogue** — conversation between two or more people — allows the narrator to recede and the characters to take center stage. When you use quotations, you — the writer — are repeating for the reader what the source said, and the reader listens to you relating what was said. But when you use dialogue, the writer disappears and the reader listens directly to the characters.

Compare these examples:

During the public hearing, Henry Lathrop accused the council of wasting taxpayers' money. "If you don't stop voting for all this spending, I am going to circulate a recall petition and get you all kicked off the council," he said.

Mayor Margorie Gold told Lathrop he was free to do as he wished. "As for us," she said, "we will vote in the best interests of the city."

That is the traditional way of presenting quotes. The reporter is telling readers what was said instead of taking readers to the council chambers and letting them listen. Here is how that account would sound handled as dialogue:

When Henry Lathrop spoke to the City Council during the public hearing, he pounded on the podium. "You folks are wasting taxpayers' money. If you don't stop voting for all this spending, I am going to circulate a recall petition and get you all kicked off the council."

Mayor Margorie Gold slammed her gavel on her desk.

"Mr. Lathrop," she said as she tried to control the anger in her voice. She looked at him directly. "You are free to do as you wish. As for us, we will vote in the best interests of the city."

At the hearing, Lathrop and Gold were speaking to each other. The second version captures the exchange without the intercession of the writer.

Dialogue is a conversation between two or more people, neither of whom usually is the reporter. This is dialogue between Cindy Martling, a rehabilitation nurse, and Mary Jo, the patient's wife, after Martling scolded the patient for feeling sorry for himself:

She wandered around a bit, then saw Mary Jo standing in the hallway. The two women went to each other and embraced. "I'm sorry," Martling said through more tears. "I didn't mean to lose control. I hope I didn't offend you."

"What you did was wonderful," Mary Jo said. "He needed to hear that. Dan is going to work through it, and we're all going to be OK."

Dialogue is a key element in creating scenes. The writer permits the characters to talk to each other.

Foreshadowing

Foreshadowing is the technique of giving hints about what's coming. Moviemakers tease you with the scenes they think will encourage you to buy a ticket. Broadcasters foreshadow to keep you from leaving during a commercial: "Coming up, there's a burglar prowling your neighborhood." Every lead foreshadows the story. The leads that not only tell but promise more good stuff to come are the most successful. Tom Koetting, then of *The Wichita* (Kan.) *Eagle*, spent nine months observing the recovery of a doctor who had nearly lost his life in a farm accident. He produced a story of about 100,000 words. The simple lead promised great things to come: "Daniel Calliendo Jr. had not expected to meet death this calmly."

A student at Florida A&M University used the same technique to invite readers to continue the story:

A North Carolina family thought the worst was behind them when they were robbed Saturday morning at a gas station just off Interstate 95.

The worst was yet to come.

The worst was yet to come. That's another way of saying, "Read on; the story gets even better."

In the next example, you see a longer opening that is packed with promises of great things to come. It also was written by a college student, this one at the University of Missouri.

Deena Borman's relationship with her roommate, Teresa, during her freshman year in college had shattered long before the wine bottle.

Weeks had gone by with Teresa drawing further and further away from Deena. Finally, after repeatedly hearing Teresa talk about suicide, Deena says, "I kept telling her how silly she was to want to die."

That made Teresa angry, so she threw a full wine bottle at Deena. It shattered against the wall and broke open the simmering conflict between them. That was when Deena tried to find out what had gone wrong with Teresa's life, and that was when Teresa told Deena that she wanted to do something to get rid of her.

And that was when Deena began to be scared of her own roommate.

The writer is promising a great story. What is wrong with Teresa? Does Teresa really try to hurt Deena? Does Deena really have something to be scared about? There is a promise of great things to come. Would you keep reading?

Anecdotes

The ultimate treats, **anecdotes** are stories embedded in stories. They can be happy or sad, funny or serious. Whatever their tone, they should illustrate a point. You are likely to remember the anecdotes more than anything else in the story. You probably remember the stories that your professors tell regardless of whether you remember the rest of the lecture. Long after you've forgotten this chapter, you will probably remember the Barney Calame anecdote and some of the other examples. Facts inform. Anecdotes inform and entertain.

Befitting something so valuable, they are hard to obtain. You can't get them by asking your source, "Got any good anecdotes?" But you can get them by asking your source for examples so you can re-create the scene.

That's what Kelly Whiteside of *USA Today* did after Michelle Snow of the Tennessee Lady Vols stole the ball, thundered the length of the court and dunked the ball two-handed during a game. Players on her team jumped and screamed; even the opposing team and its fans cheered. Five days later, Whiteside wanted to know what happened in the locker room at halftime after this historic event in women's basketball. It was only the third time in NCAA history that a woman had dunked during a game.

> "Good anecdotes — which is to say, entertaining anecdotes — stick in the mind. I rarely need to resort to my notes to recall them."
>
> — James B. Stewart, *Follow the Story*

Afterward, the Lady Vols waited for coach Pat Summitt to come into the locker room. They wondered how she would react. After all, Summitt, the John Wooden of the women's game, is a purist who always said that dunking was overrated. At halftime, the locker room door creaked open, and Summitt walked in. Her piercing blue eyes were focused intensely, and a serious look was frozen on her face. Summitt turned toward Snow.

"Nice high-post steal there, Snow," Summitt said. And everyone in the locker room dissolved in laughter as Summitt gave Snow a high-five.

If Whiteside had handled the story in typical expository fashion, she would have quoted Snow or other sources in the locker room something like this:

```
Snow said she and her teammates wondered if Coach Pat Summitt
approved of the dunk.

    "We were all sitting quietly in the locker room at
halftime," Snow said. . . .
```

Instead, Whiteside called Snow and asked her several specific questions, such as "What did you do when you got in the locker room?" and "What did Pat Summitt say?"

"She needed to be my eyes and ears," Whiteside said of Snow.

Whiteside also needed to talk to others to get more detail and to corroborate the information Snow had given her. Summitt told her that she had come into the locker room with a serious look on her face and had given Snow a high-five, two details Snow hadn't volunteered. Whiteside also talked to Debby Jennings, the Sports Information director, also present in the locker room.

"Each person added something," Whiteside said. As a result, she was able to re-create the scene rather than merely report what happened.

Phrase your questions to get stories. For example, when someone tells you that another person is a practical joker, you want to ask, "Can you give me an example of that?" Some of the best anecdotal examples come from phrasing questions in the superlative: "What's the funniest thing that ever happened to you while you were standing in front of an audience?" "What's the worst case you've ever seen come into this emergency room?" "Everyone tells me Rodney is always the first one they call when they need help on a project. Has he ever helped you?" "Can you give me an example?"

All of these elements — writing in scenes, using dialogue, foreshadowing and anecdotes — are the ingredients of narration. Most stories move from exposition to narration several times during a story. Now let's look at the structures in which you can use these techniques.

HOW TO MODIFY THE INVERTED PYRAMID

Structures change with the information. When you move out of reporting on breaking news, you probably also move out of the inverted pyramid. That requires you to report differently and use different structures.

Service Journalism

In Chapter 1, you read that one of the criteria for news is usefulness. Many, if not most, of the magazines you find on the racks appeal to readers by presenting information they might find useful. More than that, they attempt to present this useful information in the most usable way. This approach to presenting information has been called **service journalism.** Oftentimes, you see it labeled "News you can use."

Newspapers, too, are doing more service journalism. Some sections, such as travel, food and entertainment, use many techniques of service journalism. Front-page news stories, too, often contain elements of service journalism, even if it's just a box listing a sequence of events or directing readers to more information.

In this textbook, you see examples of service journalism in the pullout elements that list the learning objectives for each chapter or highlight important points. The techniques of service journalism require that you think about content and presentation even as you are reporting. Ask yourself, "What does the reader need to be able to act on this information?" The answer might range from an address to a phone or fax number to instructions on how to fix a lawnmower or make a loaf of bread. It might include directions on how to travel to a festival or where and when to buy tickets. As these examples illustrate, you move from simply talking about something to providing the information the reader needs to act on your story.

Much of the basic service journalism information can be presented as sidebars or lists or boxed material. In Figure 9.2, more information about service journalism is presented in common service journalism presentation style.

Service Journalism

In today's microwave world, in-a-hurry readers want practical information presented in the most efficient and effective way.

Bill Watterson once drew a comic strip of Calvin that shows Calvin reading the label on the package of a microwave dinner. In his classic outraged face, Calvin screams his protest: "Six minutes to microwave this?? Who's got that kind of time?!"

Perhaps the primary rule of writing today is: Did you give the message in such a way as to take the reader the least amount of time? Readers will only pay attention to what you say if you show them respect. Today you show respect by paying heed to people's lack of time.

After all, time is more than money. Time is life. You waste my time; you waste my life.

Readers are most likely to give you time if you offer them something useful. Yes, they'll read for relaxation and entertainment, but many don't turn to you for that.

Remember, **the opposite of useful is useless.**

But more than that, you must present useful information in the most usable way. You must present it in such a way that people will clip it out and stick it on the refrigerator — or bulletin board, or place it in a retrievable file. Some have called it refrigerator journalism.

What this means is that you must think not just of a message of words on paper. You must think of how these words will appear on the page. You must become concerned about presentation.

• •

Basics Service journalism is:

• **Useful.** You must inform readers, yes. But if you find ways to demonstrate how the reader can use the information, you will be more successful. You've heard of WIIFM. What's in it for me? "You" and "your" are the most used words in advertising. See how often you can get "you" in the first sentence of your copy. Using "you" will force you to consider the reader.

• **Usable.** Here's a rule. Whenever you can make a list, make a list. Lists get more attention, better comprehension and more retention. Five ways to save money. Do this; don't do that. Advantages, disadvantages. (Don't think you have to write sentences.) "Tips" is a magical word.

• **Used.** Service journalism is action journalism. You are successful only if people use the information. People stop paying attention to information they never use. You should be able to prove to advertisers and others that your readers do what you tell them to do. That means, you must devise ways to get readers to respond. To get readers involved and doing things, you must promise them something. Offer a prize; give them something free. Give a T-shirt for the best suggestion or to the first five to respond. People will kill for a T-shirt or a coffee mug.

Refrigerator Journalism
10 tips to serve today's readers

1. **Save them time.**
2. **Help them make more money, save money, get something free.**
3. **Address different levels of news interest.**
4. **Address niche audiences more effectively.**
5. **Become more personally useful.**
6. **Become more immediately usable.**
7. **Become more accessible.** Give readers your name, phone number, fax number, e-mail address.

8. **Become more user-friendly.** Learn to layer the news, use cross references, put things in the same place, color-code when you can, tell readers where to find things, use page numbers on contents blurbs—even on covers, use glossaries, show them where to find more information.

9. **Become more visual and graphic.** Use charts, infograms, pictograms because they are more effective and efficient.

10. **Become more engaging and interactive.** Use contests, quizzes, crosswords, games—make your readers do things. They remember better if they do something, if they are active rather than passive. Give awards to those who send answers in to you. Give a coffee mug to the reader with the best tip of the month. Readers who are more involved in your publication are more likely to resubscribe.

Figure 9.2

Employing the common presentation devices of service journalism — such as boxes and sidebars — this example shows how to highlight information readers can find and use easily.

Print is a hot, intense medium. Refrigerator journalism
cools off a hot medium and invites access and participation.

195

9/Beyond the
Inverted Pyramid

Other devices of service journalism

1. Use blurbs. After a title and before the article begins, write a summary/contents/benefit blurb. David Ogilvy says no one will read the small type without knowing the benefit upfront. Use the same benefit blurb in a table of contents or menu or briefs column. Every publication needs such a column. The best word in a benefit blurb is "how." How to, how you, how I, how Jane Doe did something. Be personal. Use people in your messages.

Also, use internal blurbs, little summaries, pullquotes, tips to tease and coax readers on to the page.

2. Use subheads. When you write, outline your piece to make it more coherent. Put the main points of the outline into the copy. Perhaps a better word than subhead is "entry point." Let readers enter the copy where they find something interesting.

3. Have a question-and-answer column. A Q&A format allows readers to save time by skipping over things they already know or are not interested in.

4. Repeat things in different ways for different people. Don't be afraid to say something in a box or a graphic that you have said elsewhere. Reinforcing a message and involving more of the senses aid retention.

"Never be above a gimmick."
—Dave Orman, ARCO

5. Think more visually. Stop using pictures and graphics that do not contain information. Make them useful. When you can, put information in a graphic that speaks to the subject matter it contains. Don't be afraid of gimmicks or of being too obvious. Remember, being effective and efficient is the only thing that matters.

Cliff Edom, founder of photojournalism, taught thousands of students and professionals not just how to take pictures, but to take pictures that tell or show the news. He called it photojournalism.

We used to write articles and then look for graphics or photos to enhance the message. Now, we put the information in the graphic (where it will get more attention and have more impact), and write a story to enhance the graphic. It's called "graphic journalism."

The power of the box

When you can, put some information in a box. Boxes or sidebars, like lists, get more attention, cause better comprehension and aid retention.

1. A reference box. For more information, see, read, call.

2. A note box. Take notes from your articles as if you were studying for an exam. Give them to your readers to complement, reinforce, supplement your message.

3. A glossary box. If you wonder whether all of your readers will understand all of your terms, put those terms in a glossary box. Find a way to indicate which words are defined by putting them in color or in a different typeface or underlining them. Also, teach readers how to pronounce difficult words. They will remember them better.

4. A bio box. When you are writing about a person and need to say something about where the person lived, went to school, and worked, put this information in a separate box so that your main story is not interrupted by these facts. If you have more than one person in the story, bio boxes are even more useful.

In a nutshell

4 goals of the service journalist:

1. **Attention**
2. **Comprehension**
3. **Retention**
4. **Action**

PR Tip

Newspapers, magazines and newsletters such "as pr reporter" are doing more and more service journalism. "News you can use" or "tips & tactics" has become a familiar head. Both newspapers and magazines are becoming more visual. Yet, most news releases sent out by PR professionals look the same as they did five and 50 years ago. Why not try refrigerator journalism techniques in your next news release?

News Narrative

In Chapter 7 you saw examples of inverted pyramid stories that didn't have the news in the first paragraph. But as soon as the writer set the hook, the news lead appeared and the writer arranged the rest of the story in the traditional descending order of importance. Further modification, though, offers writers more choices. For instance, when Jane Meinhardt of the *St. Petersburg Times* wrote about an unusual burglary ring, she started with a non-news lead, went to news and then went back to chronology. Let's see how it works:

Setting the scene: PALM HARBOR — They carried knapsacks and bags to tote loot. They had a screwdriver to pry open doors and windows. They used latex gloves.

They acted like professional criminals, but officials say they were teen-age burglars coached and directed by a Palm Harbor woman whose son and daughter were part of her gang.

Traditional lead: Pinellas County Sheriff's deputies arrested Rovana Sipe, two of her children and two other teens Wednesday after a series of home burglaries.

"She was the driver," said Sheriff's Sgt. Greg Tita. "She pointed out the houses. She's the one who said 'Do these.'"

Support lead: Sipe, 38, of 2333 State Road 584, was charged with two counts of being a principal in burglary. She was held Thursday in lieu of $20,000 bail.

Her daughter, Jackie Shifflet, 16, was charged with grand theft. Her son, Ryan Shifflet, 15, was charged with two counts of burglary.

Charles Ruhe, 17, of 1600 Ensley Ave., in Safety Harbor, and Charles Taylor, 16, of 348 Jeru Blvd. in Tarpon Springs, also were held on four counts of burglary each.

"They were very well-prepared to do burglaries, especially with the guidance they were given," Tita said. "We recovered thousands of dollars of stolen items. Anything that could be carried out, was."

Back to chronology: The burglary ring unraveled Tuesday, Tita said. A Palm Harbor woman saw a large, yellow car driven by a woman drop off three boys, he said. The three went to the back of her house.

They put on gloves and started to pry open a window with a screwdriver, she said. When she tapped on a window, they ran.

She called 911. As she waited for deputies, other neighbors saw the boys walk through a nearby neighborhood carrying bags.

Deputies chased the boys and caught two. The third got into a large yellow car driven by a woman.

The bags contained jewelry, a shotgun and other items deputies say were taken from another house in the neighborhood. Tita said the boys, later identified as Taylor and Ruhe, told detectives about other burglaries in Dunedin and Clearwater and who else was involved.

At Sipe's house, detectives found stolen VCRs, televisions, camcorders and other valuables. They arrested the other two teens and Sipe.

"We're very familiar with this family and its criminal history," Tita said. "We have found stolen property at the house in the past and made juvenile arrests."

This is news, but it is presented as a story rather than as a listing of facts arranged in order of most- to least-important. The traditional lead isn't in the first paragraph of Meinhardt's story, but it's not very far into the story, either. And when the writer returns to the chronology, she uses a transition that signals a story to come: "The burglary ring unraveled Tuesday, Tita said." The transition has echoes of "Let me tell you how it happened." Journalists shouldn't be afraid to experiment with different story forms.

The Focus Structure

For centuries, writers have told stories by focusing on one individual or group that represents a bigger population. This approach allows the writer to make large institutions, complex issues and seven-digit numbers meaningful. Not many of us can understand — let alone explain — the marketing system for wheat, but we could if we followed a bushel of wheat from the time it was planted until a consumer picked up a loaf of bread in the supermarket (see Figure 9.3).

The Wall Street Journal knew that not many of us would be attracted to a story about the interaction between two or more pesticides. That's why one reporter told the story of an individual to tell a story of pesticide poisoning:

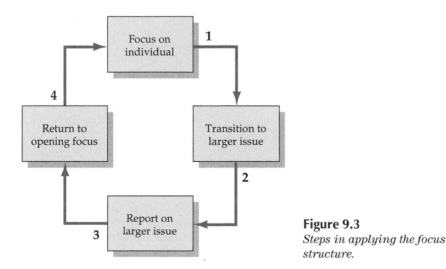

Figure 9.3
Steps in applying the focus structure.

Thomas Latimer used to be a vigorous, athletic man, a successful petroleum engineer with a bright future.

Then he mowed the lawn.

Want to read on?

Even though the Soviet dictator Joseph Stalin was hardly talking about literary approaches, he summed up the impact of focusing on a part of the whole when he said, "Ten million deaths are a statistic; one death is a tragedy." Think about that the next time you hear that a plane crash killed 300 people. You probably are not emotionally touched by the crash unless you know someone who was on the plane. If you were able to write the story of the crash by focusing on a couple of the victims, you would have a better chance of emotionally involving your readers.

Issues such as health care, budget deficits and sexual harassment don't have much emotional appeal. You make them relevant if you discuss the issue by focusing on someone affected by it. For instance, the college student who wrote this story spoke to Karen Elliott, who willingly told her story to help others with the same disease. The key word is "story." You write articles about diseases; you write stories about people:

Karen Elliott, 44, remembers the phone call from Dr. Jonathen Roberts, a general surgeon, as if it had happened yesterday. Dr. Roberts' nurse called one afternoon two years ago and told Karen to hold the line. She froze. She had just had a biopsy on her right breast because of a new lump. It's never good news when the doctor calls at home. Dr. Roberts cut to the chase.

"You have atypical hyperplasia," he said.

Being a nurse, Karen knew exactly what he meant. No number of breast self-exams could have detected this. Atypical hyperplasia is a life-long condition characterized by abnormal cells. Affecting only 4 percent of the female population, it puts Karen and others at an increased risk for breast cancer. With her family history of the disease, her risk of breast cancer jumps sky-high.

What Karen didn't know was that her pleasant life in New Bloomfield would become a roller coaster of ups and downs for the next two years, a ride that nearly destroyed her. Her husband of 19 years, Bob, and their two children, Bethany, 6, and Jordan, 8, could only watch as she struggled with the decision of whether to voluntarily have her breasts removed because Karen, and only Karen, could make that choice.

Reporters working on local stories have just as many opportunities to apply this approach as those writing national and international stories. For example, instead of keeping score on the United Way fund drive, you should focus on the people who will benefit — or fail to benefit — from the campaign. If the streets in your city are bad, write about the problem from the point of view of a driver. If Dutch elm disease is killing the trees in your city, concentrate on a homeowner who has lost several. The focus structure offers the writer a powerful method of reducing institutions, statistics and cosmic issues to a level readers can relate to and understand.

Advertising agencies use the technique, too. That's why instead of being solicited for money to help the poor and starving, you are asked to support one child for only pennies a day. The technique gives poverty and hunger a face. Millions starving is an abstraction; one starving child is a tragedy.

WRITING THE SET-UP

You've completed your reporting. You've found a person through whom you can tell your story. You have all the information about the issue. You know you are going to open with a scene or an anecdote or some other approach that will say to the reader, "I've got an interesting story to tell." Now you must finish the set-up to the story. The **set-up** consists of the transition to the theme paragraph, the theme, or nut, paragraph, foreshadowing, the "so what?" and the to-be-sure. Let's look at each of these.

Add the Transition and Nut Paragraph

When you open with a scene or an anecdote, you must construct a transition that explicitly makes the connection to the theme paragraph, commonly known as the **nut paragraph.** "Explicitly" is the key word. If you fail to help readers understand the point of the opening, however interesting it is, you risk losing them. The transition in this example is in italics:

Anita Poore hit the rough pavement of the parking lot with a thud. She had never felt such intense, stabbing pain and could barely lift her heavy head. When she reached for the car door, a police officer stared at her and asked her husband, "Is she drunk?" A wave of nausea swept over her, and she vomited.

"That's it. Get her out of here!" the officer demanded.

Poore was not drunk. She avoided jail, but she faces a life sentence of pain.

Now 25, she has suffered migraine headaches since she was in seventh grade.

Not that it is much comfort, but she's not alone. Health officials estimate that Americans miss 157 million workdays a year because of migraines and spend more than $2 million a year on over-the-counter painkillers for migraine, tension and cluster headaches. Researchers haven't found a cure, but they have found methods to lessen the pain.

The italicized transition explicitly places Anita Poore among those who miss work, buy painkillers and are still waiting for a cure. What follows is the theme.

Earlier in this chapter, you were introduced to wheat farmer Don Sheber. The sentence in italics is where the writer connected Sheber to the nut paragraph:

In a normal year, Sheber's 600 acres of farmland in Kay County should be thick with nearly waist-high wheat stalks, and by harvest's end, his grain bins should be stuffed with 20,000 bushels of golden grain.

But this is not a normal year. As Sheber finished his harvest early this week, he counted only 6,500 bushels from his shriveled crop, less than one-third his normal yield.

TIPS: The set-up
consists of

• The transition to the theme paragraph.
• The theme paragraph.
• Foreshadowing.
• The "so what?"
• The to-be-sure.

We also introduced you to Karen Elliott, who was diagnosed with atypical hyperplasia. Here again is the nut paragraph, the part of the story that states the theme:

> What Karen didn't know was that her pleasant life in New Bloomfield would become a roller coaster of ups and downs for the next two years, a ride that nearly destroyed her. Her husband of 19 years, Bob, and their two children, Bethany, 6, and Jordan, 8, could only watch as she struggled with the decision of whether to voluntarily have her breasts removed because Karen, and only Karen, could make that choice.

This is where the writer tells readers what the story is about — in this case, her struggle with her decision whether to voluntarily have her breasts removed. There are many other themes the writer could have pursued.

The nut paragraph, says Jacqui Banaszynski, Pulitzer Prize–winning writer, "is like a secret decoder ring — it lets the hapless reader know what your story is about and why they should read it." When you have involved the reader and successfully written the explicit transition to the nut paragraph, you are ready to build the rest of the set-up.

Add Foreshadowing

Foreshadowing can be done in a single line: "The killing started early and ended late." Or foreshadowing can be developed as part of several paragraphs. The goal is to assure readers they will be rewarded if they continue reading.

This is what Erik Larson of *The Wall Street Journal* promised readers of his fire investigation story:

> And so began what may well be the most intensive scientific investigation in the history of arson — not a whodunit, exactly, but a whatdunit. So far the inquiry has taken Seattle investigators places arson squads don't typically go, even to the Navy's weapons-testing grounds at China Lake in California. Along the way, the investigation has attracted a team of scientists who, likewise ensnared by the "Twilight Zone" nature of the mystery, volunteered time and equipment. At one point the investigators themselves torched a large building just to test a suspected fuel.

Add the "So What?"

The "**so what?**" tells readers explicitly why they should care. Thomas Latimer was poisoned when he mowed his lawn. So what? Sheber's harvest yield had dropped by two-thirds. So what? Anita Poore almost got arrested for having a migraine headache. Interesting, but so what?

Reporters and editors know the "so what?" or they wouldn't spend time on the story. Too often, however, they fail to tell it to readers. Latimer's story is in-

"My own bias is probably apparent by now, so I will admit it: If I could put a stake into the heart of the nut graf, I would. And yet I would have to almost immediately reinvent it, for I use it myself."

— James B. Stewart,
Follow the Story

teresting, but it's much more important when you are told why you should care. The brackets enclose the "so what?":

The makers of the pesticide, diazinon, and of Tagamet firmly deny that their products had anything to do with Mr. Latimer's condition. The pesticide maker says he doesn't even believe he was exposed to its product. And in fact, Mr. Latimer lost a lawsuit he filed against the companies. [Even so, the case intrigues scientists and regulators because it illustrates the need for better understanding of the complex interactions between such everyday chemicals as pesticides and prescription drugs.

Neither the Food and Drug Administration nor the Environmental Protection Agency conducts routine tests for such interactions. Indeed, the EPA doesn't even evaluate the synergy of two or more pesticides commonly used together. "We have not developed ways to test any of that," says an EPA spokesman. "We don't know how to do it." And a new congressional report says the FDA lacks both the resources and the enforcement powers to protect Americans from all kinds of poisons.]

The "so what?" is the impact — the relevance — to people who have no warning that two or more pesticides may interact to poison them.

In other cases, the "so what?" may be included in the theme statement. Let's look at the migraine story again:

[1] Not that it is much comfort, but she's not alone. [2] Health officials estimate that Americans miss 157 million workdays a year because of migraines and spend more than $2 million a year on over-the-

counter painkillers for migraine, tension and cluster headaches. [3] Researchers haven't found a cure, but they have found methods to lessen the pain.

The first sentence is the transition; the second is the "so what?"; the third is the theme, which includes foreshadowing. The "so what?" establishes the dimensions of the problem. When you define the "so what?" you are establishing the story's impact.

Add the To-Be-Sure

To maintain an evenhanded approach, writers must acknowledge that there are two or more sides to a story. We call this "to-be-sure," as in to-be-sure there are other opinions. We've seen in the pesticide story that the makers of the drugs and pesticides "firmly deny that their products had anything to do with Mr. Latimer's condition."

We see the technique again in an article about the impact of gambling on Tunica, Miss. Writer Jenny Deam opens with a scene in the mayor's store. The mayor says gambling is the best thing that ever happened to the town. At the front counter, a woman is asking for the $85 back she paid on furniture last week. She lost her grocery money gambling. What comes next is a combination theme and to-be-sure statement, highlighted in italics:

Writers must acknowledge that there are two or more sides to the story. Once the story is defined, the writer is ready to examine all sides of the issue.

And so is the paradox of this tiny Mississippi Delta county, now that the casinos have come to call.

On the one hand, unemployment in a place the Rev. Jesse Jackson once called "America's Ethiopia" has dropped from nearly 24 percent to a low last fall of 5 percent. Anyone who wants a job has one with the casinos. There are more jobs than people to fill them. In a county of about 8,100 people, the number of food stamp recipients fell from 4,218 before the casinos to 2,907 now.

But there is another side. New problems never before seen.

Since the first casino opened in 1992, the number of DUI arrests has skyrocketed by 400 percent. U.S. Highway 61 leading to Memphis is constantly jammed. On a busy weekend as many as 28,000 cars head toward the nine casinos now open. The criminal court system is just as overloaded. In 1992, there were 1,500 cases filed. A year later, 2,400. As of last month there had already been 6,800 cases filed for this year.

"Well," says the mayor, "it's just like anything else in life: You got to take the evil with the good."

Now that the story has been defined, the writer is ready to examine both sides of the issue.

And now that you have constructed the set-up, you are ready to enter the body of the story.

WRITING THE BODY

Think of readers as people antsy to do something else. To maintain their interest, offer them frequent examples to support your main points. In narration, you use anecdotes, scenes and dialogue to move the story line. You mix exposition (the facts) with narration (the story line). A few pages ago, we introduced you to Karen Elliott, who had just received word by telephone that she had atypical hyperplasia. The writer, Tina Smithers, has been dealing in exposition for a few paragraphs, so she shared an anecdote set in the following scene to keep the readers' interest:

Karen was walking downstairs to get the beach ball out of the summer box for Bethany's Hawaiian swim party at Kindercare. Suddenly, Karen fainted and fell down the stairs. She knew she had broken something. Coming to, she blindly made her way upstairs and lay on the bed.

"The cat was staring me in the eyes," she mumbled as Bob, fresh from the shower, grabbed ice and a pillow.

Karen noticed Bethany crying in the doorway. At this point, Karen realized she had been shouting, "Call 9-1-1! Call 9-1-1!" She didn't want her daughter to see her lose control. She quieted down and told Bethany to come to her bed.

"It's okay, honey. Mommy broke her arm, but they'll be over soon to fix it."

In the ambulance, one of the paramedics tried to cut off her yellow Tommy Hilfiger sweater.

"It's brand new," Karen shouted. "Can't you pull it off?"

They gave one small yank, and Karen immediately changed her mind. Every bump along the way was agonizing. Karen pleaded for more morphine. Her wrist, it turned out, was broken in 20 places.

Tips for Writing

Ken Fuson, 44, is a feature writer at *The Des Moines Register*. He has won several national writing awards, including an ASNE Writing Award. He offers his Top Ten hints for improving your writing:

1. *Write stories*. Write real stories — narrative stories that hook readers from the opening scene and transport them to another world. Stories that make people call out to their spouse or roommate and say, "You have got to read this." Remember: You can find these stories in the courthouse, at city hall and on the police blotter.

And they can be done on deadline.

2. *Look for conflict or drama*. Most of the best stories have a conflict and a resolution. Jon Franklin, author of *Writing for Story*, says the more basic the conflict — involving love, hate, death, triumph and travail — the better the story. Pared to its essence, the *Wizard of Oz* consists of two parts. Conflict: Dorothy loses home. Resolution: Dorothy finds home. The plot is what happens in the middle.

3. *Be there*. Put people on the scene. "Make me see," editor Henry Belk told his reporters. "You aren't making me see." Belk was blind. Even spending a half-hour with the subject of a quick-hit profile is better than just conducting a phone interview.

4. *Think scenes*. Use dialogue and descriptions to make readers feel as if they're watching the action unfold as it happens. Move your camera shots — from panning the crowd to close-ups.

5. *Write every sentence*. I'm stealing that advice from Susan Orlean, the wonderful writer for *The New Yorker*. She says we shouldn't distin-

guish between the "writerly" sentences, which we spend all our time on, and the workmanlike sentences that do all the heavy lifting. Think about every sentence. Be the reader's guide through the entire piece, not just the descriptive parts.

6. *Take ownership of a story*. Roy Peter Clark of the Poynter Institute uses music to show that different artists can sing the same song with quite different results. No matter what the assignment — even if it's that hardy perennial, the day-after-Thanksgiving shopping spree story — make it your own.

7. *Search for the universal truth*. The story about a mother who stays by her sick child's bedside isn't about health care; it's a story about devotion. The story of the priest who gives his first sermon isn't about graduating from the seminary; it's a story about faith. The story about the athlete who overcomes childhood arthritis to win an Olympic gold medal isn't about the competition; it's a story about perseverance. Constantly ask yourself: What's this story *really* about?

(continued)

Tips for Writing (continued)

8. *Look for humor opportunities.* This is the most underused tool in our writing kit. Readers love humor almost as much as they love real stories.

9. *Take risks.* I once wrote a one-sentence, one-paragraph weather story that (much to my amazement) has been reprinted several times. It's not just a matter of trying to be clever. It's a matter of doing anything to get read.

10. *Remember Tammy Gaudette.* Tammy is a housewife in Iowa who was invited to appear on a panel of newspaper readers. She was asked what she read. "Oh, I don't like the news," she said. "I like the interesting stories." Always ask yourself: Would I read this?

The outline for the body of your story should look something like this:

  I. Point A
     Support: Anecdote/scene/quotations/documents
 II. Point B
     Support: Anecdote/scene/quotations/documents

And so on. To support each point, you'd like to have anecdotes and scenes, including dialogue, as evidence. Sometimes you also offer good quotations or supporting documents. More complicated stories will have more complicated outlines. If you are telling the story chronologically, you may introduce flashbacks to present events out of sequence.

Think of your story infrastructure as an interstate highway. The highway is your narrative thread. In one story, it might be chronology. In another, it might be movement from one location to another. At times, you need to exit the highway to introduce other examples and ideas. The exits should be smooth — easy off, easy on.

WRITING THE ENDING

Stories should end, not just stop. A good technique called a **tie-back** is one of the significant differences between the inverted pyramid and the focus structure. The content of the inverted pyramid diminishes in importance and interest so that the story can be cut from the end. In contrast, the focus structure has an ending. So if the story has to be shortened, the writer or editor has to delete something other than the ending.

Writing in *USA Today*, Christine Brennan opened with this anecdote:

The late Arthur Ashe was on his second visit to South Africa in 1974 when he noticed a black boy, about 14, who day after day watched his every move around the grounds of the South African Open tennis tournament.

Finally, as Ashe wrote in his memoir, *Days of Grace*, he asked the boy why he was following him.

"Because you are the first one I have ever seen," he answered.

"The first what?" Ashe asked.

"You are the first truly free black man I have ever seen," the boy replied.

After writing about the significance of having the Presidents Cup golf matches in South Africa in 2003, Brennan concludes with this tie-back:

There is an acclaimed book about growing up black in South Africa, *Kaffir Boy*, written by Mark Mathabane. In the book, the author mentions how he started to have dreams for his own future after seeing Arthur Ashe. "How could a black man play such excellent tennis," he wrote, "move about the court with such self-confidence, trash a white man and be cheered by white people?"

In his memoir, Ashe mentioned Mathabane, with good reason. They had met before, during Ashe's historic 1974 visit to South Africa. Mathabane, you see, was the 14-year-old boy who simply couldn't let Arthur Ashe out of his sight.

The conclusion is a direct reference to the opening, which is why it is called a tie-back. Another way to end is with a summary, not of the last point in the story but of the story's theme itself. Here's Erik Larson concluding his arson story:

One thing is certain, Mr. Fowler says: "The arsonist is a professional, not a pyromaniac out to watch things burn. If this guy were crazy we'd have caught him a long time ago," he says. "But this guy is a businessman."

Anecdotes, dialogue, scenes and good quotes all can end the story. Don't just stop; construct an ending.

PUTTING IT TOGETHER

We've seen bits and pieces of narration in the focus structure. Now let's look at how a writer used narration to tell the story of a man who was abandoned in a county home, where he lived most of his life without any contact with his family. What you are about to read is an example of the use of chronology using narrative techniques and flashbacks.

Ken Fuson (**www.asne.org/kiosk/writingawards/1998/98writingawards. htm#fuson**) wrote this story for *The Des Moines Register*:

LENOX, Ia. — For the past 67 years, the only proof that anyone in his family cared about Harvey Quillin was a faded birthday card in his file at a Taylor County care center.

Dear Son:

I'm wishing you a very, very happy day and sending you my love. Will try to come see you, but don't know when we can. I hope you are well.

Love from Dad.

The card arrived in 1951.

Harvey never heard from his father — or his mother, or from any other immediate relative — again.

If this bothered Harvey, if he felt lonely, confused or bitter, he kept those emotions private. Harvey is mentally retarded. It's possible that he simply failed to comprehend the concept of family. The missed birthdays, holidays, Thanksgiving dinners — perhaps he didn't know any better.

Harvey is 77 years old. He can't read and has never held a job. He has been the responsibility of the state, or Taylor County, since he was 10 years old.

All those years, Harvey has just existed, a forgotten branch on the family tree. Finding him would require a wrinkled sheet of notebook paper, a yellowed newspaper obituary and the dogged persistence of a distant cousin who hoped to make her family whole.

What little is known about Harvey Quillin's life is contained, along with the birthday card, in his file at Taylor Ridge Estates, the residential care center in Lenox where he now lives. He was born in September 1923 in Montgomery County to Vascoe and Claudie Quillin. His parents divorced in 1934, when Harvey was 10. That year they admitted their only child to the Glenwood State Hospital-School. He was diagnosed as mildly to moderately mentally retarded.

Had Harvey been born today, he likely would have gone to school, and certainly could have learned enough skills to hold a job. Society and the law are different now. More opportunities exist for the mentally disabled.

In those days, "People thought they were possessed by devils," says Sandy Helm, the assistant administrator of Taylor Ridge Estates. "They didn't want them around. They were scared to death of them."

Parents often were ashamed of their retarded children, she says. They were advised to place the children in state institutions. Several of Taylor Ridge's older residents, like Harvey, never heard from their families again. They were abandoned.

"It's very sad," Helm says.

Nobody knows why Harvey's parents divorced, or where his mother went next. Harvey's father eventually moved to Kansas and married again, to a woman named Alice. It's her handwriting that appears on the birthday card that Harvey received in 1951, his last contact with a family member.

That same year, Harvey was transferred from Glenwood to the Taylor County Home, located in an enormous two-story house between Bedford and Lenox. Most Iowa counties had such a home — called "the poor farm" by locals — that served as the last refuge for the indigent, disabled and unwanted.

This is how a staff worker described Harvey in 1976:

"He is a rather slender man with dark hair and dark brown eyes that are lit with mischief. His face and smile express much energy that is truly delightful. From time to time, he would raise his right hand and that would then twitch."

The writer noticed something else.

"According to the staff at the County Home, Harvey talks in many voices to himself. When interrupted he will stop and acknowledge your presence. I overheard one of his conversations and it was fascinating. His voices had personalities of their own. He sounded as though he really enjoyed the companions that he had created in his mind."

Helm, too, has heard Harvey's imaginary conversations.

"You'd swear to God he was talking to a woman," she says.

She doesn't believe Harvey has a multiple personality disorder. He simply has an uncanny ability to mimic voices.

After the events of the past six months, Helm says she now thinks Harvey's conversations might have served a greater purpose than entertaining himself. "I just wonder if it was a replacement for a family that he didn't have."

In 1951, the same year Harvey moved into the Taylor County Home, a second cousin named Doris Russell left her Missouri home to follow her husband, an airman in the U.S. Air Force, around the country.

Back then, she says, "I didn't give all that much thought to my relatives. I was too busy changing diapers and wiping runny noses on my four children."

Russell's interest in genealogy began in 1990, then blossomed into a full-fledged hobby four years ago when her husband retired and they returned to Missouri. They live in Raymore, a suburb south of Kansas City.

"It's like putting a puzzle together on the table," she says. "You put one piece in, and it looks like a picture, and that makes you want to find the next piece. Then you're up until midnight, trying to put all the pieces in."

Russell, 67, was working on her mother's family tree last year when she discovered a wrinkled piece of notebook paper. On it, her maternal grandmother had listed the names of seven siblings — when they were born, when they died, how many children they had.

The grandmother's siblings included twins — Virgil and Vascoe Quillin. The list indicated Vascoe had a child, but there was no other information. A blank branch on the family tree.

"It just plagued me," Russell says. "I don't know why. That's what happens when you get into genealogy. You become obsessed with it almost. The puzzle isn't done until you've got it."

Who was this mystery child?

She questioned relatives. Several said they thought Vascoe had a son who was mentally disturbed, or got into trouble, or something. They couldn't remember. An older relative thought the son's name was Harvey, but he wasn't certain. A few relatives, including her own mother, advised Russell to quit, as they put it, "looking for the dead."

Russell pressed on. She assumed the mystery child was dead. All she wanted was to fill in the blanks — the date of birth and death — on the family tree.

She knew that Vascoe Quillin, the child's father, had died in 1955 in Chetopa, Kan., a small town on the Kansas-Oklahoma border. During a vacation last spring, Russell convinced her husband to stop there. It was a long shot, but perhaps she could find a record of Vascoe's death at the local funeral home.

Yes, the funeral home owner said, checking his records, here it is.

He referred her to the local historical society. There, Russell found a 45-year-old newspaper obituary for Vascoe that included this line: "He had a son named Harvey in Conway, Ia."

Russell says, "I went crazy, I was so excited."

Conway is so small — population 55 — that Russell had to call the post office in nearby Bedford to find someone who might remember Harvey Quillin. She was given the phone number, but not the name, of a Conway resident. She recalls their conversation:

"Did you ever know a Harvey Quillin?"

"Never heard of him."

"Did you live there in 1955?"

"Yes, I did."

Russell groaned. How could you live in a town that small and not know someone? She asked one final question.

"Was there anyone in town that took care of troubled children, or homeless children?"

"We had a county home out here, but it closed in 1981. They moved everybody to a place in Lenox."

On May 18, Russell dialed the phone number of Taylor Ridge Estates. Her fondest wish was that somebody could tell her the date when Harvey Quillin died.

T. J. Henriksen, the business manager of Taylor Ridge Estates, took the call.

"Well, we've got Harvey right here," she said.

Russell says: "I nearly fainted. I cried. I thought he'd be dead."

Sandy Helm, the assistant administrator, talked to Russell next.

"She was just screaming with excitement," Helm says. "I had goosebumps."

Word swept through the care center.

"You're not going to believe this," Helm told the nurses. "Harvey's got a family!" Everybody had tears in their eyes.

Now it was time to inform Harvey.

He is a tall, chunky man with short, coal-black hair and a face dominated by big black glasses. He will talk to people he trusts, like Helm, but when he gets nervous, Harvey's arms begin to shake and his conversation is reduced to one-word replies, usually, "Yeah."

"He just lets you know that he appreciates the things you do for him," Helm says. "I don't know if he can really express himself, but you can tell what he's thinking by the look on his face.

"When Harvey smiles, everybody in the room smiles."

Harvey likes watching baseball, playing bingo and listening to the school children when they come to sing for the 50 residents.

Only two other residents have spent more time under Taylor County's care. For birthdays, or Christmas, or the annual Family Day picnic, the 35 staff members often bought Harvey a gift. Otherwise he went without. He didn't complain. Perhaps he didn't know any better.

"Everybody enjoys Harvey," Helm says. "He's just a likeable guy."

She wondered how he would react to Russell's phone call. It had been so long since he had a family. Would he understand? Would he care?

"Harvey, I just talked to a woman who says she's a member of your family," Helm told him. "She wants to come see you."

Harvey stared blankly at her. Helm understood.

"I don't think he believed it, either."

A week after the phone call, on May 25, Russell and three relatives from Missouri arrived at the care center to visit Harvey for the first time. They brought chocolate chip cookies and a stack of black-and-white photographs.

Helm led the family into a conference room and watched.

Harvey was polite but cautious. His arms trembled. He said nothing.

Russell began showing photographs.

Harvey still said nothing.

Russell placed another old photograph on the table. It showed three young men, all wearing coats and hats.

"Harvey, do you know any of these people?"

Harvey's arms began to shake. Tears filled his eyes. With a trembling index finger, he slowly pointed to the young man sitting on the far right in the photograph. Then Harvey, who rarely talks to people he doesn't trust, said this:

"That's my dad."

He had pointed to Vascoe Quillin.

Harvey cried. Helm cried. Russell and the other relatives cried. After all those years, Harvey remembered.

"Now what does that say to you?" Russell says. "Forget genealogy. A child never forgets his parents. Sixty-seven years later, Harvey knew who his dad was. Oh, I think there's a sermon in this one."

They wondered: Is it also possible that Harvey knows that he was abandoned by his parents? That he has been holding in that hurt all this time? That he remembers more about his past than he can adequately express or that anyone has previously imagined?

"I believe it," Russell says.

Helm agrees: "It's certainly possible."

Harvey's family went to work. They replaced the stiff institutional chair in his room with a green easy chair. They filled his bare walls with family photos, postcards and greeting cards. They sent candy and gifts. They have visited four times since May, and a pre-Christmas trip is planned.

On Harvey's family tree, these relatives are distant cousins. While previous generations in the family forgot about Harvey, they embrace him. Times change. Attitudes do, too.

"Whenever they walk in, his face lights up," Helm says. "We have seen a change in him since his family found him that's for the good. He's more open. He'll talk more. He smiles more."

In September, for the care center's annual Family Day picnic, Russell and a dozen other relatives headed to Iowa to surprise Harvey with a birthday gift: His first television. He couldn't talk. He just smiled.

"This is more than a fill-in-the-blank on the family tree," Russell says. "I believe we all deserve to be loved. I just believe Harvey deserves to have a family before he dies.

"He's not forgotten. I really think he knows that, too. I may be wrong, but I think he does."

Harvey's fellow residents were thrilled for him. During the picnic, a woman born with Down syndrome cornered Russell. She was excited and out of breath.

"We didn't know Harvey had a family!" she said.

Russell replied, "Well, we didn't know there was a Harvey."

* * *

Before she left the care center, Russell approached Helm for a private meeting.

Russell knew Harvey has prostate troubles and congestive heart failure. He gets along fine now, but he's almost 80.

When Harvey dies, Russell said, there is an empty plot in Missouri where he could be buried among other relatives.

Helm presented another option.

The care center and Taylor County already had made provisions for Harvey. If the family consents, he will be buried among the other longtime residents of the county home. Like Harvey, many had been abandoned and forgotten, symbols of a long-ago time in Iowa history.

These were Harvey's friends, the people with whom he played bingo, watched baseball games and listened to school kids sing Christmas carols for the past 67 years. Russell thought that sounded appropriate.

"They and the staff people were his family for years and years," she says. "They loved him and he loved them."

All those years, everyone thought Harvey Quillin didn't have a family.

Now, it turns out, he has two.

Reread the first seven paragraphs. In the seventh, Fuson defines the story and foreshadows that it will take an unexpected turn. Is there enough foreshadowing? Fuson still agonizes about it. "I still think I might have let people know that this story was going to pack a wallop. The big problem really was the second chunk, telling about Harvey's background. If I were writing it over, I might have started in the present day, using the description of him that I include later, and then backtrack to how he got there." What do you think?

Suggested Readings

Brooks, Terri. *Words' Worth: A Handbook on Writing & Selling Nonfiction.* New York: St. Martin's Press, 1989. Full of detailed advice and examples.

Franklin, Jon. *Writing for Story: Craft Secrets of Dramatic Nonfiction by a Two-Time Pulitzer Prize Winner.* New York: Plume, 1994. If you want to write nonfiction narration, this book is must reading.

Harrington, Walt H. *Intimate Journalism.* Thousand Oaks, Calif.: Sage Publications, 1997. Harrington, a former newspaper writer and now a book author and professor, offers insights into the how and why of telling stories of common people. The book includes several of his stories and those of others with commentary on reporting and writing techniques from each of the authors.

LaRocque, Paula. *The Book on Writing: The Ultimate Guide to Writing Well.* Oak Park, Ill.: Marion Street Press, 2003. A great book for beginners, this book covers three main topics: mechanical and structural guidelines, creative elements of storytelling and grammar, usage and punctuation.

Stewart, James B. *Follow the Story: How to Write Successful Nonfiction.* New York: Touchstone, 1998. Formerly of *The Wall Street Journal*, Stewart won a Pulitzer Prize in 1988 for his reporting on the stock market crash and insider trading. He uses his work to illustrate how to write narration.

Suggested Web Sites

www.aasfe.org/index.html
The American Association of Sunday and Feature Editors posts the winning entries in its annual contest. Several great examples.

www.asne.org
The American Society of Newspaper Editors conducts a prestigious writing contest every year. Winners from six years are posted on this site. These are the best of the best. At the home page, select Archives, then ASNE Awards to go to the winning entries.

www.projo.com/words
The Providence Journal offers an excellent site full of writing and reporting tips from its staff members. Many of their stories are included as examples.

Exercises

1. Write four to eight paragraphs about how you and your classmates learned to be reporters. Pick a scene from one of your classes and re-create it. Provide the transition into the body of the story and then stop.

2. Interview a student in your reporting class. Ask questions that elicit anecdotes. Write an anecdote about the person.

3. Using a chronology, write approximately eight paragraphs of a story about some aspect of your experience in the reporting class.

4. Choose a personal experience that is worth telling in a first-person story. Write two to three pages using chronology in the first person.

5. Find examples in newspapers or magazines of service journalism and analyze them. Find an example of a story that would have benefited from service journalism techniques. Tell what you would have done to make the information more usable.

6. Analyze focus structure stories found on the front page of either *The Wall Street Journal* or *USA Today*. How many elements of the set-up can you identify? Find all the anecdotes. Identify any dialogue.

7. Write the first two pages of an event of your life. Try to include as many parts of the set-up as you can: scenes, dialogue, foreshadowing and the "so what?" statement.

I n 1998 while being interviewed on radio about his job as obituary writer for *The Washington Post*, Richard Pearson was asked whether he had written his own obituary.

"No," he answered. "There are too many people in the news room [who] would want to rush it into print."

The *Post* didn't rush his obituary into print, but when he died in 2003, colleague Claudia Levy opened his obituary this way:

Richard G. Pearson, 54, who crafted graceful obituaries for Cary Grant, George C. Wallace, Roy Rogers, Andy Warhol and thousands of other well-known and virtually unknown people, died of pancreatic cancer Nov. 11 at Virginia Hospital Center–Arlington.

As obituary editor of *The Washington Post*, Pearson chronicled masterfully the lives of movie stars, sports luminaries, senators, prime ministers, mathematicians, generals, sergeants, teachers, bus drivers, beekeepers, barbers, construction workers, cooks and housekeepers. Obit writing, he once observed, "made my life an adventure."

The *Post* has six people who write obituaries about people known and unknown These obituaries are not formulaic pieces. They are life stories.

In the online world, obituaries are big business. Newspaper Web sites sell advertising to funeral homes and auxiliary services because they have found that readers search for obituaries frequently. Even former residents of a city monitor obituaries. Some Web sites are devoted to obituaries and provide resources for readers and advertisers. One, **www.legacy.com**, is a subsidiary of two newspaper groups. It provides links and a searchable database to hundreds of newspapers and, in turn, sells advertising to the funeral industry. It also allows readers to post memorials to friends and family members who have died.

Web editors and entrepreneurs are just discovering the drawing power of obituaries, but most newspaper editors have known about obituaries for years. Chuck Ward, publisher of the *Times Herald* in Olean, N.Y., once told his readers about the time his editor asked whether they should do a special obituary on the father of one of their employees.

"My response was that unless the father (or any relative) of the employee met the criteria for a glorified obituary, the obituary should be treated as 99 percent of our obituaries are. . . ."

In this chapter you will learn:

1. How to write an obituary and what information you will need.

2. Where to get interesting material.

3. What policies newspapers may follow in printing controversial information.

He then recounted that when he went to the visitation that evening, the line extended 50 yards outside the mortuary. He returned in an hour, and the line was still long. That got Ward thinking about his question earlier in the day: "What did he do?"

"All he did, apparently, was live a wonderful, loving life with a splendid family. During the course of that life, he must have touched the lives of countless people in our community. And they all were there to say goodbye."

Ward learned that people don't have to be public figures to deserve well-reported obituaries. Too many obituaries read as if they were written by a computer program — efficient but lifeless. This persists despite readership surveys that show that about 50 percent of readers look at obituaries, about twice as many as those that look at most other features.

And obituaries are read critically. If the deceased was an Odd Fellow, you'd better not say he was an Elk. If the deceased belonged to the Shiloh Baptist Church, count on a phone call if you say she was a member of Bethany Baptist. Reporting and writing obituaries is important work.

Despite this importance, many newspapers do not publish a news obituary unless the person who dies is well-known. At many papers the advertising department handles obituaries as paid notices. Many metropolitan papers have adopted this policy because to publish obits on everyone who died in the area would require a substantial amount of space. *The Kansas City Star* published 14,600 obituaries in a year before it began charging. At papers where obits are handled as advertising, the families often write some creative and entertaining obituaries. For instance, one wrote in a Utah paper, "He had his own ideas and some worked." Another wrote, "He devoted his retirement years to amassing a fortune of four dollars and thirteen cents."

Some large papers, such as *The New York Times*, the *Philadelphia Daily News*, *The Cincinnati Enquirer*, *The Detroit News* and *The Des Moines Register*, and some small papers, such as the Guntersville, Ala., *Advertiser-Gleam* and the *Columbia Missourian*, take obituaries seriously. Ron Liebau, metro editor of the *Enquirer*, told the *Gannetteer*, "For reporters who shrug them off, I tell them they probably don't have anything more important to do."

Jim Nicholson of the New York *Daily News*, who writes obituaries full-time, won the American Society of Newspaper Editors Distinguished Writing Award. Readers want to know, he said, "How did someone live a good life? How did they get through this world?"

Even if you work at a paper where most obituaries are paid notices or are published as death notices that are written from forms filled out by the family, when a prominent person dies, the news department will want a story. Knowing how to report and write an obit is important because you may make your first impression on an editor by the way you handle the assignment. The editor will examine your work critically. Is the information correct? Is it complete? Did you check additional sources? Did you follow newspaper style? Did you follow newspaper policy? This chapter examines such questions.

BASIC OBITUARY INFORMATION AND STYLE

An obituary is a news story. You should apply the same standards to crafting a lead and building the body of an obituary as you do to other stories.

Crafting a Lead

You begin by answering the same questions you would answer in any news story: who (Michael Kelly, 57, of 1234 West St.), what (died), where (at Regional Hospital), when (Tuesday night), why (heart attack) and how (while jogging). With this information, you are ready to start the story.

The fact that Kelly died of a heart attack suffered while jogging may well be the lead, but the reporter does not know this until the rest of the information essential to every obituary is gathered. You also must know:

- Time and place of funeral services.
- Time and burial place.
- Visitation time (if any).
- Survivors.
- Date and place of birth.
- Achievements.
- Occupation.
- Memberships.

Any of those items can yield the nugget that will appear in the lead. However, if none of these categories yields notable information, the obituary probably will start like this:

```
Michael Kelly, 57, of 1234 West St., died Tuesday night at
Regional Hospital.
```

Another standard approach could be used later in the news cycle:

```
Funeral services for Michael Kelly, 57, of 1234 West St., will
be at 2 p.m. Thursday at St. Catherine's Roman Catholic
Church.
```

However, good reporters often find distinguishing characteristics of a person's life. It may be volunteer service, an unusual or important job, service in public office or even just having a name of historical significance. Whatever distinguishes a person can be the lead of the obituary. These leads demonstrate the techniques:

Michael Francis Comerford, 70, who as night metropolitan editor of *The Inquirer* orchestrated the coverage of breaking deadline stories from Abscam to the murder of mob boss Angelo Bruno, died Tuesday at Hospice of Port Orange in

---

TIPS: Five safeguards for obit writers

- Confirm spellings of names.
- Check the addresses. If a telephone book or city directory lists a different address, contact the mortuary about the discrepancy.
- Check the birth date against the age, noting whether the person's birthday was before or after the date of death.
- Verify with the mortuary or family any obituary phoned or faxed to the newspaper.
- Check your newspaper's library for stories about the deceased, but be sure you don't pull stories about someone else with the same name.

Daytona Beach Shores, Fla. Mr. Comerford suffered from heart disease. He retired in 1995 after more than 27 years at *The Inquirer.*

* * *

Jeanne Calment of France, the world's oldest person, died Tuesday at age 122.

* * *

Linda Kay Berry didn't flinch when tarantulas, black widow spiders and 3-inch-long cockroaches crawled up her arm.

The slithering sensation of a snake across her neck sent her into smiles. Even a puncture wound from a king snake didn't stop her from loving all things creepy and crawly.

Berry, an animal keeper at the Museum of Discovery in Little Rock, died Tuesday of breast cancer. She was 53 and lived in Little Rock.

Writing approaches can be as varied for obituaries as for any other news story. The following story emphasizes the personal reactions of those who knew the deceased:

"I don't write about death, I write about life."

— Michael Best,
The Detroit News

Few persons knew her name, but nearly everyone knew her face.

For 43 years, Mary Jones, the city's cheerful cashier, made paying your utility bills a little easier.

Tuesday morning after she failed to report to work, two fellow employees found her dead in her home at 432 East St., where she apparently suffered a heart attack. She was 66.

By Tuesday afternoon, employees had

placed a simple sign on the counter where Miss Jones had worked.

"We regret to inform you that your favorite cashier, Mary Jones, died this morning. We all miss her."

"She had a smile and a quip for everybody who came in here," said June Foster, a bookkeeper in the office.

"She even made people who were mad about their bills go away laughing."

Building the Story Body

Most of the obituary information is provided by the mortuary on a standard form. When the obituary is written straight from the form, this is usually what results:

Michael Kelly, 57, of 1234 West St., died Tuesday night at Regional Hospital.

Kelly collapsed while jogging and died apparently of a heart attack.

Services will be at 2 p.m. Thursday at St. Catherine's Roman Catholic Church. The Rev. Sherman Mitchell will officiate. Burial will be at Glendale Memorial Gardens in Springfield.

Friends may visit at the Fenton Funeral Chapel from 7 to 9 p.m. Wednesday.

Born Dec. 20, 1947, in Boston to Nathan and Sarah Kelly, Kelly was a mem-

ber of St. Catherine's Roman Catholic Church and a U.S. Navy veteran of the Vietnam War. He had been an independent insurance agent for the last 25 years.

He married Pauline Virginia Hatfield in Boston on May 5, 1967.

Survivors include his wife; a son, Kevin, of Charlotte, N.C.; and a daughter, Mary, who is a student at the University of North Carolina at Chapel Hill.

Also surviving are a brother, John of Milwaukee, Wis., and a sister, Margaret Carter, of Asheville, N.C.

The Kelly obituary is a dry biography, not a story of his life. There is no hint of Kelly's impact on friends, family or community. Good reporting produces stories of life, such as this one:

Jyles Robert Whittler, a World War I veteran and son of a former slave, died Monday at Truman Veterans Hospital. He was 100.

Mr. Whittler helped build the Missouri United Methodist Church in Springfield and served as its janitor for 55 years.

In 1986, the church's basement social hall was christened the Jyles Whittler Fellowship Hall in his honor.

"He's a legend in Springfield and rightfully so," said his friend Roy Smith. "He labored hard and lived well. He's in heaven."

The more traditional biographical information, along with information about visitation and funeral services, appears later in the story.

Here is another example built on good reporting:

Ila Watson Portwood died Sunday at the Candlelight Care Center of complications stemming from a stroke she suffered about two weeks earlier. She was 89.

She was born on Aug. 30, 1914, in Boone County. She graduated from Howard Payne School in Howard County and attended the University of Michigan.

She was the former owner and operator of the Gem Drug Company. She and her late husband, Carl, started as employees in 1935 and bought the business in 1962. They retired in 1981 and sold the company to Harold Earnest.

"She was a total lady," Earnest said. "I've never seen her mistreat anyone. Just the sweetest lady anyone can meet."

Mrs. Portwood volunteered from 1980 to 1986 at the Cancer Research Center's Women's Cancer Control Program and was named volunteer of the year in 1983.

"She was a people person," said Rosetta Miller, program coordinator. "Her caring personalized her commitment to the staff and patients. . . ."

Whittler and Portwood were ordinary people whose lives affected others. An obituary should celebrate that life rather than merely note the death.

Because much of the information in any obituary comes directly from the family, it is generally accurate. But you should still check the spelling of all names, addresses and the deceased's age against the birth date. You should also never print an obituary based on information offered over the phone by someone purporting to be a funeral home representative. Too many newspapers have been the victims of hoaxes. Always call the funeral home yourself to confirm the death.

Choosing Your Words

Avoid much of the language found on mortuary forms and in obituaries prepared by morticians. The phrasing often is more fitting for a eulogy than for a newspaper story.

Because of the sensitivity of the subject matter, euphemisms have crept into the vocabulary of obituary writers. "Loved ones," "passed away," "our dearly beloved brother and father," "the departed" and "remains" may be fine for eulogies, but such terms are out of place in a news story.

Watch your language, too, when you report the cause and circumstances of a death. Unless the doctor is at fault, a person usually dies not "as a result of an operation," but "following" or "after" one. Also, a person dies "unexpectedly" but not "suddenly." All deaths are sudden. Note, too, that a person dies "apparently of a heart attack" but not of "an apparent heart attack." And a person dies of injuries "suffered," not "received."

Be careful with religious terms. Catholics "celebrate" Mass; Reform Jews usually worship in "temples," whereas Orthodox and Conservative Jews do so in "synagogues." An Episcopal priest who heads a parish is a "rector," not a "pastor." Followers of Islam are called "Muslims."

Consult your wire service stylebook when you have a question.

The stylebook prescribes usage in another instance, too. A man is survived by his wife, not his widow, and a woman is survived by her husband, not her widower. In fact, you will need to consult your local stylebook often when you are writing an obit. Do you use titles such as Mr. and Mrs.? Do you mention divorced spouses, deceased spouses or live-in companions? Do you identify pallbearers? Do you say when memorial contributions are requested?

Once you have checked the spelling and corrected the language, it is time to begin gathering additional information.

TIPS: Choosing your words

- Avoid euphemisms; such terms are out of place in a news story.
- Watch your language as you report the cause and circumstances of a death.
- Be careful with religious terms.

SOURCES OF INFORMATION

TIPS: Sources for obits

- Mortuary forms.
- The newspaper.
- The newspaper's library.
- Interviews with family and friends of the deceased.

Like any news story, an obituary is more complete when the information comes from several sources. Common sources for obits include mortuary forms, death notices and news stories in the newspaper, the newspaper's library and interviews with family and friends of the deceased.

Mortuary Forms

For many newspapers the standard form from the mortuary is the primary source of information (see Figure 10.1). The mortuary can be of further help if you need more information. Does your city editor want a picture of the deceased? Call the mortuary. They usually can obtain one quickly from the family. Is there some conflicting or unclear information on the form? Call the mortuary.

Writing obituaries from the mortuary's information alone is a clerk's work. As a reporter you should go beyond the form. You should also confirm every fact on the sheet. Mortuary forms are notoriously inaccurate.

Sometimes, what the mortuary form doesn't tell you is as important as what it does say. For the writer of the following obit, the first clue that the death notice

NAME OF FUNERAL HOME: _____

PHONE: _____

PERSON TO CONTACT: _____

NAME OF DECEASED: _____

ADDRESS: _____

_____

OCCUPATION: _____

_____

AGE: _____

CAUSE OF DEATH: _____

_____

DATE AND PLACE OF DEATH: _____

_____

TIME AND PLACE OF FUNERAL SERVICES: _____

_____

CONDUCTED BY: _____

BURIAL: _____

TIME AND PLACE FOR VISITATION: _____

_____

BIOGRAPHICAL INFORMATION: _____

_____

_____

_____

_____

SURVIVORS: _____

_____

_____

_____

_____

_____

_____

Figure 10.1

A mortuary form provides basic information. However, it's not always accurate or complete, so check it against other sources.

was unusual was the age. The deceased was 12. That alone was enough for the reporter to start asking questions. The result was an obituary that moved from the records column to the front page:

Sandra Ann Hill, 12, lost her lifetime struggle against a mysterious muscle ailment Wednesday night. The day she died was the first day she had ever been admitted as a hospital inpatient.

Although they knew it was coming, the end came suddenly for Sandra's family and school friends, said her father, Lester, of 1912 Jackson St.

Just last Friday, she attended special classes at the Parkdale School. "She loved it there," Hill said. "Like at recess, when the sixth graders would come in and read to her. She always wanted to be the center of attention."

"Bright as a silver dollar" was the way one of Sandra's early teachers described her. In fact, no one will ever know. Sandra couldn't talk.

"We didn't know what she knew or didn't know," her father said. Sandra's only communication with the world around her came in the form of smiles and frowns — her symbols for yes and no.

"There were times when I'd come around the corner and kind of stick my head around and say 'boo,'" her father recalled. "She smiled. She liked that."

The care and attention Sandra demanded makes the loss particularly hard for her family to accept, Hill said. "I can't really put it into words. You cope with it the best you can, keep her com-

fortable and happy. We always took her with us."

Sandra came down with bronchitis Friday. Complications forced her to be admitted Wednesday to Lincoln County Hospital, where she died later that night.

Sandra's fight for life was uphill all the way. It started simply enough when she was four months old. Her mother, Bonnie, noticed she "wasn't holding up her head" like her other children.

Although her ailment was never firmly diagnosed, doctors found Sandra's muscles held only half the tissues and fibers in a normal child's body. The diagnosis: a type of cerebral palsy. The prognosis: Sandra had little chance to live past the age of 2. Medical knowledge offered little help.

Sandra was born in Springfield on Jan. 15, 1984. She is survived by her parents; one brother, Michael Eugene Hill; one sister, Terrie Lynn Hill, both of the home; and her grandparents, Gordon Hill of Seale, Ala., and Mrs. Carrie Harris of Phoenix, Ariz.

Services will be at 3:30 p.m. today at the Memorial Funeral Chapel with the Rev. Jack Gleason conducting. Burial will follow at the Memorial Park Cemetery.

The family will receive friends at the Memorial Funeral Home until time for the service.

The reporter who wrote this obituary obviously did a great deal of research beyond what was on the mortuary form. Because the girl was not a public figure, the reporter could not consult a reference work such as *Who's Who in America* or a national publication. But the reporter did have access to the newspaper library and could interview the girl's family and friends. These are the sources that can help make interesting copy.

One way to irritate the source and fail to get interesting copy is to ask people who are grieving, "How do you feel?" It's a question asked often by reporters at the scene of a disaster when people are waiting to hear about their relatives or friends. As one editor commented, "How the hell should they feel? Newspapers are not in the business of measuring the degree of grief. . . ."

The Newspaper

Another good source is the paid funeral notices in the newspaper. A reporter in Columbus, Ind., spotted an interesting story when he realized that an obituary notice from a funeral home was for the city's "broom man." The resulting story, which appeared on Page One, began this way:

You probably knew him.

Notice of his death Christmas Day almost seemed to fade among the others published Thursday. Ernest W. Ferrenburg, 75, of 1210 California died at 2:50 p.m. Wednesday at Bartholomew County Hospital, the notice said.

"Nobody knew him by his name. He was just the old broom salesman," said one of his six daughters, Irene Michaelis of Greenwood.

Workers and shoppers probably can recall seeing Ferrenburg standing on a street corner downtown on Washington Street, holding a generous stock of brooms of various shapes and sizes. The thin white cane he carried told passersby he had lost his sight. That happened in a gun accident when he was 19.

The story ends this way:

Ferrenburg never considered himself handicapped.

"I can hear birds sing. I can hear little children," Mrs. Michaelis said her father replied when asked whether he would rather see than hear. "I'd rather be blind anytime than deaf."

Hartford Courant reporter Leonard Bernstein wrote about another remarkable life after the obituary notice had already been published. It began this way:

For as long as anyone can remember, David Lowery had two dreams: to buy his own home and raise his own children.

For 23 years, he worked — often two jobs at a time — and finally, on Sept. 1, 1983, he bought a house in Hartford.

Within nine months, the second dream was fulfilled: On June 11, Lowery became a single father, bringing home two brothers from Massachusetts who had been seeking a family for two years.

And then it ended.

On July 8, a cool Sunday evening, Lowery was driving his new family home from church in Middletown when he pulled to the side of I-91 and told the boys he was sick. The 10-year-old flagged down a passing car; the 13-year-old climbed in to go for help.

Seven hours later, David Lowery, 44, was dead of a cerebral hemorrhage.

His death did not make the headlines. No famous people spoke at the funeral.

But David Lowery — a Big Brother for 14 years in Hartford, a member of Shiloh Baptist Church in Middletown where he sang and formed a youth choir, a regular visitor to people whom others had forgotten — was loved by many, and they still mourn.

Each of the last two stories could have been run as a combination obituary and death story if someone had pursued the obituary information when it came to the city room.

The Newspaper Library

In the newspaper library, you may find an interview with the deceased, an interesting feature story or clips indicating activities not included on the mortuary form. In an interview or feature story the person may have made a statement about a philosophy of life that would be appropriate to include in the obituary. The subject also may have indicated his or her goals in life, against which later accomplishments can be measured. You can find the names of friends and co-workers in the clips as well. These persons are often the source of rich anecdotes and comments about the deceased.

The New York Times recognized an interesting person when staff members checked the files of Thelma Koch. Writer Douglas Martin shared Koch's life story with readers:

Selma Koch, a Manhattan store owner who earned a national reputation by helping women find the right bra size, mostly through a discerning glance and never with a tape measure, died Thursday at Mount Sinai Medical Center. She was 95 and a 34B.

In the final years of her life, Mrs. Koch appeared on national television and radio programs to discuss her specialty and her occupational longevity. She relished her celebrity, but not as much as she loved guiding the generations of women who visited her store: She worked seven 10-hour days last week instead of her usual six.

Her grandson Danny said he guessed that her only regret would be not dying in the family's store, the Town Shop on Broadway at 82nd Street, something she had often said she hoped to do.

Meyer concluded the life story with this quote:

Mrs. Koch never stopped wondering why people kept asking her questions. "What's the big deal?" the small woman asked in her raspy, staccato voice. "I'm just selling bras."

Bringing Life to Obituaries

Tracy Breton is an investigative reporter for *The Providence Journal.* She specializes in writing about legal issues and the courts, and in 1994 she shared a Pulitzer Prize for investigative reporting. Breton once was called upon to write the obituary of a Superior Court judge she knew. She did such a good job that at the wake, two other judges asked if she would write their obituaries. Here is her advice:

"I like writing obits — at least obits of people I know well — because obituaries are really profiles, and in profiles, you try to capture the essence of the person. And you can bet that out of everything you write in your journalistic career, your obituaries are the stories that are most likely to be passed along for generations — yellowed and encased in plastic — by the people who have been touched by them.

"In obituaries, you are bringing the person you're writing about to life for the last time, so it's important to use all the skills you have developed as a feature writer. The use of telling detail is important. So are anecdotes and scenes that show your subject in action. If there's a quote from them that you can cull from your newspaper's archives — something they said that would provide a window into their personality — use quotes from the deceased.

"I advocate having beat reporters write obits of the people they cover. But sometimes you will be assigned to write an obit of someone you have never met, so it's important to find others who have known your subject well.

"You need to show compassion. I find that a good way to get detail is to go to the home of the deceased and try to get information from family members. Bring some Kleenex because if you are gentle and show genuine concern, you will get those who know your subject best to give you the material you need. Be sympathetic; ask how they would like their loved one to be remembered and then just sit back and listen.

"Too many obits that appear in newspapers are formulaic; the reader gets no sense of who the deceased was and what made him or her a unique personality."

Your newspaper's files are not the only source for information on people who have state or national reputations. You or your librarian should also search electronic databases for stories that have appeared in other publications.

Interviewing Family and Friends

Papers treat public figures in more detail not only because they are newsworthy but also because reporters know more about them. Even though private citizens usually are less newsworthy, many good stories about them are never written because the reporter did not — or was afraid to — do the reporting. The fear is usually unfounded. William Buchanan, who has written many obituaries for *The Boston Globe*, said his calls are almost always welcomed: "The person I called appreciated that someone cared enough to want to know more about a loved one."

That's true even in the worst of circumstances, such as a suicide. Karen Ball, a former reporter for the *Columbia Missourian*, learned that lesson when she was assigned to do a story on Robert Somers, a university professor who had committed suicide. Ball didn't look forward to calling Mrs. Somers. First, Ball talked to students, Somers' colleagues and university staff members. She even obtained a copy of his résumé.

"By knowing a lot about him — where he'd studied, what his interests were and where he worked — I knew that I could go into an interview with a bereaved relative and at least have something to talk about," she says.

Ball approached Mrs. Somers in person and explained that her husband was respected and liked. Mrs. Somers agreed to talk. To get her to elaborate on his personality and what he was like away from school, Ball prodded her with ques-

---

Allen Green, Fort Wayne—1923–2000

Allen Green, 77, of Fort Wayne, a member of First Baptist Church, died Saturday, Nov. 11, 2000, at home.

The Indian Mound, Tenn., native was a World War II Army veteran. He had worked for 31 years at Hobby Ranch House as a custodian and also at Trinity Lutheran School for 15 years.

Surviving are his daughters, Frances Green of Oklahoma and Wanda Fay Higgins of Kalamazoo, Mich.; sons Johnny of Ohio and Charles of Tennessee; stepsons George Dahl, Joseph Dahl of Castle Hayne, N.C., and Willard Dahl of Fort Wayne; stepdaughters Aira of Maryland, Audrey Sanders of Hanover, Pa., Sandra Yancey and Margaret McClellen, both of Fort Wayne; sisters Bessie L. Jackson of Pennville and Gladys Keats of Indian Mound, Tenn.; brothers Monroe L. of Zanesville, James A. of Fort Wayne and Horace L. of Hunting; 29 grandchildren; and 19 great-grandchildren.

He was preceded in death by his first wife, Nellie; his second wife, Emma; sisters Gerline Cherry and Della Jones; and a brother, Lester.

Services are 1 p.m. Wednesday at D.O. McComb & Sons Lakeside Park Funeral Home, 1140 Lake Ave., with calling from 2 to 5 and 7 to 9 p.m. Tuesday. Burial will be at Lindenwood Cemetery.

Memorials are to the family.

Figure 10.2
Beginning in 1998, The News-Sentinel *in Fort Wayne, Ind., doubled the space devoted to obituaries, added information and improved the presentation. Executive Editor Joe Weiler said his goal is "to give all people the dignity and respect they deserve, to make sure that all the vital information is included, and that bureaucratic rule making doesn't stand in the way of doing the right thing."*

tions about their children, where they had lived before and other family matters. She also talked to Somers' mother. Ball told her some of the positive things that students and faculty had said about her son. That helped the mother deal with her sorrow and helped Ball write her story. The story of Somers' life began:

Miko Somers sat at her kitchen table folding and unfolding her youngest daughter's bib as she talked about her husband.

"He could never do anything halfway," Mrs. Somers says. "He set such a high standard for himself. Whatever he did had to be the very best, and he pushed himself to make it that way."

Today Mrs. Somers buries her husband. Monday, Robert Somers, 40, her husband for 17 years, the father of their four daughters and an associate professor in the University's history department, took his life by driving his car head-on into a tree.

Karen Ball didn't know the Somers family, but she still got the story. Even when you know someone, good reporting can improve the story. Tracy Breton of *The Providence Journal* learned early one morning that a judge whom she had covered on and off for 26 years had died. Visiting the judge's home at the invitation of his wife, Tracy learned a good deal more about the man she thought she already knew.

"I was surprised at how modestly he lived," she said, "and learned some things about the judge that I didn't know — like where he played golf with his wife (the judge's golf clubs were stored in the living room, up against a wall behind the TV), the fact that he had attended a computer class that day before watching the NCAA basketball tournament on TV, and that the judge had been stressed over the trial he was presiding over. . . ."

At the judge's wake, two Superior Court judges asked Breton if she would write their obituaries when the time came.

NEWSPAPER POLICY

Newspaper policy often dictates what will — and will not — be included in an obituary. Those newspapers that do have written policies may prescribe how to handle everything from addresses to suicides.

Some newspapers, for instance, prohibit a statement such as "In lieu of flowers, the family requests donations be made to the county humane society." This prohibition is in response to lobbying from florists.

Because of threats to the safety of property and the individuals involved, in some cities even information essential to the obituary no longer appears in the paper. Some newspapers specifically tell reporters not to include the address of the deceased. Criminals have used information taken from the obituary columns to prey on survivors. Knowing the time of the funeral and the address of the deceased makes it easy to plan a break-in at the empty residence during the services. Therefore, this information may be withheld.

TIPS: Policy options

- Run an obituary that ignores any embarrassing information and, if necessary, leave out the cause of death. If circumstances surrounding the death warrant a news story, run it separate from the obituary.
- Insist on including embarrassing details and the cause of death in the obituary.
- Insist on including embarrassing details and the cause of death in the obituary only for a public figure.
- Put a limit on how far back in the person's life to use derogatory information such as a conviction.
- Print everything newsworthy that is learned about public figures but not about private figures.
- Print everything thought newsworthy about public and private figures.
- Decide each case as it comes up.

Two other kinds of information on which newspapers may have restrictive policies are the cause of death and potentially embarrassing information.

Cause of Death

If the person who dies is not a public figure and the family does not wish to divulge the cause of death, some newspapers will comply. That is questionable news judgment. The reader wants to know what caused the death. A reporter should call the mortuary, the family, the attending physician and the appropriate medical officer. Only if none of these sources will talk should the newspaper leave out the cause of death. Many newspapers require that obituaries include the cause of death in the version that the newspaper writes.

A death certificate must be filed for each death, but obtaining it often takes days, and some states do not make the cause of death public record. Even if the state lists the cause of death and the reporter has timely access to the death certificate, the information is often vague.

If the death is caused by cancer or a heart attack or is the result of an accident, most families do not object to including the cause in the obituary. But if the cause is cirrhosis of the liver brought on by heavy drinking, many families do object, and many papers do not insist on printing the cause.

If the deceased was a public figure or a young person, most newspapers insist on the cause of death.

If the death is the result of suicide or foul play, reporters can obtain the information from the police or the medical examiner. Some newspapers include suicide as the cause of death in the obituary, others print it in a separate news story, and still others ignore it altogether. This is one way to report it:

> "We write about how people lived, not how they died."
>
> — Kay Powell,
> *Atlanta Journal-Constitution*

Services for Gary O'Neal, 34, a local carpenters' union officer, will be at 9 a.m. Thursday in the First Baptist Church. Coroner Mike Pardee ruled that Mr. O'Neal died Tuesday of a self-inflicted gunshot wound.

Embarrassing Information

Another newspaper policy affecting obituaries concerns embarrassing information. When the *St. Louis Post-Dispatch* reported in an obituary that the deceased had been disbarred and that he had been a key witness in a bribe scandal involving a well-known politician 13 years earlier, several callers complained. The Reader's Advocate defended the decision to include that history in the obituary:

One who called to complain about the obit told me it reminded her of the quotation from Shakespeare's *Julius Caesar*, about how the good a man does is often buried with him and forgotten.

Yes, I said, and the first part of that quotation could be paraphrased to say that the news a man makes often lives after him.

When author W. Somerset Maugham died, *The New York Times* reported that he was a homosexual, even though the subject generally had not been discussed in public before. When Bill Mauldin, a Pulitzer Prize–winning editorial cartoonist, died in 2003, the *Chicago Sun-Times*, where he had worked for years, wrote, "In his last years, Mr. Mauldin battled alcoholism and Alzheimer's." Acquired immune deficiency syndrome (AIDS) is the latest cause of death to trouble editors. The death of actor Rock Hudson brought AIDS to the attention of many who had never heard of the disease before. Many newspapers agonized over whether to say that Hudson had AIDS. As other public figures died of AIDS, it became almost routine to report the cause of death. Because AIDS still carries a stigma, some spokespeople go out of their way to make sure people don't suspect the cause of death was AIDS.

The more AIDS or any other disease is reported as a cause of death, the more accepted it will become. Cancer once had a similar stigma. In Boise, Idaho, the newspaper reported that several people requested before they died that AIDS be listed as the cause. They did this to make others more aware of the disease. One professor who has studied AIDS coverage suggests that obituary writers ought not to soften the language or use euphemisms when reporting AIDS-related deaths; should refer to AIDS "patients" rather than "victims"; and should try to reach the family for information and confirmation.

The crucial factor in determining the extent to which you should report details of an individual's private life is whether the deceased was a public or private person. A **public figure** is someone who has been in the public eye. A participant in civic or social activities, a person who spoke out at public meetings or through the mass media, a performer, an author, a speaker — these all may be public figures. A **public official,** an individual who has been elected or appointed to public office, is generally treated like a public figure.

Whether the subject is a public figure or private citizen, the decisions newspapers must make when dealing with the obituary are sensitive and complicated. It is your obligation to be aware of the newspaper's policy. In the absence of a clear policy statement, you should consult the city editor.

> "People are a lot more open than they were, but I think that they're still not open enough when it comes to AIDS. It's been my experience that nobody will admit it unless they are in the arts. If somebody in business dies of AIDS, we may never know about it."
>
> — Irvin Horowitz,
> obituary writer,
> *The New York Times*

Suggested Readings

Casella, Peter A. "Media Mistakes Can Be Devastating." *The Bulletin*, ASNE, Sept.-Oct. 1986, p. 40. Casella, a journalist, tells about the time the broadcast media mistakenly reported that his wife had been killed in a helicopter crash.

Hart, Jack and Johnson, Janis. "A Clash between the Public's Right to Know and a Family's Need for Privacy." *The Quill*, May 1979, pp. 19–24. An account of the backlash against a newspaper that printed a syndicated story of how the daughter of a locally prominent family had died a big-city prostitute.

Hipple, John and Wells, Richard. "Media Can Reduce Risks in Suicide Stories." *Editor & Publisher*, Oct. 14, 1989, p. 72. A counselor who specializes in treating suicidal young people and a journalist combine to offer suggestions on handling stories involving suicide.

Randolph, Eleanor. "AIDS and Obituaries," *Chicago Tribune*, Sept. 24, 1989. A roundup of how various newspapers handle AIDS as a cause of death.

Robins, Wayne. "Obituaries a Staple Offline — and On." *Editor & Publisher*, July 24, 2000, p. 27. A roundup of obituaries on the Web.

Siegel, Marvin, ed., *The Last Word: The New York Times Book of Obituaries and Farewells: A Celebration of Unusual Lives*. New York: Quill, 1998. Examples of well-written and compelling obituaries from *The New York Times*.

Suggested Web Sites

www.bismarcktribune.com
Most newspapers post obituaries on their Web sites, but *The Bismarck* (N.D.) *Tribune*'s site has a searchable database of more than 9,000 obituaries. Look under "archives."

www.legacy.com
Two newspaper companies created a portal Web site to sell advertisements to the funeral industry and auxiliary services and to provide access to obituaries in hundreds of newspapers.

www.obitpage.com
This site is by and for obituary writers and readers. It includes interesting obituaries, interviews, news about conferences for obituary writers and readers and other interesting information.

www.projo.com/words/index.htm
The Providence Journal's Web site for writers includes an index of stories by staff members describing how they reported and wrote stories. Select "Index of Past Writing Tips," then "profiles." Scroll down to Tracy Breton's article, "Capturing the Essence," May 4, 2000.

Exercises

1. Which elements are missing from the following obituary information?

   a. John Peterson died Saturday at Springfield Hospital. Funeral services will be at 1:30 p.m. Tuesday. Friends may call at the Restwell Funeral Home, 2560 Walnut St., from 6 to 9 p.m. Monday. The Rev. William Thomas will officiate at services in the First Baptist Church. Burial will be at City Cemetery.

   b. Richard G. Tindall, Springfield, a retired U.S. Army brigadier general, died at his daughter's home in Summit, N.J. Graveside services will be at 2 p.m. July 3 at Arlington National Cemetery in Arlington, Va.

2. Write a lead for an obituary from the following information:

   Martha Sattiewhite, born July 2, 1974, to Don and Mattie Sattiewhite, in Springfield. Martha was killed in a car accident June 30, 1995. Funeral services will be July 2. She was president of her Springfield High School senior class and of the sophomore class at the University of Oklahoma.

3. An obituary notice comes from a local funeral home. It contains the basic information, but under achievements it lists only "former member of Lion's Club." Your city editor tells you to

228

find out more about the deceased. Whom would you call and why?

4. If George Thomas, private citizen, committed suicide while alone in his home, would you include that fact in his obituary? Why or why not?

5. A few newspapers write obituaries of notable people in advance because the time between the death and publication can be short. Some papers even interview the subject. Write a two-page advance obituary of one of the following: Condoleezza Rice, Henry Cisneros, Abe Rosenthal or Madonna. At the end, list your sources.

"A news release led me to the most important story I ever wrote," says Judd Slivka, a general assignment reporter for *The Arizona Republic*. (See "On the Job," p. 237.) Reporters do not go out and dig up all the stories they write. Many stories come to them. They are mailed, e-mailed, telephoned, faxed or hand-delivered by people who want to get something in "the news." They come from people or offices with different titles: public-relations departments, public-information offices, community-relations bureaus, press agents, press secretaries and publicity offices. The people who write them call their stories news releases or press releases; other journalists are more likely to call them handouts.

Because good publicity is so important, private individuals, corporations and government agencies spend a great deal of money to obtain it. Much of the money goes for the salaries of skilled and experienced personnel, many of whom have worked in the news business. Part of their job is to write news releases that the news media will use.

You may very well want to be among those people. You may be seeking a career in public relations or advertising, but your journalism department wisely has you begin by studying news and newswriting. Only by studying news and how news organizations handle news will you be successful in public relations or in offices of public information. Knowing how reporters are taught to deal with news releases will help you write better releases if that ever is your job. Of course, studying news also helps you enormously in the advertising world.

Skilled public-relations or public-information practitioners know how to write news, and they apply all the principles of good newswriting in their news releases. A good news release meets the criteria for a good news story.

Nevertheless, as two of the best PR professionals, Carole Howard, formerly of *Reader's Digest*, and Wilma Mathews, formerly with AT&T and now director of public relations at Arizona State University, tell us, news releases are never intended to take the place of reporters. News releases, they write in *On Deadline: Managing Media Relations*, simply acquaint an editor with the basic facts of potential stories. Those who write news releases come to accept that their carefully crafted sentences will be checked and rewritten by reporters.

In this chapter you will learn:

1. What types of news releases there are.

2. How to handle the news release.

As a reporter, you must recognize that news releases are both a help and a hindrance to a newspaper. They are a help because without them, newspapers would need many more reporters. They are a hindrance because they sometimes contain incomplete or even incorrect information. Because they are intended to promote the interests and favorable reputation of the individuals and organizations that disseminate them, news releases, by their very nature, are not objective.

Nevertheless, wise editors do not discard news releases without reading them. These editors often give them to reporters, often the newest ones, as sources for stories.

When your editor hands you a news release, you are expected to know what to do with it. You must be able to recognize the news in the release and apply all that you have learned about news values. The release may lead you to a good story. Your resourcefulness may improve your chances of being assigned to bigger things.

TYPES OF NEWS RELEASES

After you have read a number of news releases, you will notice that generally they fall into three categories:

1. Announcements of coming events or of personnel matters — hiring, promoting, retiring and the like.
2. Information about a cause.
3. Information that is meant to build someone's or some organization's image.

Recognizing the types and purposes of news releases (and recognizing that some are hybrids and serve more than one purpose) will help you know how to rewrite them.

Announcements

Organizations use the news media to tell their members and the public about coming events. For example:

> The Camera Club will have a special meeting at Wyatt's Cafeteria at 7 p.m. on Wednesday, March 20. Marvin Miller will present a slide program on "Yellowstone in Winter." All interested persons are invited to attend.

Although the release promotes the Camera Club, it also serves as a public-service announcement. Newspapers that print such announcements are serving their readers. Here is another example:

The first reception of the new season of the Springfield Art League will be on Sunday, Sept. 8, 3 to 5 p.m. in the Fine Arts Building.

Included in the exhibition will be paintings, serigraphs, sculpture, batiks, weaving, pottery, jewelry, all created by Art League members, who throughout the summer have been preparing works for this opening exhibit of the season.

The event also will feature local member-artists' State Fair entries, thus giving all who could not get to the fair the opportunity to see these works.

The exhibition continues to Friday, Sept. 13. All gallery events and exhibitions are free.

Other news release announcements concern appointments, promotions, hiring and retiring. The announcement of an appointment may read like this:

James McAlester, internationally known rural sociologist at Springfield University, has been appointed to the board of directors of Bread for the World, according to William Coburn, executive director of the humanitarian organization.

McAlester attended his first board meeting Jan. 22 in New York City. He has been on the university faculty since 1999.

Prior to that, he served as the Ford Foundation representative in India for 17 years.

The 19,000-member Bread for the World organization is a "broad based interdenominational movement of Christian citizens who advocate government policies that address the basic causes of hunger in the world," says Coburn.

The occasion is the appointment of McAlester, but the release also describes the purpose of the Bread for the World organization. By educating readers about the organization's purpose, the writer hoped to promote its cause.

Companies often send releases when an employee has been promoted. For example:

James B. Withers Jr. was named senior vice president in charge of sales of the J.B. Withers Company, it was announced Tuesday.

Withers, who has been with the company in the sales division for two years, will head a sales force of 23 people.

"We are sure Jim can do the job,"

James B. Withers Sr., company president, said. "He brings youth, intelligence and enthusiasm to the job. We're pleased he has decided to stay with the company."

Founded in 1936, the J.B. Withers Company is the country's second-largest manufacturer of dog and cat collars.

A release like this one is an attempt by the company to get its name before the public and to create employee goodwill. Written in the form of an announcement, it is an attempt at free publicity.

Cause-Promoting Releases

News releases in this category seek to further a cause. Some of these releases come from organizations whose worthwhile causes are in need of funds or volunteers. The letter reprinted here is from a county chairman of the American Heart Association to the editor of a newspaper. It is not written in the form of a release, but its effect is meant to be the same:

"Desktop publishing has dramatically increased the quantity and enhanced the quality of news releases coming into a news room. News releases from local clubs and organizations that once were written in longhand on notebook paper now rival those of professional public relations firms. The net effect: more news releases with local news than ever before. In a competitive media marketplace, smart newspapers can parlay this additional information into community pages packed with names and faces, reflecting the lives of readers in a way that other media can't."

— Ken Paulson,
senior vice president,
The Freedom Forum

The alumnae and collegiate members of the Alpha Phi Sorority have just completed their annual Alpha Phi "Helping Hearts" lollipop sale. This year Valerie Knight, project chairwoman, led sorority members to achieve record-breaking sales. The lollipop sale is a national project of the Alpha Phi Sorority.

Sunday, March 5, Valerie Knight presented a check for $1,800 to the American Heart Association, Shelby County Unit.

The contribution was presented during a reception at the Alpha Phi house. This contribution is an important part of the annual fund-raising campaign of the American Heart Association.

I wish to extend special thanks to the members of Alpha Phi and in particular to Valerie Knight for this outstanding project. In addition, I wish to thank the many merchants who participated in the project by selling lollipops in their businesses.

Heads of organizations like this attempt to alert the public to their messages in any way they can. Any release, notice or letter they can get printed without paying for it leaves money for the cause that they represent.

Image-Building Releases

Another kind of news release serves to build up some person's or some organization's image. Politicians seek to be elected or to be re-elected. They desire as much free publicity as they can get. For example:

James M. Merlin, honorary chairman of the board and director of Merlin Corporation, has been named honorary chairman of the Finance Committee, which will seek city-wide financial support for the campaign to elect Hong Xiang as Springfield's next mayor.

Merlin, a well-known civic leader and philanthropist, termed the election of Xiang "one of the most important and far-reaching decisions the voters of Springfield will make in a long time. The city's financial crisis can only be solved through the kind of economic leadership Xiang has demonstrated the past 10 years as 1st Ward councilperson."

The appointment of Merlin as honorary chairman serves only to promote the image of the candidate. The quote is self-serving.

Organizations and government agencies at all levels often try to build their public image. Many of them have local mayors proclaim a day or a week of recognition, as in the following:

Mayor Juanita Williams has proclaimed Saturday, May 11, as Fire Service Recognition Day. The Springfield Fire Department in conjunction with the University Fire Service Training Division is sponsoring a demonstration of the fire apparatus and equipment at the Springfield Fire Training Center. The displays are from 10 a.m. to 5 p.m. at 700 Bear Blvd. All citizens are urged to attend the display or visit their neighborhood fire station on May 6.

Our PRODUCT is your SAFETY.

If an editor hands you a release such as this, he or she probably has decided that it is worth using in some form. The rest is up to you.

NEWS FROM SUNSET
Contact: Shelia Gretchen
Office of Public Information
Sunset Community College
Springfield
Phone (315) 555-2231 Ext. 695

Betty S. Snead
Director of Public Information

IMMEDIATE RELEASE
November 9, 2001

Key

1. The place or institution involved.

2. The name of the contact person from whom you may secure further information.

3. The address and phone number.

4. The name of the director of information.

5. The release date, or the date on which the announcement should be printed, which is often "immediate."

6. The date on which the release was sent.

Figure 11.1
The information at the top of a news release can provide ideas and sources that will enhance your story.

HANDLING THE NEWS RELEASE

Regardless of the type of news release, be sure to read the information that appears at the top (see Figure 11.1). All of that information may be useful to you. Even so, many news releases leave unanswered questions. You probably will want to contact people other than the director of information or even the contact person if you have serious doubts about some of the data given. But for routine accuracy checks, the persons listed on the release can do the job. They may lead you to other helpful sources, too. Sometimes you may have sources of your own. And sometimes you may uncover the real story only from people who are neither connected to nor recommended by the director of information.

You may have to consult your editor regarding the release date. As a courtesy, most newspapers honor release dates. However, sometimes a morning or evening paper will publish the release early because waiting until the following day would render the information useless. Also, once a release is public knowledge, editors feel justified in publishing whatever information it contains, even prior to the suggested release date. A release date is broken for all when it is broken by one.

Rewriting the Announcement Release

Sometimes directors of information want nothing more than a listing on the record or calendar page of a newspaper. Here is an example:

TIPS: How to approach a
news release

- *Finish the reporting.*
  What questions are left
  unanswered?
- *Rewrite it.* Make sure
  that the story adheres to
  AP style.

FOR THE CALENDAR

Elisabeth Bertke, quiltmaker and designer from Salem, Massachusetts, will discuss her work at 7:00 o'clock p.m. Tues., February 7, in Charters Auditorium, Hampton College. Two quilts designed and constructed by Bertke are included in the exhibit "The New American Quilt," currently on display at the Smith Art Gallery.

"This is an exciting display," Betty Martin, president of the Smith Art Gallery board of directors, said. "You simply can't afford to miss it."

This simple release may go directly to the copy desk or to a special calendar editor.

If given to you, rewrite it. Some newspapers insist that you rewrite every news release if for no other reason than to avoid the embarrassment of running the same story as a competing newspaper. For some it is a matter of integrity and professionalism.

First, note all the violations of AP style in the preceding example:

- "Massachusetts" should be abbreviated "Mass."
- "7:00 o'clock P.M." should be "7 p.m."
- "Tues." should be spelled out "Tuesday."
- "February" should be abbreviated "Feb."
- A hyphen should be inserted in "quilt-maker."

Avoid relying on the copy desk to do your work if the rewrite is given to you.

You should check the other points as well. Confirm the spelling of Bertke's name, and see if there is an apostrophe in Charters Auditorium. The Smith Gallery may or may not be on the Hampton campus. Ask how long the exhibit will be at the gallery. Are quilts made by local people included in the exhibit? Perhaps your questions will lead to a feature story on local quilt-making.

In your rewrite, you will drop the quotation of Betty Martin. But you may insert better, less self-serving and less promotional quotes.

Here is another example:

Mr. Richard G. Hernandez has been selected as the Outstanding Biology Teacher of Nevada of the Year by the National Association of Biology Teachers. He was previously selected as Nevada Science Educator of the Year.

As an outstanding representative of good high-school biology teaching Hernandez will receive a certificate and a series 50 binocular microscope with an engraved citation. Hernandez has been teaching at Hickman High School since 1980.

The story is far from earthshaking, but the honor is statewide. In large newspapers the release may not get much play. A small community newspaper, however, will use it and perhaps enlarge upon it.

A first reading of the release tells you that it is wordy and leaves many questions unanswered. Hernandez may be an interesting fellow, but the release tells us little about him. You should approach this release in the same way you

News Releases: Diamonds in the Rough

Judd Slivka works as a general assignment reporter for *The Arizona Republic*. He has worked for the *Arkansas Democrat-Gazette, Columbia Missourian, Minneapolis Star Tribune* and *Seattle Post-Intelligencer*. His work has twice been nominated for a Pulitzer Prize.

It may surprise you to learn that Slivka says the most important story of his life came out of a news release.

"I get about 400 pieces of mail a week," Slivka says. "E-mail, snail mail, books, letters from people who hate me or hate the stories I write.

"The majority of that mail, though, is news releases. I get them from Democrats and Republicans. I get them from animal shelters. I get them from vintage clothing stores. Every person sending them has a cause to promote, and the truth is that most of the causes don't make good stories for the newspaper."

But now and then, one does, Slivka says. "And that's why I read nearly every news release."

Sometimes that policy pays off. Big-time.

An advance copy of a news release from the state health department had come across another reporter's desk. The release detailed the results of a study that found that nearly a dozen deaths over a decade at Lake Powell — a popular vacation spot along the Arizona-Utah line — were due to a design flaw in the houseboats people were using.

Carbon monoxide from houseboat generators could build up underneath an extended deck at the rear of the boat, and people swimming near it could get poisoned.

"The other reporter had gotten the news release from a friend of hers at the health department," Slivka says. "It was going to be released two days later. To speed things up, I was brought in to help."

The morning the release was officially given to the public, the paper had these four elements: a main story detailing the study, a list of victims, a detailed graphic, and stories of people who survived poisoning, including race-car driver Al Unser Jr.

The news release provided them with a start. "But the other reporter and I went well beyond it. We called experts on carbon monoxide. We called houseboat manufacturers. We called the people who did the study, and we went through the data with them line by line. We asked hard questions.

"If we had just written a story off a news release, it would have been flat and one-dimensional and not served the readers." Slivka says. "Instead, we used it as a starting point to delve into something that was much deeper and more complicated. Over the next three months, we published 25 stories detailing breakdowns in federal government oversight, the industry's ambivalence about the issue, and how families who had lost loved ones were coping."

Over time, the paper published more than 70 stories about the danger of carbon monoxide on

(continued)

237

News Releases: Diamonds in the Rough (continued)

recreational boats and followed the path of federal researchers as they've moved from houseboats to cabin cruisers. There have been congressional hearings that have quoted the paper's reports, manufacturers have been forced to change their designs, and the story has been copycatted by every major television network.

"The truth is," Slivka says, "I hate news releases. Most of them are blasted out to lists of reporters without any thought about who's on the receiving end, and thus are wastes of time. But another truth is that I read them, hoping to find a diamond of a story in the rough of unsolicited press releases."

approach any news release: Finish the reporting, and then rewrite it. News style demands a new lead to the release:

A Hickman High School science teacher has been named Outstanding Biology Teacher of the Year by the National Association of Biology Teachers.

Richard G. Hernandez, a Hickman teacher since 1980, will receive a certificate and a series 50 binocular microscope with an engraved citation.

Previously selected as Nevada Science Educator of the Year, Hernandez . . .

There the story runs out of information. You need to ask the following questions:

- Age?
- Degrees from where?
- Local address?
- Spouse, family?
- Annual award? One teacher selected from each state?
- Any previous Hickman winners? Any from local high schools?
- Year he received Nevada Science Educator award?
- Nominated for the award by whom?
- Date and place of bestowal? Public ceremony?
- Value of series 50 binocular microscope?

Then call Hernandez and find out how he feels about the award. Talk to the principal, to fellow teachers and to some of Hernandez's students. Good quotations will spice up your story.

Rewriting the Cause-Promoting Release

Newspapers generally cooperate with causes that are community-oriented. News releases like the following get attention:

A free tax clinic for low-income persons and senior citizens will be held on Feb. 9 and 10 in Springfield.

The clinic is sponsored by the Central State Counties' Human Development Corporation with the Accounting Department of the Springfield University College of Business.

Senior and graduate accounting students under the direct supervision of accounting faculty members will work with each taxpayer to help that taxpayer complete accurately his or her tax return.

The Human Development Corporation encourages persons especially to use the clinic who may be eligible for senior citizens' credits or other credits.

This is the fifth year the clinic has operated in Shelby County. Last year more than 275 persons in the eight counties served were assisted.

For information regarding the location of the clinics and to make an appointment, contact the Shelby County Human Development Corporation, 600 E. Broadway, Room 103, Springfield, 555-8376.

Again, you need more information. To begin with, you need to know more about the Human Development Corporation. A background paragraph on its origins, where it gets its money and its other areas of concern will put the story into context.

The release is unclear about who is eligible. What must your income be? How old must you be? Also, you must find out the exact locations of the clinics.

Once you have answers to all your questions, dig for some human interest. Talk to a participating faculty member and to students who helped before and will help again. Then talk to some people who were helped in the past and to some who will come for help. Obviously, you must talk to those in charge of the joint effort.

Because efforts like these are in the public interest, newspapers will give them space. They will be more critical with releases that are merely self-serving.

Rewriting the Image-Building Release

The following is a typical release from a politician:

Sen. John Choi said today that nearly $400,000 in grants have been given final approval by two departments of the state government for interlocking improvements in Springfield and Lincoln County.

Choi said, "This is something I have been working for this past year. It is a chance to show that state agencies are interested in communities. It also demonstrates that two agencies can work together to produce a coordinated, workable solution to improve a blighted area in Springfield."

The grants, Choi said, come from the State Bureau of Outdoor Recreation — $247,000 for purchasing Baltimore and Ohio railroad rights-of-way and developing a strip park — and the Department of Housing and Urban Development — $150,000 for planning the Flat Branch area. The second grant also stipulates that part of the money be used to coordinate the two projects: the B&O strip park and the Flat Branch redevelopment.

"I think residents of Springfield and Lincoln County will have a chance to help out in the planning of these two facilities. I hope this means the entire community will express opinions and come to a conclusion that will see these projects become a reality in the next two years."

The first three words of the release indicate who is being served by the release. A Springfield reporter might write the lead this way to serve the reader:

Springfield and Lincoln County will receive nearly $400,000 in state grants to fund the B&O strip park and the Flat Branch redevelopment project, Sen. John Choi said today.

The second paragraph of the release is a long and newsless quote from the senator. Probably he did not say those words at all; they were likely written by his press agent. You should eliminate them, or if you want a quote from the senator, call him and talk to him yourself.

The second paragraph of your story should indicate the source of the funding:

The grants come from two state agencies. The State Bureau of Outdoor Recreation granted $247,000 for purchasing the Baltimore & Ohio Railroad rights-of-way and for developing a strip park, and the Department of Housing and Urban Development granted $150,000 for planning the Flat Branch area. The second grant also stipulates that part of the money be used to coordinate the two projects.

You could handle Choi's last quote this way:

Choi said he hoped Springfield and Lincoln County residents will have a chance to help plan the two facilities. "I hope this means the entire community will express opinions and come to a conclusion that will see these projects become a reality in the next two years."

Like many news releases of this kind, this announcement would trigger other news stories in the local papers. This story would call for local reactions from city and county officials and from local residents. The editor might assign several stories on the matter.

Releases from organizations can also be self-serving — and sometimes misleading. Suppose you were given the following news release:

NEWS RELEASE
**Springfield Community Teachers
  Association**
Lillian A. Briggs, President
Contact: Tom Monnin, SCTA Salary
  Committee Chairman
Phone: 555-555-6794 (Central High
  School)
  555-2975-555 (home)

For Immediate Release
Springfield — Dogcatchers in Springfield make a higher starting salary than Springfield teachers, as discovered in a recent survey by the Springfield Community Teachers Association. According to their research, a new teacher in the Springfield public school system makes $25,700, while a firefighter starts at $26,676 or $976 more than a new teacher. "This is a shameful situation for an educational community," said Tom Monnin, Springfield SCTA Salary Committee chairman.

The statistics gathered by the Springfield SCTA Salary Committee indicate that police with a bachelor's degree make

$28,327. This is a $2,627 gap in starting salaries for public employees with comparable education. Following is a comparison of starting salaries of some Springfield city employees and of public school teachers for the school year:

Occupation	Starting Salary
Police officer with bachelor's degree	$28,327
Firefighter with bachelor's degree	26,676
Meter reader	20,789
Animal control officer	21,576
Bus operator	20,038
Teacher with bachelor's degree	25,700

"Springfield teachers do not think city employees are overpaid but that teachers are underpaid," Monnin said.

Even though teachers work under a 9¼-month contract, the workweek is not 40 hours. When the hours for preparing and grading, attending sports events, musical concerts, dances, other after-school activities and PTA meetings are considered, a teacher's workweek is much longer than 40 hours. Summer break is used by many teachers for advanced preparation at the university, at their own expense.

The Springfield SCTA Salary Committee will present the salary proposal at the next meeting of the Springfield Board of Education.

The Springfield SCTA represents approximately 523 members in the public school system.

Your first task is to read the release carefully. The lead cleverly suggests that dogcatchers make as much money as teachers do, although it speaks only of starting salaries. The more you read the release, the more uncomfortable you should feel with it. No one can blame teachers for wanting more money, but there are other factors to consider. What about working conditions? Teachers in Springfield's schools certainly don't have to put their lives on the line the way police officers and firefighters do. Most people do not want to spend their lives chasing stray dogs. Besides, the list of salaries in the release does not support the lead that says the starting salary of dogcatchers is higher than the starting salary of teachers.

The fact that teachers work for a little more than nine months a year is down in the fourth paragraph. The release fails to mention a two-week break over Christmas and a week off in the spring semester. Most firefighters get two weeks off per year.

Is the release trying to suggest that because teachers actually spend more than 40 hours a week working, they should not have to work more than 9¼ months? Not all teachers spend all their lives going to summer school. You probably know several who have summer jobs or who take long vacations.

Before you turn in a rewrite of the release, you have a lot of checking to do.

Reporter Melanie Davis began by calling the city of Springfield's personnel office. When asked about the $26,676 starting salary of a firefighter, the personnel officer replied: "You wouldn't begin at that salary. Everyone is hired at $25,644 for a trial period of at least six months. If you work out OK, you might jump up to $26,676. Again, there are a lot of considerations besides the college degree."

Take special care when news releases cite studies, polls or surveys. Check the source of the figures for accuracy and possible bias. If you can't confirm the figures and their reliability, don't use them.

Further checking revealed that the news release did indeed contain inaccurate information about the starting salaries of firefighters.

Davis knew she was on to something. Comparing starting salaries was one thing. But how much could a person eventually earn in a position?

She then asked about the starting salary for a police officer. "Yes," the director of personnel said, "$28,327 is the beginning salary for a police officer with a B.S. degree."

Davis then asked whether anyone could get hired at that salary if he or she had a B.S. degree.

"Most people wouldn't stand a chance of being hired," he said. "We have more than 100 applicants for every position, so we can be quite choosy. Unless a person has had some real experience as a police officer, I don't think he or she would make it."

Further questioning revealed that a top salary for a police officer was $36,841 after six years of service.

Davis then called a high-school teacher. She asked her if she had to put in more than 40 hours a week at her job.

"Oh, yes," she said. "I teach a section of English composition, and I have a lot of papers to grade. I used to spend a lot of evenings preparing for classes, but once you've taught a course, it gets easier. And then I have to go to all those football games and basketball games."

Davis then found out that she was indeed required to attend, but only because she was in charge of the cheerleaders. When Davis expressed sympathy, the teacher replied, "No, I really don't mind. After all, I get $1,500 a year extra for being in charge of the cheerleaders."

Davis then learned from someone at the Springfield Schools' personnel office that quite a few teachers received compensation for after-school activities — coaching, directing plays and musical activities, advising the staffs of the school newspaper and senior yearbook, and chaperoning dances. Teachers sponsoring class and club activities could earn from $500 to $1,500; a sponsor of the pep squad could earn up to $1,500. The top teacher's salary without any of these extras was $46,400.

Now Davis was ready to call Tom Monnin, the man whose name was on the release, for additional information. She asked if it was fair to compare a new teacher's salary with a new firefighter's salary when the top pay for a firefighter was $33,881 and the top teacher's salary was $46,400. Monnin explained that it took 17 years for a teacher with a master's degree plus 75 hours to reach that top salary. A teacher with a bachelor's degree could make $33,980 after 11 years of teaching. When Davis asked about summers off and other vacations, Monnin replied, "I figure I work a 60-hour week. That means I work 51 40-hour weeks a year."

Monnin acknowledged that many teachers got paid extra for extracurricular activities. "But not all of them do," he said. "And there are many activities we do feel the responsibility to attend."

When asked about the argument that teachers do not have to put their lives on the line the way police and fire officials and even dogcatchers do, Monnin replied: "It's debatable who has to put their lives on the line. We're not as bad off as some schools, but we often have to restrain students physically."

Only now was Davis ready to write the story. Here's what she wrote:

The Springfield Community Teachers Association said Tuesday that new firefighters earn more than new teachers.

What the teachers did not say was that a teacher eventually can earn nearly $12,000 more a year than a firefighter can.

The SCTA statement was included with a survey that lists starting teachers' salaries at $25,700. Other figures listed as starting salaries are: police officer with a bachelor's degree, $28,327; animal control officer, $21,576; meter reader, $20,789; bus operator, $20,038.

"This is a shameful situation for an educational community," said Tom Monnin, the SCTA Salary Committee chairman. "Springfield teachers do not think city employees are overpaid but that teachers are underpaid."

The association officers said that even though teachers work under a nine-month contract, extracurricular activities extend the workweek beyond 40 hours. Summer break, they said, is used for advanced study at the teachers' own expense.

"I figure I work a 60-hour week," Monnin said in an interview. "That means I work 51 40-hour weeks a year."

Some extracurricular activities, such as coaching, directing plays and supervising cheerleaders, earn extra compensation.

Teachers are not compelled to attend after-school functions, but "we do feel the responsibility to attend," Monnin said.

Teachers also feel compelled to continue their education. Top pay for a teacher with only a bachelor's degree is $33,980 after 11 years of teaching. A teacher with a master's degree plus 75 hours of classes can earn $46,400 after 17 years of teaching.

A police officer with a bachelor's degree can reach a top salary of $36,841 after six years of police work. But a person with a bachelor's degree and no police work experience is not likely to be hired, said Phil James, the Springfield director of personnel. James also said all firefighters are hired at $25,644. If a person has a bachelor's degree and stays on, he or she could make $26,676 after a six-month trial period.

Top pay for a dogcatcher is $27,626. "I sure wish I got summers off like those teachers," Tom Merell, an animal control officer, said. "I got nothing against teachers. But most of them make more money than I'll ever make. . . . Besides, students don't bite many teachers."

The SCTA Salary Committee will present its salary proposal at the next meeting of the Springfield Board of Education.

The reporter did with this news release what you should do with many of them. She was not satisfied with the way it was written or with the information it contained. By asking some important questions, she was able to put together an informative and more accurate story. Without saying that the news release was dishonest or misleading, the reporter corrected or clarified some of the information contained in it. The plight of the teacher is told clearly and objectively, but it is placed in a much better perspective than was found in the news release.

Like many news releases, this one was the basis for a story the newspaper otherwise would not have had. That is why editors pay attention to them and why reporters look for the real story.

WRITING NEWS RELEASES THAT GET ATTENTION

Even the smallest newspaper or TV or radio station gets dozens of news releases daily. How do you break through the clutter and get yours opened, or listened to, or looked at by the gatekeepers on the news desks? If you send news releases online, your problem is still the same.

Here are some guidelines to help you get your messages to the audiences you want to have them.

- *Know what news is and how to write it.* Presumably, if you are headed toward a career in public relations or public information, you are taking this newswriting course to help you understand all of the principles of news. The news media will not pay attention to copy that is laced with opinions or self-serving quotations. Worse, they will ridicule your work and discard it immediately.

  Avoid statements such as this: "Monroe College is recognized as the foremost and most prestigious college of liberal arts in the entire Midwest." Who says?

  When you are writing for most publications, certainly for newspapers, knowing how to write news means knowing Associated Press style. Correct spelling, usage and grammar is essential, of course, but just as important, write in AP style. Why should news editors have to edit your style? More than that, why should they take you seriously if you do not bother to write in the style of their publications?

  News releases are notoriously inaccurate and inconsistent. How ironic that the people most concerned with image are so careless in how they present themselves to the public!

- *Know the structure and workings of news rooms.* If you do not get actual experience of how a news room works in college, be sure you find ways to spend some time in one. In Chapter 2, you learned how news rooms are organized. Now use your public-relations skills to get inside one and to experience what goes on there.

  The most simple and important thing you can learn about news rooms is that they have deadlines. You must learn the deadlines of the various media where you work, and respect them. That means you cannot call in a story to a television news station a half-hour before broadcast time. Not only will a news station not use your story, but it will resent and not forget the interruption at a critical time. News media will tell you what time you must have a story in for it to make the news that day.

- *Know the people in the news media and the jobs they hold.* This is especially true of the newspaper. Sending a release addressed to the paper is risky and often foolish. Sending a release to the business editor or to the features editor might make more sense. Putting the name of the editor of the section you wish the release to appear in might work even better.

If people in the news media know you and trust you, you can sometimes call them with a story and let them go with it. Regardless of how you do it, your job is to help reporters write good stories. If you can help them do that and serve your interests at the same time, you will be a successful public-relations practitioner.

- *Know the style of writing that fits the medium.* Do not make the mistake of sending to the radio or TV station the same news release that you send to the newspaper. Do not expect busy newspeople to translate your newspaper release into broadcast copy. If you can write broadcast copy (see Chapter 19), you have a much better chance of getting the copy read over the air. And if you can supply video, many stations will use it in their news broadcasts.

Suggested Readings

Bivins, Thomas H. *Public Relations Writing*, Fourth Edition. Lincolnwood, Ill.: NTC/Contemporary Publishing Group, 1999. You can learn how public-relations professionals approach a wide variety of writing tasks.

Howard, Carole and Mathews, Wilma. *On Deadline: Managing Media Relations*, Third Edition. Prospect Heights, Ill.: Waveland Press, 2000. A practical book on how organizations should deal with the news media.

Wilcox, Dennis L. and Nolte, Lawrence W. *Public Relations Writing and Media Techniques*, Fourth Edition. New York: HarperCollins, 2000. Emphasizes writing, producing and distributing a variety of public-relations materials.

Suggested Web Sites

www.poewar.com
When you get to the site, go to "Writing Effective Press Releases" (listed under "The Writing Business" heading). John Hewitt describes techniques that public-relations writers use to capture a publication's attention.

www.pressflash.com/anatomy.html
You can learn from this anatomy of a news release.

www.press-release-writing.com/10_essential_tips.htm
Note these 10 essential tips for writing news releases.

Exercises

1. Read each of the following news releases. First, correct all departures from Associated Press style rules. Second, indicate the type of news release it is. Third, list questions you would have if you were to rewrite it, including the facts you would check and the sources you would turn to for the answers.

a. NEWS RELEASE

The 2004 Sheep Knowledge awards will be made on the basis of a comprehensive test over knowledge in the book, Raising Sheep the Modern Way, by Paula Simmons. Information concerning availability of this book may be obtained from libraries, bookstores, or university agriculture departments.

The test will be developed, administered, and scored by nationally known livestock specialists. The contest is being announced early to give students adequate time for preparation. The test will be given in Springfield at 8:00 P.M. on September 5. The contest will be open to any person who is not yet eighteen, on that day.

The four top winners will receive trophies and divide ten commercial ewes as follows: First, 4 ewes. Second, 3 ewes. Third, 2 ewes. Fourth, 1 ewe.

b. NEWS RELEASE

Plaza Frontenac will be filled with floral displays from 10:00 A.M. to 9:00 P.M. on Friday October 31 and 10:00 A.M. to 4:00 P.M. on Saturday November 1 as the East Central District of the Federated Garden Clubs of America, Inc. presents "Challenge," a flower show of artistic flower arrangements and outstanding horticultural specimens on both levels of the plaza.

Hundreds of entries, including table settings, arrangements featuring fresh flowers, evergreens and dried plants will offer decorating ideas for special occasions. Educational exhibits on state birds, the propagation and growing of African violets, and a patio garden of perennials designed by Doug and Cindy Gilberg of Gilberg Perennial Farms.

General co-chairmen for the event are Wilma Stortz and Kay Schaefer. In 1997 the group staged a major flower show at Plaza Frontenac and won a national award.

The show is free and open to the public. Plaza Frontenac is located on the corner of South Main and Hamilton. Shopping hours are 10:00 A.M. to 9:00 P.M. Monday through Friday.

c. NEWS RELEASE

The teaching faculty, administration and staff of The South Shore Country Day School formally began the school year Friday, August 30, with an all day workshop on curriculum planning.

This year, the School will be involved in a year long task of self evaluation. All aspects of the School's curriculum and student life will be considered and a new five year, long range plan for the curriculum will be written. The School's last major plan was constructed in 1994.

The evaluation process is designed to keep curriculum consistent with the School's educational philosophy and statement of mission. It will identify problems, strengths, and opportunities for expansion. At various stages of the process, all constituencies of the School will have an opportunity to express concerns and opinions. By the end of the school year, a new plan will be ready for integration and implementation by the School's administration.

William R. Lopez, Chairman of the School's Board of Trustees, spoke to the faculty about the upcoming project and the need to change. "We will attempt to make the current school better; we will not be creating a new school," he said.

Thomas B. Lang, the School's headmaster, emphasized the importance of total faculty participation in the formulation and execution of the mission statement. "We're all in this together." Lang said. "Curriculum is the sum of all the parts. No one teaches in a vacuum."

Among topics discussed at the workshop were: the importance of academic excellence; student social service; a need for diversity within the student body; the importance of educating the whole child; providing increased opportunity for students to participate in a variety of academic and nonacademic projects; and the ethical considerations in the School.

2. Assume you are a reporter for the Springfield paper. Your instructor will be your news source for any questions you have. Rewrite each of the following releases.

a. NEWS RELEASE

Nearly 11,000 seat belt violation warnings were issued to motorists by the State Highway Patrol during the first month the new seat belt law was in effect.

Colonel Howard J. Hoffman, Superintendent of the State Highway Patrol, reported today that 10,908 warnings were issued to motorists in passenger vehicles for not wearing their seat belts as required by State Law.

Colonel Hoffman also noted that during this same reporting period, 50 persons were killed in traffic accidents investigated by the Highway Patrol. Only two of the persons killed in these mishaps were found to be wearing seat belts.

"The value of wearing a seat belt cannot be overemphasized," Hoffman said. "We don't know how many of these investigated traffic deaths could have been avoided by the use of seat belts. It is known, however, that seat belts have saved lives and prevented serious injuries to others. We will continue to vigorously enforce the State seat belt law and hopefully more and more motorists will make it a habit to buckle their seat belts."

b. NEWS RELEASE

The Better Business Bureau serving the tri-state area has launched a fund-raising drive to finance the installation of a 24-hour computerized telephone service called Tel-Tips.

James C. Schmitt, President, said Tel-Tips is a unique consumer information and education system designed to give quick useful information about specific goods and services. Consumers would be provided with a number to call and the system will put the caller in contact with a selected pre-recorded message.

A goal of $20,000 has been established to finance installation of Tel-Tips and the physical expansion of the BBB's office.

"Despite efficient telephone communications and computer system, we expect to lose nearly 24,000 calls this year," said Schmitt. "Our operators are trained to limit time given to each caller to avoid losing callers, while at the same time attempting to provide complete information."

The Bureau is unable to respond to inquiries before and after business hours and on weekends, times many customers need BBB services.

Tel-Tips is a computerized information center that allows 114 consumer tip messages to be made instantly available to callers. This system answers incoming calls with a pre-recorded message and instructs the caller to dial the number of the message he or she wants to hear. This unit operates automatically with the use of a Touch-Tone telephone, 12 hours a day. A rotary dial telephone may be used during regular business hours with the assistance of an operator.

c. NEWS RELEASE

"Chest Pains," a film in the HEALTHSCOPE series produced by the American College of Physicians, will be shown from 7-8:30 p.m., Wednesday, Oct. 22, at St. Mary's Health Center. Springfield internist, Dr. Harold Kanagawa, will host a question-and-answer period following the film.

Although most people assume that chest pains signify a heart attack, the public is less aware that other conditions — hiatal hernia, ulcers, viral infections of the heart's membranes — can also cause pains that require prompt diagnosis and appropriate medical treatment. Designed to help increase awareness of these symptoms and their possible significance, "Chest Pains" features an internist and actual patients as they work together to resolve underlying medical problems.

In your first year or so of general-assignment reporting, you will be assigned to cover many speeches, news conferences and meetings — some routine, some of great importance. Communities often elect and re-elect their leaders on the basis of their performance at these events. Speeches, news conferences and meetings rally communities to causes and nations to war.

Before President Lyndon B. Johnson's televised address on the Gulf of Tonkin incident in 1964, a Harris Survey showed that less than half of the electorate approved of the president's Vietnam policy. After his address, a second poll indicated that 70 percent approved. Before President Richard M. Nixon addressed the nation to attempt to justify the invasion of Cambodia in 1970, a Harris Survey showed that only 7 percent of the public supported the decision. After Nixon's television address, more than 50 percent approved. A *USA Today*/CNN/Gallup poll showed that President Bill Clinton's news conference regarding his troubles with the Whitewater real estate deal raised his approval rating of how he was handling Whitewater from 39 percent to 50 percent. More recently, President George W. Bush's popularity rating rose from 50 percent to 60 percent in the days just after his first State of the Union address.

Some argue that John F. Kennedy's display of intelligence and wit at news conferences got him elected and earned him respect as president. President Nixon, in contrast, had little flair for give-and-take and less love for reporters. Consequently, his performance at news conferences added little to his popularity. President Ronald Reagan felt at home in front of cameras, and although he disliked news conferences, his televised speeches helped boost his image tremendously. Town meetings helped President Bill Clinton get to the White House. Former Vice President Al Gore's perceived stiffness on TV may have helped put George W. Bush into the White House.

Because the coverage of speeches, news conferences and meetings is similar, we examine all three in this chapter. But you should keep in mind their distinguishing characteristics.

A **speech** is a public talk. Someone speaks to an audience in person or on radio or television. Regardless of the medium, a speech is a one-way communication. The speaker speaks, and the audience listens.

Speakers are usually invited and sometimes paid to address an audience. That is not the case with those who hold a news conference.

People "call" a **news conference.** They do not send invitations to the general public, but they do alert members of the various news media. The media respond because of the importance of the person calling the news conference and because the person may have something newsworthy to say. The person holding the news conference often begins with an opening statement and usually accepts questions from reporters. A news conference is meant to be a two-way communication.

Unlike speeches and news conferences, **meetings** are not held with an audience in mind, although an audience may be present and allowed to participate. A meeting is primarily for communication among the members of a group or organization, whether a local parent-teacher association or the Congress of the United States. Reporters who are permitted to witness a meeting tell the public what is of interest and importance. This task of the news media is especially important if the participants are members of a governmental body that spends or allocates the public's money collected through taxes.

Because you will spend a great deal of time as a reporter covering speeches, news conferences and meetings, you will want to learn all you can about covering them well.

PREPARATION

Professional reporters know that preparation makes covering a story much easier. In all cases, reporters should do their homework. You prepare for speeches, news conferences and meetings in much the same way. Because these events are usually announced in advance, you have time for thorough preparation.

Preparing for the Speech Story

Not every speech will demand a great deal of research. Many speakers and speeches will be dry and routine. The person giving the speech will be someone you know or someone you covered before. At other times you may get an assignment on short notice and be forced to find background information after hearing the speech. In either case, never take the speaker or the topic for granted. Failure to get enough background on the speaker and on the speech almost guarantees failure at writing a comprehensive speech story.

The first step in your research is to identify the speaker correctly. Middle initials are important; sometimes even they are not enough. Sometimes checking the address is not enough. One reporter wrote about the wrong person because he did not know that a father and son with the same name had the same address.

USA Today had to print a "clarification" after reporting that Larry King had made a $1,000 donation to President Clinton's campaign. The donor was Larry L. King, author and playwright.

A hospital in Boston was threatened with a lawsuit after telling relatives that Robert J. Oliver had died. Robert J.'s fiancee was surprised a few days later when he called her. The man who had died was Robert W. Oliver. Robert W. was not listed in the phone book; Robert J. was.

TIPS: Technical thoughts for the television journalist

Speeches, news conferences and meetings present several technical challenges. Here are three to keep in mind:

- *Think visuals.* What will your backdrop be? Will there be signs, photos, samples, logos or flip-charts to help tell the story?
- *Think sound.* Will there be one microphone or a multi-box for you to insert your mike, or will you be free to set up your own microphone?
- *Think light.* Will the event take place outdoors or in a well-lit room, or must you bring your own lighting? How far is the camera throw (the distance from the event to your camera)? Will there be a camera platform or a set space, or will you be free to set up your camera anywhere?

Be sure you have the right person. Then, before doing research on the speaker, contact the group sponsoring the speech and ask for the topic. You might find you need to do some reading to prepare yourself to understand the subject. If you are lucky, you may get an advance copy of the speech. Also check your newspaper library to see what your paper has done on the speaker. If you have access to a data bank, use it. Visit your local library.

If the speech is important enough, you might want to contact the speaker ahead of time for a brief interview. If he or she is from out of town, you might plan for a meeting at the airport. You might also arrange ahead of time to interview the speaker after the speech. You may have questions and points to clarify.

Not every speech will demand that much effort. But even the most routine speech assignment needs preparation. Do not assume, for instance, that Gene Martin, director of the local library, is addressing the state Writer's Guild to tell members how to use the library to improve their stories. Gene Martin may also be a successful "true confessions" writer, published dozens of times in such magazines as *True Confessions* and *True Romance*. He may be telling guild members how he does it.

Sooner or later you may be called on to cover speeches by major political figures, perhaps even the president of the United States. For this task, too, you will need background — lots of it. It demands that you read the news and you know what is going on. You must keep up with current events.

Preparing for the News Conference Story

Preparing for a news conference is like preparing for a speech. You need up-to-date background on the person giving the news conference, and you must learn why the news conference is being held. Often the person holding the news conference has an announcement or an opening statement. Unless that statement is leaked to the press, you will not know its content ahead of time, but you can make some educated guesses. Check out any rumors. Call the person's associates, friends or secretary.

You and every other reporter at a news conference will have a line of questions to pursue. Your editor may want certain information, and other editors may want something else. Once the news conference begins, you will not have time to think of questions; recording responses to other reporters' questions will keep you too busy. The better prepared you are, the better chance you will have of coming away with a coherent, readable story.

It may be impossible to arrange an interview before or after the news conference. If the person holding the news conference wanted to grant individual reporters interviews, he or she probably would not have called the news conference. But you can always ask — you might end up with some exclusive information.

Preparing for the Meeting Story

You never know what to expect at a meeting, either. So you must do your best to prepare. Who are the people holding the meeting? What kind of an organization

TIPS: Preparing for the speech story

- Be sure you have the right person.
- Contact the group sponsoring the speech and ask for the topic.
- Check your newspaper library for background on the speaker.
- If the speech is important enough, contact the speaker for a brief interview.

TIPS: Preparing for the news conference story

- Get up-to-date background on the person holding the news conference.
- Learn why the conference is being held.
- Check out any rumors beforehand; call the person's associates, friends or secretary.
- Try to arrange an interview before or after the news conference.

is involved? Who are the key figures? Again, the morgue is your first stop. Then contact some of the key figures.

See if you can find out what the meeting is about. Perhaps the president or the secretary has a written agenda for the meeting. If you know the main subject to be discussed, you will be able to study and investigate the issues before arriving. Knowing what to expect and being familiar with the issues will make covering the meeting much easier.

A reporter with a regular beat — an assigned area of responsibility — usually covers meetings of the most important organizations and groups such as the city council, the school board or the county board. (Beat reporting is discussed in detail in Chapter 14.) A beat reporter has continuing familiarity with the organization and with the issues involved. Often the meetings of important organizations are preceded by an **advance** — a report outlining the subjects and issues to be covered during the upcoming meeting.

TIPS: Preparing for the meeting story

- Contact some of the key figures.
- Try to find out what the meeting is about. You can then study and investigate issues before arriving.

COVERING SPEECHES, NEWS CONFERENCES AND MEETINGS

TIPS: Achieving total coverage of content and event

- Get the content correct. Recorders can be helpful, but always take good notes. Quote people exactly and in context.
- Note the background, personal characteristics and mannerisms of the main participants.
- Cover the event. Look around the edges — at the audience (size, reactions) and sometimes at what is happening outside the building.
- Get there early, position yourself and hang around afterward.

The story is often told of a reporter who prepared well for a speech assignment, contacted the speaker, got a copy of the speech, wrote the story and spent the evening in a bar. Not until after he handed in his speech story did he find out that the speech had been canceled.

And then there's the yarn about a young reporter assigned to cover a meeting who came back and told the city editor there was no story.

"Why not?" the city editor asked.

"Because the meeting was canceled."

"Why was that?"

"Well," replied the reporter, "when the meeting started, some of the board members got into this big argument. Finally, three of them walked out. The president then canceled the meeting because there was no quorum."

Of course, the canceled meeting and the circumstances surrounding its cancellation probably were of more interest to readers than the meeting itself would have been. Preparing to cover an event is only the beginning. Knowing what to do when you get there is equally important. You must cover the entire event — the content of a speech, news conference or meeting; the time, place, circumstances and number of people involved; and possible consequences of what was said or of the actions taken.

Getting the Content Correct

You may find a tape or digital recorder useful for covering the content of speeches, news conferences and meetings. Recorders often scare people who don't work in broadcast journalism, but they should not. Indeed, at many newspapers today reporters are being asked to bring back audio for the newspaper's Web site. Practice using a recorder. Use it again and again to become familiar with its idiosyncrasies. Knowing in general how to operate recorders is not enough. You need to be comfortable with the one you are using. For example, you must be sure how sensitive the microphone is. It is sound you want, and sound you must get.

The most frequent complaint you may hear about recorders is that listening to the entire recording takes too long. You may have to listen to a whole speech just to find a certain quote you want to check. But if you have a recorder with a counter, you may avoid this problem. At any point in a speech or a meeting when something of importance is said, you need only to note the number on the counter. Finding the quotation later will then be easy.

There is one thing you must do even when you record an event: You must take notes in exactly the same way that you would if you were not recording. Malfunctions can occur, even with the best machines, at the most inopportune times.

So, with or without a recorder, you must become a proficient note taker. Many veteran reporters wish they had learned shorthand or speed-writing early in their careers. You may find it useful to buy a speed-writing manual and learn a few symbols. Sooner or later every reporter adopts or creates some note-taking shortcuts. You will have to do the same. Learn to abbreviate (*wh* for "which," *th* for "that," *bk* for "book," *st* for "street," *bldg* for "building," etc.). Make up signs (*w/* for "with," *w/o* for "without," *acc/* for "according to").

Are you one of those fortunate people with a fantastic memory? Some reporters develop an incredible knack for re-creating whole conversations with complete accuracy without taking a note. Are you instead someone who takes reams of notes (see Figure 12.1)? If you are, take them as neatly as you can. Many

TIPS: Using a tape or digital recorder

- Be familiar with the machine. Practice using it. Make sure you understand its peculiarities. Check its sound capabilities.
- Set it where you can see it's working. If it has a digital counter, note the number when you hear a quote you want.
- Take notes as if it might not be working. After all, it might not be.

Figure 12.1
A story about a speech, news conference or meeting often requires direct quotes. Whether you use a recording device or not, be sure to take proficient notes you can use while writing your story.

of us cannot read our own handwriting at times — a nuisance, particularly when a proper name is involved.

Taking notes is most crucial when you wish to record direct quotes. As you learned in Chapter 4, putting someone's words in quotation marks means only one thing: You are quoting the person word for word, exactly as the person spoke. Speeches, news conferences and meetings all demand that you be able to record direct quotes. Your stories will be lifeless and lack credibility without them. A speech story, for example, should contain many direct quotes.

Whether covering a speech, news conference or meeting, be careful to quote people in context. For example, if a speaker gives supportive evidence for an argument, you would be unfair not to report it. Quotes can be misleading if you carelessly or deliberately juxtapose them. Combining quotes with no indication that something was said in between them can lead to inaccuracies and to charges of unfairness. Suppose, for example, someone said:

> "Cutting down fuel costs can be an easy thing. If you have easy access to wood, you should invest in a good wood-burning stove. With little effort, you can cut your fuel bills in half."

A reporter who omitted the middle sentence of that quote would make the speaker look ridiculous:

> "Cutting down fuel costs can be an easy thing. With little effort, you can cut your fuel bills in half."

There is more to a speaker than the words he or she is saying. Sometimes, quoting a speaker at length or printing a speech in its entirety may be justified. But when you quote a whole speech, you are recording it, not reporting it. The overall content of the speech may or may not be news. Sometimes the news may be what a speaker left unsaid. You must decide what is newsworthy.

Describing the Participants

In addition to listening to what a speaker says, you must watch for other things. A recording misses a speaker's facial expressions and gestures. These are sometimes more important than the words themselves.

For example, you may have heard the story of how Soviet Premier Nikita Khrushchev pounded the table with his shoe in the U.N. General Assembly on Sept. 20, 1960. But you probably are unsure about what he was saying or what he was protesting. Similarly, you may remember from your American history class the setting of President Franklin D. Roosevelt's fireside chats, but you probably don't remember the content.

Simply reporting the words of a speaker (or of the person holding a news conference or participating at a meeting) does not indicate volume and tone of voice, inflections, pauses, emphases and reactions to and from those in attendance. You may note that a speaker very deliberately winked while reading a sentence. Or you may notice an unmistakable sarcasm in the speaker's voice.

Regardless of who the speaker is or where the speech is taking place, you always must note the speaker's background. A person's words often must be measured against that individual's background. For example, if an ex-Communist is speaking on communism, this fact may have a bearing on what is said. If a former CIA agent speaks about corruption in the CIA, the message would not be adequately reported if the person's background were not mentioned.

Sometimes purely physical facts about the speaker are essential to the story. A blind person pleading for funds to educate the blind, a one-armed veteran speaking about the hell of war, a gray-haired person speaking about care for the elderly — these speakers must be described physically for the story to be complete, accurate and understandable.

You also should note what the person who introduces a speaker says. This may help you understand the significance of the speaker and the importance of what he or she has to say.

Covering the Event

Keep an eye on the audience and on what's happening around the edges. You need to measure the mood of the audience by noting the tone of the questions. Are they sharply worded? Is there much laughter or applause? Perhaps members of the audience boo. Does the speaker or the person holding the news conference or the person presiding over the meeting remain calm and in control? Is there casual bantering or joking with the audience? Is the audience stacked with supporters or detractors?

Sometimes the real action takes place outside in the form of a picket line or protest. Sometimes police manage to keep protesters away from the site. Sometimes who is *not* there is news.

Don't overlook the obvious. For example, you should note the size of the audience. Reporting a "full house" means little unless you indicate the house capacity. One way to estimate attendance is to count how many people are sitting in a row or in a typical section. Then you simply multiply that number by the number of rows or sections in the hall. Use good judgment and common sense to adjust for some sections being more crowded than others.

TIPS: Covering the event

- Be sure to note what the recorder misses — gestures and facial expressions.
- Remember that a person's words often must be measured against his or her background.
- Take note of the tone of questions.
- Note the size of the audience.

Arriving, Positioning Yourself and Staying On

Most reporters arrive early. At some events they have special seating, but you should probably not count on it unless you know for sure.

At a speech, sitting in the first row is not necessarily the best thing to do. Perhaps you should be in a location that lets you see the reaction of the audience. If there is a question-and-answer period, you may want to be able to see the questioner. And you certainly want to be in a good position to ask questions yourself.

At a news conference, your location may help you get the attention of the person holding the conference. You should have your questions prepared, but preparing them is not enough. You have seen presidential news conferences on television, and you know how difficult it is to get the president's attention. Any news conference presents the reporter with the same difficulties, though on a

Speeches, News Conferences and Meetings

After receiving a master's in journalism, Barry Murov worked as an associate editor of a Washington, D.C., newsletter, where he covered federal job programs. Then after working for the *St. Louis Business Journal* for six years, first as a reporter, then as managing editor, Murov became editor of *St. Louis* magazine. Now he's employed by Fleishman-Hillard Inc., an international public-relations firm.

Murov has written and edited dozens of stories covering speeches, meetings and news conferences. Here are some tips he has for you:

"Always ask for a copy of the speech ahead of time," Murov says. "Even when you are lucky enough to get a copy, don't assume that the speaker will stick to the text."

As a consultant for Fortune 500 corporations, Murov knows that "many executives tend to tinker with their speeches, even making significant changes, up until the final minute."

Murov says you should follow along in the text to note where the actual presentation differs. "You don't want your story to include a statement from the text that the speaker deleted. Also, you may find the real news nugget buried in the speech."

Don't leave a meeting or news conference immediately. "Go up to the spokesperson or the leader of the meeting and ask a question that hasn't been covered during the actual event.

"That can benefit in two ways: One, you will have something extra for your readers. Two, it helps you build a relationship with the spokesperson that may pay off in the future."

TIPS: Five ways to master the meeting story

- Arrive early.
- Prepare your questions.
- Listen to others' questions.
- Pursue what is newsworthy.
- Don't rush off. Some of the best stories happen afterward.

smaller scale. You have seen how difficult it is for reporters to follow up on their own questions. At some news conferences you will not be called on twice.

But you must do more than try to get your own questions answered. You must listen to others' questions and be able to recognize the making of a good story. Too often a good question is dropped without follow-up because reporters are not listening carefully or are too intent on pursuing their own questions. Listen for what is newsworthy and pursue it. Sticking with an important subject will make the job of writing the story easier. Remember, when the news conference is finished, you will have a story to write. Piecing together notes on dozens of unrelated topics can be difficult, if not impossible.

At a meeting you should be able to see and hear the main participants. Ordinarily, a board or council will sit facing the audience. Before the meeting starts, you should know which members are sitting where. You may want to assign each participant a number so you do not have to write the person's name each time he or she speaks. You also can draw a sketch of where members are sitting. In this way you will be able to quote someone by number and if necessary find out his or her name later. Know who the officers are. The president or the secretary may distribute handouts before the meeting. After a meeting, the secretary may be able to help you fill in missing words or information.

As a general rule, when the speech, news conference or meeting is over, do not rush off (unless you are on deadline). Hang around. Some of the best stories happen afterward. You should have some questions to ask. You may want some clarifications, or you may arrange to interview a key spokesperson. Listen for reactions from those in attendance.

STRUCTURING AND WRITING YOUR STORY

Writing the lead for the speech, news conference or meeting story is no different from writing the lead for any other story. All of the qualities of the lead discussed in Chapter 7 are important here as well.

You must be careful not to emphasize something about the event that is of great interest or curiosity but that does not lead into the rest of your story. It is tempting, for example, to lead with a striking quote. But rarely does a speaker or someone holding a news conference highlight the content or the main point in a single, quotable sentence. As always, there are exceptions. As a lead for one of Dr. Martin Luther King Jr.'s most famous addresses, a good reporter might have begun with "I have a dream."

Because of the nature of the inverted pyramid news story, rarely should you follow the chronology of the event you are covering. But the flow of your story may demand some attention to chronology. If you pay no attention to chronology, you may distort, or cause readers to misinterpret, the meaning of the event.

Writing the Speech Story

Although you may not soon be called upon to cover the speeches of well-known politicians, you can learn a lot from the way the pros handle important political addresses. These speeches can be long and complex, such as President George W. Bush's call for democracy in the Middle East on Nov. 7, 2003. Let's study how Charlene Gubash of NBC covered the speech for the Web site MSNBC.com:

CAIRO, Egypt — President Bush's speech about the need for democracy in the Middle East was met with a mixture of rare praise and skepticism here Thursday.

While commentators condemned the U.S. leader for again, in their view, ignoring Israel's occupation of Palestinian territory, some hailed his remarks as "historic." In fact, analysts and commentators who are usually outraged over the U.S. administration's policy in the region found themselves in agreement on many points.

The president made a plea for democratic reforms in the Middle East the cornerstone of a speech dealing with democratic values across the globe.

And he acknowledged shortcomings in past policy, saying the United States and other nations shared blame for the lack of democratic freedoms in the Middle East.

"Sixty years of Western nations excusing and accommodating the lack of freedom in the Middle East did nothing to

Figure 12.2
Speech stories, such as one about George W. Bush's call for democracy in the Middle East, incorporate the same elements as other stories.

make us safe because in the long run stability cannot be purchased at the expense of liberty," Bush said.

The president spoke to the National Endowment for Democracy, a group that champions democratic gains around the world, on the same day that he was signing an $87.5 billion package approved by Congress for military and reconstruction operations in Iraq and Afghanistan.

U.S. wars in those two Islamic countries, notably to oust Saddam Hussein in Iraq, have served to seriously damage America's reputation across the Arab world. And what's seen as Washington's bias toward Israel in the conflict with the Palestinians has undermined its credibility in the Middle East.

Consequently words of praise were unexpected.

Notice how Gubash used that last paragraph to put the story into context for her readers. Doing just that is essential in almost any speech story. Also note the focus on the reactions of those who heard it:

"It is an historical speech, and I agree with what the president had to say, and this is the first time," said Hafez Abu Se'da, head of the Egyptian Organization for Human Rights.

"It is a new vision from the United States now because they focus on democracy. For a long time, they focused on economy and commercial interests. It is historical because the United States is talking about democracy and the interest of the people in these countries."

The human rights advocate also praised what Bush had to say about democracy's being compatible with Islam and Arab culture.

"I agree with him. Always we hear from the governments of this region saying our culture is not ready for democracy, that we have our own type of democracy. This is not true. Democracy is democracy, freedom is freedom. . . .

Islam is compatible with democracy and is not against democracy," Abu Se'da said.

But Abu Se'da said that just as the area needs democracy and justice, the United States has an important role to play by solving the Israeli-Palestinian problem in a just way. . . .

You also need to get reactions, and you may want to put them in a story separate from the account of the speech itself. Reaction stories often accompany stories about presidential speeches.

Writing the News Conference Story

Writing the news conference story may be a bit more challenging than writing the speech story. Because you will come to the conference with different questions in mind than your fellow reporters, you may come away with a different story. At least your lead may be different from the leads of other reporters.

A news conference often covers a gamut of topics. Often it begins with a statement from the person who called the conference.

For example, when the mayor of Springfield holds a news conference to announce her candidacy for a second term, you can be sure that she will begin with a statement to that effect. Although her candidacy might be news to some people, you may want to ask her questions about the location of a new landfill that the city is rumored to be planning. Most citizens will admit the need for landfills, but their location is always controversial. And then there's that tip you heard about the possibility of the city manager's resigning to take a job in a large city.

Other reporters will come with other questions. Will there be further cuts in the city budget? Will the cuts mean that some city employees will lose their jobs? What happened to the plans to expand the city jail?

After you come away from a news conference that covered many topics, you have the job of organizing the material in some logical, coherent order. Usually you will treat the most newsworthy subject first and deal with the other subjects in the order of their importance. Rarely would you report on them in the chronological order in which they were discussed.

Suppose you decided the location of the landfill was the most important item of the news conference — especially if the mayor revealed the location for the first time. You may begin your story this way:

The city will construct its new landfill near the intersection of State Route 53 and Route E, four miles north of Springfield, Mayor Juanita Williams said today.

"After nearly a year of discussion and the best advice we could obtain, we are certain the Route E location is best for all concerned," Williams said at a news conference.

The mayor admitted there would be continued opposition to the site by citizens living in the general area, especially those in the Valley High Trailer Court. "No location will please everyone," Williams said.

Williams called the news conference to make the expected announcement of her candidacy for a second term.

Now you have to find a way to treat the other topics of the conference. You may want to list them first in a series of bullets:

In other matters, Williams said:
- City Manager Diane Lusby will not be resigning to take another post.
- Budget constraints will not permit any new construction on the city jail this year.

- Budget cuts will not cost any city employees their jobs. However, positions vacated by retiring personnel will not be filled.

After this list, you will either come back to your lead, giving more background and citing citizens or other city officials on the subject, or go on to treat, one at a time, the matters you listed. Pay particular attention to making proper transitions from paragraph to paragraph so your story is coherent. "On other subjects, the mayor said . . . ," "The mayor defended her position on . . . ," "Again she stressed. . . ."

If one of the subjects is of special interest, you may want to write a sidebar, a shorter piece to go with your main story. For this story, you may want to do a sidebar on the mayor's candidacy, her record, her possible opponents and the like.

With a longer or more complicated story, you may want to make a summary list of all the main topics covered and place them in a box or sidebar.

Remember, your job is to give readers the news, as simply and clearly as possible. Remember, too, to cover the event as well as the content. Perhaps only three reporters turned up for the news conference, or perhaps some pickets protested the mayor's remarks about a local abortion clinic. Sometimes what happens at a news conference is more newsworthy than anything the person holding the conference says. What happens there might well be the lead of your main story, or you may want to place it in a sidebar.

Writing the Meeting Story

Readers also want you to take their place at the meeting you are covering. Let's look at a simple meeting story — in this case a meeting of a local school board:

The decision of three national corporations to protest a formula used to compute their property taxes is causing more than $264,000 to be withheld from the Walnut School District's operating budget for the 2002–2003 school year.

Superintendent Max Schmidt said at Monday's school board meeting that International Business Machines Corp., ACR Corp. and Xerox are protesting that the method used in computing their 2001 property taxes was no longer valid. Nine California counties are involved in similar disputes.

The taxes, totaling $264,688, are being held in escrow by the county until the matter is resolved. Some or all of the money eventually may be returned to the district, but the administration cannot determine when or how much.

"If we take a quarter million dollars out of our program at this time, it could have a devastating effect," Schmidt said. "Once you've built that money into your budget and you lost it, you've lost a major source of income."

Mike Harper, the county prosecuting attorney, and Larry Woods, the school district attorney, advised board members to take a "wait-and-see attitude," Schmidt said. He said that one alternative would be to challenge the corporations in court. A final decision will be made later.

The board also delayed action on repayment of $80,000 to IBM in a separate tax dispute. The corporation claims the district owes it for overpaid 1999 property taxes. The county commission has ruled the claim is legitimate and must be repaid.

A possible source of additional income, however, could be House Bill 1002, Schmidt said. If passed, this appropriations bill would provide an additional $46 million for state education, approximately $250,000 of which could go to the Walnut School District.

Charles Campbell, the district architect, said plans for the area's new vocational technical school to be built on the Rock Bridge High School campus will be given to contractors in February. Bids will be presented at the March 15 board meeting.

The board voted to have classes on Presidents Day, Feb. 15, to make up for time missed because of the teachers' strike.

The issue of the meeting was money problems — a subject that concerns every taxpayer. The writer jumped right into the subject in the lead and then in the second paragraph gave us the who, when and where. The reporter then dealt with specifics, naming names and citing figures, and quoted the key person at the meeting. In the last two paragraphs the writer dealt with other matters discussed in the meeting.

The issues discussed at a meeting are not your only considerations in covering a meeting story. Remember, too, to cover the event. Who was there? Who represented the public? Did anyone have reactions after the meeting was over?

One reporter began her meeting story in this way:

Even though they are footing the bill, only one of Boone County's residents cared enough to attend a Tuesday night hearing on the county's 2004 budget.

With an audience of one citizen plus two reporters, County Auditor June Pitchford presented her official report on the $21 million budget to the Boone County Commission in a silent City Council chamber.

Even when covering routine, boring events, you are allowed to use your imagination. In addition to getting all the facts, your job is also to be interesting, to get people to read the story. Remember, one of the criteria of news is that it be unusual. Another is that it be interesting.

Finally, you are always expected to write well — even for a common event like a speech, news conference or meeting.

Suggested Readings

Biography and Genealogy Master Index. Detroit, Mich.: Gale Research Co., 1981 to present. A compilation of a large number of biographical directories with names of people whose biographies have been written. Indicates which date and volume of those reference books to consult for the actual biography.

Biography Index. Bronx, N.Y.: H. W. Wilson Co., 1946 to present. Helps you locate biographical articles that have appeared in 2,000 periodicals and journals, as well as in biographical books and chapters from collective biographies.

Current Biography. Bronx, N.Y.: H. W. Wilson Co., 1940 to present. Monthly publication about people in the news, including a photo of each. Excellent source for people not yet or perhaps never included in more formal biographical sources.

Suggested Web Sites

www.pbs.org/greatspeeches/
This site claims it is "one of the most comprehensive on-line collections of speech texts of contemporary American history." It also gives the backgrounds of many famous speakers and their speeches and puts them in their historical context. Some speeches have audio and video links.

www.rcameron.com/journalism/citycouncil
This Web site takes you step by step through the process of covering a city council meeting.

Exercises

1. Journalist Sam Donaldson is coming to town to speak on the current U.S. president's relationship with the press. Prepare to cover the speech. Record the steps you will take to prepare for the speech and the information you have gathered on Donaldson.

2. You learn that actor Robert Redford is holding a news conference before speaking to a local group about environmental issues. You also learn that Redford is personally and actively involved in these issues. Using appropriate databanks, gather and record background information on Redford.

3. Find out when the faculty council or similar faculty representative group is having its next meeting. Record the steps you take to prepare for the meeting and the information you gather as you prepare. Then cover the meeting and write the story.

4. The following speech by Vincente Fox, president of Mexico, took place at the Camino Real Sumiya Hotel in Cuernavaca, Mexico, on June 25, 2003. He was addressing a meeting of officials discussing local development and community capacity building. Write a speech story that concentrates on the content of Fox's speech.

   Good morning. Welcome. What a pleasure it is to be with all of you. Thank you, John, director of Employment, Labor and Social Affairs, for inviting me to participate at this seminar. Thank you for holding it here in Mexico and here, in this wonderful spot, in the state of Morelos, in this beautiful city of Cuernavaca.

   Sergio, thank you, Governor, for once more inviting us to this state; this state where it can be said that today the rule of law has returned, where today security is sound, that kidnappings have practically fallen to zero, when in the past the state came to be known more for that than anything else.

The countryside is working without conflicts, working productively and growing. Likewise tourism: This city is a tourism destination that receives many visitors who today come to enjoy not only its natural beauties and climate, but its security.

The rule of law and security are the launchpad for any development process, national, global or local, so congratulations, Governor, and thank you for the invitation.

Friends:

Welcome to Mexico. I thank our Organization and especially the Local Economic and Employment Development Program for the opportunity to address you.

Congratulations to Carlos Flores, now our ambassador to the OECD. I know that he is going to do a great job because he has been a great public servant.

Well, undoubtedly one of the main challenges facing humankind is how to promote development, how to eliminate poverty, how better to distribute income. Above all, facing these challenges requires determination and will; it requires a joint effort and teamwork to bring about sustained and sustainable economic growth; but at the same time, growth with a human face, growth with equity.

In Mexico we have learned our lesson, we know all about this; we have learned that the fight for economic stability starts with an unbending and strict fiscal discipline. It is the only way to have healthy growth. Since some time ago we saw that authoritarian policies, populist policies led us to major disasters. We have not only learned in this struggle, but we have already won some important battles.

In these two and a half years we have maintained a policy, based on a solid and unbending fiscal discipline, that has brought us great stability and has protected — and this is the most important thing — the incomes of people and families, and has protected their assets.

For the first time we are enjoying inflation rates that are coming into line with those of leading economies; for the first time we are enjoying interest rates — the lowest in our history — that are coming into line with the economies we compete with.

We have the highest reserves in our history — more than $53 billion — and the foreign debt is falling each year, currently standing at a level of $76 billion. Our reserves to debt ratio is one of the best in the world. We also have a free economy; Mexico's economy is one of the most open in the world, and, undoubtedly, it has the largest number of free trade agreements.

Mexico has built a network of free trade agreements with 32 countries, and the most important of these agreements are with the world's largest markets, as is the case of NAFTA, with North America; the agreement with the European Union; the agreement we are going to sign with Japan next September; and other agreements we have with South and Central America.

This has today put Mexico in ninth place in the world in terms of the size of its economy, and seventh place in terms of the size of the balance of trade. Mexico has a balance of trade worth more than $350 billion, allowing us to buy more from many countries, allowing us to sell more to many countries.

I often remind the United States that we are not only neighbors, that we share a long border crossed every day by more than a million citizens, more than a million. We are also friends, long-standing friends, as countries and as governments; but today we are partners, and we are partners because, among other things, Mexico buys more goods and services from the United States than it buys from France, Germany, Italy, Spain and England put together. We are a real trading partner of the United States.

Over these three years stability has enabled us to do many things: to mobilize domestic savings, public and private savings for investment, and to boost productive investments, especially on the level of the citizen and communities.

Because if in the year 2000 30 percent of Mexican citizens were bankable — in other words, had a savings account or access to commercial banking — today, through the new system of social banking and micro loans and agricultural and financial cooperatives, we are ensuring 100 percent of citizens have direct access, in their communities, to financing for productive projects or for consumption, or have access to savings, to generate their own savings.

And this is how, little by little, we have been able to improve the quality of life in communities and for people thanks to which we can strengthen the domestic market; because Mexico moved its economy, over the last 10 years, in globalization, precisely through that network of trade agreements, because today those leading economies and those markets are in recession, are stagnating.

We have given the priorities in our economic strategy a major new turn: one, from outside to inside. Now we are strengthening our domestic economy, the domestic market, and strengthening the capacities of communities and families.

And the other new turn, similarly, from large to small, to that wonderful world of micro, small, and medium-sized enterprises.

In this regard, we have transformed our financial system and we have transformed the work of government and the productive apparatus.

It is surprising to see that things have changed in the last two years. For example, we realize today that the country's large companies made 800,000 workers redundant; 800,000 families who lost their incomes in those enterprises of more than 5,000 workers.

But enterprises with less than five workers generated one and a half million new jobs, formal or informal, but one and a half million new jobs all the same.

To some extent we are exchanging workers or jobs for entrepreneurs, thanks to that extension of the financial system on the local level.

Also today, thanks to stability and low inflation rates, Mexico's workers — after continuously losing purchasing power for 25 years — over these last two years have seen a 12 percent real-terms growth in their purchasing power, thanks to the formula of low inflation and better wage rises.

In social policies, we have concentrated and focused efforts on the lowest-income families, communities or municipalities. Today in Mexico, more than 20 million Mexican men and women, one in five of every Mexican men and women, are receiving direct economic support, focused, in their own name, so that that family has enough for nutrition and food, for health and for education. That program is called Opportunities and covers 4.24 million families each month in our country. And it is already bearing fruit because secondary education attendance rates among these families in country areas are growing by 25 percent a year; and attendance rates, for example, at university, through the National Scholarships and Financing System, grew from 19 percent of young people in 2000 to 22.2 percent currently in university. So we are boosting the formation of human capital to be able to promote the development of the local economy.

We are undeniably waging an all-out war against poverty in Mexico. This is an aspiration of any government: reducing poverty, the number of poor families, and distributing income better.

In these two years we have made progress in this area. In the last income-spending survey we see that the number of families in extreme poverty in Mexico fell by 16 percent, although there has not been the economic growth they would like.

And so the number of families, according to the World Bank and the United Nations measurement unit of a dollar a day, in Mexico in the year 2000 9 percent of families or people had an income of less than one dollar a day, 9 percent; in the year 2002 this figure is 6 percent, of families with an income lower than one dollar, remaining in Mexico.

Here I would like to acknowledge not only the social policies that the three tiers of government have followed, but also our beloved compatriots, those Mexican men and women who left for the United States seeking opportunities, and who have made the most of them.

Now, in the year 2002, they sent more than $10 billion to Mexico in small transfers to their families.

Undoubtedly that was a major factor in the fight against poverty here in Mexico, but there is another one: The cost of those transfers, on average between $100 and $200 and that had a cost of just over $15 per transfer, has been cut; it now costs $5 per transfer.

By having to pay less to the banks, lower transfer cost rates, there are important savings for families and people.

So this situation has allowed us to ensure that income is better distributed now in Mexico, because in the year 2000 we had a ratio of the lowest-income decile, the 10 percent of families with the lowest incomes, to the 10 percent of families with the highest incomes, a ratio of one to 25, 25 times more, now it is one, a ratio of one to 21, only 21 times is the difference between the highest-income decile and the lowest-income decile in Mexico.

So sustained progress is built in an atmosphere of intense competition, conducive to innovation and constant improvement; sustained progress is built with better planned regulations capable of liberating society's energies; sustained progress is constructed in an atmosphere of certainty that enables long-term planning.

Development is constructed through investment in education, health and nutrition, and progress is constructed through macroeconomic stability.

Without personal effort, without initiative and entrepreneurial capacity in communities and municipalities, together with local development, we would not be seeing what we have been able to see in these last two years.

Only determined local, national and global actions will allow us to promote sustained and sustainable economic growth; an environment of freedoms is essential to allow people to fully use their talents and capacities to the benefit of themselves and their communities.

Development is a shared responsibility. Solid development, over the long haul, needs policies like those we have mentioned, policies that promote local employment, that boost alliances of public and private investment, that generate growth from the bottom up, local and regional progress that can be consolidated through international cooperation.

We OECD countries have been benefiting for years from the many studies, seminars, conferences, exchanges of successful experiences that this organization has fostered. Therefore, Mexico is highly satisfied apart from being proud to belong to this organization. The rich exchange of ideas allows us to reflect upon and learn from the most successful public policy practices for our countries.

In particular, Mexico's participation in the Local Economic and Employment Development Program has especially helped us to identify and analyze and put into practice new ideas for local development.

These have been linked to the strengthening of communities; job creation through the promotion of micro, small and medium-sized enterprises.

As the only Latin American member of the OECD, Mexico wants these successful experiences to be shared by our brothers in the continent, in Latin America. So Mexico proposes, as has already been mentioned, that during this important meeting the suitability be analyzed of creating a Latin American Local Development Center, which could have its headquarters here, in the state of Morelos, already

home to important teaching and research centers and a large academic community.

We are more than ready, and make a public commitment to providing whatever contribution we should make to materialize this idea for the benefit of all Latin America.

Through this center, Mexico would reinforce its capacity as a nation for encounters, and would link our organization and cooperation with the countries of the rest of Latin America.

With your support, a Latin American Local Development Center would contribute enormously to the analysis and assessment of different local development strategies in our region and to the design of new and more effective tools to promote it.

I am certain that at this meeting many and very important strategies for local development in Latin America will be analyzed, which we will study very closely, implementing those that we feel can assist us in the task we are already undertaking.

Be assured, all of you, that I sincerely hope the work to be done over these three days is successful. And now, with your permission, I would like to ask you to stand while I formally declare this Seminar opened:

Today, on the 25th of June of the year 2003, in the city of Cuernavaca, Morelos, I declare the OECD's Local Economic and Employment Development Program's meeting on New Local Development Strategies for Latin America formally opened.

Thank you very much. I wish you every success. Congratulations!

5. Prepare for, cover and write:

a. A speech story.
b. A news conference story.
c. A meeting story.

Then compare your stories to those appearing in the local paper.

13 Other Types of Basic Stories

W hen major crimes occur in a community, interest is high among readers and viewers. That gives reporters a chance to deliver compelling accounts of what happened. Consider this example from Leonora Bohn Peter of the *Savannah* (Ga.) *Morning News:*

Tap. Tap. Tap. Tap. Pause. Tap. Tap. Tap.

Ashley Lewis hit the counter of the oak witness box with his index finger, mimicking what he heard through a crack in the bathroom window the night of Dec. 4, 1997, as he got ready for bed.

It sounded like a typewriter. But Lewis, testifying on the first day in the death penalty trial of Jerry Scott Heidler for the murder of a family in Santa Claus a year and a half ago, found it hard to believe his mother, a secretary, would break out her typewriter at almost 2 a.m. Just a half hour before, she had told him to turn the television off and go to bed.

Lewis walked to his mother's room and turned on the light. She was asleep in bed. He walked through the house, turning on other lights. Nothing.

"I got this real eerie feeling," Lewis said.

Lewis did not know it yet, but a half-mile away, four of his neighbors lay dead.

Three hours later, Toombs County Sheriff's Department Deputy Mike Harlin arrived at the doorstep of the Daniels family on Dasher Lane in Santa Claus. Just about every light in the one-story brick house was on. He thought that was odd for 5:10 a.m.

He knocked on the front door, which was slightly ajar. No answer. Through a window to the left, he noticed the arm of a small child in a bunk bed by the window.

He walked in and announced he was there. He heard a baby crying and a radio playing music. He walked toward the room with the child in it. On the top bunk, he found what was left of 8-year-old Bryant Daniels, who had been shot through the eye.

"I have a small boy myself," Harlin said, swallowing hard as he recalled the image on the witness stand Monday afternoon. "At that point, it was pretty obvious that words wouldn't help."

Harlin moved through the house, running into 4-year-old Corey Daniels near the dining room table. Harlin knelt down beside the child.

"Mama and Daddy are dead. Brother Guy shot them all," Corey said.

A baby continued to cry. The radio, obviously an alarm for early rising postal worker Danny Daniels, continued to play music.

Harlin opened the door of the master bedroom. The first thing he noticed was the gun cabinet with several empty slots where guns had been. Next he noticed a body up against the door, preventing him from opening it further. Corey showed him another entrance to the room, through a laundry room and a bathroom.

Harlin walked into the sunken bedroom and found 10-month-old Gabriel standing between his baby bed and his parents' king-sized bed, hanging onto the sheets. Beneath the sheet lay Kim Daniels, 33, who had been shot in the head. Danny Daniels, 47, also was dead on the bed. And a third body, that of 16-year-old Jessica Daniels, lay over by the door....

That interesting account won the Jesse Laventhol Prize for Deadline Reporting. Stories about crime, accidents, fires and court proceedings are often assigned to beginning reporters. Newspapers, magazines and Web sites record major events in the life of a community, and those events often call for such stories. Such stories also are the staple of a local news report on television. As a result, it's likely that as a beginning reporter you will have a chance to cover them. This chapter will help you prepare to do just that.

YOUR PREPARATION

When writing an account of a crime, an accident, a fire or a court proceeding, begin as you do any other story — with a check in the morgue. There you'll find background on the subject of an obituary. Or you'll learn whether a similar crime has occurred before, whether accidents are common at the location of the latest one, whether similar fires have occurred suspiciously often or whether a person charged with a crime has been in trouble before.

Preparing for the Crime Story

Meetings, news conferences, speeches and court proceedings usually are scheduled events, so on most occasions you should have ample time beforehand to do background research on the individual or topic to be covered. Obituaries also call for a first stop in the broadcast station or newspaper library, but crime reporting may be different. If the police radio reports a murder in your area, you may be dispatched to the scene as the story is breaking. At that point, no one will know who is involved or what happened. There will be no time to check the library, and you will have to do your initial reporting at the scene.

Most information about crimes comes from three sources:

- Police officials and their reports.
- The victim or victims.
- The witness or witnesses.

The circumstances of the crime may determine which of the three is most important, which should be checked first or whether they should be checked at all. If the victim is available, as a reporter you should make every effort to get an interview. But if the victim and witnesses are unavailable, the police and their report become primary sources.

When your editor assigns you to a crime story is important. If you are dispatched to the scene of the crime as it happens or soon afterward, you probably will interview the victim and witnesses first. The police report will have to wait; probably, it isn't even ready. But if you are assigned to write about a crime that occurred the night before, the police report is your starting point.

A police officer investigating a crime covers much of the same ground as you. The officer is interested in who was involved, what happened, when, where, why and how. Those details are needed to complete the official report of the incident, and you need them for your story. When you write about crime, always check the police report. It is often the source of basic information such as:

- A description of what happened.
- The location of the incident.
- The name, age and address of the victim.
- The name, age and address of the suspect, if any.
- The offense police believe the suspect has committed.
- The extent of injuries, if any.
- The names, ages and addresses of witnesses, if any.

The reporter who arrives at the scene of a crime as it takes place or immediately afterward has the advantage of being able to gather much of that information firsthand. When timely coverage is impossible, however, the police report allows the reporter to catch up quickly. The names of those with knowledge of the incident usually appear on the report, and the reporter uses that information to learn the story. See Figure 13.1 for an example of a police report.

Reporters sometimes write crime stories from the police report alone. For routine stories, some editors view such reporting as sufficient. Good newspapers, however, demand more because police reports frequently are inaccurate. Most experienced reporters have read reports in which the names of those involved are misspelled, ages are wrongly stated and other basic information is inaccurate. Sometimes such errors are a result of sloppy reporting by the investigating officer or mistakes in transcribing notes into a formal report. Occasionally, the officer may lie in an attempt to cover up shortcomings in the investigation or misconduct at the scene of the crime. Whatever the reason, good reporters do their own reporting and do not depend solely on a police officer's account. Remember that good editors frown on single-source stories of any kind. It's your job to do solid reporting, and you are expected to consult multiple sources.

Robert Snyder, a former history professor at Princeton University, studied U.S. crime reporting while a research fellow at the Gannett Center for Media Studies in New York. He was alarmed by what he found. Crime stories, he discovered, still rely heavily on one police source. That, Snyder insists, is a dangerous and seemingly irresponsible practice. One of journalism's founding principles is that a story's credibility is built on the number of sources used.

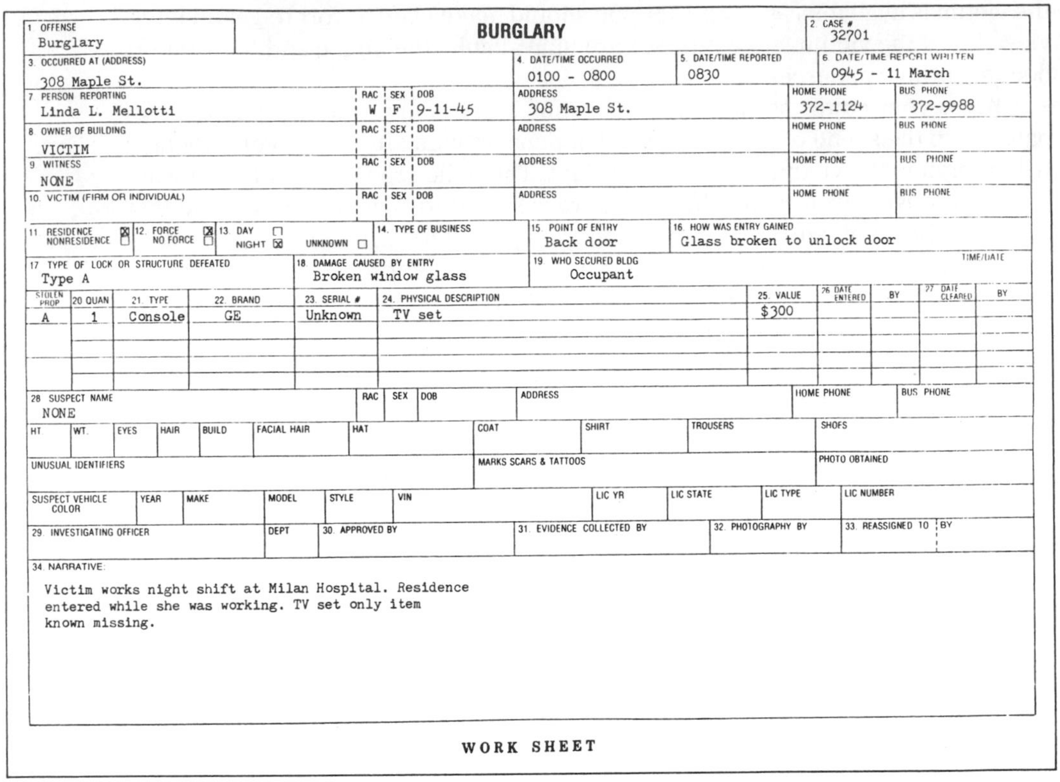

BURGLARY

1 OFFENSE: Burglary
2 CASE #: 32701
3 OCCURRED AT (ADDRESS): 308 Maple St.
4 DATE/TIME OCCURRED: 0100 - 0800
5 DATE/TIME REPORTED: 0830
6 DATE/TIME REPORT WRITTEN: 0945 - 11 March

	RAC	SEX	DOB	ADDRESS	HOME PHONE	BUS PHONE
7 PERSON REPORTING: Linda L. Mellotti	W	F	9-11-45	308 Maple St.	372-1124	372-9988
8 OWNER OF BUILDING: VICTIM						
9 WITNESS: NONE						
10 VICTIM (FIRM OR INDIVIDUAL)						

11 RESIDENCE ☒ NONRESIDENCE ☐ 12 FORCE ☒ NO FORCE ☐ 13 DAY ☐ NIGHT ☒ UNKNOWN ☐ 14 TYPE OF BUSINESS
15 POINT OF ENTRY: Back door
16 HOW WAS ENTRY GAINED: Glass broken to unlock door
17 TYPE OF LOCK OR STRUCTURE DEFEATED: Type A
18 DAMAGE CAUSED BY ENTRY: Broken window glass
19 WHO SECURED BLDG: Occupant
TIME/DATE

STOLEN PROP	20 QUAN	21 TYPE	22 BRAND	23 SERIAL #	24 PHYSICAL DESCRIPTION	25 VALUE	26 DATE ENTERED	BY	27 DATE CLEARED	BY
A	1	Console	GE	Unknown	TV set	$300				

28 SUSPECT NAME: NONE | RAC | SEX | DOB | ADDRESS | HOME PHONE | BUS PHONE
HT | WT | EYES | HAIR | BUILD | FACIAL HAIR | HAT | COAT | SHIRT | TROUSERS | SHOES
UNUSUAL IDENTIFIERS | MARKS SCARS & TATTOOS | PHOTO OBTAINED
SUSPECT VEHICLE COLOR | YEAR | MAKE | MODEL | STYLE | VIN | LIC YR | LIC STATE | LIC TYPE | LIC NUMBER
29 INVESTIGATING OFFICER | DEPT | 30 APPROVED BY | 31 EVIDENCE COLLECTED BY | 32 PHOTOGRAPHY BY | 33 REASSIGNED TO | BY

34 NARRATIVE:
Victim works night shift at Milan Hospital. Residence entered while she was working. TV set only item known missing.

WORK SHEET

Figure 13.1
This burglary report is typical of the type of report available to reporters at most police stations.

For crime stories, the background check in the morgue often is done after you return to the office. Once you have the names of those involved, for example, you can see whether the morgue reveals relevant material about them. Was the suspect arrested before? Was the store robbed before? The morgue might help answer those kinds of questions.

Preparing for Accident and Fire Stories

If you are assigned to cover an accident or fire, you can expect some of the same problems you'd encounter if covering a crime. Much depends on whether the police or fire report (see Figure 13.2) is available before or after you are assigned to the story.

If the accident or fire took place overnight, the report prepared by officials is the place to start. It will give you most of the basic information you need. It also will lead you to other sources.

If you are sent to the scene of an accident or fire, your job is to collect much of that information yourself. As for crimes, the basic information you'll need includes:

DATE | TIME | ADDRESS

PAGE OF

CASUALTY REPORT

FD-500

CHANGE 2 ☐
DELETE 3 ☐ (74)

INCIDENT NO.	EXP
8 0 9 0 5 1 3	

NAME (LAST, FIRST MIDDLE)	AGE	Time of Injury	MONTH	DAY	YEAR
SANDOZA MANUEL R	32	0945	02	08	96

HOME ADDRESS: 307 Banning Ave., Apt. 3
TELEPHONE: 555-9088

46 SEX: 1 ☒ Male; 2 ☐ Female
47 CASUALTY TYPE: 1 ☒ Fire Casualty; 2 ☐ Action Casualty; 3 ☐ EMS Casualty
48 SEVERITY: 1 ☒ Injury; 2 ☐ Death
49 AFFILIATION: 1 ☐ Fire Service; 2 ☐ Other Emergency Personnel; 3 ☒ Civilian

FAMILIARITY WITH STRUCTURE	LOCATION AT IGNITION	CONDITION BEFORE INJURY
Occupant (50)	Unknown (51)	Unknown (52)
CONDITION PREVENTING ESCAPE	**ACTIVITY AT TIME OF INJURY**	**CAUSE OF INJURY**
N/A (53)	Leaving building (54)	Falling debris (55)
NATURE OF INJURY	**PART OF BODY INJURED**	**DISPOSITION**
Broken leg (56)	Leg (57)	Hospitalized (58)

REMARKS: Occupant was leaving burning structure when burning eave fell and struck his leg.

By #31 Ambulance to General Hospital

NAME (LAST, FIRST MIDDLE)	AGE	Time of Injury	MONTH	DAY	YEAR

HOME ADDRESS
TELEPHONE

46 SEX: 1 ☐ Male; 2 ☐ Female
47 CASUALTY TYPE: 1 ☐ Fire Casualty; 2 ☐ Action Casualty; 3 ☐ EMS Casualty
48 SEVERITY: 1 ☐ Injury; 2 ☐ Death
49 AFFILIATION: 1 ☐ Fire Service; 2 ☐ Other Emergency Personnel; 3 ☐ Civilian

FAMILIARITY WITH STRUCTURE	LOCATION AT IGNITION	CONDITION BEFORE INJURY
(50)	(51)	(52)
CONDITION PREVENTING ESCAPE	**ACTIVITY AT TIME OF INJURY**	**CAUSE OF INJURY**
(53)	(54)	(55)
NATURE OF INJURY	**PART OF BODY INJURED**	**DISPOSITION**
(56)	(57)	(58)

REMARKS:

By Ambulance to Hospital

Nelson Riley
Supervisor*
*Injury reports for fire personnel, Immediate supervisor to sign here.

SIGNATURE of person completing form/DATE
John R. Sanders

Printed in U.S.A.

Figure 13.2
This casualty report is typical of those available to reporters at most fire stations.

- A description of what happened.
- The location of the incident.
- The name, age and address of the victim or victims.
- The extent of injuries, if any.
- The names, ages and addresses of witnesses, if any.

TIPS: What to do at the scene of an accident

- Question the person in charge of the investigation.
- Try to find and interview witnesses.
- Try to find friends or relatives of the victims.
- If possible, interview the victims.
- Talk with others at the scene.
- Be sensitive to victims and their families.

Preparing for the Court Story

Most court stories you are likely to cover will be follow-ups to earlier stories. If a murder suspect is appearing for a preliminary hearing, details of the crime probably were reported earlier, and a check of the morgue may give you ample background information as you prepare for your visit to the courtroom. Otherwise, a chat with the district attorney, the police chief or one of their assistants might provide ample background for writing the story.

Court stories often are difficult for beginners to write because they are unlikely to understand the complex process used in criminal prosecutions. In addition, there are civil court proceedings, lawsuits that charge an individual or company with harming another. Here's our best advice on how to approach court stories: Ask plenty of questions of the judge and attorneys before or after the court proceeding or during recesses. It's much better to admit your lack of knowledge about the court process than to make a serious error in print because you didn't understand what was happening.

WRITING THE STORY

Knowing how to organize stories about crime, accidents, fires and court proceedings is essential. It helps to have a model, and the examples that follow are designed to assist you.

The Crime Story

There is no magic formula for writing crime news. Solid reporting techniques pay off just as they do in other types of reporting; then it is a matter of writing the story as the facts demand. Sometimes the events are most effectively told in chronological order, particularly when the story is complex. More often, a traditional inverted pyramid style works best. The amount of time the reporter has to file the story also influences the approach. Let's take a look at how the newspaper accounts of two crimes were developed over time and why different writing styles seemed appropriate for each.

Gathering facts from the many sources available and sorting through conflicting information can be time-consuming tasks. Sometimes the reporter may have to write the story before all the facts are gathered. The result is a barebones account written to meet a deadline. Such circumstances often lead to crime stories written like this:

A Highway Patrol marksman shot and killed a Kansas man in a rural area south of Springfield this morning after the victim threatened to blow off the head of his apparent hostage. A hitchhiker reportedly told police earlier this morning that his "ride" had plans to rob a service station on Interstate 70. That tip apparently followed an earlier report of a van leaving a station at the Millersburg exit of I-70 without paying for gasoline.

An ensuing hour-long chase ended at 9:30 a.m. in an isolated meadow in the Pierpont area when Capt. N.E. Tinnin fired a single shot into the stomach of the suspect, identified as Jim Phipps of Kansas City, Kan.

Phipps, armed with a sawed-off shotgun, and his "hostage," identified as Anthony Curtis Lilly, 17, also of Kansas City, Kan., eluded police by fleeing into a rugged, wooded area at the end of Bennett Lane, a dead-end gravel road off Route 163.

Tinnin said he fired the shot with a .253-caliber sniper rifle when it appeared Phipps was going to shoot Lilly. Two troopers' efforts to persuade Phipps to throw down his weapon and surrender were unsuccessful, Tinnin said.

Notice that even in that bare-bones account, the available facts of the story dictated a chronological approach after a summary lead.

The reporter who produced that story for an afternoon newspaper did a good job of collecting information after a puzzling incident. Still, several words and phrases (the apparent hostage, a hitchhiker reportedly told police, a tip apparently followed) provide tip-offs that the series of events was not entirely clear.

With more time to learn the full story, a reporter for the city's morning newspaper resolved many of those conflicts. As a result, readers got a more complete account of what occurred:

James Phipps and Anthony Lilly, a pair of 17-year-olds from Kansas City, Kan., were heading west on Interstate 70 at 7:30 a.m. Friday, returning from a trip to Arkansas.

Within the next hour and a half, Phipps had used a sawed-off shotgun stolen in Arkansas to take Lilly hostage, and, after holding that shotgun to Lilly's head, was shot and killed by a Highway Patrol captain on the edge of a rugged wooded area south of Springfield.

As the episode ended, local officials had only begun to piece together a bizarre tragedy that involved a high-speed chase, airplane and helicopter surveillance, a march through a wooded ravine and the evacuation of several frightened citizens from their country homes.

As police reconstructed the incident, Phipps and Lilly decided to stop for gas at the Millersburg exit east of Springfield at about 7:30 a.m. With them in the van was Robert Paul Hudson Jr., a San Francisco-bound hitchhiker.

Hudson was not present at the shooting. He had fled Lilly's van at the Millersburg exit after he suspected trouble.

The trouble began when Lilly and Phipps openly plotted to steal some gasoline at Millersburg, Hudson told police. He said the pair had agreed to display the shotgun if trouble arose with station attendants.

Hudson said he persuaded Phipps to drop him off before they stopped for gas. He then caught a ride to Springfield and told his driver of the robbery plans he had overheard. After dropping Hudson off near the Providence Road exit, the driver called Springfield police, who picked up Hudson.

Meanwhile, Phipps and Lilly put $8.90 worth of gas in the van and drove off without paying. The station attendant notified authorities.

As he approached Springfield, Phipps turned onto U.S. 63 South, where he was spotted by Highway Patrol troopers Tom Halford and Greg Overfelt. They began a high-speed chase, which ended on a dead-end gravel road near Pierpont.

During the chase, which included a U-turn near Ashland, Phipps bumped the Highway Patrol car twice, forcing Halford to run into the highway's median.

Upon reaching the dead end, the suspects abandoned the van and ran into a nearby barn. At that point, Phipps, who Highway Patrol officers said was wanted in Kansas for escaping from a detention center, turned the shotgun on Lilly.

When Halford and Overfelt tried to talk with Phipps from outside the barn, they were met with obscenities. Phipps threatened to "blow (Lilly's) head off," and vowed not to be captured alive.

Phipps then left the barn and walked into a wooded area, pressing the gun against Lilly's head. Halford and Overfelt followed at a safe distance but were close enough to speak with Phipps.

While other officers from the Highway Patrol, the Lincoln County Sheriff's Department and Springfield police arrived at the scene, residents in the area were warned to evacuate their homes. A Highway Patrol plane and helicopter flew low over the woods, following the suspects and the troopers through the woods.

The four walked through a deep and densely wooded ravine. Upon seeing a partially constructed house in a nearby clearing, Phipps demanded of officers waiting in the clearing that his van be driven around to the house, at which time he would release his hostage. Halford said, "They disappeared up over the ridge. I heard some shouting (Phipps' demands), and then I heard the shot."

After entering the clearing from the woods, Phipps apparently had been briefly confused by the officers on either side of him and had lowered his gun for a moment.

That was long enough for Highway Patrol Capt. N.E. Tinnin to shoot Phipps in the abdomen with a high-powered rifle. It was about 8:45 a.m. Phipps was taken to Boone County Hospital, where he soon died.

The story is as complete as possible under the circumstances. The reporter who wrote it decided to describe the chain of events in chronological order because of the complexity of the story and because the drama of the actual events is most vividly communicated in a chronological narrative.

The story is also made effective by its wealth of detail, including the names of the troopers involved, details of the chase and much, much more. The reporter had to talk with many witnesses to piece together this account. The hard work paid off, however, in the form of an informative, readable story. Notice how the third paragraph sets the scene and provides a transition into the chronological account. Such attention to the details of good writing helps the reader understand the story with a minimum of effort.

If a number of people witnessed or were affected by a crime, you may supplement the main story with a sidebar that deals with the personal impact of the crime. The writer of the preceding chronological account also decided to write a separate story on nearby residents, who had little to add to the main story but became a part of the situation nonetheless:

In the grass at the edge of a woods near Pierpont Friday afternoon, the only remaining signs of James Phipps were a six-inch circle of blood, a doctor's syringe, a blood-stained button and the imprints in the mud where Phipps fell after he was shot by a Highway Patrol officer. Elsewhere in the area, it was a quiet, sunny, spring day in a countryside dotted by farms and houses. But inside some of those houses, dwellers still were shaken by the morning's events that had forced a police order for them to evacuate their homes.

Mrs. James G. Thorne lives on Cheavens Road across the clearing from where Phipps was shot. Mrs. Thorne had not heard the evacuation notice, so when she saw area officers crouching with guns at the end of her driveway, she decided to investigate.

"I was the surprise they weren't expecting," she told a Highway Patrol officer Friday afternoon. "I walked out just before the excitement."

When the officers saw Mrs. Thorne "they were obviously very upset and shouted for me to get out of here," she said. "I was here alone and asked them how I was supposed to leave. All they said was, 'Just get out of here!'"

Down the road, Clarence Stallman had been warned of the situation by officers and noticed the circling airplane and helicopter. "I said, 'Are they headed this way soon?' and they said, 'They're here,'" said Stallman.

After Stallman notified his neighbors, he picked up Mrs. Thorne at her home and left the area just before the shooting.

On the next street over, Ronald Nichols had no intention of running.

"I didn't know what was happening," Nichols said. "The wife was scared to death and didn't know what to do. I grabbed my gun and looked for them."

Another neighbor, Mrs. Charles Emmons, first was alerted by the sound of the surveillance plane. "The plane was flying so low I thought it was going to come into the house," she said. "I was frightened. This is something you think will never happen to you."

Then Mrs. Emmons flashed a relieved smile. "It's been quite a morning," she said.

The techniques of writing in chronological order and separating the accounts of witnesses from the main story worked well in the preceding case. More often, however, crime stories are written in the classic inverted pyramid style because of time and space considerations:

A masked robber took $1,056 from a clerk at Gibson's Liquor Store Friday night, then eluded police in a chase through nearby alleys.

The clerk, Robert Simpson, 42, of 206 Fourth St. said a man wearing a red ski mask entered the store at about 7:35 p.m. The man displayed a pistol and demanded that Simpson empty the contents of the cash register into a brown grocery bag.

Simpson obeyed but managed to trigger a silent alarm button under the counter.

The robber ordered Simpson into a storage room in the rear of the building at 411 Fourth St.

Officer J.O. Holton, responding to the alarm, arrived at the store as the suspect left the building and fled south on foot.

Holton chased the man south on Fourth Street until he turned west into an alley near the corner of Olson Street. Holton said he followed the suspect for about four blocks until he lost sight of him.

Simpson said receipts showed that $1,056 was missing from the cash register. He described the robber as about 5 feet 11 inches with a bandage on his right thumb. He was wearing blue jeans and a black leather coat.

Police have no suspects.

Such an account is adequate, and you can write it directly from the police report. That, of course, would be a single-source story. So a good reporter would add to the story by taking time to interview the clerk and police officer.

After filing this story for the first edition, the reporter found time to call the police officer. He had little to add. Then the reporter contacted the clerk, who had plenty to say. This was the result:

"I'm tired of being robbed, and I'm afraid of being shot," says Robert Simpson. "So I told the owner I quit."

Simpson, 42, of 206 Fourth St. quit his job as night clerk at Gibson's Liquor Store today after being robbed for the fourth time in three weeks Friday night.

Simpson said a man wearing a red ski mask entered the store at 411 Fourth St. at about 7:35 p.m. and demanded money. Simpson emptied $1,056 into a grocery bag the robber carried and was ordered into a storage room at the rear of the building.

"He said he'd blow off my head if I didn't cooperate, so I did exactly what he told me," Simpson said. "But I managed to set off the alarm button under the counter while I was emptying the cash register."

Officer J.O. Holton responded to the alarm and arrived as the robber left the store but lost him as he fled through nearby alleys on foot.

"We keep asking the cops to set up a stakeout, but they don't do anything," Simpson said. "I know they've got a lot of problems, but that place is always getting hit."

Police records revealed that Gibson's was robbed of $502 Sept. 10, $732 Sept. 14 and $221 Sept. 24. Simpson was the clerk each time.

"This may have been the same guy who robbed me last time," Simpson said, "but I can't be sure because of that mask. Last time he had a different one."

Police Chief Ralph Marshall said he has ordered patrol cars to check the vicinity of the liquor store more often and is considering the owner's request for a stakeout.

"That's just great," Simpson said. "But they can let someone else be the goat. I quit."

Simpson described the robber as a heavy man about 5 feet 11 inches tall. He was wearing blue jeans and a black leather jacket and had a bandage on his right thumb.

Police have no suspects.

The reporter took the time to get a good interview, and the direct quotes add to the appeal of the story. The reporter also recognized and brought out the best angle: the personal fear and frustration experienced by people in high-crime areas. The result is a much more imaginative use of the basic inverted pyramid formula and a much more interesting story.

The clerk, in the course of his remarks, supplied an important tip about repeated robberies at the store. Two weeks later, police arrested a man as he tried to rob the store. The earlier report was used for background, and a complete story resulted.

Accident and Fire Stories

When you are assigned to cover an accident or a fire, many of the facts and all of the color are gathered at the scene. If the accident has just taken place, a visit to the scene is essential. Being there will give you the best picture of what happened, and you will be able to write a solid story. Too many reporters cover accidents and fires as purely passive observers. Indeed, you must observe. But you must also actively solicit information from those who are present. Many of them, including those directly involved, you may never be able to find again.

When dispatched to the scene of an accident, move as quickly as possible to collect this information:

Disasters Don't Just Disappear

A year and a half after leaving journalism school, Lisa Arthur found herself covering the rebuilding of South Dade County for *The Miami Herald*. Hurricane

Andrew had struck the area on Aug. 24, 1992, and the trail of destruction was still visible 18 months later.

The experience taught Arthur that some of the most important stories in disaster reporting come months after the initial crisis.

"When I arrived, there were still hundreds of people living in trailers, and pockets of the landscape still resembled a bombed-out Beirut," she says. "People were still suffering a great psychological trauma, and they looked to the local media to deliver the message that all was not well yet. They still needed help even though the memory of the hurricane had begun to fade for people not directly affected."

Arthur has this advice for reporters covering the long-term aftermath of any disaster. First,

focus on the ordinary people and the small battles they are fighting to get their homes and lives repaired. There are still people in South Dade today who are living in trailers because contractors ripped them off or they didn't have insurance. This is fertile ground for stories that are important and can sometimes make a difference. Second, follow the money trail. Tens of millions of federal dollars flow into devastated areas. Track the money and see whether it trickles down to the people who need it. Third, look for heroes. Arthur stumbled upon a Pittsburgh philanthropist who had been quietly pumping millions of recovery dollars into South Dade. His deeds went unnoticed for two years. Arthur's story about him wound up on the front page of the *Herald*.

- The names, ages, addresses and conditions of the victims.
- Accounts of witnesses or police reconstructions of what happened.
- When the accident occurred.
- Where it occurred.
- Why or how it happened or who was at fault, as determined by officials in charge of the investigation.

If that list sounds familiar, it should. You could simplify it to read "who, what, when, where and why." As in any news story, that information is essential. You must gather it as quickly as possible after being assigned to the story. Just as important is knowing what to do when you arrive on the scene. These suggestions will help:

- *Question the person in charge of the investigation.* This individual will attempt to gather much of the same information you want. A police officer, for example, needs to know who was involved, what happened, when it happened and who was at fault. If you are able to establish a good relationship with the investigator, you may be able to secure much of the information you need from this one source, though single-source stories are usually inadequate.

Remember that the spellings of names, addresses and similar facts must be verified later. Any veteran reporter can tell you that police officers and other public officials are notoriously bad spellers and often make errors in recording the names of victims. To avoid such errors, call relatives of the victims or consult the city directory, telephone book or other sources to check your information.

- *Try to find and interview witnesses.* Police and other investigators may lead you directly to the best witnesses. The most accurate account of what happened usually comes from witnesses, and the investigators will try to find them. You should, too. A good way to do that is to watch the investigators. Listen in as they interview a witness, or corner the witness after they are finished. If there is time, of course, try to find your own witnesses. You cannot and should not always rely on investigators to do your work for you.

- *Try to find friends or relatives of the victims.* These sources are helpful in piecing together information about the victims. Through them you often get tips about even better stories.

- *If possible, interview the victims.* Survivors of an accident may be badly shaken, but if they are able to talk, they can provide firsthand details that an official report never could. Make every attempt to interview those involved.

- *Talk with others at the scene.* If someone died at the scene of the accident, an ambulance paramedic or the medical examiner may be able to give you some indication of what caused the death. At the least you can learn where the bodies or the injured will be taken. That may help, because later the mortician or hospital officials may be able to provide information you need for your story.

- *Be sensitive to victims and their families.* You have a job to do, and you must do it. That does not mean, however, that you can be insensitive to those involved in an accident.

Of course, your deadline will have a major impact on the amount of information you are able to gather. If you must meet a deadline soon after arriving at the scene, you probably will be forced to stick to the basics of who, what, when, where, why and how. Thus it is important to gather that information first. Then, if you have time, you can concentrate on more detailed and vivid information to make the story highly readable.

The following account of a tractor-trailer accident was produced in a race against the clock by the staff of an afternoon newspaper:

TIPS: Source checklist for accidents, fires and disasters

- Civilian witnesses.
- Victims of personal injury, if they are able to be interviewed.
- People who were involved but escaped injury.
- Victims of property damage, including property owners, tenants and employees.
- Neighbors and passersby.
- Relatives and neighbors of victims.
- Rescue workers (firefighters, police, EMS workers, hospital personnel, etc.).
- Government regulatory agencies (local, state and federal).

A truck driver was killed and a woman was injured this morning when a tractor-trailer believed to be hauling gasoline overturned and exploded on Interstate 70, turning the highway into a conflagration.

Both lanes of I-70 were backed up for miles after an eastbound car glanced off a pickup truck, hurdled the concrete median and collided with a tanker truck heading west.

The explosion was immediate, witnesses said. Residents along Texas Avenue reported the initial fireball reached the north side of the street, which is about 300 yards from the scene of the accident. A wooded area was scorched, but no houses were damaged.

Police evacuated the 600 block of Texas Avenue for fear that the fire would spread, but residents were returning to their homes at 12:35 p.m., about an hour after the collision. Authorities also unsuccessfully attempted to hold back the onlookers who gravitated to a nearby shopping center parking lot to view the blaze.

Police did not identify the driver of the truck, which was owned by a Tulsa, Okla., firm named Transport Delivery Co.

"Apparently it was gasoline," said Steve Paulsell, chief of the County Fire Protection District. "That's what it smelled like." Other officials reported the truck may have been hauling fuel oil or diesel fuel.

For an afternoon newspaper with an early afternoon deadline, such a story presents major problems, particularly when it occurs, as this one did, at about 11:30 a.m. Four reporters were dispatched to the scene; all of them called in information to a writer back at the office. There was little time to interview eyewitnesses. Because of the pressing deadline, the reporters were forced to gather most of their information from fire and police officials at the scene.

Writers for the morning newspaper, by comparison, had plenty of time to gather rich detail to tell the story in human terms. Much of the breaking news value was diminished by the next morning because of intense coverage by the afternoon newspaper, radio and television. It was time to tell the story of a hero:

Witnesses credited an off-duty firefighter with saving a woman's life Monday following a spectacular four-vehicle collision on Interstate 70 just east of its intersection with Business Loop 70.

The driver of a gasoline truck involved in the fiery crash was not so lucky. Bill Borgmeyer, 62, of Jefferson City died in the cab of his rig, which jackknifed, overturned and exploded in flames when he swerved in a futile attempt to avoid hitting a car driven by Leta Hanes, 33, of Nelson, Mo.

Mrs. Hanes, who was thrown from her auto by the impact, was lying unconscious within 10 feet of the blazing fuel when firefighter Richard Walden arrived at the crash scene.

"I knew what was going on," Walden recalled, "and I knew I had to get her away from there." Despite the intense heat, Walden dragged the woman to safety.

"She had some scrapes, a cut on her knee and was beat around a little bit," Walden said. "Other than that, she was fine."

Mrs. Hanes was taken to Boone Hospital Center, where she was reported in satisfactory condition Monday night.

Smoke billowing from the accident scene reportedly was visible 30 miles away. Westbound interstate traffic was backed up as far as five miles. Several city streets became snarled for several hours when traffic was diverted to Business Loop 70. The eastbound lane of I-70 was reopened about 2 p.m.; the westbound lane was not reopened until 3 p.m. . . .

"The news is no longer the news. . . . It's all about luridness. Body bags will be seen at 7, chasing ambulance at 8, victim's family at 9."

— Oliver Stone,
film director

The richness of detail in the second account and the eyewitness descriptions of what happened make the story more interesting. The importance of adding such detail is apparent.

Accidents and fires present similar problems for the reporter, but at a fire of any size you can expect more confusion than at the scene of an accident. One

Figure 13.3
Hazards at the scene of a disaster, such as this fire resulting from a Los Angeles–area earthquake, can make a reporter's job difficult and dangerous.

major difference, then, is that the officer in charge will be busier. At the scene of an accident the damage has been done and the authorities usually are free to concentrate on their investigation. At a fire the officer in charge is busy directing firefighters and probably will be unable to talk with you. The investigation will not even begin until the fire is extinguished. In many cases the cause of the fire will not be known for hours, days or weeks. In fact, it may never be known. Seldom is that the case in an accident, except perhaps for air accidents.

Another problem is that you may not have access to the immediate area of the fire (see Figure 13.3). Barriers often are erected to keep the public — and representatives of the news media — from coming too close to a burning structure. The obvious reason is safety, but such barriers may hamper your reporting. You may not be able to come close enough to firefighters to learn about the problems they are having or to obtain the quotes you need to improve your story.

These problems usually make covering a fire more difficult than covering an accident. Despite the difficulties, you cover a fire in much the same way, interviewing officials and witnesses at the scene. You also should try to interview the property owner. Moreover, because the official investigation will not have begun, you must conduct your own. When covering any fire, you must learn:

- The location of the fire.
- The names, ages and addresses of those killed, injured or missing.
- The name of the building owner or, in the case of a grass fire or forest fire, the landowner.
- The value of the building and its contents or the value of the land.
- Whether the building and contents were insured for fire damage. (Open land seldom is.)

- When the fire started, who reported it and how many firefighters and pieces of equipment were called to the scene.
- What caused the fire, if known.

As in any story, the basics are who, what, when, where, why and how. But the nature of the fire will raise other questions that must be answered. Of primary importance is whether life is endangered. If it is not, the amount of property damage becomes the major emphasis of the story. Was arson involved? Was the building insured for its full value? Was there an earlier fire at the same location? Did the building comply with fire codes? Were any rare or extremely valuable objects inside? Did any explosives inside complicate fighting the fire and pose an even greater threat than the fire itself?

Your job is to answer these questions for the readers or viewers. You will be able to obtain some of that information later on from official fire reports if they are ready before your story deadline (see Figure 13.2). But most information will come from interviews that you conduct at the scene with the best available sources. Finding your sources may not be easy, but you can begin by looking for the highest-ranking fire official. Large departments may have a designated press officer whose job is to deal with you and other reporters.

Another important source is the fire marshal, whose job is to determine the cause of the fire and, if arson is involved, to bring charges against the arsonist. You should make every effort to talk with the fire marshal at the scene, if he or she is available. In most cases, though, the marshal will be the primary source of a second-day story.

As in covering any **spot news story** — a story in which news is breaking quickly — deadlines will determine how much you can do at the scene of a fire. If your deadline is hours away, you can concentrate on the event and the people connected with it. You will have time to find the little boy whose puppy was killed in the fire or interview the firefighter who first entered the building. But if you have only minutes until your deadline, you may have to press the fire official in charge for as much information as possible. You may have to coax from that person every tidbit, even making a nuisance of yourself to gather the information you need. Through it all, you can expect confusion. There is little order to be found in the chaos of a fire.

The Court Story

Throughout complicated court proceedings (see Figure 13.4), a reporter has numerous opportunities to write stories. The extent to which the reporter does so depends on the importance of the case and the amount of local interest in it. In a major case the filing of every motion may prompt a story; in other cases only the verdict may be important. As in any type of reporting, news value is the determining factor.

Also, as in any form of reporting, accuracy is important. Perhaps no other area of writing requires as much caution as the reporting of crime and court news. The potential for libel is great.

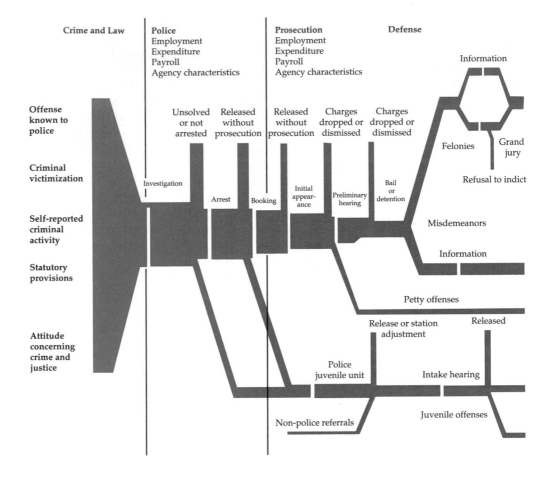

Figure 13.4

This chart shows how cases proceed through the U.S. criminal justice system.

Many courts handle both civil and criminal cases. Media coverage often focuses on criminal cases, although civil actions — lawsuits involving disputes of one type or another — often provide excellent sources of stories.

Libel is damage to a person's reputation caused by a written statement that brings the person into hatred, contempt or ridicule, or that injures a person's business or occupational pursuits (see Chapter 9). Reporters must be extremely careful about what they write. One of the greatest dangers is the possibility of writing that someone is charged with a crime more serious than is the case. After checking clippings in the newspaper library, for example, one reporter wrote:

The rape trial of John L. Duncan, 25, of 3925 Oak St. has been set for Dec. 10 in Jefferson County Circuit Court.

Duncan is charged in connection with the June 6 rape of a Melton High School girl near Fletcher Park.

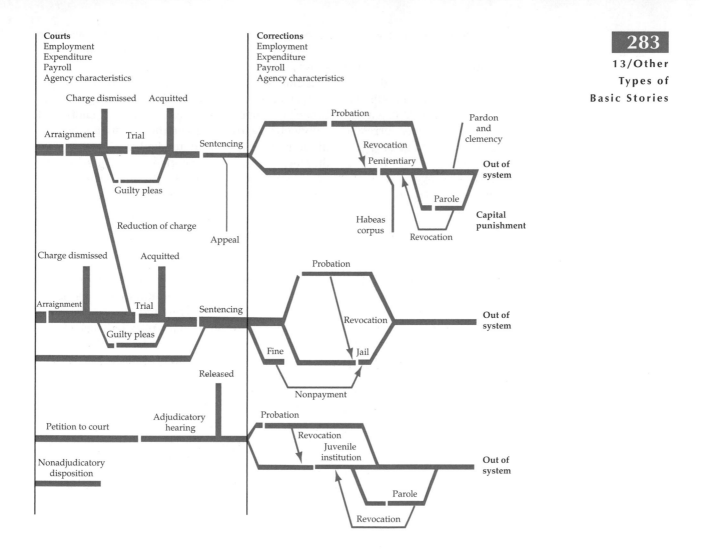

Duncan had been charged with rape following his arrest. However, the prosecutor later determined the evidence was insufficient to win a rape conviction, the charge was reduced to assault and the newspaper had to print a correction.

Any story involving arrests should raise caution flags. You must have a working knowledge of libel law and what you can and cannot write about an incident. Any reporter who would write the following, for example, is asking for trouble:

```
John R. Milton, 35, of 206 East St. was arrested Monday on a
charge of assaulting a police officer.
```

Only a prosecutor, not a police officer, may file charges. In many cases, a police officer may arrest a person with the intent of asking the prosecutor to file a certain charge, but when the prosecutor examines the evidence, the evidence may warrant only a lesser charge. For that reason, most newspaper editors prefer to print the name of an arrested person only after the charge has been filed.

Unfortunately, deadline constraints sometimes make that impossible, and many newspapers publish the names of those arrested before the charge is filed. A decision to publish a name in such circumstances requires extreme caution. If an individual were arrested in connection with a rape and the newspaper printed that information, only to learn later that the prosecutor had filed a charge of assault, a libel suit could result. Many states, however, give journalists a **qualified privilege** to write fair and accurate news stories based on police reports. Once the charge is filed, the lead should be written like this:

```
John R. Milton, 35, of 206 East St. was charged Monday with
assaulting a police officer. Prosecutor Steve Rodriguez
said. . . .
```

By writing the lead this way, the reporter shows that Milton not only was arrested but also was charged with a crime by the prosecutor. Carelessness leads not only to libel suits but also to attacks on a suspect's reputation.

Reporters who cover court news encounter many such pitfalls. They are not trained as attorneys, and it takes time to develop a working knowledge of legal proceedings. The only recourse is to ask as many questions as necessary when a point of law is not clear. It is far better to display ignorance of the law and ask questions than to commit a serious error that harms the reputation of the accused and opens the newspaper to costly libel litigation.

However, it is also important to know that anything said in open court is fair game for reporters. If, in an opening statement, a prosecutor says the defendant is "nothing but scum, a smut peddler bent on polluting the mind of every child in the city," then by all means report the comment in context in your story. But if a spectator makes that same statement in the hallway during a recess, you probably would not report it. Courts do not extend the qualified privilege to report court proceedings beyond the context of the official proceeding.

With the preceding points in mind, let's trace a criminal case from the time of arrest through the trial to show how a newspaper might report each step. Here is a typical first story:

An unemployed carpenter was arrested today and charged with the Aug. 6 murder of Springfield resident Anne Compton.

Lester L. Rivers, 32, of 209 E. Dillow Lane was charged with first-degree murder, Prosecuting Attorney Mel Singleton said.

Chief of Detectives E.L. Hall said Rivers was arrested on a warrant after a three-month investigation by a team of three detectives. He declined to comment on what led investigators to Rivers.

Compton's body was found in the Peabody River by two fishermen on the morning of Aug. 7. She had been beaten to death with a blunt instrument, according to Dr. Ronald R. Miller, the county medical examiner.

That straightforward account of the arrest was filed on deadline. Later the reporter would interview neighbors about Rivers' personality and write an im-

Lessons of the Police Beat

When the *San Diego Tribune* expanded its zoned editions in 1985, the paper hired journalism graduate James Grimaldi to cover El Cajon, Calif. His goal was to go from the suburbs to the city desk.

"The fastest way to the front page was police stories," Grimaldi says.

One Sunday, the El Cajon police discovered a quadruple homicide. Grimaldi volunteered to cover the story. By the end of the day, he had scored an exclusive jailhouse interview with the killer. Within six months, Grimaldi was promoted to police reporter.

He combed through hundreds of police reports looking for trend stories while covering internal policies of the San Diego Police Department. At that time, the force was wracked by a high officer death rate and embarrassed by a sensational, racially divisive trial of a black man acquitted of shooting to death a white police officer in what he said was self-defense.

Once, as coroners removed a charred body from a San Diego Dumpster, Grimaldi was on the scene. He later was the first to report that the death was probably the work of a serial killer. He wrote about police corruption,

including the chief's use of city-owned video equipment to tape a TV show on bass fishing.

"There's no better way to learn how to report and write than covering crime," Grimaldi says. "It is the quickest way to explore any community. There's humor and pathos, politics and social issues. Every rookie reporter should spend some time covering crime."

From the *Tribune*, Grimaldi went to *The Orange County Register* in 1989 as a general-assignment reporter. Crime stories taught Grimaldi reporting techniques he used for an investigation of medical deaths, rapes and drug-dealing at the California Institution for Women in Frontera. The Frontera stories won numerous national prizes.

In 1994, Grimaldi was named the *Register*'s bureau chief in Washington. Now at *The Washington Post*, he still relies on the reporting foundation first built on the police beat.

proved story for other editions. This bare-bones story, however, provides a glimpse of several key points in covering arrest stories. Notice that the reporter carefully chose the words "arrested and charged with" rather than "arrested for," a phrase that may carry a connotation of guilt.

Another important element of all crime and court coverage is the tie-back sentence. This sentence relates a story to events covered in a previous story — in this case, the report of the crime itself. It is important to state clearly — and near the beginning of the story — which crime is involved and to provide enough information about it so that the reader recognizes it. Clarification of the crime is important even in major stories with ready identification in the community. This story does that by recounting when and where Compton's body was found and by whom. It also tells that she died after being hit with a blunt instrument.

Court Organization and Procedure

When a suspect is apprehended and charged with a crime, the reporter's job is only beginning. Because the public wants and needs to know whether the suspect is guilty and, if so, what punishment is imposed, the media devote much time and space to court coverage of criminal charges.

At first glance reporting court news appears to be simple. You listen to the judicial proceedings, ask a few questions afterward and write a story. It may be that simple if you have a thorough knowledge of criminal law and court procedure. If you do not, reporting court news can be extremely confusing. No journalism textbook or class can prepare you to deal with all the intricacies of criminal law. That is a subject better suited for law schools. You should learn the basics of law, court organization and procedure, however. With this foundation you will be prepared to cover court proceedings with at least some understanding of what is happening. You can supplement this knowledge by asking questions of the judge and attorneys involved.

Court Organization
In the United States there are two primary court systems: federal and state. Each state has a unique system, but there are many similarities from state to state. The average citizen is most likely to have contact with city or munici-

pal courts, which have jurisdiction over traffic and other minor violations of city ordinances. News from these courts is handled as a matter of record in many newspapers.

Cases involving violations of state statutes usually are handled in the state trial courts that can be found in most counties. These courts of general jurisdiction (often called circuit or superior courts) handle cases ranging from domestic relations matters to murder. "General jurisdiction" is an important designation. It means these courts can and do try more cases, of greater variety, than any other type of court, including federal district (trial) courts. Courts of general jurisdiction handle civil cases, such as contractual disputes, as well as the criminal cases that are the primary focus of news reporters.

Federal district courts have jurisdiction over cases involving violations of federal crime statutes, interpretation of the U.S. Constitution, civil rights, election disputes, commerce and antitrust matters, postal regulations, federal tax laws and similar issues. Federal trial courts also have jurisdiction in actions between citizens of different states when the amount in controversy exceeds $50,000.

Court Procedure
Crimes are categorized under state statutes according to their seriousness. The two primary

categories of crimes are misdemeanors and felonies. Under modern statutes, the distinction between a felony and a misdemeanor turns on whether the offense is punishable by imprisonment in a state prison or in a county jail. Most state statutes describe a misdemeanor as an offense punishable by a fine, a county jail term not to exceed one year, or both. Felonies are punishable by a fine, a prison sentence of more than one year or death.

Pretrial Proceedings in Criminal Cases
A person arrested in connection with a crime usually is taken to a police station for fingerprinting, photographing and perhaps a sobriety test or a lineup. Statements may be taken and used in evidence only if the person arrested has been informed of and waives what police and lawyers call Miranda rights, so named because the requirement was imposed in a U.S. Supreme Court case involving a defendant named Miranda. Those rights include the right to have an attorney (either hired by the defendant or appointed by the court if the defendant is indigent) and the right to remain silent. Usually within 24 hours a charge must be filed or the person must be released. The time limit may vary from state to state, but all states have some limitation to prevent unreasonable detention.

Initial Appearance

If, after consulting with police and reviewing the evidence, the prosecuting (or state or circuit) attorney decides to file charges, the defendant usually is brought before a judge, is informed of the charges and is reminded of the Miranda rights. Bail usually is set at this time. If the charge is a misdemeanor and the defendant pleads guilty, the case usually is disposed of immediately, and a sentence is imposed or a fine is levied. If the plea is not guilty, a trial date usually is set.

If the crime is a felony, the defendant does not enter a plea. The judge sets a date for a preliminary hearing, unless the defendant waives the right to such a hearing. A defendant who waives this hearing is bound over to the general jurisdiction trial court. The process of being bound over means simply that the records of the case will be sent to the trial court.

A preliminary hearing in a felony case usually is held before a magistrate or a lower-level judge in state court systems. The prosecutor presents evidence to try to convince the judge that there is probable cause to believe that a crime has been committed and that the defendant committed it. The defendant has the right to cross-examine the state's witnesses, and the defendant may present evidence, but this normally is not done. Thus, because stories about preliminary hearings often are one-sided, care must be exercised to write a story that is well-balanced.

If the judge does find that there is probable cause, the prosecuting attorney must file what is called an information within a short period of time (usually 10 days) after the judge orders the defendant bound over for trial. This information must be based on the judge's findings of probable cause.

Under most state constitutions, it is possible to bring a person accused in a felony case to trial in one of two ways. One is the preliminary hearing; the other is a grand jury indictment. In federal courts, the U.S. Constitution requires indictment by a grand jury in felony cases.

Grand jury hearings are secret in some states. Jurors are sworn not to reveal information about what takes place in the grand jury room, and potential defendants are not allowed to be present when testimony is given concerning them. The prosecuting attorney presents evidence to the grand jury, which must determine whether there is probable cause to prosecute. The prosecutor acts as adviser to the grand jury.

A grand jury returns a true bill when probable cause is found. A no true bill is returned if no probable cause is found. When a grand jury finds probable cause, an indictment is signed by the grand jury foreperson and the prosecuting attorney. The indictment then is presented in open court to a trial judge.

If the defendant is not already in custody, the judge orders an arrest warrant issued for the accused. Arraignment in the trial court follows. This is the first formal presentation of the information or the indictment to the defendant. The arraignment is conducted in open court, and the defendant enters a plea to the charge. Three pleas — guilty, not guilty, and not guilty by reason of mental disease or defect — are possible.

A process known as plea bargaining sometimes is used at this point. Under this process, a defendant may change a plea from not guilty to guilty in return for a lighter sentence than may be imposed if a jury returns a guilty verdict. Typically, in such circumstances the defendant pleads guilty to a lesser charge than the one outstanding. A defendant charged with premeditated or first-degree murder, for example, may plead guilty to a reduced charge of manslaughter. The prosecutor often is willing to go along with such an arrangement if the time and expense of a trial can be saved and if justice is served.

If a guilty plea is entered, the judge may impose a sentence immediately, or a presentencing investigation of the defendant's background may be ordered to help the judge set punishment.

(continued)

Many jurisdictions require presentencing investigations, at least in felony cases. If sentencing is delayed for that purpose, a sentencing date usually is set to allow ample time for completion of the report.

If a not-guilty plea is entered, the judge sets a trial date. Most jurisdictions have statutes or court rules requiring speedy trials in criminal cases and setting time limits from the date of the charge being filed to the date of the trial.

As the prosecutor and defense attorney prepare for trial, motions may be filed for disclosure of evidence, suppression of evidence and similar rulings. Journalists will have a special interest if a defense attorney files a motion for a change of venue, which allows the trial to be conducted in a county other than the one in which the alleged crime occurred. Requests for venue changes often result from pretrial stories in the local media that may prejudice potential jurors. This was the case when the Los Angeles police officers accused of beating Rodney King were tried in Simi Valley.

The Trial
The trial starts as a jury, usually made up of 12 members and at least one alternate, is selected from a group of citizens called for jury duty. During the selection process (called *voir dire*) the prosecutor and defense attorney question the prospective jurors to identify jurors who each side hopes will be sympathetic to its position. In the federal system the judge often asks questions, but the prosecutor and defense attorneys may suggest questions for the judge to ask potential jurors.

Each attorney is allowed to eliminate a certain number of individuals from consideration as jurors without having to state a reason. Thus, either attorney can dismiss a prospective juror believed to be prejudiced against the attorney's view. Elimination of a prospective juror for cause (if, for example, he or she is related to the accused) also is permitted. An unlimited number of challenges for cause is allowed each attorney.

Once 12 jurors and one or more alternates are chosen and sworn, the prosecutor makes an opening statement. The opening statement outlines how the prosecutor, acting on behalf of the state, expects to prove each of the elements of the crime. The defense attorney may follow with an outline of the defense or may wait until after the prosecution has introduced its evidence. The defense also may waive an opening statement.

To establish what happened and to link the defendant to the crime, witnesses for the state are called to testify. During this procedure the prosecutor asks questions, and the witness responds. The defense attorney then has an opportunity to cross-examine the witness. Frequently, one attorney will object to questions posed by the other, and the judge must rule on the objection. When the defense attorney finishes cross-examination, the prosecutor conducts re-direct examination to try to clarify for the jury points that may have become confused during cross-examination and to bolster the credibility of a witness whose credibility may have been damaged during cross-examination. Then the defense attorney may conduct another cross-examination, and the prosecutor may conduct another re-direct examination. This process can continue until both sides have exhausted all questions they want to ask the witness.

After all the prosecution witnesses have testified and the state rests its case, the defense almost always makes a motion for acquittal, in which it argues that the state has failed to prove its case beyond a reasonable doubt. Almost as routinely as such motions are made, they are denied. A basic tenet of criminal law in the United States is that the prosecution must prove the defendant guilty. The defendant is not required to prove anything or to testify.

The defense then calls witnesses to support its case, and

the prosecutor is allowed to cross-examine them. Finally, when all witnesses have testified, the defense rests. The prosecutor then calls rebuttal witnesses in an attempt to discredit testimony of the defense witnesses. The defense then has the right to present even more witnesses, called surrebuttal witnesses. After the various rebuttal witnesses have testified, the judge presents instructions to the jury — what verdicts the jury can return and points of law that are key to the case. The prosecutor then makes his or her closing argument, usually an impassioned plea for a guilty verdict addressed directly to the jury. The defense attorney's closing argument follows, and the prosecutor is allowed a final rebuttal. In the federal system, closing arguments precede the judge's instructions to the jury. The jury then retires to deliberate.

Because unanimous verdicts are required for acquittal or conviction in a criminal trial, deliberations often are protracted. If the jury fails to reach a unanimous verdict (a hung jury) after a reasonable period of time, the judge may order a mistrial, in which event the entire case will be retried from the beginning of jury selection. If a verdict is reached, the jury returns to the courtroom, where the verdict is read. In some states juries are permitted to recommend sentences when guilty verdicts are reached. Sometimes a second stage of the trial occurs when the jury must decide, for example, whether to recommend life imprisonment or death. But the final decision always is made by the judge unless a crime carries a mandatory sentence. Sentencing may be done immediately, but more likely a presentencing report will be ordered and a sentencing date set.

The defense often files a motion asking that a guilty verdict be set aside. Such motions usually are denied. A motion for a new trial usually brings similar results. However, in most jurisdictions a motion for a new trial and a denial are prerequisites to the filing of an appeal. Appeals often follow guilty verdicts, so a verdict seldom is final in that sense. Except in extreme circumstances involving serious crimes, judges often permit the defendant to be released on bail pending the outcome of appeals.

The following morning the suspect was taken to Magistrate Court for his initial court appearance. Here is a part of the story that resulted:

Lester L. Rivers appeared in Magistrate Court today charged with first-degree murder in connection with the Aug. 6 beating death of Springfield resident Anne Compton.

Judge Howard D. Robbins scheduled a preliminary hearing for Nov. 10 and set bail at $10,000. Robbins assigned Public Defender Ogden Ball to represent Rivers, 32, of 209 E. Dillow Lane.

Rivers said nothing during the 10-minute session as the judge informed him of his right to remain silent and his right to an attorney. Ball asked Robbins to set the bail at a "reasonable amount for a man who is unemployed." Rivers is a carpenter who was fired from his last job in June. Despite the seriousness of the charge, it is essential that Rivers be free to help prepare his defense, Ball said.

Police have said nothing about a possible connection between Rivers and Compton, whose body was found in the Peabody River by two fishermen on the morning of Aug. 7. She had been beaten to death.

The reporter clearly outlined the exact charge and reported on key points of the brief hearing. Again, the link to the crime is important to inform the reader about which murder is involved.

Next came the preliminary hearing, where the first evidence linking the defendant to the crime was revealed:

Lester L. Rivers will be tried in Jefferson County Circuit Court for the Aug. 6 murder of Springfield resident Anne Compton.

Magistrate Judge Howard D. Robbins ruled today that there is probable cause to believe that a crime was committed and probable cause that Rivers did it. Rivers was bound over for trial in Circuit Court.

Rivers, 32, of 209 E. Dillow Lane is being held in Jefferson County Jail. He has been unable to post bail of $10,000.

At today's preliminary hearing, Medical Examiner Ronald R. Miller testified that a tire tool recovered from Rivers' car at the time of his arrest "could have been used in the beating death of Miss Compton." Her body was found floating in the Peabody River Aug. 7.

James L. Mullaney, a lab technician for the FBI crime laboratory in Washington, D.C., testified that "traces of blood on the tire tool matched Miss Compton's blood type."

In reporting such testimony, the reporter was careful to use direct quotes and not to overstate the facts. The medical examiner testified that the tire tool *could have been used* in the murder. If he had said it *had been used*, a stronger lead would have been needed.

Defense attorneys usually use preliminary hearings to learn about the evidence against their clients and do not present any witnesses. This apparently was the motive here because neither the police nor the prosecutor had made a public statement on evidence in the case. They probably were being careful not to release prejudicial information that could be grounds for a new trial.

The prosecutor then filed an *information*, as state law required. The defendant was arraigned in Circuit Court, and the result was a routine story that began as follows:

Circuit Judge John L. Lee refused today to reduce the bail of Lester L. Rivers, who is charged with first-degree murder in the Aug. 6 death of Springfield resident Anne Compton. Rivers pleaded not guilty. Re-

peating a request he made earlier in Magistrate Court, Public Defender Ogden Ball urged that Rivers' bail be reduced from $10,000 so he could be freed to assist in preparing his defense.

The not-guilty plea was expected, so the reporter concentrated on a more interesting aspect of the hearing — the renewed request for reduced bail.

Finally, after a series of motions was reported routinely, the trial began:

Jury selection began today in the first-degree murder trial of Lester L. Rivers, who is charged with the Aug. 6 beating death of Springfield resident Anne Compton.

Public Defender Ogden Ball, Rivers' attorney, and Prosecuting Attorney Mel

Singleton both expect jury selection to be complete by 5 p.m.

The selection process started after court convened at 10 a.m. The only incident occurred just before the lunch break as Singleton was questioning prospective juror Jerome B. Tinker, 33, of Woodland Terrace.

"I went to school with that guy," said Tinker, pointing to Rivers, who was seated in the courtroom. "He wouldn't hurt nobody."

Singleton immediately asked that Tinker be removed from the jury panel, and Circuit Judge John L. Lee agreed.

Rivers smiled as Tinker made his statement, but otherwise sat quietly, occasionally conferring with Ball.

The testimony is about to begin, so the reporter set the stage here, describing the courtroom scene. Jury selection often is routine and becomes newsworthy only in important or interesting cases.

Trial coverage can be tedious, but when the case is interesting, the stories are easy to write. The reporter picks the most interesting testimony for leads as the trial progresses:

A service station owner testified today that Lester L. Rivers offered a ride to Springfield resident Anne Compton less than an hour before she was beaten to death Aug. 6.

Ralph R. Eagle, the station owner, was a witness at the first-degree murder trial of Rivers in Jefferson County Circuit Court.

"I told her I'd call a cab," Eagle testified, "but Rivers offered her a ride to her boyfriend's house." Compton had gone to the service station after her car broke down nearby. Under cross-examination, Public Defender Ogden Ball, Rivers' attorney, questioned whether Rivers was the man who offered the ride.

"If it wasn't him, it was his twin brother," Eagle said.

"Then you're not really sure it was Mr. Rivers, are you?" Ball asked.

"I sure am," Eagle replied.

"You think you're sure, Mr. Eagle, but you really didn't get a good look at him, did you?"

"I sold him some gas and got a good look at him when I took the money."

"But it was night, wasn't it, Mr. Eagle?" Ball asked.

"That place doesn't have the best lighting in the world, but I saw him all right."

The reporter focused on the key testimony of the trial by capturing it in the words of the participants. Good note-taking ability becomes important here, because trial coverage is greatly enhanced with direct quotation of key exchanges. Long exchanges may necessitate the use of the question-and-answer format:

Ball: In fact, a lot of the lights above those gas pumps are out, aren't they, Mr. Eagle?

Eagle: Yes, but I stood right by him.

Q: I have no doubt you thought you saw Mr. Rivers, but there's always the possibility it could have been someone else. Isn't that true?

A: No, it looked just like him.

Q: It appeared to be him, but it may not have been because you really couldn't see him that well, could you?

A: Well, it was kind of dark out there.

Eventually, there is the verdict story, which usually is one of the easiest to write:

Lester L. Rivers was found guilty of first-degree murder today in the Aug. 6 beating death of Springfield resident Anne Compton.

Rivers stood motionless in Jefferson County Circuit Court as the jury foreman returned the verdict. Judge John L. Lee set sentencing for Dec. 10.

Rivers, 32, of 209 E. Dillow Lane could be sentenced to death in the electric chair or life imprisonment in the State Penitentiary.

Public Defender Ogden Ball, Rivers' attorney, said he will appeal.

After the verdict was announced, Mr. and Mrs. Lilborn O. Compton, the victim's parents, were escorted from the courtroom by friends. Both refused to talk with reporters.

Many other types of stories could have been written about such a trial. Lengthy jury deliberations, for example, might prompt stories about the anxiety of the defendant and attorneys and their speculations about the cause of the delay. Covering court news requires care and good reporting. As in any kind of reporting, you must be well-prepared. If you understand the language of the courts and how they are organized, your job is simplified.

Remember that annual crime statistics are a common source of stories. Reporters must take care when reporting them, however, if they involve small numbers. It is dramatic to say, "Murders increased by 300 percent in 1999," but it is misleading if the increase was from one murder to four.

To provide a more accurate picture, reporters can perform the equivalent of adding apples and oranges. "Unlike" items can be added, subtracted, multiplied and divided, if they are grouped in a category that makes them "like" items. For example, you can group murders, rapes, assaults and armed robberies in the category "violent crimes." That way, you can add murders to rapes to assaults to armed robberies. This technique can be useful if an individual category such as murder isn't large enough to provide much insight (as in many small towns). However, the larger category must be logical and meaningful.

OTHER ISSUES IN CRIME AND COURT REPORTING

The Free-Press/Fair-Trial Controversy

Covering the courts is not a simple task. If done poorly, it inevitably leads to criticism for the press, as evidenced by the 1954 murder trial of Dr. Samuel Sheppard in Cleveland. Sheppard was accused of murdering his wife. News coverage in the Cleveland newspapers, which included front-page editorials, was intense. In 1966, the U.S. Supreme Court said the trial judge had not fulfilled his duty to protect the jury from the news coverage that saturated the community and to control disruptive influences in the courtroom.

That case more than any other ignited what is known as the **free-press/fair-trial controversy.** This controversy raged during the O.J. Simpson case in the mid-1990s. On numerous occasions, Judge Lance Ito threatened to end television

Figure 13.5
*Members of the media in Wichita, Kan., photograph evidence that a jury will view
during its deliberation.*

coverage of court proceedings to protect Simpson's rights during his criminal
trial. Lawyers charged that the media ignored the Sixth Amendment right of the
accused to an impartial jury. The media countered with charges that lawyers
ignored the First Amendment.

Editors realize that coverage of a crime can make it difficult to empanel an
impartial jury, but they argue that courts have available many remedies other
than restricting the flow of information. In the Sheppard case, for example, the
Supreme Court justices said a **change of venue,** which moves the trial to a location where publicity is not as intense, could have been ordered. Other remedies
suggested by the court in such cases are to "continue" (delay) the trial, to grant a
new trial or to head off possible outside influences during the trial by sequester-
ing the jury. Editors also argue that acquittals have been won in some of the most
publicized cases in recent years.

Despite the remedies the Supreme Court offered in the Sheppard case, trial
judges continued to be concerned about empaneling impartial juries. Judges
issued hundreds of gag orders in the wake of the Sheppard case. Finally, in 1976,
in the landmark case of Nebraska Press Association vs. Stuart, the Supreme
Court ruled that a **gag order** was an unconstitutional prior restraint that violated
the First Amendment to the Constitution. The justices did not go so far as to rule
that all gag orders are invalid. But in each case, the trial judge has to prove that
an order restraining publication would protect the rights of the accused and
that no other alternatives would be less damaging to First Amendment rights.

"To make inroads into the
mind-set that 'if the press
reported it, it must be true'
is the lawyer's most challenging task."

— Robert Shapiro,
attorney

That ruling, of course, did not end the concerns of trial judges. Rather than issue gag orders restricting the press from reporting court proceedings, some attempted to close their courtrooms. In the first such case to reach the U.S. Supreme Court, Gannett vs. DePasquale, the press and public suffered a severe but temporary blow. On July 2, 1979, in a highly controversial decision, the justices said, "We hold that members of the public have no constitutional right under the Sixth and Fourteenth amendments to attend criminal trials." The case itself had involved only a pretrial hearing.

As a result of the decision and the confusion that followed, the Supreme Court of Virginia sanctioned the closing of an entire criminal trial. The accused was acquitted during the second day of the secret trial. The U.S. Supreme Court agreed to hear the appeal of the trial judge's action in a case known as Richmond Newspapers vs. Virginia. On July 2, 1980, the court said that under the First Amendment "the trial of a criminal case must be open to the public." Only a court finding of an "overriding interest," which was not defined, would be grounds for closing a criminal trial.

In Massachusetts, a judge excluded the public and press from the entire trial of a man accused of raping three teenagers. A Massachusetts law provided for the mandatory closing of trials involving specific sex offenses against minors. The U.S. Supreme Court held in 1982 in Globe Newspaper Co. vs. Superior Court that the mandatory closure law violated the First Amendment right of access to criminal trials established in the Richmond Newspapers case. The justices ruled that when a state attempts to deny the right of access in an effort to inhibit the disclosure of sensitive information, it must show that the denial "is necessitated by a compelling governmental interest." The court indicated in the opinion that in some cases in-camera proceedings (proceedings that take place in a judge's chambers outside the view of the press and public) for youthful witnesses may be appropriate.

In Press-Enterprise vs. Riverside County Superior Court, the U.S. Supreme Court ruled in 1984 that a court order closing the jury-selection process in a rape-murder case was invalid. The court ruled that jury selection has been a public process with exceptions only for good cause. In a second Press-Enterprise vs. Riverside County Superior Court case, the U.S. Supreme Court said in 1986 that preliminary hearings should be open to the public unless there is a "substantial probability" that the resulting publicity would prevent a fair trial and there are no "reasonable alternatives to closure." In 1993, the Supreme Court continued its emphasis on the importance of open court proceedings. It struck down a Puerto Rican law that said preliminary hearings "shall be held privately" unless the defendant requests a public preliminary hearing.

These cases appeared to uphold the right of the press and public to have access to criminal proceedings. Judges, however, have a duty to protect the rights of the accused, and similar situations may arise in the future. The Supreme Court of the State of Washington, in Federated Publications vs. Swedberg, held in 1981 that press access to pretrial hearings may be conditioned on the agreement of reporters to abide by voluntary press-bar guidelines that exist in some states. The decision involved a preliminary hearing in a Bellingham, Wash., murder case tied to the "Hillside Strangler" murders in the Los Angeles area. The state Supreme Court ruled that the lower-court order was "a good-faith attempt to accommodate the interests of both defendant and press." The lower court had required reporters covering the hearing to sign a document in which the reporters agreed to abide by press-bar guidelines. The state Supreme Court said the document should be taken as a moral commitment on the part of the reporters, not as a legally enforceable document.

The U.S. Supreme Court in 1982 refused to hear an appeal of that case. Fortunately, many states have statutes to the effect that "the setting of every court shall be public, and every person may freely attend the same." When such statutes are in place, the closed-courtroom controversy appears to be moot. In states that have no such statute, the result seems to be that:

- A criminal trial must be open unless there is an "overriding interest" that requires some part of it to be closed.
- Judges must find some overriding interest before closing pretrial hearings.

One effect of the Washington decision is that many media groups are withdrawing from state press-bar agreements in the few states that have such guidelines. Their reasoning is that the voluntary guidelines in effect could become mandatory.

In 1994, the U.S. Judicial Conference ended its three-year experiment on cameras in federal courts by banning cameras. In 1996, the Judicial Conference agreed to permit cameras in some lower federal courts. And 47 states do allow cameras in at least some state courtrooms. Only Indiana, Mississippi, South Dakota and the District of Columbia ban courtroom cameras. The fact remains that there are many ways for judges to protect the rights of the accused without trampling on the right of the press and public to attend trials and pretrial hearings. Indeed, most editors are sensitive to the rights of the accused. Most exercise self-restraint when publishing or broadcasting information about a crime. Most have attempted to establish written policy on such matters, although others insist that individual cases must be judged on their merits.

Reporters and editors must share with judges the burden of protecting the rights of the accused. They also must ensure that certain groups within our society are not treated unfairly, either by the courts or in the media. In his study of crime reporting at the Gannett Center for Media Studies, Robert Snyder discovered that minorities tend to be covered by the media mainly in the context of crime news. Crime reporting is a staple of urban news, and urban areas are where minorities are concentrated. In large cities such as New York and Los Angeles, some areas of the city often make news only because of crime. As it is reported now, Snyder says, crime is almost always a conversation about race. He concludes that if the media are to change that perception, they must cover minorities more broadly and sympathetically. The real story of crime, Snyder says, should be the "breaking down of communities and the real weakening of the social structure."

Many editors are concerned about the way minorities are portrayed in crime stories. Many newspapers and broadcast stations, in fact, studiously avoid gratuitous mentions of race. Their reporters are allowed to mention the race of a suspect only as part of the complete identification of a fugitive. For many years, it was common to read or hear references to a "six-foot-tall black man" wanted for a crime. Today such a description would be considered unacceptable. There are too many men who fit that description, and the racial reference merely reinforces the stereotype of African Americans as criminals. If, however, a complete description of a fugitive might help lead to an arrest, it is appropriate to mention race as a part of that description. Only when race becomes the central theme of a story should it be emphasized.

Similarly, most editors consider a person's sexual orientation off limits unless the story focuses on heterosexuality or homosexuality. Increasingly, though, gays and lesbians are willing to talk openly about their sexual orientation as a means of advancing the cause of gay rights. Such issues cannot and should not be ignored by the media. But tastefully handling crime news involving homosexual murders often proves to be difficult. This was never more true than in the sensational murder trial of Milwaukee's Jeffrey Dahmer, convicted of sexually molesting young boys and men, killing them and eating parts of their bodies. In such cases, the press walks a fine line between responsibly informing the public and pandering to its seemingly insatiable appetite for sensational crime news.

Megan's Law

Effective October 1997, federal law requires each state to have a version of Megan's Law in place or lose federal anticrime money. Megan's Law is named for Megan Kanka, a 7-year-old girl raped and strangled in New Jersey in July 1994 by a man who had two prior convictions for sexually assaulting young girls and who moved to a house across the street from Megan. In June 1997, her killer, Jesse Timmendequas, received a death sentence.

The federal Megan's Law requires a person convicted of violent sexual crimes to register a current address with local law-enforcement agencies and to register a change of address within 10 days of moving into a new neighborhood. Failure to register is a crime. The federal law also requires states to perform yearly "verification." But federal law merely requires that a "designated state law-enforcement agency shall mail a nonforwardable verification form to the last reported address of the person" and that person shall sign and return the form within 10 days. While the signed form will say that the person resides there, the federal law requires no independent verification.

In addition, the federal law requires that the designated law-enforcement agencies "release relevant information that is necessary to protect the public concerning a specific person required to register. . . ." However, the details of this release of information are left up to the states. Some states release information on all registered sex offenders. Other states allow law-enforcement agencies to release information only when they consider a particular person to pose a risk.

A problem for newspapers trying to decide whether to print information made available under the applicable Megan's Law of their states is the accuracy of the information. Of course, convictions are a matter of public record and verifiable through court records. But addresses are not so easily verified. Even if a state declares that the addresses are a matter of public record, the problem remains that the information may be incorrect. Publication of incorrect information may receive protection from libel damages under a qualified privilege to make a fair and accurate report based on public records. Appropriate attribution to the public record, of course, would be necessary. But still the publication of an unverified address might potentially pose a legal problem. For instance, if publication posed a reasonable foreseeable risk of physical harm, and that harm occurred, the publisher might be sued for negligence. A reasonable person might foresee a risk of physical harm to Jimmy Jones living at 803 Mill Creek, an address erroneously given as the home of sex offender John Doe.

Even if the legal risks to a publisher are nonexistent, ethics should dictate careful reporting of addresses of sex offenders. These addresses may be self-reported, may not be independently verified, and will certainly be constantly changing. Such knowledge should give responsible publishers pause about reporting particular addresses, let alone lists of registered offenders' addresses, without first using standard reporting techniques to verify accuracy.

Negligence and Crime Reporting

The key to liability in negligence cases is "foreseeability." If an individual engages in conduct that could foreseeably create harm, and that harm then occurs, the individual may be liable for negligence. Foreseeability refers to what a "reasonably prudent person" would "reasonably" foresee under similar circumstances.

The first major negligence suit against the media for the bodily harm or risk of bodily harm by a third party started in Columbia, Mo. According to Sandra Hyde, as she walked down the main street of Columbia after midnight in August 1980, a man with a red beard and red hair, driving a red Mustang, pulled alongside her. He allegedly opened his door, leveled a sawed-off shotgun at her, and ordered her to get in. She did. He then demanded, "You will do what I want you to do or I will blow your brains out." As he drove around a corner, Hyde jumped out of the car and ran to safety in a nearby disco.

Hyde reported the incident to the police. Of course, she gave her name and address — a couple of facts that her assailant didn't have until a *Columbia Daily Tribune* reporter got a copy of the report from the police and the newspaper published her name and address the next day. Then, according to Hyde, the man started terrorizing her, stalking her at her home and workplace and making phone calls to give her messages such as, "I'm glad you're not dead yet; I have plans for you before you die" and "I wanted to refresh your memory of who I am before I kill you tonight."

Hyde sued, alleging negligence by the city in disclosing her name and address. The defendants countered that the information disclosed was a public record under Missouri's Sunshine Law. The trial court ruled in favor of the defendants, accepting the public-record defense. However, on appeal, the Court of Appeals for the Western District of Missouri ruled that Sandra Hyde did indeed have valid grounds to sue for negligence. The Court of Appeals concluded, "[I]t was reasonably foreseeable that the publication of the name and address of the victim, while the assailant was still at large, was a temptation to [the assailant] to inflict an intentional harm upon the victim — a foreseeable risk the. . . defendants had a duty to prevent."

In flatly rejecting the "Sunshine Law" defense, the court used the following *reductio ad absurdum* argument:

> To construe the Sunshine Law to open all criminal investigation information to anyone with a request . . . courts constitutional violations of the right of privacy of a witness or other citizen unwittingly drawn into the criminal investigation process. . . . Such a construction leads to the absurdity . . . that an assailant unknown as such to the authorities, from whom the victim has escaped, need simply walk into the police station, demand name and address or other personal information — without possibility of lawful refusal, so as to intimidate the victim as a witness or commit other injury.

To avoid what the court called an "absurd" conclusion, it held that "the name and address of a victim of crime who can identify an assailant not yet in custody is not a public record under the Sunshine Law."

In 1983, the U.S. Supreme Court let the Hyde case stand. In doing so, the court sent the message that newspapers could be found liable for printing a news story that exposed a specific victim to an unreasonable, foreseeable risk of harm — even though the defendant arguably was using public records.

A California appeals court cited Hyde when it let a woman sue the *Los Angeles Times* after the paper reported her name in connection with her discovery of the dead, nude body of her roommate who had been beaten, raped and strangled. The reporter, a summer intern, had gotten the name through the coroner's office. Again, the court did not accept the public-record defense.

Issues of Taste and Ethics

Some of the major issues involving taste and ethics in crime and court reporting are these:

- When should the media reveal details of how a murder or another crime was committed?
- When should the media reveal details about sex crimes or print the names of sex-crime victims?
- When should the media reveal a suspect's confession or even the fact that the suspect confessed?
- When should the media reveal a defendant's prior criminal record?
- When should the media reveal the names of juveniles charged with crimes?

None of these questions can be answered to everyone's satisfaction, and it is doubtful whether rules can be established to apply in all such situations. There have been charges that when the media reveal details of a murder, some people use the techniques described to commit additional murders. This charge is directed most frequently at television, but newspapers have not been immune.

As in the Dahmer case, the reporting of sex crimes often causes controversy. Most editors think of their publications as family newspapers or broadcasts and are properly hesitant about reporting the lurid details of sex crimes. What began as an interesting murder case in one college town turned into grist for the scandal mill. A college professor murdered one of his students who had asked for after-hours tutoring. When police unraveled the morbid tale of the professor, a homosexual necrophiliac, knowing what to write for the family newspaper became a major problem for the reporter. The newspaper provided information to the public on what had happened but deliberately avoided sensationalism. Even during the trial, specifics were avoided in favor of testimony that revealed the nature of the case in general terms:

> "He lived in a world of fantasies," the doctor said. "He spent much of his time daydreaming about homosexual, necrophilic, homicidal, suicidal and cannibalistic fantasies."

To have been more specific would have been revolting to many of the newspaper's readers.

A related problem is the question of how to handle rape reports. Too often, rapes are not reported to police because victims are unwilling to appear in court to testify against the suspects. Defense attorneys sometimes use such occasions to attack the victim's morals and imply that she (or he) consented to sexual relations. Many victims decline to press charges because of fear that their names will be made public in newspapers and on radio and television. Both of these things happened to the woman who accused NBA star Kobe Bryant of rape. There is, after all, still a lingering tendency to attach a social stigma to the rape victim, despite increasing public awareness of the nature of the crime.

In some states, "rape shield" statutes prohibit a defendant's attorney from delving into the rape victim's prior sexual activity unless some connection can be shown with the circumstances of the rape charged.

Many editors will not publish or broadcast details of a suspect's confession in an effort to protect the suspect's rights. Revealing such information blocks the way for a fair trial perhaps more easily than anything else the media can do. Some newspapers and broadcast stations, however, continue to reveal assertions by police or prosecutors that a confession was signed. Many question whether such information isn't just as prejudicial as the confession statement itself.

Occasionally, the question arises of whether to suppress an unsolicited confession. After a youth was charged with a series of robberies and was certified to stand trial as an adult, a newspaper reporter phoned the youthful defendant, who was free on bail, for an interview. The result was interesting. The defendant admitted to two other robberies in what amounted to a confession to the newspaper and its readers. The editor, who would not have printed a simple statement by police that the defendant had confessed to the crime, printed this one. Why? The editor reasoned that information about a confession to police amounts to secondhand, hearsay information. The confession to a reporter, however, was firsthand information obtained by the newspaper directly from the accused.

Lawyers also view as prejudicial the publication of a defendant's prior criminal record. Even if authorities refuse to divulge that information, much of it may be in the morgue. Should it be published? Most editors believe it should be, particularly if a prior conviction was for a similar offense. Most attorneys disagree.

Whether to use the names of juveniles charged with crimes is a troublesome issue as well. Most states prohibit law-enforcement officers and court officials from releasing the names of juveniles. The reasoning of those who oppose releasing juveniles' names is that the publicity marks them for life as criminals. Those who hold this view argue that there is ample opportunity for these individuals to change their ways and become good citizens — if the media do not stamp them as criminals. Others argue that juveniles who commit serious offenses, such as rape and armed robbery, should be treated as adults.

Questions such as these elicit divergent views from editors, some of whom regularly seek the advice of their lawyers. Little guidance for the reporter can be offered here. Because the decision to publish or not to publish is the editor's, not the reporter's, consultation is necessary. Each case must be decided on its merits.

Suggested Readings

Buchanan, Edna. *The Corpse Had a Familiar Face.* New York: Random House, 1987. The first of two books by one of America's best crime reporters.

Buchanan, Edna. *Never Let Them See You Cry.* New York: Random House, 1992. An excellent description of covering crime in Miami.

Center on Crime, Communities and Culture and *Columbia Journalism Review. Covering Criminal Justice.* New York: Graduate School of Journalism, Columbia University, 2000. A manual listing resources to help reporters covering crime and the courts.

Giles, Robert H. and Snyder, Robert W., eds. *Covering the Courts: Free Press, Fair Trials and Journalistic Performance.* Piscataway, N.J.: Transaction Publishers, 1998.

Pulitzer, Lisa Beth. *Crime on Deadline: Police Reporters Tell Their Most Unforgettable Stories.* New York: Boulevard Books, 1996. Real stories from nine of the nation's top crime reporters.

Siegel, Marvin, ed. *The Last Word: The New York Times Book of Obituaries and Farewells: A Celebration of Unusual Lives.* New York: Quill, 1998. Examples of well-written and compelling obituaries from *The New York Times.*

Singer, Eleanor and Endreny, Phyllis M. *Reporting on Risk: How the Mass Media Portray Accidents, Diseases, Disasters and Other Hazards.* New York: Russell Sage Foundation, 1993. A critical look at media reporting of accidents and disasters.

Suggested Web Sites

www.fbi.gov
The FBI Web site provides useful information about crime coverage.

www.fema.gov
The Federal Emergency Management Agency, part of the U.S. Department of Homeland Security, provides assistance during major emergencies.

www.ntsb.gov
The National Transportation Safety Board is an excellent source of accident information.

www.supremecourtus.gov
The Supreme Court of the United States is the nation's highest court. The court's Web site outlines its operation.

Exercises

1. Find an accident story in a local newspaper. List all the obvious sources the reporter used in obtaining information for the story. List additional sources you would have checked.

2. Talk with a firefighter in your local fire department about the department's media policy at fire scenes. Based on what you learn, write instructions for your fellow reporters on what to expect at fires in your city or town.

3. Make a list of at least 10 federal agencies that may be of help in reporting accident, fire and disaster stories. Also list the telephone numbers of the agency offices nearest to you.

4. Cover a session of your local municipal court. Write a story based on the most interesting case of the day.

5. Find a court story in a local newspaper. Determine what sources the reporter used in the story, and tell how the story could have been improved.

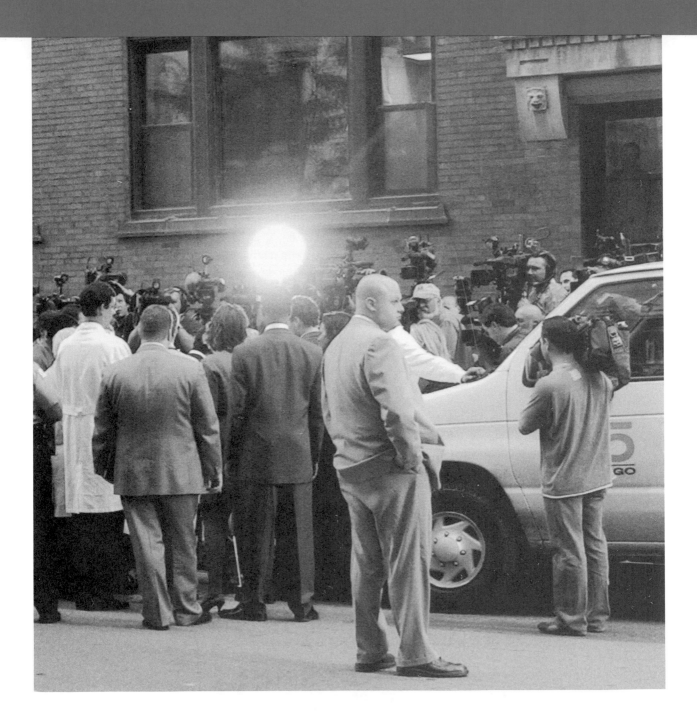

When she was a journalism student, Karen Brooks dreamed of someday becoming editor in chief of *Rolling Stone*. Instead, like many reporters fresh out of school, she felt fortunate to get a job covering cops. She loved it, and she was good at it. She learned the special language and the tribal customs of the civil servants we pay to protect us. Then, after 18 months, her bosses at the Corpus Christi, Texas, *Caller-Times* wanted to reward her hard work and bring her energy to covering local politics. She made the switch, she recalls, "kicking and screaming, because I wanted to do cops forever."

A few years later, another paper, the *Fort Worth Star-Telegram*, asked her to learn another new language and a new set of customs. This time, the language was Spanish. Her new beat was 1,000 miles long — the U.S.–Mexican border. She loves this one, too, although her office is in her home, hundreds of miles from the news room. And some things don't seem to change. Not long ago, she found herself in Mexico City, working on a story involving murder and political corruption.

Through it all, Karen says, "Most of what the editors and teachers taught me in J school was right on the money. The reporting and writing techniques pretty much put me ahead." She adds, "What I think helped me the most in each step was a willingness to try new things and take chances on accepting assignments that I didn't know anything about."

That mix of strong basic skills and an appetite for trying new things has never been more important, as new issues and new technology require constant change even at the core of reporting: beat coverage. Beats — specific areas of responsibility — form the backbone of most newspaper journalism. Increasingly, television news rooms are developing area specialists, too, although smaller staffs and time pressures seldom permit the same degree of concentration. Online opportunities also are altering responsibilities and expectations.

That's true, for example, at the *Rochester* (N.Y.) *Democrat and Chronicle*. The paper is owned by Gannett, one of America's biggest media chains. Jane Sutter is the managing editor. She directs the news coverage.

"Our convergence commitment has definitely changed reporters' work," she says. "Now, reporters are expected to file a few paragraphs from the scene of a press conference, fire, accident, etc., or write those up as soon as they come back to the office. We know that we get our greatest number of online readers early in the morning, at lunchtime,

In this chapter you will learn:

1. Basic principles for covering any beat.

2. How to apply those principles to some of the most common beats.

and between 4 and 5 p.m., so it's very important that we update the Web site continuously throughout the day." Reporters are equipped with cell phones, and photographers have laptop computers to permit posting of pictures shot digitally.

The *D&C* also has a partnership with the Rochester ABC affiliate. Newspaper reporters are regularly interviewed on Channel 13. ("And they do dress up," Sutter says.) For the 11 p.m. news program, the paper even provides exclusive summaries of stories that will appear in the next morning's paper. The station gets stories its broadcast competitors don't have, and the newspaper gets wider exposure for its work.

Not only the technology has changed. You saw in Chapter 1 how the definition of news itself is broadening. That change extends the range of beats. Along with such standard beats as local government, police, business and sports, cultural beats reflect the interests and activities of a changing America. Some beat reporters cover shopping malls. Some cover commuting. Some cover spiritual life. Some cover cyberspace.

Increasingly, beat reporters tell their audiences not only what is happening but also how to get involved. Stories include telephone numbers and e-mail addresses along with the names of decision-makers. Much of the most useful reporting is done in advance of public meetings, with the goal of enabling citizens to become participants instead of passive onlookers. Readers are regularly invited to use e-mail or online bulletin boards to speak up on public issues.

With all these changes, though, beat reporters remain the eyes and ears of their communities. They are surrogates for their readers, keeping track of government, education, police, business and other powerful institutions that shape readers' lives.

The principles of good reporting apply to the coverage of any beat. The same principles also apply to specialized publications, including those aimed at particular ethnic groups, industries or professions. A reporter for *Women's Wear Daily* may cover designers. A reporter for *Diario las Americas* in Miami may cover Cuban exile politics. But each is doing the same job: discovering and writing news that's relevant and useful to the publication's readers.

Many news organizations are responding to audience interests by creating teams of reporters to cover interrelated topics instead of institutions. One team may write about issues of home and family life. Another may cover the arts and popular culture. Another team may focus on the problems and opportunities of urban living.

Editors and audiences expect reporters on these new beats, like those in more traditional assignments, to provide information and understanding that will help readers improve the quality of their lives. That's important work. It's rewarding work. But it's not easy.

PRINCIPLES FOR REPORTERS ON A BEAT

Whether you cover the public library or the Pentagon, the county courthouse or the White House, the principles of covering a beat are the same. If you want to succeed as a reporter, you must be prepared, alert, persistent and wary. And, on any beat, you must be there.

That checklist will help you win the trust of your sources, keep up with important developments on your beat and avoid the trap of writing for your sources instead of your readers. Let's take a closer look at what each of those rules means in practice.

Be Prepared

Where should preparation begin? For you, it has already begun. To work effectively, any journalist needs a basic understanding of the workings of society and its various governments. You need to know at least the rudiments of psychology, economics and history. That is why the best education for a journalist is a broad-based one, providing exposure to the widest possible sampling of human knowledge. But that exposure will not be enough when you face an important source on your first beat. You will need more specific information, which you can acquire by familiarizing yourself with written accounts or records or by talking to sources.

TIPS: The successful beat reporter is

- Prepared.
- Alert.
- Persistent.
- There.
- Wary.

Reading for Background

In preparing to cover a beat, any beat, your first stop should be the newspaper library (see Chapter 5). The library of the newspaper is likely to have computer access not only to material that has appeared in that newspaper but also to worldwide networks of information on nearly any topic. You can often access the contents of major newspapers, magazines, research publications and other reference libraries without regard to physical distance. Use the Internet as a tool to acquire background and to understand the context of local events and issues. For example, if your new beat is medicine or science, you might begin with the Web site of the Association of Health Care Journalists (**www.ahcj.umn.edu**) or the National Association of Science Writers (**www.nasw.org**). If your new beat is the Mexican border, you might be surprised at the valuable background information to be found on Mexico at **www.cia.gov**. The Central Intelligence Agency Web site includes reliable historical, economic and political data on every country.

In your local research, make notes of what appear to be continuing issues, questions left dangling in previous stories or ideas for stories to come. Go back several years in your preparation. History may not repeat itself, but knowledge of it helps you assess the significance of current events and provides clues to what you can expect.

Library research is only the start of your preparation. You must become familiar with the laws governing the institution you cover. If a governmental organization is your beat, find the state statutes or the city charter that created the agencies you will be covering. Learn the powers, duties and limitations of each official. You may be surprised to discover that someone is failing to do all that the law requires. Someone else may be doing more than the law allows.

Look at your state's open-meeting and open-record laws, too. Every state has such laws, although they vary widely in scope and effectiveness. Knowing what

TIPS: Preparing to cover a beat

- Use the Internet to acquire background information and understand context.
- Make note of continuing issues or ideas for stories to come.
- Become familiar with the laws governing the institution you cover.
- Look at your state's open-meeting and open-record laws.

information is open to the public by law can be a valuable tool for a reporter dealing with officials who may prefer to govern privately.

Talking to Sources

Now you're ready to start talking to people. You should conduct your first interviews in the news room with your predecessor on the beat, your city editor and any veterans who can shed light on the kinds of things that rarely appear in statute books or newspaper stories. Who have been good sources in the past? Who will lie to you? Who drinks to excess? Who seems to be living extravagantly? Whose friends are big land developers? Who wants to run for national office? Who has been hired, fired or promoted? Who has moved to a competing company? Remember that you are hearing gossip, filtered through the biases of those relating it. Be a little skeptical.

Some understanding of the workings of your own news room won't hurt, either. Has your predecessor on the beat been promoted? Has he or she been transferred because of unsatisfactory performance? Will an introduction from your predecessor help you or hurt you with your sources? And what are your city editor's expectations? Is your assignment to report almost every activity of government, or will you have time to do some investigative work and analysis? Trying to live up to your boss's expectations is easier if you know in advance what they are.

Only after gaining as much background as possible are you ready to face the people you will be covering. A quick handshake and a superficial question or two may be all you have time for in the first encounter, but within a week you should arrange for sit-down conversations with your most important sources. These are get-acquainted sessions. You are trying to get to know the sources, but don't forget that they need to know you, too, if they are going to respect and trust you.

You may have noticed that the preparation for covering a beat is similar to the preparation for an interview or for a single-story assignment. The important difference is that preparing for a beat is more detailed and requires more time and work. Instead of just preparing for a short-term task, you are laying the foundation for an important part of your career. A beat assignment nearly always lasts at least six months and often two years or more. Understanding that will help shape your first round of meetings with sources.

A story may emerge from those first interviews, but their purpose is much broader. You are trying to establish a relationship, trying to convert strangers into helpful partners in news gathering. To do that, you should demonstrate an interest in the sources as people as well as officials. Ask about their families, their interests, their philosophy, their goals. Make clear with your questions that you are interested rather than ignorant. (Don't ask if the source is married. You should already know. Say, "I understand your daughter is in law school. Is she going into politics, too?" Similarly, don't ask if your source has any hobbies. Find out beforehand. Say, "So you collect pornographic comic books. Sure takes your mind off the budget, doesn't it?")

And be prepared to give something of yourself. If you both like to fish, or you both went to Vassar, or you both have children about the same age, seize on

---

TIPS: Talking to sources

- Talk to your predecessor on the beat, your city editor and veterans in the news room for background.
- Understand your editor's expectations.
- Establish a relationship with sources — demonstrate interest in them.

those ties. All of us feel comfortable with people who have something in common with us. This is the time, too, to let your sources know that you know something about their work and that you're interested in it.

Was your source elected as a reformer? Ask about the opposition she is encountering. Has your source complained that he lacks the statutory power to do a satisfactory job? Ask if he's lobbying to change the law. Has the industry become more competitive? Ask about her strategies for meeting the challenge. Is it budget time? Let him know you're aware of the problems with last year's budget. Nothing does so much to create a warm reporter-source relationship as the reporter's demonstrated knowledge of and interest in the beat.

Solid preparation will help you avoid asking stupid questions. More important, it will help you make sure you ask the right questions. And because you have taken the trouble to get to know your sources, you are more likely to come away with responsive answers.

Be Alert

Lisa Arthur learned her way around schools in three years on the education beat for *The Miami Herald*. When she was assigned to cover the shooting of a teacher, she was ready for any possibility. The shooting had attracted national attention, so a throng of journalists gathered outside the building. School officials announced that only a small group of reporters, called a **pool,** would be allowed inside. Faced with head-to-head competition from a Fort Lauderdale *Sun-Sentinel* reporter, Lisa thought fast.

Let her tell the story:

"So I said, I covered schools in Broward for three years, and there are dozens of schools I have still never seen the inside of. Have you ever actually been to this school?

"She says no. (The mind reels. If there ever was a time to flat-out lie, this was it.)

"I said, Look, no offense, but if you knew them that well, they would have just picked you as the pool reporter and not sent you over here to fight it out with us folks they've never seen before. . . . My suggestion is we flip a coin.

"She said okay. . . .

"I flip. She calls heads. It lands in my palm ever-loving tails side up. . . .

"We ended up being in there for about 30–40 minutes only. The leash was more like a choke chain. But it was understandable. I got lucky because the guy in there coordinating the mental health team was a psychologist from the Miami-Dade school district. So he was extremely helpful and went as far as he could.

"Afterwards I had to give a debriefing to every outlet that wanted it. I literally gave everyone everything in my notebook . . . and all the quotes I used. But nobody could write the inside-the-school story the way we could without giving it a 'from pool report' byline. . . .

"I could have explained not getting in there to my bosses. No one expected me to. Just getting to the coin toss was a major victory for us. I don't know how she explained it."

Sometimes, being alert means thinking fast and seizing opportunity. Sometimes, it means recognizing an important story when others don't. Important stories are seldom labeled as such. In many cases the people involved may not realize the significance of what they are doing. Probably more often they realize it but hope nobody else will. The motivation for secrecy may be dishonesty, the desire to protect an image or a conviction that the public will misunderstand.

If your beat is a government agency, you will find that many public officials and public employees think they know more about what is good for the public than the public does. The theory of democratic government is that an informed citizenry can make decisions or elect representatives to make those decisions in its own best interests. If you are the reporter assigned to city hall, the school board or the courthouse, you carry a heavy responsibility for helping your readers put that theory into practice. To discharge that responsibility, you must probe beneath the surface of events in search of the "whys" and "hows" that lead to understanding.

When you are presented with a news release or hear an announcement or cover a vote, ask yourself these questions before passing the event off in a few paragraphs:

- *Who will benefit from this, and who will be hurt?* If the tentative answer to the first part suggests private interests, or the answer to the second part is the public, some digging is in order.
- *How important is this?* An event that is likely to affect many people for good or ill usually deserves more explanation than one affecting only a handful.
- *Who is for this, and who is against it?* Answers to these questions often are obvious or at least easy to figure out. When you know them, the answers to the first two questions usually become clearer.
- *How much will this activity cost, and who will pay?* An architect's design for renovating downtown may look less attractive when the price tag is attached. The chamber of commerce's drive to lure new industry may require taxpayers to pay for new roads, sewers, fire protection, even schools and other services for an increased population.

Once you have asked the questions and gotten answers, the story may turn out to be about no more than it appeared to be on the surface. But if you don't ask them, you — and your readers — may find out too late that more was there than met the eye. The answers allow you to judge that most important element of news value — impact.

Be Persistent

Persistence means two things to a reporter on a beat. First, it means that when you ask a question, you do not give up until you get an answer (see Figure 14.1). Second, it means that you must keep track of slow-developing projects or problems.

Figure 14.1
Skilled reporters are persistent interviewers and insist on responsive answers. Make sure your questions are answered satisfactorily.

Insisting on a Responsive Answer

One of the most common faults of beginning reporters is that they give up too easily. They settle for answers that are unresponsive to their questions, or they return to the news room not sure they understand what they were told. In either case the result is an incomplete, confusing story.

"Why is it that our fourth-graders score below average on these reading tests?" you ask the school superintendent.

He may reply, "Let me first conceptualize the parameters of the socioeconomic context for you."

The real answer probably is "I only wish I knew."

Your job is to cut through the jargon and the evasions in search of substance. Often that is not an easy task. Many experts, or people who want to be regarded as experts, are so caught up in the technical language of their special field that they find it almost impossible to communicate clearly. Many others seek refuge in gobbledygook or resort to evasion when they don't know an answer or find the answer embarrassing. Educators and lawyers are particularly adept at such tactics.

Listen politely for a few minutes while the school superintendent conceptualizes his parameters. Then, when he finishes or pauses for breath, lead him back toward where you want to go. One way is to say, "It sounds to me as if you're saying . . ." and rephrase what he has told you in plain English. At those times when you simply are in the dark — and that may be often — just confess your puzzlement and ask for a translation. And keep coming back to the point: "But how does all that affect reading scores?" "How can the problem be solved?" "What are you doing about it?"

The techniques you have learned for preparing for interviews and conducting them will help you. Your preparation for the beat will help, too. Probably most helpful, though, are the questions you keep asking yourself rather than your source: "Does that make sense to me?" "Can I make it make sense to my

TIPS: Insisting on a responsive answer

- Cut through the jargon and evasions in search of substance.
- Rephrase technical language in plain English.

readers?" Don't quit until the answer is yes. You should not be obnoxious, but you do have to be persistent.

Following Up Slow Developments

Persistence is also required when you are following the course of slow-developing events. Gardeners do not sit and watch a seed germinate. They do, however, check every few days, looking for the green shoots that indicate that growth is taking place as it should. If the shoots are late, they dig in to investigate.

Beat reporting works much the same way. A downtown redevelopment plan, say, or a revision in a school's curriculum is announced. The story covers the plans and the hoped-for benefits. The seed is planted. If it is planted on your beat, make a note to yourself to check on it in a week or two. And a week or two after that. And a month after that. Start a file of reminders so you won't forget. Such a file often is called a **tickler** because it serves to tickle your memory.

Like seeds, important projects of government or business take time to develop. Often what happens during the long, out-of-public-view development is more important than the announcements at the occasional news conferences or the promises of the promotional brochures. Compromises are made. Original plans turn out to be impractical or politically unpalatable. Consultants are hired. Contracts are signed. Public money is spent. The public interest may be served, or it may not.

Sometimes the story is that nothing is happening. At other times the story may be that the wrong things are happening. Consulting contracts may go to cronies of the mayor. Redevelopment may enhance the property values of big downtown landowners. Curriculum revisions may be shaped by some influential pressure groups.

Even if nothing improper is taking place, the persistent reporter will give the readers an occasional update. At stake, after all, are the public's money and welfare.

Be There

In beat reporting there is no substitute for personal contact. Trying to do it all by telephone or e-mail won't work. The only way to cover a beat is to be there — every day, if possible. Joking with the secretaries, talking politics with council members and lawyers, worrying over the budget or trading gossip with the professional staff — you must make yourself a part of the community you are covering.

Remember that the sources who are most important to you probably are in great demand by others, too. They have jobs to do. Maneuver to get as much of their time as you need, but don't demand too much. Do your homework first. Don't expect a school superintendent to explain basic concepts of education. You can learn that information from an aide or from reading. What you need to learn from the superintendent is how he or she intends to apply those concepts, or why they seem to be inapplicable here. Find out what a "Class I felony" is before asking the police chief why they are increasing. You will get the time you need more readily if busy sources know their time will not be wasted.

Life of a Happy Beat Reporter

Mary Jo Feldstein was taking a chance when she took a job at a newspaper she'd never heard of in a Pennsylvania city she'd never visited. Less than two years later, she was as happy as a young reporter is ever going to be. She was also moving up, to a job at the *St. Louis Post-Dispatch*. Here's her report on life on the beat at the Scranton *Tribune:*

"At 10 a.m. you're patiently, compassionately interviewing a patient who overcame the limita-tions of medical science to prove the spirit of humanity. The next hour, you're analyzing hundreds of pages of Medicare cost reports with a bunch of hospital-finance geeks. In the afternoon, you're schmoozing with politicians, chasing down a tip that the gov-ernor met with policy wonks to lay out his medical malpractice reform package.

"At the end of each day, you'll likely have an A1 candidate to write. You always have a story because it's your responsibility to explain the most rapidly chang-ing industry and the most press-ing social problem in our nation.

"You marvel at other reporters' ability to focus, work on a pro-ject and go for days, maybe weeks, without a fast-breaking story. News happens constantly on your beat, and there's always some issue begging for the clarifi-cation and context a more in-depth piece provides.

"You're a health-care reporter."

She admits she's biased, but she argues that no beat is more challenging or complex. Her assignment "requires an under-standing of numbers and politics and people," she says. Gaining that understanding took plenty of background reading. As a place to start, Mary Jo recommends the Web site of the Association of Health Care Journalists.

Already, she has broken dozens of important stories, including one that led an insurer to change its policy on terrorism coverage and a series that inspired merger talks among the community's financially strug-gling hospitals.

She's proud of that series and warmed by her continuing connection with one of the ordi-nary people she included. Joe Piechota's wife, Joyce, died after her cancer treatment was delayed.

Mary Jo says, "Joe and I met about 10 times before the story ran, sometimes for interviews . . . other times because he was lonely and just needed to talk. Joe once told me that having his wife's story told might encourage change and that helped him heal.

"Joe still calls. He says it's just to see how I'm doing. I say it's to remind me why I'm doing this."

There are other simple techniques you can use to build and maintain good relationships with the people on your beat. Here are some of them:

- *Do a favor when you can.* As a reporter you spend much of your time asking other people to do favors for you — giving you their time, sharing informa-tion they need not share, looking up records and figures. If a source needs a favor in return, don't refuse unless it would be unethical. The favors asked usually are small things, such as getting a daughter's engagement picture or a club announcement in the paper, procuring a print of a picture taken with the governor to decorate the official's wall, bringing in a few copies of a favorable feature you wrote.

- *Don't shun good news.* One ill-founded but common complaint is that news media report nothing but bad news. Admittedly, there is usually no story when people are doing what they are supposed to do. Sometimes there should be, if they do their duty uncommonly well or have done it for a very long time or do it under the burden of some handicap. Sources like these "good news" stories and so do readers.

- *Protect your sources.* Many people in government — politicians and bureaucrats alike — are willing to tell a reporter things they are not willing to have their names attached to in print or otherwise. The same is true of people in private business, who may fear reprisals from their employer, co-workers or competitors. Sometimes such would-be anonymous sources are trying to use you to enhance their own positions. You have to protect yourself and your readers against that possibility. Confer with an editor if you have doubts. Most papers are properly wary of relying on unnamed sources. Sometimes, though, the requests for anonymity are valid, necessary to protect the source's career. Once you have agreed to protect a source, you must do it. Don't tell anyone but your editor. An inability to keep your mouth shut can cost you more than a source. It can cost you your reputation. (The protection of sources has legal as well as ethical implications. So-called shield laws in some states offer limited exemptions for journalists from legal requirements to disclose sources — see Chapter 21. But there are no blanket exemptions. In one effort to resolve such problems, some news organizations try to negotiate written agreements obligating a source to come forward if continued secrecy might cost a reporter a jail term or the newspaper a loss in a lawsuit.)

- *Above all, be accurate.* Inaccurate reporting leads first to loss of respect from sources, then to loss of the sources themselves and finally to loss of the job. If you are a good, tough reporter, not all your contacts on your beat will love you. But if you are an accurate reporter, they will respect you.

The best way to assure accuracy is to check and double-check. Many of the stories you will write are likely to be complicated. You will be expected to digest budgets, master plans, legal opinions and complicated discussions, and to translate these into language your readers can understand. When in doubt, ask somebody. If you are unclear about the city manager's explanation of the budget before the council, arrange a meeting afterward and go over it. If a company's brief in a legal case has you confused, call the lawyer who wrote it. If the new master land-use plan strikes you as vague, consult with the planner. If you are writing a story on a subject you feel tentative about, arrange to read it back to the sources when it is complete. Not all experts relish being asked to translate their jargon into English, so in some cases you will have to insist, politely. The best persuader is the assurance that it is far better for your sources to take a few minutes to explain now than to see themselves misrepresented in print.

Remember, beat reporting is a lot like gardening. Both require you to be in the field every day, cultivating. And in both, the amount of the harvest is directly proportional to the amount of labor invested.

Be Wary

The point of all this effort — the preparation, perceptiveness, persistence and personal contact — is to keep your readers informed. That is an obvious statement, but it needs to be made because every reporter on a beat is under pressures that can obscure the readers' importance. You must be wary of this problem.

You will have little to do with 99.9 percent of your readers. They will not write you notes when you have done a story they like or call you when they dislike what you have written. They will not offer to buy you a cup of coffee or lunch, or stop you in the hall to urge you to see things their way. But your sources will.

If you write that city council members are thinking about raising the property-tax rate, you probably will hear complaints from council members about premature disclosure. If you write that the police department is wracked by dissension, expect a less-than-friendly reaction from the chief. If you write that the CEO of a major business is looking for a new job, the chances are that he or she will deny it even though the story is true.

All sources have points of view, programs to sell, careers to advance, opponents to undercut. It is likely and legitimate that they will try to persuade you of

Figure 14.2
A TV crew covers a press conference featuring a man who rode his horse from Montana to Crawford, Texas, to protest President George W. Bush's policies.

the merit of their viewpoint, try to sell their programs through the columns of your newspaper, try to shape the news to help their careers.

Be wary of sources' efforts to use you. You can lose the critical distance a reporter must maintain from those being covered. When that happens, you start thinking like a participant rather than an observer. You begin writing for your sources rather than your audience. This is a real danger. No one can spend as much time as a reporter on a beat does with sources or devote as much effort to understanding them without becoming sympathetic. You may forget that you are writing for the outsiders when you associate so closely with the insiders.

Many veteran police reporters, for example, begin thinking like those they cover, some of them even adopting the common police officer's suspicion of journalists. The police reporter for one big-city radio station first took to carrying a gun, then quit reporting altogether to do public-relations work for the sheriff's department.

ONLINE COVERAGE

Before we apply those principles to specific beats, let's look briefly at the opportunities and challenges online journalism presents to beat reporters. At the beginning of this chapter, you got a glimpse of those opportunities and challenges at the *Rochester Democrat and Chronicle.* First is the opportunity for instant reporting. With cell phones, digital cameras and laptop computers, reporters can and do file short stories and even photographs for posting on the Web site as the story unfolds. For newspaper reporters, this is a high-tech return to the distant days of multiple editions, when instead of one deadline a day journalists had many. For radio and television reporters, the online opportunities match those of live reporting over the air. Research shows that increasing numbers of online readers rely on Web sites to stay in touch with news as it happens.

Online, you're expected to gather and present to readers more information, more detail and more points of view than either print or broadcast permits. Readers who care enough to follow an issue online want and expect to see the source documents you use — and that the policy-makers use. They want and expect links to other Web sites that offer related information or further background.

The *Democrat and Chronicle* has a weekly award for staffers who seize the opportunities of convergence. Called the Golden Tater award, it is a humorous way of making a serious point. The news room's daily electronic newsletter announced one award this way:

The Golden Tater for above-and-beyond service to new media goes this week to Sue McNamara, Paulina Garces-Reid, Matt Leingang, Jamie Germano and Tricia Powers for their outstanding multimedia effort "Matters of the Heart."

This is Sue's second TV-Web-print triple play. She oversaw the Guantanamo Bay series and came to the new-media department with "Heart" during the reporting phase. Matt recorded audio, told viewers about the reporting process during a strong appearance on Channel 13's morning show and suggested a novel idea — that we should host a live online chat with the transplant team and patient. Paulina worked long hours over several weeks to create a multimedia presentation, and Tricia reworked her graphics — a case study in how to present something that would be a long print narrative in a Web-friendly, interactive piece. . . .

That example shows another important opportunity offered online — interactivity. As you already know, interactivity is what really sets online media apart. It is a term with two practical meanings. First, online journalism permits readers to interact with the information you post. With the proper software, readers can search your Web site's restaurant reviews, lists of dangerous intersections or any other information that can be tailored to individual needs.

The second type of online activity is between journalists and readers. During the Iraq War, for example, www.washingtonpost.com regularly arranged online conversations between reporters in Baghdad and readers anywhere in the world. Such conversations give readers a chance to ask follow-up questions and reporters a chance to clarify or personalize the news. Some traditional reporters find this prospect terrifying. They're more comfortable in a world of one-way communication, reporter to reader. That world is fast disappearing.

COVERING THE MOST IMPORTANT LOCAL BEATS

Your political science courses will introduce you to the structure of government, but from a reporter's viewpoint, function is usually even more important than structure. You must learn who holds the real power, who has the most influence on the power holders and who are the most likely sources of accurate information. The specifics vary from city to city, but there are some general principles that will help you in covering any form of state or local institution.

- *Information is power.* The holder of information may be a professional administrator — the city manager, school superintendent, police chief or court clerk — or it may be an elected official — the mayor, chair of the county commission or chair of the school board. The job title is unimportant. Find the person who knows in detail how any organization really works, where the money goes and how decisions are made. Get to know that person because he or she will be the most important person on your beat.
- *The budget is the blueprint.* This principle is a corollary of the first. Just as detailed knowledge of how an organization works is the key to controlling that organization, a budget is the blueprint for the organization's activities. The budget tells where the money comes from and where it goes. It tells how many people are on the payroll and how much they are paid. It tells what programs are planned for the year and how much they will cost. Over several years' time, the budget tells where the budget makers' priorities are, what they see as their organization's role in the community.

TIPS: Crucial factors and practical principles for beat reporters

- *Power:* Information is power.
- *Money:* The budget is the blueprint.
- *Politics:* Distributing power and money is politics.

So, find copies of the last two or three years' budgets for your beat. Try to decipher them. Learn all you can from your predecessor and from newspaper clips. Then find the architect who drew up this blueprint — the budget director or the clerk or the assistant superintendent — and get a translation. Ask all the questions you can think of. Write down the answers.

When budget-making time arrives, follow every step. Attend every public hearing and every private discussion session you can. In those dollar figures are some of the most important stories you will write — stories of how much your readers will be paying for schools and roads and garbage pickup, stories of what they will get for their money. (For a guide to understanding budgets see Chapter 6.)

- *Distributing power and money is politics.* While looking for your beat's power centers and unraveling its budget mysteries, you will be absorbing as well the most interesting part of beat reporting — politics.

At any organizational level in any form, power and money go hand-in-hand with politics. Politics provides the mechanisms through which limited resources are allocated among many competing groups. Neither elections nor political parties are necessary for politics. You will have to learn to spot more subtle forms of political maneuvering.

If you are covering city hall, for example, pay close attention as the city budget is being drafted. You may find the mayor's pet project being written in by the city manager. Nobody elects the city manager, but it is good politics for him or her to keep the mayor happy. Are the builders influential in town? If so, you will probably find plenty of road and sewer projects in the budget. Are the city employees unionized? Look for healthy wage and benefit increases if they are. Is there a vocal retirees' organization? That may account for the proposed senior citizens' center. None of those projects is necessarily bad just because it is political. But you and your readers ought to know who is getting what and why.

Now suppose an election is coming up, and the builders' campaign contributions will be heavy. A councilman who is running for mayor switches his vote from money for parks to money for new roads. Has a deal been made? Has a vote been sold? That's politics, too. Some digging is in order.

Power, money and politics are the crucial factors to watch in any beat reporting. With this in mind, let's take a closer look at the most important local beats.

City and County Government

Most medium-sized cities have council-manager governments. The mayor and council members hire a professional administrator to manage the day-to-day affairs of the city. The manager, in turn, hires the police and fire chiefs, the public works director and other department heads. Under the city charter the council is supposed to make policy and leave its implementation to the manager. Council members usually are forbidden to meddle in the affairs of any department.

What does it mean to write for your readers instead of your sources? It means that you must follow several important guidelines.

Translate.

The language of bureaucrats, educators, scientists or lawyers is not the same language most people speak. You need to learn the jargon of your sources, but you also need to learn how to translate it into standard English for your readers. The city planning consultant might say, "Preliminarily, the concept appeared to permit attainment of all our criteria; but, when we cost it out, we have to question its economic viability." Your lead could translate that to:

The proposed plan for downtown redevelopment looks good on paper, but it may cost too much, the city's planning consultant said today.

Make your writing human.

In big government and big business, humanity often gets lost in numbers. Your readers want and need to know the impact of those numbers on real people. How many people will be displaced by a new highway? And who are they? Who will be affected by a school closing or a welfare cut? When a police report announced that burglaries were up by 35 percent in the last two months, an enterprising reporter told the story through the eyes of a victim. It began this way:

Viola Patterson picked her way through the shattered glass from her front door, passed the table where her television used to sit, and stopped before the cabinet that had held her family silver.

She wept.

Mrs. Patterson, 72, is one of the more than 75 people victimized by burglars in the last two months.

Think of the public pocket-book.

If the tax rate is going up 14 cents, how much will it cost the average homeowner? If employees of a firm are seeking a 10 percent raise, how much will that cost the employer? How much of that increase will be passed on to customers? If garbage collection fees are about to be increased, how do they compare to fees in comparable cities?

The city manager proposed "adjusting" the price of electricity to lower the cost to industrial customers and raise rates to private homes. The city hall reporter did a quick survey of comparable cities around the state. Then she wrote:

City residents, who already pay more for their electricity than residents of eight similar-sized cities around the state, would be charged an average of $4 per month more under a proposal announced Tuesday by City Manager Barry Kovac.

Industrial users, whose rate now is about average among the nine cities, would enjoy the second-lowest rate under Kovac's proposal.

Kovac defended his plan as "equitable and necessary to ensure continued economic growth for the city."

Get out of the office.

City council votes are important, but far more people will have personal contact with government in the form of a police officer, a clerk or a bus driver than with a council member. Go to where government meets its constituents. Ride a bus. Visit a classroom. Patrol with a police officer. Not only will you get a reader's-eye view of your beat, but you may also find some unexpected stories.

Ask the readers' questions.

"Why?" "How much will it cost me?" "What will I get out of it?" You are the public's ombudsman.

Remember, a good beat reporter has to be prepared, be alert, be persistent and be there. If you always keep in mind the people you are writing *for*, you'll keep the customers — and the editors — satisfied.

317

Some cities have governments in which the mayor serves as chief administrator. Rudy Giuliani, mayor of New York when the terrorists attacked in 2001, became a national hero for his take-charge approach. Whatever the structure, you will have a range of good sources to draw on.

Subordinate administrators. They know details of budgets, planning and zoning, and personnel matters. They are seldom in the spotlight, so many of them welcome a reporter's attention so long as the reporter does not get them into trouble. Many are bright and ambitious, willing to second-guess their superiors and gossip about politics, again providing you can assure them that the risk is low.

Council members. Politicians, as a rule, love to talk. What they say is not always believable, and you have to be wary of their attempts to use you, but they will talk. Like most of us, politicians are more likely to tell someone else's secret or expose the other guy's deal. So ask one council member about the political forces behind another member's pet project while asking the other about the first's mayoral ambitions. That way you probably will learn all there is to know.

Pressure groups. You can get an expert view of the city's land-use policies from land developers and a different view from conservationists. The manager or the personnel director will tell one side of the labor-management story. The head of the employees' union tells the other. How about the school board's record in hiring minorities? Get to know the head of the NAACP or of the Urban League chapter. Public officials respond to pressure. As a reporter you need to understand those pressures and who applies them.

Public citizens. Consumer advocate Ralph Nader made the term "public citizens" popular, but every town has people — lawyers, homemakers, business executives, retirees — who serve on charter commissions, head bond campaigns, work in elections and advise behind the scenes. Such people can be sources of sound background information and useful assessments of officeholders.

Opponents. The best way to find out the weaknesses of any person or program is to talk with an opponent. Seek out the board member who wants to fire the school superintendent. Look up the police captain demoted by the new chief. Chat with the leader of the opposition to the new hospital. There are at least two sides to every public question and every public figure. Your job is to explore them all.

Once you have found the sources, keep looking, listening and asking for tips, for explanations, for reactions, for stories. The fun is just starting.

Covering a city is very much like covering a county government. In both cases you deal with politicians, with administrators, with budgets, with problems. The similarities may be obscured by differences in structure and style, however.

Cities are more likely to have professional administrators, for example. The administration of county governments is more likely to be in the hands of elected commissioners, supervisors or judges. Counties, too, are more likely to have a multitude of elected officials, from the sheriff to the recorder of deeds. City governments are more likely to be bureaucracies. One way to generalize about the differences is to say that city governments often are more efficient and county governments are more responsive.

These differences frequently mean, for a reporter, that county government is easier to cover. More elected officials means more politicians. That, in turn, can mean more talkative sources, more open conflict, more points at which constituents and reporters alike can gain access to the governmental structure.

The principles and the problems of reporting are the same. The budget remains the blueprint whether it is drafted by a professional administrator or an elected officeholder. Knowledge is power whether it is the city manager or the elected county clerk who knows where the money goes. Politics is politics.

The Schools

No institution is more important to any community than its schools. None is worse covered. And none is more demanding of or rewarding to a reporter. The issues that arise on the school beat are among the most important in our society. If it is your beat, be prepared to write about racial tensions, drug abuse, obscenity versus free speech, religious conflict, crime, labor-management disputes, politics, sex — and yes, education.

The process of learning and teaching can be obscured by the furor arising from the more dramatic issues. Even when everyone else seems to have forgotten, though, you must not forget that all those are only side issues. The most important part of the school beat is what goes on in the classroom.

Whether those classrooms hold kindergartners or college students, the principles for covering education remain the same. For the most part, so do the issues. When the schools are private rather than public, you have fewer rights of access.

The classroom is not an easy place to cover. You may have trouble getting into one. Administrators frequently turn down such requests on the grounds that a reporter's presence would be disruptive. It would be, at first. But a good teacher and an unobtrusive reporter can overcome that drawback easily. Many papers, at the start of the school year, assign a reporter to an elementary school classroom. He or she visits frequently, gets to know the teacher and pupils, becomes part of the furniture. And that reporter captures for readers much of the sight and sound and feeling of education.

There are other ways, too, of letting readers in on how well — or how badly — the schools are doing their job. Here are some of them:

- *Examine standardized test scores.* Every school system administers some kind of standard tests designed to measure how well its students compare either with a set standard or with other students. The results of such tests

TIPS: Keeping up with issues on the education beat

- Subscribe to trade newsletters and magazines.
- Remember the most important part of the beat — what goes on in the classroom.
- Understand what standard test scores mean.
- Get to know teachers, administrators and students.

are or ought to be public information. Insist on learning about them. Test scores are an inadequate measure of school quality, but they are good indicators. When you base a story on them, be sure you understand what is really being compared and what factors outside the schools may affect the scores. Find out what decisions are made on the basis of standardized test scores. For example, do schools whose students' average scores are relatively low get additions to their faculty? Do they get special-education teachers?

- *Be alert to other indicators of school quality.* You can find out how many graduates of your school system go to college, how many win scholarships and what colleges they attend. You can find out how your school system measures up to the standards of the state department of education. Does it hold the highest classification? If not, why not? National organizations of teachers, librarians and administrators also publish standards they think schools should meet. How close do your schools come?
- *In education, as in anything else, you get what you pay for.* How does the pay of teachers in your district compare with pay in similar-sized districts? How does the tax rate compare? What is the turnover among teachers?
- *Get to know as many teachers, administrators and students as possible.* You can learn to pick out the teachers who really care about children and learning. One way to do that is to encourage them to talk about their jobs. A good teacher's warmth will come through.

One reason schools are covered poorly is that the beat often does not produce the obvious, easy stories of politics, personalities and conflict that the city hall or police beats yield. School board meetings usually produce a spark only when a side issue intrudes. Most school board members are more comfortable talking about issues other than education itself, which often is left to the professionals.

The politics and the budgets of schools are very much like those of other institutions. The uniquely important things about the school are the classroom and what happens inside it. Your reporting will suffer if you forget that fact. So will your readers.

The Police Beat

The police beat probably produces more good, readable stories per hour of reporter time than any other beat. It also produces some of the worst, laziest reporting and generates many of our most serious legal and ethical problems. It is the beat many cub reporters start on and the beat many veterans stay on until they have become almost part of the force. It offers great frustration and great opportunity. All these contradictions arise from the nature of police work and of reporting.

If you are going to be a police reporter — and nearly every reporter is, at least briefly — the first thing you have to understand is what police officers are and what they do. We hire police officers to protect us from each other. We require them to deal every day with the dregs of society. Abuse and danger are parts of the job, as is boredom. We pay police officers mediocre wages and accord them little status. We ask them to be brave but compassionate, stern but tolerant. Very often what we get is less what we ask for than what we should expect. Police work seldom attracts saints. Police officers are frequently cynical, often prejudiced, occasionally dishonest.

When you walk into a police station as a reporter for the first time, expect to be met with some suspicion, even hostility. Young reporters often are perceived by police as being radical, unkempt, anti-authority. How closely does that description fit you or your classmates?

Police departments are quasi-military organizations, with strict chains of command and strong discipline. Their members are sworn to uphold the status quo. The reasons that police and young reporters are mutually suspicious should be clear by now.

Then how do you cover these people? You do so by using the techniques Karen Brooks applied in Corpus Christi — the same tricks of the trade she later used to cover politics and the border.

- *Educate yourself in police lore.* Take a course in law enforcement, if you can, or take a course in constitutional law. You also might read Joseph Wambaugh's novels for a realistic portrait of the police.
- *Try to fit in.* Keep your hair neat, dress conservatively and learn the language. Remember that police officers, like the rest of us, usually are quicker to trust people who look and act the way they do.
- *Lend a sympathetic ear.* You enjoy talking about yourself to somebody who seems to be interested; so do most police officers. They know they have a tough job, and they like to be appreciated. Open your mind, and try to understand even the points of view with which you may disagree strongly.
- *Encourage gossip.* Police officers may gossip even more than reporters do. Encourage such talk over a cup of coffee at the station, while tagging along in a patrol car or over a beer after the shift. The stories will be one-sided and exaggerated, but you may learn a lot. Those war stories are fascinating, besides. Just don't print anything you haven't verified.
- *Talk with other police-watchers.* Lawyers can be good sources, especially the prosecutors and public defenders who associate every day with the police. Other law-enforcement sources are good, too. Sheriff's deputies, for example, may be eager to talk about dishonesty or inefficiency in the city police department, and city police may be eager to reciprocate.

One important reason for all this work is that little of the information you need and want as a police reporter is material you are entitled to under public records laws. By law you are entitled to see only the arrest sheet (also called the arrest log or blotter). This record tells you only the identity of the person arrested, the charge and when the arrest took place. You are not entitled by law to see the arrest report or to interview the officers involved.

Writing a story depends on securing more than the bare-bones information. Finding out details depends on the goodwill you have generated with the desk sergeant, the shift commander and the officers on the case. The dangers — of being unfair, of damaging your and your paper's or broadcast station's reputation — are ever-present. Good reporting requires that you know what the dangers are and how to try to avoid them.

The greatest danger arises from the one-sidedness and frequent inaccuracy of police reports. At best, the reports represent the officer's viewpoint. Particularly in cases involving violence, danger, confusion or possible repercussions, there may be plausible viewpoints different from that of the police officer. Conflicting interpretations of the same situation lead many times to the dropping of charges.

To protect yourself, and to be fair to the accused, always be skeptical. Attribute any accusatory statement to the officer who made it. If the room for doubt is great enough, talk to the accused, his or her relatives or lawyer, and any witnesses you can find. The result is almost sure to be a fairer, more complete story.

Sometimes the story is that the police officers themselves are misbehaving. Jo Craven McGinty was fresh out of journalism graduate school and new to the computer-assisted reporting staff of *The Washington Post*. That didn't prevent her from suggesting that the *Post* follow up on something she had spotted at the National Institute for Computer-Assisted Reporting. A first run through the data was promising, and soon a team was studying the rate at which Washington, D.C., police shot civilians. It was far higher than the national average. Before the team was finished, a system of deadly carelessness and corruption was exposed. And the *Post* won a Pulitzer Prize for the rookie's idea.

The Courts

One way to begin trying to understand the American judicial system is to think of it as a kind of game. The opposing players in a criminal case are the state, which is the accuser, and the defendant, who is the accused. In a civil case the opponents are the plaintiff and the defendant. Each player is represented by a lawyer, who does everything possible to win for his or her client. The judge referees the contest, insisting that all players abide by the rules. At the end, the judge (sometimes with a jury) decides who won.

Such an irreverent description grossly oversimplifies a system that, because of its independence and usual honesty, stands second only to a free press in protecting the liberty of Americans. But it may help in demystifying a system that also can overawe a beginning reporter.

There is a great deal in courts and the law to inspire awe. Black-robed judges and learned attorneys speak a language full of Latin phrases and highly specialized terms. Written motions, arguments and decisions are laden with convoluted sentences and references unintelligible to the uninitiated. A court can protect your money or your freedom or deprive you of them.

You can hardly cover the courts aggressively while standing awestruck, though, so here are some tips that may help restore your working skepticism:

- *Never trust a lawyer unless you know him or her very well.* Although most lawyers are honest, all lawyers are advocates. Consequently, everything they write or say must be interpreted as being designed to help their client and hurt their opponent. That is true whether the lawyer represents the defense or the prosecution in a criminal case or represents either side in a civil lawsuit. Bar association codes of ethics forbid it, but many lawyers will try to use reporters to win some advantage. Be suspicious.
- *A judge's word may be law, but it isn't gospel.* Not every judge is a legal scholar. Most judges are, or have been, politicians. All judges are human. They are subject to error, capable of prejudice. Some are even dishonest. Otto Kerner was a judge of a federal appeals court when he was convicted of corruption that occurred while he was governor of Illinois. Abe Fortas was a justice of the U.S. Supreme Court, a close adviser of President Lyndon B. Johnson, and Johnson's nominee for chief justice when a reporter disclosed he was receiving regular payments from a man convicted of violating federal law. Fortas resigned from the court.
- *Truth and justice do not always prevail.* Prosecutors sometimes conceal evidence favorable to the defense. Defense lawyers sometimes seize on technicalities or rely on witnesses they know to be unreliable in order to win acquittals. Judges sometimes misinterpret the rules or ignore them. Innocent people do go to jail, and guilty ones go free. Courts are no more perfect than are newspapers. The two combined can produce frightening scenes, such as the one in Cleveland in 1954 when the newspapers screamed for blood and a political judge denied Dr. Sam Sheppard the most basic rights before convicting him of murdering his wife. The Supreme Court decision overturning that conviction became a landmark in spelling out proper trial procedures. In other cases, the press helped correct miscarriages of justice. Reporter Gene Miller won two Pulitzer Prizes for winning freedom for persons wrongfully imprisoned after unjust murder convictions.

The judicial system is not exempt from honest and critical reporting. And the sources of that reporting — just as in city hall or the police station — are records and people. First, a few words about court records, where to find them and how to use them.

Court Records

Whenever a case is filed in court — whether it is a criminal charge or a civil lawsuit — the court clerk assigns it a number. It also has a title. In the case of a criminal charge, the title will be "State vs. Joe Doakes," or something similar. (The "vs." is short for "versus," the Latin word meaning "against.") A civil case — a lawsuit seeking damages, for example — could be "Joe Doakes vs. John Doe." Doakes would be the plaintiff, the party filing the suit. Doe would be the defendant. In order to secure the records from the clerk, you must know the case number or case title, which lawyers also call the "style" of the case.

You can follow a case by checking the file. At least in the more important criminal cases, however, you usually keep track by checking with the prosecutor and defense lawyers.

Once a civil suit has been filed, the defense files a reply. The plaintiff may file a motion seeking information. The defense may file a motion to dismiss the suit, which the plaintiff will answer. The judge rules on each motion. You can follow it all by checking the file regularly. Except in rare cases, all motions and information filed with the court become public records. Often information from lawsuits can provide you with interesting insights into the otherwise private affairs of prominent persons or businesses.

Many lawsuits never go to trial before judge or jury. It is common procedure for lawyers to struggle for advantage over a period of months, filing motions and countermotions to gain the best position or to sound out the other side's strength. Then, after a trial date has been set, one side or the other will propose a settlement, which is negotiated. The case is dropped. One reason for that course of action is that the details of an out-of-court settlement need not be made public, unlike the outcome of a trial.

Human Sources

If a case goes to trial, you cover civil and criminal proceedings in much the same way. You must listen to testimony and, during breaks, corner lawyers for each side to seek explanation and elaboration, while filling in the background from court records and your morgue. Your personal contacts are important sources of information during this process.

Lawyers. Remember the warning to be leery of lawyers. However, despite the self-serving nature of many of their comments, lawyers are likely to be the best sources on the court beat. Every courthouse reporter needs to win the confidence and goodwill of the prosecutor and his or her staff. Not only can they keep you abreast of developments in criminal prosecution, they often can — because assistant prosecutors generally are young, political and ambitious — keep you tuned in to all sorts of interesting and useful courthouse gossip. They are good sources for tips on who the best and worst judges are, which local officials may be on the take, which defense lawyers are less than upright. Like all gossip, such tips need careful handling and thorough checking. But the raw material is often there.

Lawyers in private practice can be grouped, from a reporter's viewpoint, into two classes: those who will talk and those who won't. The former class usually includes young lawyers, politically ambitious lawyers and criminal defense lawyers, all of whom often find publicity helpful. Cultivate them. Lawyers have egos only slightly smaller than those of reporters. Feed those egos. Encourage them to talk about themselves, their triumphs, their ambitions. You will reap story possibilities, background information and gossip to trade with other sources.

Judges. Don't ignore judges as sources, either. Some are so conscious of their dignity and their images that they have no time for reporters. Remember, though, that most judges in most states are elected to their jobs. That makes them politicians, and it is a rare politician who slams the door on a friendly reporter. Even many federal judges, who are appointed by the president, have done a stint in politics and still have their taste for newspaper ink. Judges' egos may be even bigger than reporters'. Treat every judge accordingly.

Other court functionaries. Many other court functionaries can be helpful sources. Police officers and sheriff's deputies or U.S. marshals assigned to court duty often are underworked and glad of a chance to talk about whatever they know, which may turn out to be good backstage stuff. The bailiffs who shout for order in court and help the judge on with a robe may be retired police officers or small-time politicians and also talkative. And secretaries, as everywhere, are good to know and even better to have know you.

You cover the courts, then, as you cover any other beat. You learn the language, figure out the records and develop your sources.

Religion

If you ever doubted the importance of religion in the world or in the news, just do a quick Google search for the terms "Islamic fundamentalists" and "pedophile priests." Whether your beat is the Pentagon or the police station, you're more likely than ever to find yourself covering stories with a connection to religion. Indeed, the dark side of religion news has become so prominent that it's easy to forget that religion has always been more important to everyday people than journalists seem to think.

More Americans attend religious services than attend college football games. More Americans are active in religion than in politics. Overwhelming majorities of Americans say that religion is important in their lives. However, you'd never guess any of those realities from reading or viewing most news reports. The typical newspaper offers a weekly Religion page, usually published on Saturday, when circulation and readership are low. The typical television news coverage of religion is even less, often nonexistent.

There are some signs that journalism is waking up. Some papers, large and small, are expanding religion reporting beyond the weekly page. Some have expanded their definitions of the subject to include broader issues of spirituality and ethics. Others are recognizing the role of religion beyond formal worship. That's not surprising. Just consider the stories:

In *social issues*, religion plays a role in the continuing debate over sex education, AIDS research and treatment, abortion, homosexuality, and an almost-endless variety of other policy questions.

In *politics*, religion has become a key to campaigning and to governing. Presidents from both major political parties proclaim themselves born-again

**TIPS: Look for religion
stories in**

- Social issues.
- Politics.
- Law.
- International affairs.
- Everyday life.

Christians. Candidates at all levels solicit the support of the religious right or, in fewer cases, make the most of their independence from it. In campaigns throughout the country, well-organized and well-financed religious organizations, usually conservative in their theology and their politics, exert influence even beyond their numbers. In major cities, candidates court Jewish and Muslim support.

In *law*, constitutional questions continue to cloud the relationship of church and state. The U.S. Supreme Court is asked to decide whether inclusion of the phrase "under God" in the Pledge of Allegiance is a violation of the First Amendment. President George W. Bush made news when he urged federal financial support for the social welfare programs of religious organizations. The hierarchy of the Catholic Church angered many of the faithful when it failed to report to law-enforcement agencies accusations of sexual abuse by priests.

Since Sept. 11, 2001, reporters accustomed to writing about *international affairs* have found themselves required to explain Islam, the religion of one-fifth of the world's population. While political leaders struggled with unfamiliar names and previously unknown organizations, journalists had to learn the differences between Sunni and Shiite, the role of religion in the politics of Pakistan, and the geography and theology of the world's fastest-growing faith.

In *everyday life*, religion-based charities assume increasing importance as the American economy leaves behind growing numbers of the unskilled and uneducated. The "Religion Calendar" for just one week in a Midwestern college town includes activities that range from the African Methodist Episcopal women's group to the pagan Wiccan circle to meditation practice at the Zen Center.

So how does a reporter cover such a range of issues, personalities and events?

First, prepare. Read as widely as you can. A good place to start is with a booklet called *Deities & Deadlines*. Its subtitle tells its purpose: *A Primer on Religion News Coverage*. Written for the Freedom Forum by a veteran religion news reporter, John Dart, this little guide is full of specific, helpful advice and information. It includes brief descriptions of the major faiths, summaries of issues and a list of sources, complete with telephone numbers. You can order it from the Freedom Forum First Amendment Center at Vanderbilt University in Nashville, Tenn.

The best-informed coverage of religion and related issues can be found in such magazines as *Cross Currents*, *Christianity Today*, *National Catholic Reporter*, *Christian Century*, *Worldview* and other publications you'll find indexed at your local public or university library. Every major faith today has a Web site.

For theological expertise and local comment on major stories about religion, consult faculty members at the nearest Religious Studies department or seminary. But beware of their possible biases. Get to know your local religious activists, in the clergy and outside. Who are the rebels and the questioners? Who are the powers behind the pulpit quietly raising money, directing spending and guiding policy?

Remember that religion is also big business. Public records and computer databases can help you trace property ownership and finances. Religious organizations often own commercial property, housing, parking lots, educational facilities. Typically, they pay no taxes, but their economic impact can be great, and it isn't always positive. Churches have been found to be slumlords.

Religious organizations pay no income taxes, either. But they are required to file federal tax forms — Form 990 — to maintain their tax-exempt status. These Internal Revenue Service forms are the only income tax forms that are public by law. You'll find readers interested in the finances as well as in the good works of religion.

In addition to ignorance, other obstacles impede effective coverage of religion. Many reporters and editors are reluctant to subject religious leaders and institutions to the same scrutiny as their counterparts in business or politics. Remember that religious leaders are human. They are often good, sometimes devious, occasionally corrupt. Be respectful, but remember that a member of the clergy who demands deferential treatment might be hiding something behind that ecclesiastical smile.

Another special problem in covering religion is the emotional intensity with which many people hold to their beliefs. If you do serious reporting, you will not be able to avoid arousing somebody's wrath. You can avoid arousing it needlessly, however, by doing your homework.

Do not confuse a Southern Baptist with an American Baptist, or a Lutheran of the Missouri Synod with a Lutheran of the Evangelical Lutheran Church of America. You will not get very far interviewing a Jesuit if you ask him what denomination he belongs to. But not every Roman Catholic priest is a Jesuit. Don't attribute the same beliefs to Orthodox, Conservative and Reform Jews. And remember that Jews and Christians, although they dominate American religious life, are only a fraction of the world's religious believers.

Some stories about religion are uplifting. They tell of selfless service to the poor, the sick, the forgotten and abandoned. They illustrate values other than money or power. They describe the courage of people who put lives and property on the line for human rights or in opposition to war. Other stories are not so uplifting. Parishes run up huge debts. Parochial schools hire badly trained, poorly paid teachers. Blacks are refused admission. Women are refused ordination.

Stained-glass windows are no barrier to politics. Religious issues, such as abortion, homosexuality and capital punishment, are often also political issues. Churches may use their economic clout to combat injustice or to support it. Belief can be blind.

Whatever side of religion it explores, a good story about religion will wind up on the front page along with the best of the city hall or medical stories. The techniques for getting those stories are no different, either.

The Environment, Science and Medicine

In surveys, newspaper readers say they want more and better coverage of the environment. That feeling is especially strong among younger readers (and nonreaders, too). Environment stories are as close as your city parks, the public landfill or the local water supply. Expert sources are as close as the nearest university or state natural resources agency. Well-informed, passionate advocates are as close as the local chapter of the Sierra Club, the Audubon Society or nearly any developer of subdivisions or defender of property rights.

Emilia Askari, then president of the Society of Environmental Journalists, prepared some suggestions for editors on responding to reader interest. Her tips offer useful starting points for would-be environment writers:

- *Define the beat broadly.* The environment includes urban as well as wilderness issues. Think of abandoned buildings, old service stations and sewer systems as well as wetlands and endangered species.
- *Spend time on the beat.* Cultivate sources among experts and activists. Read what they read.
- *Expect pressure and controversy.* Land use, preservation, property rights and economics all can generate emotion as well as interest. You'll be under critical scrutiny by all sides of every issue you cover.
- *Look beyond purely local issues.* Such broader issues as global warming, deforestation and overfishing have local angles as close as the weather and the grocery store.
- *Educate yourself.* Look for opportunities to attend conferences on topics and techniques. Learn computer-assisted reporting. Take a course or more at the nearest college.
- *Write for kids.* They're interested; they're active; they're the readers and the citizens of tomorrow. Besides, there's no better way to make sure you really understand a complex issue than to explain it successfully to a youngster.
- *Watch for reports of scientific studies and translate them into everyday language.* Many of the best environment stories begin with research reports in scientific journals. Often those reports are picked up first in the specialized publications mentioned below. Make sure you know, and tell readers, the funding sources and any other possible bias in the studies you report.

Askari also offers a good source of information and professional guidance — her society. The SEJ home page can be found at **www.sej.org**. Information from and about the quarterly *SEJournal* can be accessed from this site.

Many of the techniques, the problems and the possibilities of environment reporting are paralleled in reporting on science and medicine.

On these beats there will be fewer meetings to attend or offices to visit than on a city hall or school beat. More of the stories here are likely to be generated by your own enterprise or by applying the local touch to a national story. You can find out what a new pesticide ban will mean to local farmers, for instance. Or you can determine whether local doctors are using a new arthritis treatment, or what a researcher at the state university is learning about the effects of alcohol on rats.

Where can you look for story ideas? Specialized publications are good places to start. Read the *Journal of the American Medical Association*, the *New England Journal of Medicine* and *Medical World*. New developments and issues in medicine are covered in news stories. *Scientific American* and *Science News* are informed but readable sources of ideas in all the sciences. For environmental issues, read *Natural History* magazine. Your state's conservation department may put out a publication. Get on the mailing lists of the National Wildlife Federation, the Sierra Club, the Audubon Society and Friends of the Earth.

Nearly every community has human sources, too. In medicine, these include members of the local medical association, the administrator of the hospital and public health officials. In the sciences, look for local school or college faculty, employees of government agencies such as extension or research centers, even interested amateurs such as those in astronomy societies. In the area of the environment, there usually is no shortage of advocacy groups or of industries that want to defend their interests. State and federal regulatory and research agencies are helpful, too.

The special problems posed by scientific beats begin with the language your sources use. It is a language full of Latin phrases, technical terms and numbers. You will have to learn enough of it both to ask intelligent questions and to translate the answers for your readers. A good medical dictionary and science dictionary are invaluable. Use them and continue asking for explanations until you are sure you understand.

Another problem may be convincing scientists and physicians to talk to you in any language. Many of them have had little contact with reporters. Much of the contact they have had probably has been unpleasant, either because it arose from some controversy or because the reporter was unprepared. Reluctant sources are much more likely to cooperate if you demonstrate that you have done your homework, so you have at least some idea of what they are talking about. Promise to check your story with the sources. Accuracy is as much your goal as theirs.

In medicine a concern for privacy may deter some sources from talking freely. A physician's allegiance is, and should be, to the patient. As a reporter you have no legal right to know a patient's condition or ailment. That is true even if the patient is a public official. In fact, most information about a person's medical history and condition is protected by law from disclosure by government record keepers. When the mayor goes to the hospital, then, and you want to know why, your only tools are your persuasiveness and the goodwill you have built up with hospital officials, the attending physician or the mayor's family.

Sources also may be guarded in comments about their work. Most researchers in medicine and science are cautious about making any claims about the significance or certainty of their work. Some are not so cautious. You must be. Check and double-check, with the researcher involved and with others knowledgeable in the field, before describing any development as "important" or "dramatic" or "frightening." Overstatement will damage your credibility with sources and readers.

Sometimes a researcher will be reluctant to discuss his or her work until it has been published in a professional journal or reported at a convention. Such presentation may be more important to the scientist than any newspaper publicity. Funding and fame are high-stakes issues for research scientists. Many, justifiably afraid of having unscrupulous fellow researchers claim credit for their work, maintain secrecy until a study is complete. A researcher's agreement to give you first notice when he or she is ready to go public may be the best you can hope for in this circumstance.

Despite difficulties, the coverage of science, medicine or the environment offers great challenges and rewards. The challenge is discovering and explaining developments and issues that are important to your readers. The rewards, as in all other areas of reporting, can be prizes, pay raises or — most important — recognition by your sources and peers of a job well done. The key to success in covering these beats is the same as for any other beat: Be prepared, be alert, be persistent, be there and be wary.

Suggested Readings

Dart, John. *Deities & Deadlines: A Primer on Religion News Coverage*, Second Edition. Nashville, Tenn.: The Freedom Forum First Amendment Center, 1998. This booklet is a primer on covering news of religion.

Houston, Brant, ed. *The Investigative Reporter's Handbook*, Fourth Edition. New York: Bedford/ St. Martin's, 2002. The first comprehensive guide to using public records and documents, written by members of Investigative Reporters and Editors. A must for serious reporters. See also the readings at the end of Chapter 18, "Investigative Reporting." They'll be useful in beat reporting, too.

Royko, Mike. *Boss*. New York: New American Library, 1971. A classic, brilliantly written study of urban machine politics.

Suggested Web Sites

www.journalismnet.com
A great source for journalists. Go to the topics list on the right side of the home page. You'll find sources for almost any subject.

www.poynter.org
We list this site repeatedly because it is so useful in so many ways. One feature is its links to nearly every professional journalism organization. See also the bibliography for sources and examples.

www.scout.cs.wisc.edu
The Scout Report is a weekly publication offering a selection of new and newly discovered Internet sources of interest to researchers and educators.

www.stateline.org
This site provides story tips and background information on state government and state-level issues.

Exercises

1. You've been assigned to cover city government. Do some background reading in your local newspaper and the other sources described in this chapter. Then write a memo describing what you expect to be the most important issues on your new beat and who you expect to be your most important human sources.

2. In the library or in a computer database, look up three recent national or international stories about a religious issue. Write a memo explaining how you would localize each story for your city. Include possible sources.

3. Using Nexis or another public computer database, examine how two or three major newspapers cover a national beat, such as Congress or a federal agency. What similarities and differences do you see between that work and local coverage? The topics will be different, but what about sources? Do you see any different focus on reader interests?

4. Analyze a local news story about science, medicine or the environment. Identify the sources. If you were reporting this story, what other sources would you consult? What specific questions would you try to get answered?

Here's the introduction to a report from the business news task force of the Associated Press Managing Editors:

> If the business of America is indeed "business," then the business of American newspapers is definitely business news coverage.
>
> Across the nation, newspaper editors are adding staff, increasing newshole and giving new prominence to business journalism that just a few years ago was relegated to a small section or a few pages back behind the Sports.
>
> What's going on?
>
> To some extent, newspapers are merely catching up with their readership. . . .

Scandals on Wall Street and a volatile stock market have made business news a Page One staple. Even as recently as 20 years ago, the business section was a few columns of stocks and business briefs. But now, stories about the Federal Reserve lowering or raising interest rates frequently lead the evening newscasts. Why? Because readers and viewers want to know where interest rates are headed before they buy a car or invest in a house or in stocks.

Since 60 percent of Americans now own stock, often through Individual Retirement Accounts or 401(k) funds, millions of news consumers are focused on the ups and downs of the Dow Jones Industrial Average or the performance of individual stocks or mutual funds.

Because of this surge of interest in business news, even politics reporters have had to learn the basics of business. The relative health of the U.S. economy played a major role in the 2000 and 2004 election campaigns, from the debate over the loss of jobs overseas to medical benefits for seniors.

Any story can be a business story. Yet many business desks of the past limited themselves to movements in stock prices or the Consumer Price Index. They put many readers to sleep and ignored most of the potential audience.

Stock prices are still important, of course. Many investors and business people consult their daily newspapers for just those numbers. But today, more newspapers are focusing on what those numbers mean to the reader. Business journalists are also cutting out a lot of the jargon that often confused potential readers. Instead, they are explaining things

In this chapter you will learn:

1. How to prepare to cover business news.

2. Where to find business news.

3. How to understand the numbers of business.

4. How to find and report consumer news.

in commonsense language that most people understand. As a result, readership — and the amount of space publishers are willing to give business news — is on the rise.

So are stories about how to spend, save and invest money. Consumer and personal finance stories, which include everything from how to save money on car repairs to how to invest an inheritance, are common.

The number of jobs in business journalism is growing. The most spectacular growth has been in the broadcast and online worlds. Many online organizations, such as CNET.com, specialize in covering some slice of the business world for a narrow but affluent audience. Web portals like CBS Marketwatch and MSN Money have large staffs devoted to covering corporate news.

In the broadcast world, television networks, especially cable, are also expanding their coverage. CNN, Bloomberg and CNBC, for example, devote hours of air time to consumer and economic news.

Newspapers, as that APME report suggests, also are responding to reader demand. Many have weekly business sections, as well as special sections that focus on specific issues such as real estate or automobiles. With the baby boom generation nearing retirement, dozens of magazines are devoted to personal finance and investing. There also is a broad selection of trade publications that focus on specific industries.

To get a job on any business desk, however, you need to understand basic business terminology and basic math. You also need to learn how to read financial statements, which is surprisingly easy. Beyond that, you need the skills of any journalist: perseverance, curiosity and an ability to ask questions and get answers.

PREPARING TO COVER BUSINESS NEWS

The range of business stories can be as broad as the range of business itself. Business stories may be about a company's promotions and retirements. Or they may concentrate on a company's potential profits, of interest to investors and potential investors in that company. Other business stories can cover personal finance issues that are of interest to lay readers rather than investment community insiders. Such stories explore issues such as these: Which are better investments, 15- or 30-year mortgages? Is art a good investment? Which mutual funds are high performers? Personal finance news is so popular that some business desks, like the one at *The Kansas City Star*, produce personal finance sections every week.

A business story might also be about a new kind of digital camera that would interest not just shareholders of the company but potential buyers as well. It could deal with the economic effects of mad cow disease on McDonald's stock and on Iowa beef producers. It can also be about the global economy, such as how high-tech customer service jobs are fleeing to Bombay, or how the Chinese company Haier Inc. is expanding its refrigerator factory in South Carolina.

Those stories have obvious local angles. Sometimes, though, the local angle is not so obvious. A story about a decision by the Federal Reserve Board's Open Market Committee to expand or tighten the money supply may seem far removed from your audience. But that decision can affect the rate your readers pay for a car or mortgage loan. Or it can affect them in how it adds to or subtracts from inflation. News of a sizable trade deficit for the United States may weaken the value of the dollar and increase the price of a Sony TV, a Volkswagen or a bottle of Cutty Sark Scotch whiskey. It takes skill, but a good business journalist can make these seemingly esoteric stories clear and relevant to the audience. And the clearly written explanation can land on Page One.

Many major corporate and economic decisions that affect us all are made in Washington, New York, Chicago and a few other major metropolitan centers. But those cities do not have a monopoly on the creation and coverage of business news. Even in towns of a few thousand residents, businesses will be opening or closing, and manufacturing plants will be increasing or decreasing production, hiring or firing employees. Local residents will be spending money for houses, cars, ski trips or new laptop computers, or socking it away in the town's banks or savings and loan associations. There is a business story in every such development.

Business stories can be as bright and as interesting as any story in any other section of the paper. That is demonstrated regularly in such publications as *The Wall Street Journal*, *The New York Times*, the *Chicago Tribune*, *Business Week* and *Forbes*. Here, for example, is the beginning of a *York* (Pa.) *Daily Record* story about a drive to increase financial regulation of cemeteries:

When Miriam Speck buried her husband Kenneth on Feb. 28, it was a sad day made sadder by the poor condition of the cemetery.

Her husband's grave at Suburban Memorial Gardens had been dug that morning, and fresh, soggy equipment tracks were still visible near the grave when the family gathered around it.

"We literally stood there with mud gushing up over our shoes," said Speck's daughter Donna Sharp. Her mother sat in the only chair provided for the service. It, too, was sinking down in the mud.

It was a lousy way to say good-bye to a husband and father. But the unnecessary grief was not over. It would drag on several more weeks, only to be punctuated by one final — and expensive — indignity.

During weekly visits to Kenneth's grave, Speck and her daughter noticed it was not being maintained. The ground over the grave had sunk about a foot and

water was standing in it. The fill-in dirt was still piled off to the side.

So, two months after the burial, when the ground had thawed, mother and daughter took matters into their own hands. On a beautiful spring day they took a shovel to the cemetery to finish filling the grave themselves.

"It was horrible," Sharp recalled. "It was terrible."

While the two women were standing around the grave, the cemetery's caretaker drove up, Sharp said. He explained to them the bitter history of the cemetery, how the former owner, Don Snyder, had died last year leaving virtually no money to run it, and how the new owner was taking over.

The women were pleased that someone would be rescuing the cemetery, which is on Bull Road in Conewago Township. But their joy turned to anger once again when they found out the bronze grave marker the Specks had bought for $450 in 1977 was nowhere to be found.

Not only that, if her mother wanted a marker for her husband's grave, she would have to buy one — for the second time — from the new owner.

Sadly, Snyder had died owing more than $350,000 in personal debt that was secured by the cemetery. He had also failed to set aside funds to cover purchases of vaults and grave markers he had sold to people before they were needed. Similar situations around the state have led the state legislature to consider greater regulation of cemeteries and funeral homes.

Small news organizations, as well, can have a big impact when covering large companies based in their communities. Jeff Zimmer, business editor of the Durham, N.C., *Herald-Sun* routinely has won awards for his newspaper's investigative coverage of Blue Cross–Blue Shield of North Carolina and its efforts to take the health insurer from a nonprofit company to a public company.

How to Report Business Stories

What separates a business story from a soccer story — or, for that matter, a soccer story from a story about atomic particles — is the knowledge and language required to ask the right questions, to recognize the newsworthy answers and to write the story in a way that the reader without specialized knowledge will understand. A reporter who understands the subject can explain what the jargon means.

For example, if banks change their prime rates, the personal finance reporter might be the person to write the story explaining that an increase of one percentage point could result in higher interest rates for car or home loans.

If West Coast longshoremen go on strike, one reporter covering local corporations might explore the impact on the supplies for a local manufacturer, whereas a retail reporter might talk to store owners about whether they'll have the right toys on their shelves in time for Christmas. With terrorism continuing to affect the airline and travel markets, labor and transportation reporters at *The Orlando Sentinel* often work together on a story about how security alert levels affect local employment.

Business reporters must use understandable language. But oversimplifying can turn readers off. *The Wall Street Journal* avoids both traps by shunning jargon as much as possible and explaining any technical terms essential to the story. In one story, for example, the *Journal* explained the terms "Federal Open Market Committee," "federal funds rate," "M1," "M2" and "free-reserve position." Sophisticated readers might know what those terms mean, but many of the paper's readers would not.

A 2001 study by the American Press Institute on business journalism training needs confirmed what business people and business journalists alike have long suspected: Top business executives think that journalists overall don't do a very good job of covering the complexities of business.

Another study, conducted in 2002 by the University of Missouri School of Journalism, found that business journalists were more skeptical of information from business sources than other sources.

Translating Business into English

Nik Deogun didn't set out to be a business reporter. It took an internship with *The Wall Street Journal* to change his mind. True, he had studied economics as an undergraduate, but his reporting courses in his master's program in journalism school had emphasized government and education. He sought the internship not because of the *Journal's* niche in business coverage but because he hoped for the chance to do the kinds of news features that appear on its front page.

He got hooked on business. "This is where the power lies, and not many people are writing about it," he says. "Money is the source of all power, the source of all evil" — and thus the source of good stories.

Deogun thinks his generalist background, both in liberal arts and in journalism, prepared him well. Business writers need to understand the social and political context in which their subjects operate.

"I use here the same reporting skills you'd use on any beat," he says. "If tomorrow I had to go cover fly-fishing, I wouldn't know diddley. But I'd learn. You read a lot and ask people questions."

Too much specialization in a field such as business can even be a handicap. The *Journal* serves an audience more involved in business than the audiences of most daily papers or broadcast outlets, but a reporter's job still includes a great deal of translating from the jargon of the specialist into everyday English.

Now the deputy bureau chief in Washington, D.C., for the *Journal*, Deogun understands he must be able to speak the technical language without falling into the trap of also writing it. "Most of your readers don't know that much about business," he observes.

Clear thinking and clear writing remain essential.

Sourcing presents a major challenge for business reporters: how to get information from someone who does not legally have to tell you anything. It often takes much more clever reporting skills to coax a story out of a business source than it does out of a government official. After all, almost all government information is open to the public. Many business records are not.

On the one hand, as John Seigenthaler, founder of the First Amendment Center, pointed out, "There is a feeling [among business executives] that the profit motive simply isn't understood as being as American as apple pie by numbers of journalists."

On the other hand, among journalists, he said, "There's a strong sense that business executives malinger, are not responsible and for the most part misrepresent and even more often refuse to communicate."

TIPS: How to report
business stories

- Use language readers will understand, but don't oversimplify.
- Always be fair. You can win the trust and confidence of business people — or at least their grudging respect.
- Appearances count. It may help you to dress as business people do.
- The more you can demonstrate that you understand a business, the more likely you are to generate trust that will draw out the information you seek.
- Get to know as many company executives as you can.
- Always remember that a company, government agency or pressure group may be using you to plant stories that serve some special interest.

The mistrust that many business people have of the press can make it difficult to cover stories adequately, even when it would be in the business's interest to see that the story is told. Even if executives are willing to talk, they may become angry if the reporter quotes an opposing point of view or points out a wart on the corporate visage.

The best antidote a reporter can use against this animosity is to report fairly and accurately what a business is doing and saying. By always being fair, you can win the trust and confidence of business people — or at least their grudging respect.

Because business executives tend to be cautious when it comes to talking with reporters, it may help you to dress more like a business manager than a concert reviewer. Appearances count, and business people, like reporters, plumbers, generals and linebackers, feel more comfortable with their own kind.

The more you can demonstrate that you understand their business, the more likely you are to generate the trust that will draw out the information you seek. "Understanding" is not synonymous with "sympathy," but ignorance usually means a reporter is likely to misinterpret what is said.

Public-relations people often are helpful in providing background information and directing you to the executives who can provide other comment and information, but you should try to get to know as many company executives as you can. Sometimes you can do this best through a background interview, one not generated by a crisis but intended simply to provide information about what the company is doing. Perhaps you can arrange to have lunch to see what the managers are thinking about and to give them a chance to see you are probably not the demon that they may have thought you to be.

Always remember that a company, government agency or pressure group may be trying to use you to plant stories that serve some special interest. Companies want a story to make them look promising to investors with the hope of driving up the price of the stock or to make them attractive merger partners. If you are suspicious, do some digging; talk to competitors and analysts, and ask detailed questions. Just because a company or some other group is pushing a story does not mean you have to write it. The best place for some interview notes is the wastebasket.

Conflict-of-interest issues challenge business journalists because they often write stories, some of which are unfavorable, about advertisers. Business editors across the country have become increasingly concerned as advertisers threaten to pull advertising over unfavorable coverage. For instance, in 2003 a story in *The Orlando Sentinel* on the shoddy practices of home builders cost the newspaper $700,000 in canceled advertisements.

Auto dealers and grocers, both traditionally large advertisers, have worked together to pressure other newspapers. While newspapers make a show of not caving in to such pressures, advertiser threats can produce a chilling effect in the news room.

It is challenging to cover business. To do so effectively, a business reporter should be all the things any good reporter is — honest, fair, alert to possible new stories and to new angles on old stories. Business writing can be rewarding, both financially (because specialists usually earn premium pay) and intellectually.

Where to Find Business Stories

The starting point in writing a business story is similar to the first step in reporting any story — understanding the subject you're writing about. For the business reporter, that almost always means some basic research into the subject. For openers, check your organization's library to learn what's been written locally about your topic or company.

Then turn to your computer. There is a broad spectrum of databases that provide lists and summaries of stories published on a wide range of subjects. The truly adept can plumb raw data, including stock market transactions, to track the impact of announcements, mergers and promotions on stock. But everyone can use simple Internet searches to access annual reports, stock analyses, press releases and other announcements.

Of growing importance are computer searches of databases that provide lists and summaries of stories published on a range of topics. Newsearch, Standard & Poor's, Predicasts, Dow Jones and Disclosure Inc. are some of the companies providing these data. Reuters, Dow Jones (Factiva) and Bloomberg Business News also provide background information on companies and securities, historical prices and real-time news on business and economic issues. Likewise, Business Wire, PR Newswire, Tribune Business News, all major newspapers and magazines, and the Associated Press all provide online business information.

Many of the paper information sources discussed below are also available online. The good business reporter knows how to use the *Readers' Guide to Periodical Literature*, the *Business Periodicals Index*, *The New York Times Index*, *The Wall Street Journal Index* and perhaps the *National Newspaper Index* (which indexes the *Times*, the *Journal*, the *Los Angeles Times* and *The Washington Post*). These indexes will tell you where to find stories about your business or industry.

Another valuable secondary source for business reporters is *Predicasts' F & S Index of Corporations and Industries*, considered by many to be the best index for company and industry information. *Predicasts* indexes a broad range of business, financial and industrial periodicals, plus a few reports by brokerage houses. For information on foreign companies, see *Predicasts' F & S Index International*. The *Public Affairs Information Service Bulletin* is a less inclusive index from the area of economics, social conditions, public administration and international relations.

Records and Reports

Here are some good sources of information that you will find invaluable when writing business stories. Remember, many of these can be accessed through various online databases. That means you can decide on a question, log on and have the information you need right away.

>   *Corporate data.* Basic information on corporations can be found in three directories published annually. Your university or public library probably has all three. *Dun & Bradstreet's Million Dollar Directory* includes almost

TIPS: Where to find business stories

- Conduct some basic research into the subject. Check your paper's library to learn what's been written locally about the topic or company.
- Turn to your computer. From a broad spectrum of databases you can obtain lists and summaries of stories published on a wide range of subjects.
- Print sources will tell you where to find stories about your business or industry.

40,000 U.S. companies worth $1 million or more. It lists officers and directors, products and services, sales, number of employees and addresses and telephone numbers. The *Middle Market Directory* profiles companies worth $500,000 to $999,999. The three-volume *Standard & Poor's Register of Corporations, Directors and Executives* provides similar information for about 36,000 U.S. and Canadian companies. Volume 2 lists executives and directors with brief biographies. The third directory is the *Thomas Register of American Manufacturers* and the *Thomas Register Catalog File*. The 11 volumes are more comprehensive than the other two directories.

Investment data. To get specific information about the financial performance of a company or an industry, check reports prepared by Standard & Poor's (especially valuable is S&P's Compustat Services Inc.), Moody's, Dun & Bradstreet or Value Line Investment Survey. These reports also discuss company prospects and major trends. Also helpful are annual corporate scoreboards prepared by *Fortune, Business Week* and *Forbes* magazines. *Business Week* uses S&P's Compustat to prepare its scoreboard. You would be wise to buy and file those issues for future reference.

Financial ratios. To assess a company's financial picture and management, you should compare your subject's financial ratios with the averages for other firms in the same industry. Industry ratios and averages can be found in reports prepared by Dun & Bradstreet, Moody's, and S&P's Compustat and in a number of trade journals.

Company filings. For years the Securities and Exchange Commission operated under the guiding principle that companies should make available a maximum amount of information so that stockholders could make the most informed decisions regarding management's performance. The SEC preferred to keep out of corporate affairs and to let the stockholders provide necessary discipline. Much of that information was made public through SEC filings. In recent years the SEC has required less information, but corporate filings remain a valuable source of information for reporters. You should start with the annual report, which will give you an attractively packaged overview of the company's operations and finances. The 10-K, a more detailed document required by the SEC, also will give you the number of employees, a list of major real estate and equipment holdings, and any significant legal proceedings. Many other important documents, such as labor contracts, are listed by reference and can be acquired through the company, a Freedom of Information Act request or a private service such as Disclosure Inc. The proxy statement, which goes to shareholders before the annual meeting or other important meetings, provides an outline of issues to be voted on, as well as executive salaries and information on the company's board of directors. The proxy also sometimes contains leads about the company's business dealings. Interesting nuggets are found under mundane headings such as "other matters" or "legal proceedings." For example, now-bankrupt Enron Corp. did disclose some hints about its offshore partnerships in the footnotes of the Houston company's SEC filings. Those footnotes did generate some stories, but company officials did not disclose the true extent of the company's financial problems. In any filing, always read anything pertaining to lawsuits. That, in turn, can lead you to public documents regarding a particular suit.

Many companies are quite willing to send you their annual report, 10-K and proxy statement. They may even send you the other documents outlined above. To keep up with SEC filings, you may want to follow the *SEC News Digest* at your local library, or use the SEC's online EDGAR service. To obtain specific filings, you can contact an organization such as 10K Wizard, which, for a fee, will alert you to new reports filed with the SEC by public companies.

Trade press. Beyond the newspapers and magazines you already know and read is another segment of journalism known as the **trade press.** In these journals and house organs you will find grocers talking with grocers, undertakers talking with undertakers and bankers talking with bankers. You will learn the important issues in a field, how an industry markets its products and services, and what legislation it fears and favors. Interested in health care and physicians? Try *Medical Economics*, where investigative reporter Jessica Mitford predicts you will find "many a crass and wonderfully quotable appeal to the avarice of the practitioners of the healing arts." When Chris Welles wrote a piece on the health hazards of modern cosmetics, much of his best information came from trade magazines. He found the specific periodicals by looking in the *Drug & Cosmetics Periodicals Index* and the *F & S Index of Corporations and Industries.*

A number of trade publications are independent and objective. Among them are *Advertising Age, Aviation Week & Space Technology, Institutional Investor, American Banker, Medical World News* and *Variety.* Many more, however, are practically industry public-relations organs. But even they can be valuable for learning about current issues, marketing and lobbying strategies, and even market shares. To find trade publications, consult the *Standard Periodical Directory, Ulrich's International Periodicals Directory, Standard Rate & Data Service: Business Publication Rates and Data,* and *Gale Directory of Publications and Broadcast Media.* Many trade publications offer online versions, like **www.ogi.com**, the online version of the comprehensive trade publication *Oil & Gas Journal.*

Newsletters. Newsletters have become an important source of inside information in recent years. Some are purely ideological, but others can be valuable. Among the best are *Energy Daily, Nucleonics Week, Education Daily, Higher Education Daily* and the *Washington Report on Medicine.* For example, the *Friday Report,* published by Institutional Shareholder Services, explores proxy issues of U.S. companies and is a must-read for professional investors who need to know what issues are facing corporate boards. To find newsletters, consult *The Newsletter Yearbook Directory.*

Directories. Directories can be an invaluable tool for locating information on companies, organizations or individuals. You can use them to learn who makes a certain product, to identify company officers or directors or to find an expert source for an interview. Basic directories include *Who's Who, Directory of Directories, Guide to American Directories, Consultants and Consulting Organizations Directory, Directory of Special Libraries & Information Centers, Research Centers Directory, Consumer Sourcebook, Statistical Sources* and *Directory of Industrial Data Sources.* To contact companies by phone or mail, look in the *National Directory of Addresses and Telephone Numbers,* published by Concord Reference Books Inc.

Court records. Most companies disclose only information required by the SEC. But when a corporation sues or is sued, an extensive amount of material becomes available. Likewise, criminal action against principals in a firm can provide the lead to a good story. It is important to check court testimony and records at all levels, including those of bankruptcy and divorce court.

Local regulators. Frequently, businesses want to enlarge their facilities or expand into new markets. To do so, a business may seek funds from an industrial bond authority, which helps the company obtain large sums of money at below-market rates. Or when an institution such as a hospital wants to expand its services, often it must make a case for the expansion before a regional or local agency. In either case, documents filed to support the requests may be revealing and may put into the public record information that previously was unobtainable.

Others. The preceding lists are certainly not exhaustive. Other relevant materials may be found at local tax and record-keeping offices, as well as in filings with the Federal Trade Commission, the Federal Communications Commission, the Food and Drug Administration, the Interstate Commerce Commission, the Bureau of Labor Statistics and various state agencies. *Crain's Chicago Business* used Census Bureau figures as the basis of a story on retail sales trends. The *U.S. Government Manual* lists and describes government agencies, including their functions and programs. Don't overlook the Federal Reserve system, which employs scores of economic analysts at each of its 12 regional banks. Eight times a year, the Fed publishes a comprehensive book of regional statistics and analysis, nicknamed the "Beige Book," available online at **www.federalreserve.gov**. The *Consumer Confidence Index*, a survey of 5,000 sample households by the Conference Board, gauges consumer sentiment on the U.S. economy. This is an important monthly index, followed by market watchers as well as the Federal Reserve in setting interest rates.

A number of private firms specialize in economic analysis, such as the WEFA Group and Data Resources Inc. In writing about the benefits OPEC could reap from oil company mergers, *The Wall Street Journal* cited figures generated by WEFA.

Online sources abound with reams of corporate news and financial information, such as Yahoo! Finance, MSN Money and CBS Marketwatch, among others. The sites offer historical stock price information, lists of corporate compensation, links to SEC filings and corporate news releases.

The following is a list of places to look for publicly held companies' SEC filings:

- *13-D.* Lists owners of more than 5 percent of the voting stock. Filed within 10 business days. Must report increases and decreases of holdings.
- *13-F.* Quarterly report of ownership by institutional investors. Includes holders of less than 5 percent of the company.
- *8-K.* Report of significant incident.

- *10-Q.* Quarterly financial statement.
- *10-K.* Annual financial statement. Includes number of employees, lists of major real estate and equipment holdings, significant legal proceedings. Many other important documents, such as labor contracts, are listed by reference and can be acquired through the company, Freedom of Information Act request or private service.

- *Proxy statement.* Contains information on executive salaries, director information, shareholder voting issues.
- *Annual report to shareholders.* May lack much of the data found in the 10-K.
- *Securities registration statement/prospectus.* Submitted when new stock is to be issued; usually contains same information as 10-K and proxy but is more up to date.

Don't overlook documents and testimony from congressional hearings. Chris Welles drew much of the best material for his book on the ending of fixed brokerage commissions, *The Last Days of the Club*, from 29 volumes of hearings and reports that came out of several years of investigations by two congressional subcommittees.

Human Sources

Who are the people you should talk to on the business beat? Here are some who are important sources of information:

Company executives. Although many public-relations people can be helpful, the most valuable information probably will come from the head of the corporation or the heads of its divisions. Chief executive officers are powerful people, either out front or behind the scenes, in your community. They are often interesting, usually well-informed. Not all of them will be glad to see you, although many executives value open communication with the press. In 2000, in an effort to tighten up information that could lead to illegal stock trading based on inside information, the SEC adopted Regulation FD (Fair Disclosure). It governs how corporate executives release information about corporate finances and other material information. Although Regulation FD has an exemption for journalists, it has caused executives to be more cautious in releasing information. As a result, many companies now release quarterly financial information at Web-based conference calls that journalists can listen to and ask questions of executives.

Public-relations sources. Don't automatically assume the public-relations person is trying to block your path. Many people working in corporate communications are truly professional, and providing information to journalists is part of their job. Remember, though, that they are paid to make the company look good, so they will likely point you in the direction of the company's viewpoint. Public-relations professionals aren't objective, but that doesn't mean that the information they provide is untrue. Instead, you should assume that it is being packaged to show the company in its best light.

Academic experts. Your college or university will have faculty members with training and experience in varying areas of business and economics. Often they are good sources of local reaction to national developments or analysis of economic trends. They are usually happy to cooperate. Many university public information offices prepare lists of their nationally or regionally known experts and their phone numbers. The lists are available for the asking.

Associations. Although trade associations clearly represent the interests of their members, they can provide expert commentary on current issues or give explanations from the perspective of the industry. When *The New York Times* reported on the revival of the moving industry, the Household Goods Carriers Bureau, a major trade group, proved to be an important source. *The Wall Street Journal* found the National Association of Realtors a valuable source for a story on housing costs. To find trade associations, look in the *Encyclopedia of Associations* or the *National Trade and Professional Associations of the United States.*

Chamber of commerce officials. Their bias is clearly pro-business, and they will seldom make an on-the-record negative comment about business, but they usually know who is who and what is what in the business community. The chamber may be involved in such projects as downtown revitalization and industry recruiting. State and regional areas all have economic development agencies that receive tax funds and are required to file reports of their recruitment activities.

Former employees. The best business reporters say that frequently their most valuable sources are former employees of the company they're profiling. Writes Welles, "Nobody knows more about a corporation than someone who has actually worked there." He warns, "Many, probably most, have axes to grind, especially if they were fired; indeed, the more willing they are to talk, the more biased they are likely to be." The good reporter will show care in using materials thus gained.

Labor leaders. For the other side of many business stories and for pieces on working conditions, contracts and politics, get to know local union officials (see Figure 15.1). The workings, legal and otherwise, of unions make good stories, too.

Others. Don't overlook the value of a company's customers, suppliers and competitors. You also may want to consult with local bankers, legislators,

Figure 15.1
*Union meetings, such as
this one of the United Food
and Commercial Workers in
Los Angeles, can be excellent sources of labor stories.*

legislative staff members, law-enforcement agencies and regulators, board
members, oversight committee members and the like.

Announcements and Meetings

The source of much business news, and the starting point for many good stories,
is the announcement by a company of a new product or the firm's reaction to
some action by a government agency. Such announcements should be treated
like any news release. The same standards apply to judging newsworthiness, and
the same reporting techniques come into play.

The news may come in a news conference, which may be called to respond
to a general situation such as a strike or takeover attempt. Or it may be called to
try to add some glitter to a corporate announcement the company feels will be
ignored if made in news releases alone. You can almost tell how newsworthy
something is going to be by the amount of paraphernalia on hand in the news
conference room. The more charts, graphs, enlarged photos, projectors and
screens in the room, the more likely you are to be dazzled instead of enlightened.
These presentations should not be ignored, however, because you can never be
sure in advance that something newsworthy will not be said.

If you work in a city where one or more corporations are based, you may
have the opportunity to cover an annual meeting, which invariably produces

some news. Although some meetings are more lively and more newsworthy than others, all say something about the state of the company's business and provide an opportunity for shareholders to ask management questions about the company's performance. The time leading up to the annual meeting also can produce drama, as key players jockey for position.

Here, for example, is a story from the *Columbia* (Mo.) *Daily Tribune* about managerial maneuverings at a local company:

Tomorrow morning, about 270 stockholders will vote to settle a vicious feud over one of Columbia's crown jewel companies. The dispute became a civil war this year, with friends of 20 years taking sides against each other, co-founder of the company against co-founder, former mentor against student, even brother against brother.

At stake is control of Analytical Bio-Chemistry Laboratories Inc., better known as ABC Labs. The company's shareholders will meet tomorrow at the Holiday Inn Executive Center to choose six directors for the nine-member board.

Those elected will control the future of a firm whose sales last year reached $21 million, up from $7 million four years ago. Also at stake is the livelihood of some 370 employees of the environmental testing firm, about half of whom are highly skilled scientists and technicians.

The battle has very little to do with business and everything to do with personality conflicts, hurt feelings and control. There is little dispute between the groups over the future of the firm, the general philosophy for growth or the business opportunities available for the rapidly growing company. Instead, the battle is over who will sit in the board seats and call the shots.

Reporter Enterprise

As in other areas of journalism, often the best business news stories are generated by a reporter's own initiative, sparked by a hunch or a tip passed along by an editor, a shareholder or a disgruntled employee or customer. Sometimes a self-promoting source can lead to a good story. When the president of a commodity options firm called *The Boston Globe* to suggest a story on her company, reporter Susan Trausch was dispatched. It was a new company and headed by a woman. The reporter quickly became suspicious of some things she saw and was told. The investigation that followed produced a series on abuses in an unregulated industry and won several national prizes. The original caller got her name in the paper all right, but hardly as she had expected.

In other cases a news release may raise questions that turn into stories. For example, a routine announcement of an executive appointment may lead a curious reporter to a story about the financial problems that produced the changes in leadership. A stockholder's question may result in a story about a new trend in corporate financing or a shift in emphasis on operations within the company. Sometimes, an offhand comment at lunch about what one executive has heard about another company will lead to a front-page story after you do some digging. Or a former employee's call that a company is quietly laying off workers may produce a story about the firm's declining fortunes.

Most major business stories are developed by using a combination of human and documentary sources. The techniques are no different from those of covering city hall, sports or science.

Looking at the Numbers

Although most reporters find accounting about as appealing as quantum physics or microbiology, an understanding of the numbers that a business generates is essential to any intelligent analysis of a company or an industry. The most complete summary of the financial picture of a business is found in the annual report and the 10-K.

An annual report may be viewed as a statement of the image a company wants to project. Some companies print their reports on the highest-quality paper and fill them with big, brightly colored pictures; others try to project an image of dignity. Occasionally an annual report's presentation reflects the financial health or illness of a company. The 1980 Chrysler Corp. report remains a classic; the company reported a net loss of $1.7 billion in a black-and-white report that was 32 pages long, on plain paper stock and without a single photograph. The next year Chrysler reported a loss of "only" $475 million in a report on heavier paper and with 16 color pictures of its best-selling products. In 1982 Chrysler touted a profit of $170 million in a splashy, multicolored report that included a color portrait of then-chairman Lee Iacocca.

More than 100 million copies of annual reports are pumped out each year at a cost of $1 to $6 each. They can be valuable tools, but you should realize that they are not written to be read like a magazine. Rather, annual reports should be approached by sections and with specific goals in mind. Accountants suggest that readers skim sections and move from point to point. They note that the process is less like reading and more like digging out information.

Most veteran reporters start with the auditor's statement, which is generally located near the back of the annual report, together with basic financial data, explanations of footnotes and supplementary financial information. The basic auditor's report, ranging from one long paragraph to three or four paragraphs, states that the material conforms to generally accepted auditing standards and that it fairly presents the financial condition of the company.

Until recently, an auditor's report longer than two paragraphs indicated trouble. Now, however, reporters must read the entire report closely because auditors tuck warnings of trouble in the middle of the standard language they use in all reports.

Next, move on to the footnotes, where the seeds of many fascinating stories may be germinating among the innocuous prose and numbers that follow and supplement the company's basic financial data. Then, flip back to the front of the annual report and find the report from the chairman or chairwoman. It is usually addressed "To our shareholders" and should give an overview of the company's performance.

Warren Buffett, chairman of Berkshire Hathaway Inc., is legendary for his straightforward assessment of company performance. Buffett's letters to

TIPS: Cautionary tips when examining an annual report

- The numbers on an annual report are not definite.
- Look at the company's numbers in the context of both its industry and several years' performance.
- Use the knowledge you gain in this chapter to reach preliminary conclusions that you can pursue with experts and company officials.

shareholders can run to 20 pages; include references to investment guru Ben Graham, Adam Smith and Karl Marx; and offer lessons in investment theory. His letters have been compiled and make fascinating reading.

Next, take a few minutes to examine the company's operations divisions to get an idea of its different products. You should look for areas that will help the company in the future. Perhaps a new product has been developed or another company has been acquired that will boost profits.

After that you're ready to look at the numbers. Here are a few things to watch for:

Balance sheet. This is a snapshot of the company on one day, generally the last day of the fiscal year. The left side of the balance sheet lists the assets, or what the company owns. On the right side are the liabilities, or what the company owes, and the shareholders' equity, or the dollar value of what stockholders own. The two sides must balance, so the balance sheet can be summarized as assets equal liabilities plus shareholders' equity. The balance sheet shows how the year in question compares with the previous year. Reporters should note any significant changes worth exploring for a possible story.

Income statement. This report, also referred to as an earnings statement or statement of profit and loss, answers this key question: How much money did the company make for the year? Look first at net sales or operating revenues and determine if they went up or down. If they increased, did they increase faster than they did last year and faster than the rate of inflation? If sales lagged behind inflation, the company could have serious problems.

Return on sales. Company management and financial analysts calculate a number of ratios to gain better insights into the financial health of an organization. One important test of earnings is the relation of net income to sales, which is obtained by dividing net income by sales. This will tell you how much profit after taxes was produced by each dollar of sales. Reporters should remember that percentages can vary widely by industry.

Return on equity. This ratio, which shows how effectively a company's invested capital is working, is obtained by dividing net income minus preferred dividend by the common stockholders' equity for the previous year. Every year since 1997, Standard & Poor's Equity Research staff has compiled a list of the best returns on equity by U.S. companies of various sizes. Those are available in *Business Week* magazine every January or on **www. businessweek.com**. *Business Week* and S&P are owned by McGraw-Hill, the information publishing company.

Dividends. These are declared quarterly and generally are prominently noted in the annual report. Dividends are an inducement to shareholders to invest in the company. Because companies want to see dividends rise each quarter, they sometimes go so far as to change their accounting or pension assumptions so enough funds will be available to increase dividends. Other companies, such as Berkshire Hathaway Inc., declare no dividends because they prefer to reinvest profits internally. Shareholders of Microsoft Corporation complained for years that the software giant was holding on to too much cash and urged the board to return more money to its investors through higher dividends.

Now that you have an idea of how to examine an annual report and its numbers, it is time for some important words of caution. First, the numbers in an annual report, though certified by an auditor and presented in accordance with Securities and Exchange Commission regulations, are not definite because they are a function of the accounting assumptions used in their preparation. That leads to the second and third points: Look at a company's numbers in the context of both its industry and several years' performance. To understand how well a firm is performing, examine the numbers along with those of other firms in the same industry. For example, the debt-equity ratios of utilities are much higher than those of most manufacturing companies, such as auto manufacturers. Look at how the company has performed for the last five to 10 years. Then you will discern trends instead of basing your conclusions on one year's performance, which may be atypical.

The next caution: Don't think that reading this section or passing an accounting course makes you qualified to analyze a company's finances. Rather, use the knowledge you gain in this chapter to reach some preliminary conclusions that you can pursue with the experts and then with company officials. Only the best reporters are qualified to draw conclusions from company financial data — and then only after years of study and practice.

CONSUMER NEWS

The phrase "consumer news" is in its broadest sense arbitrary and redundant. All news is, directly or indirectly, about consumers. And many business stories could just as easily be called consumer stories. A story about the stock market may affect or be of interest to "consumers" of stocks and bonds even though those items aren't "consumed" in the same sense as corn flakes. A story about the price of crude oil affects consumers of gasoline and many other products refined from crude oil. A story about a drought that may drive up the price of wheat has an impact on consumers of hamburger buns. And a story that beef prices are increasing affects the consumer of the hamburger that goes with the bun. The person who has purchased the newspaper in which your stories run is a consumer of newspapers.

Consumer news deals with events or ideas that affect readers in their role as buyers of goods and services in the marketplace. Although news of that kind has existed for as long as there have been newspapers and was spread by word of mouth long before that, its development as a conscious area of coverage generally began in the mid-1960s with the rise of vocal consumer groups. The consumer movement was helped along immeasurably by Ralph Nader's 1965 book *Unsafe at Any Speed,* an attack on the Chevrolet Corvair. General Motors Corp.'s subsequent attempts to spy on Nader and the ensuing publicity when the matter went before Congress also generated interest.

In many ways consumerism is as much a political as an economic movement. The wave of federal, state and local regulations promulgated in the 1960s and 1970s attests to that fact. Such legislation has affected producers of goods not only in the area of safety but also in the realms of finance, labeling and pricing.

The media have played such a major role in publicizing crusaders such as Nader and their causes that in many respects the consumer movement is a creature of the media. Those who espouse consumer causes recognize the power public exposure can bring them. What this means to you as a reporter is that although consumer groups may be friendlier than business people, they too will try to use you to their advantage.

Where to Find Consumer News

Sources of consumer news fall into three general categories: government agencies, quasi-public consumer groups and private businesses. Let's consider each of these groups.

Government Agencies

Many municipalities, especially large cities, have a public consumer advocate who reports to the mayor and calls public attention to problems that affect consumers. Most county prosecuting attorneys' offices also have someone — or even a whole department — to challenge business practices of questionable legality. Cases of consumer fraud — in which people pay for something they do not receive or pay for something of a certain quality and receive something less — are handled by these offices.

At the state level, most states have a consumer affairs office to investigate consumer problems and to order or recommend solutions. In addition, state attorneys general investigate and prosecute cases of consumer fraud. Most states also have regulatory commissions that represent the public in a variety of areas. The most common commissions regulate insurance rates and practices, rates and levels of service of utilities and transportation companies, and practices of banks and savings and loan associations.

At the federal level, government regulatory agencies involved in consumer affairs have the power to make rules and to enforce them:

- The Federal Trade Commission oversees matters related to advertising and product safety.
- The Food and Drug Administration watches over prices and safety rules for drugs, foods and a variety of other health-related items.

Figure 15.2
*A public consumer activist group holds a sign on Capitol Hill proclaiming that
Congress is "For Sale."*

- The Securities and Exchange Commission oversees the registration of securities for corporations and regulates the exchange, or trading, of those securities.
- The Interstate Commerce Commission regulates prices and levels of service provided by surface-transportation companies in interstate commerce.
- The Federal Energy Regulatory Commission regulates the rates and levels of service provided by interstate energy companies.
- The Occupational Safety and Health Administration has inspectors who routinely visit and report on safety in workplaces and factories, as well as investigate workplace accidents.

Nearly every other federal agency or cabinet office deals with some form of consumer protection, ranging from banking and finance to education to housing to highway and vehicle safety. These agencies are useful to reporters in several ways. First, they are good sources of background information and data of almost every conceivable form. Second, they are good sources of "hard" information, such as the results of investigations, cautionary orders and the status of legislation affecting their area of expertise. Also, public-information officers of these offices, regulatory agencies and even members of Congress usually are accessible and helpful in ferreting out information for reporters. You may have to make

A Business Mini-Glossary

Bonds
Governments and corporations issue bonds to raise capital. The bonds pay interest at a stated rate and are redeemable on a predetermined maturity date.

Constant dollars
Because of inflation, $10 doesn't buy in 2004 what it did in 1984. Constant dollars take inflation into account by figuring their value compared with a base period.

Consumer Price Index
A measure of the relative price of goods and services, the CPI is based on the net change compared with a base period. An index of 115 means the price has increased 15 percent since the base period. Thus, to report the significance of a rise or drop in the CPI, you need to know the base year.

Dow Jones Industrial Average
This is the principal daily measure of stock prices. It is based on the combined value of 30 major stocks. It exceeded 10,000 for the first time in 2001.

IRA (Individual Retirement Accounts)
These are savings accounts whose earnings (as well as some contributions) are tax-free until withdrawal. They generally can't be accessed until retirement.

Mutual funds
These are collections of bonds, stocks and other securities managed by investment companies. Individuals buy shares in them much as they buy shares of stock, but mutual funds provide more diversity.

Stocks
A share of stock represents a piece of a company. The price varies from day to day.

---

several calls to Washington to get plugged into the right office, but many federal agencies have regional offices in major cities.

Consumer Groups

Nongovernment consumer groups are composed of private citizens who have organized to represent the consumer's interest. They, too, are often good sources of background information or comment.

Common Cause, which lobbies for federal and state legislation, and Consumers Union, which publishes the popular *Consumer Reports*, are general in nature. Many states have public-interest research groups. Other organizations are specialists, such as the Sierra Club, which concentrates on environmental matters. Still other groups may be more local in scope. They may try to enact such legislation as returnable-bottle ordinances or to fight what they perceive as discrimination in the way banks and savings and loan associations make housing loans.

These groups, through their ability to attract the attention of the media and to find sympathetic ears in Washington and the state capitals, have a greater impact on legislation and news coverage than their numbers would suggest. It is always a good idea to try to determine whom a particular group represents and how broad its support is, especially in cases where the group has not already established its legitimacy. The group may be an association with many members or merely a self-appointed committee with little or no general support. One person, under the guise of an association or committee, can rent a hotel meeting room and call a news conference to say almost anything. Such is the nature of the media that in most cases at least one reporter will attend the news conference and write something about it. The broader a group's support, the greater is the impact of its statement. If *Consumer Reports* says an auto model is dangerous, that judgment is national news. If an individual says the same thing, nobody pays any attention.

Private Businesses

Almost all large corporations and many smaller ones have public-relations departments. They try to present their company in the most favorable light and to mask the scars as well as possible when the company is attacked from the outside, whether by the press, the government or a consumer group.

Because of the successes of the consumer movement, a number of companies have taken the offensive and have instituted programs they deem to be in the public interest. We see oil companies telling drivers how to economize on gasoline, electric utilities telling homeowners how to keep their electric bills at a minimum, banks suggesting ways to manage money better, and telephone companies pointing out the times it is least expensive to make long-distance calls.

Corporate public-relations people can be valuable sources for a variety of stories by providing background information or comments and reactions to events affecting their company. Also, they may help a reporter place an event in perspective, as it affects a company or industry, for example. Sometimes they are good primary sources for feature stories about products or personalities.

How to Report Consumer Stories

Consumer stories may be exposés, bringing to light a practice relating to consumers that is dangerous or that increases the price of a product or service. Research for such stories can be simple and inexpensive to conduct, and the findings may arouse intense reader interest. The project can be something as simple as buying hamburger at every supermarket in town to see if all purchases weigh what they are marked. Or it may be something that takes more time and work, such as surveying auto repair shops to see how much unnecessary repair work is done or how much necessary repair work is not diagnosed. Deborah Diamond of *Ladies' Home Journal* took a VCR that had been rigged to need minor repairs to three different repair shops. She came back with three vastly different diagnoses and a wide range of repair estimates. Only one of the repair shops identified and repaired the actual problem, which led to a story on how to protect yourself from this type of fraud.

Consumer stories also may be informational, intended to help readers make wiser or less expensive purchases. In 2003, *The New York Times* published a story on what parts of Manhattan were relative bargains for renters. You may want to discuss the advantages and disadvantages of buying a late-model used car instead of a new one. Or you can point out the advantages and disadvantages of buying term life insurance instead of whole life insurance.

Other consumer stories can be cautionary, warning readers of impending price increases, quality problems with products or questionable practices of business or consumer groups. Such stories can have great impact. A Houston television station's reports about Firestone tire deficiencies led to a massive recall. Sometimes newspapers, magazines and broadcast outlets act as surrogates for consumers. One example of this is the "Action Line" kind of question-and-answer column published in many newspapers. A column like this has the power of the paper behind questions to companies and thus often is more successful than an individual in reaching satisfactory settlements on questions of refunds, undelivered purchases and other consumer complaints. The past few years have seen an explosion in television programs in which reporters go undercover with hidden cameras and act like consumers. Such stories have revealed such diverse scandals as what really happens in a day-care center after the parents leave and where the septic tank company actually dumps sewage. Also, dozens of magazines and books focus on consumer news, from stories on what to look for when building a new house to how to select a good nursing home.

Consumer stories can be dangerous, though. It was a consumer story about how to get the best deal on a used car that led to the massive advertising boycott — and the loss of $200,000 in ad dollars — at the *San Jose Mercury News*. A consumer story led to a lawsuit against *The Denver Post* when it published a story about a dry cleaner that consistently lost customers' clothes.

Consumer and business news stories can provide valuable information not only to readers who are consumers but to readers who are producers and financiers and regulators as well. But they must be carefully reported and compellingly written.

One especially valuable source of information for consumer stories is the *Consumer Sourcebook*, published by Gale Research Co. The two-volume book describes more than 135 federal and 800 state and local agencies and bureaus that provide aid or information dealing with consumers.

Suggested Readings

Goodman, Jordan and Bloch, Sonny. *The Dictionary of Finance and Investment Terms*. Chicago: Dearborn Financial Publishing, 1994. A necessary desk reference book for any financial writer.

Houston, Brant, ed. *The Investigative Reporter's Handbook: A Guide to Documents and Techniques*. New York: Bedford/St. Martin's, 2002. See chapter on Business.

MacDougall, A. Kent. *Ninety Seconds to Tell It All: Big Business and the News Media*. Homewood, Ill.: Dow Jones–Irwin, 1981. An examination of the business-press relationship.

Mitford, Jessica. *Poison Penmanship: The Gentle Art of Muckraking*. New York: Vintage Books, 1957. A classic introduction on sources, especially the trade press. Includes 17 investigative pieces with commentary on the reporting techniques.

Schmertz, Herbert. *Good-Bye to the Low Profile: The Art of Creative Confrontation*. Boston: Little, Brown, 1986. Mobil executive touts the merits of public-relations hardball.

Woodward, Bob. *Maestro: Greenspan's Fed and the American Boom*. New York: Simon & Schuster, 2000. A primer on the power of the Federal Reserve and the economic clout of its chairman, Alan Greenspan.

Suggested Web Sites

www.bea.doc.gov and **www.bls.gov**
These sites, from the U.S. Department of Commerce and the U.S. Department of Labor, respectively, offer overviews of the U.S. economy and exhaustive studies about each segment of the economy.

www.business.com
A directory of business Web sites with information about individual companies and industries.

finance.yahoo.com
This portal is an accessible and free index of corporate financial filings, stock prices and corporate news.

www.nicar.org
The National Institute for Computer-Assisted Reporting provides access to databases and training in how to use them to analyze business, economic and regulatory information.

www.sabew.org
The Society of American Business Editors and Writers can be a good source for contacts and story ideas.

Exercises

1. Find five stories in the local newspaper that ran outside the business section and explain how they could have been turned into business stories.

2. Sign up for a stock market game that allows students to invest play money in real stocks. There are several offered online. Look at **money central.msn.com/investor**.

3. Send away for a prospectus on a mutual fund and study its investment rationale. Or send away for a prospectus on a stock offering and study its price-earnings ratio, yield dividends and other value indicators. Look up commentary on the fund or stock on the Web and explain the fund's or stock's performance.

4. Use Nexis or the SEC's EDGAR Online service to find the 10-K report on a publicly traded company with a local operation.

In sports, the stories are usually on the field of play. But not always. Sometimes, the big story is in the stands, among the fans. And sometimes, the reporter covering that story isn't even a sportswriter. That was the case in Chicago, during the 2003 National League Championship Series, when the Cubs were on the verge of ending a 58-year drought and finally returning to the World Series. They were within one game, five outs, when a Florida Marlins player hit a foul fly ball into the stands. Cubs outfielder Moises Alou reached for the ball, but a fan deflected it. Given a second chance, the Marlins hitter started the game-winning rally. The Cubs' jinx continued, and the attention of the sports world focused on the fan, who fled the stadium, hiding his face to conceal his identity. His anonymity didn't last long. Anne Sweeney, a young general assignment reporter for the *Chicago Sun-Times*, takes up the story:

> The city desk got a tip after the game. Several phone calls and searches tracked the guy down. I was called at 1 a.m. and was told to head in his general direction as early as possible the next day. I was there by 7 a.m. AP was there. . . . Because I was there, I got the neighbor first and caught the dad coming home from a business trip. They never answered the door again.
>
> With the neighbor, I just approached him on his doorstep and said gee, what a terrible situation this is, but is it really your neighbor? How awful that must be. He bit and started talking.
>
> The dad tried to blow me off, but I just called out to him politely and he turned around and tossed out the one comment I thought was the best — that he did a good job teaching his son how to catch a baseball.

Sweeney's story was the first to identify the fan. It was a controversial decision and led to days of debate on talk radio, sports Web sites and in newspaper columns. The *Sun-Times* staff, Sweeney pointed out, talked about the ethics of the story before publishing it:

> There were very intense discussions early in the day. We moved it on our Web site first, which shortened the time we had to decide. . . . I was initially very concerned about what we were doing. One real concern was the fact that he lived with his family. They really had nothing to do with it, but because they lived with him, were being dragged into it. . . .
>
> I think we did the right thing. After discussing it with editors, I understand that, like it or not, Steve Bartman ended up in the middle of

In this chapter you will learn:

1. How to apply the techniques of beat reporting to the special challenges of sports.

2. How to cover sports events.

3. How to use the techniques of good writing to write well about sports.

a major news story. We don't really serve anybody to leave parts of the story out. But what really calmed me was a comment from our metro editor, who kindly reminded me it is simply dangerous for newspapers to be in the business of censoring information about news events (outside of the obvious: we don't name people until charged, we don't name juveniles, etc.). He told me we would set ourselves up for having to make that decision again and again, and he didn't want to do that, nor did he think it was our job.

Sports is often derided as the "toy department of journalism." This story and many others, however, demonstrate that writing about sports is writing about life, with all the challenges and satisfactions of any other form of reporting. Both the principles and the techniques of good reporting apply — in the stadium or on a stakeout.

COVERING THE SPORTS BEAT

What young sports fan doesn't dream of someday writing about sports? Not T.J. Quinn. After graduating from journalism school with a news-ed emphasis, he took a job covering local government on a suburban newspaper. Not until four years later, accepting an unexpected job offer, did he turn to sports. Eight years into his career, he was covering major league baseball for the New York *Daily News*. He considers it a good job but hardly a dream. Here are a few of the lessons he has learned along the way:

- "It's a lot harder to come up with a fresh angle on a mid-August baseball game when the team is out of the pennant race than it is to write about a fire."
- "Stories about sports are stories about the people who play them. Sports writing tells you who won the race. Good sports writing tells you how they got there and makes you care about the people who ran."
- "The best sportswriters are the best sports reporters and hold themselves to the same standard as any political writer worth his or her salt. Journalism is journalism."
- "There are elements in sports writing that are vastly different from news, of course. Talking to large, naked men is one. Having to duck out of the way of foul balls is another. Getting vicious hate mail because you think Greg Maddux is the most successful right-hander since Walter Johnson is yet one more."

A good sports reporter is a good reporter. That's not always obvious, especially to beginners, because the love of sports lures them to the field in the first place. Most sports reporters were sports fans before they were journalists. That's not typical of other specialties. Reporters who cover government seldom attend city council meetings for fun. Medical reporters don't usually spend their days off observing operations. (Instead, they may watch a sports event.)

As a sports reporter and writer, you will likely find your workplace organized in much the same way as the news department. Typically, in the sports department of a newspaper, there will be reporters, copy editors and an editor. The difference is likely to be the scale. On small papers, the sports editor may double as writer and may even take the photographs, too. On midsized papers, the sports reporters usually don't specialize as the news reporters may. One day you may be covering high school swimming; the next, football or a visiting rodeo.

In broadcasting, at small and medium-sized stations, a "sports department" is likely to consist of one person who serves as writer, photographer and sports anchor at various times of the day or night. The big crews, the "guys in the truck" you hear mentioned on ESPN, are at the network level. At most local stations, you'll be expected to report, to write, to photograph and to deliver your work on camera. Sometimes, when time pressure is great or the game is big, you'll go on the air live, summarizing a game that has just ended or that may even be in progress. Then your skills at ad-libbing will be tested, a challenge print reporters don't face.

One more thing: Don't confuse sports reporters with play-by-play announcers. The latter may be reporters in a literal sense, but they usually aren't journalists. Their skill is in instant description, not the behind-the-scenes digging or the after-the-fact analysis expected of print or broadcast reporters. Often they are hired by the teams they follow or the sponsors they serve instead of by the station carrying their work. When you're a beginning reporter, the principles that follow apply to any medium and any sport.

In Chapter 14, we discussed the techniques employed by all successful beat reporters. Review them. They apply to coverage of sports as well as to politics or education or science. Now we will see how they can help you meet the special challenges of reporting sports.

Be Prepared

Before you even thought about sports reporting, the chances are that you were reading, watching and playing sports. In that sense, at least, preparing to be a sports reporter is easier than preparing to cover city hall. But there is more to preparation than immersing yourself in sports. Competition pushes people to their limits, bringing out their best and worst. So you need to know some psychology. Sports has played a major role in the struggles of blacks and women for equality. So you need to know some sociology and history. Sports, professional and amateur, is big business. So you need a background in economics. Some of our greatest writers have portrayed life through sports. So you need to explore literature.

This paragraph by Grantland Rice, for example, may be the most famous lead ever written for a sports story:

Outlined against a blue-gray October sky, the Four Horsemen rode again. In dramatic lore, they are known as Famine, Pestilence, Destruction and Death. These are only aliases. Their real names are Stuhldreher, Miller, Crowley and Layden. They formed the crest of the South Bend cyclone before which another fighting Army football team was swept over the precipice at the Polo Grounds yesterday afternoon as 55,000 spectators peered down on the bewildering panorama spread on the green plain below.

Sports Reporting Is Beat Reporting

After graduating from journalism school, T.J. Quinn began his career covering several towns in the southern suburbs of Chicago. He recalls that he wrote about council meetings, murders, fires, politics and "the occasional feature about a spectacular schnauzer."

He became a sportswriter on a whim, his fiancée's whim. After she and T.J. left Chicago for the *Salt Lake City Tribune*, she was visiting the old paper when the editor mentioned an opening on the White Sox beat. She said T.J. might be interested. He was. From covering the Sox for the *Daily Southtown*, he moved to the *Bergen* (N.J.) *Record* to cover the New York Mets. A couple of years later he moved up again, this time to the New York *Daily News*, still on the Mets beat.

Except for "talking to large, naked men" and ducking foul balls, covering baseball isn't so different from covering politics, he has found. "There are two sides; someone is going to win; someone is going to lose; and everyone is going to speak in clichéd sound bites."

He reminds young fans who want to be sportswriters, "Sports entertainment is a multibillion-dollar business that requires some knowledge of local and state governments, taxes and business. There are payrolls to calculate, salary caps to consider and contracts to dissect. And half the time it seems like athletes are covered in the courtroom more often than on the court. It helps if a sportswriter knows how and where to get arrest reports and how to read them."

The special challenge of writing about sports, he says, "is taking a sport like baseball or basketball or volleyball, attending a match and then finding a way to distinguish it from the zillions of games played in that sport before."

The secret: "As the esteemed Rick Reilly says to young writers, 'Never write a sentence you've read before.' Stories about sports are stories about the people who play them. There are plenty of heartwarming tales of athletes who overcame tremendous personal hardship, and there are plenty more who are immature, greedy narcissists. But they are almost all heroes, because they all have to follow a hero's path. They have goals, they seek to achieve them and they have to overcome obstacles to get there. Some make it; some don't."

And a final word of advice: "After a while, those hot dogs get pretty nasty. Better to pack a sandwich."

Grantland Rice, the most famous American sportswriter in the first half of the 20th century, graduated Phi Beta Kappa from Vanderbilt University, where he majored in Latin and Greek. His prose may seem overblown by today's standards, but he wrote some memorable poetry, too. And he knew who the Four Horsemen of the Apocalypse were.

Be Alert

Here's T.J. Quinn again: "The myth of the job is that sportswriters sit in the press box, eat hot dogs, live on expense accounts and get to travel all over the country. Mostly true. But covering a beat means keeping track of which players are doing what, who's injured, what a team needs to get better and where they might get it, who wants a contract, who's going to be a free agent, which pitcher is experimenting with a new grip on his slider, which coach is feuding with the owner, which power forward is angry with the point guard because she doesn't pass to the low post enough."

And here's the top of a story that resulted from that kind of paying close attention:

Mike Hampton was already a professional athlete the first time he beat his father at basketball.

Until that day, as an 18-year-old minor leaguer, he was oh-for-life against Mike Sr., never walking off the driveway of their Homosassa, Fla., home with so much as a gift win.

When Little Mike was 8 years old, Big Mike blocked his shots. When Little Mike tried to drive the lane, Big Mike would put his body in front of the boy and put him on the ground. The boy bled often but learned to cry less and less. His eyes puffy, his breath short, he would sometimes storm off, but he always came back to play the next day.

"It was gross how tough he was," the new ace of the Mets pitching staff said. "You fall down, get a scratch. 'Get up. It'll stop hurting. Get up; let's go.'"

Big Mike knew it was cruel, and wonders still whether he pushed the boy too hard. But the boy needed to learn that winning meant taking something, not waiting for a handout. . . .

That is a story that entertains while it informs. It shows readers something of the character of an athlete and the meaning of tough love. Here are a few tips to help you be alert to stories that get beyond the cliché:

- *Look for the losers.* Losing may not — as football coaches and other philosophers like to assert — build character, but it certainly bares character. Winners are likely to be full of confidence, champagne and clichés. Losers are likely to be full of self-doubt, second-guessing and surliness. Winners' dressing rooms are magnets for sportswriters, but you usually can tell your readers more about the game and those who play it by seeking out the losers.
- *Look for the bench warmers.* If you follow the reporting crowd, you'll end up in front of your local version of Alex Rodriguez or Venus Williams every time. Head in the other direction. Talk to the would-be football player who has spent four years practicing but never gets into a game. Talk to the woman who dreams of being a professional golfer but is not yet good enough. Talk to the baseball player who is growing old in the minor leagues. If you do, you may find people who both love their sport more and understand it better than do the stars. You may find less press agentry and more humanity.
- *Look beyond the crowds.* Some of the best, and most important, sports stories draw neither crowds of reporters nor crowds of fans. The recent and

rapid growth of women's sports is one example. Under the pressure of federal law — the "Title IX" you read and hear about — the traditional male dominance of facilities and money in school and college athletics is slowly giving way to equal treatment for women. From junior high schools to major universities, women's teams now compete in nearly every sport except football. With better coaching, and more incentive, the quality of performance is increasing, too. The results of this revolution are likely to be felt far beyond the playing fields, just as the earlier admission of African-Americans to athletic equality advanced their standing in other areas. Male-run sports departments, like male-run athletic departments, can no longer overlook women athletes.

The so-called minor sports and participant sports are other largely untapped sources of good stories. More Americans watch birds than play football. More hunt or fish than play basketball. More watch stock-car races than watch track meets. But those and similar sports are usually covered — if at all — by the newest or least talented reporter on the staff. Get out of the press box. Drop by a bowling alley, a skeet-shooting range, the local college's Ultimate Frisbee tournament. Anywhere you find people competing — against each other, against nature, against their own limits — you can find good stories.

Be Persistent

It was a big story. A sports agent had told another newspaper that he had given money to and arranged travel for a star college basketball player before and during the player's senior season. The agent saw it as no big deal. He had done the same for players at universities across the country as he tried to win their allegiance for life in the professional leagues. But for the university, his allegations, if true, could mean at least embarrassment and at most the forfeiting of NCAA tournament games in which the player had participated.

It was a big problem. The agent had been willing, even eager, to talk to reporters at the metropolitan newspaper that broke the story. He was available to other reporters at other papers with which he was familiar. But he had no time for student reporters at the newspaper of the university most involved. His attitude was discouraging for the reporters, frustrating for their editors and baffling for their readers.

The reporters refused to give up. They got the agent's home phone number, in a city across the continent, from the reporter who had discovered his role. They left message after message. While they waited for his call, they worked at the story from the edges by talking to people less directly involved but more accessible. The player himself, of course, was unavailable to any reporters. Finally, after a week of reading other versions of the story they wanted, the student reporters got a payoff for their persistence. The agent called. Using what they had gleaned from other interviews and previous stories, the students were able to write a story that offered readers a few new tidbits:

Nate Cebrun on Thursday described prospective agents' year-long courtship of former university basketball player Jevon Crudup as an "out-of-control bidding war."

Cebrun, a self-described middleman, said his dealings with Crudup and his mother, Mary, probably netted them only about $5,000 in cash and other gifts. But sports agents Michael Harrison and Raul Bey must have spent even more money on Crudup, Cebrun said.

"I saw Jevon's mother at Missouri's game against Arizona in tournament action. And I know she wasn't able to afford that with the money she makes," Cebrun said in a phone interview from his Las Vegas home. "But if I were a betting man, I'd almost guarantee Harrison paid for her to go to L.A."

In that case, the reward for persistence was catching up on an important story. In other cases, the reward may be a story that otherwise wouldn't be done at all. That was so when a sports reporter at the *St. Paul* (Minn.) *Pioneer Press* learned of a university secretary who said she had written term papers for University of Minnesota basketball players. Weeks of cajoling her to talk, checking

Figure 16.1

The recent rapid growth of women's sports has generated much public interest and media attention. Here Demya Walker of the Sacramento Monarchs, goes up for a shot against Lisa Leslie of the Los Angeles Sparks.

out her accounts, prying loose supporting documents and withstanding pressure even from the state's governor yielded stories that stunned Minnesota and won for the paper a Pulitzer Prize.

The most important reward of persistence, though, is the loyalty of readers who feel well-served.

Be There and Develop Contacts

Being there, of course, is half the fun of sports reporting. You're there at the big games, matches and meets. You're there in the locker rooms, on team buses and planes, with an inside view of athletics and athletes that few fans ever get. And you should be there, most of the time. If you are to answer your readers' questions, if you are to provide insight and anecdote, you must be there, most of the time.

Sometimes you should try being where the fans are. Plunk down $20 (of your boss's money) for an end-zone seat and write about a football game from the average fan's point of view. Cover a baseball game from the bleachers. Cold hot dogs and warm beer are as much a part of the event as is a double play. Watch one of those weekend sports shows on television and compare the way a track meet or a fishing trip is presented to the way it is in person. Join a city league softball team or a bowling league for a different kind of inside view.

A sports reporter must develop and cherish sources just as a city hall reporter must. You look for the same kinds of sources on both beats. Players, coaches and administrators — like city council members and city managers — are obvious sources. Go beyond them. Trainers and equipment managers have insiders' views and sometimes lack the fierce protectiveness that often keeps players, for example, from talking candidly. Alumni can be excellent sources for high school and college sports stories. If a coach is about to be fired or a new fund drive is being planned, important alumni are sure to be involved. You can find out who they are by checking with the alumni association or by examining the list of major contributors that every college proudly compiles. The business managers and secretaries who handle the money can be invaluable for much-needed but seldom-done stories about the finances of sport at all levels. Former players sometimes will talk more candidly than those who are still involved in a program. As on any beat, look for people who may be disgruntled — a fired assistant coach, a benched star, a big contributor to a losing team. And when you find good sources, cherish them. Keep in contact, flatter them and protect them. They are your lifeline.

Be Wary, and Dig for the Real Story

It is even harder for a sports reporter than it is for a political or police reporter to maintain a critical distance from the beat. The most obvious reason is that most of the people who become sports reporters do so because they are sports fans. To be a fan is precisely the opposite of being a dispassionate, critical observer. In addition, athletics — especially big-time athletics — is glamorous and exciting.

The sports reporter associates daily with the stars and the coaches whom others, including cynical city hall reporters and hard-bitten managing editors, pay to admire at a distance. Finally, sports figures ranging from high school coaches to owners of professional baseball teams deliberately and persistently seek to buy the favor of the reporters who cover their sports.

We are taught from childhood that it is disgraceful to bite the hand that feeds you. Professional teams and many college teams routinely feed reporters. Major-league baseball teams even pay reporters to serve as official scorers for the game. In one embarrassing incident, the reporter-scorer made a controversial decision that preserved a no-hit game for a hometown pitcher. His story of the game made little mention of his official role. The reporter for the opposition paper wrote that if it had been his turn to be scorer, he would have ruled the other way.

Sports journalism used to be even more parasitic toward the teams it covered than is the case now. At one time, reporters routinely traveled with a team at the team's expense. Good newspapers pay their own way today.

Even today, however, many reporters find it rewarding monetarily as well as psychologically to stay in favor with the teams and athletes they cover. Many teams pay reporters to write promotional pieces for game programs. And writing personality profiles or "inside" accounts for the dozens of sports magazines can be a profitable sideline.

Most sports reporters, and the editors who permit such activities, argue that they are not corrupted by what they are given. Most surely are not. But temptation is there for those who would succumb. Beyond that, any writer who takes more than information from those he or she covers is also likely to receive pressure, however subtle, from the givers.

Every sports reporter is given a great deal by high school and college coaches or publicity agents, who feed reporters sheets of statistics, arrange interviews, provide space on the team bus or plane, and allow access to practice fields and locker rooms. And what do they want in return? They expect nothing more than an unbroken series of favorable stories. Too often, they get exactly that. Only the names have been changed in this excerpt from a metropolitan newspaper:

The State U. troops reported today to begin three weeks' tune-up before the Fighting Beagles invade Western State.

Offensive commander Pug Stanley had some thoughts available Thursday before some 90-odd players arrived.

"We really made some strides this year," Stanley declared. . . . Charlie Walker, he said, is no longer feeling his way around at quarterback. The Beagle pass catchers are hardly old men, but the top four targets are two juniors and two sophomores rather than two sophomores and two freshmen.

State U.'s heaviest artillery is located behind Charlie Walker. Beagle runners ranged from good to outstanding a year ago. Most are back, with a season's more experience.

"Our runners keep on getting better," commented their attack boss. "Our backfield has to be our biggest plus. We're going to burn some people with it this year."

TIPS: Digging for the real story

- Maintain your distance from the people you cover.
- Keep readers in mind.
- Answer readers' questions about the story behind the story that too often goes unanswered:
  - Money.
  - The real "why."
  - The real "who."

The story did not mention that State U., which had managed only a 6–5 record the previous year against weak opposition, was universally picked to finish in the second division of its second-rate conference. That's not only bad writing, but bad reporting.

Anywhere athletics is taken seriously, from the high schools of Texas to the stadiums of the National Football League, athletes and coaches are used to being given special treatment. Many think of themselves as being somehow different from and better than ordinary people. Many fans agree. Good reporters, though, regard sports as a beat, not a love affair.

Those sports reporters maintain their distance from the people they cover, just as reporters on other beats do, by keeping their readers in mind. Readers want to know who won, and how. But they also want to know about other sides of sports, sides that may require some digging to expose. Readers' questions about sports financing and the story behind the story too often go unanswered:

Money. Accountants have become as essential to sports as athletes and trainers. Readers have a legitimate interest in everything from ticket prices to the impact of money on the actual contests.

The Real "Why." When a key player is traded, as much as when a city manager is fired, readers want to know why. When athletes leave school without graduating, find out why. When the public is asked to pay for the expansion of a stadium, tell the public why. One of the attractions of sports is that when the contest is over, the spectators can see who won and how. Often that is not true of struggles in government or business. The "whys" of sports, however, frequently are as hard to discover as they are in any other area.

The Real "Who." Sports figures often appear to their fans, and sometimes to reporters, to be larger than life. In fact, athletics is an intensely human activity. Its participants have greater physical skills, and larger bank accounts, than most other people, but they are people. Probably the two best descriptions of what it is really like to be a major-league athlete were written by athletes — *Ball Four* by Jim Bouton and the novel *North Dallas Forty* by Pete Gent. Still, some of the best sports writing results from the continuing effort by reporters to capture the humanity of games. Roger Kahn, in perhaps the finest baseball book ever written, *The Boys of Summer,* needed only two inches of type to capture Carl Erskine, the old Dodger pitcher, in this scene with his wife and their mentally handicapped son:

Jimmy Erskine, nine, came forward at Betty's tug. He had the flat features and pinched nostrils of Mongolism [the then-popular term for Down syndrome].

"Say, 'Hello, Roger,'" Betty said.

Jimmy shook his head and sniffed.

"Come on," Carl said.

"Hosh-uh," Jimmy said. "Hosh-uh. Hosh-uh."

"He's proud," Carl said, beaming. "He's been practicing to say your name all week, and he's proud as he can be." The father's strong right hand found Jimmy's neck. He hugged the little boy against his hip.

Figure 16.2
To get to the why *and* how *of a game's outcome, reporters need to dig beneath the mere results. Getting out of the press box to find an interesting story angle or to secure compelling quotes from players and coaches can bring a story to life.*

COVERING THE CONTESTS

A major part of any sports reporter's job, however, is covering the games, matches or meets. That task is harder than it might seem. You have the same problems you would have in covering any event, from a city council meeting to a riot. You must decide what to put in your lead, capture the most interesting and significant developments, find some good quotes, answer as many of your readers' probable questions as you can and meet your deadline. But a reporter covering a football game, for instance, has a major concern that a reporter writing about a council meeting does not have. Most of the readers of your football story already know a great deal about the game. Many were there. Others saw it on television or listened on radio. They know *what* happened. They expect you to tell them *why* and *how*.

In sports writing, as elsewhere in journalism, the inverted pyramid structure has given way in many cases to an alternate approach. (You learned about these alternatives in Chapter 9.) Your goals for the opening of any story about a sports event should be twofold:

- *Focus on the unique element.* No sporting event is quite like any other. A perceptive reporter picks out what made this game different and shares it with the reader. The unique element may be a single play, a questionable ruling by an official, an untimely injury, or a missing player. Find that unique element and you have found the key to your story. Your lead may be a quote, the description of a scene, an analysis by some expert observer or your own summary of the contest's high point. Whatever opening device you choose, be sure the facts support it. A summary or an analysis based on fact is permissible in a news story. Reliance on your own opinion is not.

- *Tell the reader who won.* No description is so compelling and no analysis so astute that a reader will forgive you if you forgot to say at the start what the outcome of the event was. The basic who, what and where must never be left out or buried in the body of your story. The story is, after all, about the contest.

The body of your story should develop the unique angle brought out in the lead. This writing technique gives a unified focus and maintains the reader's interest. In the course of the story, you should also meet three other objectives:

- *Describe what happened.* In addition to knowing the outcome, your audience will want to read at least the highlights of how it was reached, if only to savor them again. Analysis and background are hollow without the solid descriptive core of what happened.
- *Answer readers' questions.* The story should supply the explanation — or part of it, at least — of why the game turned out as it did. It should tell readers something they could not have discovered easily for themselves. Rarely should you have to rely on your own expertise to answer the questions of why and how. Experts abound at practically every sports event. Assistant coaches or scouts sit in the press box. The coaches and players directly involved are available after the game. Alumni, supporters or former players can be found if you look for them. The most important question for you to ask as a reporter is what your readers will want to know. Then try to find the answers for them.
- *Get the competitors into the story by using good quotes.* Your audience usually wants to know what the competitors think about what they have done. When winners exult, when losers cry, put your audience in the scene. That is part of the attraction of sports. The hours spent getting to know athletes pay off when they share with you — and your audience — what the contest was really like.

The preparation and techniques of interviewing are essentially the same in a locker room as in a politician's office, although you seldom have occasion to interview a mayor who is wearing only a towel. The reward for a good job in either situation is the same, too. You get lively quotes that provide some insight.

FOLLOWING THE MONEY

If your assignment includes a professional team, you'll quickly learn to think in terms of signing bonuses, salary caps and the seven-figure contracts of major-

"Slowly, but ever so surely, is vanishing the notion that the sports department's job is to cover the games and perpetuate the image that sports are pure, its participants are All-American boys, and its pages [are] places simply to report the game and what was said after it was over.

"And who knows, maybe someday we'll even achieve equal status in job title. Through the years, it has always been 'reporter' on the news side, sports 'writer' in my world.

"I'm beginning to discover more sports reporters."

— Tom Tuley, executive
sports editor,
The Cincinnati Post

league stars. But even during your student days, while you're covering your college teams, money talks. If you listen, and if you follow the money trail, you'll help your readers understand the business behind the games.

Here's some advice from Mike McGraw of *The Kansas City Star*. McGraw isn't a sportswriter. He's an investigative reporter with a share of a Pulitzer Prize to his credit. He gave these tips to a conference of Investigative Reporters and Editors. He notes that some college football teams are worth more than some pro franchises. He also notes that most major college athletic programs, while earning millions every year, wind up losing money. Inevitably, at least some of those losses are made up from money taken, directly or indirectly, from the academic programs of the institution. McGraw suggests you examine:

The perks coaches receive, from free cars to huge shoe contracts. The NCAA requires that coaches get written permission from their institution's president before making those lucrative deals. Ask to see those records.

Budgets. Athletic departments typically have separate budgets. At state-supported schools, those budgets are public records. Look especially for any subsidies to athletics from academics.

Gender equity issues. Federal law now requires schools receiving federal funds to file reports listing coaches' salaries, athletic budgets, recruiting costs and other expenditures by gender. Those reports are public records.

Booster clubs. Many are incorporated as nonprofit organizations. If so, they're required to file Form 990 — the only federal tax form that is open to public inspection. Look for extra payments to coaches and others.

Stadium and arena financing. For tax-supported schools, state open-records laws give you access to numbers on operating costs, financing and such sensitive matters as personal seat licenses.

Academics. Student records are protected by the Buckley Amendment. However, budgets can show spending on the often-elaborate tutoring programs for athletes. You may be able to get documents showing courses or degree programs recommended to the athletes, and you can get statistics on overall academic performance.

Enforcement issues. Open-records laws give you access to documents such as any self-reported violations of NCAA rules.

Conferences. You can also get copies of Form 990 for the athletic conference your school belongs to. These forms show both revenue and such expenditures as salaries of top officials.

McGraw's tips may not win you a Pulitzer, but they will help you help your readers understand the bottom line of sports.

WRITING ABOUT SPORTS

Many sports journalists think of themselves more as writers than as reporters. This chapter is intended to help you become a sports reporter. But good writing is an important part of any top reporter's skills, and sports offers abundant material for good writing.

Good writing is precise, conveying what the author means to say and nothing else. It is descriptive, re-creating for the reader the sights, the sounds, the smells of the event. It is suited in pace and in tone to the story — lively for an exciting game, somber for the reflections of a loser.

Consider, for example, the possibilities offered a writer by one of the most common but least-valued contributors to sports: mud (see Figure 16.3).

```
The ball skittered across the cleat-torn field, slithering
through the slop of mud and water.
     Two players raced after it, but their legs tangled. They
fell into the muck and slid out of bounds.
     It was a beautiful day for Cougar soccer on Friday. The
Cougars are American Midwest Conference champions after
defeating Lindenwood 3-1.
```

Or you could try a summary lead and then let an athlete do the talking:

```
What a mess.
     The Springfield cross-country team knew it would be facing
the best runners in the state on Saturday. But the team didn't
know the Class 4A state championships would turn into a mudfest.
     "It was awesome," said Springfield junior Nathan Mechlin.
"I sank into the mud about ankle-high. It was fun. I loved it."
```

You can almost feel the mud between your toes, or in your eyes. The ball went "slithering through the slop." Two players, legs tangled, "fell into the muck." A teenage runner, mud-covered, exults, "It was awesome."

Good writing captures the environment and the emotions. It is based on detailed observation and full of imaginative word choices. It doesn't require elaborate settings or major-league athletes. It requires you to use the tools of the craft.

Here, for example, is narrative, used to capture the key moment in a championship high school softball game:

The bottom of the 15th inning would be as tense as the rest of the game.

Hickman managed to load the bases with one out on singles by Janet Reilly and Jessica Barton and on an error by Jays third baseman Gretchen Snodgrass.

With junior first baseman Kelly Simmons, who had two hits already, coming up, the Hickman fans sensed imminent victory. However, Simmons was called out on strikes, watching a changeup sneak by her.

This brought up junior second baseman Lauren Kriegbaum, whose day had

TIPS: Remember, you produce a good game story by

- Doing your homework before the game.
- Spotting the unique element and building the story on it.
- Telling your readers who won and how.
- Answering readers' questions.
- Getting the participants into the story.

Figure 16.3
"The ball skittered across the cleat-torn field, slithering through the slop of mud and water." Use descriptive language to re-create the sights, sounds and smells of a sporting event.

consisted of no hits, a strikeout with the bases loaded to end the fourth inning and a popout with the winning run on second base in the seventh.

With a 1–1 count, Kriegbaum hit a grounder to third. First baseman Chrissy Armstrong was unable to hang onto Snodgrass' throw, allowing pinch runner Denise Brixton to come home with the winning run.

Brixton's run set off a wild celebration among the Hickman players, who piled on one another at the pitcher's mound in a victory scrum.

From the foreshadowing in the first paragraph through the buildup of tension, the unlikely hero and the celebratory term borrowed from the sport of rugby, this writing employs the classic tools of storytelling.

One of the best contemporary sports reporters and writers is Thomas Boswell of *The Washington Post*. He has won the Best Newspaper Writing award of the American Society of Newspaper Editors. Here are a few samples of his work. First, the opening of a story about aging baseball players:

The cleanup crews come at midnight, creeping into the ghostly quarter-light of empty ballparks with their slow-sweeping brooms and languorous, sluicing hoses. All season, they remove the inanimate refuse of a game. Now, in the dwindling days of September and October, they come to collect baseball souls.

Age is the sweeper, injury his broom.

Mixed among the burst beer cups and the mustard-smeared wrappers headed for the trash heap, we find old friends who are being consigned to the dust bin of baseball's history. If a night breeze blows a back page of the *Sporting News* down in the stadium aisle, pick it up and squint at the one-time headline names now just fine print at the very bottom of a column of averages.

Notice the imagery, as gloomy as the subject matter. Notice the pacing, with long, complex sentences slowing the eye to match the mood of sadness. Notice the metaphor: age as the sweeper, injury the broom. But notice, too, the sharp-eyed description that must ring true to anyone who has ever seen or thought about the debris cast aside by a baseball crowd. A little later in the same story:

"I like a look of Agony," wrote Emily Dickinson, "because I know it's true." For those with a taste for a true look, a glimpse beneath the mask, even if it be a glimpse of agony, then this is the proper time of year. Spring training is for hope, autumn is for reality. At every stop on the late-season baseball trail, we see that look of agony, although it hides behind many expressions.

Familiarity with the classics of literature did not die with Grantland Rice. Boswell not only finds the line, he makes it work.

From another story, this one about a championship boxing match, comes a short paragraph that is equally powerful but sharply different in tone:

Boxing is about pain. It is a night out for the carnivore in us, the hidden beast who is hungry.

Later in that story, Boswell returns to the theme:

But boxing never changes. One central truth lies at its heart and it never alters: Pain is the most powerful and tangible force in life.

The threat of torture, for instance, is stronger than the threat of death. Execution can be faced, but pain is corrosive, like an acid eating at the personality.

Pain, as anyone with a toothache knows, drives out all other emotions and sensations before it. Pain is priority. It may even be man's strongest and most undeniable reality.

And that is why the fight game stirs us, even as it repels us.

From the poetry of aging to the brutality of pain, Boswell matches his images, his pace and his word choice to the subject matter. The principles of careful observation and clear writing cover all occasions.

There is one thing that sets a writer like Boswell apart from many lesser writers. It is his attitude toward his readers. That may be worth copying, too. After winning the ASNE award, he told an interviewer:

We vastly underestimate our audience in newspapers. In 11 years I have never had one letter from anybody saying, "What's all this highfalutin talk?" I get the most touching letters from people who seem semi-literate but who really appreciate what you're doing. I think the fact that people are capable of understanding the Bible, or sensing the emotion in Shakespeare, just proves how far they are above our expectations.

TIPS: Working with sports statistics

- Perspective is vital. A 400-meter dash time of 52 seconds is poor for a collegian but outstanding for a freshman in high school.
- Don't repeat in a story what already is included in box scores or other statistical listings.
- If you have a list of figures in your story, consider presenting it in graph or chart form.
- Avoid using statistics you don't understand. If you don't know what earned-run averages mean, don't refer to them.

Suggested Readings

Feinstein, John. *A Season on the Brink*. New York: Macmillan, 1986. This chronicle of a year with Indiana basketball coach Bobby Knight entertains while explaining much about the high-pressure world of big-time college sports.

Flood, Curt. *The Way It Is*. New York: Trident Press, 1971. The first-person story of the baseball player whose challenge to the reserve clause revolutionized professional sports in America. Also noteworthy are the caustic comments on sportswriters.

Kahn, Roger. *The Boys of Summer*. New York: New American Library, 1973. One of the best sports books ever written.

Sports Illustrated. Continuously features the best examples of how sports should be reported.

Wolff, Alexander and Keteyian, Armen. *Raw Recruits*. New York: Pocket Books, 1990. A hard look at college basketball recruiting written by two veterans of *Sports Illustrated*.

Suggested Web Sites

www.espn.com
The king of sports on television (and on the Web), ESPN shows you the competition, gives you ideas and provides background on every sport that's played for money. (**www.cnnsi.com** is similar, but it draws content from *Sports Illustrated* magazine and CNN television.)

www.ncaa.org
Here you'll find the rules of the game for upper-level college teams, plus lots of background.

Every college and every pro team now has its own Web site, usually packed with all the trivia a fan or a writer could desire.

Exercises

1. Go back to Anne Sweeney's assignment that began this chapter. What do you think of the newspaper's decision to identify the fan who got caught up in the game? What do you think of Sweeney's editor's justification?

2. You have been assigned to cover your college's men's basketball team. Write a memo describing at least five likely sources and listing at least five story ideas.

3. Now do the same for the women's basketball team. Compare facilities, funding, fan interest and actual coverage. Be prepared to discuss your findings.

4. Select a "minor" sports event, such as a wrestling meet or a volleyball game. Prepare for and cover the event. Write the story.

5. Choose one of the story ideas in exercise 1 or 2. Report and write it.

6. Compare the coverage of a major event in your local newspaper and in *Sports Illustrated*. Which seems better written? Why?

7. Compile an inventory of the online sources available to fans and reporters in your area. What story possibilities does your list suggest?

In the movie *Absence of Malice*, Paul Newman plays a contractor under investigation by a reporter. In frustration and outrage, Newman erupts, "You don't write the truth. You write what people say." Every thoughtful journalist recognizes the reality revealed in that complaint. A serious limitation of most journalism is that reporters are no better than their sources. Most sources are people, and much — too much — of journalism consists of repeating what those people say.

That's a limitation that cuts into journalists' ability to provide their readers and viewers with the best obtainable version of the truth. Increasingly, however, the best reporters are using more reliable tools for gathering and analyzing information. Those are the tools of science. Journalists don't usually regard themselves as scientists. Many would resist the very suggestion. But the best reporting has a great deal in common with the work of political scientists, historians and sociologists. Like social scientists, reporters frame research questions or hypotheses. They seek answers to their questions by the careful accumulation of reliable data and the use of scientific formulas and statistics to analyze the information they've gathered. They double-check their findings for reliability. Then they report clearly and carefully what they have learned.

Here's an example: the *Omaha* (Neb.) *World-Herald* wanted to reveal the best obtainable version of the truth about one of the most important and least examined institutions of modern life — high school. First, *World-Herald* reporters followed eight ordinary students through a year of school, recounting in narrative form the triumphs and tragedies, academic and social, of teenagers learning to be adults.

Sure, critics said, you may have captured those individual stories, but you haven't told us how well the schools are doing at their main job of educating. So Mike Reilly, assistant managing editor for investigations, and his team persuaded the University of Nebraska to release statistics on the performance of freshmen at the main campus, in Lincoln. No names but thousands of numbers — test scores, university grades, academic status and the Nebraska high schools from which those freshmen had graduated.

Using the skills of computer-assisted reporting, the newspaper staff analyzed all that data and reported the results in a four-day series of front-page stories. Those results were stunning: The statistics demonstrated that graduates of some of Omaha's, and the state's, most highly regarded high schools wound up on academic probation at rates far higher than graduates of lesser-known schools. The statistics also showed that female students succeeded at a significantly higher rate than males.

This wasn't just reporting what somebody said, or even what a reporter had observed. This was new knowledge, developed by the newspaper and presented to readers who had no way, on their own, of learning what they, and policymakers, needed to know. This is social science reporting.

The social science tool that journalists use most often is the public opinion survey. It is also the tool they most often misuse. Here's an example from the Associated Press:

ST. LOUIS — Vice President Al Gore has a slight lead over Texas Gov. George W. Bush in Missouri, according to a poll published in Sunday's *St. Louis Post-Dispatch*.

Gore, the Democratic nominee, has the backing of 44.6 percent of those polled, compared with 39.7 percent for Bush, the Republican nominee. The poll of 601 likely voters was taken Tuesday through Thursday of last week and has a margin of error of 4.1 percent.

See the problem? Many readers wouldn't. That last phrase — "margin of error of 4.1 percent" — means that the first paragraph is plain wrong. Any scientist would tell you that a 4 percent margin of error means that the poll really shows that Mr. Gore's support is somewhere in the range of 40.6 percent to 48.6 percent and Mr. Bush's support is between 35.7 and 43.7 percent. Bush might actually be ahead of Gore. The lead should have said that the race was too close to call.

These examples show both the power and the pitfalls of using the research tools of social science in reporting. The increasing complexity of the world around us requires the journalists of today and tomorrow to learn tools adequate to the task of understanding and explaining that world. Often the most useful tools turn out to be those developed and regularly used by social scientists. In unskilled hands, however, sharp tools can be dangerous.

COMPUTER-ASSISTED REPORTING

American journalism — print, broadcast and online — relies on computers. Reporters write on computers. Photographers edit and transmit their pictures by computer. The almost unlimited storage capacity of computers, and the flexibility of digital technology, enables online journalists to combine text and video with links to original documents and to related information stored anywhere in the world. Increasingly, journalists are also using computers to analyze data, to do what the *World-Herald* team did and create knowledge that nobody knew before.

Computers assist reporting in two main ways. First, journalists can access digital information from databases on the Internet. (You learned about these resources and how to tap them in Chapter 5.) Second, journalists become knowledge creators by compiling and analyzing information that was previously not collected or not examined. That's what the Nebraska reporters did.

David Herzog, director of the National Institute of Computer-Assisted Reporting, teaches University of Missouri students and hundreds of practicing journalists from all over the world how to use their computers as more than word processors. His students learn how to acquire data from government agencies, nonprofit organizations and other researchers. Then they learn to use the techniques of statistical analysis to pull important patterns, developing trends and good stories from the numbers.

Take, for instance, the topic of guns. Jo Craven McGinty was a graduate student at Missouri who mastered analytical techniques and worked part-time for NICAR helping professional journalists tell statistics-based stories. She came across an FBI database on the use of weapons by police officers. When she took an internship at *The Washington Post*, she took with her that knowledge and a story idea. Months later, as part of the *Post*'s investigative team, she helped tell the story that Washington, D.C., police used their guns to shoot civilians more often than police in any other city. The story won a Pulitzer Prize for the *Post*.

Not all computer-assisted reporting leads to Pulitzers, but much of it reveals important information that otherwise would remain hidden in bureaucratic files. Sometimes those stories are hidden in plain sight, and the data just demands arranging in order to be understood. Herzog is an expert in computer mapping, the use of special software programs to display information in maps that reveal significant patterns. Instances of crime, for example, can be mapped to show what truly are the dangerous areas of a city. Outbreaks of disease can be mapped to help identify sources of infection. Patterns of immigration or unemployment or voting can be demonstrated more clearly by electronic maps than words alone could describe.

To learn more, or to get help with your own reporting, go to **www.nicar.org**. You might call that connection computer-assisted learning.

PARTICIPANT OBSERVATION

Audiences around the world watched in real time as America's war with Iraq unfolded. Viewers saw desert terrain jump across their screens as cameras mounted on military vehicles captured the progress of American and British troops toward Baghdad. Correspondents wearing camouflage uniforms often slipped into the first-person plural as they described the experiences of the soldiers they were accompanying. The military term for those reporters was that they were "embedded" with their units. A social scientist would say that they were engaged in "participant observation."

Participant observation is a tool long used by anthropologists and sociologists to learn about unknown societies by becoming part of the scene they are studying. War correspondents have used it for just as long to provide firsthand accounts of campaigns. Other journalists have employed participant observation for **undercover reporting,** to expose crimes or social ills from the inside. All participant observers get close-up views of their subjects, insights not obtainable from studying statistics or formal interviewing. Facts and feelings can be captured that otherwise would remain unknown.

TIPS: Participant observation problems to consider

- Sensitivity is essential, especially when people you write about may be embarrassed or have their jobs placed in jeopardy.
- Make sure not to become so involved that you change the course of the events you're observing.
- Don't assume that the people you're observing feel as you do.
- Remember that participant observation is a good but limited tool. It usually works best as a supplement to interviewing and examining documents.

Along with its unique advantages, participant observation also poses some unique problems. These problems may have no clear solutions, but you and your editors need at least to consider them before you set out to become an ambulance attendant or a migrant worker.

The problem of invasion of privacy. Unless you identify yourself as a reporter, you are, in effect, spying on people — an ethically questionable activity. But if you do identify yourself, the advantages of participant observation can be lost. Sensitivity is essential, especially when the people you write about may be embarrassed or have their jobs placed in jeopardy.

The problem of involvement. There are two things to watch out for. First, do not become so involved that you change the course of the events you are observing. You may be on stage, but you are not the star performer. Second, do not assume that the people you are observing feel the same way you do. No matter how hard you work at fitting in, you remain an outsider, a visitor. The view from inside a migrant workers' camp or a psychiatric hospital is different when you know you will be there for two weeks instead of two years or a lifetime. This was the problem that drew the most criticism of the embedded reporters in Iraq. Their perspective on the war was necessarily that of the units to which they were attached. One reporter for *USA Today* even wrote a column in which he described how, during a battle, he was requested to help a medic who was treating a wounded soldier. The reporter told how he put his "objectivity" aside to save the life of a man who might have saved the reporter's life if the fight had turned out differently.

The problem of generalizing. Scientists know well the danger of generalizing from limited observations. Reporters don't always recognize that danger, or sometimes they forget it. Keep in mind that although participant observation yields a detailed picture of a specific situation, it tells you nothing reliable about any other situation. Participant observation is a good tool, but it is a limited one. It usually works best as a supplement to the standard techniques of interviewing and examining documents. This, too, was true of the war reporting. As the embedded journalists pointed out, theirs was not the only angle from which the war was reported. Other reporters at military headquarters, back home or even in besieged Baghdad all contributed to the overall account. That's a lesson to keep in mind.

SYSTEMATIC STUDY OF RECORDS

The example at the beginning of this chapter relied on the systematic study of records. Kathleen Kerr and Russ Buettner of *Newsday* faced the same sort of problem. Their goal was to discover whether New York City's criminal justice system discriminated against the poor. Their method was to acquire computer databases of city and state records on 27,810 prisoners and then to use their own computer to sort those cases by race and other criteria. They found that the poor, especially minorities, often were denied bail and forced to wait in jail for trials that often found them not guilty. No amount of traditional interviewing and observing could have produced such credible stories.

Scholars long have used the systematic study of records in their research. Its use by reporters is still limited but growing. The advantage of detailed analysis of court records, budgets, voting records and other documents is that it permits reporters and readers to draw conclusions based on solid information. The widespread availability of powerful personal computers and easy-to-use analytical programs brings the systematic study of records within the reach of any news organization.

The main obstacles to such study are shortages of time and money. Major projects for a large metropolitan daily often require months of work by one or more reporters. On small papers, especially, you may have trouble freeing yourself for even several days. And reporters' time and computer time both cost money. Editors and publishers must be convinced that the return will be worth the investment before they will approve. You probably should have at least some clues that wrongdoing, injustice or inefficiency exists before launching a systematic study.

Once you have begun a study, make sure that it is in fact systematic. Either examine all the pertinent records or choose the ones you examine in such a way that they will be truly representative of the rest. Be sure to ask the right questions, and record the information necessary to answer them. A computer can perform complicated analyses very quickly, but it cannot analyze facts that have not been fed into it. People who use computers have a word for that problem: GIGO, an acronym for "Garbage In, Garbage Out."

Don't set out on a systematic study without assurances of time and money, a clear idea of what you're looking for and expert technical advice. If the expertise is unavailable at your newspaper, look to the nearest college.

TIPS: Once you begin a study . . .

- Make sure it is systematic. Either examine all the pertinent records or choose the ones you examine in such a way that they are truly representative of the rest.
- Be sure to ask the right questions and record the information necessary to answer them.
- Remember that a computer can perform complicated analyses very quickly but cannot analyze facts that have not been fed into it.

FIELD EXPERIMENTS

Here's a test you can do. Say you want to find out whether landlords in your town discriminate against nonwhite would-be renters. Send out teams of different races to visit the same rental agencies or to respond to the same advertisements. Then compare the results. Did the all-white teams receive more welcoming treatment than others? A scientist conducting that kind of test would call it a **field experiment.** In all such experiments researchers take some action in order to observe the effects.

Reporters may not think of themselves as scientists, but they conduct a great many experiments. A common one is to examine the honesty of auto mechanics by taking a car in perfect condition to several shops and reporting what "defects" each finds. Consumer reporters also commonly check weights and measures: Does a "pound" of hamburger really weigh a pound? Or they test for discrimination by having an African American reporter and a white reporter apply for the same insurance policies or mortgages.

Computer-Assisted Reporting Wins Awards

Not many reporters win the Pulitzer Prize in their first job after journalism school. Jo Craven McGinty did, as a key member of an investigative team at *The Washington Post*. She'd be the first to tell you that the secret of her success was computer-assisted reporting.

Jo already had several years of experience on small newspapers when she decided to return to graduate school. She began learning computer-assisted reporting and became a graduate research assistant at the National Institute for Computer-Assisted Reporting (NICAR).

In that job, she recalls, "I implemented my new skills in computer-assisted reporting which I had learned in the classroom. And, while preparing the FBI's annual release of the Uniform Crime Report database, I noticed something: It appeared that the FBI tracked police shootings but did not release the records. I knew that I would pursue those records when the time was right."

That time came when Jo was hired in a temporary position to work on computer-assisted reporting at the *Post*. She picks up the story: "I obtained several years of the FBI records on computer tape. They revealed that D.C. police had shot and killed more people than any other big-city police department at that time."

The *Post* team, led by investigations editor Jeff Leen, discovered that a flood of new police hires had swamped the department's training program and failed to receive proper instruction. Many officers skipped required handgun training. Some bad shootings were covered up. Poor record-keeping meant that the police department's top brass didn't even know how many people their officers were killing — until the reporters told them.

The five-day series that resulted saved lives, generated reforms and won for the *Post* the Pulitzer gold medal for public service, the highest award in American journalism.

Now Jo is working at *Newsday*, where she is again putting to good use the principles and techniques of social science she learned in grad school.

If reporters' field experiments are to be successful, they must follow the same guidelines — and avoid the same pitfalls — that scientists' experiments must. A little scientific jargon is necessary here. It is fairly straightforward, though, and will be useful if you ever have the opportunity to set up an experiment.

Your field experiment must have a *hypothesis*, a statement of what you expect to find. Your hypothesis must be stated clearly and simply. When it is, it will help focus your attention on the two elements of the experiment: the independent variable and the dependent variable. The *variables*, just as their name implies, are the things that change during the experiment. The *independent variable* is what you think may be a cause. You change it and observe what happens to the *dependent variable*, the effect.

Get your facts first, and then you can distort them as much as you please.

— *Mark Twain*

Sometimes reporters distort the facts without even trying.

The *San Jose* (Calif.) *Mercury News* reported that women are "10 times more likely to be represented on the Supreme Court of the United States than on the average board of directors for a company in Silicon Valley." The *Mercury News* based that statement on the fact that 22.2 percent of the justices were women, compared with 2.9 percent of Silicon Valley directors.

But there were about 135 million women in the United States; two of them were Supreme Court justices and 30 of them were Silicon Valley directors. Thus, despite the paucity of women on Silicon Valley boards, the likelihood of a woman being represented there was actually 15 times greater than on the Supreme Court.

In its effort to illustrate a point, the *Mercury News* stumbled into an error that is common in newspapers. It generalized to the entire population (all U.S. women) from figures that applied only to subpopulations (women on the Supreme Court and Silicon Valley boards). What the *Mercury News* should have said was that the "ratio of women to men on the Supreme Court is nearly 10 times greater than on the boards of directors of Silicon Valley companies."

The lesson from the *Mercury News* story is that even when you think you're comparing apples to apples, make sure you don't have some oranges in there. You must have the same base population for a comparison to mean anything.

Here are some other ways statistics can deceive:

Bias can influence the credibility of a survey. For example, a national survey on sexual behavior indicated that 1 percent of 3,321 men questioned said they were gay, compared with the 10 percent commonly accepted as constituting the gay population. When reporting the survey results, *Time* magazine pointed out that people might be reluctant to discuss their sexual orientation with a "clipboard-bearing stranger."

One year does not a trend make. A large increase in the number of rapes merits a story, but it might represent a fluctuation rather than a trend. Depending on the subject matter, you need to study at least five to 10 years of data to determine whether there is a significant shift.

The way organizations compile figures can change and that can distort comparisons. In the late 1980s, the formula for compiling AIDS cases among heterosexuals was changed. The figures skyrocketed, as did the number of media reports on the spread of AIDS to the general population. Not all the reports noted the change in compiling the statistics.

Conclusions that sound credible might not hold up under the scrutiny of cause and effect. Advocacy groups that call for less violence on television say studies show TV violence causes violence in children. They cite research at Yale showing that prolonged viewing of violent programs is associated with aggressive behavior among children. But the association could be that children who tend to be aggressive watch more violent programming, not the other way around.

Let's look again at the search for bias in renting. As a social scientist, you would state the hypothesis you're testing: "Landlords in our town discriminate against renters of color." The independent variable is race. The dependent variables are the forms of security, the kinds of identification and the rents charged to each team. You're looking to see how differences in the variable of race affect the dependent variables.

381

There are two other steps you must take to ensure a successful experiment. First, you must *control* the experiment. Every aspect of the experiment must be carefully structured to make sure that any change you observe is caused only by the independent variable you want to test. For example, your teams of would-be "renters" must be as much alike as possible in the financial details they provide, the way they dress, their gender and their age. Otherwise, any differences in the responses by the landlords might be due to something other than race, the variable you are interested in. Also, the applicants should visit the same landlords and speak to the same officials. Without careful control of the experiment, you may end up unable to say with certainty that you have proved or disproved your hypothesis. Then you've got no story.

The other step is called *randomization*, or *random selection*. In a small town you could run your experiment with every landlord. But in a big city that would be impossible. So if you want to be reasonably sure that the results of the experiment apply to all the landlords in town, you must choose at random the ones to approach. Randomization allows you to assume that what you select — 10 rental agencies, for instance — is representative of the whole — the total number of landlords in the city.

Choosing anything at random simply means that you employ a method for choosing that gives every bank or every name an equal chance of being picked. The procedure for making a random selection is beyond the scope of an introductory reporting text. The Suggested Readings at the end of the chapter include several books in which you can find that and other material relating to the concepts introduced here. Much of that other material deals with statistics. Many experiments require statistical analysis to ensure that what you have found is significant. Most polls and surveys require some statistical analysis, too. Explanations of the fairly simple math involved also can be found in the books listed in Suggested Readings.

PUBLIC OPINION POLLS

Surveying is a powerful journalistic tool. At the beginning of the chapter, we examined an example of its misuse. Despite such problems, more journalists, politicians, businesses and scholars are using poll results because they show more reliably than anecdotes or ordinary interviews what the public thinks about important issues. Many news organizations now go beyond reporting the findings of national polling firms such as the Gallup and Louis Harris organizations to conducting or commissioning their own surveys. Several journalism schools — including those at the universities of Alabama, Florida, North Carolina and Missouri — have developed scientific polling operations staffed by faculty and students to serve newspapers and broadcasters.

When polls are conducted properly and reported carefully, they can be both interesting and useful, telling people something they could not know otherwise and perhaps even helping to produce wiser public policies. But when they are badly done or sloppily reported, polls can be bad news for journalists and readers alike.

Figure 17.1
Polling voters on election day is an excellent way to forecast election results. However, polls must be conducted properly and interpreted carefully to produce reliable information.

We've seen how a set of poll numbers from the 2000 presidential campaign was misused. Here's another set of poll results from 2003, when Democratic candidates were fighting for the right to run against Bush in 2004. These come from the Pew Research Center for the People and the Press (**www.people-press.org**):

Bush vs. Gephardt   Bush vs. Dean
49   43   52   41

Bush vs. Kerry   Bush vs. Lieberman
50   42   53   41

Bush vs. Clark
51   42

To interpret these results correctly, you need one more number: the margin of error. In this survey, the margin of error was 2.5 percent. So what does social science tell you about the early presidential race? President Bush was indeed leading all the most likely Democratic challengers, but there was no real difference in strength among the challengers. All their standings fell within the margin of error. Just one more thing: Any reputable pollster would warn that a survey produces a snapshot, a limited picture of attitudes at the moment the question was asked. Unless you have multiple surveys showing a statistically significant trend, you shouldn't use polling numbers to make predictions.

The chances are good that sometime in your reporting career you will want to conduct an opinion poll or at least help with one your newspaper is conducting. The Suggested Readings listed at the end of the chapter will tell you much of what you need to know for that. Even if you never work a poll, you almost certainly will be called on to write about the results of polls. What follows will help you understand what you are given and help you make sure your readers understand it, too.

Requirements for Sound Polling

The Associated Press Managing Editors Association prepared a checklist of the information you should have and should share with your audience about any poll on which you are reporting. Several of those points require some explanation.

Identity of the sponsor. The identity of the survey's sponsor is important to you and your readers because it gives some clues to possible bias. Most people would put more trust in a Gallup or Harris poll's report that, for instance, Smith is far ahead of Jones in the presidential campaign than they would in a poll sponsored by the Smith for President organization.

Exact wording of the questions. The wording of the questions is important because the answer received often depends at least in part on how the question was asked (see Chapter 3 on interviewing for more detail). The answer might well be different, for example, if a pollster asked, "Whom do you favor for president, Jones or Smith?" rather than "Wouldn't Jones make a better president than Smith?"

Population. In science, the **population** is the total number of people — or documents or milkweed plants or giraffes — in the group being studied (see Chapter 6). For an opinion survey the population might be all registered voters in the state, African American males under 25 or female cigarette smokers. To understand what the results of a poll mean, you must know what population was studied. The word "sampled" refers to the procedure in which a small number — or sample — of persons is picked at random so as to be representative of the population.

Sample size and response rate. The sample size is important because — all other things being equal — the larger the sample, the more reliable the survey results should be. The response rate is especially important in surveys conducted by mail, in which a low rate of response may invalidate the poll.

Margin of error. The **margin of error** of any survey is the allowance that must be made for the possibility that the opinion of the sample may not be exactly the same as the opinion of the whole population. Another name for it is "sampling errors." The margin of error depends mainly on the size of the sample. For instance, all other things being equal, a sample of 400 would have a margin of error of 5 percent, and a sample of 1,500 would have a margin of error of 3 percent. If, with a sample of 1,500, the poll shows Jones with 60 percent of the votes and Smith with 40 percent, you can be confident that Jones actually has between 57 and 63 percent and Smith actually has between 37 and 43 percent. The laws of probability say that the chances are 19 to 1 that the actual percentages fall within that range. Those odds make the information good enough to publish.

Which results are based on part of the sample. The problem of sampling error helps explain why it is important to know which results may be based on only part of the sample. The smaller that part is, the greater the margin of error. In political polls it is always important to know whether the results include

---

TIPS: "Average" can mean different things to different people

In reporting statistics, be certain you know the "average" involved. All of the following are averages:

- *Mean:* The arithmetic average, found by adding all the figures in a set of data and dividing by the number of figures. The mean of 2, 4 and 9 is 5 (2 + 4 + 9 = 15; 15 ÷ 3 = 5).
- *Median:* The middle value in a set of figures. If there is no middle value because there is an even number of figures, average the two middle numbers. The median of 2, 4 and 9 is 4. The medians of 5, 7, 9 and 11 and of 3, 7, 9 and 15 both are 8 (7 + 9 = 16; 16 ÷ 2 = 8).
- *Mode:* The most frequent value in a set of figures. The mode of 2, 5, 5, 5, 15 and 23 is 5.

"Next question: I believe that life is a constant striving for balance, requiring frequent tradeoffs between morality and necessity, within a cyclic pattern of joy and sadness, forging a trail of bittersweet memories until one slips, inevitably, into the jaws of death. Agree or disagree?"

Figure 17.2
Some pollsters' questions seem designed to elicit a desired response.

responses from all eligible voters or only from individuals likely to vote. The opinions of the likely voters are more important than others' opinions.

When the interviews were collected. When the interviews were collected may be of critical importance in interpreting the poll. During campaigns, for example, the candidates themselves and other events may cause preferences to change significantly within a few days. Think of presidential primaries. As candidates join or drop out of the race, support for each of the other candidates changes. A week-old poll may be meaningless if something dramatic happened after it was taken. Candidates have been known to use such outdated results to make themselves appear to be doing better than they really are, or their opponents worse. Be on guard.

How the interviews were collected. When the poll is your newspaper's, the obligation remains to let your readers know how it was taken. It is also incumbent on the paper to reveal how reliable the poll is.

The Need for Caution in Interpreting Polls

Whether you are helping to conduct a survey or only reporting on one produced by someone else, you must exercise caution. Be on guard for the following potential problems:

- *The people interviewed must be selected in a truly random fashion if you want to generalize from their responses to the whole population.* If they are not, you have no assurance that the interview subjects are really representative. The old-fashioned people-in-the-street interview is practically worthless as an indicator of public opinion for this reason. The man or woman in the street probably differs in important ways from all those men and women who are not in the street when the questioner is.

  Also invalid are such "polls" as the questionnaires members of Congress mail to their constituents. Only strongly opinionated — and therefore unrepresentative — people are likely to return them. For the same reason the "question-of-the-day" feature that some newspapers and broadcast stations carry tells you nothing about the opinions of the great mass of people who do not respond. Even worse are the TV polls that require respondents to call a 900 number to register their opinions. Because there is a charge for such calls, these pseudo-polls produce not only misleading results but profits that encourage their use.

- *The closer the results, the harder it is to say anything definitive.* Look again at the example of the Smith-Jones campaign. Suppose the poll showed Smith with 52 percent and Jones with 48 percent of the vote. Smith may or may not be ahead. With the 3 percent margin of error, Smith could actually have only 49 percent, and Jones could have 51 percent. All that you could report safely about those results is that the race is too close to call. Many reporters — and pollsters — are simply not careful enough when the outcome is unclear.

- *Beware of polls that claim to measure opinion on sensitive, complicated issues.* Many questions of morality, or social issues such as race relations, do not lend themselves to simple answers. Opinions on such matters can be measured, but only by highly skilled researchers using carefully designed questions. Anything less can be dangerously oversimplified and highly misleading.

Surveying, like field experiments, systematic analysis and participant observation, can help you as a reporter solve problems you could not handle as well by other techniques. But these are only tools. How effectively they are used — or how clumsily they are misused — depends on you.

Suggested Readings

Campbell, Donald and Stanley, Julian. *Experimental and Quasi-Experimental Designs for Research.* Skokie, Ill.: Rand McNally, 1966. A classic guide to field experimentation that is also useful in providing a better understanding of scientific research.

Demers, David Pearce and Nichols, Suzanne. *Precision Journalism: A Practical Guide.* Newbury Park, Calif.: Sage Publications, 1987. A primer for students and journalists, simply written and complete with examples.

Houston, Brant. *Computer-Assisted Reporting*, Third Edition. New York: Bedford/St. Martin's, 2004. A practical introduction to data analysis and field reporting.

McCombs, Maxwell, Shaw, Donald L. and Grey, David. *Handbook of Reporting Methods*. Boston: Houghton Mifflin, 1976. Offers examples of real-life uses of social science methods in journalism but does not provide enough on statistics to serve as a guide in employing the methods.

Meyer, Philip. *Precision Journalism*, Fourth Edition. Lanham, Md.: Rowman & Littlefield, 2002. A detailed introduction to surveying, conducting field experiments and using statistics to analyze the results by a reporter who pioneered the use of these methods in journalism. The theoretical justification of the techniques is included as well.

Seltzer, Richard A. *Mistakes That Social Scientists Make*. New York: St. Martin's Press, 1996. A useful book about the kinds of errors often made by social scientists during their research.

Williams, Frederick. *Reasoning with Statistics*. New York: Holt, Rinehart and Winston, 1979. A nonintimidating but sufficiently complex guide to using mathematical tools.

Suggested Web Sites

www.aejmc.org

The Association for Education in Journalism and Mass Communication is the professional organization of journalism teachers and researchers. For a journalist or journalism student, perhaps the most useful contents of this site are the links to the research publications of the organization. Many of the reports in those publications use, and explain, the techniques discussed in this chapter.

www.gallup.com

The Gallup organization is and for years has been one of the most reputable of the national polling companies. This site contains results of a wide variety of public polls, along with their methodology.

www.people-press.org

This is the site of the Pew Research Center for the People and the Press. Here you'll find not only poll results but explanations of methodology and limitations.

Exercises

1. Find a newspaper story that reports on the results of a public opinion survey. Analyze the story using the guidelines discussed in this chapter.

2. Using the technique described by Philip Meyer in *Precision Journalism* (see the Suggested Readings), design a simple survey. Write a memo outlining your plan.

3. Design a field experiment: State your hypothesis, identify the dependent and independent variables, and describe the controls you will use.

4. As a class project, carry out one of the surveys designed in response to exercise 2.

5. Analyze the data you collected in exercise 4 using SPSS or a similar software package. As a final step, write the story of your findings.

nvestigative reporters aren't always digging into crime and corruption. Sometimes they perform a public service by examining our most trusted institutions. The *Dayton Daily News* in Ohio, for example, took a look behind the benign image of the Peace Corps. Nearly two years of relentless reporting required travel around the world, interviews with former volunteers and foreign officials, and lawsuits to force the organization to release internal documents. The result was a week-long series that exposed for the first time the carefully concealed hazards of Peace Corps service. The *Daily News* found that dozens of volunteers have been raped or robbed. Some have been murdered — and the Peace Corps has hidden that information from family members, the public and even law-enforcement agencies.

Like many investigative reporters, the *Daily News* team relied on a mix of traditional techniques and computer-assisted reporting, plus the leverage of the Freedom of Information Act to pry loose essential documents.

Mei-ling Hopgood was one of two lead reporters on the series. She is the Washington reporter for the *Daily News*. She reflected on the work as the series appeared. "For about a year, the agency wouldn't cooperate at all. Finally we filed a lawsuit, and they gave up FOIA info and databases on crime and death. . . . It was a mix of CAR and A LOT of shoe-leather reporting. We had to make call after call to identify and get to victims. We used Autotrack a lot. But each death, each incident was a mini-investigation, so it was very time-intensive. We filed more than 75 FOIA requests."

The series attracted national attention. "We have gotten tons of reaction," Hopgood said. "The AP preview ran all over the nation. Our story ran in most of the Cox Newspapers in some form. We've gotten many, many letters and e-mails. . . . You can also see the debate, more productive and balanced, on **peacecorpsonline.com**. They posted all our stories. The Senate may call hearings. We're waiting to see."

That's investigative reporting in the 21st century. Good reporters use technology and the law, along with shoe-leather reporting to tell an important, hidden story. The Internet spreads the story around the world and permits instant response. Stakeholders use a Web site for passionate debate. The public is both informed and involved. Public policy may change. Mei-ling Hopgood, her colleague Russell Carollo and

In this chapter you will learn:

1. The process of investigative reporting.

2. How to find and use human and written sources.

3. The obstacles you will face as an investigative reporter.

389

thousands of other journalists are doing difficult, important work. They're serving society.

Investigative reporting has a rich tradition in American journalism. The fiercely partisan editors of the Revolutionary era dug for facts as well as the mud they hurled at their opponents. In the early 20th century, investigative reporting flowered with the "muckrakers," a title bestowed with anger by Theodore Roosevelt and worn with pride by journalists. Lincoln Steffens explored the undersides of American cities, one by one, laying bare the corrupt combinations of businessmen and politicians that ran them. Ida Tarbell exposed the economic stranglehold of the oil monopoly (see Figure 18.1). Theodore Dreiser, Upton Sinclair and Frank Norris revealed the horrors of working life in factories and meatpacking plants.

Their professional heirs today bring to the work the same commitment to exposure and reform. They use refinements of many of the same techniques: indepth interviews, personal observation, analysis of documents. But modern muckrakers have a powerful tool their predecessors didn't dream of: The computer allows reporters today to compile and analyze masses of data, to perform complicated statistical tests, and to create charts and graphs to enhance un1derstanding. This tool, in turn, requires of reporters numeracy as well as literacy. It requires the addition of another set of skills to every serious journalist's repertoire.

Figure 18.1
Ida Tarbell, one of the original muckrakers, helped set the pattern for investigative reporting with her exposé of Standard Oil.

Computer-assisted reporting gives young reporters the opportunity to be admitted to the major league of journalism. If you learn computer skills along with the techniques taught in this chapter, you will be equipped for the 21st century.

THE PROCESS

Most investigations start with a hunch or a tip that something or someone deserves a close look. If a preliminary search bears out that expectation, a serious investigation begins. When enough information has been uncovered to prove or modify the reporter's initial hunch, it's time to analyze, organize and write the story.

Beginning the Investigation

No good reporter sets out on an investigation unless there is some basis for suspicion. That basis may be a grand jury report that leaves something untold or a tip that some public official is on the take. It may be a sudden upsurge in drug overdoses, or it may be long-festering problems in the schools. Without some idea of what you're looking for, an investigation is too likely to turn into wild-goose chasing.

Acting on the tip or suspicion, together with whatever background material you have, you form a hypothesis. Reporters hardly ever use that term, but it is a useful one, because it shows the similarity between the processes of investigative reporting and scientific investigation (see Chapter 17). In both, the **hypothesis** is the statement of what you think is true. Your hypothesis may be "The mayor is a crook" or "The school system is being run incompetently." It is a good idea to clearly state your hypothesis when you begin your investigation. By doing so, you focus on the heart of the problem and lessen the possibility of any misunderstanding with your editor or other reporters who may be working with you.

Once the hypothesis is stated, the reporter — like the scientist — sets out to prove or disprove it. You should be open to the possibility of disproof. Reporters — like scientists — are not advocates. They are seekers of truth. No good reporter ignores or downplays evidence just because it contradicts his or her assumptions. In journalism, as in science, the truth about a situation is often sharply different from what is expected. Open-mindedness is an essential quality of a good investigative reporter. Remember, too, that you may have a good story even if your hypothesis is disproved.

Carrying Out the Investigation

The actual investigative work usually proceeds in two stages. The first is what Robert W. Greene, a legendary reporter and Pulitzer Prize–winning editor for *Newsday*, named the **sniff.** In this stage you nose around in search of a trail worth following. If you find one, the second stage, serious investigation, begins.

Preliminary checking should take no more than a day or two. Its purpose is not to prove the hypothesis but to find out the chances of proving it. You make that effort by talking with the most promising source or sources, skimming the most available records, consulting knowledgeable people in your news room. The two questions you are trying to answer at this stage are (1) "Is there a story here?" and (2) "Am I going to be able to get it?" If the answer to either question is no, there is little point in pursuing the investigation.

When the answer to both questions is yes, however, the real work begins. It begins with organization. Your hypothesis tells you where you want to go. Now you must figure out how to get there. Careful organization keeps you on the right track and prevents you from overlooking anything important as you go. Many reporters take a kind of perverse pride in their illegible notebooks and cluttered desks. As an investigative reporter you may have a messy desk, but you should arrange your files of information clearly and coherently. Begin organizing by ask-ing yourself these questions:

- Who are my most promising sources? Who is likely to give me trouble? Whom should I go to first? Second? Last?
- What records do I need? Where are they? Which are public? How can I get to the ones that are not readily accessible?
- What is the most I can hope to prove? What is the least that will still yield a story? How long should the investigation take?

Then draw up a plan of action. Experienced reporters often do this mentally. But when you are a beginner, it's a good idea to write out a plan and go over it with your editor. The editor may spot some holes in your planning or have some-thing to add. And an editor is more likely to give you enough time if he or she has a clear idea of what has to be done.

Carry out your plan, allowing flexibility for the unexpected twists that most investigations take. During your first round of interviews, keep asking who else you should talk to. While you are checking records, look for references to other files or other persons.

Be methodical. Many investigative reporters spend an hour or so at the end of every day adding up the score, going through their notes and searching their memories to analyze what they have learned and what they need next. Some develop elaborate, cross-indexed files of names, organizations and incidents. Others are less formal. Nearly all, however, use a code to disguise the names of confidential sources so that those sources will remain secret even if the files are subpoenaed. The method you use isn't important as long as you understand it. What is vitally important is that you have a method and use it consistently. If you fail to keep careful track of where you're going, you may go in the wrong direc-tion, or in circles.

Getting It Right

The importance of accuracy in investigative reporting cannot be overstated. It is the essential element in good journalism of any kind. But in investigative reporting especially, inaccuracy leads to embarrassment, to ruined reputations and, sometimes, to lawsuits. The reputations ruined often are those of the careless reporter and newspaper. Most investigative stories have the effect of accusing somebody of wrongdoing or incompetence. Even if the target is a public official whose chances of suing successfully for libel are slim (see Chapter 22), fairness and decency require that you be sure of your facts before you put them in print.

During the Watergate investigation, *The Washington Post* followed the policy of requiring verification from two independent sources before an allegation could be published. That is a good rule to follow. People make mistakes. They lie. Their memories fail. Documents can be misleading or confusing. Check and double-check. There is no good excuse for an error.

Writing the Story

Most investigative stories require consultation with the newspaper's lawyer before publication. As a reporter you will have little or nothing to say about the choice of your paper's lawyer. That lawyer, though, will be an important part of your investigative career. The lawyer advises on what you can print safely and what you cannot. Most editors heed their lawyer's advice. If you are lucky, your paper's lawyer will understand and sympathize with good, aggressive journalism. If he or she does not, you may find yourself forced to argue for your story. You will be better equipped for such an argument — few reporters go through a career without several — if you understand at least the basics of the laws of libel and privacy. Chapter 22 outlines those laws, and several good books on law for journalists are listed in the Suggested Readings at the end of that chapter.

The last step before your investigation goes public is the writing and rewriting. After days or weeks of intense reporting effort, the actual writing strikes some investigative reporters as a chore — necessary but unimportant. That attitude is disastrous. The best reporting in the world is wasted unless it is read. Your hard-won exposé or painstaking analysis will disappear without a trace unless your writing attracts readers and maintains their interest. Most reporters and newspapers that are serious about investigative reporting recognize this. They stress good writing almost as much as solid reporting.

How do you write the results of a complicated investigation? The general rule is, as simply as you can. One approach is to use a **hard lead,** displaying your key findings in the first few paragraphs. Another choice, often used, is to adopt one of the alternative approaches to storytelling explained in Chapter 9.

We've met Mei-ling Hopgood, who helped report and write the *Dayton Daily News* investigation of the dangers of the Peace Corps. Here's how that series began:

"Go to the scene of the disaster and don't let the breaking story stop you from thinking ahead. There, you will find almost all of the sources to tell you what went wrong in responding to the disaster. Though you will have to get your proof through public-record requests, you will get your leads at the scene."

— James Grimaldi,
The Washington Post

AGUA FRIA, El Salvador — On a clear Christmas night near a moonlit stretch of Pacific beach, a man with a pistol came from the darkness and forced Diana Gilmour to watch two of her fellow Peace Corps volunteers being gang-raped while a male volunteer was pinned helpless on the ground.

One of the men — his breath reeking of alcohol — raped Gilmour, too. Then the attackers herded the volunteers at gunpoint to a field of high grass where they feared they would be executed.

"I was constantly waiting to hear a shot in the dark," Gilmour said.

Suddenly another volunteer approached with a flashlight, and the attackers fled.

The best stories usually are about people, and this one is no exception. The drama of one case introduces readers to the bigger story. A few paragraphs later Hopgood and colleague Russell Carollo show that big picture:

Records from a never-before-released computer database show that reported assault cases involving Peace Corps volunteers increased 125 percent from 1991 to 2002, while the number of volunteers increased by 29 percent, according to the Peace Corps. Last year, the number of assaults and robberies averaged one every 23 hours.

The *Dayton Daily News* spent 20 months examining thousands of records on assaults on Peace Corps volunteers occurring around the world during the past four decades. . . .

Moving from the particular to the general is both a logical progression and an effective way to show readers the humanity and the full scope of the investigation. Notice that the last paragraph also lets readers know something about how the information was developed. That's important, too, if you want to be believed. (In this case, the paper's editor also wrote a column explaining both motivation and methods of the investigation. That's another good idea. You owe it to your audience to be as open as possible about not only what you know but how you know it. In this era of diminished credibility, it's especially important to do everything you can to be honest and open about your work.)

Writing an investigative story so that it will be read takes the same attention to organization and to detail as does any good writing. Here are a few tips that apply to all types of writing but especially to investigative stories:

- *Get people into the story.* Any investigation worth doing involves people in some way. Make them come alive with descriptive detail, the kind we were given in the Peace Corps story.
- *Keep it simple.* Look for ways to clarify and explain complicated situations. When you have a mass of information, consider spreading it over more than one story — in a series or in a main story with a sidebar. Think about how charts, graphs or lists can be used to present key facts clearly. Don't try to print everything you know. Enough to support your conclusions is sufficient; more than that is too much.
- *Tell the reader what your research means.* A great temptation in investigative reporting is to lay out the facts and let the reader draw the conclusions. That is unfair to you and your reader. Lay out the facts, of course, but tell the reader what they add up to. A reporter who had spent weeks investigating the deplorable conditions in his state's juvenile corrections facilities wrote this lead:

Florida treats her delinquent children as
if she hated them.

Then he went on to show the reality that led to that summary. If the facts are
there, drawing the obvious conclusions is not editorializing. It is good and
helpful writing.

- *Organize.* Careful organization is as important in writing the investigative
  story as in reporting it. The job will be easier if you have been organized all
  along. When you are ready to write, examine your notes again. Make an outline. Pick out your best quotes and anecdotes. Some reporters, if they are
  writing more than one story, separate their material into individual folders,
  one for each story. However you do it, know what you are going to say
  before you start to write.
- *Suggest solutions.* Polls have shown that readers prefer investigative stories
  that show how to correct the problems described in the stories. Many of
  today's best newspapers are satisfying readers' demands by going beyond
  exposure in search of solutions. Are new laws needed? Better enforcement
  of present laws? More resources? Better training? Remember that the early-
  20th-century Progressive movement of which the original muckrakers were
  a part produced reforms, not just good stories.

Think of writing as the climax of a process that begins with a hypothesis,
tests that hypothesis through careful investigation, checks and double-checks
every fact, and satisfies the concerns of newspaper editors and lawyers. Every
step in that process is vital to the success of any investigative story.

THE SOURCES

Investigative reporters — like other reporters — get their information from
people or documents. The perfect source would be a person who has the pertinent documents and is eager to tell you what those documents mean. Don't
count on finding the perfect source. Instead, count on having to piece together
the information you need from a variety of people and records — some of the
people not at all eager to talk to you and some of the records difficult to obtain
and, if you do gain access to them, difficult to understand. Let's consider human
sources first.

Human Sources

Suppose you get a tip that the mayor received campaign contributions under the
table from the engineering firm that just got a big city contract. Who might talk?

Enemies. When you are trying to find out anything bad about a person, his or
her enemies are usually the best sources. More often than not, the enemies

of a prominent person will have made it their business to find out as much as possible about that person's misdeeds and shortcomings. Frequently, they are happy to share what they know with a friendly reporter.

Friends. Friends are sometimes nearly as revealing as enemies. In trying to explain and defend their friend's actions, they may tell you more than you knew before. Occasionally you may find that someone your target regards as a friend is not much of a friend after all.

Losers. Like enemies, losers often carry a grudge. Seek out the loser in the last election, the losing contender for the contract, the loser in a power struggle. Bad losers make good sources.

Victims. If you are investigating a failing school system, talk with students and their parents. If your story is about nursing home abuses, talk with patients and their relatives. The honest and hard-working employees caught in a corrupt or incompetent system are victims, too. They can give you specific examples and anecdotes. Their case histories can help you write the story.

Experts. Early in many investigations, there may be a great deal that you don't understand. You may need someone to explain how the campaign finance laws could be circumvented, someone to interpret a contract, someone to decipher a set of bid specifications. Lawyers, accountants, engineers or professors can help you understand technical jargon or complicated transactions. If they refuse to comment on your specific case, fit the facts you have into a hypothetical situation.

Police. Investigative reporters and law-enforcement agents often work the same territory. If you are wise, you will make friends with carefully selected agents. They can — and frequently will — be of great help. Their files may not be gold mines, but they have investigative tools and contacts you lack. When they get to know and trust you, they will share. Most police like seeing their own and their organization's names in the paper. They know, too, that you can do some things they cannot. It takes less proof for you to be able to print that the mayor is a crook than it may take to convince a jury. Most police investigators want to corner wrongdoers any way they can. You can use that attitude to your advantage.

People in trouble. Police use this source and so can you, although you cannot promise immunity or a lesser charge, as the police can. A classic case is the Watergate affair. Once the Nixon administration started to unravel, officials trying to save their careers and images began falling all over each other to give their self-serving versions of events. People will react similarly in lesser cases.

As an investigative reporter, you cultivate sources in the same ways a reporter on a beat does. You just do it more quickly. One excellent tactic is to play on their self-interest. Losers and enemies want to get the so-and-so, and thus you have a common aim. (But don't go overboard. Your words could come back to haunt you.) Friends want their buddy's side of the story to be explained. So do you. If you keep in mind that no matter how corrupt your target may be, he or she is still a human being, it may be easier to deal sympathetically with that person's friends. That attitude may help ensure that you treat the target fairly as well.

Experts just want to explain the problem as you present it. And you just want to understand. People in trouble want sympathy and some assurance that they still merit respect. No reporter should have trouble conveying either attitude.

Another way to win and keep sources is to protect them. Occasionally a reporter faces jail unless he or she reveals a source. Even jail is not too great a price to pay in order to keep a promise of confidentiality. More often, the threats to confidentiality are less dramatic. Other sources, or the target of the investigation, may casually ask, "Where'd you hear that?" Other reporters, over coffee or a beer, may ask the same question. Hold your tongue. The only person to whom a confidential source should ever be revealed is your editor.

Human sources pose problems as well as solve them. To get at an enemy or protect a friend, to make themselves look better or someone else look worse — and sometimes simply for fun — people lie to reporters. No reporter is safe and no source is above suspicion. They may use you, too, just as you are using them. The only reason most people involved on any side of a suspicious situation will talk about it is to enhance their own position. That is neither illegal nor immoral, but it can trip up a reporter who fails to take every self-serving statement with the appropriate grain of salt.

Sources may change their stories as well. People forget. Recollections and situations change. Pressures can be applied. Fear or love or ambition or greed can intrude. A source may deny tomorrow — or in court — what he or she told you today.

Finally, sources will seldom want to be identified. Even the enemies of a powerful person often are reluctant to see their names attached to their criticisms in print. So are friends. Experts, while willing to provide background information, often cite their codes of ethics when you ask them to go on the record. Stories without identifiable sources have less credibility with readers, with editors, even with colleagues.

Written Sources

Fortunately, not all sources are human. Records and documents neither lie nor change their stories, they have no axes to grind at your expense, and they can be identified in print. Many useful documents are public records, available to you or any other citizen on request. Others are nonpublic but still may be available through your human sources.

Public Records

As the examples earlier show, a great deal can be learned about individuals and organizations through records that are available for the asking, if you know where to ask. Let's take a look at some of the most valuable public records and where they can be found.

Property records. Many investigations center on land — who owns it, who buys it, how it is zoned, how it is taxed. You can find out all that information and more from public records. Your county recorder's office (or its equivalent) has on file the ownership of every piece of land in the county as well as the history of past owners. Most such offices have their files cross-indexed so that you can find out the owner of the land if you know its location, or the location and size of the property if you know the owner. Those files also will tell you who holds a mortgage on the land. The city or county tax assessor's office has on file the assessed valuation of the land, the basis for property taxes. Either the assessor or the local zoning agency can tell you for what use the property is zoned. All requests for rezoning are public information, too.

Corporation records. Every corporation must file with the secretary of state a document showing the officers and principal agent of the company. The document must be filed with every state in which the company does business. The officers listed may be only "dummies," stand-ins for the real owners. Even if that is the case, you can find out at least who the stand-ins are. But that is only the beginning. Publicly held corporations must file annual reports with the Securities and Exchange Commission in Washington. The reports list officers, major stockholders, financial statements and business dealings with other companies owned by the corporation. Nonprofit corporations — such as foundations and charities — must file with the Internal Revenue Service an even more revealing statement, Form 990, showing how much money came in and where it went. Similar statements must be filed with the attorneys general of many states. Corporations often are regulated by state or federal agencies as well. They file regular reports with the regulating agency. Insurance companies, for instance, are regulated by state insurance commissioners. Nursing homes are regulated by various state agencies. Broadcasters are overseen by the Federal Communications Commission, truckers by the Interstate Commerce Commission. Labor unions must file detailed statements showing assets, officers' salaries, loans and other financial information with the U.S. Department of Labor. Those statements are called "5500 Forms."

Once you have such corporation records, you must interpret them. Your public library has books that tell you how. Or your newspaper's own business experts may be willing to help.

Court records. Few people active in politics or business go through life without some involvement in court actions. Check the offices of the state and federal court clerks for records of lawsuits. The written arguments, sworn statements and answers to questions (interrogatories) may contain valuable details or provide leads to follow. Has your target been divorced? Legal struggles over assets can be revealing. Probate court files of your target's deceased associates may tell you something you need to know.

Campaign and conflict-of-interest reports. Federal — and most state — campaign laws now require political candidates to disclose, during and after

One newspaper exposed
the ugly truth about
pollution in Puget Sound.

Reporter: Robert McClure
Reporter: Lisa Stiffler
Photographer: Paul Joseph Brown

For 150 years, Puget Sound has provided the Seattle area with food, jobs and commerce as well as recreation and inspiration. In return, the region has treated the sparkling blue waters of the Sound like a sewer. Until recently, nobody paid much attention to the consequences of that destructive pattern. Then, in November, the Seattle Post-Intelligencer published a five-part series called "Our Troubled Sound."

For the first time, area residents became aware of the size and severity of the crisis. The series led to a public outcry for the government to take action. As a result, state and federal officeholders have vowed to stop the pollution and begin clean-up programs. This time, the eyes of the region will be on them.

Making waves when public health and natural resources are at risk is another way Hearst Newspapers make a positive contribution to their communities . . . and that's what excellence in journalism is all about.

To read more on the series go to www.seattlepi.com/specials/sound

Hearst Newspapers

Figure 18.2
Investigative reporters have uncovered scandals, illegal activity, and raised public awareness of issues such as water pollution.

each campaign, lists of who gave what to whom. Those filings can yield stories on who is supporting the candidates. They also can be used later for comparing who gets what from which officeholder. Many states require officeholders to file statements of their business and stock holdings. These can be checked for possible conflicts of interest or used as background for profile stories.

Loan records. Commercial lenders usually file statements showing property that has been used as security for loans. Known as Uniform Commercial Code filings, these can be found in the offices of state secretaries of state and, sometimes, in local recorders' offices.

Minutes and transcripts. Most elected and appointed governing bodies, ranging from local planning and zoning commissions to the U.S. Congress, are required by law to keep minutes or transcripts of their meetings.

Using and Securing Public Records

The states and the federal government have laws designed to ensure access to public records. Many of those laws — including the federal **Freedom of Information Act,** which was passed to improve access to government records — have gaping loopholes and time-consuming review procedures. Still, they have been and can be useful tools when all else fails. Learn the details of the law in your state. You can get information on access laws and their interpretations by contacting the Freedom of Information Center at the University of Missouri, 127 Neff Annex, Columbia, Mo. 65211.

Nonpublic Records

Nonpublic records are more difficult, but often not impossible, to obtain. To get them, you must know that they exist, where they are and how to gain access. Finding out about those things requires good human sources. You should know about a few of the most valuable nonpublic records:

Investigative files. The investigative files of law-enforcement agencies can be rich in information. You are likely to see them only if you have a good source in a particular agency or one affiliated with it. If you do obtain such files, treat them cautiously. They will be full of unsubstantiated allegations, rumor and misinformation. Be wary of accepting as fact anything you have not confirmed yourself.

Past arrests and convictions. Records of past arrests and convictions increasingly are being removed from public scrutiny. Usually these are easier than investigative files to obtain from a friendly police or prosecuting official. And usually they are more trustworthy than raw investigative files.

Bank records. Bank records would be helpful in many investigations, but they are among the most difficult to get. Bankers are trained to keep secrets. The government agencies that regulate banks are secretive as well. A friend in a bank is an investigative reporter's friend indeed.

Income tax records. Except for those made public by officeholders, income tax records are guarded carefully by their custodians, and properly so. Leaks are rare.

Credit checks. Sometimes you can get otherwise unavailable information on a target's financial situation by arranging through your newspaper's business office for a credit check. Credit reports may reveal outstanding debts, a big bank account, major assets and business affiliations. Use that information with care. It is unofficial, and companies that provide it intend it to be confidential.

Problems with Written Sources

Even when you can obtain them, records and other written sources present problems. They are usually dull. Records give you names and numbers, not anecdotes or sparkling quotes. They are bare bones, not flesh and blood. They can be misleading and confusing. Many highly skilled lawyers and accountants spend careers interpreting the kinds of records you may find yourself pondering without their training. Misinterpreting a document is no less serious an error than misquoting a person. And it's easier to do.

Documents usually describe without explaining. You need to know the "why" of a land transaction or a loan. Records tell you only the "what."

Most investigative reporters use both human and documentary sources. People can explain what records cannot. Documents prove what good quotes cannot. You need people to lead you to documents and people to interpret what the documents mean. And you need records to substantiate what people tell you. The best investigative stories combine both types of sources.

NEW TOOLS, TRADITIONAL GOALS

As you've seen, the computer is the most important new tool of investigative reporting. Once you know how to use it, the computer allows you to obtain, analyze and present information in ways that would have been impossible a few years ago, let alone in the era of the original muckrakers. But useful as it is, the computer is only a tool. Many modern investigative reporters are guided by goals that their predecessors of a century ago would easily recognize.

Today's investigators, like the original muckrakers, often are not satisfied with uncovering individual instances of wrongdoing. They tend to want to look at organizations as a whole, at entire systems. They seek not only to expose but to explain. In many cases they also seek to change the problems and abuses they reveal. Many, perhaps most, investigative reporters think of themselves as more than chroniclers of fact or analysts. They also see themselves as reformers. This, too, was true of the muckrakers.

In Chapter 17, you met Jo Craven McGinty, who used her computer-assisted reporting skills to help *The Washington Post* win a Pulitzer Prize for a team investigation of the misuse of firearms by police. In this chapter, the On the Job feature introduces Karen Dillon, whose lengthy investigation of the trickery that allowed police agencies to keep millions of dollars that should be going to public schools combined the tools of computer analysis with the passion for reform.

This drive to expose abuses is something the public welcomes and expects from journalists. Studies have shown that the consumers of journalism support investigative reporting when it leads to reforms. There's no conflict between investigative reporting and the journalistic standard of objectivity, either. You'll remember from Chapter 1 that objectivity doesn't have to mean neutrality. In journalism as in science, objectivity is the method of searching for the truth. Just as scientists are not expected to be neutral between disease and cure, journalists don't have to be neutral between good and evil. What objectivity requires of both scientists and journalists is honest, open-minded investigation and truthful reporting of the results of that investigation.

Leading Readers Through the Maze

Karen Dillon entered journalism through the back door — literally. She began in the backshop of a small paper in Iowa. After working her way into the news room, she decided to go to college, where she earned degrees in political science and journalism. After school, she got a job covering the police in Florida. For the past seven years, she has been at *The Kansas City Star*, on the special projects desk.

"In that time I have noticed one overarching theme," she says. "Many public agencies are doing something their leaders don't want the public to know about. In other words, public agencies can be anything but. The luxury — and the burden — of my job is that I am given the time and means to become the public's microscope. I question the bureaucrats, follow the money and take our readers into the sometimes-working maze of their governments."

She began following the money into the maze of drug-law enforcement after she spotted a case in which the Missouri Highway Patrol stopped a vehicle on Interstate 70 and found a large amount of cash. The Patrol seized the money, saying it was the proceeds from drug sales, even though no drugs were ever found and no one was charged. Then the Patrol turned the money over to the federal Drug Enforcement Administration, which kept 20 percent and returned the rest to the Patrol, which kept it.

The Missouri Constitution, like laws in other states, requires such seized money to be used for public education. Karen decided to investigate the frequency of such financial sleight-of-hand between law enforcement agencies. "Pulling reports in more than 200 seizure cases in Missouri, we found that the I-70 case was typical — police usually circumvented the law when they seized cash and gave it to the feds without getting court approval."

Her stories prodded Missouri lawmakers to act, filing bills to plug the loophole. The U.S. attorney, embarrassed, called a press conference to attack her work. Karen and the *Star* were not deterred.

Karen broadened her reporting, using the Internet to access forfeiture laws in all 50 states. She used Justice Department statistics to build a database showing that millions of dollars were involved. She learned that local law enforcement agencies across the country were getting federal help to circumvent state laws and use seized cash to finance their own activities. In 35 states, that was against the law.

The national story, titled "To Protect and Collect," drew widespread public response. Meanwhile, a Missouri appeals court ruled that the police were, indeed, breaking the law.

And Karen is leading her readers through other mazes.

THE OBSTACLES

You have seen now why investigative reporting is important and how it can be done. The picture would not be complete, though, without a brief look at the reasons why not every newspaper or broadcast organization does investigative reporting. As a reporter you will face certain obstacles. You and your editors will have to overcome them if you are to do real investigative reporting. Good newspapers and news broadcasters do overcome such obstacles.

Money and Staffing

The first obstacle is money. Investigative reporting is the most expensive kind of reporting. It takes time, and time is money. *Newsday*'s investigative team spent nine months on a series about heroin traffic. Two *Miami Herald* reporters spent most of their time for more than two years on an investigation of corruption in a federal housing program. Usually the reporters doing investigations are the paper's or station's best and highest-paid. Frequently, fees for experts are involved. Lawyers charge for looking over a story and much, much more if a suit is filed. Space to publish the results costs money, too.

The second obstacle is staffing. Most newspapers and broadcast organizations, large or small, are understaffed. When a reporter is devoting time to an investigation, somebody else must be found to fill the gap. Many editors are unable or unwilling to adjust for prolonged absences by a key reporter. You may be able to get around that obstacle by doing your investigating in bits and pieces, keeping up with routine assignments all the while. That kind of part-time probing requires a high level of dedication from you and your editor. Such commitment is hard to sustain over long stretches of time.

Lack of Courage

The third obstacle is a lack of courage. This is the great inhibitor. Investigative reporting means disturbing the status quo. It *means* poking into dark corners, asking hard questions about controversial, sensitive affairs. Investigative reporting upsets people. If you are looking into the right things, the people who get upset are likely to be important.

Violence or the threat of violence directed toward reporters and newspapers in this country is rare. The 1975 murder of investigative reporter Don Bolles in Phoenix was shocking partly because such things hardly ever happen. In many other countries, investigative reporters routinely risk death or imprisonment. Every year, the Inter-American Press Association publishes a list of journalists in the Americas who were killed in the line of duty. Colombia and Mexico are especially dangerous. In the United States, economic or social pressure, usually applied to your editor or publisher, is common enough. It takes courage to stand up to such pressure.

The Nixon administration threatened the lucrative television licenses of the Washington Post Co. during the Watergate investigation. The federal government sued the *New York Times*, *Boston Globe* and *St. Louis Post-Dispatch* to prevent publication of the *Pentagon Papers*. FBI and CIA agents investigated newspapers and harassed reporters during the era of Vietnam and Watergate. Those were dramatic cases. The papers involved were big and rich, and they resisted.

Other pressures are directly economic. After the *San Jose* (Calif.) *Mercury News* published a buyer's guide to getting the best deals on cars, automobile dealers pulled ads worth millions of dollars. The paper's publisher issued an apology, although there were no serious inaccuracies in the report. You can imagine how the newspaper's staff felt.

More common and less visible are the social pressures and social influence of editors' and publishers' peers. It is common for the top executive of a newspaper to associate socially with the political and business leaders who may be the targets of investigative reporting. It is also common for the reporters who work for those executives to be pulled off such stories.

If you find yourself on a paper lacking money or staff, you can still find ways to do investigative reporting, at least part-time, if you want to badly enough. But if you find yourself on a paper lacking courage, you have only two choices: give up or leave.

Fortunately, investigative reporting is so important and its rewards are so substantial that more reporters than ever are finding the support to do it. You can, too.

Suggested Readings

Downie, Leonard Jr. *The New Muckrakers*. New York: New Republic Book Co., 1976. Personality sketches and descriptions of how some of the best investigative reporters work.

Houston, Brant. *Computer-Assisted Reporting*, Third Edition. New York: Bedford/St. Martin's, 2004. Invaluable how-to guide for using the newest and most powerful reporting tool. Houston is executive director of Investigative Reporters and Editors Inc.

Houston, Brant. *The Investigative Reporters' Handbook*, Fourth Edition. New York: Bedford/St. Martin's, 2002. Tells you how to get and how to use the most important records and documents.

The IRE Journal. Publication of Investigative Reporters and Editors Inc., 138 Neff Annex, Missouri School of Journalism, University of Missouri, Columbia, Mo. 65211. Every issue has articles on investigations, guides to sources and documents, and a roundup of legal developments. Edited transcripts of IRE conferences also are available.

Rose, Louis J. *How to Investigate Your Friends and Enemies*. St. Louis: Albion Press, 1981. Very good on the nuts and bolts of investigating.

Williams, Paul. *Investigative Reporting and Editing*. Upper Saddle River, N.J.: Prentice Hall, 1978. A classic, good on both how and why to investigate.

Suggested Web Sites

www.ire.org
Begin here. Investigative Reporters and Editors, headquartered at the University of Missouri, is the world's leading source of expertise, story ideas and professional and personal support for investigative reporters.

www.nicar.org
The National Institute for Computer-Assisted Reporting, a partnership of IRE and the Missouri School of Journalism, teaches the skills and provides the consulting you'll need to get and analyze the data for richer, more revealing stories.

www.opensecrets.org
The Center for Responsive Politics specializes in collecting, analyzing and making available information on money and politics. The center's handbook, "Follow the Money," is an invaluable resource for any reporter interested in the impact of money on self-government.

Exercises

1. School board member Doris Hart reported at last week's meeting of the board that major flaws, including basement flooding and electrical short circuits, have shown up in the new elementary school. She noted that this is the third straight project designed by consulting architect Louis Doolittle in which serious problems have turned up. School Superintendent Margaret Smith defended Doolittle vigorously. Later, Hart told you privately that she suspects Doolittle may be paying Smith off to keep the consulting contract, which has earned the architect more than $100,000 per year for the past five years.

   Describe how you will investigate:

   a. The sniff.
   b. Human sources. Who might talk? Where should you start? Whom will you save for last?
   c. What records might help? Where are they? What will you be looking for?
   d. What is the most you can hope to prove? What is the least that will yield a story?

2. Choose a public official in your city or town and compile the most complete profile you can, using only public records.

3. Use one or more of the computer databases described in Chapter 5 to learn as much as you can about your representative in Congress. Write the most complete investigative profile you can from the databases. In a memo, explain what additional information you'd need to complete your story and where it might be found.

19 Writing News for Radio and Television

When hijacked planes struck the World Trade Center in New York City on Sept. 11, 2001, few people learned about it first in the newspapers.

Radio and television did what they do best: They told the world the details of what happened. Moreover, they were able to repeat their reports and update their audience as the news developed. If you tuned in to CNN, you not only saw what happened and listened to commentary, you also saw additional headlines streaming below the picture on a ticker tape. Like online news, the station provided up-to-date coverage and gave you the choice to watch the news you were most interested in. At times you probably heard the anchor on television say that you should go to the network's or station's Web site for more information.

Of course, radio and television reporters are not always present to record the news while it is happening. Much of the time, these journalists must write and report news after it has occurred. Many, if not most, radio and television stations provide at least some news that is written by journalists working for the wire services, such as the Associated Press or Reuters.

Selecting and writing news for these media is different from selecting and writing news for print. This chapter explores the differences and discusses news reporting and writing for television and radio. Even if your primary emphasis is not radio and television news, in this day of converging media in news rooms, you may be called upon to work with radio and television reporters and even to prepare copy for their reports. And if you are writing for radio or television news, almost certainly you will be called upon to contribute to the station's Web site. Radio and television stations have expanded their news operations to give background for stories they don't have time to air. Rather than interrupt programming when new facts arrive on a developing story, they often send listeners and viewers to their Web sites.

CRITERIA FOR SELECTING RADIO AND TELEVISION NEWS

All of the news criteria you have learned so far apply to the selection of print and broadcast news. However, four criteria distinguish radio and

In this chapter you will learn:

1. How the selection of radio and television news differs from that of print news.

2. How to write radio and television news.

3. How to prepare radio and television news copy.

television news selection from print news: These newswriters emphasize timeliness above all other news values, information more than explanation, news with audio or visual impact, and people more than concepts.

Timeliness

The radio and television newswriter emphasizes one criterion of news value more than any other: timeliness. *When* something happens often determines whether a news item will be used in a newscast. The breaking story receives top priority.

Radio and television news "goes to press" many times a day. If an event is significant enough, regular programming can be interrupted. The sense of immediacy influences everything in radio news, from what is reported to how it is reported. Often this is true of television news. Even when television and radio air documentaries or in-depth segments, they typically try to infuse a sense of urgency, a strong feeling of the present, an emphasis on what's happening now.

Information

Timeliness often determines why a news item is broadcast; time, or lack of it, determines how it is reported. Because airtime is so precious, radio and television reporters are generally more concerned with information than with explanation. Most stories must be told in 20 to 30 seconds; rarely does a story run longer than two minutes. A minute of news read aloud is only 15 lines of copy, or about 150 words. After you subtract time for commercials, a half-hour newscast has only 22 minutes of news, which amounts to about one-half of the front page of a newspaper. Although radio and television newswriters may never assume that their audience knows anything about a story, they may often have to assume that listeners or viewers will turn to newspapers, newsmagazines or the Internet for further background and details.

Of course, because of the long success of *60 Minutes* and because of relatively low production costs, newsmagazine formats such as *20/20*, *48 Hours* and *Dateline/NBC* continue to proliferate. *Dateline/NBC* now runs twice a week, and there's even a *60 Minutes II*. These programs represent a somewhat different challenge to television newswriters, but even in a newsmagazine format, the writing resembles that done for television news.

Audio or Visual Impact

Another difference between radio and television and print news results from the technologies involved. Some news is selected for radio because a reporter has recorded an on-the-scene audio report. Some news is selected for television because it is visually appealing or exciting. For this reason, news of accidents or of fires that may get attention only in the records column of the newspaper may get important play on a television newscast. If a television crew returns with good pictures of an event, that event often receives prominence in the next newscast.

People

Another important difference between radio and television and print news selection is that radio and television more often attempt to tell the news through people. They follow the "classic writing formula" described by Rudolf Flesch in *The Art of Readable Writing:* Find a problem, find a person who is dealing with the problem, and tell us how he or she is doing. These journalists look for a representative person or family, someone who is affected by the story or who is a chief player. Thus, rather than using abstract concepts with no sound or visuals, television in particular humanizes the story. You can't shoot video of an issue.

WRITING RADIO AND TELEVISION NEWS

Radio and television writing emphasizes certain characteristics that newspaper and online writing do not, and story structure may vary.

Characteristics of Radio and Television Newswriting

Because of the emphasis on timeliness, radio and television newswriters, like online writers, must emphasize immediacy and try to write very tightly and clearly. However, radio and television newswriters must work harder at achieving a conversational style.

Immediacy

Radio and television newswriters achieve a sense of immediacy in part by using the present tense as much as possible. Note the use of present-tense verbs (italicized) in this Associated Press story:

The cost of a college education *is going* up.

A study released today *says* declining tax revenues and the weak economy have led to tuition and fee increases at two- and four-year institutions this school year.

Those increases *average* more than five percent.

The figures were released by the nonprofit College Board, which *owns* the SAT college exam.

The board *says* tuition and fees at four-year public institutions now *average* over four thousand dollars a year. But College Board President Gaston Caperton *says* public colleges and universities *are* "still a remarkable value."

The average yearly cost at a four-year private college also went up more than five percent to about 18 thousand dollars. Financial aid *is* also *growing*. The board *says* a record 90 (b) billion dollars in financial aid — including loans — was handed out during the 2003–2004 school year.

Notice that the verb "is going" in the lead is the progressive form of the present tense. Radio and television writing often uses the progressive form to

> "Good television journalism presents news in the most attractive and lucid form yet devised by man."
>
> — Bill Small, veteran broadcaster, former president of CBS News

TIPS: Radio and television newswriting

- Emphasizes immediacy.
- Has a conversational style.
- Is tightly phrased.
- Is clear.

Figure 19.1
*MSNBC is one of the 24-hour cable news networks. This format allows for immediate
broadcast of breaking stories.*

indicate continuing action. Of course, to be accurate, the past tense is sometimes
necessary, as in the sentence beginning: "A study *released* today . . ." and
"declining tax revenues and the weak economy *have led.* . . ." Try to use the
present-perfect tense ("have led") more than the past tense because, again, the present perfect indicates past action that is continuing. It's what's happening *now*.

Sometimes you stress immediacy by saying, "just minutes ago" or, on a
morning newscast, "this morning." If there is no danger of inaccuracy or deceit,
though, you can omit references to time. For example, if something happened
yesterday, you may report it today like this:

```
The latest rash of fires in southern California is under
control.
```

But if you use the past tense in a lead, you should include the time element.

```
The legislature sent a welfare reform bill to the governor
late last night. It finished just in time before the spring
recess.
```

The best way to avoid the past tense is to avoid yesterday's story. You can do that by updating yesterday's story. By leading with a new development or a new fact, you may be able to use the present tense.

Remember, radio and television are "live." Your copy must convey that important characteristic.

Conversational Style

Although "write the way you talk" is questionable advice for most kinds of writing, with some exceptions, it is imperative for radio and television writing. "Read your copy aloud" is good advice for most kinds of writing; for radio and television writing, that's what it's all about.

Write so that your copy *sounds* good. Use simple, short sentences, written with transitive verbs in the active voice. Transitive verbs do things *to* things; they demand an object. People rarely use verbs in the passive voice when they talk; it usually sounds cumbersome and awkward. You don't go around saying, "Guess what I was just told by somebody." "Was told" here indicates the passive voice; the subject is being acted upon. Note the preposition "by" also tells you the verb is in the passive voice. "Guess what somebody just told me" is active and more natural, less wordy and stronger. "Told" is in the active voice; the subject is doing the acting.

Because casual speech contains contractions, an occasional contraction is OK, too, as long as your pronunciation is clear. The negative "not" is more clearly understood than when you use it as a contraction. Conversational style also permits the use of occasional fragments. Sentences are sometimes strung together loosely with dashes and sometimes begin with the conjunction "and" or "but," as in the following example from the Associated Press:

> (Spring Lake, North Carolina) — Aubrey Cox keeps giving police the slip. But he's had lots of practice — he's been doing it for 41 years.

Writing in conversational style does not mean that you may use slang, colloquialisms or incorrect grammar. Nor does it mean that you can use vulgar or off-color expressions. Remember that your audience includes people of all ages, backgrounds and sensitivities.

Tight Phrasing

You must learn to write in a conversational style without being wordy. That means you must condense. Cut down on adjectives and adverbs. Eliminating the passive voice gets rid of a couple of words. Make each word count.

Keeping it short means selecting facts carefully because often you don't have time for the whole story. Radio and television newscasters want good, tight writing that is easy to follow. Let's look at how a wire story written for newspapers can be condensed for radio and television. Here are the opening paragraphs of a 10-paragraph story from the AP newspaper wire:

DENVER (AP) — Teachers seeking better working conditions and a greater role in school governance struck today for the first time in 25 years, setting up picket lines outside the city's 107 public schools.

Officials worked to keep classes running for the district's 63,000 students with substitute teachers, administrators and regular teachers who declined to strike.

Picket lines went up at daybreak, less than 12 hours after teachers voted to go on strike by a nearly 2-to-1 margin. Talks had broken off Saturday.

Union President Leonard Fox estimated 3,000 of the district's 3,800 teachers stayed away from class. It was not immediately clear to what extent classes were disrupted.

There were no reports of violence. School superintendent Irv Moskowitz said all schools were open and administrators were working to bring in more substitutes to staff more classes Tuesday.

"As time goes on, you'll see our programs become more efficient," Moskowitz said.

The story goes on to quote a picketing teacher and a sympathetic high-school student and ends with lots of dollar figures regarding salaries, raises and the pay package.

Here's how the story appeared on the Associated Press broadcast wire in its entirety:

(Denver) — Denver school officials say all public schools are open today despite a strike by teachers.

Officials say the district's 63 thousand students are being taught by a combination of administrators, substitute teachers and regular teachers crossing the picket lines.

The union estimates three thousand of the district's 38 hundred teachers are on strike.

The teachers voted by nearly a two-to-one margin last night to reject a one-year contract offer.

This is the first teachers' strike in Denver in 25 years.

In the radio version, listeners are given the bare facts. They must turn to their newspapers or online news source for the details. One newspaper story is often two or three broadcast stories and can sometimes be a half dozen online stories.

In radio and television news, tight writing is important even when there is more time. These writers usually strive to waste no words, even in documentaries, which provide in-depth coverage of events.

Clarity

"Short words are best, and old words, when short, are best of all."

— Winston Churchill

Unlike readers of newspaper and Internet news sources, television and radio news audiences can't go back over the copy. They see or hear it only once, and their attention waxes and wanes. So you must try hard to be clear and precise. However, all of the emphasis on condensing and writing tightly is useless if the message is not understood.

Clarity demands that you write simply, in short sentences filled with nickel-and-dime words. Don't look for synonyms. Don't be afraid to repeat words or phrases. Oral communication needs reinforcement. Avoid foreign words and phrases. Avoid phrases like "the former" and "the latter." Repeat proper names in the story rather than use pronouns. The listener can easily forget the name of the person to whom the pronoun refers.

When you are tempted to write a dependent clause in a sentence, make it an independent clause instead. Keep the subject close to the verb. Close the gap between the doer and the activity. This version doesn't do that:

```
A man flagged down a Highway Patrol officer near Braden,

Tennessee, today and told him a convict was hiding in his

house. The prisoner, one of five who escaped from the Fort

Pillow Prison on Saturday, surrendered peacefully.
```

The second sentence contains 12 words between the subject, "prisoner," and the main verb, "surrendered." By the time the broadcaster reaches the verb, many listeners will have forgotten what the subject was. The story is easier to understand this way:

```
A man flagged down a Highway Patrol officer near Braden,

Tennessee, today and told him a convict was hiding in his

house. The prisoner surrendered peacefully. He's one of five

who escaped from the Fort Pillow Prison on Saturday.
```

The third sentence is still a complex sentence, but it is easily understood. The complex sentence is often just that — complex — only more so in oral communication.

Clarity also requires that you resist a clever turn of phrase. Viewers and listeners probably are intelligent enough to understand it, but a good figure of speech takes time to savor. If listeners pause to savor it (if they grasped it in the first place), they will not hear what follows. Clever columnists often fail as radio commentators.

Even more dangerous than figures of speech are numerical figures. Don't barrage the listener or viewer with a series of numbers. If you must use statistics, break them down so that they are understandable. For example, it is better to say that one of every six Americans smokes than to say there are 45 million smokers in the United States. You may be tempted to say how many billion dollars a federal program will cost, but you will help listeners understand if you say that it will cost the average wage earner $73 for each of the next five years.

Story Structure

Now that you know the characteristics of radio and television writing, let's examine the story structure. Writers must craft television and radio leads somewhat differently from the way they cast print and online leads. They also must construct special introductions and conclusions to video or audio segments and synchronize their words with taped segments.

Writing the Radio and Television Lead

Like newspaper reporters, television and radio reporters must grab the attention of their audience. Much of what you learned in Chapters 6 and 7 applies to radio

Writing News for Radio and Television

Bernard Choi works as the government reporter and fill-in anchor for KWCH (CBS) in Wichita, Kan. Before that, he spent two years on the education beat at KWCH. During the summer of his sophomore year in college, he interned at WPSD (NBC) in Paducah, Ky. There he won first place in the Randolph Hearst Journalism Awards in television news. He also won first place in the Education Writers Association's Television Hard News category.

"I was a wide-eyed reporter straight out of college," Choi says. "When my new boss offered me a full-time on-air reporting position, I jumped at the chance. The excitement apparently paralyzed my hearing, as I failed to listen to his one condition: I would have to cover a beat, the education beat.

"I had never covered a beat. I never took a beat-reporting class. I didn't know what covering a beat entailed."

Three years, two beats and countless mistakes later, Choi says, "I realized I was in way over my head. But I'm glad no one caught on and that they gave me the chance to discover the most rewarding type of journalism. It allows you to dig the story up from the ground before it appears in a news release or the news wires.

"When other television reporters in the market scrambled when a story hit the newspaper, I was already on it. It's not because I am a better journalist. It's because I did all the hard work and legwork that led up it."

Covering a beat involves all the mundane tasks: reading city-council agendas, reading planning reports and zoning regulations, trying to decipher state and district test scores, keeping up with boring school newsletters, reading state laws. You don't always get rewarded with a great story, Choi says, but it's the breath of knowledge and expertise you develop in an area that pay off in the long run.

The most important lesson Choi learned from covering a beat is you have to talk to people.

"I'm generally a shy person with people I don't know. In the past two years, I have had to force myself to walk up to strangers and chat. Stories are about people, and what better way to find a story than to talk to people. More often than not, you will get a story from someone who is plugged in a lot faster than trying to search public records."

A good example came one lazy afternoon. "I already had a story for the day, and I had time to spare at City Hall. I had made a personal resolution to talk more often with the city-council members. Because I had an hour to spare, I went to the council office to hunt a council member down. Once I got there I was told everyone had gone to lunch. Disappointed, I started walking to my car. Then I turned back and headed up to the cafeteria, where I spotted one council member. I hesitated at the door. I had already eaten, and I didn't want to interrupt. After five minutes of internal debate, I bought a lunch and sat next to the council member and started making small talk.

Thirty minutes later, Choi found out the U.S. Attorney's Office was in town covertly investigating former council members for questionable oversight; the city was ready to offer incentives to bring in a major corporation; a top city official was steering business to his wife's firm; and the council member's daughter was headed off to a prestigious college on the East Coast.

"There have been other conversations that netted absolutely nothing," he says. "I've wasted many a precious hour talking with an official and wasted many a night looking through agendas. But I've learned it's that one conversation, it's reading an extra page of a city report, it's that extra phone call that makes the difference. I've learned this because I've also been on the losing end."

The people, the organization, the beat you cover will appreciate the extra work. When you go the extra step to really understand the issue, they know. They can tell when you've done your homework and when you're slacking off. You are dealing with their lives. They don't owe you anything. If you don't take them seriously, they will treat you in kind. It's not just makeup and hairspray. This is a serious enterprise.

Choi's final advice: Journalists should say thanks every now and then.

and television leads. But be aware that people tend to be doing other things when listening to radio or watching television, so when you write for them, you strive to attract their attention in different ways.

One way is by preparing your audience for what is to come. You cue listeners to make sure they are tuned in. You introduce the story with a general statement, something that will pique the interest of the audience; then you go to the specifics. For example:

```
Things are far from settled for Springfield's teacher strike.
School officials and union representatives did not agree on a
contract yesterday. They will not meet again for at least a
week.
```

Sometimes the opening sentence will cover a number of news items:

```
There were several accidents in the Springfield vicinity
today.
```

"Cuing in" is only one method of opening a radio or television story. Other leads go immediately into the what and the who, the where and the when. In radio or television news the what is most important, followed by who did the what. The time and place may be included in the lead, but seldom is the why or the how. If time permits, the why and the how may come later in the story, but often they are omitted.

The first words of the lead are the most important. Don't keep the listener guessing as to what the story is about. Don't begin with a dependent clause or with prepositional phrases, as in this example:

```
With the strong backing of Governor Minner, a second state
spending-limit bill is scheduled for final Senate action
today.
```

Figure 19.2
Christiane Amanpour is CNN's chief international correspondent. Her authoritative reports from around the world have informed millions.

The opening words are meaningless without what comes later. The listener may not know what you are talking about. Here is a better way to introduce this story:

```
The Senate will vote today to make deeper cuts in state
spending — with the strong backing of Governor Minner.
```

Be sure to "tee up," or identify, an unfamiliar name. By introducing a person, you prepare listeners for the name they otherwise may miss. Do it this way:

```
Veteran Kansas City, Kansas, businessman and civic leader
Ivar Larson died yesterday in a nursing home at age 83.
```

Don't mislead. The opening words must set the proper tone and mood for the story. Attract attention; tease a little. Answer questions, but don't ask them. Lead the listener into your story.

Writing Lead-Ins and Wrap-Ups

Radio and television journalists must learn how to write a **lead-in** that introduces a taped excerpt from a news source or from another reporter. The functions of a lead-in are to set the scene by briefly telling the where, the when and sometimes the what, and to identify the source or reporter. The lead-in should contain something substantive. Here's an example:

```
A grand jury has decided not to charge a Springfield teenager
in the killing of his father. Jan Morrow reports the panel
believes the death was an accident.
```

Lead-ins should generate interest. Sometimes several sentences are used to provide background, as in the following:

```
We'll all be getting the official word this morning on how
much less our dollars bought last month. The consumer price
index for March is expected to show another sharp rise in
retail prices. The rate of inflation was one percent in
January and one-point-two percent in February. Here's more on
our inflation woes from Bill McKinney.
```

Be careful not to include in the lead-in what is in the story. Just as a headline should not steal word for word the lead of a newspaper story, the lead-in should not rob the opening words of the correspondent. The writer must know the contents of the audio report in order to write a proper lead-in.

After the recorded report, you may want to wrap up the story before going on to the next item. The **wrap-up** is especially important in radio copy because there are no visuals to identify the person just heard. If the story reported by Evelyn Turner was about a meeting to settle a strike, you might wrap up Turner's report by adding information:

```
Turner reports negotiations will resume tomorrow.
```

A wrap-up such as this gives your story an ending and clearly separates it from the next story.

"Writing a silence is as important as writing words. We don't rely on video enough."

— John Hart, veteran NBC broadcaster

Writing for Videotape

Writing for a videotaped report begins with the selection of the subject and deciding how it is to be videotaped. The writing continues through the editing process and is done with the pictures clearly in mind.

Words and pictures must be complementary, never interfering with each other, never ignoring each other. Your first responsibility is to relate the words to the pictures. If you do not, viewers will not get the message because they will be wondering what the pictures are about.

You can, however, stick too closely to the pictures by pointing out the obvious in a blow-by-blow account. You need to avoid both extremes and use what Russ Bensley, formerly of CBS News, calls the "hit-and-run" technique. This means that at the beginning of a scene or when a scene changes, you must tell the viewer where you are or what is happening. Once you are into the scene, the script may be more general and less closely tied to the pictures.

Suppose the report concerns the continuation of a hospital workers' strike and the opening scene shows picketers outside the hospital. You can explain the tape by saying:

```
Union members are still picketing Mercy Hospital today as the
hospital workers' strike enters its third week.
```

Viewers now know two things that are not obvious in the tape: who is picketing and where. If the tape switches to people sitting around a table negotiating, you must again set the scene for viewers:

```
Meanwhile, hospital administrators and union leaders are
continuing their meetings — apparently without success.
```

Once you have related the words to the pictures, you may add other details of the strike. You must not only comment on the tape but complete it as well. Part of completing it is giving the report a wrap-up or a strong ending. Don't be cute, and don't be obvious, but give the story an ending. Here's one possible ending for the strike story:

```
Strikers, administrators, patients and their families agree
on one sure effect of the strike — it's a bad time to be sick.
```

Now that you know some principles of writing radio and television news, let's learn how to prepare the copy.

PREPARING RADIO AND TELEVISION COPY

Preparing copy to be read by a newscaster is different from preparing it for a typesetter. Your goals are to make the copy easy for the newscaster to read and easy for the audience to understand. What follows will help you accomplish these two goals.

Format

Most radio and television news editors want triple-spaced copy. Leave two to three inches on the top of the page and one to two inches on the bottom.

For radio copy, set your computer so that you have 70 characters to a line. Each line will average about 10 words, and the newscaster will average 15 lines per minute. Start each story on a separate piece of paper. That way, the order of the stories can be rearranged, and stories can be added or dropped easily. If a story goes more than one page, write "MORE" in parentheses at the bottom of the page.

Write television copy on the right half of the page in a 40-character line. Each line will average about six words, and the newscaster will average about 25 lines per minute. Use the left side of the copy for audio or video information. This information, which is not to be read by the newscaster, is usually typed in all caps. The copy that is read generally appears upper- and lowercase. In television copy, number the stories, and start each story on a separate page. If a story goes more than one page, write "MORE" in parentheses at the bottom of the page.

Do not hyphenate words, and be sure to end a page with a complete sentence or, if possible, with a complete paragraph. Then if the next page should be missing in the middle of a newscast, the newscaster could at least end with a complete sentence or paragraph.

At most stations, you prepare copy for a videoprompter, an electronic device that projects the copy over the camera lens so the newscaster can read it while appearing to look straight into the lens.

Date the first page of your script, and type your last name in the upper left-hand corner of every page. Stations vary regarding these directions. The newscast producer determines the **slug** for a story and its placement. Some producers insist that the slug contain the time of the broadcast. If a story continues to a second page, write under the slug "first add" or "second add," or "page 2," "page 3" and so forth.

Stations with computerized news rooms may use scripting software that alters these formats somewhat. For information about how a television station works, tips about writing and all other aspects of television news, take a look at **www.scripps.ohiou.edu/actv-7/manual**, a guide used by television students at Ohio University's E. W. Scripps School of Journalism's television station.

slug ⟶	west broadway
time of newscast ⟶	12-30
date of broadcast ⟶	1-11-99
reporter's name ⟶	flanagan

Members of Citizens for the Preservation of West Broadway

plan to gear up their petition drive again this weekend. The group

began circulating petitions <u>last</u> weekend.

The petitions request the City Council to repeal all previous

ordinances and resolutions on the widening. Many residents of the

West Broadway area complain that the proposed widening project will

damage its residential nature.

Petition-drive coordinator Vera Hanson says the group is pleased

with the show of support from residents all over Springfield . . .

but it won't know exactly how many signatures it has until next week.

Figure 19.3
Sample of radio copy.

"jorgenson" is the name of the reporter.

"six" is the time of the newscast.

"6-17" is the day of the broadcast.

"art" is the slug for the story.

"MOC:" means the person is live on camera with audio from his or her microphone.

"SOT:27" means there is sound on the tape lasting 27 seconds.

"NAT SND UNDER" means the tape sound should be kept at a low level.

"VOICE OVER" means the voice is from the anchorperson in the studio speaking over the tape that is being shown.

"SUPER: BUCHANAN HIGH SCHOOL" indicates the title that should be shown over the tape.

":00–:05" indicates that the title should be shown five seconds after the report of this news item begins.

Figure 19.4
Sample of television copy.

```
jorgenson           six            6-17           art


MOC: JORGENSON                  A lesson in art and architecture paid

                            off for some Buchanan High School students

SOT     :27                 today.  Ribbons were the prizes for winning
NAT SND UNDER
VOICE OVER                  entries in a sketch exhibit of scenery and

SUPER: BUCHANAN HIGH SCHOOL buildings in the capital city area.
       :00-:05
                                The Springfield art club sponsored the

                            show and called in Springfield College art

                            professor Bill Ruess to judge the artwork.

                                Ruess says he was impressed by the

                            students' skills, especially those who tried

                            their hand at the different art media for

                            the first time.
```

Names and Titles

In radio and television style, unlike that followed by newspapers, well-known names, even on first reference, are not given in full. You may say Senator Dole of North Carolina or Governor Napolitano of Arizona. Don't use middle initials unless they are a natural part of someone's name (Edward R. Murrow) or unless they are necessary to distinguish two people with the same first and last names, as with George W. Bush.

Titles should always precede names so that listeners are better prepared to hear the name. When you use titles, omit the first name and middle initial. For example, you would say Federal Reserve Chairman Greenspan and Justice Ginsburg.

Pronunciation

You must help the newscaster pronounce the names of people and places correctly. To do this, write out difficult names phonetically in parentheses. MSNBC has its own reference list, and many individual stations have their own handbooks. Look up difficult names in unabridged dictionaries. If you don't find the name there, call the person's office, or the consulate or embassy. If the name is of a U.S. town, try calling someone in that town. There is no rhyme or reason to the way some people pronounce their names or to the way some names of places are pronounced. Never assume. Never guess. Find out. Here's an example of how you should write out difficult names:

```
(Zamboanga, Philippines — AP) — There's been another deadly
bombing in the Philippines.
    A bomb exploded near a Roman Catholic church in the
southern city of Zamboanga (zahm-BWAHNG'-gah), killing one
person and injuring 12.
```

Perhaps most people would know how to pronounce Lima (LEE-mah), Peru, but not everyone would correctly pronounce Lima (LIE-mah), Ohio. You must note the difference between NEW-erk, N.J., and new-ARK, Del., both spelled Newark. And who would guess that Pago Pago is pronounced PAHNG-oh PAHNG-oh?

Abbreviations

Generally, do not use abbreviations in your copy. It is easier to read a word written out than to read its abbreviation. Do not abbreviate the names of states, countries, months, days of the week or military titles.

When you do abbreviate a name or phrase, use hyphens instead of periods to prevent the newscaster from mistaking the final period in the abbreviation for the period at the end of the sentence. You may abbreviate United States when you use it as an adjective — U-S would be the correct form. If an abbreviation is well known — U-N, G-O-P, F-B-I — you may use it. Hyphens are not used in acronyms such as NATO and HUD that are pronounced as one word.

You may use the abbreviations Dr., Mr., Mrs. and Ms., and a.m. and p.m.

Symbols and Numbers

Do not use symbols in your copy because newscasters can read a word more easily than they can interpret a symbol. Never use such symbols as the dollar sign ($) and the percent sign (%). Don't even use the abbreviation for number (no.).

Numbers can be a problem for both the announcer and the listener. As in newspaper style, write out numbers one through nine. Also write out eleven, because 11 might not be easily recognized as a number. Use figures for 10 and

from 12 to 999. The eye can easily take in a three-digit number, but write out the words thousand, million and billion — for example, 3,800,000 becomes three million, 800 thousand. Write out fractions (two-and-a-half million dollars) and decimal points (three-point-two percent).

Some stations have exceptions. Figures often are used to give the time (3:20 a.m.), sports scores (ahead 5 to 2) and statistics, market reports (an increase in the Dow Jones Industrial Average of 2-point-8 points) and addresses (3-0-0-2 Grand Street; in common speech no one would give an address as three thousand two).

Ordinarily, you may round off big numbers. Thus, 48-point-3 percent should be written "nearly half." But when dealing with human beings, don't say "more than one hundred" if 104 people died in an earthquake.

Use *st*, *nd*, *rd* and *th* after dates: August 1st, September 2nd, October 3rd, November 4th. Make the year easy to pronounce: June 9th, 1973.

Quotations and Attributions

Rarely use direct quotations and quotation marks. Because it is difficult and awkward to indicate to listeners which words are being quoted, use indirect quotes or a paraphrase instead.

If it is important for listeners to know the exact words of a quotation (as when the quoted words are startling, uncomplimentary or possibly libelous), introduce the quote by saying "in his words," "with these words," "what she called" or "he put it this way." Most writers prefer to avoid the formal "quote" and "unquote," though "quote" is used more often than "unquote." Here's an example:

```
In Smith's words, quote, "There is no way to undo the harm
done."
```

When you must use a direct quotation, the attribution always should precede the quotation. Because listeners cannot see the quotation marks, they will have no way of knowing the words are a direct quote. If by chance they did recognize the words as a quote, they would have no idea who was being quoted. For the same reason, the attribution should precede an indirect quote as well.

If you must use a direct quotation, keep it short. If the quote is long and it is important to use it, use a tape of the person saying it. If you are compelled to use a quote of more than one sentence in your copy, break it up with phrases such as "Smith went on to say" or "and still quoting the senator." For television, put longer or more complicated quotes on a full-screen graphic display as you read it.

Punctuation

In radio and television copy, less punctuation is good punctuation. The one exception is the comma. Commas help the newscaster pause at appropriate places. Use commas, for example, after introductory phrases referring to time and place, as in the following:

```
In Paris, three Americans on holiday met their death today
when their car overturned and caught fire.
```

```
Last August, beef prices reached an all-time low.
```

Sometimes three periods are used in place of a comma. Three periods also take the place of parentheses and the semicolon. They signal a pause and are easily visible. The same is true of the dash — typed as two hyphens. Note the dash in the following example:

```
But the judge grumbled about the news coverage, and most
prospective jurors agreed -- saying the news coverage has
been prone to overstatement, sensationalism and errors.
```

The only punctuation marks you need are the period, comma, question mark, dash, hyphen and, rarely, quotation marks. To make the copy easier to read, add the hyphen to some words even when the dictionary does not use it: anti-discrimination, co-equal, non-aggression.

Stations vary in writing style and in the preparation of copy. But if you learn what is presented here, you will be well-prepared. Differences will be small, and you will adapt to them easily.

Suggested Readings

Bliss, Edward Jr. and Hoyt, James L. *Writing News for Broadcast*, Third Edition. New York: Columbia University Press, 1994. A classic text that excels in good writing.

Block, Mervin. *Writing Broadcast News — Shorter, Sharper, Stronger*, Second Edition. Chicago: Bonus Books, 1997. An excellent book by a former network newswriter.

Freedman, Wayne. *It Takes More Than Good Looks*. Chicago: Bonus Books, 2003. A book packed with practical, down-to-earth advice by a man called "the best local TV news feature reporter in the country."

Stephens, Mitchell. *Broadcast News*, Fourth Edition. New York: Holt, Rinehart and Winston, 1998. Covers all aspects of broadcast writing and the business of broadcast news.

White, Ted. *Broadcast News Writing, Reporting and Producing*, Third Edition. Boston: Focal Press, 2001. The best book on all aspects of broadcast newswriting.

Exercises

1. Watch a local evening television newscast. Make a simple list of the news stories. Then try to find those stories in the next morning's local newspaper and compare the coverage.

2. Check to see if the following AP stories written for broadcast follow acceptable broadcast style. Are they technically correct? Do they emphasize immediacy? Change the copy where you think necessary.

   a. (Nice, France-AP) — Positive thinking might make cancer patients feel better, but it won't help their chances of surviving the disease.

   A new study finds that a positive outlook won't improve a person's survival rate.

   The British study looked at whether psychologist-run support groups kept patients alive.

   Researchers analyzed eleven studies that included a total of 15 hundred patients.

   The lead researcher says there was no evidence at all that support groups prolong life in cancer patients.

   However, experts say it's still worthwhile for patients to try to improve their mindsets, perhaps by joining a cancer support group, because it does make them feel better.

   The findings were presented today at a meeting of the European Society of Medical Oncology in Nice, France.

   b. (Atlanta-AP) — Before heading to jail, an Atlanta pastor used his last sermon to encourage his flock to continue whipping disobedient children.

   The Reverend Arthur Allen Junior — convicted of cruelty to children — took off his belt and waved it behind a 14-year-old boy as part of a mock whipping at the House of Prayer.

   Allen and four church members were found guilty Thursday of aggravated assault and cruelty to children for whipping two boys in front of the congregation in February of 2001. The defendants received prison sentences ranging from 20 to 90 days, plus fines and mandatory parenting classes.

   The pretend whipping yesterday mocked a judge's order that Allen and his followers use only an open hand on their own children's buttocks.

3. Rewrite the following AP newspaper briefs in broadcast writing style. Assume that the news is current and that you have time for one paragraph of four or five lines for each story.

   a. ZURICH, Switzerland (AP) — Thieves have stolen seven Picasso paintings worth more than $40 million from an art gallery, police said today.

   Zurich police said the break-in occurred over the weekend through the cellar of a neighboring house.

   A police statement said two works, "Seated Woman" and "Christ of Montmartre," were the most valuable of the paintings stolen. Both paintings were stolen in 1991 from a Zurich gallery and were recovered the following year.

b. SEAL BEACH, Calif. (AP) — State authorities have disputed a retirement community's rules on keeping its pools and golf courses off-limits to underage users — whom it defines as being under 55.

The State Fair Employment and Housing Department filed a complaint against Leisure World after Alfred and Mary Gray objected last year to a no-access policy for younger spouses at Leisure World's recreational facilities. Mary Gray was 51 at the time.

Operators of Seal Beach Leisure World, whose 9,000 residents comprise one-third of the city's population, have decided to contest the federal Unruh Civil Rights Act cited by state officials, administrator Bill Narans said.

4. Read a copy of a current newspaper; then write a five-minute newscast. Pay special attention to lead-ins and wrap-ups. (Do not include sports material in your broadcast.)

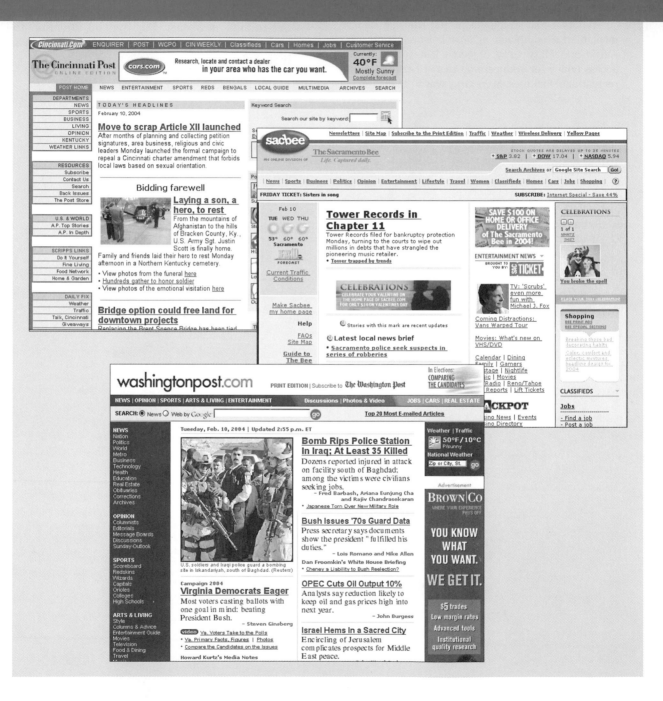

When the United States invaded Iraq in early 2003, journalists ushered in a new era in war reporting. While incredible new technologies helped reporters file traditional reports for newspapers, magazines, and radio and television newscasts, no medium broke more new ground than the Internet.

While millions of viewers were glued to their television sets for the latest live reports from Fox, CNN, MSNBC and the other networks and cable news channels, millions more turned to their computers for a real-time display of contemporary reporting. Among the groundbreaking experiments born in Iraq:

- CNN.com offered an interactive map showing where CNN correspondents and anchors were stationed throughout the Middle East. Clicking on the correspondent's icon called up his or her latest video and audio reports.
- *St. Petersburg Times* staff photographer John Pendygraft was "embedded" with a Marine helicopter squad on missions in and around Kuwait and Iraq, and used a high-speed satellite phone to transmit powerful photos and words to a Weblog.
- NBC and MSNBC teamed up to provide dispatches from the front, nicely supplementing the networks' broadcast reports.
- The *Star Tribune* of Minneapolis produced audio, video and photo reports from its reporters in the Gulf.
- Newspaper conglomerate Knight Ridder produced War Watch, a Weblog of news and commentary edited by SiliconValley.com editors John Murrell and John Paczkowski. Knight Ridder provided links to it on many of its local news sites (such as **philly.com** and **herald.com**).

The Internet has not only changed war reporting, it has changed the entire field of journalism. Almost every newspaper and television station now has its own Web site. You can link to most newspaper sites at **news paperlinks.com** and other media at **newslink.org**. And no longer can anyone say that no one is making money online. According to a study by the World Association of Newspapers in Paris, 38 percent of newspapers make money, 26 percent break even and 36 percent lose money. A Borrell Associates report, based on an analysis of more than 250 dailies, says that newspapers can generate as much as $650 million in annual revenue by 2005 "through reorganization, improved database infrastructure and a Web-focused sales team."

Newspapers have an annual Interactive Newspapers Conference and Trade Show and an annual competition that rewards the best overall U.S. and non-U.S. newspaper online service; best news, sports, business, entertainment, special and classified sections; best design and best use of interactivity. Radio and television stations and cable outlets also have Web sites, some of them, such as ESPN.com, among the best that exist. All kinds of magazines and newsletters also have a presence online. The American Business Press, for example, has become the American Business Media, and its Neal awards include the best Web site. The Newsletter Publishers Association became The Newsletter and Electronic Publishers Association.

Online journalism allows readers, not editors, to be in charge. Readers go online because they want the most up-to-date news as quickly as possible. On the Internet they don't have to wait until the radio or television anchors get around to telling them about aspects of the news they want to learn. Online news consumers get only the information they want and spend as little or as much time as they like. And like print, if you miss something, you can go back and read it again.

Unlike print, however, online news is updated continually, and other related stories can be added. Online media not only keep readers up-to-the minute with the news, they also keep a record of all that went before the latest bulletin. They connect readers to other sites that give background on breaking news. They include still photographs that the paper has no room to print, and many offer audio and video that can be listened to or viewed on demand. They can fill readers in on anything they may have missed while reading or viewing traditional news coverage.

Not only is online news current, it's also geographically indifferent. While readers of the printed version of the *Seattle Post-Intelligencer* are found mostly in the Seattle metropolitan area, readers of its Web site can be found worldwide. You didn't have to live in Seattle to read the work of *Post-Intelligencer* reporter M.L. Lyke and photographer Grant M. Haller, who were among a group of journalists "embedded" with U.S. forces on board the aircraft carrier USS *Abraham Lincoln*. Lyke wrote a continuous Weblog for seattlepi.com about her experiences, called "Aboard the USS Abraham Lincoln." All of it was conveyed at the time and place of the reader's choosing, under his or her direction.

No wonder an increasing number of news consumers often turn first to the Internet for news, especially for breaking news. A report of Minnesota Opinion Research Inc. indicated that 62 percent of 2,000 general Internet users surveyed choose an online newspaper for local news. An online survey of 12,429 current online newspaper users found that 86 percent of this group prefers Internet newspapers for local coverage.

But news consumers are not the only ones using online information. Journalists everywhere have had to learn to find and confirm information on the Internet. A study by George Washington University's Graduate School of Political Management of 271 political reporters revealed that they "read political coverage, research candidates' backgrounds, locate sources and experts, follow poll results and monitor candidate messages online," reports an Ifra Trend Report.

You must know how and where to access information on the Internet, and, most important, which sources you can trust. The publication you work for may have a list of reliable URLs (uniform resource locators). In most cases, you can trust information more if it has a byline you know or a byline that is further identified. Better, you can trust the validity of information on the Web if you know the sponsoring organization that is hosting the information. The publisher of the information, of course, should be neutral and have nothing to sell and no cause to promote. Several books, such as Alison Cooke's *Authoritative Guide to Evaluating Information on the Internet*, and Web sites, such as **http://thorplus.lib.purdue.edu/rguides/studentinstruction/evaluation/evaluating websites.html**, help you evaluate the quality and reliability of Web sites.

The problem is that people "publish" on the Web without the normal copy editing that's done with print-based publications. The result is that you find a lot of misspelled names, incorrect titles, wrong dates, and so forth — even on pages from reliable organizations.

Some would argue that there is even an evolving ethic on the Web that accuracy of information is less important. Some have personal rules that say never attribute information on the Web unless you have confirmation from a person able to confirm the attribution.

One further caution: You need to be conscious of the massive amount of dated material on the Web. What reads like new information might be years old. Be sure to check the creation date of the material you are citing.

Although you need to remain skeptical about Web reliability, Steve Outing, new-media writer and columnist for *Editor & Publisher* magazine, says that more and more content from Internet-originated sources is appearing in reputable newspapers. "Where once print editors distrusted content originating from online content companies, now there is much more acceptance that online content can be every bit as good, if not better, than content acquired from traditional media sources," Outing writes.

As has been described elsewhere in this text, you soon may be required to be versatile in using various media in covering a story. You may have to decide whether the online story should be video, audio, print — or all three. As John Pavlik writes in *Introduction to Online Journalism* by Roland De Wolk, "In this world of on-demand media, journalism will feature a rich blend of text, audio, video and interactivity to tell virtually any story. To work effectively in this environment, journalists will need to be comfortable with, if not fluent in, the grammar of all media modalities."

"Computers can:

- Look things up for us.
- Navigate for us ('Please turn to page . . .')
- Link words to other words.
- Remember where we were and take us back there.
- Play audio, video, and animation.
- Organize and present information according to a nonlinear structure."

— Andrew Bonime and Ken C. Pohlmann, *Writing for New Media*

HOW TO WRITE ONLINE

Regardless of the medium for which you work, you will need to know how to write online. At a growing number of newspapers, even veteran journalists are

The Associated Press Managing Editors association amended its bylaws in 2001 to fill one seat of its board of directors with a supervisor of an online news operation, and in 2002, Ken Sands, interactive editor of *The Spokesman-Review*, Spokane, Wash., was elected to the board.

being asked to turn in two versions of their stories, one for the newspaper and one for the paper's Web site. At the *St. Paul Pioneer Press*, all print reporters must file a Web story within 30 minutes after witnessing an event or learning about the news. Today, cyberspace has turned newspapers into 24-hour competitive news machines, and print-only reporters are rapidly becoming a disappearing species.

At *The Tampa Tribune*, where convergence is a mantra, Donna Reed, the managing editor, insists that the newspaper's most valuable staffers are those who can produce material for multiple media. "I can send one sports reporter to the Super Bowl, and he can cover for the newspaper, the Web site and even television," Reed says.

Good online writing has many of the characteristics of other forms of effective writing. Much of what you have read so far about newswriting applies to online journalism; what you've learned about news gathering and reporting, either in print or broadcast, applies here. The demand for accurate, simple, clear and concise writing is the same for all the media.

Nevertheless, the online journalist must be aware of some fundamental differences. These differences result in stories that look quite different from the stories published on paper or broadcast. One sure way to drive away online readers is to give them **shovelware** — stories as they appeared in print. Hundreds of publications continue to do that: shovel their print stories into a whole new medium, a medium that has its own demands, strengths and even some weaknesses. Most online readers refuse to be buried in shovelware — unless they have a real need for in-depth information.

Admittedly, also, there are readers who want the stories as they appear in the newspaper and not rewritten in some other form. They want shovelware because they want to know what other readers are seeing. Newspapers can serve this segment of the audience with shovelware. Or as *The New York Times* has done, they put out online versions that look exactly like the newspaper. Most readers, however, prefer Web sites that play to the medium's strengths: frequent updates, links to Web sites, and audio and video clips. Perhaps no one has better defined the medium than ESPN's Web site, espn.com. Take a look at that site, and you get a good idea of what's possible. Text, audio, video and even databases work together to give consumers the ultimate interactive experience.

Still, writing for online publication remains in an experimental stage. Researchers have yet to establish what works best in this race to capture today's hurried readers.

This chapter does not attempt to teach you Web coding. That's best learned in a computer class, rather than by reading about it. You may want to check a couple of tutorials such as "webmonkey" (**hotwired.lycos.com/webmonkey**). This chapter, however, does explain the best current thinking and practice in online writing. You will learn a different way to think about writing and some rules that apply more to online writing than to other forms.

Let's begin with these three principles:

- The reader rules.
- The writing is nonlinear.
- Structure is everything.

The Reader Rules

Unlike print journalists writing for newspapers and magazines, where narrative works fine, newswriters online should keep no secrets from readers; they should not try to withhold information until later in the story. In short, when writing online you should surrender control of the story's sequence to the reader. Online, authors lose their "position of central authority," writes David Weinberger, author/editor of the *Journal of the Hyperlinked Organization,* a newsletter that considers the Web's effect on how business works. Every reader is different; every reader has different needs. Every reader, therefore, not only will pick and choose what to read but also will choose a path that best meets those needs.

Also, readers can come from anywhere in the world, not just from a local audience. And because of the enormous archive retrieval functions of the Internet, readers can come in at any time. As Prof. Phil Brooks of the Missouri School of Journalism tells his students, "Today becomes yesterday tomorrow." In other words, he says, when writing for the Web you are writing history to an international audience.

You should think of ways to present different information for different people at different times. Unlike newspapers and magazines, which must decide how long to make a story, you should layer information in such a way that readers can choose the amount they need at any given time.

You have learned to write the inverted pyramid story. This much of the traditional news story remains the same. The lead in an online story becomes even more important because the lead literally may be all that appears on the screen. Readers may have to click to get more of the story. The lead must nail the "what?" or the "so what?" to get the full attention of the reader. In fact, it is similar to the anchor's introduction to a television news story.

The lead is also important because for most search engines, the lead will be the only information provided for the link to the story. You would be wise to include key words such as "Maine" and "governor" in the lead about a story concerning the Maine governor.

Sometimes the lead appears like an extended headline, followed by two or three statements that also read as headlines. After the lead, little is the same as the traditional news story. Readers often can click on the hyperlinked headlines to read the full version of the story on another page within the Web site.

Note also that the reader is active, not passive. Steve Outing writes on poynter.org:

> If I gave you an assignment to look at the content of 100 news Web sites, you'd probably find that 95 percent of them don't ever go beyond routine presentation of text, images and the occasional audio or video clip. It's still the rare few that craft content in such ways that go beyond what would be possible in print or broadcast. Rare is the story that uses online interactive techniques that help the user understand the story best by letting him or her interact with and manipulate elements of the story — to experience it, not just read about it.

Outing writes that good Internet writing says to the reader, "Don't read —do!" It does this because it plays to the essential nature of the Internet: that it is interactive.

According to the Newspaper Association of America, the U.S. Internet audience had 174 million users in 2004. Users in 2002 spent more time online at home than ever before — three and a half hours per month compared with two hours and 45 minutes during 2001. These same people spent less time with other media, notably 23 percent less time with television and 20 percent less time with magazines.

The search engine Google, founded in 1998, now gets 150 million queries a day from more than 100 countries, according to a story in *The New York Times.*

The Writing Is Nonlinear

Because most people don't think linearly, writing online is more in line with the way people think. It's even more in line with the way today's readers read. Break the story into short, digestible pieces. Rather than stringing together a long story and trying to get readers to read the whole thing in the order you presented it, keep in mind that many readers don't want to read everything you have to tell them. You must give them choices and let them decide what to read and in what order. Stories that require multiple screens turn off many readers immediately.

Many readers hate to scroll on screen. Some exit even before they get to the bottom of the screen. Few will take the time to read a lot of text in one clump. Note, of course, that this is not true of highly motivated readers who crave your information. At times you may want to send them to reliable databanks where they can read the whole story and get all the facts — preferably, of course, within your own site.

Structure Is Everything

Some who write online forget entirely about structure. That's a huge mistake. Even though an online story takes on an entirely different structure, it still must be organized in a logical, coherent way. The online reader does not revel in chaos. Even though the story may appear on the screen as a mosaic, the way that mosaic is composed will help attract readers, keep readers and help readers follow what for them is the most logical path.

The online writer must present information in layers. Remember, no two readers are alike. You may present the same information with different degrees of detail and support. The first layer is information that is immediately available to readers — no action or effort is demanded. A second layer, a more substantial read, could be reachable easily by moving the cursor or by scrolling. A third layer may require readers to click on a link that opens up still more information, perhaps audio, video or a source document.

When you write for print, you need to be concerned with continuity, with themes, with working in all aspects of the story while remaining clear and coherent. When you write online, you need to worry not about the structure or flow of the whole piece but rather about the relationships of the levels and parts. You need to help readers navigate from place to place to get the information they want. That means you must have clear entrances and exits.

Sometimes you have to give clear directions. For example, if you include a hyperlink in your story, more readers will "click here" if you tell them to do so than if you don't. Sometimes you may take readers down one path that branches into several others. Some call this technique "threading." A plane crash can lead to various threads — the airline and its record of crashes, the plane itself and the record of that type of plane, the place of the accident, the people involved, and so forth.

An Online Career

Troy Wolverton says that when he was studying journalism in graduate school, he "quickly fell in love with the Internet." He took every course available in new media, as well as newspaper reporting, basic photojournalism and broadcast journalism. He freelanced for *The New York Times* Web site and taught a class in Internet basics. He left graduate school to take a job at the *San Jose* (Calif.) *Mercury News* as an online editor.

After two years, he began working as a reporter for CNET News.com, a technology-news Web site. There he covered e-commerce companies such as Amazon.com, online auctioneer eBay and online brokerage E*Trade. Troy is now on his third online job, as a reporter at TheStreet.com, where he covers the retail industry both online and off.

"I was trying to figure out where I wanted to go when I left CNET. Many online reporters I know — the few of us who are left — have a desire to get back to print. In fact that's the route several of my former News.com colleagues have taken.

"I probably wouldn't turn down *The New York Times* if they came calling, but I really enjoy working online. I love the immediacy of the medium. By the time a newspaper is delivered to a reader's door, many of the stories in it have been online for hours.

"Writing for an online publication brings you closer to your readers. When I wrote for a newspaper, I felt as if my stories were floating out into the ether. I had no idea whether people were reading them. I know how much people are reading my News.com articles by how many e-mail responses I receive.

"Life hasn't been easy online. A number of publications closed their doors, and lots of people had a difficult time finding work. And the demands can be overwhelming. As I was leaving CNET, the editors there were asking reporters to write at least two headline stories a day and to be working on larger enterprise stories at the same time.

"Despite the downfalls and the downsizing, I still feel as if this is the place to be. More and more people are getting their news online. If anything, the online medium will become more dominant in the future as the Internet becomes more prevalent and news becomes increasingly available on cell phones, PDAs and the like."

You need not be concerned about some repetition. Remember, readers choose what parts to read. Besides, a certain amount of repetition or of stating things in different ways, perhaps visually, increases retention. Readers, after all, online or elsewhere, process information differently.

There is no need to show an example of what the stories in Figure 20.1 would have looked like in the traditional newspaper. You have seen lots of stories like them. Study here how they appeared online.

Figure 20.1
The Cincinnati Post (www.
cincinnatipost.com) *uses
bulky leads throughout its
Web site. The site allows
readers to find the what or
the so-what without reading
the entire story.*

GUIDELINES FOR WRITING ONLINE

Readers online are surfers or scanners, much more so than readers of print, perhaps because it takes 25 percent longer to read online than it does in print. Researchers Jakob Nielsen and John Morkes found that 79 percent of those they tested scanned a new page they came across; only 16 percent read the copy word for word.

Online expert Shel Holtz says you want readers to dive, not to surf. Surfing is what frustrated readers do. Here are 10 ways to make divers out of surfers — or at least to hold their attention long enough to get your message across.

1. Think Immediacy

Although you must first make sure what you write is accurate, the Internet can deliver news when it is brand-new. Writing online is like writing for the wire services. Everyone on the Internet is now like a wire-service subscriber. Keeping readers with you means keeping readers up-to-the-minute. You must expect to update breaking stories quickly and to add depth whenever it is available. But just because you can easily correct mistakes does not mean you are allowed to make them. Reporter David Broder of *The Washington Post* warned at the

Figure 20.2
This front-page story on
The Sacramento Bee's *Web
site* (**www.sacbee.com**) *has
a headline with a long lead.
In addition, a statement
that also reads as a headline
accompanies the lead.*

annual National Roundtable sponsored by the Scripps Howard Foundation that posting news quickly could sacrifice quality and damage credibility.

Nevertheless, newspapers are now using their Web sites to break news. For example, when *The Financial Times* learned that Iranian security forces held a son of Osama bin Laden, it reported the news on its Web site on Saturday because it doesn't publish on Sunday. The Ft. Lauderdale *Sun-Sentinel* partners with radio and television, and it may break a story on any of the media. It's usually a matter of timing.

2. Save Readers Time

What most readers do not have is time. Whatever you can do to save readers' time is worth *your* time. It's been said by various people in different ways since philosopher Blaise Pascal first said it: "Excuse me for this long letter; I don't have time to write a short one." For many stories, if not most, perhaps your chief concern should be this: Have I presented this information in such a way as to cost readers the least amount of time?

The best way to save readers' time is to be clear. Choose the simple word; vary the length of sentences but keep them short; write short paragraphs. Help readers. Emphasize key words by highlighting them or by putting them in color.

Figure 20.3
*This article on CNN.com
appears as a lead on the first
screen, but readers can click
on "Full Story" for more.
The complete story follows
the lead and has sidebars
providing more links for
further information on the
subject. CNN.com is one of
the most popular sites on
the Internet.*

From an interview with Kerry Northrup, executive director of Ifra Center for Advanced News Operations, in *EPN World Reporter:*

"A lot of people who are journalists today simply cannot be journalists tomorrow. They can't grasp the changes in how people get and use news and information. They won't adapt to thinking in terms of multiple media rather than being concerned only about their personal area of specialization. They are media bigots, for want of a better term, insisting past reason that print is print, broadcast is broadcast, Web is Web, and never will they mesh.

"The idea of blending formats to create a story greater than the sum of its parts remains foreign to them. Perhaps the kindest and most effective approach for an editorial organization to deal with this situation is to create new jobs that reflect the new requirements, the new skills, the new compensations, the new realities, and then let those that will evolve into them, and those that won't phase out."

As an interesting side note to the above, Ifra reports that in the United Kingdom, the BBC and its trade union have a new video-journalist classification with salary increases for journalists "who retrain to report, film and edit their own news stories."

Another reason to write simply, using simple words and simple sentences, is for the auto-translation programs used by some search engines to translate a page. The simpler the words and sentences, the more likely a foreign-language translation of the story will be accurate and understandable.

3. Provide Information That's Quick and Easy to Get

The overall organization of your story must say to the reader that getting this information is going to be quick and easy. Online readers have zero tolerance for confusion and no time at all to be led astray. It's too easy to click on something else.

Don't get carried away by your own eloquence. Be guided by what your readers want or need to know. Make it easy for them. Write short paragraphs with one idea per paragraph.

4. Think Both Verbally and Visually

In the past, writers for print thought little about how their stories were going to appear. Their job was to write the story — period. The designer's job was to make the story fit on the page in some meaningful way. Writers did not worry about headlines, subheads, summary quotes, photos, illustrations or anything but the story.

Television newswriters know that they must write to the pictures. Good television has good video; the visual medium tries to show rather than to tell. Words complement pictures; they say what the pictures do not. Many times, of course, the writer does not make the pictures and is not responsible for getting them.

Online journalists may not have to do it all by themselves, but they must think verbally and visually. From the outset, you must be concerned about the most effective and efficient way for the information to appear on the screen. You have to think not only about the organization of the page, but also about ways to use graphics, to be interactive and to use online tools.

No one doubts that photos and graphics grab readers' attention. That's why you see more icons and infographics in magazines and newspapers, and that's why you must think, perhaps with the help of graphic designers, of ways to use graphic elements online.

In short, if you are writing online, you have to be much more than a wordsmith. You must have a pocketful of other skills. Writing online demands a great deal of collaboration and not just with other writers. Working closely with those more expert than you in design and photography becomes crucial from the outset.

5. Cut Copy in Half

You probably don't have to be told that writing online must be concise. But you do need to be told to cut your copy in half. Years ago writing expert William Zinsser recommended that writers take their eight pages and cut them to four. Then, he wrote, comes the difficult part: cutting them to three. And that was for print!

Most online readers simply will not read long stories. Even veteran computer users find reading on screen somewhat difficult, even unpleasant, says Jakob Nielsen. Perhaps this will change when larger screens and high-resolution screens become more common by becoming less expensive.

Studies contradict each other about people's aversion to scrolling. In the not-so-distant past, some experts advised getting the whole story on one screen. Because some screens are small, they advised not writing more than 20 lines of text. Now, because of the proliferation of larger and less-irritating screens, some readers are finding it easier and less frustrating to scroll for more information.

As in broadcast newswriting, there's little room online to be cute or even literary. Be crisp and clear.

6. Use Lots of Lists and Bullets

Often you can cut copy by putting information into lists. As in service journalism, whenever you can make a list, do so. Lists get more attention, better comprehension and more retention than normal sentences and paragraphs. Bulleted or numbered lists are scannable. Readers can grasp them immediately. Think of information on the Web as a database. That's how people use their computers, and that's how they use the Web.

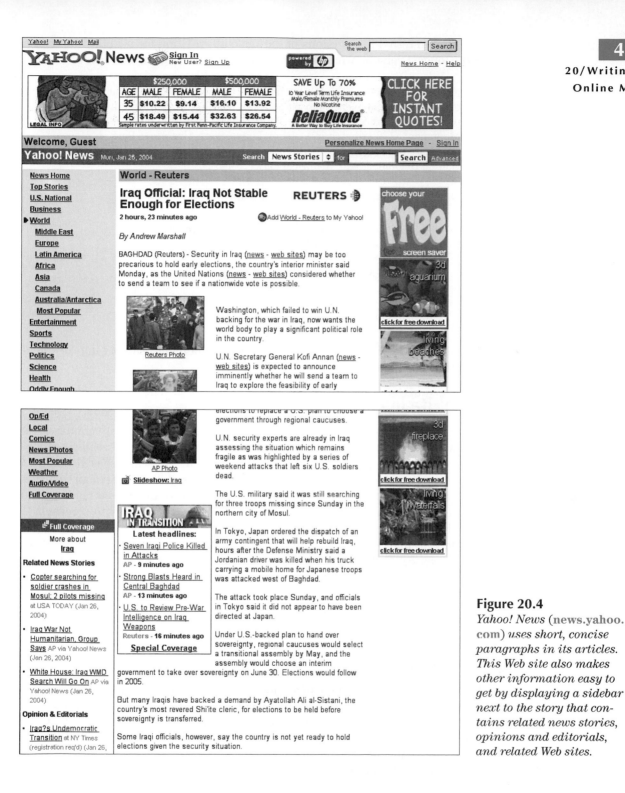

Figure 20.4

*Yahoo! News (*news.yahoo. com*) uses short, concise paragraphs in its articles. This Web site also makes other information easy to get by displaying a sidebar next to the story that contains related news stories, opinions and editorials, and related Web sites.*

Nielsen tested five versions of the same information for usability. Look first at the longest version, what he calls promotional writing, his control condition:

> Nebraska is filled with internationally recognized attractions that draw large crowds of people every year, without fail. In 1996, some of the most popular places were Fort Robinson State Park (355,000 visitors), Scotts Bluff National Monument (132,126 visitors), Arbor Lodge State Historical Park & Museum (100,000), *Carhenge* (85,598), Stuhr Museum of the Prairie Pioneer (60,002), and Buffalo Bill Ranch State Historical Park (28,446).

Now look at this same material in list form.

> In 1996, six of the most visited places in Nebraska were:
> - Fort Robinson State Park.
> - Scotts Bluff National Monument.
> - Arbor Lodge State Historical Park & Museum.
> - *Carhenge*.
> - Stuhr Museum of the Prairie Pioneer.
> - Buffalo Bill Ranch State Historical Park.

The list version of the information scored a 124 percent usability improvement over the first version.

7. Write in Chunks

When you can't put things into lists, you can still organize them into chunks of information. Put information into sidebars or boxes. Readers will read more, not less, if you break up the information into small bites. Research has also shown that putting some information in a sidebar can give readers better comprehension of the subject. But the main objective here is to write for diverse readers who want to get only the information they want in the order they want to receive it.

Think of your story as having parts. When writing a story for a newspaper, you need to think of ways to join the various parts of the story, you should craft transitions carefully and you may even add subheads. When writing a story online, rather than writing subheads, make each segment of the story a separate story. Be sure that each part can stand on its own enough to be comprehensible and to make your point. Again, remember the importance of a strong lead in the best inverted pyramid form.

8. Use Hyperlinks

To understand the Web, think of a spider web. The Web, says David Weinberger, is a place of connection; it is a connective place; it is a place where we go to connect. Users of the Internet feel connected. If you want them to read your copy and come back for more, you must satisfy and enhance that sense of being connected.

Being connected means being interactive. Web users want to be actively involved in what they are reading. They are not passive observers. Like video-game

"We have derived three main content-oriented conclusions from our four years of Web usability studies:

- Users do not read on the Web; instead they scan the pages, trying to pick out a few sentences or even parts of sentences to get the information they want.
- Users do not like long, scrolling pages; they prefer the text to be short and to the point.
- Users detest anything that seems like marketing fluff or overly hyped language ('marketese') and prefer factual information."

— John Morkes and Jakob Nielsen (1997), "Concise, SCANNABLE, and Objective: How to Write for the Web," useit.com

The 3-2-2-1 Format

After spending 25 years as a professional newsman, the last four of those as a general manager, Associate Professor Clyde Bentley now teaches classes in online journalism and other courses at the University of Missouri. In one class, students take stories from the newspaper and rewrite them for the online version. Bentley calls them online "producers" rather than reporters.

"I was surprised at the resistance my students had to changing the copy of reporters," Bentley says. "They preferred the 'shovelware' concept so they would not tamper with the prose of their friends."

In frustration, he instituted what he called a "3-2-2-1" format. "It was a way to force my young journalists to take on a new process."

Here's what the numbers mean:

- *3 subheads.* By inserting three subheads, the producers "chunk" the story into four pieces. "This is easier to read than one long, scrollable piece of text," Bentley says. The subdivisions can be as simple as "who, what, when . . ."
- *2 external links.* These are directions to further information posted outside the story (to the left of the text in our site, often at the bottom in other sites). "For instance, in a story about the local dog pound, we might have external links to the ASPCA and the American Kennel Club."
- *2 internal links.* These are explanatory links tied to text within the story. "In the pound story," Bentley explains, "the word 'Doberman' might be a link that takes one to a breeder's site that explains the Doberman Pinscher."
- *1 piece of art not available in the print edition.* Print publications limit art primarily because of space limitations. There are no such limits on the Web. "If a photographer shoots 20 shots, we can run more than one," Bentley says. "More commonly, however, the producers insert mug shots of people mentioned in the story. There is no reason not to run mugs of everyone who is mentioned in a story."

players, they want to be in control of where they are going and how they get there. Your copy must be interactive both internally and externally.

Internal Connections

The most challenging and necessary aspect of online writing is making the copy interactive. You begin that process by streamlining your copy by not including everything. Create **hyperlinks,** and allow readers to click on information elsewhere on your site.

One of the most perplexing problems writers face is deciding when to include the definition of a word. Will you insult some readers by including the definition? Will you leave others behind if you do not define the term? A similar problem is whether to tell who a person is. Many readers may wonder how stupid you think they are for telling them that actor Fred Thompson was a former Republican senator from Tennessee. Other readers may need or want that information.

Web expert Jakob Neilsen argues that Web sites must employ scannable text using:

- Highlighted keywords, including hypertext links.
- Meaningful subheads.
- Bulleted lists.
- One idea per paragraph.
- Half the word count of conventional writing.

Figure 20.5
*Perhaps better than any other site, ESPN (**msn.espn. go.com**) uses hyperlinks throughout its stories. The hyperlinks lead surfers to related stories, player profiles and even audio and video files.*

Among other rules for writing online, Ellen Schindler, a senior account executive at Berry Associates, recommends the following:

- Double-space between paragraphs. Leave two spaces after periods.
- Avoid serif type. Serifs get lost on the screen.
- Make the text black. It's easier to read.
- Simple is best.

The online writer can simply hyperlink the word or name to a different page or pop-up box. Readers need only click on the word to find its meaning or read more about it. No longer do writers have to write, "For more information, see. . . ." Academic writers use footnotes. **Hypertext,** and now **hypermedia,** linking readers to audio, video and pictures, are much more convenient.

Writing concisely has never been easier. Rather than defining words, going into long explanations, giving examples or elaborating on the story itself, you can stick to the essentials and make the rest of the story available to readers who need or want it. A story about a homicide can link to a map where the crime took place, to a chart showing the numbers of homicides this year as compared to last year, to a piece about friends of the victim, to information about violent crimes nationally, and so forth.

Remember, too, that unlike the newspaper that may be short of space, and unlike radio and television where you may be short of time, online you have unlimited space and time to run photos and aspects of stories that could be of real interest to some readers. Sports fans, for example, would probably enjoy seeing a whole gallery of shots from Saturday's championship game. They would read interviews from all of the stars of the victory — or of the defeat.

External Connections

Of course, you can do much more. You can hyperlink to different Web sites. Academic writers include bibliographies. Print journalists often identify sources

in their stories. Other writers simply say to readers, "That's all I know about the subject. I'm not telling you where I obtained my information, and I'm not telling you where you can find more information." Hypertext and hypermedia have changed all that. Not only can you hyperlink online, but readers expect that you will.

Obviously, you are not expected to draw readers away from your site to a competitor, especially on a breaking story. Nevertheless, readers will come to rely on your site to help them find more information about subjects that interest them greatly.

To find appropriate external hyperlinks, you need to know how to use search engines such as Yahoo! (**www.yahoo.com**) and Google (**www.google.com**). Check out "How to Search the Web: A Guide to Search Tools," by Terry A. Gray at Palomar College (**daphne.palomar.edu/TGSEARCH**).

9. Give Readers a Chance to Talk Back

A big part of being interactive is allowing readers to talk back. The Internet has leveled the playing field. Everyone is an owner or a publisher. Everyone feels the right, and often the need, to write back — if not to the writer of the piece, then to other readers in chat rooms. The wonderful thing about allowing readers to talk back is that they do. When they do, they will revisit the site again and again. Online readers want to be part of the process. Feedback, yes, instantly! Readers

Figure 20.7
This article on The Washington Post's *Web site* (**www.
washingtonpost.com**) *discusses the first photos
of Mars sent by the rover
Spirit. To the right are
links to more information
(shown below), including
3-D images of Mars taken
by Spirit.*

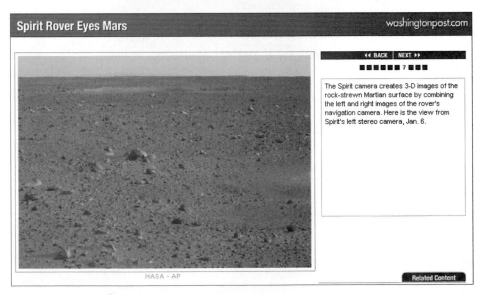

love it when newspapers such as *The Miami Herald* include the reporter's e-mail address in the byline, and many of them respond.

A word of caution: Including e-mail addresses on the Web leaves you open to operations that use a program called an e-mail syphon that scans Web site pages for e-mail addresses that are then used for spam. Depending on your mail-server provider's antispamming capabilities, putting your e-mail address in a news story or magazine article can subject you to a deluge of spam. One alternative is, rather than your permanent personal address, include in your stories a different address that you change from time to time.

Never has it been easier to find out what is on the minds of your readers. Print and broadcast have always been mainly one-way communication. Now, not only can you get opinions easily and quickly, but you can incorporate them into your story or at least hyperlink to them. Letters to the editor have always been among the best-read sections in newspapers and magazines. Many readers, especially those reading online, not only want to express their own opinions but love to read the opinions of others. Be sure, however, that you use the same strict standards for publishing others' remarks on your Web site that you use for publishing in your newspaper or magazine. Even e-mail polls can and have been flooded by advocacy groups. Reporting their results can be meaningless and misleading and certainly unprofessional unless they are monitored carefully.

10. Don't Forget the Human Touch

Veteran correspondent Helen Thomas told a convention of newspaper interactive editors on Feb. 9, 2000: "I do hope the human touch remains in the robotic scheme of things. Human beings still count."

Remember, people make the news. Facts are just facts unless you relate them to people.

LEGAL AND ETHICAL CONCERNS

Online journalists have the same legal and ethical concerns as other journalists (see Chapters 22 and 23). Libel is still libel, and plagiarism is still plagiarism. Just because you are not "in print" doesn't mean that you can destroy someone's reputation or distort the truth. You always must be aware that what is on the Internet is not yours, even though the very design of it allows you to download words and images. If you use someone else's words, put quotation marks around them, and cite the source.

Although the Internet makes it easier to find and steal someone else's work, it also makes it easier to get caught doing it. There have been several cases where Web readers of local columnists or reviewers have turned in a writer for plagiarism.

Plagiarism is not the only danger. Some areas of ethics are even more touchy and difficult to solve for online journalists.

- *Privacy.* Web sites exist that have files on almost everyone. Some allow everyone to see what anyone has ever posted on a chat box. What may journalists use? Most everyone agrees that private e-mail is off limits. But what about material sent to corporate intranets?
- *Advertising.* Newspapers and magazines generally try to label advertising as advertising, and they have rules that require ads to use typefaces different from those the publication uses. There also are rules about the placement of ads.

Online ads regularly break up the copy of news stories or pop up over news stories. There is no separation of ads from editorial content and no attempt to make any separation. Why don't the same rules that apply to print apply online? Note what the code of the American Society of Magazine Editors says:

> The same ASME principles that mandate distinct treatment of editorial content, advertisements, and special advertisements, and special advertising sections ("advertorials") in print publications also apply to online editorial projects bearing the names of print magazines or offering themselves as electronic magazines. The dynamic technology of electronic pages and hypertext links creates a high potential for reader confusion. Permitting such confusion betrays reader trust and undermines the credibility not only of the offending online publication or editorial product, but also of the publisher itself. It is therefore the responsibility

Figure 20.8
Many Web sites offer a chance for reader feedback, whether it's a chance to send a letter to the editor or to report a technical problem. The Los Angeles Times *(www.latimes.com) encourages feedback with several links to help readers send a letter to specific news departments or to help answer readers' questions.*

of each online publication to make clear to its readers which online content is editorial and which is advertising, and to prevent any juxtaposition that gives the impression that editorial material was created for — or influenced by — advertisers.

The code then goes on to spell out 10 specific ways to carry out these general guidelines.

The code of the American Society of Business Press Editors says simply:

On all such papers, editors should ensure that a clear distinction is made between advertising and editorial content. This may involve type faces, layout/design, labeling, and juxtaposition of the editorial materials and the advertisement.

The ASBPE code adds this important sentence: "Editors should directly supervise and control all links that appear with the editorial portion of the site."

- *Manipulating photos*. Print has not dealt with this problem well either. *New York Times* photographer Fred Ritchin proposed using an icon to flag a digitally altered photo. But how will readers know how much it has been altered? Will readers trust what they see?
- *Concealing your identity*. It's so easy to conceal your identity as a reporter on the Web. Certainly there is a time when you may be doing undercover investigative reporting, but the time to reveal yourself as a reporter is usually at the outset of your questioning people online, not after you have gotten to a certain point in your story.
- *Corrections*. Some online news sites act as if they never make mistakes. They simply post new stories with updated information. Surely you owe it to readers to tell them that the story has changed or has been updated with new information and how that was done. Such notice of correction or updating will not be done unless the news site has a clear policy requiring it.

Forbes.com erroneously quoted former Disney Chairman Michael Eisner as saying he didn't think his company's network, ABC, would be operating "in four to five years." In the update to the story, the changed headline read, "Clarification: Eisner Discusses the ABC Brand and Other Brands." In addition to correcting the story, Forbes.com put asterisks next to the changed sentences and included explanations at the bottom of the story such as: "The original version of this story incorrectly stated that Eisner did not see the third-ranked network being around in four to five years." In his column in *The Washington Post*, Howard Kurtz reported that Forbes.com editor Paul Maidment said his reporter had "extrapolated" without the "broader context."

- *Hyperlinks to external sites*. Is raw data journalism? How much and how often may you use raw data, and with what warnings or interpretations?

   Also, a new question has arisen about linking to external sites. National Public Radio has banned anyone from linking to its Web pages. What does that mean? Does it have the power to do that? Is it now unethical to do so?

TOMORROW'S READERS

Writing online is still in its infancy. Print has been around for centuries, and we are still figuring out ways to use it effectively. Like all good writers, online journalists must be students of writing. Both writers and readers are still learning the most effective uses of the newest medium, which is a sum of all media that is greater than its parts. The new media are more about showing than telling, about our audience experiencing rather than witnessing, about the audience actively participating rather than being passive, about the audience doing rather than merely reading. Perhaps never have writers been more challenged.

Suggested Readings

Bonime, Andrew, and Pohlmann, Ken C. *Writing for New Media.* New York: John Wiley & Sons, 1998. A thorough guide for anyone wanting to learn to write for interactive media, CD-ROMs and the Web.

De Wolk, Roland. *Introduction to Online Journalism: Publishing News and Information.* Boston: Allyn & Bacon, 2001. A short, simple and readable text with a wonderful glossary of terms.

Killian, Crawford. *Writing for the Web* (Writers' Edition). Bellingham, Wash.: Self Counsel Press, 2000. Excellent guidelines on writing for the Web.

Outing, Steve. "Report Once, Write Twice — for Print and Web." *Editor & Publisher Interactive.* Available from **www.mediainfo.com/ephome/news/news** **htm/news.htm**; Internet. A discussion of how *The Times Record News* in Wichita Falls, Texas, got its writers to supply on its Web site original content that is appropriate online.

Rich, Carole. *Creating Online Media: A Guide to Research, Writing and Design on the Internet.* New York: McGraw-Hill, 1999. A book that is as comprehensive as the title suggests by an author of other well-regarded journalism texts.

Ward, Mike. *Journalism Online.* Oxford: Focal Press, 2002. A nondogmatic, commonsense approach to all matters regarding online journalism, including good advice for writers.

Exercises

1. Choose a major national story from a recent newspaper or newsmagazine. Then visit two newspaper Web sites and compare the treatment of the story. Write a 300-word critique of the online writing techniques that the Web sites used.

2. Visit your local newspaper or television station and interview individuals who do the news online. Find out how they were trained and what major challenges they face.

3. The professor will assign you a newspaper story. Rewrite it for online use, and indicate any hyperlinks that you might include.

4. Visit five newspaper or magazine Web sites. Then pick the one that does the best job of using online writing techniques, and write a 200-word report on your findings.

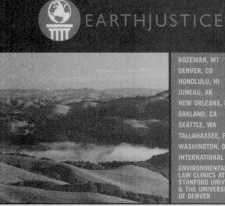

You may not be planning a career in news — you may know already that you are headed toward some area of public relations. Or, as happens to many people, perhaps you will work in news organizations for a while, but at some point in your career you may decide to switch to public relations. Or perhaps you already are writing for public relations.

Few disagree that the skill most required of public-relations people is good writing. Your writing skills should include newswriting, and you should be familiar with the way news operations work. That's why journalism schools traditionally require a course in newswriting for students interested in public relations, and that's why many public-relations professionals like to hire people with some news experience. Only by studying news and how news organizations handle it will you be successful in public relations or in offices of public information. Knowing how reporters are taught to deal with news releases will help you write better releases. Of course, studying news also helps you enormously in the advertising world and in what is now frequently called strategic marketing or strategic communications.

Skilled public relations or public information practitioners know how to write news, and they apply all the principles of good newswriting to their news releases. A good news release should meet the criteria of a good news story.

These same professionals know that working for an organization and doing internal and external communications demand a perspective different from a news perspective and, in many cases, a kind of writing different from newswriting. In many ways, of course, good writing is good writing, and what you have learned so far about newswriting also applies to public-relations writing. However, in public relations you also will be called upon to do writing that is different from the kinds of writing done by those who work for news organizations.

PUBLIC-RELATIONS WRITING — A DIFFERENT APPROACH

Let's begin with a few definitions and distinctions. Rex Harlow, the "father of public relations-research" and perhaps the first full-time

In this chapter you will learn:

1. **Various types of public-relations writing.**

2. **Guidelines for persuasive writing.**

3. **Different approaches to writing news releases.**

public-relations educator, claimed to have found 472 definitions of "public relations." The 1978 World Assembly of Public Relations in Mexico came up with this definition: "Public relations is the art and social science of analyzing trends, predicting their consequences, counseling organizational leaders and implementing planned programs of action which will serve both the organization's and public interest."

According to authors Wilcox, Ault, Agee and Cameron, these key words are found in all the definitions of "public relations":

- *Deliberate* — the "activity is intentional . . . designed to influence, gain understanding, provide feedback, and obtain feedback."
- *Planned* — "organized . . . systematic, requiring research and analysis."
- *Performance* — "based on actual policies."
- *Public interest* — "mutually beneficial to the organization and to the public."
- *Two-way communication* — "equally important to solicit feedback."
- *Management function* — "an integral part of decision-making by top management."

Public relations, then, is not just publicity, which seeks to get the media to respond to an organization's interests. Nor is it advertising, which pays to get the attention of the public, or marketing, which combines a whole host of activities to sell a product, service or idea. Advertising and marketing are concerned with sales.

If you wish to write in the field of public relations, you will have many areas to choose to work in. Here are some of the specialties:

- Media relations — seeking publicity and answering questions posed by the media.
- Government affairs — spending your time with legislatures and regulatory agencies and doing some lobbying.
- Public affairs — engaging in matters of public policy.
- Industry relations — relating to other firms in your industry and to trade associations.
- Investor or financial or shareholder relations — working to maintain investor confidence and good relationships with the financial world.

And the list goes on. Whoever said public-relations writing was dull knew nothing of the various worlds these professionals inhabit.

We must introduce one more term before proceeding. More and more today you see the term **"strategic communication"** replacing "public relations." Some have said that one simple reason for this is that the term "public relations" has always suffered a "PR" problem. It is true that many people have had a negative view of public relations, but, of course, the problems are much more serious than that.

The demands made of public-relations professionals are greater today than they were a generation ago. As Ronald Smith explains in *Strategic Planning for Public Relations:*

No longer is it enough merely to know *how* to do things. Now the effective communicator needs to know *what* to do, *why* and how to *evaluate* its effectiveness. public relations professionals used to be called upon mainly for tasks such as writing news releases, making speeches, producing videos, publishing newsletters, organizing displays and so on. Now the profession demands competency in conducting research, making decisions and solving problems. The call now is for strategic communicators.

In short, the strategic communicator must take a more scientific approach, do some research, make careful choices, and, when finished, evaluate the effectiveness of the completed program. Such a communicator would certainly be expected to write clearly and precisely, but differently from reporters.

Journalists will debate forever whether anyone can be truly objective when writing a story. Most settle the argument by saying what is demanded is a verifiable method of reporting. Nevertheless, in traditional reporting, writers should strive not to have a point of view. Reporters should not set out to prove something. Certainly they should not be an advocate for a point of view. They should get the facts and let the facts speak for themselves.

By contrast, columnists have a point of view, and good ones find ways to support it convincingly. Editorial writers use facts to persuade people to change their minds, or to confirm their opinions, or to get people to do something, or to stop doing something.

That's also what public-relations writers do. Although sometimes they wish only to inform their audiences, more often they want to do what editorial writers do: persuade the audience to a particular position.

However, there's one major difference: Journalists serve the public. public-relations writers work for an organization or for a client other than a news operation. Their job is to make that organization or client appear in the best possible light. Effective public-relations writers do not ignore facts, even when they are harmful or detrimental to the cause they are promoting. But they are promoting a cause or looking out for the best interests of the people for whom they are working. As a result, they will interpret all news, even bad news, in the most favorable light.

Public-relations writers work much the way attorneys work for clients — as advocates. They don't lie or even distort, but perhaps they play down certain facts and emphasize others. In its "official statement of public relations," the Public Relations Society of America states: "Public relations helps our complex, pluralistic society to reach decisions and function more effectively by contributing to mutual understanding among groups and institutions. It serves to bring private and public policies into harmony. . . . The public-relations practitioner acts as a counselor to management and as a mediator, helping to translate private aims into reasonable, publicly acceptable policy and action."

For a good discussion of what public relations is, check the Web site of the Public Relations Student Society of America at **www.prssa.org**. The Public Relations Society of America has a "Code of Professional Standards for the Practice of Public Relations." The code requires members to "adhere to the highest standard of accuracy and truth, avoiding extravagant claims or unfair comparisons and giving credit for ideas and words borrowed from others." It also requires members not to "knowingly disseminate false or misleading information." See www.prsa.org/profstd.html for the rest of the code.

PUBLIC-RELATIONS WRITING — A DIVERSITY OF TASKS

Like all good communicators, public-relations personnel are concerned with three things: the message, the audience and the media to deliver the message.

The Message

Like a good reporter writing a well-written story, you must know the message your organization wants to send. That message may be a product, a program or the organization itself. For every message you work on, you must first know what you hope to accomplish, even if your purpose is just to inform.

That's why it is so important for you to be a reporter first, to know how to gather information and to do so quickly. Like any reporter, you may be called upon in an instant to become something of an expert on a topic that you may never have heard of before. The public-relations staff on the *Disney Magic* of the Disney Cruise Lines may never have heard of the Norwalk virus, but suddenly 104 of the 2,485 passengers and 19 of the 1,003 crew members were suffering from nausea, vomiting, diarrhea, abdominal pain, fever and headache. All at once, one would expect, all of the skills of the public-relations professional were called into service.

This incident followed the news of another ship, the *Amsterdam*, of the Holland America line, which was being disinfected in Port Everglades in Fort Lauderdale, Fla., after more than 500 passengers and crew members succumbed to the Norwalk virus on its last four cruises.

Perhaps it was the result of some public-relations effort that caused this lead to appear in a *New York Times* story: "Despite recent outbreaks of gastrointestinal illness on cruise ships, federal health officials pronounced the ships safe yesterday and said they would not advise people to delay or avoid taking cruises."

The Audience

Almost as important as knowing all you can about the message is knowing the audience to whom you are directing it. The better you target your audience, the more effective you will be. As in advertising, demographics and psychographics determine the way you write your message, the language you choose, and the simplicity or complexity of the piece you are creating (see Figures 21.1 and 21.2).

Who are those people, what are their attitudes, and what do they do for work and recreation? You will answer these questions somewhat differently if you write for internal audiences (employees or the managers of those employees)

> ## Preamble
>
> Public Relations Society of America Member Code of Ethics
>
> - Professional Values
> - Principles of Conduct
> - Commitment and Compliance
>
> This Code applies to PRSA members. The Code is designed to be a useful guide for PRSA members as they carry out their ethical responsibilities. This document is designed to anticipate and accommodate, by precedent, ethical challenges that may arise. The scenarios outlined in the Code provision are actual examples of misconduct. More will be added as experience with the Code occurs.
>
> The Public Relations Society of America (PRSA) is committed to ethical practices. The level of public trust PRSA members seek, as we serve the public good, means we have taken on a special obligation to operate ethically.
>
> The value of member reputation depends upon the ethical conduct of everyone affiliated with the Public Relations Society of America. Each of us sets an example for each other — as well as other professionals — by our pursuit of excellence with powerful standards of performance, professionalism, and ethical conduct.
>
> Emphasis on enforcement of the Code has been eliminated. But, the PRSA Board of Directors retains the right to bar from membership or expel from the Society any individual who has been or is sanctioned by a government agency or convicted in a court of law of an action that is in violation of this Code.
>
> Ethical practice is the most important obligation of a PRSA member. We view the Member Code of Ethics as a model for other professions, organizations, and professionals.

Figure 21.1
The preamble to the Public Relations Society Code of Ethics.

or external audiences (the media, shareholders, constituents, volunteers, consumers or donors).

The first concern of the Disney public-relations staff was the people on the *Disney Magic*. They needed to communicate with the passengers, of course, but just as crucially, they needed to communicate with the staff to tell them how to deal with the situation, how to keep from getting ill themselves, what to say, and what not to say. And then there were all of the other media bombarding them with questions, and it wasn't just the news media, but travel magazines, Web sites, newsletters and cruise magazines.

And, of course, there were the moment-by-moment decisions of what to do with the people on board. How do you tell people to be careful (people stopped shaking hands when introducing themselves and touched elbows instead) without making them panic? How many extra perquisites do you offer them? For example, Disney offered to fly sick passengers home, but only one couple accepted. How many people would be demanding their money back or some other compensation? How many lawsuits would there be?

Fighting Hunger with Technology

Next week, as millions of families gather for their Thanksgiving feasts, many other Americans will go without. According to the United States Department of Agriculture, more than 12 million households lack enough food for everyone in their family at some time during the year — including holidays.

Hunger is surprisingly widespread in our country—one of the world's wealthiest — yet the government estimates that we waste almost 100 billion pounds of food each year, more than one-quarter of our total supply.

Reducing this tragic misallocation of resources is a goal of America's Second Harvest, the nation's largest domestic hunger-relief organization. Last year, it distributed nearly 2 billion pounds of food to more than 23 million people in need.

America's Second Harvest is a network of 214 affiliated food banks and other organizations that gathers surplus food donated by growers, processors, wholesalers, grocery stores and restaurants. In turn, the network distributes food to some 50,000 soup kitchens, homeless shelters, seniors' centers and other charities in every county of every state.

For instance, as part of a national program that America's Second Harvest launched in 1993, hungry children receive free meals and nutrition education at more than 1,200 Kids Cafés, operated by local Boys and Girls Clubs, schools and other community facilities.

Vast logistical challenges are involved in distributing tons of food, much of it perishable, from thousands of donors to thousands of small, nonprofit organizations. Until a few years ago, America's Second Harvest affiliates lacked any comprehensive way to manage their inventory. Without accurate and timely information, soup kitchens' pantries sometimes went bare while food was left to spoil on donors' loading docks or left unaccounted for in food banks.

In 2000, America's Second Harvest began to use a new inventory and financial-management system developed in collaboration with its affiliates, the firm eSoftware Professionals and Microsoft. Together, we created Ceres.

Ceres is software tailored specifically for hunger-relief operations. It is used by more than 100 affiliates of America's Second Harvest to track food from donation to distribution. Some affiliates have used Ceres to develop their own customized solutions, such as to bar code inventory and enable soup kitchens to order food online.

Innovation Helps Feed Families in Need

Affiliates say Ceres has helped them reduce spoilage and optimize food allocation. An evaluation found that the software streamlined food banks' operations by 23 percent in the first year alone.

Ceres saves time, freeing staff members to focus on finding new donors. The promise of more efficient use of donations, supported by more accurate and timely reports, helps bolster relationships with contributors.

Hunger in America remains troubling and perplexing, a social problem that is symptomatic of many others. Technology alone cannot solve them, but in the hands of organizations such as America's Second Harvest, it is a powerful tool that is helping to make a difference — and helping more Americans to join in the feast.

Learn more at microsoft.com/issues
Microsoft

Figure 21.2
This is a traditional news release, many of which can be found online.

Common Public-Relations Activites

Public Relations: Strategies and Tactics, by Wilcox, Ault, Agee and Cameron, lists these activities as common to those who work in public relations. Notice how many of these involve writing either directly or indirectly.

Advise management on policy

Participate in policy decisions

Plan public-relations programs

Sell programs to top management

Get cooperation of middle management

Get cooperation from other employees

Listen to speeches

Make speeches

Write speeches for others

Obtain speakers for organizational meetings

Plan and conduct meetings

Prepare publicity items

Talk to editors and reporters

Hold press conferences

Write feature articles

Research public opinion

Plan and manage events

Conduct tours

Write letters

Plan and write booklets, leaflets, reports and bulletins

Attend meetings

Plan films and videotapes

Plan and prepare slide presentations

Plan and produce exhibits

Take pictures or supervise photographers

Make awards

Design posters

Greet visitors

Screen charity requests

Evaluate public-relations programs

Conduct fund-raising drives

After 14 hours of cleaning at Port Canaveral, Fla., the *Disney Magic* set sail again with 2,400 passengers and 800 crew members. Three days into the cruise, 85 passengers were ill. A Disney Cruise Lines spokesperson told *The Orlando Sentinel*, on Nov. 27, 2002, "Federal health inspectors didn't really expect the illness to be completely gone after we cleaned last Saturday. You can't turn this on and off like a faucet."

Did they tell the passengers that before embarking?

On the previous *Disney Magic* cruise, sick passengers were charged $90 for a suppository and a shot, so some did not go for treatment. On this cruise, the national Centers for Disease Control and Prevention was providing free medical care, although David Forney, a supervisor at the CDC, said that Disney "was not real proactive in making sure passengers knew that."

The *Sentinel* story concluded: "Jaronski (the Disney spokesperson) said late Tuesday that he couldn't immediately comment on the issue of medical care last week."

The cruise ended three days early with 218 stricken with the virus. This time, Disney said it was canceling the ship's next cruise and giving it a week for a thorough cleanup.

Nevertheless, on the Disney Web site, nothing was said about the problems the cruise line was having until a couple of weeks later. Then a response to a question in the FAQ (Frequently Asked Questions) assured readers not to be afraid to take a cruise.

Carnival Cruise Lines was similarly silent. On the same day the Carnival ship the *Fascination* disembarked 200 sick passengers and crew members, its Web site — including the "Press Room," "News Releases," "Virtual Press Kit" and "Carnival Facts" sections — made no mention of the Norwalk virus.

The Media

Once you have mastered the message or product and targeted the audience, you then have to choose the best media by which to deliver the message to the audience. For a message that nearly everyone wants or needs to know, television may be your best medium. Procter & Gamble spends millions advertising soap on television because everyone needs soap. Television offers color and motion; television can show rather than just tell.

Radio listeners are usually loyal to one radio station. They will listen to your message over and over. The more often they hear it, the more likely they are to retain it.

Print is better for complicated messages and sometimes for delicate messages. Some argue that print still has more credibility than other media and that people can come back again and again to a print message.

More and more people are getting the information and products they need online, where you have all the media in one medium. Remember, people who are online generally are better educated and more affluent than those who are not. They love the control they have over the messages they find there. They can "click here" on only the information they want, and they can do so in any order they choose.

What is so wonderful (and so frightening) about "new media" is that you are dealing with a mass medium that is highly individualized; you are in the world of what has been called "mass-customization." You must present the message

Figure 21.3

Many corporations and organizations have newsletters for their employees, such as this prize-winning publication of Merck & Co., Inc., edited by Sharyn Bearse. Merck also publishes The Daily *each working day and has an intranet that is accessible only to employees. Bearse is also in charge of producing the company's annual report.*

Journalists, especially television journalists, are sometimes accused of creating stories by their very presence or, at least, of exacerbating situations, of fanning the flames. However, it is not in their job description to "create" news. A large part of doing public relations is to do just that — to create news. Here's a list of how to do that from the text of Wilcox, Ault, Agee and Cameron:

1. Tie in with news events of the day.
2. Cooperate with another organization on a joint project.
3. Tie in with a newspaper or broadcast station on a mutual project.
4. Conduct a poll or survey.
5. Issue a report.
6. Arrange an interview with a celebrity.
7. Take a part in a controversy.
8. Arrange for a testimonial.
9. Arrange for a speech.
10. Make an analysis or prediction.
11. Form and announce names for committees.
12. Hold an election.
13. Announce an appointment.
14. Celebrate an anniversary.
15. Issue a summary of facts.
16. Tie in with a holiday.
17. Make a trip.
18. Make an award.
19. Hold a contest.
20. Pass a resolution.
21. Appear before a public body.
22. Stage a special event.
23. Write a letter.
24. Release a letter you received (with permission).
25. Adapt national reports and surveys for local use.
26. Stage a debate.
27. Tie in to a well-known week or day.
28. Honor an institution.
29. Organize a tour.
30. Inspect a project.
31. Issue a commendation.
32. Issue a protest.

at different levels to different people so that different people feel they have choices, so that everyone feels as if you are writing only to him or her. It's all about individual choices and involving your readers so they interact with you. Just remember, communicating online ideally means that you have all the advantages and disadvantages of communicating all in one medium.

If you work in internal communications, you may decide to publish a newsletter or magazine. A large number of corporations communicate with employees throughout the day by an intranet, an internal online service accessible only to them. As a result, a surprisingly large number of organizations have ceased to regularly publish internal print publications.

For messages that need more explanation, such as health-care matters, perhaps a printed brochure will best do the job. Externally, for matters that may concern the community, you may want to use billboards in addition to paid ads in publications or radio and television. Or you may choose to write news releases and leave it to others to interpret your message.

Sometimes, however, there's no quick fix. What took a long time to build can come tumbling down quickly, and then a long rebuilding process is necessary.

The cruise industry became incredibly popular in a relatively short time due to a top-rated television program called *The Loveboat.* For years, the industry could not build ships fast enough to fill the demand. Fear of terrorism slowed down the demand somewhat, and perhaps now the fear of contagious disease will slow it down some more. How will public-relations professionals use the media to bring back the industry? Most likely, it will be through a long, organized campaign.

The Media Campaign

Research shows that the more media you use, the better chance you have to succeed. That's why effective public-relations people, like those in advertising, think in terms of campaigns and strategies. A campaign assumes that you can't just tell an audience only once what you want them to learn, retain and act on. You need a strategy to reach a goal that may take days, weeks, months or even years to attain. Which medium do you use to introduce the subject, which media will you engage for follow-up and details, which aspects of the message are best suited for which media? You accomplish little by sending out the message once and in only one medium. If you send the message in a mix of media, in a carefully timed or orchestrated way, the results will be exponentially greater.

Public-relations writers adapt messages to the whole spectrum of media available. To do this, you must learn what each medium does best. Perhaps Marshall McLuhan was exaggerating when he wrote that the medium is the message, but no one doubts there is a great deal of truth to his statement.

You may be hired as a speechwriter or do something as specialized as writing an organization's annual report. Corporations and institutions such as hospitals and universities hire thousands of communicators to get their messages out to the public. Or you may work for a public-relations agency that is hired to do this work for organizations.

Regardless of the means or media you choose to use, your job is to have good relations with the public. You do that best by trying to establish mutually beneficial relationships and by trying to set up win-win situations. All of this is best achieved when you make two-way communications possible. You must allow and encourage your various publics to have a voice in what you are trying to achieve. If you involve your audience in what you are trying to achieve, your chances of achieving it increase. Establishing a Web site is an excellent way to get people's ideas and reactions. Of course, you must find ways (notices on bulletin boards, brochures, newsletters, etc.) to make your Web site known.

PUBLIC-RELATIONS WRITING — A MATTER OF PERSUASION

Most of the time, your writing will attempt to persuade people. You need to study the techniques of persuasion and use them carefully. To persuade people, you need to believe three things:

1. *People are essentially good.* You need to be convinced of that and to appeal to people's basic goodness and fairness.
2. *People are intelligent or at least educable.* Don't talk down to people; don't assume that you can trick or fool them.
3. *People are changeable.* You must believe not only that people are changeable but also that you can change them.

First, more than anything else, you need to establish and maintain your credibility and the credibility of the organization you represent. Aristotle wrote that the character of the speaker is the most essential and powerful component of persuasion. Without a doubt, character is the most important thing public-relations people need to have and to develop. A sterling reputation takes a long time to build — and can be lost in an instant.

Second, you must assume goodwill on the part of your audience. You cannot persuade people by beating up on them, by calling them names or by considering them the enemy. This is particularly true regarding your attitude toward the press. Too many public-relations professionals consider the press the enemy, not to be trusted with the truth, to be stonewalled at every opportunity.

If you or your family had turned to the Disney or Carnival Web sites to book a cruise in November or December 2002, you would have seen "business as usual." There was no information about problems of illness and no warnings whatsoever. If you had not been reading Florida newspapers or paying special attention to the news, you might not have heard of the problems the cruise lines were having. (This despite the fact that the Centers for Disease Control reported that the virus might have been brought onto the ships by passengers who were not feeling well before the ship set sail but did not admit it for fear of not getting their fares refunded.)

Contrast this with what Princess Cruises did in September 2003. On Sept. 3, newspapers picked up a story about 300 passengers and crew members becoming sick on a cruise across the North Atlantic. On Sept. 4, an extensive news release appeared on the company's Web site explaining what happened on the *Real Princess* and detailing everything involved in the sanitation of the ship. The release also said that the company had gotten in touch with all the passengers who were booked for the next cruise, told them what had happened and asked them to contact the company with any concerns.

Another good example is what the University of North Carolina–Chapel Hill did when it learned that People for the Ethical Treatment of Animals had planted a spy in one of its animal-research facilities. The woman had worked there for eight months and secretly videotaped animals and the staff at work. PETA's goal was to defeat the Helms amendment to the 2002 farm bill that would have extended USDA authority for animal welfare to cover laboratory mice, rats and birds. That change, according to those opposed to it, would have meant a great deal more paperwork for the research team and little improvement in animal care. PETA held a press conference and set up a Web site showing lurid photos and making claims of animal cruelty and neglect.

"Desktop publishing has dramatically increased the quantity and enhanced the quality of news releases coming into a news room. News releases from local clubs and organizations that once were written in longhand on notebook paper now rival those of professional public-relations firms. The net effect: more news releases with local news than ever before. In a competitive media marketplace, smart newspapers can parlay this additional information into community pages packed with names and faces, reflecting the lives of readers in a way that other media can't."

— Ken Paulson, former senior vice president, The Freedom Forum, and now editor, *USA Today*

The university's response was rapid, candid and forthright. On the same day PETA broke the story, Tony Waldrop, vice chancellor for research, and other university officials held a press conference, promised a thorough investigation and opened the facility in question to reporters. The university did not attempt to deny or discredit the PETA claims. With no hint of a coverup to feed upon, university officials, at least, considered media coverage to be fair and factual, and the story faded from the news in just a couple of days. The farm bill passed with the Helms amendment intact.

Meanwhile, the university lived up to its promise to investigate. It spent several thousand hours in internal investigations, and Waldrop commissioned a panel of three outside experts to do an independent review. The university then presented a 40-page report to the federal Office of Laboratory Animal Welfare, and the local press summarized it — again, in a fair, evenhanded manner. The report was then published in the university's research magazine: a candid account of what PETA claimed, what the university found in its investigations, and what it did to correct the problem.

That's how public relations can, should and does work.

WRITING NEWS RELEASES
THAT GET ATTENTION

Even the smallest newspaper and radio or TV station gets dozens of news releases daily. How do you break through the clutter and even get listened to or looked at by the gatekeepers on the news desks? If you send news releases online, your problem is still the same.

Here are some guidelines to help you get your messages to your intended audiences:

- *Know what news is and how to write it.* If you are headed toward a career in public relations or public information, you probably are taking this newswriting course to help you understand the principles of news. The news media will not pay attention to copy that is laced with opinion or self-serving quotations. Worse, they will ridicule your work and discard it immediately.

  Avoid statements such as this: "Monroe College is recognized as the foremost and most prestigious college of liberal arts in the entire Midwest." Who says?

  To write for most publications, certainly for newspapers, you need to know Associated Press style. Correct spelling, usage and grammar is essential, of course, but just as important is AP style. Why should news editors take you seriously if you do not bother to write in the style of their publications?

  News releases are notoriously inaccurate and inconsistent in style and grammar. How ironic that people so concerned with image are so careless in how they present themselves to the public.

- *Know the structure and operations of news rooms.* If you do not get actual experience in a news room in college, find ways to spend some time in one. In Chapter 2, you studied how news rooms are organized. Now use your public-relations skills to get inside one and to experience what goes on there.

  The most simple and important thing you can learn about news rooms is that they have deadlines. Learn the deadlines of the media where you work, and respect those deadlines. That means you cannot call in a story to a television news station a half hour before broadcast time. Not only will the station not use your story, but station employees will resent you and not forget the interruption at a critical time. News organizations will tell you what time you must submit a story to make the news that day.

- *Know the people in the news media and the jobs they hold.* This is especially true of newspapers. Sending a release addressed simply to a newspaper can be a waste of your time and make you look as if you do not know what you are doing. Sending a release to the business editor or to the features editor makes more sense. Addressing by name the editor of the section in which you wish the release to appear works best.

  At a packed meeting of the Publicity Club of New York, features editor of the *New York Post* Faye Penn told her audience to stop sending her news releases. First, she said she could not possibly read them all, and second, many of them were about things her section never covered. Later, she backed down from her position and admitted that she looked to see who sent the release.

  If people in the news media know and trust you, they are more likely to read your releases, and you can sometimes call them with a story and let them write their own stories. There's nothing writers like more than to get wind of good stories. At the Publicity Club of New York meeting, however, features editor Barbara Schuler of *Newsday* warned that she never answers her phone but does read all news releases and faxes. She stressed the importance of getting the release into the right hands, and she handed out a sheet with the names, phone numbers and beat assignments of the reporters on *Newsday*. You need that list for each medium you cover.

  Just remember, your job is to help reporters write good stories. If you can help them do that and at the same time serve your client's interests, you will be a successful public-relations practitioner.

- *Know the style of writing that fits the medium.* Do not make the mistake of sending the same news release to the radio or TV station that you send to the newspaper. Do not expect busy newspeople to translate your newspaper release into broadcast copy. If you can write radio or television copy (see Chapter 19), you have a much better chance of getting the copy read over the air. And if you can supply video, many stations will use it in their newscasts.

  Of course, none of the above media, including the largest newspapers or radio or television networks, can reach as many people as online media. Millions of Web sites know practically no limits. First, you must establish your own credible, up-to-date, interactive Web site. Second, you must be thoroughly familiar with Web sites such as **www.online-pr.com, www.prnewswire.com** or **www.medialink.com** so you can distribute your releases

> "If you don't understand good journalistic style and format (who, what, when, where and why) for writing a press release, you harm your company and yourself."
>
> — G. A. Marken, president of Marken Communications, Inc., *Public Relations Quarterly*

News Releases

Jo Johnston has gone from reading news releases to writing them and sending them to the media.

After college, Johnston worked as a reporter and managing editor for *The Maryville* (Mo.) *Daily Forum* before becoming editor of *The Examiner* in Independence, Mo. She then left newspapers for corporate public relations with AT&T, where she's worked for more than 10 years.

Back when she was in the news room, she says, "We opened and read every release in the daily mail." That's not the way it is today. One reporter told her recently he doesn't have enough time to open all the overnight-delivery packages he receives.

Today's reporters are more likely to receive releases by wire service. Only a grabbing headline or lead will get the reporter to take a second look before hitting the delete key.

Once you get the reader's attention, Johnston says, your job has just begun. Reporters are usually on deadline. "So anything you can do to make the reporter's job easier will increase the odds of getting ink or airtime," Johnston says.

She tries to give technical information in simple language. "First, what's new, and so what, followed by simple descriptions and a complete story that doesn't leave the audience with unanswered questions."

Most of all, she says, "We absolutely refuse to bow to the company's pressure to include 'fluff' in a news release. After all, we're building relationships with reporters, and our reputations are at stake."

online and keep up with what's happening in public relations. Third, you must become expert yourself at using new media (note the plural) to get across your organization's messages. (See Chapter 20.)

TYPES OF NEWS RELEASES

News releases generally fall into three categories:

1. *Announcements of coming events or personnel matters — hiring, promoting, retiring and the like.* Newspapers often have a calendar where they place events of interest to their readers. Communities are interested in people's jobs — when they start, when they are promoted and when they retire.
2. *Information about a cause.* Organizations try to be good community members. Often their people do volunteer work such as holding blood drives and

raising money for children's hospitals. Organizations such as the American Heart Association find ways to get the community involved in events that raise money for the association.

3. *Information that is meant to build someone's or some organization's image.* Politicians seek to be elected or to be re-elected, so they need to be in the news. Organizations and government agencies often try to burnish their images by promoting some cause or event that demonstrates how they serve the community.

APPROACHES TO WRITING THE NEWS RELEASE

The Inverted Pyramid

The straight, no-nonsense inverted pyramid news release remains the staple of the public-relations professional. Many believe that any other approach will not be taken seriously by news professionals.

Here's an example. Notice the address and phone number of the organization putting out the release and the name of a contact person. If the news is for immediate release, say so. Otherwise, indicate a release date.

NEWS RELEASE

Missouri Department of Natural Resources

P.O. Box 176, Jefferson City, Missouri 65102 (573-751-3443)

For further information, contact: Mary Schwartz

(For immediate release)

JEFFERSON CITY, MO., FEB. 25, 2003 — The winter solitude of Roaring River, Bennett Spring and Montauk state parks will be shattered by about 8,000 fishing enthusiasts expected to participate in the annual trout opening March 1 in Missouri State Parks.

The start of trout-fishing season in these parks marks the beginning of the vacation season in Missouri state parks, which are administered by the Missouri Department of Natural Resources. The Department also administers 30 other state parks and 22 historic sites, which officially open on April 15.

"Trout opening is definitely a big event for fishermen in Missouri," said John Karel, director of state parks. "But, it's also a big day for state parks since it traditionally marks the beginning of the upcoming vacation season."

Karel notes that park visitors to Montauk, Roaring River and Bennett Spring state parks will be greeted by a number of new construction and major renovation projects. . . .

The release goes on to talk about the projects and about how many trout tags were sold. It's a traditional approach, although the lead attempts to be a bit creative with the "winter solitude" being "shattered." The lead jumps to a quote from an authority, John Karel, the director of the state parks, and uses him as the source throughout.

Wilma Mathews is the consummate public-relations professional. Her 30-year career includes 15 years with AT&T and 10 years with Arizona State University. Her background includes work with a magazine and a newspaper and at a medical center and a chamber of commerce. She is a Fellow of the International Association of Business Communicators.

In her position as director of public relations at Arizona State University, her work crosses the borders of legislative affairs, community relations, media relations, events planning, marketing, advertising, employee communication, presidential support and the ever-famous "other duties as assigned."

This particular day points out the variety of problem-solving and opportunity-snatching that comes with a job of this scope. Here she speaks of a typical day.

A Wednesday . . .

Four meetings crowded this day and took precedence over the smaller issues that came up between them.

A colleague at one of our campuses had noticed that the advertising rate issued to us at the *Arizona Republic* newspaper was based on the nonprofit status that assumed about $150,000/year in advertising. Since that rate was set, some years ago, many things have changed, and it appeared that ASU's cumulative advertising is closer to about $500,000/year, an amount that

would qualify the university for a better rate.

I presided at a meeting that included the advertising manager and two representatives from the newspaper and representatives from the major Arizona State University advertiser organizations: athletics, public events (Broadway and other performances), extended education and the College of Business and Public Affairs.

The hour-long meeting confirmed that (a) university units are collectively advertising far more than realized; (b) there is no single representative for the university at the newspaper, so individual departments are quoted rates by whatever representative they happen to get; (c) the university had not done a good job of routinely working with the newspaper's advertising department.

Results of the meeting: We agreed to get a three-year look at ASU's advertising, allow the advertising manager and staff to present next month to all ASU public relations people both the new rate and other advertising opportunities, to have one advertising rep to serve as the coordinator among reps at the newspaper, and to help the paper develop a more accurate list of ASU advertisers.

From that meeting, I went to one of the Sun Devil Advocates, an organization run by the ASU Alumni Association, to help build support for ASU's legislative agenda. The conversation focused on the need to have more face-to-face presentations within the university to departments and leadership about the serious and critical situation the university will

be in for the second half of this fiscal year as well as fiscal '04 and '05. It appears that other channels of communication about the situation have not worked, and only face-to-face is getting people's attention.

I had to leave that meeting early in order to drive to a meeting in downtown Phoenix with Arvizu Advertising and Public Relations, an agency selected just a few days before to help ASU reach the Hispanic and other minority audiences in January and February with face-to-face and print presentations about the state universities' request to increase tuition by 44 percent while also increasing financial aid significantly. The agency is being asked to turn around an estimate in less than three working days and a draft plan in six working days in order to get as much accomplished as possible during the year-end holidays. I will be coordinating this program and working with the agency.

After returning to the office, I e-mailed a summary of the meeting to the provost, vice presidents and directors who are part of the planning group on this issue.

I then left the office for a meeting in Scottsdale with United Blood Services, the organization that conducts blood drives on our campuses. ASU is large enough to warrant a single representative from UBS to schedule the drives, find volunteers to help with the drives, develop blood drive "sponsors" from within the university to host drives, and report functionally to me about the program. ASU is one of the largest suppliers of blood in the Valley and has the ability to conduct two to three drives each month at various locations. This meeting approved the development plan and goals for the coming year.

In between meetings, I made appropriate notifications within the university and with police regarding two young men soliciting funds in various neighborhoods in the Valley who claimed to be students from our West campus. This required multiple voice mails and explanations and carried over into the next day while I was traveling to Chicago.

I also completed work as a survey participant for a graduate student's paper on crisis communications involving racial disturbances, wrote thank-you notes to two speakers who had presented at the monthly internal public relations meeting, and wrote and got approved a letter from the president regarding the United Way campaign.

At day's end, I completed what I needed to do for a trip to Chicago and a presentation I was to make there.

A normal day? Yes.

Getting Beyond the Inverted Pyramid

Let's look now at a different approach; some would call it a feature approach (the information at the top of the release stays the same).

When the siren sounds at 6:30 a.m., March 1 in Bennett Spring State Park near Lebanon, Bill Brooks will be there. He'll be standing knee-deep in icy water as he's done every March 1 since 1970.

Brooks, known in fishing circles as Big Trout, will join an expected 8,000 other Missouri fishing enthusiasts for the opening of trout-fishing season in Missouri State Parks. Missouri's other trout-fishing state parks are Roaring River, near Cassville, and Montauk, near Salem.

Brooks can't imagine anything, short of a death in the family, that would keep him away. "This is just a tradition for me. I'm already making wagers and getting together my equipment."

As an extra measure, Brooks has made a special trip from his Marshfield home to the park just to check stream conditions.

After 32 years of opening days, Brooks has seen some changes. "I guess you could say they've gotten stricter on us. Things used to be a lot wilder down there in the old days, until they stopped us from gambling and stopped selling beer. . . ."

The release then introduces fishing expert Jim Rogers, who runs concessions at both Bennett Spring and Roaring River. Rogers tells with specific numbers how he has sold more than double the number of trout tags that he sold just eight years ago.

In this approach, the writer uses a "real person," a long-time fisherman, to introduce the story — rather than a person in authority. By using Brooks and Rogers, the writer tells a story and still gives important information, but in an interesting and appealing way.

Now suppose the writer accompanied this story with a photo from the year before of Big Trout standing knee-deep in icy water. Public-relations professionals

"Promotions into high office are newsworthy not just to the business, financial or trade press, but also to the person's hometown papers, alumni magazines and professional society journals. Notices of service anniversaries, training courses completed, retirements and honors received are welcome at various publications; the trick is to match the medium with the message. Some of these items, depending on visual appeal, could interest television as well."

— Carole Howard and Wilma Mathews, *On Deadline: Managing Media Relations*

467

Figure 21.4
*Photos like this one, provided by the Missouri State Department of Conservation, can
accompany press releases promoting trout fishing in Missouri.*

know that releases accompanied by photos or art of some kind get more attention and more play.

Some professionals have also begun to place attention-grabbing headlines
on top of their releases. Others accompany the head with a summary/contents/
benefit blurb. Why should the editor or the intended audience have to read the
entire release to find out what it's about?

You might want to go a step further. Why not do some service journalism?
Put the parks, their locations and the opening dates in a separate box. How
about a map of how to get there? Perhaps you could make a list of the top-10
things to remember on opening day. Maybe you could create an infographic indicating where to get trout tags. Some news organizations will use just one sidebar
or graphic of what you send. But the important thing is that if you give them
choices, you have a better chance of getting some of your information used.

In the past, some public-relations professionals shied away from what they
thought of as gimmicks, for fear that editors would not take them seriously. What
they didn't see was the way newspapers were changing, especially some sections.

Why not experiment? Attention is harder and harder to get. Don't be afraid to
try a "you" lead or even a question — for example, "Are you ready for opening

day at Bennett Spring?" Remember to get to the "so what" quickly — not your organization's but the audience's. What's in it for the reader or listener? Most readers don't care whether Comcast has announced the purchase of another company. (Some companies seem never to do anything but "announce" things in news releases.) Readers do care about how this sale might affect them and their cable bills.

Remember, too, that a film clip of Big Trout will more likely be used by a television news producer than will a written release, and a recorded interview might get played on your local radio station.

Even if none of these media uses your material the way you presented it, perhaps you will succeed in grabbing the attention of an editor or reporter. If that person is inspired to pursue the story, you'll still get the information to the public.

Be sure that you make yourself available — by cell phone, e-mail, fax, Web site, in person — 24 hours a day. A reporter on deadline will write the story with or without you. It's better that you talk — it's *always* better that you talk — to the reporter.

Remember, your job is not just to write news releases. Your job is to get information from your organization to the public. Writing news releases is only one means to that end. As a public-relations writer, you will use your writing skills in myriad ways in all media to serve your clients well.

Tips for Writers of News Releases

1. Follow an accepted journalistic style of writing. Use AP style.
2. Go easy on length. Hold it to two double-spaced, typewritten pages.
3. Avoid breaks. Don't hyphenate words at the ends of lines, and don't split a sentence at the bottom of a page.
4. Write clearly. Avoid corporate jargon, legalese or other alien language.
5. Remember the pyramid. But don't put all the w's in the lead.
6. Beware of adjectives. Especially avoid superlatives.
7. Make it local.
8. Attribute news to a person, not to a company or an organization.
9. Indent the paragraphs.

— Carole Howard and Wilma Mathews,
On Deadline: Managing Media Relations

Suggested Readings

Bivins, Thomas H. *Public Relations Writing*, Fourth Edition. Lincolnwood, Ill.: NTC/Contemporary Publishing Group, 1999. Covers a wide variety of writing expected of public-relations professionals.

Holtz, Shel. *Public Relations on the Net.* New York: Amacom, 1999. Anything Shel Holtz says or writes about online subjects is worth paying attention to. See also www.holtz.com.

Horton, James L. *Online Public Relations.* Westport, Conn.: Quorum Books, 2001. A superb primer and more, beginning by explaining terminology and ending with 85 industry and general information topics on placing news and gathering information.

Howard, Carole and Mathews, Wilma. *On Deadline: Managing Media Relations*, Third Edition. Prospect Heights, Ill.: Waveland Press, 2000. A practical book on how organizations should deal with the news media.

Newsom, Doug and Carrel, Bob. *Public Relations Writing, Form and Style*, Sixth Edition. Australia: Wadsworth, 2001. A truly thorough classic. It even has a section on grammar, spelling and punctuation.

Smith, Ronald D. *Strategic Planning for Public Relations.* Mahwah, N.J.: Lawrence Erlbaum Associates, 2002. An up-to-date text that emphasizes "strategic" planning for public-relations professionals.

Wilcox, Dennis L. *Public Relations Writing and Media Techniques*, Fourth Edition. New York: Longman, 2001. Filled with practical tips in all areas of public-relations writing; handy boxes and sidebars.

Suggested Web Sites

www.instituteforpr.com
Provides information about public-relations research, measurement, programs, seminars, publications, scholarship, and so on.

www.online-pr.com
An amazingly helpful site for anyone interested in public relations. A source for loads of useful Web sites.

www.prsa.org
Site of the Public Relations Society of America. Has general information about the society, lists its chapters and sections, has publications, membership and accreditation information, recognitions and awards, conferences and seminars.

www.prssa.org
Site of the Public Relations Student Society of America. Contains news for members and leaders of the organization, as well as job listings and a calendar of events.

www.silveranvil.org
Site of the Silver Anvil awards — annual awards to public-relations practitioners who "in the judgment of their peers, have successfully addressed a contemporary issue with exemplary professional skill, creativity and resourcefulness."

1. Visit the public relations or public affairs department of your university or of a major employer in your community. Do a report on what the staff does and what public-relations materials they produce.

2. A classmate was killed in a car accident. A couple of thousand dollars have been raised to set up a scholarship to honor his memory, but much more money is needed to endow the scholarship. Several students in the class have been training to run in the Chicago marathon. A group decides to solicit money for each mile the students complete. Organize a campaign on your campus to get people to pledge or donate money. Answer these questions:

   a. What are your target audiences?
   b. Which media will you use?
   c. What print materials will you develop?

   Then write a news release for the local media.

3. Read the following news release, and note any deviations from AP style. Also note any content that news organizations might object to.

   NEWS RELEASE
   "Chest Pains", an excellent film in the HEALTHCARE series produced by the American College of Physicians, will be shown from 7:00–8:30 P.M., Wednesday, October 22, at St. Mary's Health Center. Springfield internist Dr. Harold Kanagawa will host a question-and-answer period following the film.

   Although most people assume that chest pains signify a heart attack, the public is less aware that other conditions — hiatal hernia, ulcers, viral infections of the heart's membranes — can also cause pains that require prompt diagnosis and appropriate medical treatment. Designed to help increase awareness of the symptoms and their possible significance, "Chest Pains" features an internist and actual patients as they work together to resolve underlying medical problems.

   Through a warm and engaging human-interest style of presentation, each twenty-five-minute documentary encourages people to take an increased responsibility for their own well-being by establishing healthy habits and assuming a more active role in disease prevention.

   The HEALTHCARE series is produced under an educational grant from the Elsworth Company of Midland, Michigan. Other films in this superb, highly acclaimed series cover "Aches, Pains and Arthritis", "Diabetes", and "Abdominal Discomfort".

   Doctor Kanagawa, a renowned specialist in internal medicine, is 1 of fifty-thousand members of the American College of Physicians. Founded in 1915, the College is the largest medical specialty society in the U.S. and one of the most prestigious. It represents doctors of internal medicine, related non-surgical specialists, and physicians-in-training.

   To register or for more information, contact the Women's Life Center.

4. Interview a student from a small town. Then write a news release about his or her life and activities at the university, and send it to the town's newspaper.

5. Study the Web site of the college or university you attend. Then write a news release for your local paper describing the information and services found on the Web site.

When a cattle rancher turned vegetarian appeared on Oprah Winfrey's TV show and told her about "mad cow" disease, she replied, "It has just stopped me cold from eating another burger!" Apparently, when Oprah talks, people listen. Cattle future prices dropped 10 percent the next day. Texas cattle producers sued Oprah for libel, but a jury deliberated less than two hours before deciding in Oprah's favor.

After winning, Oprah exclaimed, "Free speech not only lives, it rocks."

Free speech not only rocks, but it also raps. The rapper Eminem won a libel suit brought by childhood classmate DeAngelo Bailey, who said Eminem's song "Brain Damage" defamed him as a school bully. Michigan judge Deborah Servitto issued her ruling in the form of a rap:

> Mr. Bailey complained his rep is trash, so he's seeking compensation in the form of cash.
> Bailey thinks he's entitled to some monetary gain, because Eminem used his name in vain.
> The lyrics are stories no one would take as fact; they're an exaggeration of a childish act.
> It is therefore this court's ultimate position that Eminem is entitled to summary disposition.

But free speech does have its limits. For example, it was acceptable to report that Richard Jewell, a security guard at first hailed as a hero following a bomb explosion at the Atlanta Olympics, had then become an FBI suspect. However, it was not acceptable to state flatly that Jewell was the bomber. Such overstatement led to out-of-court settlements by CNN, NBC, the *New York Post* and WABC radio for a reported $2 million total. Jewell's suit against the *Atlanta Journal-Constitution* was still ongoing in early 2004.

YOUR RIGHTS

The Constitution ratified in Philadelphia in 1787 did not contain explicit protections of freedom of speech and freedom of the press. Those protections were added four years later in the First Amendment, which states:

Congress shall make no law respecting an establishment of religion, or prohibiting the free exercise thereof; or abridging the freedom of speech, or of the press; or the right of the people peaceably to assemble, and to petition the Government for a redress of grievances.

Read that again: "Congress shall make no law . . . abridging the freedom of . . . the press." No other business in the United States enjoys that specific constitutional protection, unless you consider religion a business.

Why should there be such protection for the press? The Supreme Court gave an eloquent answer to that question in a 1957 obscenity decision. The press is protected, the court ruled, to ensure the "unfettered interchange of ideas for bringing about the political and social changes desired by the people."

The free flow of ideas is necessary in a democracy because people who govern themselves need to know about their government and about those who run it, as well as about the social and economic institutions that greatly affect their day-to-day lives. Most people get that information through newspapers, radio, television and the Internet.

In 1966 Congress passed the Freedom of Information Act to assist anyone in finding out what is happening in federal agencies. This act, which was amended in 1996 by the Electronic Freedom of Information Act to improve access to computerized government records, makes it easier for you to know about government business. All 50 states have similar **open-records laws.** Though of great assistance to the press, these laws also are used by individuals and businesses to gain information previously kept secret by the government. There are other laws ensuring access to government transactions. The federal government and all the states have **open-meetings laws** — often called "sunshine laws" — requiring the public's business to be conducted in public. However, all of these access laws contain exemptions that keep some meetings private.

The First Amendment, the Freedom of Information Act and the sunshine laws demonstrate America's basic concern for citizen access to information needed for the "unfettered interchange of ideas." Nevertheless, there are laws that reduce the scope of freedom of the press.

> "The government's power to censor the press was abolished so the press would remain forever free to censure the government."
>
> — Hugo Black,
>   U.S. Supreme Court
>   Justice

LIBEL

Traditionally, most of the laws limiting the absolute principle of freedom of the press have dealt with libel. These laws result from the desire of legislatures and courts to help individuals protect their reputations. Their importance was explained by U.S. Supreme Court Justice Potter Stewart in a 1966 libel case.

> The right of a man [or woman] to the protection of his [or her] own reputation from unjustified invasion and wrongful hurt reflects no more than our basic concept of the essential dignity and worth of every human being — a concept at the root of any decent system of ordered liberty.

The Keys to Avoiding Libel

Ken Paulson earned a law degree after graduating from journalism

school. He then practiced journalism for 18 years. After several years as senior vice president of the Freedom Forum in Arlington, Va., and executive director of The First Amendment Center at Vanderbilt University, he was appointed editor of *USA Today* in 2004.

"Having a law degree has been helpful as a journalist," he says, "but the key to avoiding libel suits really boils down to a few fundamentals."

The keys to avoiding a libel suit are rooted in professionalism and common sense. He suggests that journalists ask themselves these questions:

• Have I reported fully?

• Have I reported factually?
• Have I reported fairly?
• Have I reported in good faith?

"If you can answer those four questions in the affirmative, the law will take care of itself," he says. Joining the Gannett Co. in 1978, Paulson has been executive editor of *Florida Today* in Melbourne, Fla.; editor of the *Green Bay* (Wis.) *Press-Gazette*; managing editor of the *Bridgewater* (N.J.) *Courier-News;* and executive editor of Gannett Suburban Newspapers in the New York counties of Westchester, Rockland and Putnam.

Protection for reputations dates back centuries. In 17th-century England, individuals were imprisoned and even disfigured for making libelous statements. One objective was to prevent criticism of the government. Another was to maintain the peace by avoiding duels. Duels are rare today, and government is freely criticized, but the desire to protect an individual's reputation is just as strong.

Two cases concerning generals, government and reputations are of special interest to journalists and helpful in understanding libel. These extensively covered trials were held in the winter of 1984–1985 in the same federal courthouse in Manhattan.

In one, against CBS correspondent Mike Wallace and producer George Crile, Gen. William C. Westmoreland said a 1982 report by CBS accused him, as commander of U.S. forces in Vietnam, of participating in a "conspiracy at the highest levels of American military intelligence" to underreport enemy troop strength in 1967. The purpose of the alleged underreporting, CBS said, was to create the impression that the United States was winning the war.

The other case was based on a 1983 *Time* magazine cover story, "Verdict on the Massacre," about Israel's 1982 judicial inquiry into the massacre of several hundred civilians in two Palestinian refugee camps in Lebanon. The *Time* article

was about Israeli Gen. Ariel Sharon's conversations with the Gemayel family on the day after Bashir Gemayel's assassination. *Time* said Sharon had "reportedly discussed with the Gemayels the need for the Phalangists to take revenge for the assassination of Bashir."

Libel is damage to a person's reputation caused by exposing a person to public hatred, contempt or ridicule. Both generals sued because they considered the

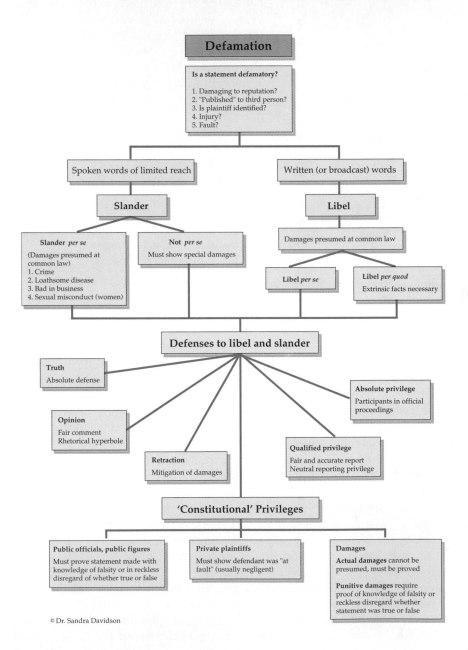

Figure 22.1

*An understanding of libel
and related concepts is
essential for journalists.*

reporters' statements to be serious attacks on their reputations, not just unpleasant comments. Their attorneys knew they would have to show that the generals had suffered hatred, contempt or ridicule.

Westmoreland was concerned that the CBS broadcast about a "conspiracy" to underreport enemy troop strength would lead people to believe he had deceived President Lyndon Johnson about the enemy. Sharon's concern was that the *Time* report suggested he had allowed, even encouraged, "revenge" killings of hundreds of civilians while he was in command in Lebanon.

The Westmoreland case ended before being submitted to the jury when both parties signed a joint statement announcing an out-of-court settlement on Feb. 19, 1985. The sudden and surprising end to the case has been attributed to the damaging testimony of two former subordinates, one a former classmate of Westmoreland at West Point. In the joint statement CBS said it made no concessions and paid no money to Westmoreland. Both parties said they were satisfied "that their respective positions have been effectively placed before the public for its consideration and that continuing the legal process at this stage would serve no further purpose." Legal fees in the case amounted to an estimated $8 million to $10 million.

The Sharon case is more helpful for understanding the complexities of libel. The jury's decision was in three parts. The first part of the verdict was in answer to the question: Was the paragraph concerning Sharon defamatory? The jury said it was. This means the *Time* article had damaged Sharon's reputation and brought him into hatred, contempt or ridicule.

The second question for the jury was this: Was the paragraph concerning Sharon and revenge false? Again the jury answered affirmatively. If the answer had been no, the case would have ended there. Truth is a complete defense for libel.

The third question for the jury was: Was the paragraph published with "actual malice" — with knowledge that it was false or with reckless disregard of whether it was false ("serious doubt" that it was true)? The jury answered no. Thus the trial ended in favor of *Time* magazine, despite the jury ruling that the article was defamatory.

Courts define four categories of defamation to help jurors like those in the Sharon case decide if someone's reputation has been damaged because of exposure to public hatred, contempt or ridicule. They are:

1. Accusing someone of a crime. (This may have been the basis for the Sharon suit.)
2. Damaging a person in his or her public office, profession or occupation. (Even if the statements by CBS and *Time* against Westmoreland and Sharon did not accuse them of crimes, the statements did damage them in their profession as military men.)
3. Accusing a person of serious immorality (such as accusing a spouse of infidelity). Many states have statutes that make an accusation of unchastity a cause of action in a libel suit.

"Journalists don't believe . . . the Freedom of Information Act was created to be turned on us as an excuse to hide information."

— Sarah Overstreet, columnist

Truth is a complete defense for libel.

4. Accusing someone of having a loathsome (i.e., contagious) disease. This category was fading as a source of defamation; however, the AIDS epidemic helped it reappear.

This does not mean you never can say a person committed a crime, was unethical in business, was adulterous or had a loathsome disease. It does mean you must be certain that what you write is true.

A misleading headline can also lead to a defamation suit, even though the story is correct. In a case involving Brian "Kato" Kaelin, who lived at O.J. Simpson's home at the time of the knifing deaths of Nicole Simpson and Ronald Goldman, the Ninth Circuit Court of Appeals ruled on a *Globe* headline that said, "COPS THINK KATO DID IT!" The headline was "not necessarily cured" by a nondefamatory story, the court decided. The significance for journalists is that an inaccurate headline can create legal problems, even if the story itself is faultless.

Libel Suit Defenses

There are three traditional defenses against libel: truth, privilege, and fair comment and criticism. Two other constitutional defenses — the actual malice and negligence tests — also help libel defendants.

Truth

Truth is the best defense against libel. However, knowing the truth is one thing; proving it is another. In April 1986, the Supreme Court ruled that a person who sues for libel must prove that the news account was false. This judgment sets a uniform rule for all 50 states: The burden of proof in libel cases involving matters of public concern is on the plaintiff. This decision, however, does not change the responsibility of the reporter to seek the truth in every possible way.

You cannot be certain, for example, whether a person charged with arson actually started the fire. Who told you that Joe Jones started the fire? The first source to check is the police or fire report. If a police officer or fire marshal says that Jones started a fire, you can report not that Jones did it but that he has been accused of doing it. Unless you have information you would be willing to present in court, you should go no further.

Be sure you report no more than what you know is true. You might, for instance, learn that Helen Greer has not paid any of her bills for two years, and the only way she can get merchandise is to pay cash when goods are delivered. Who gave you this information? If the truth is that a former employee of Ms. Greer told you, that is all the truth you have. The truth, then, is not that Helen Greer has not paid any of her bills for two years and has a bad credit rating. The only truth is that she was accused of bad business practices by a former employee.

Without supporting evidence for charges like those, careful journalists will not print or broadcast the charges. If you do and your employer is sued for damaging Helen Greer's reputation, you would have to try to convince the court that the charge was true. But what if Ms. Greer presents canceled checks and calls suppliers who deny that she owes them money? You would lose the libel suit. You must be able to prove that Helen Greer really is a credit risk before you print or broadcast that she is.

When a newspaper in Oklahoma reported that a wrestling coach had been accused of requiring a sixth-grader, who wanted to rejoin the team, to submit to a whipping by his fellow students while crawling naked through the legs of team members, the coach sued. He claimed damage to his reputation.

In cases like this, the reporter has to be certain not just that one or more participants told of the incident but also that the statements were true. In court, some participants might testify to an occurrence and others might testify the incident never took place. A jury would have to decide on the credibility of the participants.

Although you must always strive for absolute truth in all of your stories, the courts will settle for what is known as **substantial truth** in most cases. This means that you must be able to prove the essential elements of all you write.

Privilege

In addition to truth, the courts traditionally have allowed another defense against libel: **privilege.** This defense applies when you are covering any of the three branches of government. The courts allow legislators, judges and government executives the **absolute privilege** to say anything — true or false — when acting in their official capacities. The rationale is that the public interest is served when an official is allowed to speak freely and fearlessly about making laws, carrying them out or punishing those who do not obey them. Similarly, a participant in a judicial proceeding, such as an attorney, court clerk or judge, is absolutely privileged to make false and even defamatory statements about another person during that proceeding.

In the executive branch it isn't always clear whose statements are privileged and when. The head of state and the major officers of executive departments of the federal and state governments are covered. However, minor officials might not enjoy the protection of absolute privilege.

As a reporter you do have a qualified privilege, sometimes called "neutral reporting" or "conditional privilege," to report what public officials say. Your privilege is conditioned on your report's providing full, fair and accurate coverage of the court session, the legislative session or the president's press conference, even if any one of the participants made defamatory statements. You can quote anything the president of the United States says without fear of losing a libel suit, even if the president is not acting in an official capacity. Reporters have a qualified privilege to report unofficial statements. But there are many other levels of executives in federal, state and local government. Mayors of small towns, for instance, often hold part-time positions. Although you are conditionally privileged to report on what those officials say when they are acting in their official capacities, a problem can arise when the part-time mayor says something defamatory when not acting in an official capacity. Courts in some jurisdictions might grant a qualified privilege; some might not.

Fair Comment and Criticism

In some writing you may be commenting or criticizing rather than reporting. The courts have protected writers who comment on and criticize the public offerings of anyone in the public eye. Included in this category are actors and actresses, sports figures, public officials and other newsworthy persons. Most often, such writing occurs in reviews of plays, books or movies, or in commentary on service received in hotels and restaurants.

The courts call this **fair comment and criticism.** You are protected as long as you do not misstate any of the facts on which you base your comments or criticism, or as long as you do not wrongly imply that you possess undisclosed, damaging information that forms the basis of your opinion. Merely labeling a fact as an opinion will not result in opinion protection, the U.S. Supreme Court ruled in 1990.

The Actual Malice Test

A reporter who has tried diligently to do all possible research for a story will be able to meet the actual malice test and win a libel action. The key is verification: checking the information with as many sources as possible.

It was a small but momentous step from fair comment and criticism to the case of *The New York Times* vs. Sullivan. In 1964 the U.S. Supreme Court decided that First Amendment protection was broader than just the traditional defenses of truth and privilege and that the press needed even greater freedom in coverage of public officials.

The case started with an advertisement for funds in *The New York Times* of March 29, 1960, by the Committee to Defend Martin Luther King Jr. and the Struggle for Freedom in the South. The advertisement contained factual errors concerning the police, according to Montgomery, Ala., Commissioner L.B. Sullivan. He thought the errors damaged his reputation, and he won a half-million-dollar judgment against *The New York Times* in an Alabama trial court.

The Supreme Court said it was considering the case "against the background of a profound national commitment to the principle that debate on public issues should be uninhibited, robust and wide open." Thus Justice William Brennan wrote that the Constitution requires a federal rule prohibiting a public official from recovering damages from the press for a defamatory falsehood relating to his or her official conduct, unless the public official can prove the press had knowledge that what was printed was false or that the story was printed with reckless disregard of whether it was false.

The justices thereby gave you protection to write virtually anything about officeholders or candidates unless you know that what you are writing is false or you recklessly disregard the truth of what you write. They called this the **actual malice test.**

The actual malice test was applied later in a case involving a story on CBS's *60 Minutes* about a retired Army officer. Col. Anthony Herbert contended the broadcast falsely portrayed him as a liar. He tried to prove that producer Barry Lando recklessly disregarded whether or not it was a false broadcast. Herbert asked some questions that Lando claimed were protected by the First Amendment because they inquired into his state of mind and into the editorial processes during the production of the program.

The Supreme Court said in 1979 that the "thoughts and editorial processes of the alleged defamer would be open to examination." The court pointed out that protecting the editorial process "would constitute a substantial interference with the ability of a defamation plaintiff to establish . . . malice" as required by the *New York Times* case. The press greeted the ruling with displeasure, though some attorneys noted that the inquiry into the editorial process could help journalists as much as hurt them. It could help by permitting journalists and their attorneys to demonstrate how careful they were in gathering and selecting the information printed.

Assume, for example, you are told that years ago your town's mayor had been involved in a bootlegging operation. Your source is a friend of the mayor who knew him 30 years ago in Idaho. You print the story. After it is published, you find it was not the mayor but his brother who was the bootlegger. The mayor sues. You are in trouble. You must try to convince the court that you should have been able to trust your source and that you did not act with actual malice. If the source had given you many valid stories in the past, you might be able to convince the court that you had good reason to believe what you were told. You also would have to show what else you did or failed to do before you printed the story. Did you call anyone in Idaho to check? Did you talk to the mayor? Did you try other ways to verify the information? All these questions could be asked as the court tries to decide whether you recklessly disregarded the truth.

Usually a reporter who has tried diligently to do all possible research for a story will be able to meet the actual malice test and win a libel action. The key is verification: checking the information with as many sources as possible.

The decision in the Sharon case discussed earlier in the chapter is an example of the burden of proving actual malice against the press. The jury decided that *Time* did not know at the time the article in question was printed that its statement about Gen. Sharon was false.

In 1991, the Supreme Court decided Masson vs. *The New Yorker*, the so-called "fabricated quotes" case. Overruling a lower court's decision that journalists could fictionalize quotations by making rational interpretations of speakers' remarks, the Supreme Court protected the sanctity of quotation marks. But the court also made clear that not every deliberate change in a quotation is libelous. Only a "material change in the meaning conveyed by a statement" poses a problem.

Although Masson won the right to try his case, he lost against all defendants. Janet Malcolm, the journalist who misquoted Masson, won in 1994.

Standards Applicable to Public Figures

The actual malice protection was expanded in two cases in 1967 to include not only public officials but also public figures — persons in the public eye but not in public office.

The first case stemmed from a *Saturday Evening Post* article that accused Coach Wally Butts of conspiring to fix a 1962 football game between Georgia and

Alabama. At the time of the article, Butts was the athletic director of the University of Georgia. The article, titled "The Story of a College Football Fix," was prefaced by a note from the editors of the *Post* stating:

Not since the Chicago White Sox threw the 1919 World Series has there been a sports story as shocking as this one. . . . Before the University of Georgia played the University of Alabama . . . Wally	Butts . . . gave (to Alabama's coach) . . . Georgia's plays, defensive patterns, all the significant secrets Georgia's football team possessed.

The *Post* reported that, because of an electronic error about a week before the game, George Burnett, an Atlanta insurance salesman, accidentally had overheard a telephone conversation between Butts and the head coach of Alabama, Paul Bryant.

Coach Butts sued Curtis Publishing Co., publishers of the *Post*, and won a verdict for $60,000 in general damages and $3 million in punitive, or punishment, damages. Curtis Publishing appealed the case to the Supreme Court and lost. The trial judge reduced the amount of the damages to $460,000.

The second case was decided the same day. Gen. Edwin Walker sued the Associated Press for distributing a news dispatch giving an eyewitness account by an AP staffer on the campus of the University of Mississippi in the fall of 1962. The AP reported that Gen. Walker personally had led a student charge against federal marshals during a riot on the Mississippi campus. The marshals were attempting to enforce a court decree ordering the enrollment of a black student.

Walker was a retired general at the time of the publication. He had won a $2 million libel suit in a trial court. However, the Supreme Court ruled against him.

In both cases the stories were wrong. In both, the actual malice test was applied. What was the difference between the Butts and Walker cases?

The justices said the football story was in no sense "hot news." They noted that the person who said he had heard the conversation was on probation in connection with bad-check charges and that *Post* personnel had not viewed his notes before publication. The court also said, as evidence of actual malice on the part of the *Post*, that no one looked at the game films to see if the information was accurate; that a regular staffer, instead of a football expert, was assigned to the story; and that no check was made with someone knowledgeable in the sport. In short, the *Post* had not done an adequate job of reporting.

The evidence in the Walker case was considerably different. The court said the news in the Walker case required immediate dissemination because of the riot on campus. The justices noted that the AP received the information from a correspondent who was present on the campus and gave every indication of being trustworthy and competent.

In an earlier case, the Supreme Court had defined a public official as a government employee who has, or appears to the public to have, substantial responsibility for or control over the conduct of governmental affairs. In the Butts and Walker cases the court used two definitions of "public figure":

1. A person who, like Butts, has assumed a role of special prominence in the affairs of society — someone who has pervasive power and influence in a community.
2. A person who, like Walker, has thrust himself or herself into the forefront of a particular public controversy in order to influence the resolution of the issues involved.

There are other examples of public figures. A college professor who has become involved with any public controversy ranging from grading practices to gay rights may have made himself or herself a public figure. A police officer who is the leader of the Police Association may be a public figure because of his or her power and influence.

In the 1970s the Supreme Court decided three cases that help journalists determine who is and is not a public figure. The first case involved Mrs. Russell A. Firestone, who sued for libel after *Time* magazine reported that her husband's divorce petition had been granted on grounds of extreme cruelty and adultery. Mrs. Firestone, who had married into the Firestone Tire and Rubber Co. family, claimed that those were not the grounds for the divorce. She also insisted that she was not a public figure with the burden of proving actual malice.

The Supreme Court agreed. Even though she had held press conferences and hired a clipping service, the court ruled that she had not thrust herself into the forefront of a public controversy in an attempt to influence the resolution of the issues involved. The court admitted that marital difficulties of extremely wealthy individuals may be of some interest to some portion of the reading public but added that Mrs. Firestone had not freely chosen to publicize private matters about her married life. The justices said she was compelled to go to court to "obtain legal release from the bonds of matrimony." They said she assumed no "special prominence in the resolution of public questions." The case was sent back to Florida for a finding of fault, and a new trial was ordered. Eventually, the case was settled out of court.

The second case involved Sen. William Proxmire of Wisconsin, who had started what he called the Golden Fleece Award. Each month he announced a winner who, in his opinion, had wasted government money. One such winner was Ronald Hutchinson, a behavioral scientist who had received federal funding for research designed to determine why animals clench their teeth. Hutchinson had published articles about his research in professional publications. In deciding that Hutchinson was not a public figure, the court ruled that he "did not thrust himself or his views into public controversy to influence others." The court admitted there may have been legitimate concerns about the way public funds were being spent but said this was not enough to make Hutchinson a public figure.

The third case concerned an individual found guilty of contempt of court in 1958 for his failure to appear before a grand jury investigating Soviet espionage in the United States. Ilya Wolston's name had been included in a list of people indicted for serving as Soviet agents in a 1974 book published by the Reader's Digest Association. Wolston had not been indicted, and he sued.

The Supreme Court, in deciding that he was not a public figure, found that Wolston had played only a minor role in whatever public controversy there may have been concerning the investigation of Soviet espionage. The court added that a private individual is not automatically transformed into a public figure merely by becoming involved in or being associated with a matter that attracts public attention.

Lower courts have ruled that in other situations individuals have become public figures by the nature of their activities. These include an attorney in local practice for 32 years who was involved in major disputes and social activities, a newspaper publisher who regularly took strong public stands on controversial issues, and a college dean who had attempted to influence the proposed abolition of his position.

Assume you are covering a proposal to fluoridate the water of your town. Among the individuals you may write about are:

- The mayor (or town or county supervisor), who obviously is a public official.
- A doctor who has a private medical practice but is so concerned about the effects of fluoridation that he has made many public speeches. He has become a public figure because he has thrust himself to the forefront of the fluoridation controversy.
- A former state senator who now owns a radio station and is well-known in the community. She, too, is a public figure because of her prominence in the affairs of the city.

How about the attorney who is handling the litigation for the individuals opposed to fluoridation? If he also is a spokesman for this group, he may be treated as a public figure. But if he does no more than file the legal papers with the courts and leaves the press conferences and public appearances to others, he has not thrust himself to the forefront of the controversy. Do you have the same protection from a libel action when you write about him as you do when you write about the persons you are certain are public figures or public officials?

A 1974 Supreme Court decision says the answer usually is no. In the landmark Gertz vs. Welch case, the justices said states may give more protection to private individuals if a newspaper or radio or television station damages their reputations than if the reputations of either public officials or public figures are damaged.

Standards Applicable to Private Citizens

Private citizens who sue for punitive damages must meet the same actual malice test as public officials and public figures do. Because of the Gertz case, states have been allowed to set their own standards for libel cases involving private citizens who sue only for actual damages. Roughly 20 states and the District of Columbia have adopted a **negligence test,** which requires you to use the same care in gathering facts and writing your story as any reasonable reporter would use under the same or similar circumstances. If you make every effort to be fair and answer all the questions a reasonable person may ask, you probably would pass the negligence test.

One state, New York, has adopted a "gross irresponsibility test." A few states have established a more stringent standard that requires private citizens to prove actual malice. In some states the matter is unsettled because of conflicting cases or cases that are still pending, or because there have been no cases to resolve the issue.

Libel Remains a Danger

Despite all the available defenses, libel remains a serious risk to journalists' financial health, as the following examples demonstrate:

In 1995, ABC paid an estimated $15 million to $20 million in attorney fees to Philip Morris tobacco company and issued an apology to settle a suit for broadcasting on *Day One* that the cigarette maker added nicotine to its cigarettes.

In 1997, a Texas jury awarded a record $222.7 million to a defunct bond-brokerage firm against Dow Jones & Co., which owns *The Wall Street Journal*. The judge threw out $200 million in punitive damages but let stand the $22.7 million in actual damages for a *Journal* story about "bond daddies."

On the other hand, appellate courts have also been rigorous in striking down libel judgments. For example, in 1999, the Eleventh Circuit Court of Appeals struck down a $10 million judgment awarded by a Florida jury to Bank Atlantic and its chief executive, Alan Levan, for a *20/20* segment featuring investors who claimed they were cheated. Based on the large number of sources it interviewed, ABC entertained no serious doubts about the truth of its broadcast, the appeals court ruled. In 2000, the Supreme Court let that decision stand.

In 2002, the Sixth Circuit Court of Appeals reversed a $10.7 million verdict awarded by a Tennessee jury. *Sports Illustrated* had said under the heading "The Fix Was In" that a former professional boxer, Randall "Tex" Cobb, had fixed a boxing match and then used drugs. The appeals court agreed with the magazine that even if its story was wrong, the magazine did not act with actual malice because it had no particular reason to entertain serious doubts about the veracity of the story based on interviews with the boxer's opponent and a boxing expert. The Supreme Court also let that judgment stand.

The Internet is not immune to libel suits either.

In 1991, CompuServe won a libel suit brought against it in a New York federal trial court. CompuServe had contracted with another company to provide a daily newspaper about journalism for CompuServe subscribers. That second company used a third company to provide the newsletter, and CompuServe made no attempt to review the newsletter's contents.

The court referred to CompuServe as a "high technology" company that is part of the "information industry revolution," but then applied old law. Because CompuServe did not try to exercise any editorial control, the court let CompuServe off the hook in the libel case. In effect, the court shoved CompuServe into a safe pigeonhole — that of libraries, news vendors or bookstores that are unaware of libelous material in the information they sell. No library can be held responsible if a book the librarian did not review contains libelous material. CompuServe, the court said, was merely providing an "electronic, for-profit library."

In 1995, Prodigy found itself in a different pigeonhole — that of a publisher. Prodigy controlled the content of its computer bulletin boards in an effort to promote itself as "family oriented." It used an automatic software screening program to look for forbidden words, and its editorial staff deleted allegedly offensive notes. Unfortunately for Prodigy, no list of software-generated words could screen for libel. The New York trial court hearing the case ruled that by exercising editorial control, Prodigy was "expressly differentiating itself from its competition and expressly likening itself to a newspaper." Thus Prodigy could be held responsible for libel.

In 1996, however, Congress effectively overturned the Prodigy decision by passing legislation that protects Internet service providers that engage in "'good Samaritan' blocking and screening of offensive material." Congress proclaimed, "No provider or user of an interactive computer service shall be treated as the publisher or speaker of any information provided by another information content provider."

INVASION OF PRIVACY

"There are only two occasions when Americans respect privacy. . . . Those are prayer and fishing."

— Herbert Hoover,
31st U.S. president

Libel is damage to an individual's reputation. **Invasion of privacy** is a violation of a person's right to be left alone.

As a reporter, you may be risking an invasion of privacy suit under any of these circumstances:

- You physically intrude into a private area to get a story or picture — an act closely related to trespass.
- You publish a story or photograph about someone that is misleading and thus you portray that person in a "false light."
- You disclose something about an individual's private affairs that is true but also is offensive to individuals of ordinary sensibilities.

Invasion of privacy may also be claimed if someone's name or picture is used in an advertisement or for similar purposes of trade. Called "appropriation," this does not affect you when you are performing your reporting duties.

Consent is a basic defense in invasion of privacy suits. Make sure, however, that your use of the material does not exceed the consent given.

Another basic defense in an invasion of privacy suit is that you're a reporter covering a newsworthy situation. The courts usually protect the press against invasion of privacy suits when it is reporting matters of legitimate public interest. There are exceptions, however.

Trespassing

One exception arises when you invade someone's privacy by entering private property to get a story. You cannot trespass on private property to get a story or take a picture even if it is newsworthy. The courts will not protect you when you are a trespasser. Two *Life* magazine staffers lost an invasion of privacy suit because, posing as patients, they went into a man's home to get a story about a faith healer. They lost the case even though they were working with the district attorney and the state board of health.

You may enter private property only when you are invited by the owner or renter. In 1999, the court effectively prohibited the common practice of allowing journalists to accompany police on raids onto private property.

Portraying in a "False Light"

The courts also will not protect you if you invade someone's privacy by publishing misleading information about that person. For example, a legal problem arises if a photograph or information from a true story about a careful pedestrian struck by a careless driver is used again in connection with a story, say, about careless pedestrians. The pedestrian who was hit could file a lawsuit charging libel, "false light" invasion of privacy or, in some states, both.

Some states do not recognize "false light" invasion of privacy and insist that libel is the appropriate form of suit. But "false light" suits can cover situations where a picture or story is misleading but not defamatory. Even flattering material can place a person in an unwanted, false light.

Causing Unwanted Publicity Offensive to a Person of Ordinary Sensibilities

The third type of invasion of privacy that the courts recognize — unwanted publicity — arises from stories about incidents that, because they are true, are not defamatory but can be offensive to a person of ordinary sensibilities. An example is a picture published by *Sports Illustrated* in which a football fan's pants zipper was open. The fan sued for invasion of privacy but lost.

The courts say that in order for privacy to be invaded, there must be a morbid and sensational prying into private lives. Merely being the subject of an unflattering or uncomfortable article is not enough. For example, the Supreme Court held in 1975 and again in 1989 that truthfully reporting the name of a rape victim is permitted. In 1976 and in 1979 the justices upheld the right of the press to publish the names of juveniles involved with the law because the information was truthful and of public significance.

HIDDEN CAMERAS AND NEWS-GATHERING

Increasingly, stories in which journalists use hidden cameras have been causing problems for journalists and the courts. Jurists seek to answer this question: Under what circumstances does a person have a "reasonable expectation of privacy"?

In 1994, an ABC reporter hired by the Psychic Marketing Group videotaped two psychics, Mark Sanders and Frank Kersis, surreptitiously in a busy workroom.

The reporter produced a news story that cast doubt on the validity of the psychics' advice. If the two men were indeed psychic, the reporter suggested, why didn't they know they were being videotaped? Kersis subsequently died, and his parents filed a lawsuit charging ABC with wrongful death. The news story, they argued, had caused their son, a recovering alcoholic, to start drinking again, leading to his death.

A California jury awarded Sanders, the surviving psychic, $1.2 million for a violation of "the right to be free of photographic invasion." A California appeals court overturned that award on grounds that Sanders had no reasonable expectation of privacy in the busy workplace area. But the California Supreme Court reversed that decision and argued that Sanders did have a reasonable expectation of privacy from a television audience. The case never went back to trial. In February 2000, ABC settled out of court for more than $900,000.

In 1995, ABC won a fraud, trespass and invasion of privacy suit involving a *PrimeTime Live* hidden-camera report on ophthalmic clinics. Perhaps that gave *PrimeTime Live* the confidence to do a 1997 hidden-camera report on unsanitary food conditions at a Food Lion grocery store. But that report led to a suit for fraud, trespass and breach of duty or loyalty. The case resulted in a jury verdict of $5.5 million in punitive damages, later reduced to a nominal amount. The trial judge said two reporters provided false information to Food Lion when applying for the jobs that gave them access to the allegedly unsanitary area. One reporter indicated on her job application that she had prior experience as a meat wrapper, a statement that was false. In awarding damages, the judge cited those untruthful claims as a contributing factor.

In 1997, ABC prevailed over Beverly Deteresa, an attendant on a flight taken by O.J. Simpson shortly after the deaths of Nicole Brown Simpson and Ronald Goldman. Five seconds of a secretly taped interview, shot outside her condominium on a public street, aired on *Day One*. The Ninth Circuit found an "insubstantial impact on privacy interests. Deteresa does not dispute that she was videotaped in public view by a cameraperson in a public place."

In 2002, the Ninth Circuit Court of Appeals found no reasonable expectation of privacy after *PrimeTime Live*, which was covering faulty testing on Pap smears, broadcast footage obtained in a medical lab by reporters who used a camera hidden in a wig.

A local television station lost a suit because it aired a videotape of a car-accident victim in a rescue helicopter. The California Supreme Court concluded, "Although the attendance of reporters and photographers at the scene of an accident is to be expected, we are aware of no law or custom permitting the press to ride in ambulances or enter hospital rooms during treatment without the patient's consent."

PROTECTION OF SOURCES AND NOTES

Another area you must know about is your ability — or inability — to protect your sources and notes. The problem may arise in various situations. A grand jury that is investigating a murder may ask you to reveal the source of a story you wrote about the murder. You may be asked to testify at a criminal or a civil trial. Or the police may obtain a warrant to search the news room, including your desk.

The conflict that arises is between a reporter's need to protect sources of information and the duty of every citizen to testify to help the courts determine justice. Your work as a reporter will take you to events that are important and newsworthy. Anyone wanting the facts about an event can subpoena you to bring in all the details. Journalists usually resist. They work for their newspaper or radio or television station, not a law-enforcement agency. Their ability to gather information would be compromised if sources knew that their identities or their information would go to the police.

Some protection against testifying — shield laws — has been adopted by these 31 states:

Alabama	Kentucky	New York
Alaska	Louisiana	North Carolina
Arizona	Maryland	North Dakota
Arkansas	Michigan	Ohio
California	Minnesota	Oklahoma
Colorado	Montana	Oregon
Delaware	Nebraska	Pennsylvania
Florida	Nevada	Rhode Island
Georgia	New Jersey	South Carolina
Illinois	New Mexico	Tennessee
Indiana		

"[The media] seek to maintain a balance on the constantly shifting tightrope of personal privacy, access to information and government accountability."

— John R. Finnegan Sr., former newspaper editor

Congress had not acted in this area in part because journalists themselves were divided about the desirability of such legislation.

However, Congress did pass the **Privacy Protection Act** of 1980. Under that act, federal, state and local law-enforcement officers generally may not use a search warrant to search news rooms. Instead, they must get a subpoena for documents, which instructs reporters and editors to hand over the material. Officers may use a warrant to search news rooms only if they suspect a reporter of being involved in a crime or if immediate action is needed to prevent bodily harm, loss of life or destruction of the material.

The difference between a search warrant and a subpoena is great. Officers with a search warrant can knock on the door, enter the news room and search on their own. A subpoena does not permit officers to search the news room. A subpoena for specific documents requires reporters to turn over the material to authorities at a predetermined time and place. In addition, it gives reporters time to challenge in court the necessity of surrendering the material.

Even in states with shield laws, judges in most criminal cases involving grand juries will not allow you to keep your sources secret. In other criminal cases, courts may allow confidentiality if a three-part test is met. Supreme Court Justice Potter Stewart suggested this test in his dissent in Branzburg vs. Hayes, decided in 1972:

Government officials must, therefore, demonstrate that the information sought is clearly relevant to a precisely defined subject of government inquiry. . . . They must demonstrate that it is reasonable to think the witness in question has that information. . . . And they must show that there is not any means of obtaining the information less destructive of First Amendment liberties. . . . In civil litigation you may be permitted to keep sources confidential in most cases unless the court finds that the information sought is unavailable from other sources and highly relevant to the underlying litigation or of such critical importance to the lawsuit that it goes to the heart of the plaintiff's claim.

If you are sued for libel, you will find it difficult both to protect your sources and to win the lawsuit. The court might well rule against you on whether a statement is true or false if it came from a source you refuse to name. Branzburg vs. Hayes decided that reporters are obliged to respond to grand jury subpoenas as other citizens do and to answer questions relevant to the investigation of a crime. According to the court, then, reporters cannot protect their sources before a grand jury. In other words, criminal prosecutions carry more weight than civil cases. For example, William Farr spent 46 days in near solitary confinement in a Los Angeles jail in 1971 for refusing to disclose to a judge his source for a newspaper article about the trial of Charles Manson, the mass murderer (see Figure 22.2).

The principle of relevancy extends back to the Marie Torre case in 1958. Torre spent 10 days in jail in New York for refusing to disclose a confidential source the court said was relevant in a libel action by Judy Garland against CBS. Others have been jailed or threatened with jail by judges since John Peter

Figure 22.2
After refusing to disclose to a judge his source for a 1971 article about the trial of mass murderer Charles Manson, reporter William Farr was taken to jail in this police van.

Zenger, editor of the *New York Weekly Journal,* refused to reveal the name of the author of a letter published in the *Journal* in 1735.

In Texas, a federal judge found freelance writer Vanessa Leggett in contempt of court because she refused to turn over her notes to a grand jury investigating the shooting death of Houston socialite Doris Angelton. Leggett went to jail and stayed there until Jan. 4, 2002 — a total of 168 days.

The only way to avoid such confrontation with the courts is not to promise a source you will keep his or her name confidential. Only for the most compelling reason should you get yourself into this judicial conflict between the First Amendment right of a free press and the Sixth Amendment right to a fair trial.

In 1991, the U.S. Supreme Court ruled in Cohen vs. Cowles Media Co. that the First Amendment does not prevent a source from suing a news organization if a reporter has promised the source confidentiality but the newspaper publishes the source's name anyway.

ACCESS TO COURTS

Judicial acknowledgment of the right of access to courtrooms has had a sudden, cometlike history since 1979. The Supreme Court held in 1979 that "members of the public have no constitutional right" under the Sixth Amendment to attend criminal trials. In a reversal exactly one year later, the justices held that the public and the press have a First Amendment right to attend criminal trials, although not an absolute right. Trial judges could close criminal trials when an "overriding interest" justified such closure. Judges' basic concern when they close trials is to protect the right of the accused person under the Sixth Amendment to an "impartial jury" — often translated by attorneys as "a fair trial."

The First Amendment prevents the government from conducting business — even trials — in secret. In the Richmond Newspapers case in 1980, Chief Justice Warren Burger traced the unbroken and uncontradicted history of open judicial proceedings in England and the United States. He concluded that there is a "presumption of openness" in criminal trials and pointed out the important role of the news media as representatives of the public.

The next question for the justices was the role of state legislatures in closing trials. A statute in Massachusetts mandated closure of the courtroom during trials for specified sexual offenses involving a victim under 18. The Supreme Court said in 1982 that the mandatory closure statute violated the First Amendment right of access to criminal trials, even though safeguarding the physical and psychological well-being of a minor was a compelling concern. The court said it was up to the state trial judge to decide on a case-by-case basis whether closure is necessary to protect the welfare of a minor victim. The trial court should weigh the minor's age, psychological maturity and understanding, the nature of the crime, the desires of the victim and the interests of parents and relatives.

By 1984 the Supreme Court had decided that openness in criminal trials "enhances both the basic fairness of the criminal trial and the appearance of fairness so essential to public confidence in the system."

But when does a trial actually begin? At what point does the presumption that trial proceedings should be open first apply? Is there a right of access to jury-selection proceedings? The justices said in 1984 that jury selection is a matter of importance "not simply to the adversaries but to the criminal justice system." In writing the majority opinion, Chief Justice Burger said openness has what can be described as "community therapeutic value," after especially violent crimes. He said seeing that the law is being enforced and the criminal justice system is functioning can provide an outlet for the public's understandable reactions and emotions.

Public proceedings assure victims and the community that offenders are being brought to account for their criminal conduct "by jurors fairly and openly selected." Jury selection could be closed, the chief justice said, only when a trial judge finds that closure preserves an "overriding interest" and is narrowly tailored to serve that interest.

Judges are using that option. For instance, when John Gotti was convicted of Mafia activities in New York, the jurors' names were kept secret. Gotti's attorneys unsuccessfully challenged their anonymity. Jurors' names in the Rodney King case, which resulted in riots in Los Angeles in 1992, were also withheld.

In 1986 the Supreme Court decided the issue of right of access to a preliminary hearing. A California court had held a 41-day closed preliminary hearing on the pretext of protecting the accused's Sixth Amendment right to an impartial jury. Chief Justice Burger said the right of the accused to a "fair trial" and the public right of access "are not necessarily inconsistent." He added, "As we have repeatedly recognized, one of the important means of assuring a fair trial is that the process be open to neutral observers." The chief justice acknowledged that some government operations "would be totally frustrated if conducted openly" — a classic example is grand jury proceedings. However, "other proceedings plainly require public access," he said.

Finally, the chief justice said that only an overriding interest found by a trial judge can overcome the presumption of openness of criminal proceedings. Today, 47 states allow cameras in at least some state courtrooms. However, cameras are permitted in only some lower federal courts and are excluded from the U.S. Supreme Court.

Increasingly, courts are using the Internet to post court information. Judge Susan Webber Wright did so in the sexual harassment case that Paula Jones brought against then-President Bill Clinton. Such postings help prevent reporter rushes on the courthouse and make information widely available to the public. (See Chapter 13 for more on crime and the courts.)

COPYRIGHT AND FAIR USE

The purpose of copyright law is to ensure compensation to authors for contributing to the common good by publishing their works. The Constitution provides for this in Article 1, Section 8, by giving Congress the power to secure "for limited times to authors and inventors the exclusive right to their respective writing and discoveries." The same section indicates that this provision is intended "to promote the progress of science and useful arts" for the benefit of the public. Copyright laws protect your work and prohibit you from using significant amounts of others' writings without permission and, in some cases, a fee.

Key elements of copyright law include the following:

- Copyrightable works are protected from the moment they are fixed in tangible form, whether published or unpublished.
- Copyright protection begins with a work's "creation and . . . endures for a term consisting of the life of the author and 70 years after the author's death."
- Works for hire and anonymous and pseudonymous works are protected for 95 years from publication or 100 years from creation, whichever is shorter.
- There is a "fair use" limitation on the exclusive rights of copyright owners. In other words, it may be permissible to quote small excerpts from a copyrighted work without permission. According to the Supreme Court, these factors govern fair use:
  1. The purpose and character of the use.
  2. The nature of the copyrighted work.
  3. The substantiality of the portion used in relationship to the copyrighted work as a whole.
  4. The effect on the potential market for or value of the copyrighted work.

Although a work is copyrighted from the moment it is fixed in tangible form, the copyright statute says certain steps are necessary for the work to receive statutory protection. The author or publisher must:

- Publish or reproduce the work with the word "copyright" or the symbol ©, the name of the copyright owner and the year of publication.
- Deposit two copies of the work with the Library of Congress within three months of publication. Failure to do so will not affect the copyright but could lead to the imposition of fines.
- Register the work at the Library of Congress by filling out a form supplied by the Copyright Office and sending the form, the specified number of copies (usually one copy of an unpublished work and two copies of a published work), and a $30 fee to the Copyright Office. The copies and registration fee may be sent together and usually are.

Copyright law has a special provision for broadcasters of live programs. Broadcasters need only make a simultaneous tape of their live broadcasts in order to receive copyright protection. The tape fulfills the requirement that a work be in a "fixed" form for copyright protection. Because a digital form is a "fixed" form, editors of online newspapers already meet that copyright requirement.

Some aspects of U.S. copyright law changed in 1989, when the United States finally joined the 100-year-old Berne Convention, an international copyright treaty, primarily to prevent the pirating of American film productions in other countries. The changes include the following:

- *Placing a copyright notice on a work is no longer necessary to protect a copyright after publication.* This is in line with the Berne Convention principle that the copyright protection should not be subject to formalities. The copyright notice, however, is still widely used because it acts as a bar to an infringer's claim of innocent infringement.
- *Copyright registration is no longer a prerequisite for access to the federal courts for an infringement action.* But registration is required for a copyright owner to recover statutory damages. (Without registration, the copyright owner can recover only the damages he or she can prove, court costs and "reasonable" attorney's fees.) The amount of statutory damages, generally between $750 and $30,000, is determined by the judge. If the infringer was not aware he or she was infringing a copyright, the court may award as little as $200. If the infringement was willful, the court can award up to $150,000. Thus, like the copyright notice, copyright registration remains highly advisable.

In 1990, Congress extended copyright protection to visual artists to protect the integrity of their works. The Internet has provided a rich field for copyright invasion. Copyright law does apply to the Internet, however, and many copyright victims, including *Playboy* magazine, have successfully sued violators.

The Recording Industry Association of America has pursued its copyright rights against file-sharing companies such as Napster and even against students.

Obviously, both case law and statutes that affect the media are constantly changing. It's important for reporters and editors to be aware of those changes. Only if they are will they remain aware of their rights and be able to protect themselves and their companies from costly libel and invasion of privacy litigation.

Suggested Readings

Carter, T. Barton, Franklin, Marc A. and Wright, Jay B. *The First Amendment and the Fourth Estate*, Eighth Edition. Westbury, N.Y.: Foundation Press, 2000.

Holsinger, Ralph and Dilts, Jon Paul. *Media Law*, Fourth Edition. New York: McGraw-Hill, 1997.

Middleton, Kent R., Trager, Robert and Chamberlin, Bill F. *The Law of Public Communication*, Sixth Edition. Boston: Allyn & Bacon, 2003.

Overbeck, Wayne. *Major Principles of Media Law.* Toronto: Thomson Wadsworth, 2004.

Pember, Don R. *Mass Media Law*, Thirteenth Edition. Dubuque, Iowa: McGraw-Hill, 2003.

Teeter, Dwight L. Jr., Le Duc, Don R. and Loving, Bill. *Law of Mass Communications*, Tenth Edition. New York: Foundation Press, 2002.

Suggested Web Sites

www.firstamendmentcenter.org
A wonderful chronology of the "significant historical events, court cases and ideas that have shaped our current system of constitutional First Amendment jurisprudence," presented by the Freedom Forum. Also, stories, commentaries and roundups of First Amendment disputes.

www.firstamendmentcenter.org/sofa_reports/ index.aspx
The First Amendment Center posts online the annual report on the State of the First Amendment. The report discusses the public's ambivalence about First Amendment issues.

www.ldrc.com
Site of the Libel Defense Resource Center Inc., "a nonprofit information clearinghouse organized in 1980 by leading media groups to monitor and promote First Amendment rights, in the libel, privacy and related fields of law." Includes a 50-state survey of media libel law.

www.rcfp.org
The Reporters Committee for Freedom of the Press maintains online "publications and topical guides on First Amendment and Freedom of Information issues." Current hot stories, plus archives and much more.

Exercises

1. Which defense for libel discussed in this chapter would you have used to defend *Time* magazine in the lawsuit filed by Gen. Ariel Sharon? Why?

2. *The New York Times* vs. Sullivan, 376 U.S. 254 (1964), was significant as a landmark decision in favor of the press. Discuss what the consequences for the press might have been if the decision had been different.

3. You are on an assignment with your photographer, who enters a house without permission and photographs the sale of illegal drugs. Discuss the issues raised by the circumstances and explain why you would or would not publish the pictures.

4. Using the Lexis database, determine how the U.S. Supreme Court has used Richmond Newspapers vs. Virginia, 448 U.S. 555 (1980), in later cases dealing with openness in criminal proceedings.

23 Ethics

- From ESPN.com: "A veteran *Sacramento Bee* sports reporter was fired because he hid the fact that he did not file a story about a San Francisco Giants' game from the ballpark. . . ." Jim Van Vlket had watched the game on television. He also used unattributed quotes from other news sources. He was fired.
- Jayson Blair, young star reporter of *The New York Times*, plagiarized (that's how he got caught), made up scenes and sources, said he was in places he never was, made all kinds of errors — and bragged about fooling the best of them. He was fired, and top *Times* bosses, Executive Editor Howell Raines and Managing Editor Gerald Boyd, resigned.
- Pulitzer Prize–winning *New York Times* reporter Rick Bragg boasted about using details in a story — and not giving the stringers any credit. The *Times* accepted his resignation.
- From *Wired News:* "Noted War Blogger Cops to Copying." Sean-Paul Kelley, so well known for his comments on the war in Iraq that he was interviewed by *The New York Times*, NBC's *Nightly News*, *Newsweek Online* and National Public Radio, copied word-for-word from Stratfor, the Austin, Tex.-based commercial intelligence company.
- Avid Chicago Cubs fan Steve Bartman reached out for a ball that left-fielder Moises Alou could have caught. The Florida Marlins, losing 3-0 in the eighth inning, went on to score eight runs and win. Despite threats to his life, not only did news media name Bartman, but many also ran his picture and address.
- When superstar Los Angeles Laker Kobe Bryant was arrested for sexual assault, not only did some media outlets name the accuser, but some ran her picture and gave personal details of her life, including the state of her mental health.
- The California *North County Times* apologized to readers for running a photo that had been digitally altered to remove words from the back of a player's uniform. Said the paper in an editorial: "Such a change to a photograph violated the truth as captured by the camera and is a falsification that breaks the ethical standards of this newspaper."
- From Tom Walter on commercialappeal.com: A news report on WREG-TV in Memphis began this way: "The grainy, jerky black and

white pictures set you on edge. The camera focuses on a door knob. A clock radio on it, a glowing computer monitor. It lands on a person sleeping in a single bed." WPTY-TV and WMC-TV also re-created parts of the same story. It was a dramatization. But those words never appeared on the screen.

These are just a few recent well-known transgressions of journalists, and yet, arguably, journalism has never been practiced in a more ethical way in this country. How can that be? The answer is simple: Today, responsible journalism discusses openly its failings. So — watch out!

Journalism as a profession has been slow to establish a mandatory and enforced code because of a fear that it might in some way infringe upon freedom of the press.

In other professions, enforcing a code means the profession must have the power to keep people from practicing unless they have membership or a license to practice. That also means that the profession must have the power to suspend a license and to keep members from practicing if they violate the code of the profession.

For some professions, the state requires a license to practice. If as a condition of keeping that license, people may not express certain ideas, that is a form of censorship. Because journalists are not licensed by states, it is difficult to determine who is a journalist. In fact, the Supreme Court has said that it does not want to define a journalist.

Therefore, government does not keep anyone from practicing journalism, although individual news organizations have established and enforced codes of ethics that have restricted journalists from practicing journalism in their organizations. For example, some journalists who have plagiarized have been suspended or fired from their news organizations.

Because of the wide range of the First Amendment and its relatively few legal restraints, perhaps no profession has a greater need to discuss proper means of conduct than journalism. As the Commission on Freedom of the Press concluded in 1947, unless journalists set their own limits on what is acceptable and responsible, government will eventually and inevitably do it for them.

Associations of journalists such as the Society of Professional Journalists do have codes of conduct. Of course, journalists do not have to belong to such organizations to practice journalism, but at least half of all newspapers and television stations now have written codes of ethics. Larger news organizations are more likely to have them.

Critics of journalism codes of ethics condemn them for being hopelessly general and therefore ineffective or for being overly restrictive. Advocates argue that strict codes might improve journalists' credibility. Those who disagree say they merely make journalists easier targets for libel suits.

Whether your organization has a code of ethics or not, you should develop your own ethical values and principles. Your upbringing, and perhaps your religious training and education, have already helped prepare you to do that.

THREE ETHICAL PHILOSOPHIES

Your personal ethics may derive from the way you answer this fundamental question: Does the end always justify the means? Should you ever do something that is not good in itself in order to achieve a goal that you think is good?

If you answer "no" to that question, you are in some sense an absolutist or a legalist, and you are likely to subscribe to *deontological* ethics. If you answer "yes" to that question, you are more of a relativist and are likely to subscribe to *teleological* ethics. If you answer "maybe" or "sometimes," you subscribe to *situation* ethics.

Don't be put off by the philosophical jargon. To understand ethical thinking, to be able to discuss ethics and to solve ethical dilemmas that arise on the job, you need to learn the vocabulary of ethicists.

Deontological Ethics

Deontological ethics is the ethics of duty. According to this philosophy, you have a duty to do what is right. Deontologists believe that some actions are always right and some are always wrong, that there exists in nature (or, for those with religious faith, in divine revelation) a fixed set of principles or laws from which there should be no deviation. For a deontologist, the end never justifies the means. That belief is why some refer to this ethical philosophy as **absolutism** or legalism.

An absolutist or legalist sees one clear duty: to discover the rules and to follow them. If it is wrong to lie, it is always wrong to lie. Suppose a stranger comes to your door and asks where your roommates are so that he can murder them. If you were an absolutist, you would not lie to save their lives. An absolutist or legalistic ethical philosophy could induce a conscientious objector not only to refuse to take up arms but also to refuse to go to war even as a medic. The deontologist believes that if war is absolutely wrong, to participate in war in any way is absolutely wrong.

One such absolutist was Immanuel Kant (1724–1804). Kant proposed the "categorical imperative," a moral law that obliges you to do only those things that you would be willing to have everyone do as a matter of universal law. Once you make that decision, you regard it as "categorical" and without exception, and it is imperative that you do it.

Many people draw support for their absolutism or legalism from their religious beliefs. They cite the Bible, the Koran or some other book they believe to be divinely inspired. If they themselves cannot resolve an ethical dilemma, they turn to their minister, priest, rabbi or imam for the answer. The absolutist is concerned only with doing the right thing and needs only to discover what that is.

The absolutist journalist is concerned only with whether an event is newsworthy. If it is interesting, timely, significant or important, it is to be reported, regardless of the consequences. The duty of the journalist is to report the news. Period. Walter Cronkite once said that if journalists worried about what all the

"Statement of Shared Purpose" from the Committee of Concerned Journalists: "The central purpose of journalism is to provide citizens with accurate and reliable information they need to function in a free society." The Committee listed nine principles to accomplish this:

1. Journalism's first obligation is to the truth.
2. Its first loyalty is to citizens.
3. Its essence is a discipline of verification.
4. Its practitioners must maintain an independence from those they cover.
5. It must serve as an independent monitor of power.
6. It must provide a forum for public criticism and compromise.
7. It must strive to make the significant interesting and relevant.
8. It must keep the news comprehensive and proportional.
9. Its practitioners must be allowed to exercise their personal conscience.

possible consequences could be for reporting something, they would never report anything.

What happens when journalists have knowledge of something, some corruption in government or marital infidelity of a political candidate, and do not report it? What happens when the public learns that journalists knew but did not let the public know? What happens to public trust? The public relies on the news media to keep them informed. That is why journalists enjoy First Amendment privileges.

This deontological philosophy was best enunciated by Charles A. Dana, who in 1868 began a 29-year career as editor of the *New York Sun*. Dana said, "Whatever God in his infinite wisdom has allowed to happen, I am not too proud to print."

Absolutists discount any criticism of the press for printing or broadcasting certain stories. Stop blaming the messenger, they say. We don't make events happen; we just report them.

When a television news producer was asked why he telecast the confession of a suspect, he replied, "Because it's news."

Many journalists find the deontological philosophy attractive because it provides a rationale for full disclosure, for never withholding anything newsworthy from the public. In the end, these journalists believe, journalists are unethical only when they withhold the news. Publishing without fear of the consequences or without favoring one group's interests over another's is, to them, highly ethical behavior.

Teleological Ethics

Teleological ethics is the ethics of final ends. According to this philosophy, what makes an act ethical is not the act itself but the consequences of the act. Teleologists believe that the end can and often does justify the means. In this philosophy, ethics are more relativistic than absolutist or legalistic.

From a teleological perspective, stealing, for example, may not always be wrong. In some cases, it may be the right thing to do. A mother who steals food for her starving child would be performing a good act. A person who lies to save someone's life would be acting ethically. A person who kills to protect his or her own life would be acting morally.

An important consideration in teleological ethics is the intention of the person performing the act. What one person would declare unethical, another person would do for a good purpose or a good reason. For example, police often work undercover, concealing their identity in order to apprehend criminals. If in the course of that work they must lie or even get involved in criminal activity, the teleological response would be: So be it. Their purpose is to protect the public; their intention is to work for the good of society. The end justifies the means.

Some journalists would not hesitate to do the same. Some would require certain conditions be in place before they would steal or use deceit, but then they would proceed. They believe their purpose is to be the watchdog of government, to protect the common good, to keep the public fully informed. Whatever they must do to accomplish these goals, they argue, is clearly ethical.

Figure 23.1
Jayson Blair may forever be the symbol of unethical journalism. He not only disgraced himself and one of the world's greatest newspapers, but he also brought about the resignation of The New York Times' *top bosses, Executive Editor Howell Raines and Managing Editor Gerald Boyd.*

The most extreme expression of the notion that the end justifies the means was written centuries ago by the Italian political theorist Niccolò Machiavelli (1469–1527). In the 20th century, the American philosopher and educator John Dewey (1859–1952) revealed teleological leanings in his philosophical pragmatism — whatever works is ethical.

A pragmatic approach is common in business generally and in the business of journalism. If a proposed negative story about a local grocery brings threats of withdrawing advertising, some editors will decide against publishing it. If a proposed favorable story brings pledges of more advertising dollars, they will publish the story. They'll generally do whatever works.

Situation Ethics

Situation ethics is the ethics of specific acts. When asked whether the end justifies the means, a person subscribing to situation ethics would reply, "It all depends." Here are eight philosophies that use some form of situation ethics.

Antinomianism

Antinomianism is the belief that there are no moral absolutes and that there is only one operative principle — namely, that every person and every ethical situation is unique, and to solve an ethical dilemma by applying principles held by others or principles that apply in other cases is unethical. An antinomian believes that because each situation is unique, each ethical problem must be judged entirely on its own merits.

"The primary function of newspapers is to communicate to the human race what its members do, feel and think." — from the American Society of Newspaper Editors in 1923. To do this, the ASNE issued the following guidelines (quoted from *Digital Dilemmas: Ethical Issues for Online Media Professionals* by Robert I. Berkman and Christopher A. Shumway):

Responsibility. The right of a newspaper to attract and hold readers is restricted by nothing but considerations of public welfare.

Freedom of the press. Freedom of the press is to be guarded as a vital right of mankind.

Independence. Freedom from all obligations except that of fidelity to the public interest is vital.

Sincerity, truthfulness, accuracy. Good faith with the reader is the foundation of all journalism worthy of the name.

Impartiality. Sound practice makes clear distinction between reports and expressions of opinion. News reports should be free from opinion or bias of any kind.

Fair play. A newspaper should not publish unofficial charges affecting reputation or moral character without opportunity given to the accused to be heard; right practice demands the giving of such opportunity in all cases of serious accusation outside judicial proceedings.

Decency. A newspaper cannot escape conviction of insincerity if, while professing high moral purpose, it supplies incentives to base conduct, such as are to be found in details of crime and vice, publication of which is not demonstrably for the general good.

This does not mean that an antinomian has no core values. It does not mean that an antinomian is always willing to lie or cheat or steal. In some instances, an antinomian journalist would not hesitate to pose as someone else in an attempt to gather information. In other instances, the antinomian would decline to do so. The determining factor would be the situation itself, because no two situations are alike.

John Merrill's Deontelics

Other proponents of situation ethics are not as extreme as the antinomians. Some ethicists shy away from absolutism and say that one must consider both the act and the consequences of the act. Journalism scholar and ethicist John Merrill calls such ethics **deontelics** — a word he coined combining deontological and teleological ethics. To act responsibly, Merrill says, journalists must consider more than just the ethics of the act, although they dare not ignore that some acts are by their very nature unethical in most cases.

For a journalist, telling the truth is paramount, and lying is unethical — in most cases. According to deontelic theory, there may be a rare time when lying is

Figure 23.2
The Chicago Cubs were five outs away from their first World Series in 58 years when Cubs fan Steve Bartman (wearing headphones) interfered with a ball that left-fielder Moises Alou could have caught. The Florida Marlins, losing 3-0, went on to score eight runs and to win the game. News media ran Bartman's name, his picture and even his address. Bartman received death threats.

justifiable for a good purpose. For example, an investigative reporter might justify lying about his or her identity as a journalist if that is the only way to get information for an important story.

Mixed-Rule Deontology

Similar to deontelics is what other ethicists, such as Edmund Lambeth, call mixed-rule deontology. These ethicists believe that journalists have a duty to consider both the act itself and possible consequences of the act. Although not claiming to be a relativist, Lambeth sets forth certain guidelines that make some acts, usually considered unethical, ethical in certain situations. We'll see some of those guidelines and the guidelines of the Society of Professional Journalists when we discuss journalists' use of deceit later in this chapter.

Love of Neighbor

A fourth type of situation ethics has been described by Joseph Fletcher, author of *Situation Ethics*. Fletcher bases his philosophy on love of neighbor as articulated in the Golden Rule and the maxim "You shall love your neighbor as yourself." He presents his ethics from a Christian perspective with roots in Judaic teaching, but one need not profess Christianity to share the conviction that all principles are relative to one absolute: love of neighbor. Indeed, many religions, as well as secular humanism, hold human values as the highest good.

Although persons who subscribe to this belief understand and accept other ethical maxims and weigh them carefully when facing an ethical decision, they must be prepared to set them aside completely if love of neighbor demands it. In a broad sense, followers of Fletcher's form of situation ethics always place people first. In every ethical dilemma, they always do what is best for people. Sometimes they must choose between love for one person and love for a larger community of people.

Utilitarianism

The thinking that Fletcher advocates leads to another form of situation ethics: **utilitarianism.** From the utilitarian perspective, your choices are ethical if you always choose the action that is likely to bring the most happiness to the greatest number of people. This theory, formulated by John Stuart Mill (1806–1873) and Jeremy Bentham (1748–1832), was later modified to emphasize the greatest good rather than the greatest happiness. Some utilitarians also add the words "over a long period of time," because some actions may seem wrong if one looks merely at the present situation.

For example, some ABC *PrimeTime Live* reporters lied to get jobs as meat inspectors at a Food Lion supermarket. Not only that, to get their story they themselves deliberately did not detect and discard bad meat. They did all of this, of course, for the greater good of protecting the public from putrid meat.

Most journalists, perhaps, would not go that far but probably do subscribe to a utilitarian philosophy. They know, for example, that publishing a story about the infidelities of a public figure may destroy the person's reputation, hurt his or her family and perhaps even lead to suicide, but — taking a utilitarian view — they would decide that for the greater good, the public should have this information. The decision to publish would seem even more justifiable if the public official were involved in embezzlement or bribery.

Former Cleveland talk-show host Joel Rose committed suicide the same day *The Plain Dealer* published a story that he was being investigated for harassing several women. The public overwhelmingly blamed the newspaper for Rose's death, but *The Plain Dealer* maintained that Rose was a public figure and that the paper merely reported the fact that Rose was a suspect.

Some journalists who would agree that publishing pretrial publicity may endanger a defendant's right to a fair trial also believe that by keeping an eye on the police and the courts, they are ensuring that all people in the long run have a better chance for a fair trial.

Critics of journalists and utilitarianism say this philosophy is too easy to practice and too vague to be useful. Some journalists respond that it is the only practical philosophy in a hurry-up, deadline-focused world. They believe that achieving the greatest good for the greatest number calls for a general operating principle: When in doubt, unless some clear circumstance dictates against it, it is best to report the news. Otherwise, the public will not be able to rely on its news agencies, the role of the press in a democracy will be undermined and perhaps democracy itself will be abolished. Democracy, after all, practices a form of utilitarianism — one called majority rule.

Ayn Rand's Rational Self-Interest

Ayn Rand's ethics of rational self-interest is the opposite of utilitarianism and certainly of Christianity or any form of altruism. Someone subscribing to her notion of **ethical egoism** would never sacrifice himself or herself for the good of others. An ethical egoist always looks out for his or her own self-interest first, believing that if everyone acted in this manner, everyone would be better off.

Journalists who are ethical egoists would not mind using people for stories, even if the people they use have no idea how embarrassing the story may be to them. Photographers would take pictures of dying or dead children and of their grieving parents. Broadcasters would not hesitate to telecast people committing suicide. In their opinion, whatever helps them get good stories and thus advance in the profession is ethical.

Some critics accuse journalists of embracing rational self-interest merely to sell newspapers or to increase ratings. However, on many occasions journalists report stories that anger both their readers and their advertisers.

> "Ethics is a system of principles, a morality or code of conduct. It is the values and rules of life recognized by an individual, group or culture seeking guidelines to human conduct and what is good or bad, right or wrong."
>
> — Conrad C. Fink, professor of media ethics

John Rawls's Veil of Ignorance

A different form of rational self-interest is manifested in the ethical philosophy of John Rawls. His "veil of ignorance" would have you treat all people the same, as if there were no differences in social or economic status. Race, gender, age, looks — behind the veil, all people are equal; all are to be treated the same. If there is any unequal treatment, it must benefit the least advantaged persons.

Rawls argues that these considerations would make people act more in tune with their rational self-interest. People would be more likely to look out for themselves if they placed themselves in the position of others.

In our society, research indicates that wealthy white men and poor African-American men who commit the same crimes seldom receive the same sentences. This disparity is especially apparent among those who receive the death penalty. The "veil of ignorance" would help judges and juries to disregard racial and other differences.

Journalists often treat famous people — especially politicians — more harshly than they treat average citizens. If journalists placed themselves with politicians behind the veil, perhaps their adversarial attitude would dissipate somewhat.

> "I tell the honest truth in my paper, and I leave the consequences to God."
>
> — James Gordon Bennett, newspaper publisher, 1836

Aristotle's Golden Mean

Another form of situation ethics derives from Aristotle's notion of the **golden mean,** a moderate moral position that avoids extremes. Aristotle believes that after considering the extremes, a person is likely to find a rational and moral position somewhere in between — and not necessarily in the middle.

Journalists make choices ranging from running no photographs of a tragedy to running the most graphic display of violent death. A person who subscribes to the ethics of the golden mean would try to run a photo that indicates the horror of the tragedy without offending the sensibilities of the audience or of the family involved.

The *Detroit Free Press* tried to do this when it ran a front-page photograph of a Wayne County Medical Examiner's Office worker holding a plastic bag with the body of a 7-month-old baby inside (see Figure 23.3). The story ran on Sept. 15, 2000, and the paper received many calls and letters protesting the photo. The strong criticism lessened once the paper explained its reason for running the photo. Deputy photography director J. Kyle Keener said the photo was chosen because it showed "the extent of how poorly our children are treated." In a letter to readers the following day, executive editor Robert G. McGruder stated, "It was not our intention to offend, alienate and even lose some readers, but we knew that might happen. We weighed that against telling our readers about a horrific story that took place in our community."

SOLVING ETHICAL DILEMMAS

Unless you are an absolutist, ethical reasoning can take many forms. You may adopt one or more of the ethical stances just discussed, and they will guide your day-to-day ethical decision making. What is paramount is that you engage in what Lambeth and others have called **principled reasoning.** You must deliberate by reflecting on ethical principles — principles that will help you decide proper or moral ways to act.

Principled reasoning assumes that you are not acting ethically if you do something simply because you have been told to do it or because that's what everyone else does. You are not ethical if you report the story just to beat the competition.

Suppose you had received the FBI leak of Richard Jewell's name as the suspect in the Atlanta Olympics bombing (see Figure 23.4). (Jewell was subsequently cleared of all charges.) Suppose NBC had announced the suspect's name. Suppose *The New York Times* had printed the suspect's name. How would you have gone about making a rational, ethical decision?

To help journalists and others make ethical decisions, ethicists Clifford Christians, Kim Rotzoll and Mark Fackler have adapted a model of moral reasoning

Figure 23.3
Decisions on whether to publish certain photographs cause more controversy than nearly any story newspapers print. The Detroit Free Press *had to weigh whether the community would benefit from the shock of the photo.*

Figure 23.4
*Richard Jewell became the
FBI's prime suspect in
Atlanta's Centennial
Olympic Park bombing
in 1996. He was subse-
quently cleared of all
charges but not before
having his name leaked
to the press. On July 30,
1996, the* Atlanta Journal-
Constitution, *citing unidentified law enforcement
sources, published a special
edition saying the FBI considered him a suspect.*

devised by Dr. Ralph Potter of the Harvard Divinity School. Called the **Potter
Box** (see Figure 23.5), the model has four elements:

1. *Appraising the situation.* Making a good ethical decision begins with good
   reporting. You need all the facts from a variety of sources. Reaching a decision
   without trying to know all the facts makes any ethical decision impossible.

   Did Tom Brokaw of NBC have all the facts before he named Richard
   Jewell as the suspect in the Atlanta Olympics bombing?
2. *Identifying values.* What are your personal values, your news organization's
   values, your community's values, the nation's values? You may place high
   value on your personal credibility and that of your news organization. Certainly, freedom of the press is a value prized by this nation. You value your
   audience's right to know, but you may value a person's right to a fair trial
   more. You also value your independence and not being used by the police
   department or by the prosecution or by the defense.
3. *Appealing to ethical principles.* You need to look at the ethical principles
   discussed previously. The principles are not meant to be a shopping list from
   which you pick and choose items that serve your personal interest. To be
   ethical, you may have to choose a principle or principles that are far from
   expedient. Even if you choose a utilitarian solution, Aristotle's golden mean

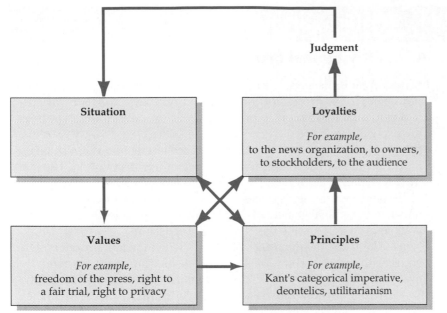

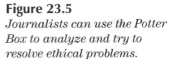

Figure 23.5

Journalists can use the Potter Box to analyze and try to resolve ethical problems.

may keep you from going to extremes, and Kant's categorical imperative may keep you from doing anything at all.

You have a duty to your audience to present them with the news. Not broadcasting Richard Jewell's name may result in some loss of credibility, especially since a network newscast named Jewell. Aristotle's golden mean might incline you not to broadcast Jewell's name but rather to report that the FBI had leaked a name. Kant's categorical imperative might lead you to believe that to jeopardize a person's right to a good name is always wrong.

4. *Choosing loyalties.* You owe a certain loyalty to your news organization, yes, but you must also be loyal to your readers, listeners or viewers. And what about loyalty to your sources and to the people about whom you are reporting?

As mentioned above, you have a duty to serve your audience. Not broadcasting Richard Jewell's name may cause people to turn elsewhere for the news. Can you completely ignore the fact that another station chose to broadcast it? You also must consider your loyalty to your station's owners and stockholders.

Usually there is no one clear answer to a difficult ethical dilemma. Seldom do the most reasonable and experienced news veterans agree completely. But principled reasoning at least makes an ethical decision possible.

The four elements in the Potter Box need not be considered in any particular order. Also, don't stop reasoning after you have touched upon the four elements. Principled reasoning should continue, even to another discussion of another ethical dilemma.

A Healthy Ethical Process

"Every journalist must 'do ethics' in every story," says Kelly McBride. "Young journalists make a common mistake when they fail to identify everyday decisions as ethical choices. Journalists of all experience levels make an even bigger mistake: They assume they should know the answer to every ethical question. Both mistakes undermine a healthy ethical process."

As a teacher of ethics at the Poynter Institute, McBride spends most of her time fostering "a healthy ethical process." McBride has an undergraduate degree in journalism (1984) and a master's degree in religion from Gonzaga University (2000). She spent 14 years as a reporter at *The Spokesman-Review* in Spokane, Wash.

"Young journalists have more power than they imagine in this process," McBride says. "As a newcomer to the profession, or to a particular news room, you are expected to figure out how things get done."

The best tool to accomplish this? "Curiosity," McBride says. "Use your reporting skills to understand the ethical climate of your news room. Observe the signs. Where do the important conversations occur and who is involved?

"Test your observations. Ask colleagues involved in a specific decision to describe the process. In your own work, bounce your decisions off your supervisor and your peers. Invite key editors to tell you what they like about the best stories in the paper or on the air.

"Ask this question over and over again: Why do we do it this way? This simple question will force your co-workers to articulate their news rooms' values. It may help some people see the gaps between the way things are and the way they ought to be."

These are the things McBride did while a reporter. She observed. "From my desk in the back corner of the news room," she says, "I could see decisions being made. In fact, I could see through the decisions to the very structure, the skeleton if you will, that supported the decision-making process."

She learned that in a healthy news room, reporters constantly turn to each other for exchanges, McBride says. The pathways between the editors' and reporters' desks are busy, two-way streets. At the intersections, journalists cluster in conversation. The most encouraging sign of all occurs when a huddle briefly loosens up and more people are invited into a discussion.

"When the news room is sick, decisions are made in secret, behind closed doors," McBride says. "Surprises show up in the paper or on the air without explanation, and no one knows how the decisions were made. People are afraid to ask questions. There is very little talking."

Now from her desk at the Poynter Institute, McBride gets a larger view. "I get to peer into news rooms around the country," she says. "Part of my job is to offer counseling to journalists trying to make better decisions."

The phone calls and visits reinforce what she first learned about ethical decision making by sitting in the back of the news room and watching the process. "There are three components to any decision in the news room: the individual, the institutional values and the culture," McBride says. People call her when one of these components is out of kilter.

You can e-mail questions to her at kmcbride@poynter.com and sign up for her regular columns at **www.poynter.org**.

This continuing ethical dialectic or dialogue helps create ethical journalism and ethical journalists. Journalists should not simply reflect society. They should present a reasoned reflection. Journalism should be done by people who make informed, intelligent and prudent choices.

The main objection to the Potter Box is that using it takes too much time and is impractical in the deadline-crazed business of journalism. However, as you become better acquainted with ethical principles and more practiced at principled reasoning, you will be able to make ethical decisions much more quickly and reasonably.

Although each case is different and you must always know the situation, you need not always start from the beginning. After a while you know what your values are, where your loyalties lie and which principles will most likely apply.

ETHICAL PROBLEMS

Journalism ethicist Ralph Barney says that journalists must always be concerned with protecting the First Amendment, "which allows them to push the envelope for the good of society." Because of the First Amendment, society has fewer "rules" for journalists in spite of the special problems they face. The following sections discuss some of those problems.

Deceit

Perhaps the most bothersome of ethical problems facing journalists involves using deceit of some kind to get a story. Deceit covers a wide range of practices. When may you lie, misrepresent yourself, use a hidden tape recorder or camera? When may you steal documents? For the absolutist, the answer is simple — never! But for the rest of us, the answer is not easy.

Ethicist Edmund Lambeth has written that for deceit to be used the abuse must be in immediate need of correction and the news media must be the only means to correct it.

Obviously, police often work undercover. Many journalists do the same — especially if it is to expose police malfeasance. Shouldn't journalists, like other citizens, call the police when they see that the law is being broken — rather than broadcast a story about it on the evening news?

Journalists use deceit most often in consumer reporting. For example, the journalists who exposed a computer repair shop that charged $500 for minor repairs could hardly have done so by revealing that they were journalists. Is there any way other than deceit to expose a crooked dentist who puts unnecessary crowns on people's teeth?

Conflicts of Interest

Reporting generally assumes that the reporter starts out with no point of view, that the reporter is neither out to get someone nor to get something out of the story. This basic tenet is the foundation for any and all credibility.

TIPS: Three guidelines

- *Be free of obligations* to anyone or to any interest except the truth. As scholar John Merrill has written, the primary obligation of the journalist is to be free.
- *Be fair.* Even children know when you treat them unfairly or when they are being unfair. So do you.
- *Remember good taste.* Some actions and stories may be ethical, but they may be in bad taste.

Ethicist Jay Black reports that most news-media ethics codes devote the bulk of their substance to determining what constitutes a conflict of interest. And well they should.

Friendship

Perhaps the most obvious, the most frequent and yet the most overlooked source of a conflict of interest confronting journalists is friendship. Professor Paul Fisher, founder of the Missouri Freedom of Information Center, called friendship the greatest obstacle to the flow of information. No one knows whether friendship causes more stories to be reported or more stories to be killed. Either way, it sets up a powerful conflict of interest.

Sometimes reporters get too close to their sources. That's why, in some news organizations, beat reporters are shifted around.

Friendship can involve one's family, or a friend of one of the family. In smaller communities especially, editors and producers dine with members of the chamber of commerce, the Kiwanis, the Kings Daughters, the country club. Sometimes a story involves a close acquaintance of a co-worker or a member of one's church.

If you ever find yourself covering a story that involves a personal acquaintance, ask your supervisor to assign the story to someone else.

Payola

Journalists may not accept payment for writing a story from anyone other than their employer. *The Honolulu Advertiser* suspended a freelance columnist when it learned he had accepted $500 to write an article favorable to the dairy industry. *The Kansas City Star* fired a veteran outdoors writer for mentioning the name of a van he had received for free.

News organizations frown on reporters doing promotional work for people they cover. For example, when Lou Dobbs was managing editor of Cable News Network business news, he was reprimanded by CNN for making promotional videos for Wall Street firms.

Other conflicts of interest are not so obvious. The *San Jose Mercury News* prohibits its business news reporters and editors from owning stock in local companies.

Will news agencies prohibit journalists from accepting speakers' fees? Will Congress attempt to legislate full disclosure of journalists' income and associations? Ken Auletta quoted then-Sen. Robert G. Torricelli of New Jersey in *The New Yorker* magazine: "What startles many people is to hear television commentators make paid speeches to interest groups and then see them on television commenting on those issues. It's kind of a direct conflict of interest. If it happened in government, it would not be permitted."

Auletta reported that ABC's Sam Donaldson attacked the Independent Insurance Agents of America for treating congressional staff to a Key West junket. That same group had paid Donaldson $30,000 to lecture to them several months earlier.

> "Journalists demean themselves and damage their credibility when they misrepresent themselves and their work to news sources and, in turn, to the public at large."
>
> — Everette E. Dennis, executive director, Freedom Forum Media Studies Center

What about the reporters who spout their opinions on Sunday morning talk shows and then "objectively" report on those same matters on Monday?

For example, ABC commentator Cokie Roberts, who seems to cover everything political in the nation's capital, accepted President George W. Bush's appointment to the President's Council on Service and Civic Participation. Is there such a thing as a nonpolitical government commission — especially when there is huge government funding involved?

Freebies

- "Whoever said there's no free lunch was obviously not a sports reporter," writes Laura Shutiak in the *Calgary Herald*. Sports reporters are not the only journalists who are wined and dined by those seeking publicity.

- "Put a movie star in a room with 100 journalists armed with knives and forks and some might say you've got a fair fight," writes Dan Cox in *Variety*. "If you're a studio chieftain, however, those are the kind of odds you like, because you know that when the day is done, your latest pic is in for a stupendously inordinate amount of 'safe' press coverage — or, as some marketing whizzes maintain, free advertising." Cox quotes a senior VP of marketing for a film company saying, "Now it seems they have a press junket for nearly every film." Why? As advertising costs increase, executives work harder for free advertising.

- In summer 1997, Iomega, maker of computer disks and drives, held a party for 60 guests, 35 of whom were journalists. Iomega promised each of them a free hardware/software package called Buz, which had a value of $199. Most of the journalists signed up for the freebie.

- Auto shows, such as the North American International Auto Show, provide valuable press kits and sometimes other keepsakes for journalists. Not only do journalists accept them, but they have begun selling them on eBay. *Detroit News* reporter Mark Truby quotes journalism ethics professor William McWhirter: "It's probably a new low for all of us."

- "Many travel writers have long accepted free trips in return for writing favorable stories," writes James S. Hirsch in *The Wall Street Journal*, "but now a new twist has emerged in the cozy ties between the travel industry and the trade press. International journalists attending a travel conference in Miami this week have been issued an edict: Submit published stories about the conference or forfeit your place at the table next year."

A new twist indeed. But freebies have always come with a price:

- Can reporters remain objective?
- Do reporters write stories they would otherwise not write?
- Does the public perceive the reporter who has accepted or is suspected of accepting freebies as objective?

It is the perception of conflict that bothers most news organizations. Some argue that the least reporters must do is disclose prominently in their stories any freebies they have accepted. As in any case of deceit, reporters must disclose how they were able to get the story and why accepting freebies was necessary. For example, small news outlets cannot afford to send their travel writers on expensive tours.

When the Poynter Institute's Kelly McBride did a workshop for members of the American Association of Sunday and Feature Editors, she mentioned that she refused to accept freebies. She reports: "I was losing the battle. They were ready to string me up by the chandeliers, toss me into the Gulf of Mexico. They thought I was nuts." Even when she told them to tell the readers about the freebies, she received resistance. The reason? "Many editors thought such disclosure would further undermine credibility, not strengthen it. Others said the readers already know." It was clear that they thought the features department was different from the city desk.

Nevertheless, most news organizations have rules against accepting freebies. The Scripps-Howard newspaper group says, "When the gifts exceed the limits of propriety, they should be returned." The Society of Professional Journalists says, "Nothing of value shall be accepted." Is a cup of coffee something of value? The Associated Press expects its staff members to return gifts of "nominal value." Is a baseball cap of nominal value?

The ethics code of *The Orange County* (Calif.) *Register* says reporters may accept free meals and drinks only if the meal itself or the events surrounding it are of news value. The code also allows tickets or passes to cultural and athletic events only for the purpose of covering those events.

At the *Chicago Tribune*, staff members can accept nothing over the value of a simple keychain.

The *San Jose Mercury News* "will pay for meals and drinks shared with news sources, for luncheons or dinners which are covered as news events and for restaurant meals reviewed." It prohibits free tickets to sports events, movies, fairs, amusement parks and all entertainment that has a charge.

Some news organizations allow reporters to accept freebies — but the reporters turn them in for an annual auction with the proceeds going to charity.

You must learn the ethics code of your news organization. Sometimes, your personal code may be more stringent than that of your organization. In that case, follow your own code. Remember, you may not think a freebie will influence your reporting. But does your audience think it might?

And if you choose a career in public relations, remember that the code of the Public Relations Society of America states that you are to do nothing that tempts news professionals to violate their codes.

Checkbook Journalism

Will the audience believe your story if you paid your source for it? Should you always report that you had a paid source? Is it ethical to pay a source for an exclusive story? Should newspeople be in the business of keeping other newspeople from getting a story?

In the O.J. Simpson case, "journalists" paid witnesses for their stories. Those deals subsequently caused the witnesses' testimony to be tossed out of court.

Are paid sources likely to have an ax to grind? Do they come forward only for financial gain?

The terrible consequence of checkbook journalism is that even legitimate news professionals may be cut off from sources who want and expect pay. Some sources have begun asking for a fee even for good news. The increase in tabloid journalism, both in print and in broadcast, has brought the opportunists out in droves.

The networks say they do not pay for interviews, but the tabloids say payments to the networks are disguised as consultant fees, writes Richard Zoglin in *Time* magazine. He reports that the traditional stigma against checkbook journalism may be fading away. He quotes Everette Dennis, senior vice president and executive director of the Freedom Forum International Consortium of Universities, who says, "It's hard to argue that the ordinary person shouldn't share in the benefit of what's going to be a commercial product."

The New York Times reported what NBC, ABC and CBS did to get an exclusive interview with Pfc. Jessica Lynch after she had been rescued from an Iraqi hospital. CBS dangled much more than a two-hour documentary. The *Times* quotes a letter from Betsy West, a CBS News senior vice president, to Lynch's military representatives: "Attached you will find the outlines of a proposal that includes ideas from CBS News, CBS Entertainment, MTV networks and Simon & Schuster publishers." A possible movie, book, guest appearances — who could resist?

CBS did some of the same with Aron Ralston, the hiker in Utah who had to cut off his arm to get out from under a boulder.

Surely, good reporting demands that you pay sources only when necessary and only if you can get other sources to corroborate your findings. You'd also better be sure that your bosses know that you're doing it.

Participation in the News

You'd also better let your bosses know which organizations you belong to. When *The Fairfield* (Iowa) *Ledger* fired two reporters who had joined a local church-sponsored pro-life group, the two reporters filed a $250,000 lawsuit charging the paper with religious discrimination and with violation of their civil rights.

The Washington Post issued a memo to staffers that barred any reporters who had participated in a pro-abortion rights march in Washington "from any future participation in coverage of the abortion issue." Don Kowet reported in *The Washington Times* that the same memo prohibited any "news room professional" from participating in such a protest.

But what about participating in a political campaign? Or running for office? William J. "B.J." Laurie, editor of the *Courier Journal* in Crescent City, Fla., opted to run for city commissioner.

And must a religion reporter be an atheist? Must reporters set aside personal religious convictions?

According to Kowet, Richard Harwood, *Washington Post* **ombudsman** at the time, told a conference of journalists: "You have every right in the world to run for office, or participate in a political activity or lobbying activity. You don't have the 'right' to work for *The Washington Post*."

"But I don't believe that paying sources is unethical, as long as it's disclosed to the reader; in some cases I think it makes for better journalism. It gives a fair share of the profits to sources who spend time and take risks."

— John Tierney, from "Newsworthy," reprinted from The New York Times Company

"If you're not involved in the community at all and you're totally neutralized, you end up not knowing enough about the community, not being able to get enough leads and so on in order to do your job."

— Tony Case, quoting ethicist Louis W. Hodges in *Editor & Publisher*

Nevertheless, some worry that uninvolved journalists will be uninformed journalists, an unconnected group of elitists. The problem is compounded when editors and even news organizations are involved in community projects. May the editor join the yacht club? May the station support the United Way? Is *The New York Times'* coverage of the Metropolitan Museum of Art influenced by its generous support of that institution? May an HIV-positive journalist report on AIDS?

The second war in Iraq gave the word "embedded" a new meaning for journalists. Those covering the war underwent Pentagon training for their work there. When in Iraq, they accompanied soldiers in an officially sanctioned role never experienced by reporters covering previous wars. Most of those who participated felt they benefited from the training and that they were better reporters for it. Will we ever know?

Jules Crittenden, an embedded reporter for the *Boston Herald*, called American soldiers' attention to a bevy of Iraqis who were firing at a U.S. battalion. In his *Embedded Journal* written for Poynter, Crittenden said he was sure that some would question his ethics or objectivity. His answer: "Screw them, they weren't there. But they are welcome to join me next time if they care to test their professionalism."

Reporters have accompanied police on raids for years, but when the World Trade Organization met in Miami in December 2003, Associated Press reporter Rachel La Corte wrote that Police Chief John Timoney wished to embed journalists in order to place "them on the front lines of a protest expected to draw tens of thousands of people." Would you have participated? Under what circumstances?

Should journalists demand of themselves what they demand of politicians — full disclosure of their financial investments and memberships, as well as public knowledge of their personal tastes, preferences and lifestyles?

Surely if you own stock in a company, you must at least tell your editor and make a full disclosure. Better, you should not report on the stock at all. Mark Glaser reported in the USC Annenberg Online Journalism Review:

> CNBC glamour anchor Maria Bartiromo recently took flack for an on-air disclosure that she owned stock in Citigroup — just before interviewing Sanford Weill, the company's CEO.
>
> Then, before you could say "online angle," CBS MarketWatch star columnist Thom Calandra touted stock in Ivanhoe Energy Inc. on "CBS MarketWatch Weekend" while making an on-air disclosure of stock ownership. Then the show's anchor, Susan McGinnis, disclosed that she owned shares in Ivanhoe as well. The Monday after the report aired, Ivanhoe's stock shot up 26.7 percent to a new 52-week high.

Advertising Pressure

It's quite possible that you won't work long at a news organization before you realize some subjects are taboo and others are highly encouraged. If you are lucky, you will work for a paper, station, magazine or Web site that still has a solid wall of separation between editorial and advertising.

However, in some places, advertising salespeople are allowed to peek over that wall and see what the publication, station or Web site is planning to run. That information might help sell some advertising. Some say, what could be wrong with that?

The next step is for the advertising manager to climb over the wall and suggest that editorial do a story on some subject so that advertising can be sold.

And then the next step isn't far away. Advertising sits at your desk and begins to dictate what must or must not be printed or broadcast and even what must and must not be said. In print and online media, advertising may want the layout, design and type of ads or sections to look like the publication's normal layout, design and typefaces.

Probably, though, on a day-to-day basis, advertising has more to do with what stories will *not* be run. You may learn quickly that you are not to do a story critical of the local grocery store. Chinese journalist Y.Y. Zhang reports that the oral decree of the *Guangzhou Daily*'s publishers has been carried out loyally: "Never write any stories about the shortcomings of our city's real estate developers because they provide us with 30 percent of advertising."

One small paper lost $50,000 a year in advertising for criticizing a local theater that was part of a big chain of theaters and owner of several other theaters in town. Research has shown that magazines that continue to receive millions in cigarette advertising have carried few or no articles about the health hazards of tobacco. Car buff magazines carry more articles about the cars they advertise than about unadvertised vehicles.

Although some newspaper companies have allowed advertising and news personnel to become a bit chummier, some magazines have gone much further. The Southern Progress Corp., for example, a big moneymaker for Time Warner and publisher of *Southern Living*, *Southern Accents*, *Progressive Farmer*, *Cooking Light* and other successful magazines, has stopped worrying about the separation of advertising and editorial. In a *Wall Street Journal* story by Matthew Rose, former Southern Progress editor Michael Carlton said, "There is no church and state. They all sit in the same church, maybe in different pews." In the same story, another former chief executive of the Southern Progress unit is quoted as saying, "For me, the acid test was: Am I serving the reader well?"

Not only does Southern Progress tip off advertisers as to what editorial is going to do, but it also sometimes allows advertisers into planning sessions and to make suggestions.

With Southern Progress boasting high renewal rates and high profits, is this the future? In the Nashville *Scene*, Matt Pulle quotes from the Meredith Corp.'s 2003 annual report: "Now everyone at each station, including news anchors and other on-air personalities, is playing a role in generating advertising revenues or supporting sales operations."

Even the tabloids check with Wal-Mart, reports AdAge.com. David Pecker, chairman-CEO of American Media, publisher of the *Star*, *Globe*, and *National Enquirer*, tabloids that sell a combined 2.8 million copies on newstands weekly, says, "We work with Wal-Mart." If there is "a very controversial cover, we will call and say, 'This is what we are doing.'" That's to keep those tabloids selling at

Wal-Mart and not banned like *Maxim* and *Stuff*. When someone approached Jack Kliger, president-CEO of Hachette Filipacchi Media, with "a somewhat sexy idea for a magazine," the person had a solution to "the Wal-Mart-sex question" — use "toned-down covers for copies that Wal-Mart will sell." That example, reports AdAge.com, shows the power of Wal-Mart, the largest single retailer for magazines' on-the-rack sales.

The question of advertisements online is dealt with in Chapter 20. Radio newscasters generally separate themselves from the commercials. Yet popular long-time commentator Paul Harvey and, more recently, Rush Limbaugh and Charles Osgood, have not refrained from reading the commercials with the same gusto with which they say everything else. What has it done to their credibility? Television suffers the same advertising pressures as print with the added problems that there are only so many minutes in a newscast. How ethical is it to cut a complicated international story to 90 seconds just to make time for one more commercial?

Although CBS denied giving in to advertising pressure, it canceled its miniseries on Ronald Reagan due to pressure from viewers and advertisers — who had not even seen the series.

It's only fair to point out, of course, that news media have rejected advertising pressure, sometimes at the cost of millions of dollars. For example, during Super Bowl XXVIII in February 2004, which boasted the highest television advertising fees of the year, CBS decided not to air an ad by the political activist group MoveOn.org that criticized President Bush, saying they wouldn't run "issue" ads.

On the flip side of this issue, if you are going into advertising, you need to look at advertising codes of ethics that sometimes state explicitly that enticing or pressuring news media to violate their codes is unethical.

Invasion of Privacy

Most journalists would cry out against an invasion of their own privacy. Yet many of them argue for a vague "right to know" when they report on others, especially if those others are public officials or public figures. The head-on collision of the right to know and the right to privacy will confront you every day of your reporting lives. The Constitution mentions neither "right."

The most obvious and talked-about issue pertaining to the right to privacy is naming crime victims, especially rape and abuse victims. Florida legislated against publishing rape victims' names, only to have the law struck down by a Florida District Court. The U.S. Supreme Court has held that news agencies cannot be punished for publishing lawfully obtained information or information from a public record. Meanwhile, state legislators are looking for ways to close the records on rape and to punish police, hospitals, court clerks and other officials for releasing victims' names.

So it comes down to a matter of ethics, and, as usual, there is no complete agreement. But most news outlets will not publish a rape victim's name without the victim's permission. The same is true of the names of juvenile victims of sex crimes. The obvious reasons are that the victim has suffered greatly and that public knowledge of the crime may stigmatize the victim. Even though the reporting of incidents of rape has risen from 10 percent of all such crimes to 20 percent, most victims do not come forward because of the stigma attached.

Some argue that it is equally unfair to name the accused as it is the accuser. Here are some possible guidelines:

1. Name the accuser and the accused only when charges are filed, not at the accusation or arrest stage. This stage at least says the prosecuting attorney believes there is enough evidence to support going forward.
2. Name the accuser only if the person agrees. That requires that you make contact directly or through intermediaries to ask the question.

Many disagree. Charles Gay, editor and publisher of *The* (Washington State) *Shelton-Mason County Journal*, is one of them. Reporter Beth Kaiman quotes Gay in seattletimes.com: "I just can't bring myself to be part of a journalistic fraternity that says there's something wrong with you and we're not going to print your name. I want to get rid of the stigma, not perpetuate it."

Geneva Overholser, former editor of *The Des Moines Register*, former ombudsman of *The Washington Post* and now a professor at the Missouri School of Journalism, has long believed in revealing the names of rape victims. In her electronic newsletter from the Poynter Institute, she argues that most discussions about this matter center on broader sociological questions, not on journalistic questions. She writes:

> While I recognize the good intentions of those who seek to protect rape victims, I believe that much of the effort has had contrary results — and that there is little evidence that it has helped rape victims or furthered social understanding. But these views of mine — and the views of others — on these questions are fundamentally beside the point journalistically.
>
> When it comes to asking whether to use people's names, the journalistic ethic is clear: We name names. We do this for reasons of credibility and fairness. To my mind, protecting children is the one valid exception.

But even the question of naming juvenile offenders has no easy or universal answer. Traditionally, news organizations have held that juveniles are juveniles and are entitled to make juvenile mistakes, even if those mistakes are crimes. Juvenile court records are, after all, sealed. But the courts have upheld the right to publish juvenile offenders' names on the public record.

Some media critics, such as former *Fresno Bee* ombudsman Lynne Enders Glaser, applaud the publication of the names of juvenile offenders. Glaser wrote: "It doesn't take a rocket scientist to figure out that more and more violent crimes are being committed by young people. And in increasing numbers, *Bee* readers have challenged the law and the media to stop protecting the identity of criminals because of their age."

Regardless of the stigma forever attached to the juvenile offender's name and the embarrassment of his or her parents and family, some worry that in some groups a youth's notoriety will encourage other young people to violate the law. Others argue that the prospect of public humiliation will make other juveniles think twice before committing crimes.

Reporting on crime victims and reporting on juvenile crimes are just two of the myriad privacy issues you will face. Journalists are still protected when writing about public officials and public figures — most of the time. But what about the children of politicians or celebrities?

Photographers and videographers must be especially concerned with privacy. "Lead with blood" is not an uncommon dictum in TV news rooms. But how much blood? And how often and under what circumstances do we stick cameras into people's grieving and anxious faces? When may we ask, if at all, "How did you feel when you saw your daughter get hit by a car?"

When a reporter asked former President Harry Truman how he felt when he heard that President John Kennedy was killed, Truman answered, "It's none of your damn business."

When is privacy paramount, and under what circumstances do you fail as a journalist to keep your audience informed?

You should keep one thing in mind: Is secrecy better than disclosure? Is it better to have people whispering names to each other, even guessing who the involved person is, than dispelling all rumors with the facts?

Withholding Information

May you ever withhold information from the news organization for which you work? If you are writing what you hope to be a best-selling book, may you save some "news" until the book is published?

If you work as a journalist, are you ever off-duty? A doctor isn't. Doctors take an oath to treat the sick. If you witness something at a friend's house or at a party, do you tell your news director about it?

One reporter was fired when his boss discovered that he attended a post-concert party of a rock band where lines of cocaine were openly available. The reporter did not include this information in his coverage of the band. His defense was that if he reported the drug abuse, he would never get interviews or get close to other rock groups, and he would be finished as a music critic. His defense didn't work.

If you learn that a political candidate is "sleeping around," would you withhold that information? Would you do so even if you knew that if the public had that information, the candidate would not be elected? Suppose after the election it became clear that you had had the information before the election but did not publish it? *The Oregonian* apologized to its readers for not publishing reports about Sen. Bob Packwood's alleged sexual-harassment charges until after he was re-elected.

The *Los Angeles Times* received all kinds of criticism (one reader wrote about the *Times'* "sleazy hatchet job") for publishing the sexual-harassment complaints of 16 women against then candidate-for-governor Arnold Schwarzenegger in the final week of the campaign in California's special recall election in 2003. Eleven of the women went on record with their names. Schwarzenegger won anyway.

Sometimes there's more than an election at stake. St. Louis WKBQ general manager Bill Viands did not apologize when a popular St. Louis meteorologist

"Journalism, to a considerable degree, has ceased to be the profession of intelligent, idealistic and charming gentlemen. It has become the profession of public office seekers, title hunters, social pushers, dollar diddlers, mountebanks and cads."

— Columnist
H.L. Mencken
in 1924

committed suicide after WKBQ aired intimate messages left on the answering machine of a woman who said he had been harassing her. In a *Chicago Tribune* story by Staci D. Kraemer, WKBQ producer Courtney Landrum said, "I couldn't believe [the airing of messages] was unethical in any way, shape or form. . . ."

Leading politicians in France blamed negative reporting that questioned the integrity of Prime Minister Pierre Beregovoy for his suicide. Press critics blamed the media treatment of Vince Foster, counselor to President Bill Clinton, for his suicide. Foster's suicide note lamented that ruining people's lives was sport in our nation's capital.

Sometimes the press withholds information. In El Paso, Tex., the media held a story of the kidnapping of two boys for two days because of threats, relayed by the FBI, that the kidnappers would kill the boys if the kidnapping were publicized. The boys eventually were freed unharmed.

Sometimes a news organization withholds information to protect its reporters and to maintain access to news sources. Eason Jordan, CNN's chief news executive, shocked the journalistic world with his candid admission in a *New York Times* op-ed piece that CNN often did not report Iraqi government atrocities in Iraq — even when its own reporters were the victims. Reporter Peter Johnson quoted CNN spokesperson Matthew Furman as saying that "you do what you have to do to protect your people." Columnist Eric Fettmann wrote in the *New York Post:* "It's like saying that the best interests of journalism would have justified suppressing stories on the Holocaust in order to keep a U.S. News bureau in Berlin to tell Nazi Germany's side."

Sometimes the press doesn't withhold anything. Sometimes it comes down to what ethicist Edmund Lambeth calls "humaneness." You never do needless harm to an individual or inflict needless pain or suffering. It is better that you do the least harm possible. You certainly don't do harmful stories deliberately to harass someone or without a good reason. No one likes a bully.

Plagiarism

No one wants you to use his or her work as if it were your own. No one condones plagiarism. The problem is defining what constitutes plagiarism. You probably know when you do it even if no one else does.

If you read Jim Romenesko's blog (and you should) on the Poynter Web site (**www.poynter.org/medianews**), it seems that nearly every other day there is a story about some reporter admitting to plagiarism. Even *New York Times* Hollywood correspondent Bernard Weinraub admitted to "screwing up." A graduate student in the Gaylord College of Journalism and Mass Communication at the University of Oklahoma lifted several paragraphs from a Web site. Lauren Cavagnolo, writing in oudaily.com, quoted the editor of *The Oklahoma Daily*, where the column ran, as saying: "This is troubling news. There is nothing more damaging to a paper's credibility than to have a reporter plagiarize and have it published."

In the daily practice of journalism, reporters, consciously or unconsciously, deal with many situations that could involve plagiarism. Roy Peter Clark of the Poynter Institute has listed them (see box on page 522). It is not unusual for a writer to plagiarize and have absolutely no idea that he or she is doing it.

Beware of Plagiarism!

- *Taking material verbatim from the newspaper library.* Even when the material is from your own newspaper, it is still someone else's work. Put it in your own words or attribute it.
- *Using material verbatim from the wire services.* Sometimes writers take Associated Press material, add a few paragraphs to give some local flavor, and publish it as their own work. Even though it is a common practice, it is not right.
- *Using material from other publications.* Some blame electronic databases for a whole new explosion of plagiarism. Sometimes writers steal the research of others without attribution. And sometimes they use others' work without realizing it.
- *Using news releases verbatim.* The publicists are delighted, but you should be ashamed — especially if you put your name on an article. Rewrite it, except perhaps for the direct quotations, and use them sparingly. If you use a whole release, cite its source.
- *Using the work of fellow reporters.* If more than one reporter works on a story, if you use a byline on top, put the other names at the end of the story.
- *Using old stories over again.* Columnists, beware! Your readers have a right to know when you are recycling your material. Some of them might catch you at it, and there goes your credibility.

— Roy Peter Clark,
The Poynter Institute

Apparently, sometimes something one has read becomes so familiar to the reader that the reader later considers it his or her own.

When the *Indianapolis Star/News* fired TV writer Steve Hall in 1999 for plagiarism, Hall stood by his work and maintained that if he had in fact plagiarized, he had done so unconsciously. Hall said he might have unknowingly used information he had read elsewhere. He also said that if plagiarism occurred, it was because of his heavy workload.

Nevertheless, you must fight every impulse, question and check any doubts, avoid any hint of plagiarism. As William A. Henry III wrote in *Time* magazine, a reporter has a First Amendment bond with the public. "Plagiarism," he wrote, "imperils that bond, not because it involves theft of a wry phrase or piquant quote, but because it devalues meticulous, independent verification of fact — the bedrock of a press worth reading."

That bond is not just with the public. It's with your fellow workers and the news organization for which you work. Your personal ethics will safeguard and nurture that bond. Once it is broken, so are you.

Suggested Readings

Beckman, Robert I. and Shumway, Christopher A. *Digital Dilemmas: Ethical Issues for Online Professionals.* Ames: Iowa University Press, 2003. A superb review of ethical principles for journalists of all kinds, including a discussion of who is a journalist in the Internet age, privacy, speed and accuracy, advertising and editorial independence.

Christians, Clifford, Rotzoll, Kim and Fackler, Mark. *Media Ethics, Cases and Moral Reasoning,* Sixth Edition. New York: Longman, 2001. Applies the Potter Box method of principled reasoning to dozens of journalism, advertising and public-relations cases.

Day, Louis Alvin. *Ethics in Media Communications,* Fourth Edition. Belmont, Calif.: Wadsworth, 2003. Begins with a superb discussion of ethics and moral development, ethics and society, and ethics and moral reasoning, and goes on to discuss nearly every problem facing journalists, accompanied by actual cases.

Fletcher, Joseph. *Situation Ethics: The New Morality.* Philadelphia: Westminster Press, 1966. A classic work on Christian situation ethics.

Lambeth, Edmund B. *Committed Journalism,* Second Edition. Bloomington: Indiana University Press, 1992. Creates an ethics code specific to the practice of journalism.

Merrill, John. *The Imperative of Freedom: A Philosophy of Journalistic Autonomy.* New York: Hastings House, 1974; Lanham, Md.: University Press of America, 1990. Establishes freedom as the primary imperative of the journalist.

Merrill, John. *Journalism Ethics: Philosophical Foundations for News Media.* New York: St. Martin's Press, 1997. Provides in-depth understanding of the philosophical and theoretical underpinnings of journalism morality.

Wilkins, Lee and Patterson, Philip. *Media Ethics: Issues and Cases,* Fourth Edition. Dubuque, Iowa: McGraw-Hill, 2002. An excellent discussion of journalism ethics with up-to-date cases.

Suggested Web Sites

www.elon.edu/andersj/ethics.html
A Web page for online news ethics by Janna Quitney Anderson, from the Elon School of Communications.

www.journalism.indiana.edu/ethics
This Web site from Indiana University School of Journalism provides an extensive database of ethics cases in journalism.

www.rtnda.org/ethics/coe.shtml
The Radio-Television News Directors Association Journalism Ethics program put together this site.

www.spj.org
The Society of Professional Journalists makes available to journalists ethics news, an ethics hotline, an ethics listserv and other resources.

www.poynter.org/medianews
Poynter Online, Jim Romenesko's blog, or Web journal, providing "your daily fix of media industry news, commentary, and memos."

www.poynter.org
The Poynter Institute provides a file of articles written about ethical issues in journalism.

1. You learn that the daughter of a local bank president has been kidnapped. The family has not been contacted by the kidnappers, and police officials ask you to keep the matter secret for fear the abductors might panic and injure the child. Describe how a deontologist, a teleologist and a situation ethicist would make their decisions about how to handle the situation.

2. Would a travel writer ever be justified in accepting a free trip? Explain your answer by using various theories of situation ethics.

3. You are a photographer for a newspaper. On your way back from a track meet, you see a man who looks as if he is thinking about jumping off a bridge. You have a camera with motor-drive action, which permits you to take pictures in rapid-fire sequence. Which of the following would you do? Justify your response.

   a. Shoot pictures from a distance.
   b. Approach the man slowly, take pictures and try to talk him out of jumping.
   c. Step out of his sight and radio to the newspaper to send police.
   d. Take some other action.

4. For at least a year, on four or five occasions, reporters on your paper have heard rumors that a residence for the aged is negligent in its care of the elderly. Your editor asks you to get a job there as a janitor and report what you find. What would be your response?

5. A Christian minister is running for mayor of your city, which is a conservative, traditional community. You learn that he and his wife of 18 years have a son who was born four months after they were married. Using the Potter Box, decide whether you would release that information.

6. Do a computer search of articles written in the past three years on whether journalists should publish the names of rape victims. Then write a brief summary of your findings.

APPENDIX 1   Twenty Common Errors of Grammar and Punctuation

Grammar provides our language's rules of the road. When you see a green light, you proceed on faith that the other driver will not go through the red light. Drivers have a shared understanding of the rules of the road. Writers have a shared understanding of the grammar rules that ensure we understand what we are reading. Occasionally, as on the road, there is a wreck. We dangle participles, misplace modifiers and omit commas. If we write "Running down the street, his pants fell off," we are saying a pair of pants ran down a street. If we write "He hit Harry and John stopped him," the missing comma changes the meaning to "He hit Harry and John."

To say what you mean — to avoid syntactical wrecks — you must know the rules of grammar. We have compiled a list of 20 common errors that we find in our students' stories and in the stories of many professionals. Avoid them, and you'll write safely.

To take quizzes based on this list of 20 common errors of grammar and punctuation, go to Exercise Central for Associated Press Style at bedfordstmartins.com/apexercises.

1. Incorrect comma in a series in Associated Press style

Use commas to separate the items in a series, but do not put a comma before *and* or *or* at the end of the series unless the meaning would be unclear without a comma.

INCORRECT COMMA BEFORE "AND"	**The film was fast-paced, sophisticated, and funny.**
CLEAR WITHOUT COMMA	**The film was fast-paced, sophisticated and funny.**
UNCLEAR WITHOUT COMMA	**He demanded cheese, salsa with jalapeños and onions on his taco.**

A comma before *and* would prevent readers from wondering if he demanded salsa containing both jalapeños and onions or if he wanted the salsa and the onions as two separate toppings.

COMMA NEEDED
BEFORE "AND"

He demanded cheese, salsa with jalapeños, and onions on his taco.

2. Run-on sentence

An independent clause contains a subject and a predicate and makes sense by itself. A run-on sentence — also known as a *comma splice* — occurs when two or more independent clauses are joined incorrectly with a comma.

RUN-ON

John Rogers left the family law practice, he decided to become a teacher.

You can correct a run-on sentence in several ways. Join the clauses with a comma and one of the coordinating conjunctions — *and, but, for, nor, or, yet* or *so* — or join the clauses with a semicolon if they are closely related. Use a subordinating conjunction such as *after, because, if* or *when* to turn one of the clauses into a dependent clause. Or rewrite the run-on as two separate sentences.

CORRECTING A RUN-ON WITH A COMMA AND A COORDINATING CONJUNCTION

John Rogers left the family law practice, for he decided to become a teacher.

CORRECTING A RUN-ON WITH A SEMICOLON

John Rogers left the family law practice; he decided to become a teacher.

CORRECTING A RUN-ON BY MAKING ONE INDEPENDENT CLAUSE A DEPENDENT CLAUSE

John Rogers left the family law practice when he decided to become a teacher.

CORRECTING A RUN-ON BY WRITING TWO SEPARATE SENTENCES

John Rogers left the family law practice. He decided to become a teacher.

3. Fragment

A fragment is a word group that lacks a subject, a verb or both, yet is punctuated as though it were a complete sentence. Another type of fragment is a word group that begins with a subordinating conjunction such as *because* or *when*, yet is punctuated as though it were a complete sentence.

FRAGMENTS

After she had placed her watch and an extra pencil on the table.

Without feeling especially sorry about it.

Correct a fragment by joining it to the sentence before or after it or by adding the missing elements so that the fragment contains a subject and a verb and can stand alone.

After she had placed her watch and an extra pencil on the table, the student opened the exam booklet.

CORRECTING A FRAGMENT BY TURNING IT INTO A SENTENCE

She apologized to her boss for the outburst without feeling especially sorry about it.

4. Missing comma(s) with a nonrestrictive element

A nonrestrictive element is a word, phrase or clause that gives information about the preceding part of the sentence but does not restrict or limit the meaning of that part. A nonrestrictive element is not essential to the meaning of the sentence; you can delete it and still understand clearly what the sentence is saying. Place commas before and (if necessary) after a nonrestrictive element.

UNCLEAR	**The mayor asked to meet Alva Johnson a highly decorated police officer.**
CLEAR	**The mayor asked to meet Alva Johnson, a highly decorated police officer.**
UNCLEAR	**His wife Mary was there.**
CLEAR	**His wife, Mary, was there.**

5. Confusion of *that* and *which*

The pronoun *that* always introduces restrictive information, which is essential to the meaning of the sentence; do not set off a *that* clause with commas. The pronoun *which* introduces nonrestrictive, or nonessential, information; set off a nonrestrictive *which* clause with commas.

INCORRECT	**The oldest store in town, Miller and Company, that has been on Main Street for almost a century, will close this summer.**
CORRECT	**The oldest store in town, Miller and Company, which has been on Main Street for almost a century, will close this summer.**
INCORRECT	**The creature, which has been frightening residents of North First Street for the past week, has turned out to be a screech owl.**
CORRECT	**The creature that has been frightening residents of North First Street for the past week has turned out to be a screech owl.**

6. Missing comma after an introductory element

A sentence may begin with a dependent clause (a word group that contains a subject and a verb and begins with a subordinating conjunction such as *because* or *when*), a prepositional phrase (a word group that begins with a preposition such as *in* or *on* and ends with a noun or pronoun), an adverb such as *next* that modifies the whole sentence, or a participial phrase (a word group that contains a past or present participle, such as *determined* or *hoping*, that acts as an adjective). Use a comma to separate these introductory elements from the main clause of the sentence.

DEPENDENT CLAUSE	**After the applause had died down, the conductor raised his baton again.**
PREPOSITIONAL PHRASE	**Without a second thought, the chicken crossed the road.**
ADVERB	**Furthermore, the unemployment rate continues to rise.**
PARTICIPIAL PHRASES	**Waiting in the bar, José grew restless.**
	Saddened by the news from home, she stopped reading the letter.

Although it is always correct to use a comma after an introductory element, the comma may be omitted after some adverbs and short prepositional phrases if the meaning is clear:

Suddenly it's spring.

In Chicago it rained yesterday.

Always place a comma after two or more introductory prepositional phrases.

In May of last year in Toronto, Tom attended three conventions.

Here are more examples:

INCORRECT	**Shaking her head at the latest budget information the library administrator wondered where to find the money for new books.**
CORRECT	**Shaking her head at the latest budget information, the library administrator wondered where to find the money for new books.**
INCORRECT	**After a week of foggy, rainy mornings had passed he left Seattle.**
CORRECT	**After a week of foggy, rainy mornings had passed, he left Seattle.**

7. Missing comma(s) between coordinate adjectives

Adjectives are coordinate if they make sense when you insert *and* between them or place them in reverse order.

COORDINATE ADJECTIVES	**The frightened, angry citizens protested the new policy.**
	The frightened and angry citizens protested the new policy.

The adjectives make sense with *and* between them, so they are coordinate.

The angry, frightened citizens protested the new policy.

The adjectives make sense in reverse order, so they are coordinate. Separate coordinate adjectives with commas.

INCORRECT	**The gaunt lonely creature was also afraid.**
CORRECT	**The gaunt, lonely creature was also afraid.**

8. Missing comma(s) in a compound sentence

Two or more independent clauses — word groups containing a subject and a verb and expressing a complete thought — joined with a coordinating conjunction (*and, but, for, nor, or, yet* or *so*) form a compound sentence. Place a comma before the conjunction in a compound sentence to avoid confusion.

UNCLEAR	**She works as a pharmacist now and later she plans to go to medical school.**
CLEAR	**She works as a pharmacist now, and later she plans to go to medical school.**

9. Misused semicolon

In a compound sentence that has a coordinating conjunction joining the clauses, place a comma before the conjunction, not a semicolon.

INCORRECT	**The Chicago Cubs did not play in the World Series; but they did win their division.**
CORRECT	**The Chicago Cubs did not play in the World Series, but they did win their division.**

10. Misplaced or dangling modifier

Modifiers are words or phrases that change or clarify the meaning of another word or word group in a sentence. Place modifiers immediately before or directly after the word or words they modify. A *misplaced* modifier appears too far from the word or words it is supposed to modify in the sentence. A *dangling* modifier appears in a sentence that does not contain the word or words it is supposed to modify. A modifier at the beginning of a sentence should refer to the grammatical subject of the sentence.

MISPLACED MODIFIER	*subject* **Having predicted a sunny morning, the downpour surprised the meteorologist.**
CORRECT	*subject* **Having predicted a sunny morning, the meteorologist did not expect the downpour.**

	subject
DANGLING MODIFIER	**Working in the yard, the sun burned her badly.**
	subject
CORRECT	**Working in the yard, <u>she</u> became badly sunburned.**

11. Missing or misused hyphen(s) in a compound modifier

A compound modifier consists of two or more adjectives or an adjective-adverb combination used to modify a single noun. When a compound modifier precedes a noun, you should hyphenate the parts of the compound unless the compound consists of an adverb ending in -*ly* followed by an adjective.

INCORRECT	**His over the top performance made the whole film unbelievable.**
	The freshly-printed counterfeit bills felt like genuine dollars.
	The local chapter of Parents without Partners will sponsor an open toga party on Saturday.
CORRECT	**His over-the-top performance made the whole film unbelievable.**
	The freshly printed counterfeit bills felt like genuine dollars.
	The local chapter of Parents without Partners will sponsor an open-toga party on Saturday.

12. Missing or misused apostrophe

Do not confuse the pronoun *its*, meaning "belonging to it," with the contraction *it's*, meaning "it is" or "it has." The possessive form of a noun uses an apostrophe; possessive pronouns never take apostrophes.

INCORRECT	**The car is lying on it's side in the ditch.**
	Its a blue 1999 Ford Taurus.
	That new car of her's rides very smoothly.
CORRECT	**The car is lying on its side in the ditch.**
	It's a blue 1999 Ford Taurus.
	That new car of hers rides very smoothly.

For clarity, avoid using the contraction ending in -*'s* to mean "has" instead of "is."

UNCLEAR	**She's held many offices in student government.**
CLEAR	**She has held many offices in student government.**

13. Incorrect pronoun case

A pronoun that is the subject of a sentence or clause must be in the subjective case (*I*, *he*, *she*, *we*, *they*). A pronoun that is the direct object of a verb, the indirect object of a verb, or the object of a preposition must be in the objective case (*me, him, her, us, them*). To decide whether a pronoun in a compound construction — two or more nouns or pronouns joined with *and* or *or* — should be subjective or objective, omit everything in the compound except the pronoun and see whether the subjective or objective case sounds correct.

INCORRECT   **He took my wife and I to dinner.**

(Try that sentence without the first part of the compound, *my wife and.*)

CORRECT   **He took my wife and me to dinner.**

INCORRECT   **Her and her family donated the prize money.**

(Try that sentence without the second part of the compound, *and her family.*)

CORRECT   **She and her family donated the prize money.**

The pronouns *who* and *whom* often cause confusion. *Who* (or *whoever*) is subjective; *whom* (or *whomever*) is objective. If the pronoun appears in a question, answer the question using a pronoun (such as *I* or *me*) to determine whether to use the subjective or objective form.

INCORRECT   **Who does Howard want to see?**

Answering the question — *Howard wants to see me* — reveals that the pronoun should be objective.

CORRECT   **Whom does Howard want to see?**

When *who* or *whom* is not part of a question, it introduces a dependent clause. Determine the case of the pronoun in the clause by removing the clause from the sentence and replacing *who* or *whom* with *I* and *me* to see which form is correct.

INCORRECT   **She welcomed whomever knocked on her door.**

The clause is *whomever knocked on her door.* Replacing *whomever* with *I* and *me — I knocked on her door; me knocked on her door* — reveals that the subjective form *whoever* is correct.

CORRECT   **She welcomed whoever knocked on her door.**

14. Lack of agreement between pronoun and antecedent

Pronouns must agree in number (singular or plural) and person (first, second or third) with their *antecedents* — the nouns or pronouns to which they refer. Do not shift, for example, from a singular antecedent to a plural pronoun, or from a third-person antecedent to a first- or second-person pronoun.

INCORRECT   **The class must check their work.**

CORRECT   **The class must check its work.**

                   Class members must check their work.

15. Biased language

Avoid stereotypes and biased language. Take special care to avoid gender-specific pronouns.

BIASED	**A reporter must always check his work.**
ACCEPTABLE	**Reporters must always check their work.**
	If you are a reporter, you must always check your work.
BIASED	**Local politicians and their wives attended a dinner in honor of the visiting diplomat.**
ACCEPTABLE	**Local politicians and their spouses attended a dinner in honor of the visiting diplomat.**

16. Lack of agreement between subject and verb

Subject and verb must agree in number. Use the form of the verb that agrees with a singular or plural subject. Be especially careful to identify the subject correctly when words separate subject from verb.

INCORRECT	**The bag with the green stripes belong to her.**
CORRECT	**The bag with the green stripes belongs to her.**

A compound subject with parts joined by *and* is always plural. When parts of a compound subject are joined by *or*, make the verb agree with the part of the compound closest to the verb.

INCORRECT	**A mystery writer and her daughter lives in the house by the river.**
CORRECT	**A mystery writer and her daughter live in the house by the river.**
INCORRECT	**Either Mike or his sisters has the spare key.**
CORRECT	**Either Mike or his sisters have the spare key.**

17. Incorrect complement with linking verb

A linking verb such as *be, appear, feel* or *become* links a subject with a word or words that identify or describe the subject. When the identifying word — called a *subject complement* — is a pronoun, use the subjective case for the pronoun.

INCORRECT	**That was him on the telephone five minutes ago.**
CORRECT	**That was he on the telephone five minutes ago.**

When a word or words describing the subject follow a linking verb, the word or words must be adjectives.

INCORRECT	**She feels terribly about the things she said.**
CORRECT	**She feels terrible about the things she said.**

18. Incorrect use of subjunctive mood

Conditions contrary to fact require a verb to be in the subjunctive mood. Apply this rule in stories about all pending legislation at all levels of government. Use the subjunctive mood in "that" clauses after verbs of wishing, suggesting and requiring; in other words, use the subjunctive in clauses, dependent or independent, that do not state a fact.

INCORRECT	**The bylaws require that he <u>declares</u> his candidacy by April 10.**
CORRECT	**The bylaws require that he <u>declare</u> his candidacy by April 10.**
INCORRECT	**The bill <u>will</u> require everyone to register for the draft at age 18.**
CORRECT	**The bill <u>would</u> require everyone to register for the draft at age 18.**

19. Wrong word

Wrong-word errors include using a word that sounds similar to, or the same as, the word you need but means something different (such as writing *affect* when you mean *effect*) and using a word that has a shade of meaning that is not what you intend (such as writing *slender* when you want to suggest *scrawny*). Check the dictionary if you are not sure whether you are using a word correctly.

INCORRECT	**Merchants who appear <u>disinterested</u> in their customers may lose business.**
CORRECT	**Merchants who appear <u>uninterested</u> in their customers may lose business.**
INCORRECT	**The guests gasped and applauded when they saw the <u>excessive</u> display of food.**
CORRECT	**The guests gasped and applauded when they saw the <u>lavish</u> display of food.**

20. Incorrect verb form

Every verb has five forms: a base form, a present-tense form, a past-tense form, a present-participle form used for forming the progressive tenses, and a past-participle form used for forming the passive voice or one of the perfect tenses.

Dropping the ending from present-tense forms and regular past-tense forms is a common error.

| INCORRECT | **The police are <u>suppose</u> to protect the public.** |
| CORRECT | **The police are <u>supposed</u> to protect the public.** |

Regular verbs end in *-ed* in the past tense and past participle, but irregular verbs do not follow a set pattern for forming the past tense and past participle, so those forms of irregular verbs are frequently used incorrectly. Look up irregular verbs if you are uncertain of the correct form.

INCORRECT	**The manager was not in the restaurant when it was robbed because he had <u>went</u> home early.**
CORRECT	**The manager was not in the restaurant when it was robbed because he had <u>gone</u> home early.**
INCORRECT	**The thieves <u>taked</u> everything in the safe.**
CORRECT	**The thieves <u>took</u> everything in the safe.**

APPENDIX 2   Wire Service Style Summary

Most publications adhere to rules of style to avoid annoying inconsistencies. Without a stylebook to provide guidance in such matters, writers would not know whether the word *president* should be capitalized when preceding or following a name, whether the correct spelling is *employee* or *employe* (dictionaries list both), or whether a street name should be *Twelfth* or *12th*.

Newspapers use the wire service stylebooks to provide such guidance. For consistency, the Associated Press and United Press International collaborated in establishing style, and rules of the two services differ in only minor ways. Most newspapers follow one of those stylebooks, although the Associated Press dominates.

This section is an abbreviated summary of the primary rules of wire service style. This summary should be helpful even for those without a stylebook, but we provide it assuming that most users of this book have one. Why? Because this section includes only the rules used most frequently, arranged by topic to make them easier to learn. Only about 10 percent of the rules in a stylebook account for 90 percent of the wire service style you will use regularly. You will use the rest of the rules about 10 percent of the time. It makes sense, therefore, to learn first those rules you will use most often.

ABBREVIATIONS AND ACRONYMS
Punctuation of Abbreviations

- Generally speaking, abbreviations of two letters or fewer have periods:
  600 B.C., A.D. 1066
  8 a.m., 7 p.m.
  U.N., U.S., R.I., N.Y.
  8151 Yosemite St.
  EXCEPTIONS: *AM radio, FM radio, 35 mm camera, the AP Stylebook, "LA smog," D-Mass., R-Kan., IQ, TV.*
- Generally speaking, abbreviations of three letters or more do not have periods:
  CIA, FBI, NATO
  mpg, mph
  EXCEPTION: *c.o.d.*

Symbols

- Always write out *%* as *percent* in a story, but you may use the symbol in a headline.
- Always write out *&* as *and* unless it is part of a company's formal name.
- Always write out *¢* as *cent* or *cents*.
- Always use the symbol *$* rather than the word *dollar* with any actual figure, and put the symbol before the figure. Write out *dollar* only if you are speaking of, say, the value of the dollar on the world market.

Dates

- Never abbreviate days of the week.
- Don't abbreviate a month unless it has a date of the month with it: *August 2004; Aug. 17; Aug. 17, 2004.*
- The five months spelled with five letters or fewer are never abbreviated: *March; April 20; May 13, 2004; June 1956; July of that year.*
- Never abbreviate *Christmas* as *Xmas*, even in a headline.
- *Fourth of July* is written out.

People and Titles

- Some publications still use courtesy titles (*Mr., Mrs., Ms., Miss*) on second reference in stories, although most seem to have moved away from them as sexist. Many publications use them only in quotations from sources. Others use them only in obituaries and editorials, or on second reference in stories mentioning a husband and wife. In the last case, other newspapers prefer to repeat the person's whole name or, especially in features, use the person's first name. The Associated Press suggests using a courtesy title when someone requests it, but most journalists don't bother to ask.
- Use the abbreviations *Gov., Lt. Gov., Rep., Sen.* and *the Rev.*, as well as abbreviations of military titles, on first reference; then drop the title on subsequent references. Some titles you might expect to see abbreviated before a name are not abbreviated in AP style: *Attorney General, District Attorney, President, Professor, Superintendent.*
- Use the abbreviations *Jr.* and *Sr.* after a name on first reference if appropriate, but do not set them off by commas as you learned to do in English class.

Organizations

- Write out the first reference to most organizations in full rather than using an acronym: *National Organization for Women.* For *CIA, FBI* and *GOP*, however, the acronym may be used on the first reference.
- You may use well-known abbreviations such as *FCC* and *NOW* in a headline even though they would not be acceptable on first reference in the story.
- Do not put the abbreviation of an organization in parentheses after the full name on first reference. If its abbreviation is that confusing, don't use an abbreviation at all but rather call it something like "the gay rights group" or "the bureau" on second reference.
- Use the abbreviations *Co., Cos., Corp., Inc.* and *Ltd.* at the end of a company's name even if the company spells out the word; do not abbreviate these words if followed by other words such as "of America." The abbreviations *Co., Cos.* and *Corp.* are abbreviated, however, if followed by *Inc.* or *Ltd.* (and, by the way, these latter two abbreviations are not set off by commas even if the company uses them).

- Abbreviate political affiliations after a name in the following way:
  Sen. Christopher Bond, R-Mo., said . . .

Note the use of a single letter without a period for the party and the use of commas around the party and state.

- Never abbreviate the word *association*, even as part of a name.

Places

- Don't abbreviate a state name unless it follows the name of a city in that state:
  Nevada; Brown City, Mich.
- Never abbreviate the six states spelled with five or fewer letters or the two noncontiguous states:
  Alaska, Hawaii, Idaho, Iowa, Maine, Ohio, Texas, Utah
- Use the traditional state abbreviations, not the Postal Service's two-letter ones:
  Miss., not *MS*

EXCEPTION: Use the two-letter postal abbreviations when a full address is given that includes a ZIP code.

Here are the abbreviations used in normal copy:

Ala.	Md.	N.D.
Ariz.	Mass.	Okla.
Ark.	Mich.	Ore.
Calif.	Minn.	Pa.
Colo.	Miss.	R.I.
Conn.	Mo.	S.C.
Del.	Mont.	S.D.
Fla.	Neb.	Tenn.
Ga.	Nev.	Vt.
Ill.	N.H.	Va.
Ind.	N.J.	Wash.
Kan.	N.M.	W. Va.
Ky.	N.Y.	Wis.
La.	N.C.	Wyo.

- Use state abbreviations with domestic towns and cities unless they appear in the wire service dateline list of cities that stand alone. Many publications add to the wire service list their own list of towns well-known in the state or region. Use nations' full names with foreign towns and cities unless they appear in the wire service dateline list of cities that stand alone. Once a state or nation has been identified in a story, it is unnecessary to repeat it unless clarity demands it.

The lists of cities in the United States and the rest of the world that the wire services say may stand alone without a state abbreviation or nation are too lengthy to include here. Consult the appropriate stylebook. A handy rule of thumb is if it's an American city and has a major sports franchise, it probably stands alone. Likewise, if it's a foreign city most people have heard of, it probably stands alone.

- Don't abbreviate the names of thoroughfares if there is no street address with them:
  Main Street, Century Boulevard West.

- If the thoroughfare's name has the word *avenue, boulevard, street* or any of the directions on a map, such as *north* or *southeast*, abbreviate those words with a street address: *1044 W. Maple St., 1424 Lee Blvd. S., 999 Jackson Ave.*
- In a highway's name, always abbreviate *U.S.* but never abbreviate a state's name. In the case of an interstate highway, the name is written in full on first reference, abbreviated on subsequent ones:
  U.S. 63 or U.S. Highway 63, Massachusetts 2
  Interstate 70 (first reference), *I-70* (second reference)
- Never abbreviate *Fort* or *Mount.*
- Always use the abbreviation *St.* for *Saint* in place names. Exceptions: *Saint John* in New Brunswick, *Ste. Genevieve* in Missouri, *Sault Ste. Marie* in Michigan and Ontario.
- Abbreviate *United States* and *United Nations* as *U.S.* and *U.N.* when used as adjectives, but spell them out as nouns.

Miscellaneous

- Use the abbreviation *IQ* (no periods) in all references to *intelligence quotient.*
- Abbreviate and capitalize the word *number* when followed by a numeral: *No. 1.*
- Use the abbreviation *TV* (no periods) only in headlines, as an adjective and in constructions such as *cable TV.* Otherwise, spell out *television.*
- Use the abbreviation *UFO* in all references to an *unidentified flying object.*
- Use the abbreviation *vs.*, not *v.*, for *versus.*

CAPITALIZATION

- Proper nouns are capitalized; common nouns are not. Unfortunately, this rule is not always easy to apply when the noun is the name of an animal, food or plant or when it is a trademark that has become so well-known that people mistakenly use it generically.
- Regions are capitalized; directions are not:
  We drove east two miles to catch the interstate out West.
  - Adjectives and nouns pertaining to a region are capitalized: *Southern accent, Western movie, a Southerner, a Western.*
  - A region combined with a country's name is not capitalized unless the region is part of the name of a divided country: *eastern United States, North Korea.*
  - A region combined with a state name is capitalized only if it is famous: *Southern California, southern Colorado.*
- When two or more compound proper nouns are combined to share a word in common made plural, the shared plural is lowercased:
  Missouri and Mississippi rivers
  Chrisman and Truman high schools
- Government and college terms are not always as consistent as you might think:
  - *College departments* follow the animal, food and plant rule: Capitalize only words that are already proper nouns in themselves: *Spanish department, sociology department.* By contrast, always capitalize *a specific government department*, even without the city, state or federal designator, and even if it's turned around with *of* deleted: *Police Department, Fire Department, State Department, Department of Commerce.*
  - *College and government committees* are capitalized if the formal name is given rather than a shorter, descriptive designation: *Special Senate Select Committee to Investigate Improper Labor-Management Practices; rackets committee.*

- *Academic degrees* are spelled out and lowercased: *bachelor of arts degree, master's degree.* Avoid the abbreviations *Ph.D., M.A., B.A.,* etc., except in lists.
- Always capitalize (unless plural or generic) *City Council* and *County Commission* (but alone, *council* and *commission* are lowercased). *Cabinet* is capitalized when referring to advisers. *Legislature* is capitalized if the state's body is formally named that. *Capitol,* the building, is capitalized, but *capital,* the city, is not.
- Never capitalize *board of directors* or *board of trustees* (but *Board of Curators* and *Board of Education* are capitalized). *Federal, government* and *administration* are not capitalized. *President* and *vice president* are capitalized only before a name.
- *Military titles (Sgt., Maj., Gen.)* are capitalized before a name, as are *Air Force, Army, Marines* and *Navy* if referring to U.S. forces.
- *Political parties* are capitalized, including the word *party: Democratic Party, Socialist Party.* Be sure, however, to capitalize words such as *communist, democratic, fascist* and *socialist* only if they refer to a formal party rather than a philosophy.
- Religious terms are variously capitalized and lowercased:
  - *Pope* is lowercased except before a name: *the pope, Pope Gregory.*
  - *Mass* is always capitalized.
  - Pronouns for *God* and *Jesus* are lowercased.
  - *Bible* is capitalized when meaning the Holy Scriptures and lowercased when referring to another book: *a hunter's bible.*
  - Sacraments are capitalized if they commemorate events in the life of Jesus or signify his presence: *Baptism, Communion.*
- Actual race names are capitalized, but color descriptions are not:
  Caucasian, Mongoloid, Negro
  white, red, black
- Formal titles of people are capitalized before a name, but occupational titles are not:
  President George W. Bush, Mayor Dennis Archer, Coach Roy Williams, Dean Fred Wilson, astronaut Mary Gardner, journalist Fred Francis, plumber Phil Sanders, pharmacist Roger Wheaton

Some titles are not easy to tell apart: *managing editor, chief executive officer.* When in doubt, put the title behind the name, set off with commas, and use lowercase.

- Formal titles that are capitalized before a name are lowercased after a name:
  George W. Bush, president of the United States
  Dennis Archer, mayor of Detroit
  Roy Williams, coach of the Kansas Jayhawks
  Fred Wilson, dean of students
- Formal titles that are abbreviated before a name are written out and lowercased if they follow a name:
  Gov. Bob Holden; Bob Holden, governor of Missouri
  Rep. Lindsey Graham of South Carolina or *Lindsey Graham, representative from South Carolina*
- The first word in a direct quotation is capitalized only if the quote meets all these criteria:
  - It is a complete sentence. Don't capitalize a partial quote.
  - It stands alone as a separate sentence or paragraph, or it is set off from its source by a comma or colon.
  - It is a direct quotation (in quotation marks).
- A question within a sentence is capitalized:
  My only question is, When do we start?

NUMBERS

- Cardinal numbers (numerals) are used in:
  - Addresses. Always use numerals for street addresses: *1322 N 10th St.*
  - Ages. Always use numerals, even for days or months: *3 days old; John Burnside, 56.*
  - Aircraft and spacecraft: *F-4, DC-10, Apollo 11.* Exception: *Air Force One.*
  - Clothes size: *size 6.*
  - Dates. Always use the numeral alone — no *nd, rd, st* or *th* after it: *March 20.*
  - Decades: *the '80s.*
  - Dimensions: *5-foot-6-inch guard* (but no hyphen when the word modified is one associated with size: *3 feet tall, 10 feet long*).
  - Highways: *U.S. 63.*
  - Millions, billions and trillions: *1.2 billion, 6 million.*
  - Money. Always use numerals, but starting with a million, write like this: *$1.4 million.*
  - Numbers: *No. 1, No. 2.*
  - Percentages. Always use numerals except at the beginning of a sentence: *4 percent.*
  - Recipes. All numbers for amounts take numerals: *2 teaspoons.*
  - Speeds: *55 mph, 4 knots.*
  - Sports. Use numerals for just about everything: *8–6 score, 2 yards, 3-under-par, 2 strokes.*
  - Temperatures. Use numerals for all except *zero.* Below zero, spell out *minus: minus 6,* not *–6* (except in tabular data).
  - Times: *4 a.m., 6:32 p.m., noon, midnight, five minutes, three hours.*
  - Weights: *7 pounds, 11 ounces.*
  - Years: Use numerals without commas. A year is the only numeral that can start a sentence: *1988 was a good year.*
- Numerals with the suffixes *nd, rd, st* and *th* are used for:
  - Political divisions (precincts, wards, districts): *3rd Congressional District.*
  - Military sequences: *1st Lt., 2nd Division, 7th Fleet.*
  - Courts: *2nd District Court; 10th Circuit Court of Appeals.*
  - Streets after *Ninth.* For *First* through *Ninth,* use words: *Fifth Avenue, 13th Street.*
  - Amendments to the Constitution after *Ninth.* For *First* through *Ninth,* use words: *First Amendment, 16th Amendment.*
- Words are used for:
  - Numbers less than 10, with the exceptions noted above: *five people, four rules.*
  - Any number at the start of a sentence except for a year: *Sixteen years ago. . . .*
  - Casual numbers: *about a hundred or so.*
  - Fractions less than one: *one-half.*
- Mixed numerals are used for fractions greater than one: *1½*
- Roman numerals are used for a man who is the third or later in his family to bear a name and for a king, queen, pope or world war:
  John D. Rockefeller III, Queen Elizabeth II, Pope John Paul II, World War I

Suggested Web Site

www.ap.org
The Associated Press provides wire news through sites of its member newspapers.

Society of Professional Journalists' Code of Ethics

PREAMBLE

Members of the Society of Professional Journalists believe that public enlightenment is the forerunner of justice and the foundation of democracy. The duty of the journalist is to further those ends by seeking truth and providing a fair and comprehensive account of events and issues. Conscientious journalists from all media and specialties strive to serve the public with thoroughness and honesty. Professional integrity is the cornerstone of a journalist's credibility. Members of the society share a dedication to ethical behavior and adopt this code to declare the society's principles and standards of practice.

SEEK TRUTH AND REPORT IT

Journalists should be honest, fair and courageous in gathering, reporting and interpreting information.

Journalists should:

- Test the accuracy of information from all sources and exercise care to avoid inadvertent error. Deliberate distortion is never permissible.
- Diligently seek out subjects of news stories to give them the opportunity to respond to allegations of wrongdoing.

Sigma Delta Chi's first Code of Ethics was borrowed from the American Society of Newspaper Editors in 1926. In 1973, Sigma Delta Chi wrote its own code, which was revised in 1984 and 1987. The present version of the Society of Professional Journalists' Code of Ethics was adopted in September 1996.

- Identify sources whenever feasible. The public is entitled to as much information as possible on sources' reliability.
- Always question sources' motives before promising anonymity. Clarify conditions attached to any promise made in exchange for information. Keep promises.
- Make certain that headlines, news teases and promotional material, photos, video, audio, graphics, sound bites and quotations do not misrepresent. They should not oversimplify or highlight incidents out of context.
- Never distort the content of news photos or video. Image enhancement for technical clarity is always permissible. Label montages and photo illustrations.
- Avoid misleading re-enactments or staged news events. If re-enactment is necessary to tell a story, label it.
- Avoid undercover or other surreptitious methods of gathering information except when traditional open methods will not yield information vital to the public. Use of such methods should be explained as part of the story.
- Never plagiarize.
- Tell the story of the diversity and magnitude of the human experience boldly, even when it is unpopular to do so.
- Examine their own cultural values and avoid imposing those values on others.
- Avoid stereotyping by race, gender, age, religion, ethnicity, geography, sexual orientation, disability, physical appearance or social status.
- Support the open exchange of views, even views they find repugnant.
- Give voice to the voiceless; official and unofficial sources of information can be equally valid.
- Distinguish between advocacy and news reporting. Analysis and commentary should be labeled and not misrepresent fact or context.
- Distinguish news from advertising and shun hybrids that blur the lines between the two.
- Recognize a special obligation to ensure that the public's business is conducted in the open and that government records are open to inspection.

MINIMIZE HARM

Ethical journalists treat sources, subjects and colleagues as human beings deserving of respect.

Journalists should:

- Show compassion for those who may be affected adversely by news coverage. Use special sensitivity when dealing with children and inexperienced sources or subjects.
- Be sensitive when seeking or using interviews or photographs of those affected by tragedy or grief.
- Recognize that gathering and reporting information may cause harm or discomfort. Pursuit of the news is not a license for arrogance.
- Recognize that private people have a greater right to control information about themselves than do public officials and others who seek power, influence or attention. Only an overriding public need can justify intrusion into anyone's privacy.
- Show good taste. Avoid pandering to lurid curiosity.
- Be cautious about identifying juvenile suspects or victims of sex crimes.
- Be judicious about naming criminal suspects before the formal filing of charges.
- Balance a criminal suspect's fair trial rights with the public's right to be informed.

ACT INDEPENDENTLY

Journalists should be free of obligation to any interest other than the public's right to know.

Journalists should:

- Avoid conflicts of interest, real or perceived.
- Remain free of associations and activities that may compromise integrity or damage credibility.
- Refuse gifts, favors, fees, free travel and special treatment, and shun secondary employment, political involvement, public office and service in community organizations if they compromise journalistic integrity.
- Disclose unavoidable conflicts.
- Be vigilant and courageous about holding those with power accountable.
- Deny favored treatment to advertisers and special interests and resist their pressure to influence news coverage.
- Be wary of sources offering information for favors or money; avoid bidding for news.

BE ACCOUNTABLE

Journalists are accountable to their readers, listeners, viewers and each other.

Journalists should:

- Clarify and explain news coverage and invite dialogue with the public over journalistic conduct.
- Encourage the public to voice grievances against the news media.
- Admit mistakes and correct them promptly.
- Expose unethical practices of journalists and the news media.
- Abide by the same high standards to which they hold others.

APPENDIX 4   Crisis Coverage: An Interactive CD-ROM Journalism Simulation

A s mentioned in Chapter 13, crime and accidents, fires and disasters are staples of news reporting. Almost every journalist working on a newspaper will write these types of stories, and many cover such stories frequently. Unfortunately, gaining real-world experience with this reporting is almost impossible in the introductory news-writing class. Robberies, house fires and car accidents do not fit neatly into a syllabus, nor does listening to a police scanner and driving to such events fit neatly into a student schedule.

The exercises in Chapter 13 of the *Workbook for News Reporting and Writing* provide a good starting ground for learning the fundamentals of crime and accident, fire and disaster reporting, but they can't simulate the news-gathering process. To help prepare you better for both the crime and the accident/fire/disaster genres, we provide a CD-ROM simulation of an actual tragedy, the shooting of a police officer and four bystanders in St. Joseph, Mo.

TIPS FOR USING THE PROGRAM

The simulation program puts you in the news room the night of the shooting. After a brief introduction and opening segment, you begin your news-gathering at your desk in the news room. Your job is to get information from paper, human and electronic sources as the night progresses and then write a story as more information becomes available (see the section "Types of Articles and Assignments" for possible stories/assignments). The simulation progresses from approximately 5 p.m. until deadline, at 11 p.m.

The main interface is the news room cubicle. On and around your desk are items to click on to get information, as the accompanying screen capture illustrates.

545

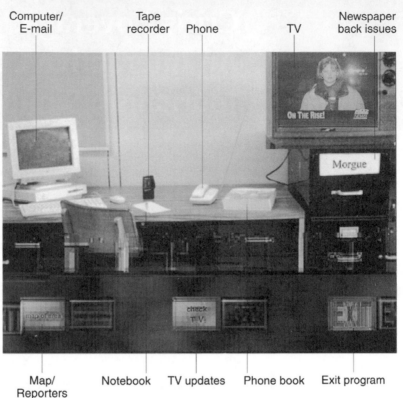

Computer/ E-mail • Tape recorder • Phone • TV • Newspaper back issues

Morgue

Map/ Reporters on scene • Notebook • TV updates • Phone book • Exit program

Clicking on the Desk Items

Just as in real-world reporting, sources develop over the course of the story, and some will not be immediately available to you. For example, when the scenario first begins, the reporters dispatched to the scene (under Map of Area) will not be ready to talk to you yet, nor will a phone call to the police station or hospital give you any information. Be sure to check back with these sources multiple times as the night progresses and more bits of news become available. The sources include the following:

- **Television.** You will watch actual news broadcasts from the night of the shooting.
- **Phone book.** Good reporters make good use of the phone. You will call some of your sources, and they will give you quotes and information.
- **Phone.** Sources will call you with updated information throughout the night.
- **Morgue.** Background research is crucial to quality reporting, and you will want to check to see if there are any related articles from back issues of the newspaper.
- **Map/Reporters.** Three reporters will be on the scene, and they will give you updates and quotes from eyewitnesses.
- **Notebook.** Reporters will bring back their notebooks with interview notes for you to use in your story.
- **Tape recorder.** One reporter will bring back a tape-recorded interview from the scene.

- **Computer/E-mail.** There will be e-mail and Web sources for you to use. In addition to the information provided on the CD-ROM, you may wish to do additional Web research.

Because these sources will be available at different times, be sure to click on all of the buttons in the time periods between the TV clips.

Pacing Yourself

The simulation covers a period of approximately six hours, but it will likely take you only between 30 and 60 minutes to run through the scenario. If you are running the program during a 75-minute or longer class, you should not have much difficulty in finishing the simulation during a full class period. If you are trying to complete the program within a 50-minute class period, be sure to be in class on time or early, take notes quickly and make good decisions about what information you will likely not need to copy down. Remember the principles of newsworthiness and definitions of "news" outlined in Chapter 1, and consider what information your readers will be interested in knowing.

Taking Notes

We pointed out in Chapter 1 that accuracy is a cornerstone of good journalism. Accuracy is especially important — and difficult — in breaking news stories about tragedies, stories that often are at the top of Page One and will be read by almost all of your audience. So be sure to take very careful notes. This is not like a book exercise for which you can easily copy down notes and double-check them at a later time. Just as in real-world reporting, for many of these sources you will have only one opportunity to get the information right and to decide what information and quotes to include in your notes. If you're using the TV sources, you won't be able to replay those segments, so take good shorthand and reconstruct your notes after each segment, as we suggested in Chapter 3.

For your notes, you may wish to use a legal pad or a reporter's notebook. Depending on your writing and typing skills, you may prefer to take notes on the computer, especially since you can later cut/copy/paste segments from your computer notes into your final draft. In order to take the computer notes, you'll want to open up a word processing program before starting the simulation and move the program's window to the side of the screen so you can click back and forth between the simulation program and the word processing window when taking notes. Be sure to save your computer notes often in case your computer crashes.

Using the TV

Good news reporters watch their broadcast colleagues — and competitors — all the time, especially during tragedies. You'll be watching several clips from the local TV station, which include selections from the local 6 p.m. and 10 p.m. newscasts and cut-ins with breaking news before and after those newscasts. In all, there are 10 video clips, some of which play automatically and some that play when you click on the *Check TV* button. *Be sure to try all of your other sources before you click on the Check TV button*, since the TV segment will jump you to a later part in the scenario.

Typically, a print journalist will not use quotes from radio or TV broadcasts. Before you begin the simulation, be sure to check with your instructor about using quotes from the TV in your story. Your instructor may forbid you from using any TV quotes or allow you to cite such quotes sparingly (ex: "In an interview with KQ2 TV last night, witness James Smith said, . . ."). He or she may allow you to quote the sources (not the reporters or anchors) as if you were interviewing them yourself. You need to know your instructor's wishes *before* you start the simulation so you know how carefully to take notes during the TV segments. You won't have a chance to hear and see those segments again.

Adjusting Sound and Using Headphones

Before you begin the scenario, you'll want to test the sound levels of your computer and make sure the sound is working because you'll need to hear all the audio and video clips in order to write your story. In addition, you may want to bring headphones that fit your computer port, to keep sound levels in the room down and to muffle the sound coming from nearby computers. Then again, the wide array of sounds and voices coming from a dozen or more computers does help mimic the bedlam found in a news room near deadline.

Quitting/Restarting the Program

Because the program replicates the timing and flow of information in a tragedy, you will not be able to jump around in the program or quit and later restart the program where you left off. If you have to restart the program, you will be placed back at the very beginning of the scenario. So be absolutely sure you want to quit before you click on the red EXIT button. Likewise, to prevent the program from crashing and thus prevent you from needing to start over, make sure you are working on a reliable computer with sufficient RAM available.

For this assignment, your instructor may want you to run through the program only once because you would get only one shot at gathering information under deadline in any crime or accident, fire or disaster story. Or your instructor may allow you to run through the program multiple times to make sure you find all of the sources.

TIPS FOR WRITING YOUR ARTICLE

Keep in mind one key tip in newswriting: Listen carefully to your editor — or in this case, your instructor — about what type of article he or she wants you to write. For a spot news story like this, neither you nor your editor would have time to do a rewrite.

In addition, make sure you understand the nature of the publication and your audience. If you are wishing to replicate the actual situation, assume you are writing for the *St. Joseph News-Press*, an independently owned daily that has a circulation of approximately 40,000 and serves the 70,000 residents of St. Joseph as well as people in the surrounding counties in northwest Missouri. Your instructor may prefer you to write the story for a larger paper, such as the *Kansas City Star*, or for a small, nearby weekly or for the Associated Press or another wire service. Which publication you write for will help determine how you write your story and what information you include.

Because most people will be writing an inverted pyramid account of the main story, the majority of the other tips in this section are geared toward that type of story. If you are writing a different type of story, you may want to refer to the sections of the book that address that type of story in more detail.

Rank Your Information in Order of Importance

You will have a lot of information to deal with and try to fit into your story. To write an inverted pyramid story, you may want to rank or mark each fact or quote to help you decide what material will go near the beginning, the middle and the end of the story and what information you probably won't need to use.

Prepare Information for a Summary Lead

You may not end up using a summary lead in your final draft, but drafting such a lead will help you write the rest of the story. Using the ranking mentioned above, write down the key answers to these questions:

Who?
What?
When?
Where?
Why?
How?

Decide which of these items need to be in the lead (the "why," for example, might not be necessary or may be unknown). Put the most important of the 5W's and H at the beginning of the lead. As mentioned in Chapter 7, try to keep the lead to 25 or 30 words and preferably to one sentence.

Write Several Alternate Leads

Even if you think you are going to use a straight summary lead, you should try other types of leads as well because you may discover one of those other leads works much better. Given the complexity of the situation, you may decide to use a multiple-element lead. Maybe the best choice will be a delayed identification. If you are writing for the St. Joseph community, you may realize an immediate-identification lead is most appropriate. After trying several lead types, you may find that a flair lead that contains elements of description or narration would work best.

Draw a Map

Drawing a map of the scene or the area on a piece of paper can help you organize your thoughts and better understand what happened, especially if you are a visually oriented person.

Make a Chronology

Even if you don't use a chronological format for your article, a timeline of the events will help you understand the events and write your article.

TYPES OF ARTICLES AND ASSIGNMENTS

In a situation such as this tragedy, the entire reporting and editing staff is mobilized. Those who were off for the day or who had already put in their hours are called back, and the whole staff works together to produce the in-depth coverage the readership will want and expect. Some reporters go to the scene and collect information. Others are stationed at the police department, city hall or hospital, while still other staffers may research information in the morgue or online. Using all of these resources, the staff produces not only one main article but also three, four or more sidebars to accompany it.

The simulation program lends itself well to writing a variety of different stories and sidebars. Before you begin the simulation, you'll need to be clear about exactly what type of article or articles your instructor wants you to write because the article's focus will affect what notes to take and what sources to pay especially close attention to.

The most typical assignment is covering the main story and using the inverted pyramid, the organizational format most often used for hard news stories like crime and accidents, fires and disasters. Before you write such a story, be sure to reread Chapter 7 to review the principles for writing inverted pyramid stories. Carefully consider what information is most important, and put that information early in the story. Don't bury key information that may end up getting cut or not getting read.

Using the inverted pyramid is not the only way to tell the story. In Chapter 13 the example of the Kansas man who was killed by a police marksman illustrates how a chronological approach sometimes works better. Your instructor may choose to have you write a chronological story instead of — or in addition to — an inverted pyramid account. To do this, you probably will want to reconstruct a timeline and reorganize your notes to represent the order in which events happened instead of the order in which the information became available to you. Your instructor may also assign you or give you the freedom to use one of the other alternatives to the inverted pyramid outlined in Chapter 9.

Regardless of which story type you are assigned, you'll want to remember to include the key information and sources for crime and accident, fire and disaster stories:

- Eyewitnesses.
- Police or other officials in charge of handling the situation.
- Victims and friends and relatives of the victims (when possible and appropriate).

Chapter 13 also stresses the importance of obtaining official documents for these types of stories, such as an accident report, a fire marshal's casualty report or a police report. For this simulation, however, an official document is not available before your deadline.

Your instructor may give you a word limit for your article, in the same way a managing editor, news editor or copy editor might tell a reporter in this situation, "Make it x inches, no more, no less," because the number of column inches allotted to the story might already be set by the time the writer finishes the story. The editors and layout personnel would likely have been scrambling to assemble all of the new shooting-related articles, photos and informational graphics. The main story may be held until the last minute so that the most current information will appear in the next day's paper. Consequently, there may be precious little leeway given for the length of the article.

A word or inches limit is a restriction for the print newspaper only, of course. Chapter 1 illustrates how the space limitations of the physical newspaper don't apply in an online environment. The print newspaper may have space for only a 700-word article and two photos, but the online edition could have 1,000-plus words and virtually unlimited photos and graphics.

Your instructor may choose one of the following articles or exercises or may choose yet another possible assignment.

Main Story

Inverted Pyramid

Write a main news story that contains all of the important facets of the story. This is the story to run under the headline at the top of Page One if you were writing for the local newspaper (see notes in the previous section about what publication you are writing for).

Alternative Organization

Consulting Chapter 9, use a different organizational method for writing the story, such as narration (chronological), vivid scenes, a focus structure or anecdotes.

Early Online Edition

Readers in the community and across the state or country who heard about the shooting are not going to be content to wait until the next morning to find out more. As suggested on the first page of this book, the reporter will need to create text — and perhaps prepare multimedia — for the newspaper's Web site so readers can access that information shortly after the incident. They may return several times in the next 24 hours, expecting updates.

There are two places in the CD-ROM simulation where you will be able to stop and write a story and an update for the online edition.

Wire Story

Assume that you are responsible for writing a story that will go out on the Associated Press wire and will likely be picked up by many of the daily newspapers across the state. Write a 750-word story.

Sidebar Stories

Shooting Injuries

Write a sidebar about the people injured. As detailed in Chapter 13, be sure to include the names, ages, addresses and conditions of the victims.

Neighbor/Witness Accounts

Write a sidebar that focuses on the eyewitnesses and includes quotes and anecdotes about the shooting and the shooter.

Killing the Shooter

Write a sidebar about the killing of the shooter, making sure to include details about the event, eyewitness quotes and information about police procedures and policy during and after a shooting.

Historical/Contextual Piece

This type of sidebar could take one of several different paths. It could look at the history of officers killed in the line of duty in the area. It could look at other mass shootings in the area. Or it could look at police officer deaths from a national perspective, requiring you to go online and research statistics.

Practice and Follow-Up

Writing Leads

Write a variety of leads for a main story, following the advice in Chapter 7 when composing an immediate-identification lead, a delayed-identification lead, a multiple-element lead and one or more flair leads.

Interviewing

Pick two sources mentioned in the simulation that you would like to be able to interview in greater depth, and write up 10 questions for each person. As you learned in Chapter 3, you'll want to phrase and order those questions carefully because this situation is sensitive. Because you will be wanting detailed quotes, make sure that at least seven of the questions are open-ended.

Ethics

Interviewing

After reading Chapter 23 and the section in Chapter 13 about victims/witnesses in the accidents, fires and disasters section, write a pro or con essay about calling to interview the wife of the slain police officer. If you would call the wife, explain why and describe the approach you would take. If you would not call the wife, explain why and cite examples from the ethical codes to support your decision.

Photos

On the CD is a folder titled "Photos." Look at the photos and put yourself in the position of a managing editor who has to decide what photos to include in the newspaper. Which photo would you put on the front page? Which photo(s) would you not print at all, and why? If the shooting had happened in another part of the state, would that location affect what photos you would not print? Write an essay explaining your choices.

GLOSSARY

absolute privilege   The right of legislators, judges and government executives to speak without threat of libel when acting in their official capacities.

absolutism   The ethical philosophy that there is a fixed set of principles or laws from which there is no deviation. To the absolutist journalist, the end never justifies the means.

actual malice   Reckless disregard of the truth. It is a condition in libel cases.

actual malice test   Protection for reporters to write anything about an officeholder or candidate unless they know that the material is false or they recklessly disregard the truth.

ad   An advertisement.

add   A typewritten page of copy following the first page. "First add" would be the second page of typewritten copy.

advance   A report dealing with the subjects and issues to be dealt with in an upcoming meeting or event.

advertising department   The department of the newspaper responsible for advertisements. Most advertising departments have classified and display ad sections.

anchor   One in the television studio who ties together the newscast by reading the news and providing transitions from one story to the next.

anecdotal lead   A newspaper story beginning that uses humor or an interesting incident.

anecdote   An informative and entertaining story within a story.

angle   The focus of, or approach to, a story. The latest development in a continuing controversy, the key play in a football game, or the tragedy of a particular death in a mass disaster may serve as an angle.

antinomianism   The ethical philosophy that recognizes no rules. An antinomian journalist judges every ethical situation on its own merits. Unlike the situation ethicist, the antinomian does not use love of neighbor as an absolute.

AP   The Associated Press, a worldwide news-gathering cooperative owned by its subscribers.

APME   Associated Press Managing Editors, an organization of managing editors and editors whose papers are members of the Associated Press.

arraignment   A court proceeding at which a defendant is informed of the charge. At the proceeding, the defendant is asked to enter a plea, and bail may be set.

average   A term used to describe typical or representative members of a group. In mathematical terms, it refers to the result obtained when a set of numbers is added together, then divided by the number of items in the set.

background   Information that may be attributed to a source by title, but not by name; for example, "a White House aide said."

backgrounder   Story that explains and updates the news.

beat   A reporter's assigned area of responsibility. A beat may be an institution, such as the courthouse; a geographical area, such as a small town; or a subject, such as science. The term also refers to an exclusive story.

blotter   An old-fashioned term for the arrest sheet that summarizes the bare facts of an arrest. Today this information is almost always kept in a computer.

books   Assembled sheets of paper, usually newsprint, and carbon paper on which reporters prepare stories. Books are not used with modern computerized processes.

brightener   A story, usually short, that is humorous or pleasing to the reader. It is also called a *bright*.

bureau   A news-gathering office maintained by a newspaper at a place other than its central location. Papers may have bureaus in the next county, in the state capital, in Washington, D.C., or in foreign countries.

bureau chief   The director of a newspaper's news operations in a remote site or bureau.

business department   The newspaper department that handles billing, accounting and related functions.

byline   A line identifying the author of a story.

chain   Two or more newspapers owned by a single person or corporation. Also known as a *group*. The American chain owning the most newspapers is Gannett.

change of venue   An order transferring a court proceeding to another jurisdiction for prosecution. This often occurs when a party in a case claims that local media coverage has prejudiced prospective jurors.

circulation department   The department responsible for distribution of the newspaper.

city editor   The individual (also known as the *metropolitan*, or *metro*, *editor*) in charge of the city desk, which coordinates local news-gathering operations. At some papers the desk also handles regional and state news done by its own reporters.

civil law   Statutes under which an individual or a group can take action against another individual or group.

clips   Stories clipped from your own or other newspapers.

closed-ended question   A direct question designed to draw a specific response; for example, "Will you be a candidate?"

conditional privilege   See *qualified privilege*.

Consumer Price Index   A tool used by the government to measure the rate of inflation. CPI figures, reported monthly by the Bureau of Labor Statistics of the U.S. Department of Labor, compare the net change in prices between the current period and a specified base period. Reporters should use this data to accurately reflect the actual costs of goods and services.

contributing editor   Magazine columnist who works under contract and not as an employee of the magazine.

control   The process of structuring an experiment so that the only forces affecting the outcome are the variables you are observing.

copy   What reporters write. A story is a piece of copy.

copy desk   The desk at which final editing of stories is done, headlines are written and pages are designed.

copy editor   A person who checks, polishes and corrects stories written by reporters. Usually copy editors write headlines for those stories, and sometimes they decide how to arrange stories and pictures on a page.

cover   To keep abreast of significant developments on a beat or to report on a specific event. The reporter covering the police beat may be assigned to cover a murder.

criminal law   Statutes under which a grand jury or an officer of the court can take action against an individual.

cub   A beginning reporter.

cutline   The caption that accompanies a newspaper or magazine photograph. The term dates from the days when photos were reproduced with etched zinc plates, called cuts.

database   A computerized information bank, usually accessed by newspapers on a subscription basis.

deadline   The time by which a reporter, editor or desk must have completed scheduled work.

deep background   Information that may be used but that cannot be attributed to either a person or a position.

delayed-identification lead   Opening paragraph of a story in which the "who" is identified by occupation, city, office or any means other than by name.

dependent variable   See *variable*.

desk   A term used by reporters to refer to the city editor's or copy editor's position, as in, "The desk wants this story by noon."

desk assistant   Entry-level position in television news rooms. Desk assistants handle routine news assignments such as monitoring wire services and listening to police scanners.

developing story   One in which newsworthy events occur over several days or weeks.

dialogue   A conversation between two or more people, neither of whom normally is the reporter.

dig   To question or investigate thoroughly, as in, "Let's do some digging into those campaign reports."

documentary   In-depth coverage of an issue or event, especially in broadcasting.

editor   The top-ranking individual in the news department of a newspaper, also known as the *editor in chief*. The term may refer as well to those at any level who edit copy.

editorial department   The news department of a newspaper, responsible for all content of the newspaper except advertising. At some papers this term refers to the department responsible for the editorial page only.

editorialize   To inject the reporter's or the newspaper's opinion into a news story or headline. Most newspapers restrict opinion to analysis stories, columns and editorials.

editorial page editor   The individual in charge of the editorial page and, at larger newspapers, the op-ed (opposite editorial) page.

executive producer   The television executive with overall responsibility for the look of the television newscast.

fair comment and criticism   Opinion delivered on the performance of anyone in the public eye. Such opinion is legally protected if reporters do not misstate any of the facts on which they base their comments or criticism, and it is not malicious.

felony   Serious crime punishable by death or imprisonment.

field experiment   A research technique in which the reporter deliberately takes some action to observe the effects. For example, a perfectly tuned automobile could be taken to several repair shops to find out if the mechanics would invent problems that required fixing.

field producer   Behind-the-scenes television reporter who often does much of the field work for a network's on-camera correspondents.

follow   A story supplying further information about an item that has already been published; *folo* is an alternate spelling.

foreshadowing   A technique of teasing readers with material coming later in the story as a way of encouraging them to keep reading.

Freedom of Information Act   A law passed in 1966 to make it easier to obtain information from federal agencies. The law was amended in 1974 to improve access to government records.

free press–fair trial controversy   The conflict between a defendant's right to an impartial jury and a reporter's responsibility to inform the public.

futures file   A collection, filed according to date, of newspaper clippings, letters, notes and other information to remind editors of stories to assign.

general manager   The individual responsible for the business operations of a newspaper. Some newspaper chains award this title to the top-ranking local executive.

graf   A shortened form of *paragraph*, as in, "Give me two grafs on that fire."

graphics editor   Usually, the editor responsible for all nonphotographic illustrations in a newspaper, including information graphics, maps and illustrations.

handout   See *news release*.

hard lead   A lead that reports a new development or newly discovered fact. See also *soft lead*.

hard news   Coverage of the actions of government or business; or the reporting of an event, such as a crime, an accident or a speech. The time element often is important. See also *soft news*.

human-interest story   A piece valued more for its emotional impact or oddity than for its importance.

hypothesis   In investigative reporting the statement a reporter expects to be able to prove, as in, "The mayor took a bribe from that massage parlor." In an experiment the statement of what a researcher hopes to find.

immediate-identification lead   The opening paragraph of a story in which the "who" is reported by name.

independent variable   See *variable*.

indictment   A document issued by a grand jury that certifies there is sufficient evidence against a person accused of a crime to warrant holding that person for trial.

inflation   A term that describes the rising cost of living as time goes by. See also *Consumer Price Index*.

information graphic   A visual representation of data.

invasion of privacy   Violation of a person's right to be left alone.

inverted pyramid   The organization of a news story in which information is arranged in descending order of importance.

investigative reporting   The pursuit of information that has been concealed, such as evidence of wrongdoing.

IRE   Investigative Reporters and Editors, a group created to exchange information and investigative reporting techniques. IRE has its headquarters at the University of Missouri School of Journalism.

lay out (v.)   The process of preparing page drawings to indicate where stories and pictures are to be placed in the newspaper.

layout (n.)   The completed page drawing, or page dummy.

lead   (1) The first paragraph or first several paragraphs of a newspaper story (sometimes spelled *lede*); (2) the story given the best display on Page One; (3) a tip.

lead-in   An introduction to a filmed or recorded excerpt from a news source or from another reporter.

lead story   The major story displayed at the top of Page One.

libel   Damage to a person's reputation caused by a false written statement that brings the person into hatred, contempt or ridicule, or injures his or her business or occupational pursuit.

maestro   The leader of a news-gathering team. Reporters, copy editors, editors and graphic designers work with a maestro to create special reports.

managing editor   The individual with primary responsibility for day-to-day operation of the news department.

margin of error   (also called sampling error) In surveys, the range within which you can be confident of accuracy. A survey with a margin of error of 3 percent, for example, typically has a 95 percent chance of being accurate within 3 percent above or below the exact result. An allowance must be made in any survey for the possibility that the sample questioned may not be exactly like all other members of the population. The margin of error varies with the size of the sample population, and should be reported in every news story about a survey.

median   The middle number in a series arranged in order of size; it is often used when an average would be misleading. (If the series has an even number of items, the median consists of the average of the two "middle" numbers.)

misdemeanors   Minor criminal offenses, including most traffic violations, which usually result in a fine or brief confinement in a local jail.

more   Designation used at the end of a page of copy to indicate there are one or more additional pages.

morgue   The newspaper library, where published stories, photographs and resource material are stored for reference.

multiple-element lead   The opening paragraph of a story that reports two or more newsworthy elements.

narration   The telling of a story, usually in chronological order.

negligence test   The legal standard that requires reporters to use the same care in gathering facts and writing a story as any reasonable individual would under similar circumstances.

network correspondent   A television reporter who delivers the news on camera. Network correspondents may or may not do the actual news-gathering for their stories.

new media   The emerging forms of computer-delivered news.

news conference   An interview session, also called a *press conference*, in which someone submits to questions from reporters.

news director   The top news executive of a local television station.

news editor   The supervisor of the copy desk. At some newspapers, this title is used for the person in charge of local news-gathering operations.

news release   An item, also called a *handout* or *press release*, that is sent out by a group or individual seeking publicity.

news room   The place, sometimes called the *city room*, where reporters and editors work.

news story   A story that emphasizes the facts, often written in inverted pyramid style.

news value   How important or interesting a story is.

not for attribution   Information that may not be ascribed to its source.

nut paragraph   A paragraph that summarizes the key element or elements of the story. Usually found in a story not written in inverted pyramid form. Also called a *nut graf*.

obscenity   A word or phrase usually referring to sexual parts or functions in an offensive way.

off-camera reporter   One who gathers news for television but does not report on the air.

off the record Usually means, "Don't quote me." Some sources and reporters, however, use it to mean, "Don't print this." Phrases with similar, and equally ambiguous, meanings are "not for attribution" and "for background only."

op-ed page The page opposite the editorial page, frequently reserved for columns, letters to the editor and personality profiles.

open-ended question One that permits the respondent some latitude in the answer; for example, "How did you get involved in politics?"

open-meetings laws State and federal laws, often called *sunshine laws*, guaranteeing access to meetings of public officials.

open-records laws State and federal laws guaranteeing access to many — but not all — kinds of government records.

page designer One who designs newspaper or magazine pages.

parallelism A technique of presenting ideas in similar grammatical forms.

paraphrase A paraphrase digests, condenses and clarifies a quotation to convey the meaning more precisely or succinctly than the way in which the speaker's words express it. Quotation marks are eliminated.

participant observation A research technique in which the reporter joins in the activity he or she wants to write about.

payola Money or gifts given in the expectation of favors from journalists.

per capita Latin term meaning "by heads." It is determined by dividing a total figure — such as a budget — by the number of people to which it applies.

percentage Mathematical way to express the portion of a whole. Literally means a given part of every hundred. Determined by taking the number of the portion, dividing by the number of the whole, and moving the decimal two places to the right.

photo editor The individual who advises editors on the use of photographs in the newspaper. The photo editor also may supervise the photography department.

piece See *story*.

plagiarism Using any part of another's writing and passing it off as your own.

play A shortened form of *display*. A good story may be played at the top of Page One; a weak one may be played inside.

poll The measurement of opinion by questioning members of some small group chosen at random so as to be representative of the entire group. A poll is also referred to as a *survey* or *public opinion poll*. See also *randomization*.

population In scientific language, the whole group being studied. Depending on the study the population may be, for example, voters in St. Louis, physicians in California or all residents of the United States.

preliminary hearing A court hearing held to determine whether there is probable cause that a defendant committed a crime and whether the defendant should be bound over for grand jury action or trial in a higher court.

press The machine that prints the newspaper. Also a synonym for journalism, as in the phrase "freedom of the press." Sometimes used to denote print journalism, as distinguished from broadcast journalism.

press agent A person hired to gain publicity for a client. The tactics used, often called *press agentry*, might include the staging of interviews or stunts designed to attract the attention of reporters.

press box The section of a stadium or arena set aside for reporters.

press conference See *news conference*.

press release See *news release*.

privilege A defense against libel that claims the right to repeat what government officials say or do in their official capacities.

production department The department of the newspaper that transforms the work of the news and advertising departments into the finished product. The composing room and press room are key sections of this department.

profanity A word or phrase contemptuously referring to the deity or to beings regarded as divine; a sacrilegious expression.

profile A story intended to reveal the personality or character of an institution or person.

proportion Puts something in proper relation to something else — explains specific numbers in the news by relating them to the size or magnitude of the whole.

public figure A person who has assumed a role of prominence in the affairs of society and who has persuasive power and influence in a community or who has thrust himself or herself to the forefront of a public controversy. Courts have given journalists more latitude in reporting on public figures.

public journalism The new (or rediscovered) approach to journalism that emphasizes connections with the community rather than separation from it. Among the newspapers best known for practicing public journalism are the *Wichita* (Kan.) *Eagle* and *The Charlotte* (N.C.) *Observer.*

publisher The top-ranking executive of a newspaper. This title often is assumed by the owner, although chains sometimes designate as publisher the top local executive.

Pulitzer Prize The most prestigious of journalism awards. It was established by Joseph Pulitzer and is administered by Columbia University.

qualified privilege The right to report what government officials say or do in their official capacities if the report is full, fair and accurate. Also called *conditional privilege.*

quote As a noun, the term refers to a source's exact words, as in, "I have a great quote here." As a verb, it means to report those words inside quotation marks.

randomization The mathematical process used to assure that every member of a population being studied has an equal chance of being chosen for questioning or observation. See also *poll.*

rate The amount or degree of something measured in relation to a unit of something else or to a specified scale. In statistics, rate often expresses the incidence of a condition per 100,000 people, such as a murder or suicide rate. Rate also can reflect the speed at which something is changing, such as inflation or the percentage increase in a budget each year. See also *per capita.*

records column The part of the newspaper featured regularly that contains such information as routine police and fire news, births, obituaries, marriages and divorces.

reporter A person whose job it is to gather and write the news for a publication or a broadcast outlet.

rewrite To write a story again in an effort to improve it. It also means to take information over the telephone from a reporter in the field and mold it into a story.

roundup A story including a number of related events. After a storm, for example, a reporter might do a roundup of accidents, power outages and other consequences of the storm.

sample A portion of a group, or population, chosen for study as representative of the entire group.

scenic lead A lead that concentrates on a description of an environment.

second-cycle story A second version of a story already published, also called a *second-day story.* It usually has new information or a new angle.

senior editor One who edits sections of major magazines.

senior writer A title reserved for a magazine's best and most experienced reporters.

series   Two or more stories on the same or related subjects, published on a predetermined schedule.

service journalism   An aspect or type of journalism that recognizes usefulness as one of the criteria of news. Taking into consideration content and presentation, service journalism presents useful information in a usable way, for instance, placing key information in a list or graphic box.

set-up   In broadcasting, an introductory statement to pique the interest of listeners or viewers.

shield laws   Legislation giving journalists the right to protect the identity of sources.

show producer   Television news specialist who produces individual newscasts and reports to the executive producer.

sidebar   A secondary story intended to be run with a major story on the same topic. A story about a disaster, for example, may have a sidebar that tells what happened to a single victim.

situation ethics   The philosophy that recognizes that a set of rules can be broken when circumstances dictate the community will be served better by it. For example, a journalist who believes it normally unethical to deceive a news source may be willing to conceal his or her identity to infiltrate a group operating illegally.

slug   A word that identifies a story as it is processed through the newspaper plant. It is usually placed in the upper left-hand corner of each take of the story. See also *take*.

sniff   The preliminary phase of an investigation.

soft lead   A lead that uses a quote, anecdote or other literary device to attract the reader. See also *hard lead*.

soft news   Stories about trends, personalities or lifestyles. The time element usually is not important. See also *hard news*.

sources   People or records from which a reporter gets information. The term often is used to describe persons, as opposed to documents.

spot news   A timely report of an event that is unfolding at the moment.

spreadsheet   Computer program adept at managing numbers. Often used for budgets.

story   The term most journalists use for a newspaper article. Another synonym is *piece*, as in, "I saw your piece on the mayor." A long story may be called a *takeout* or a *blockbuster*.

stylebook   A book of standard usage within newspaper text. It includes rules on grammar, punctuation, capitalization and abbreviation. The AP and UPI publish similar stylebooks that are used by most papers. (Portions of the AP and UPI stylebooks are reprinted in Appendix 2 of this book.)

substantial truth   The correctness of the essential elements of a story.

summary lead   The first paragraph of a news story in which the writer presents a synopsis of two or more actions rather than focusing on any one of them.

sunshine laws   See *open-meetings laws*.

take   A page of typewritten copy for newspaper use.

30   A designation used to mark the end of a newspaper story. The symbol # is an alternate designation.

tickler   A file of upcoming events kept on paper or computer at the assignment desks of most news organizations. See also *futures file*.

tie-back   The sentence or sentences relating a story to events covered in a previous story. Used in follow-up or continuing stories or in parts of a series of stories. Also, the technique of referring to the opening in the ending of the story.

tip   A fragment of information that may lead to a story; also called a *lead*.

transition   A word, phrase, sentence or paragraph that moves the reader from one thought to the next and shows the relationship between them.

undercover reporting   A technique in which a reporter pretends to be someone else in order to gain access to otherwise unobtainable information.

universal desk   A copy desk that edits material for all editorial departments of a newspaper.

update   A type of follow that reports on a development related to an earlier story.

UPI   United Press International, a worldwide news-gathering organization that is privately owned.

variable   In an experiment, one of the elements being observed. The independent variable is what is thought to be a cause; the dependent variable is the effect of that cause.

videographer   A television camera operator.

videoprompter   A mechanical or electronic device that projects broadcast copy next to the television camera lens so that a newscaster can read it while appearing to look straight into the lens.

vulgarity   A word or phrase dealing with excretory matters in a less-than-polite way.

wrap-up   The completion of commentary that comes at the end of a taped segment in broadcasting; a strong ending to a report.

Acknowledgments

"TIPS: Audiences of the 21st century" from *Undercovered: Reaching the New U.S.A.* Published by New Directions for News. Copyright © New Directions for News 2001. Funded by The Freedom Foundation. Reprinted by permission.

Figure 2.2. Adapted from *Facts About Newspapers*, 2003. By permission of the Newspaper Association of America, Reston, Va.

Figure 2.4. MSNBC #1 News Site. © 2004 Microsoft Corporation. All rights reserved. Reprinted by permission from Microsoft Corporation.

April M. Eaton, host, Urban Outlook, News Channel 5 Network. Extreme Communication Consultant, AllState Insurance Company. Reprinted by permission.

Figure 2.11. Bloomberg.com Web site. © 2004 Bloomberg L.P. Reprinted by permission. All Rights Reserved.

George Dohrmann, *Pioneer Press* staff writer, "U basketball program accused of academic fraud" from the *St. Paul Pioneer Press*, March 10, 1999. By permission of *St. Paul Pioneer Press*.

Figure 5.1. Files from DIALOG/Periodical Abstracts Plustext. Copyright © 2001 by UMI Company. All Rights Reserved. Reprinted by permission.

Figure 5.2. *The Mercury News* home page. © 2004 The Mercury News. Reprinted by permission. All Rights Reserved.

Tracy van Moorlehem and Heather Newman. MEAP story from the *Detroit Free Press*. Reprinted by permission of the publisher.

Stan Ketterer. "Guidelines for Assessing Credibility and Accuracy of Information on the Web." Reprinted by permission.

Figure 6.1. "Ranking the supes" photos from the *San Francisco Independent*, Tuesday, Aug. 5, 1997. Copyright © 1997 San Francisco Independent. Reprinted by permission.

David Ho, Associated Press writer. AP story about largest-ever product recall. Reprinted with permission of The Associated Press. Additional AP lead paragraphs. Reprinted by permission of The Associated Press.

Blake Morrison. "A fatal mystery shrouds flight 1763." From *USA Today*, Dec. 18, 2000. Copyright 2000, USA TODAY. Reprinted by permission.

Jane Meinhardt. Story about unusual burglary ring from the St. *Petersburg Times*, Oct. 21, 1994. Reprinted by permission.

Ken Fuson. Story from *The Des Moines Register.* "Top ten tips for writing." Reprinted by permission.

Leonard Bernstein. Excerpt from article about David Lowery's remarkable life by Leonard Bernstein, reporter for *The Hartford Courant*, Aug. 19, 1984. Reprinted by permission.

Leonora Bohn Peter. "Trial of Jerry Scott Heidler" from the *Savannah Morning News.* © 2001 Savannah Morning News. Reprinted by permission from the *Savannah Morning News.*

Poll checklist data prepared by the Associated Press Managing Editors Association. Copyright © 2001 by the APMEA. All rights reserved.

The Cincinnati Post **Web site.** Front-page screen shot. Copyright 2001 The Cincinnati Post, an E.W. Scripps newspaper. Reproduced by permission.

SacBee.com Web site. Front-page screen shot. Copyright © 2001 The Sacramento Bee. Reproduced by permission.

Washingtonpost.com Web site. "Major changes afoot at Pentagon" by Thomas E. Ricks and Walter Pincus from *The Washington Post*, May 7, 2001. Copyright © 2001 The Washington Post Company. Reproduced by permission.

Orlando.Sentinel.com Web site. Front-page screen shot. Copyright © 2001 OrlandoSentinel.com. Executive Producer: Mike Dame. Site Design: Ed Moss and Ray Villahobos. Reproduced with permission.

Projo.com Web site. Front-page screen shot. Lead story, "Gasoline prices climb for third straight week — pummeled at the pump" by Zachary Block, *The Providence Journal*, May 2, 2001. Copyright © 2001 The Providence Journal Company. Reproduced with permission.

BayArea.com Web site. Front-page screen shot. "Top Stories" posted Friday, May 4, 2001. Copyright © 2001 *San Jose Mercury News.* All rights reserved. Reproduced with permission.

"Would buying boycott help lower California's electricity bill?" San Francisco (AP) lead wire story posted on BayArea.com. Front-page screen shot, "Top Stories," Friday, May 4, 2001. Reprinted with permission of The Associated Press.

Detroit Free Press Web site. Front-page screen shot. www.freep.com. Copyright © 2001 Detroit Free Press, Inc. All rights reserved. Reproduced with permission.

Figure 20.1. *The Cincinnati Post* online.com Web site. Two front-page screen shots, Jan. 20, 2004, and Feb. 10, 2004. © 2004 The Cincinnati Post. Reprinted with permission. All rights reserved. www.cincypost.com.

Figure 20.2. *The Sacramento Bee* Web site. Two front-page screen shots, Jan. 26, 2004, and Feb. 10, 2004. © 2004 The Sacramento Bee. Reprinted with permission. All rights reserved.

Figure 20.3. AP photo on CNN.com Web site. © 2004 AP/Wide World Photos. Reprinted with permission. All rights reserved. CNN.com Web site. © 2004 CNN. Reprinted by permission. www.cnn.com.

Figure 20.4. *YAHOO! News* Web site. Screen shot, January 26, 2004. © 2004 Yahoo! Inc. All Rights Reserved. Reprinted by permission. www.yahoo.com. Photo from Reuters. © Reuters America LLC. Reprinted by permission. All rights reserved. www.reuters.com.

Figure 20.5. *ESPN.com* Web site. Front-page screen shot, Jan. 29, 2004. © 2004 ESPN, Inc. Reprinted by permission. All rights reserved. www.mspn.go.com.

Figure 20.6. *BostonHerald.com* Web site. Front-page screen shot, Jan. 26, 2004. © 2004 Boston Herald. Reprinted by permission. All rights reserved. www.bostonherald.com.

Figure 20.7. *Washingtonpost.com* Web site. Two front-page screen shots, Jan. 16, 2004, and Feb. 10, 2004. © 2004, The Washington Post. Reprinted with permission. www.washingtonpost.com.

Figure 20.8. *Latimes.com* Web site. Front-page screen shot. © Los Angeles Times. Reprinted with permission. www.latimes.com.

Earthjustice homepage Web site. Reprinted by permisson.

Figure 21.1. Preamble to the Member Code of Ethics of the Public Relations Society of America. Courtesy of PRSA.

INDEX

Page numbers in *italics* indicate material presented in boxes. Page numbers followed by an italicized *f* or *t* indicate figures and tables, respectively. Page numbers in **boldface** indicate terms that appear in the Glossary.

575